For Sean Mayes, a much missed friend

Published by
Adelita Ltd
www.adelita.co.uk

This edition published 2010

Author: Kevin Cann
Designer: Melissa Alaverdy (thedesignwhisperer.com)
Publisher: Jenny Ross

Cover photography credits:
Front and Spine: Duffy © Duffy Archive
Back: Left: Kenneth Pitt. Right (from top to bottom): George Underwood; Dezo Hoffmann/Rex Features;
Denis Taylor; Denis Taylor; Kenneth Pitt; Keith MacMillan/David Bowie Collection; Brian Ward/David Bowie Collection
Front flap: Kevin Cann collection. Back flap: (top) Kate Chertavian; (bottom) Mark Hayward
Inside front cover and flap: ITV/Rex Features
Inside back cover and flap: Byron Newman

Page 1: Photography by Brian Ward/David Bowie Collection. Artwork exclusively for *Any Day Now* by Terry Pastor

All other photography/artwork: see credits on page 330

ISBN: 978-0-9552017-7-6

Repro by DL Imaging, London
Printed and bound in China

David Bowie

ANY DAY NOW

The London Years: 1947-1974

Kevin Cann

THANK YOU

THANKS TO THOSE WHO HAVE PERSONALLY TAKEN THE TIME TO HELP ME, NAMELY:

Fiona Adams, Rolf Adlercreutz, Roy Ainsworth, Bernie Andrews, Adam Ant, Michael Armstrong, Tom Ayres, Max Batten, David Bebbington, Kenny Bell, Barry Bethell, Rodney Bingenheimer, Joe Blackadder, Trevor Bolder, Terry Bolton, Derek Boyes, Angela Bowie, Jochem Brouwer, Winifred Bunting, Mary Burrett, Steve Burrett, Woolf Byrne, John Cambridge, Dave Cash, Clem Cattini, Michael Chapman, Chris Charlesworth, Leee Black Childers, Nita Clarke, Les Conn, Terry Cox, Lol Coxhill, Jojanneke Claassen, Dave Clark, Celestino Coronada, Brian Davies, Dai Davies, Kiki Dee, Vernon Dewhurst, Jeff Dexter, Richie Dharma, Gus Dudgeon, Brian Duffy, Chris Duffy, John Eager, Ian Ellis, Derek Fearnley, Jude Fearnley, Julie Felix, Mary Finnigan, Matthew Fisher, Helene Lancaster, Herbie Flowers, Clive Frampton, Michael Garrett, Ron Geesin, Stuart George, Dana Gillespie, Bob Grace, Nicky Graham, Jeff Griffin, Stuart Grundy, David Hadfield, Bosse Hansson, Steve Harley, Bob Harris, Bill Harry, Nick Hedges, Tony Hill, Nicky Horne, Simon House, Kevin Howlett, Harry Hughes, Ian Hunter, John Hutchinson, Barrie Jackson, Lindsay Kemp, Rick Kemp, Haruya Kikuchi, Jak Kilby, Tony King, Victor Konn, Natasha Kornilof, Marty Kristian, Phil Lancaster, Barry Langford, Calvin Mark Lee, Lulu, Geoff MacCormack, Ralph Mace, Keith MacMillan, Alan Mair, Benny Marshall, Rosemary Mason, Sean Mayes, Paul McCartney, John Mendelssohn, Hugh Mendl, Barry Morgan, Charles Shaar Murray, Bob Musel, Laurence Myers, Bill Nelson, Anthony Newley, Paul Nicholas, Ron Oberman, Will Palin, Gabi Pape, Alan Parker, Daniella Parmar, Terry Pastor, Stella Patton, Elizabeth Peellaert, Guy Peellaert, Celia Philo, Kenneth Pitt, David Platz, Tim Renwick, Sandra Nelson, Norman Odam, Christina Ostrom, Mark Pritchett, Linda Pritchett, David Rider, Billy Ritchie, Graham Rivens, Mick Rock, Sheila Rock, Paul Rodriguez, Mick Ronson, Maggi Ronson, Minnie Ronson, Nicholas Ronson, Suzi Ronson, Ken Scott, Ken Simmons, Bob Solly, Ray Stevenson, Masayoshi Sukita, David Screaming Lord Sutch, Denis Taylor, Shaw Taylor, John Tobler, Simon Turner, Shirley Wilson, George Underwood, Birgit Underwood, Penny Valentine, Cherry Vanilla, Mike Vernon, Justin de Villeneuve, Tony Visconti, Johnny Walker, Hank Wangford, Mick Wayne, Tim Whitnall, Roy Williams, Anya Wilson, Woody Woodmansey, Kansai Yamammoto, Tony Zanetta.

FOR INVALUABLE ASSISTANCE FROM ESSENTIAL FILES:

Suet-Ming Lau, Bob Harris and Frank Richmond at Essex Music. Malcolm Bucklan and Andrew Jackson at Chrysalis. Stephen Nam at BBC Worldwide, Hal Shaper and Stella Groves at Sparta Florida. For Decca archives: John Tracey at Phonogram, Joe Black at Universal & Tris Penna, Tim Chacksfield at EMI. *The Bromley Times* and *Beckenham Journal*. Jeff Rougvie at Ryko and to Castle Communications. Innumerable newspapers, but mainly the great British music press: *Melody Maker*, *New Musical Express*, *Record Mirror*, *Disc*, *Sounds*, *Q*, *Mojo*, *Record Collector* and *US cousin's*, *Rolling Stone* and *Creem*.

This book would be far poorer without the excellent insights of my friend Tristram Penna, for which many thanks. Tris also untiringly read through various early manuscripts and offered much valued advice.

The brilliant Pete Frame, who waded with considerable authority through an early draft of an uncertain manuscript, adding some essential nuggets. John Cambridge, who has really helped unravel some of the mysteries and has a great memory, as has John 'Archie' Eager who was an enormous help with everything Buzz shaped. To the late-great Derek Fearnley, a humble man and sorely missed. To Jude and Helen Fearnley. Trevor and Shelly Bolder. For Lower Third assistance; Denis Taylor, Phil and Helene Lancaster, Graham Rivens and Terry Bolton.

Thanks for everything George: (georgeunderwood.com).

For Terry Pastor for kindly supplying the opening page artwork.

Thanks to Henry Wrenn-Meleck @ RZO Music.

To many friends at EMI, especially Nigel Reeve, Steve Davies and Drew Lorrimer.

I have been greatly assisted on archive information at BBC radio by Phil Lawton, Brigitte Kamper at ZDF, Beckenham Library and the heavenly sanctuary of the British Library at Colindale (almost my second home during research) and the Bournemouth Pavilion. John Kirkham at Barnardo's archive and Christopher Murray, Dave Warwick, Bob Greaves.

Many thanks to my old friend Mark 'Blam' Adams, sterling news administrator and sage at BowieNet (davidbowie.com), David's personal website.

To Ray Stevenson for some excellent photos and for being a trusted friend. For Chris Duffy, for all of his help and assistance. And to Kevin Howlett.

Gerald and Irene Fearnley for all of your help and belief with this project. Equally to Dave Hadfield for some extra Konrads insights, and to John Hutchinson.

Thanks to Nick Dumper and Ravens Wood School, Bromley.

To all at Adelita, namely Jenny Ross, Paul Gorman, Melissa Alaverdy, Pat Morgan, Chris Brockhurst, Geraldine Beare, Caz Facey, Imad & all at DL, Gareth Jones & all at Colorprint. Plus the Ross clan for their support.

For initial help in 1981/82: Brian Lane (Bromley Tech), Peter Noone and my commissioning editor at Vermilion, Susan Hill.

For belief and encouragement with *Any Day Now*, special thanks to the dearly missed Brian Roylance and to Oliver Craske. Thanks also to Catherine and Nick Roylance, to Robby Elson and everyone at Genesis (genesis-publications.com).

To David Buckley for general help and encouragement.

Thanks to Martin Clarkson, John Court and Eagle Vision, Alan Reynolds, Sunset and Vine Post Production.

To Paul Kinder, who created and faithfully maintains the excellent website, Bowiewonderworld.com.

To Martin Argent for his kind help and assistance and Peter Fittock, whose early years Bowie research was extremely helpful. Similarly, the work of Alex Alexander and Pete Foulstone.

General thank yous to Lin Barkass, Canadian Lana Topham, Spizz, Judy and Molly, Chris Carter, Mark Hayward, Davide De Leo, Ma & Pa, Simon and Sue, Melanie and Chas, Maggi May, Hannah and Amelia, Ronno's Mum Minnie, Russell Ford, Gordon Templeton,

Andy Fearon, Steve Ward, Mark Moxon.

Many thanks to Maxine and Howard Marshall, ex of MainMan for all your help.

To good friends Kazuya Yoshii, Hideaki Kikuchi, Youichi Hirose and Eiji Kikuchi from the excellent Yellow Monkey, whose support and generosity for the Mick Ronson Memorial projects and their love and appreciation for Michael was heartfelt.

Also, huge thanks to the late Mr and Mrs Fussey (Suzi's parents) who always helped keep me in contact with Ronno wherever he travelled, and also to (Stiff Little Fingers) Mick Rossi, who introduced me to Michael in the first place.

To Peter and Leni Gillman for the great research work on their excellent book *Alias David Bowie*.

A special thanks to my old school buddy Clive Norris, wife Angela and children Sean, Anna and Kate. You're the best.

To those I may have missed I apologise (a laptop theft some years ago annoyingly took with it important additional names, for example the lady who gave me copies of her photos of David arriving and leaving the *Mike Douglas Show* in 1973).

HOW TO USE THIS BOOK:

To differentiate live performance dates from ordinary dates and events, entries are prefixed thus (▌).

An arrow (▶) prefixing an abbreviated date indicates that there is further reading or a connection here with the item you have just read.

Dates are abbreviated by dd-mm-yy.

Most of David's appearances with The Konrads were undocumented. Many were private bookings and were not publicised.

During much of 1969 David made regular weekly appearances at the Beckenham Arts Lab. Unless reported in the local press, all of these performances were also undocumented. Those who worked closely with David at the time are agreed that he faithfully attended most weeks, sometimes twice weekly. When he was working elsewhere, or was out of the country, this is acknowledged, otherwise those evenings are listed as Beckenham Arts Lab only, with a more-than-favourable chance that David was also performing.

The Lab was quickly renamed Growth, but it is generally referred to today as the Beckenham Arts Lab and that is how it is generally listed in this book.

INTRODUCTION

David and Tony Visconti at Trident Studios, the day they began work on 'Running Gun Blues' and 'Saviour Machine', 4 May 1970.

IF you are reasonably new to David Bowie and know little about his career, you may not know the name Rodney Bingenheimer. Rodney is now officially known – after being immortalised in a film of his life and career in 2003 – as *The Mayor of Sunset Strip*.

Rodney first met David when he arrived in LA for a promotional visit in February 1971. His first gift to David was to introduce him to RCA staffer Tom Ayres (who immediately recognised David's talent and began to encourage him to look towards RCA for his next deal). After David had spent nearly a month lodging at Holiday Inns across the US, Tom invited him to stay at his home and also gave him access to recording facilities.

The reason I mention Rodney and Tom Ayres here (both of them are documented elsewhere in this book) is because it helps highlight the spirit and generosity of the many, many people who have helped me while I slowly pieced together this book.

I initially spoke to Tom on the phone as he sat on the porch of his house in Oil City, Louisiana. I keenly listened as he rendered a detailed description of his immediate view across the swamps in the balmy twilight. His many anecdotes collected from a life spent in the music business were fascinating. Without hesitation he sent me some private recordings David made while staying with him, particularly eager that I should try and identify one of the incomplete recordings David left behind. There was an instant trust and connection.

I recently called Rodney and we talked about Tom, who died in 2000: the times they worked together at Rodney's English Disco and the period David spent at Tom's home. I had written that the house was on Sunset Boulevard, based on a story Tom had told me, but Rodney had a different recollection, although he couldn't remember the exact road name. "I'm just off out to eat. I'll drive that way and check it out and will let you know," he said, at the same time promising to send me copies of two of the photos he took of David in London in 1971.

I have known Rodney for nearly 25 years but his generosity, and memories of that of Tom Ayres, brought home to me how lucky I have been to be given a chance to meet, speak with and get to know so many fascinating and interesting people. Not only to receive unconditional help but often true friendship. The above is a story I could repeat many times over.

In the limited space I have here I would like to highlight just a few of the many people who have been kind enough to help me.

Ken Pitt has been a huge influence, not only for this book but on my life. After more than 30 years David Bowie only occasionally enters our conversations, but a shared love of Victorian literature and particularly its artists more than makes up for it.

The following also deserve a special mention: Trevor and Shelly Bolder, Mary Burrett, Gus Dudgeon, John Eager and Derek Fearnley, Anthony Newley, Lindsay Kemp, Natasha Kornilof, Marty and Carol Kristian, Geoff MacCormack, Will Palin, Terry Pastor, Guy Peellaert, Mark and Linda Pritchett, Mick Rock, Maggi Ronson, Mick Ronson, Bob Solly, Ray Stevenson, Masayoshi Sukita, George and Birgit Underwood and Anya Wilson. I can't thank them enough for all of the help they have given. These sentiments are also extended to the many people who are listed opposite.

For 26 years, London was the centre of David Bowie's world. The highly respected artist he became was fully established in that time, and it makes a fascinating and inspiring story.

How does someone become as successful as David Bowie? It's all here, but you will have to factor in the esoteric and unique genius for yourself.

Director Stanley Kubrick, whose effect on David's career at various key times was profound, once succinctly commented when asked about his films: "The ideas have to be discovered by the audience, and their thrill in making the discovery makes these ideas all the more powerful."

It is in that spirit that I wrote this book. Thank you David, for a fascinating journey.

CONTENTS

KENNETH PITT

FOREWORD

DAVIE Jones was very much a progressively charismatic child of the 60s but, because of the tenacious hold the top 20 system had on an artist's career, it was not until the decade's end that he became a star – and then only just!

As a publicist who sometimes found himself managing his client, I had become part of that obscure world where publicity and management merge. When Davie Jones came to me, the first service I rendered him was to tell him to change his name. He became David Bowie. Then the name had to be publicised and this was partially done by the now famous Deram LP, which proved to be a huge morale-builder for David, giving him the opportunity to choose and record the songs he had been writing at that time. He was not well known so it didn't sell many copies, but it turned out to be an effective CV and opened many doors. One of those doors was that of Lindsay Kemp, who David would later claim to have been one of the two most influential people in his career. And the other? It was Lou Reed.

I met Lou Reed at Andy Warhol's studio, The Factory, in 1966. Andy and Tom Wilson had put singer/songwriter Lou together with a group of musicians and had produced an album with them, tracks of which were playing and and could be heard above The Factory's hubbub. It had been given the name *The Velvet Underground and* [incidentally] *Nico*. Nico I already knew, having met her in Bob Dylan's suite at the Savoy Hotel in London when I was representing him in 1964. The album had yet to be released but I enthused about it so much that I was given an acetate demo copy. I said to Nico: "I know someone in London who will love this." And love it he did, saying it was "the album that changed my life". In 2002 David told *Mojo* magazine: "Everything I both felt and didn't know about rock music was opened to me on one unreleased disc. It was *The Velvet Underground And Nico*."

To keep up the momentum of interest caused by the Deram LP, I decided to make a film of David acting out his songs from it, Decca having given me permission to use the backing tracks and remix them. I would then show this film to those producers, BBC and others, who having shown little interest in the sound of David might be attracted to the sight of him.

We were shooting the film at Greenwich Studios and it soon became obvious to me that we needed something extra, a new, very special song that was not on the Deram LP. I asked David if he could come up with something. He did. It was called 'Space Oddity'.

When released as a single, the success of 'Space Oddity' led to the trebling of David's fees for gigs, new album *David Bowie* (SBL 7912), in which he again displayed his remarkable songwriting skills, and a series of singles. Although these recent releases received lively, usually commendable, comments from the critics, the buying public showed little interest, throwing David into frequent fits of despondency and causing him to look for someone to blame. It was not a happy time.

The good news was that David's recording company, Mercury of Chicago, said it would like another album for US release. He began work on what was to become *The Man Who Sold The World*. Having previously given Tony Visconti the responsible job of producing David's recordings, I arranged with him 11 recording sessions to take place between April and May. Ambitious plans were also being laid for me to take David to Chicago, where we would join Ron Oberman, Mercury's Director of Publicity, to promote the album. It seemed to me I had done everything possible to promote David's career, but he begged

David with Ken Pitt on the roof of Pitt's Manchester Street home.

to differ. On 27 April 1970 I received a letter from him in which he wrote: 'I have been advised that you have not performed your part of our Agreement by using your past endeavours to further my career thereunder...' He went on to say that he no longer considered me to be his Personal Manager. I felt that there was no point in David and me continuing our professional relationship if he was unhappy with it, so it ended on 7 May. Forty years on, we remain good friends.

The Man Who Sold The World was long delayed, finally being released in the UK in April 1971, with Tony Visconti lamenting, "With no plans for promoting the album, David's career seemed to be in a state of limbo." He considers it to be one of his top three Bowie albums, and as recently as 2006 Morrissey said: "Today it still stands as David Bowie's best work."

This long delay prevented Mercury from keeping to its original timetable, so the album was released in the US in November 1970. Early in 1971 David finally had his long-planned meeting with Ron Oberman in Chicago, where, for the second time in his career, he was presented with two records that were to greatly enhance that career. To quote David: "In early 71 Mercury executive Ron Oberman took me to one side just before my departure from the States back to the UK and furtively pressed a couple of singles into my hand. 'Play these,' he said, 'you will never be the same again.' Back home I choked on 'Paralyzed', gasped in awe at 'Down In The Wrecking Yard' and fell all about the floor at 'I Took A Trip On A Gemini Spaceship'. It was the laugh of love. I could not believe that such a talent was unrecognised. The integrity, honesty and innocent, brutal focus entranced me. I became a lifelong fan and Ziggy got a surname."

The recordings were of Norman Carl Odam, who said that he was The Legendary Stardust Cowboy. And so Ziggy Stardust, the magical character that would rocket David to worldwide fame, was born.

The day would come when it seemed that every publishing house had its own Bowie book. In 1986 music journalist Dave Thompson wrote in *Record Collector* magazine: 'There will soon be no room left on the bookshelf for any more Bowie books and, with three more due out over the next six months, and twice that many having appeared over the last six, the potential purchaser needs to look carefully before making his decision.'

Today, a quarter of a century later, there are still Bowie books in the pipeline, but their authors would be well advised to study this remarkable encyclopedia, compiled by Kevin Cann, who is now recognised as the world's most reliably informed student of the life and work of David Bowie. He is particularly noted for his powers of investigative research. So meticulous is he that one day he phoned me and said: "In your book (*The Pitt Report*), you say that you went to Hamburg with David for four days. You say what you did on the first and second days; what did you do on the third and fourth days?"

More than once, when being interviewed by a journalist, I have not known the answer to a particular question so I have said: "Why don't you ask Kevin Cann?"

Have a good read.

PROLOGUE

DAVID Bowie's father, Haywood Stenton Jones, was born on 21 November 1912 at 41 St Sepulchre Gate, in Doncaster, Yorkshire.

In 1933 Haywood, or John as he was to be known throughout his life, struck out for London with an inheritance of £3,000, determined to make a name for himself in showbiz.

One of the characters he encountered as he endeavoured to make his way in the capital was music-hall performer James Sullivan, whose 25-year-old daughter Hilda Louise was a singer working in nightclubs in Vienna. The victory of the Nazi party in Austria's election in March 1933 prompted a mass exodus, which she joined. On her arrival at central London's Charing Cross railway station, Hilda Sullivan was met by her father and his new acquaintance, John Jones.

The young couple took up with each other, and were married on 19 December 1933 in London.

Intent on realising his show business dreams by promoting his new bride's career as a singing star, Jones invested no less than £2,000 of his inheritance on a touring revue to showcase her talents. This was called 11.30 Saturday Night, after a popular dance number of the time.

But the tour, although short, was a disaster; Hilda later said that the chosen venues, in Dudley in the west Midlands and Croydon and Chelsea in outer and inner London, were "dead places".

Such was Jones's determination, however, that back in London he ploughed the remaining £1,000 of his inheritance into opening a piano bar called The Boop-a-doop in Charlotte Street, on the borders of bohemian Bloomsbury and Soho. Hilda fronted the venture as resident performer in the guise of chanteuse Cherie, The Viennese Nightingale.

Again, this was not a financial success, mainly due to Jones's retiring personality. He simply wasn't cut out to be a 'hail fellow, well met' promoter. The Boop-a-doop closed within a year and Jones was left penniless. These forays into the entertainment industry were to inform the caution Jones expressed when his youngest son embarked on a career in pop in the 60s.

David has said that the nightclub had been "gangster and wrestling orientated. I don't know how my father got involved in that. Then he went into the army."

In fact, on 4 September 1934 Jones took up full-time employment as a clerk at the children's charity Dr Barnardo's Homes, in Elephant & Castle, south London.

Later, Jones moved with the charity to its headquarters, Barnardo's House in Stepney Causeway, just to the east of the City of London, occupying the job of public relations officer.

By all accounts, married life was soured by the failure of the couple's show business ambitions and lack of money, compounded by the loss of Jones's inheritance in his attempts to make his wife a star.

The couple separated in 1935 but two years later made another go of it. Shortly after they got back together, John spent a short while working for Dr Barnardo's in Birmingham, and had a brief affair during which his lover became pregnant. Her identity has never been revealed.

When Jones informed Hilda about these developments, his wife accepted the

David's father and mother, Haywood Stenton Jones and Margaret Mary Burns, better known as John and Peggy Jones.

situation. The child, Annette, was born in January 1938, and adopted by Jones and his wife despite their faltering relationship.

They separated again later that year.

At the outbreak of war in September 1939, with Annette being raised by Hilda, Jones – already a keen marksman in the Territorial Army – enlisted as a regular. He joined the Royal Fusiliers and went on to see action in North Africa, Sicily and Italy as part of the Eighth Army.

Late in 1945, not long after his return from war, the demobilised Jones met 31-year-old Margaret Burns at the Ritz Cinema, Church Road, Royal Tunbridge Wells, Kent, where she was working as a waitress.

Born on 2 October 1913 in a military hospital at Shorncliffe Army Camp, near Folkestone, Kent, Margaret Mary Burns (or Peggy, as she was known) had borne two children by the time she met Jones.

Her eldest, Terence Guy Adair Burns, was born on 5 November 1937; his father was a Frenchman named Jack 'Wolf' Rosemberg, who abandoned the relationship, which is why the infant was granted his mother's surname.

Peggy Burns gave birth to her second child on 29 August 1943. Christened Myra Ann, she was given up for adoption at nine months of age. The identity of the father has never been revealed.

Soon after their meeting in Tunbridge Wells, John Jones and Peggy Burns took the step of moving into their first home together – a house in Hilldrop Crescent, Kentish Town, north London.

The following year, the couple purchased a three-storey terraced house for under £500 at 40 Stansfield Road, on the borders of inner-city neighbourhoods Stockwell and Brixton in south London.

Jones was evidently still in contact with his wife Hilda, from whom he was not yet divorced (the marriage would be annulled the following year). In an unusual arrangement, Hilda agreed to the money being taken from her and her ex-partner's joint savings from his wartime pay on condition that the house (or proceeds if sold) would go to their daughter Annette on her 21st birthday.

Previously a teetotaller, during the war years Jones had become a heavy drinker, which eventually led to him being hospitalised. On recovery, he renounced alcohol for the rest of his life.

In the latter half of 1946, the couple had good cause to feel secure after the turmoil of the war years and the failure of their previous relationships. Not only did they have a new house, a loving relationship and in, John Jones's case, a steady job and recovered health, but Peggy Burns was pregnant…

1947–1963

DAVID Robert Jones is born on 8 January 1947, in Brixton, south London. He grows up in a secure environment, the household also containing his half-brother Terry Burns, who will play an important role in David's creative development.

When David is six the family moves to Bromley in Kent, on the south-eastern outskirts of London.

When cousin Kristina Paulsen arrives with her copy of Elvis Presley's 'Hound Dog', David is smitten by rock'n'roll, particularly after he witnesses a performance by pop star Tommy Steele. His fascination for music is encouraged by friendship with schoolmate George Underwood, with whom he makes his performance debut.

At secondary school, David is encouraged in artistic pursuits by teacher Owen Frampton, father of Peter.

David has a taste for fashion, and his obsession with music and art disrupts his studies, leading to conflict at home.

He absorbs influences including those of singer/performer Anthony Newley and beat writer Jack Kerouac, and in 1961 is bought a saxophone.

A playground fight with Underwood over a girl causes permanent dilation of his left pupil, leaving David with his distinctive eyes.

He takes sax lessons and is invited to join Underwood's beat group, The Konrads. They perform covers at teen dances; David occasionally slips away to see new groups like The Rolling Stones. On leaving school, he takes up a position in the art studio of a London ad agency.

The Konrads fail an audition for Stones co-manager Eric Easton, and David becomes disillusioned with the routine of performing cover versions.

On New Year's Eve 1963, David plays his last gig with The Konrads, and resolves to form a grittier, blues-influenced outfit with George Underwood.

1947

Wednesday 8 January

David Robert Jones is born at nine o'clock in the morning in a terraced house at 40 Stansfield Road, London SW9.

"This child has been on this earth before," says the midwife to mother Peggy Burns. "It's in his eyes; they're so knowing."

British law stipulates that births should be registered within 42 days, but David's is not until 1960 (when he needs his first passport for a family holiday).

During the first months of 1947 Britain endures its hardest winter since records began. These are the early stages of post-war recovery; rationing will remain in force for seven more years and London, especially those areas close to the River Thames such as Brixton, is scarred by the intensive bombing of the war years.

Monday 11 August

John Jones and Hilda Sullivan are divorced on the grounds of the former's adultery.

Friday 12 September

John Jones, 35, and Peggy Burns, 34, marry at Brixton Register Office.

1948-1950

At the beginning of 1948 Margaret Jones' first-born, David's 10-year-old half-brother Terry Burns, joins the family at 40 Stansfield Road. Later in the year he attends Henry Thornton School, a short distance away near Clapham Common.

Terry's surname is changed by deed poll to Jones

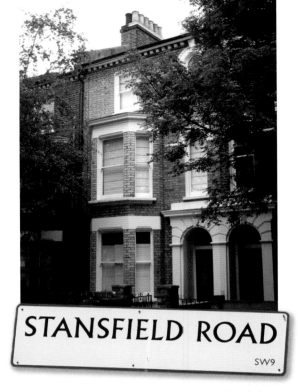

STANSFIELD ROAD

SW9

by his stepfather, though John Jones is not fond of his stepson and on coming of age Terry will switch his surname back to Burns.

At Stansfield Road, tension between John and Terry has a profound effect on the boy, who is already troubled and will develop both schizophrenic tendencies and bipolarity later in life. Terry – who shares the ground-floor bedroom with David – confides to his Aunt Pat (his mother's sister), "I hate John Jones."

To supplement their income, Mr and Mrs Jones let out a room to a lodger named Anne McLachlan.

"I had a very reserved, respectable childhood," David later told his cousin Kristina Paulsen. "Nothing really happened to me that one would consider freaky."

Although in 2003 he said: "The very first memory I have is of being left in my pram in the hallway of 40 Stansfield Road, facing the stairs. It seemed to be a very, very long time and I was very scared of the stairs. They were dark and shadowy."

In a rare interview in 1986, Mrs Jones remembered one incident in particular: "When he was about three years old he put on make-up for the first time," she said. "We had tenants in the house and one day he went missing upstairs and found a bag of lipstick, eye-liner and face-powder, and decided it would be a good idea to plaster his face with it. When I finally found him, he looked for all the world like a clown. I told him he shouldn't use make-up, but he said, 'You do, Mummy.' I agreed, but pointed out that it wasn't for little boys."

Peggy is not prone to displays of physical affection ("a compliment from her was very hard to come by," David would later say). John Jones also finds it difficult to express his feelings towards his son. "I can't remember him ever touching me. He was never able to hug me," David recalled in 1993.

1951

Monday 12 November

David's first day at Stockwell Infant School, on the corner of Stansfield Road and Stockwell Road, just two hundred yards from his home.[1]

The first day at school is always terrifying and, although David wets himself, he has picked up enough confidence by the time he gets home to inform his mother that he will walk to school unaccompanied in future.

For the school's Nativity play, David dresses up for a stage performance for the first time. "I made him a robe and head-dress and his father made him a crook," Mrs Jones said. "He absolutely loved it. It was then that we realised that there was something in David. If there was anything that caught his ear (on the radio) he would tell everyone to be quiet and listen, and then fling himself about to the music. In those days we thought he might become a ballet dancer."

According to David, his musical career almost ended before it had begun: "I was thrown out of Stansfield Road Junior School [sic] choir for making too much noise. I was always singing and joking."

1. In 1991, David and his band Tin Machine performed at the Brixton Academy, just 100 yards south of where the school still stands.

1952

Hans Christian Andersen, starring Danny Kaye, is released in the US. The film will stimulate David's already burgeoning interest in music and song construction. In 1999 he said of the musical's most popular tune: "'Inchworm' is a very important song to me. 'Two and two are four... four and four are eight...' I love the effect of two melodies together. That nursery rhyme feeling shows itself in a lot of songs I've written, like 'Ashes To Ashes'."

David also listens as his mother sings along to radio broadcasts of boy soprano Ernest Lough's rendition of 'Hear My Prayer'. Written by Felix Mendelssohn and librettist William Bartholomew, the Christian anthem is famous for one particular line.

"My mother didn't realise what she was starting," said David in 2002. "She would always say at breakfast, 'Oh, I could have been a singer you know,' and then she'd sing.

"There was this thing on radio, *Two-Way Family Favourites*, I remember. Every Sunday without fail this thing by Ernest Lough was sung, and it was 'O For The Wings Of A Dove'.

"And my mother would [sings] 'O for the wings, for the wings of a dove! Far away, far away...' and she was really good. And I thought, maybe she would be a singer, be a great singer. So that was like, one of my first influences, Ernest Lough."

During this period David holidays at his uncle Jimmy Burns' farm in Yorkshire since John Jones is briefly seconded to the Harrogate branch of Dr Barnardo's. The family also visits John's sister Rhona, who lives in the Dales, north of York.

On one occasion David encounters the newly proclaimed Queen Elizabeth and Prince Philip, who are attending a local agricultural show. David inadvertently wanders close to the Queen, who stops to speak to him.

"She said, 'Oh, hello little boy,' and I became a picture in the newspaper – 'Little boy wanders into area where Queen is'." David said in 2003.

Even though David later romanticises the effects of the time spent on his uncle's farm, the holidays from inner-city Brixton do appear to have given him happy memories.

1953

At the beginning of the year the Joneses sell 40 Stansfield Road and move to 106 Canon Road, Bickley, in the outer south-east London suburb of Bromley.

Terry does not join them; the rift is such between him and his stepfather at this stage that he takes lodgings next door to the former family home in Stansfield Road.

In this year...

1947

Wednesday 8 January

ON the day of David's birth, Elvis Aaron Presley celebrated his 12th birthday 4,362 miles away in Memphis, Tennessee. The coincidence was significant for David, who saw Elvis' worldwide stature as the model for his own early success.

Although they never met, David witnessed a Presley performance and came close to producing a song – 'Golden Years' from *Station To Station* – for The King in 1975.

Also on this day, the founding father of abstract expressionism, Jackson Pollock, began his first 'action painting'. On his 55th birthday in 2002, David revealed in his internet journal: "He (Pollock) painted his first 'dribble' painting on my day of birth, 1947, so I can identify pre- and post-drips at forty paces."

Wednesday 5 February

BIRTH of George Underwood, Bromley, Kent. Underwood would become one of David's closest friends and earliest musical collaborator.

Monday 21 April

BIRTH of James Newell Osterberg, Muskegon, Michigan. Later known as Iggy Pop, with whom David collaborated in the 70s and 80s.

Tuesday 30 September

BIRTH of Mark Feld, Hackney, London. Better known as Marc Bolan, he was David's friend, rival and sometime collaborator up until his death in 1977.

1948

Saturday 15 May

BIRTH of Brian Peter George Eno, Woodbridge, Suffolk. St John le Baptiste de la Salle was added to his name when he attended Catholic school. A founder member of Roxy Music, solo recording artist, visual artist and writer, Eno collaborated on three of David's LPs between 1977 and 1979 as well as other projects in the 90s.

1953

PUBLICATION of Robert A. Heinlein's sci-fi novel *Starman Jones*. Heinlein also wrote *A Stranger In A Strange Land* – David was considered for an acting role when a film version was mooted in the mid-70s. *Starman Jones* was a follow-up to Heinlein's 1952 novel *The Rolling Stones*, and David's single 'Starman' provided the breakthrough for his Ziggy Stardust persona on release in 1972.

1954

Sunday 4 July

END of food rationing in Britain after 14 years.

1955

Monday 25 July

BIRTH of Iman Abdul Majid in Somalia. David married Iman in 1992. Their daughter Alexandra Zahra Jones (nicknamed Lexi) was born on 15 August 2000.

1956

Tuesday 14 August

DEATH of dramatist and social activist Bertolt Brecht (born 19 February 1898). David played the lead in Brecht's play *Baal* in a BBC TV dramatisation in 1982. This led to the EP *David Bowie In Bertolt Brecht's Baal*, also released in 1982. David's version of 'Alabama Song' (from Brecht and Kurt Weill's 1930 opera *The Rise And Fall Of The City Of Mahagonny*) reached number 23 in the UK charts in 1980.

David becomes a pupil at Raglan Primary School, Raglan Road, south Bromley.

"I left Brixton when I was still quite young, but that was enough to be very affected by it," David said many years later when discussing a charity performance at the Hammersmith Odeon for the Brixton Neighbourhood Community Association. "It left strong images in my mind."

1954

The Jones family move to 23 Clarence Road, Bromley. They are joined by David's half-sister Annette, who had also occasionally lived with them in Stansfield Road. At 16 she is studying to become a nurse and while Peggy Jones is away for a spell recuperating from an operation, Annette looks after David. However, Annette remains a remote figure in David's life story, emigrating to Canada within three or four years.

Her father keeps in touch, as his Dr Barnardo's secretary Winifred Bunting recalled: "I would regularly despatch parcels to Annette."

1955

In June, the Joneses settle at 4 Plaistow Grove, a small, terraced house in Sundridge Park, Bromley, behind The Crown pub in Plaistow Lane and next to Sundridge Park railway station.

David's bedroom is at the rear of the building, overlooking the back of the pub. There is no bathroom but a portable tin bath in the kitchen, not unusual for the period. The house is to remain their home for the next 15 years.

Terry rejoins the family, taking a small bedroom next to David's. Nearly ten years David's senior, Terry plays an important role in David's early creative development, though he is around infrequently.

Monday 20 June

David starts at Burnt Ash Junior School in Rangefield Road, a mile or so from his new home, joining the A-stream.

Burnt Ash headmaster George Lloyd is noted in the teaching profession for his unique 'movement training'. Pupils are divided into groups of four and equipped with percussive instruments. They are instructed to move around and express the rhythm of the triangles and tambourines they are playing. Lloyd, who died in 1980, described David to a colleague as a "sensitive and imaginative boy".

David befriends classmate Dudley Chapman and spends much of his spare time at the Chapmans' family home in nearby Lake Avenue, taking advantage of opportunities for games of Cowboys & Indians in the large garden. Chapman – who lost touch with David when they went to different secondary schools – recalled in 1986 how, even at that age, David was enthusiastic about particular subjects, not just the skiffle music sweeping Britain's youth at that time. Among his abiding interests are modern America and its history (particularly the Wild West), Japan and martial arts.

The form teacher is the formidable Edith Baldry, known among pupils as The Bulldozer. She is remembered for the cane she carried under her arm, though today David has only fond recollections of his old teacher.

In this period a lifelong friendship is forged with another schoolmate, Geoffrey MacCormack, who lives in neighbouring Cambridge Road.[1]

1. In the years since, David has included MacCormack in some of his own triumphs, with his friend carrying out vocal duties on two tours and a number of recordings in the 7Cs in the guise of Geoffrey Alexander, Mac Cormack and Warren Peace.

November

Terry Burns leaves the family home to begin his National Service with the Royal Air Force. Signing up for one year longer than the mandatory two, he receives slightly better pay and deployments and is posted to Malta and Libya.

1956

Sunday 2 December

With David's 14-year-old cousin Kristina Paulsen visiting Plaistow Grove for an extended stay, John Jones ferries the two children to a concert by popular British singing star Tommy Steele at the Finsbury Park Empire.

Afterwards, they are taken to meet Steele backstage where they collect his autograph. David is mightily impressed and Paulsen believes this event is the first to whet his desire to become a star.

Back at home, David is amazed when Paulsen plays her copy of Elvis Presley's 'Hound Dog' (released just three months previously and by that time featured in Steele's set) and dances along to it. He eagerly swaps his copy of 'Love Me Tender' for her 'Hound Dog'.

In 1986 she remembered David having a tin guitar and a record player "when no one else had one".

1957

The beginning of the year is auspicious: David meets George Underwood, when the pair of 10-year-olds enrol with the 18th Bromley Wolf Cubs at St Mary's church hall, College Road (where the scout troop convenes on Friday evenings).

"We got on really well from the start," said Underwood in 1993. They become inseparable. Underwood is undoubtedly David's closest friend during their childhood and teenage years, and the affinity they feel borders on the telepathic. They still have alternative names for each other: David is Robert and George is Michael.

Yet the ambidexterity they share – both play guitar and other instruments with their right hands but write with their left – prompts a difficult spell for David at his school, he later revealed. "I spent a whole miserable year having to write with my right hand at Burnt Ash," he said in 1994. "It was the worst year. I got really mixed up."

Monday 15 April

David accompanies Kristina Paulsen to a local screening of *The Hunchback of Notre Dame*, starring Charles Laughton. On returning to Plaistow Grove, Mrs Jones informs Paulsen that her mother – David's aunt Una Burns – has died earlier that day.

Summer

Along with Dudley Chapman, George Underwood and others in the cub scout troop, David attends summer camp on a farm near Bognor Regis in West Sussex.

For a brief period David sings in St Mary's choir, along with Underwood and MacCormack, though formal Christianity does not loom large at home. "My father was one of the few I knew who had a lot of understanding of other religions," David said in

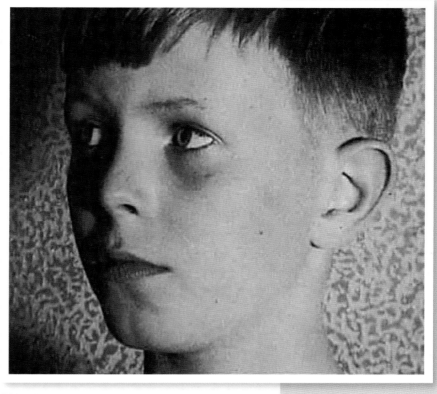

1994. "He – this is an abuse of the word – 'tolerated' Buddhists or Muslims or Hindus or Mohammedans, whatever. And he was a great humanitarian in those terms. I think some of that was passed on to me, and encouraged me to become interested in other religions. There was no enforced religion, though he didn't particularly care for English religion – Henry's religion. Oh God!"

September

David begins his final year at Burnt Ash Junior School.

In adult life, David has never shown any interest in football, but as a 10-year-old he makes the Burnt Ash first 11.

OPPOSITE PAGE

TOP: Burnt Ash school picture, 1955.

BOTTOM: Raglan Primary School, Bromley.

THIS PAGE

TOP: At home in Plaistow Grove, 1957.

BOTTOM LEFT: Plaistow Grove, David's family home for over 15 years.

BOTTOM RIGHT: David's elder half-brother, Terence Guy Adair Burns.

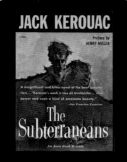

JACK KEROUAC

The Subterraneans

1958

PUBLICATION of Jack Kerouac's novella *The Subterraneans*. In 1977 David released an instrumental titled 'Subterraneans' on his album *Low*.

March

RELEASE of Chuck Berry's single 'Johnny B. Goode'/ 'Around And Around' in the US. The B-side was covered by David and considered for inclusion on the 1972 album *Ziggy Stardust*, but was replaced during the final track selection. It was issued as 'Round And Round' on the B-side of 'Drive-In Saturday' in 1973.

Saturday 22 December

BROADCAST begins on BBC TV of Nigel Kneale's six-part sci-fi serial *Quatermass And The Pit*, a favourite of David's. He created his own version of the programme's music on stage in the mid-60s when he and group The Lower Third performed the *Quatermass* theme 'Mars, The Bringer Of War'.

TOP: Mrs Baldry's class of 1957–1958, Burnt Ash Junior School. David Jones third from right, back row.

RIGHT: Burnt Ash Junior School first 11 football team, 1958. David Jones seated second row, extreme left.

BOTTOM: St Mary's, Bromley, the scene of David's first paid performance for singing – in the church choir – and the location of his first encounter with George Underwood.

Burnt Ash Junior

1958

January

David sits his 11-plus exams for selection for his secondary education starting in the autumn.

Monday 19 May

Kent Education Committee notifies John Jones that his son has a choice between Bromley Grammar and the new Bromley Technical School which is to open that autumn. David and his father visit both schools (Mr Jones' initial choice is the Grammar) but David prefers Bromley Tech and revealed in April 2001: "So, with no real battle, I got my choice."

Monday 14 July

David is interviewed by Bromley Council's education officer to determine not only his suitability for Bromley Tech, but also his future career plans.

Thursday 24 July

On leaving Burnt Ash Junior School, David is chosen to present his teacher Mrs Baldry with a class-bought gift of a garden seat. This farewell gesture makes her cry, much to her pupils' surprise.

August

As members of the cub scout troop, David and George Underwood join a summer camp on the Isle of Wight. One evening they perform their favourite songs, David on a skiffle-style string bass made from a tea-chest and Underwood on ukulele.

The songs comprise hits of the day: 'Tom Dooley', 'Putting On The Style', 'Gambling Man', 'The Ballad Of Davy Crockett' and '16 Tons'.

One of the scouts was neighbour Barrie Jackson, who lived opposite David at 23 Plaistow Road. "I felt protective towards him," said Jackson in 1992. "He was very small and when all the boys gathered together in the tent telling rude jokes, David sat aside in the corner most disgruntled, not at all impressed."

September

David starts at the all-boys Bromley Tech, which is situated in Oakley Road, Keston, a couple of miles from the town centre. This necessitates a journey on the 410 bus each day, usually in the company of Underwood.

Attendance at Bromley Tech (now Ravens Wood School for Boys) marks a change in David's outlook; youthful rebellion sets in and David's budding

interest in music and fashion diverts attention from schoolwork.

As David's musical interests blossom, he buys *Melody Maker* and *New Musical Express* every week, keeping copies in a pile in the narrow downstairs hallway.

As well as recording at home, David develops an interest in art; later occupants of the house found an early self-portrait on the back of a cupboard.

David's bedroom proves to be his sanctuary. "People who have had parents who have been hard on them have to fight to prove themselves, to gain affection, approval," he said much later. "When I lived there I would get my paints out and all she [his mother] could say was, 'I hope you're not going to make a mess.'

"And I wanted to be a fantastic artist, see the colours, hear the music, and they just wanted me turned down. I had to grow up feeling demoralised and thinking, 'They are not going to beat me'. I had to retreat into my room; so you get in the room and you carry that ruddy room around with you for the rest of your life."

Mrs Jones becomes particularly concerned and arguments between mother and son are frequent, with Mr Jones often having to intervene.

At one stage he incurs his mother's wrath when he and school-friend Alan Gonzalez decorate his bedroom walls with cave paintings copied from an encyclopaedia. "I don't think it was appreciated," Gonzalez later recalled.

Many hours are spent at Underwood's home at 69 Murray Avenue, Bromley, where David and his closest friend listen to records and talk about life and their musical ambitions. As George Underwood remembers: "Our enthusiasm was bursting at the seams, talking for hours about music, fashions, the latest fads, all things American, girls, sex and what we would become one day."

November

Terry Burns returns to Bromley, having completed three years' national service. He takes employment as an accounts clerk for publisher Amalgamated Press in Farringdon Road, close to the City of London.

There are already signs of Terry's incipient schizophrenia, which is later diagnosed as being coupled with manic depression. The 21-year-old is soon to be prescribed strong medication.

Terry's condition and later spells in psychiatric hospitals informed songs by David, such as 'All The Madmen' (1970) and their relationship is reflected in 'The Bewlay Brothers' (1971).

David has admitted that he has mythologised Terry in interviews over the years, though it is certain that his half-brother steered him towards jazz and the Beat writers of the 50s; Jack Kerouac and William Burroughs were to have the longest-lasting influence, particularly after Terry gives his half-brother a copy of Kerouac's 1957 classic *On The Road*.

1959

During his childhood, David visits John Jones' office at Dr Barnardo's headquarters in Stepney Causeway on numerous occasions, mainly to attend events his father has organised. Often accompanied by Underwood, he meets such popular entertainers of the day as TV ventriloquist Terry Hall and his puppet character Lenny The Lion.

It seems that even at this stage David's father had not entirely given up the hopes of involvement in the entertainment industry which had been dashed before the war; on Hall's death in 2007, an obituary noted that David's father worked on Hall's 1962-1963 BBC TV children's show and that he had also run the Lenny The Lion Fan Club.

On another occasion at Dr Barnardo's, David and Underwood meet US TV star Duncan Renaldo in his guise as The Cisco Kid.

"We had a wicked day," said Underwood. "The Cisco Kid was a big star with children; we watched his show faithfully every week. He told us great stories about the real Cisco Kid, who was actually – in real life – the guy who played his sidekick Pancho. For us it was quite an event."

1960

Monday 4 April

David's mother registers David's birth by declaration (since the family now lives in a different district to that in which he had been born). It is likely that this was done to provide David with a passport for a family trip to France.

September

At the start of the school year David is joined in class 3A by George Underwood and new form master Owen Frampton is appointed. Frampton is

In this year...

1959

RELEASE of Jacques Brel's album *La Valse A Mille Temps*. Tracks include 'La Mort' ('My Death'), performed by David in the early 70s (utilising the English translation by Mort Shuman and Eric Blau) and a highlight of his filmed 'retirement' concert at London's Hammersmith Odeon on 3 July 1973.

PUBLICATION of Colin MacInnes' novel of social observation *Absolute Beginners*. In 1986 the book became the basis for Julien Temple's film musical, starring David as advertising executive Vendice Partners.

Contributions to the soundtrack included the title song which reached number 2 in the UK singles chart that year.

Tuesday 3 February

DEATH of Buddy Holly in a plane crash aged 22. Holly fan, George Underwood, is devastated. "I didn't want to go to school when I heard the news. I was upset for a long time." Underwood had met Holly the previous year on the Texan's first and only UK tour, getting his autograph outside the Trocadero in Elephant & Castle, south London.

March

RELEASE of Chuck Berry's single 'Almost Grown'/'Little Queenie' in the US. The A-side was covered by David and Geoff MacCormack for a BBC radio session in 1971.

Monday 14 December

DEATH of British artist Sir Stanley Spencer (born 30 June 1891). David narrated a BBC TV *Omnibus* documentary about Spencer in March 2001.

LEFT: Photo of David retained in the school files, aged 12, in his first year at Bromley Tech, early 1959.

1960   Registered at G

DAVID (13) LEADS SPORT REVOLUTION

MEMBERS of the U.S. Navy, stationed in London, are helping the underdog side in a minor English sport revolution. And if the influence of the revolution's leader, 13-year-old David Jones, of Plaistow-grove, Bromley, is felt, English rugby could be joined by American football.

It all started when David's father, Mr. Heywood Jones, purchased a short-wave radio with evenings of musical relaxation in mind for the family. Once his son David discovered that the U.S. Armed Forces Network in Germany broadcast recorded American football games, the wireless was put to far different use. David would not miss a game.

He wrote to the U.S. Navy's London headquarters recently telling of his passion for football, and asking if someone could send him some magazines about it. He not only received the magazines, but was invited to visit the headquarters to watch football

movies. As he watched them, Petty Officers Stan Lucas, the captain of the Navy rugby team in London, and Larry Farmer stood by to tell him the finer points and explain rules.

Then, much to his amazement, David was presented with a helmet, set of shoulder pads and a football, all of which had been donated by a local Air Force base.

Lucas and Farmer took David, with equipment on, to Grosvenor-square, and ran him through several plays. His father, who comes from a family of avid rugby enthusiasts, stood by scratching his head, perplexed.

When asked if he might try organising a team, David said he didn't think so because equipment was too expensive. He said he plays rugby at school—scrum half-back, a near equivalent to the American football quarter-back position.

It is a safe bet that the people of Bromley may soon be scratching their heads, too, when David introduces "sand-lot football" to the youngsters in one of the parks.

NO COMMENT !

TOP RIGHT: David and George Underwood in front of the American Embassy, Grosvenor Square, with the captain of the US Navy rugby team, petty officer Stan Lucas, 1960. Note David's winkle-pickers and Underwood's Hy-Poynters.

ABOVE: Front page, *Bromley & Kentish Times*, 11 November 1960.

an art teacher with a fresh approach to secondary education whose son Peter will go on to make his own mark in popular music.[1]

David has described Owen Frampton as "an inspiration to all. It was an experiment for him to try and get us involved in art at a younger age. I think three-fourths of our class actually did go on to art school, which is a hell of a proportion."

Owen Frampton (who died in 2005) remembered David as "a quiet, well-mannered boy with a tightly knit group of school friends. [He] worked well at his art and always enjoyed his artwork."

Frampton establishes a new art stream for students interested in visual creativity. "I went to one of the first art-oriented high schools in England, where one could take an art course from the age of 12-13, as opposed to waiting until 17, when you go to art school," David said in 1998. "There was a strong bias towards art from when I was quite young."

His sports master, the late Ted Ward, remembered David's strength as a sprinter and his above-average abilities as a hurdler and basketball player.

By this time David is experimenting with looks and styles of haircut and attire, often modifying the school uniform. Buying the latest modes of shoes and boots, particularly the highly fashionable Denson's Hy-Poynters, David starts a school fad for tapered trousers, until even Frampton, the most liberal of the school's teachers, calls a halt with a class lecture on how adaptation of regulation clothing will not be tolerated.

David also routinely changes the colour of his hair. "It was probably only food dye or something removable," said music teacher Brian Lane. "The next day he would put the colour right, when asked to."

At the same time as Owen Frampton joins the staff, his son Peter (three years David's junior) begins schooling at Bromley Tech. Soon he comes into contact with David, and later recalled them singing and playing guitar together on the stairs in the block which housed the art department.

Underwood participated: "There was a stairway leading from our form room which had good acoustics and we'd sit on the steps. I'd be playing guitar and David would sing. We did Buddy Holly and Everly Brothers stuff. He was a good harmoniser."

1. Peter Frampton (born 1950) became a major pop star as a member of The Herd and Humble Pie (with another of David's friends, Steve Marriott) and carved out a successful solo career which peaked in the mid-70s with the release of double live album *Frampton Comes Alive!* In 1987 Frampton joined David as guitarist on his Glass Spider tour. To announce this, they appeared together at a press conference at London's Players Theatre on 20 March 1987, attended by Peter's father.

November

David uses a long-wave radio to pick up US Armed Forces broadcasts of music and sports events. This leads to his first significant press coverage, as the subject of a front-page article in the *Bromley & Kentish Times*.

He writes to the US Embassy in Grosvenor Square, central London, about his interest in American football, and is invited along to learn more on the subject accompanied by his father and Underwood.

"He'd been listening to the American football results on Forces radio and got the bug, so wrote to the Embassy for more information," said Underwood. "They were under the impression he was well into it but, in fact, it was only a couple of weeks before that he'd become keen."[1]

David is presented with a football outfit and helmet, which he takes to school the following day. "While everyone else was kicking a soccer ball around, there was this little boy in the playground, in big padded shoulders and a helmet and carrying an American football; it was quite bizarre really," said Underwood.

In the photograph which appears in the local paper, David sports the cool collegiate look, with a haircut mimicking that of new US President John Kennedy.

"David was a real JFK fan and he went to the barber's and asked for what was then called the JFK Cut," said Underwood. "It was a popular haircut at the time."

1. David's fascination with American sport didn't end there; he later became involved with a UK-based American baseball team (▸ Summer 1962). In 1965 David told his girlfriend Dana Gillespie of his interest in American football, showing her a scrapbook of local newspaper reports featuring himself. Among US historical figures of interest to David were the frontiersmen Davy Crockett and, of course, Jim Bowie.

FAR LEFT: John and Peggy Jones.

LEFT: John Jones picks up a cheque for Dr Barnardo's at a car showroom in east London in the late 50s.

ABOVE: *Strange People* by Frank Edwards, first published 1961.

1961

Friday 31 March – Monday 3 April

David takes part in an Easter holiday school trip to a hotel in Exmouth, south Devon. He wins the inter-school table tennis tournament.

Summer

Tension at home between David and his mother peaks over the fact that his all-consuming interests in music and art have elbowed aside time for other schoolwork. As a solution, David stays with his Aunt Pat and her husband Tony Antoniou in their house in Ealing, west London, during the school summer break. Terry also moves in; he is to be given much generous support and care by the Antonious during his troubled life.

Around this time David's attention is captured by Frank Edwards' *Strange People*, a collection of stories about malformed individuals and characters with inexplicable powers. David will explore such misfits in his later work, such as albums *Diamond Dogs* (1974), *Scary Monsters* (1980) and *1. Outside* (1995). In the early 80s he will also portray one of the most notable of these unfortunates, Joseph Merrick, in Bernard Pomerance's play *The Elephant Man*.

Thursday 20 July

The musical *Stop The World, I Want To Get Off* opens at the Queen's Theatre, London.

A visit to the show, starring all-rounder Anthony Newley in the role of Little Chap, is one of David's earliest theatrical experiences and proves revelatory, particularly Newley's use of mime to enhance his performance.[1] The minimal stage set design by Sean Kenny, who David will later encounter, also makes an impression.[2]

1. David recalled the impact of the production in 1972: "He [Newley] kept saying 'Stop the world', and the cast would freeze, and he'd come forward and rap to the audience. Then he'd say 'OK' and they'd start moving again. The girls were like machines, lifting their arms and legs up and down like clockwork. It just blew me over and I knew I wanted some of that, but I didn't know what exactly. That's when I started formulating my own style."

2. David consulted Sean Kenny in 1972 for lighting ideas for his brief UK tour of Top Rank venues. (▸ 1.9.72)

Autumn

George Underwood is invited to become the singer in popular local beat group The Konrads, replacing another vocalist (whose name is lost in the mists of time).

Formed the previous year, The Konrads consist of guitarists Neville Wills and Alan Dodds, drummer Dave Crook and bassist Rocky Chaudhari, who goes by the stage name Rocky Shahan after an actor in the TV series *Rawhide*.

Underwood also brings to the group a valuable asset: his amplifier.

Meanwhile David is developing a growing interest in the saxophone, a product of his abiding fascination with the Beats and in particular Little Richard's band.

David later claimed that Kerouac's *On The Road* provided the impetus: "That's why I bought a sax," he said. "The whole thing just fitted together so well. I wanted to be just like (the novel's central characters) Sal Paradise and Dean Moriarty and I almost made it, as much as one can within the confines of Bromley."

On occasional weekends, David travels to central London's beatnik haunt Trafalgar Square to talk to the denizens about Kerouac and the Beat movement

In this year...

1960

Thursday 21 July
RELEASE of Hollywood Argyles' single 'Alley Oop'. The song included the line 'Look at those cavemen go', which David would later appropriate for his song 'Life On Mars?'.

Saturday 22 October – Saturday 26 November
BROADCAST of *The Strange World Of Gurney Slade*, starring Anthony Newley, on ITV. David was inspired by the series, particularly the performance by Newley which influenced both his singing style and use of mime.

Thursday 22 December
BIRTH of visual artist Jean-Michel Basquiat, Brooklyn, New York.
David played the role of Warhol in Julian Schnabel's 1995 film *Basquiat*. Basquiat died the year after Warhol, in 1988.

1961

RELEASE of The Flares' single 'Footstompin'' in the US. In 1974 David performed the song on The *Dick Cavett Show* on TV. With contributions from John Lennon and Carlos Alomar, including an adjusted melody and new lyric, the song provides the basis the following year for David's first US number 1 single 'Fame'.

ABOVE AND RIGHT: Author Jack Kerouac. Kerouac's novel *On the Road*, first published in 1957.

In this year...

1962

Monday 1 January
UNSUCCESSFUL audition by The Beatles for a Decca contract with a test-recording session at the record company's studios in Broadhurst Gardens, West Hampstead, north London. The following year David and his fellow members in The Konrads failed a similar audition at the same studios.

Sunday 25 March
BROADCAST of *Pop Goes The Easel*, BBC TV documentary directed by Ken Russell about four exponents of English pop art: Peter Phillips, Peter Blake, Pauline Boty and Derek Boshier. David later bought paintings by Boshier. He also asked Boshier to create sets for his 1978 world tour, although they were eventually unused, and he contributed to the sleeves of albums *Lodger* (1979) and *Let's Dance* (1983).

generally. He later told a friend that he pestered them so much they would chase him away.

David is already an avid reader, encouraged by his father who also enjoys literature. "My father opened up my world because he taught me the habit of reading," David recalled in 1993. "I got so much information; so many of the things I wanted to do came from books."

While he is undeniably a sociable and outgoing teenager, this underlines David's insular qualities, as noted many years later by his friend George Underwood.

"He didn't actually go out very much, but preferred to stay home," said Underwood. "I'd often invite him to a party and he would say, 'No, I'm going to stay in, I've got some work to do.' No doubt that's why he became so successful!"

In 2002, David spoke about this insularity: "I was a kid that loved being in my room reading books and entertaining ideas. I lived a lot in my imagination. It was a real effort to become a social animal."

Friday 25 December

David's Christmas present from his father is a white, injection-moulded acrylic Grafton saxophone with gold keys. He sets about learning the accompaniment to a favourite Little Richard single.

1962

January

David persuades his father to help him acquire another saxophone. David, accompanied by his father, buys his second saxophone on hire purchase (a form of layaway) at a store in Tottenham Court Road in London's West End.

This is the Conn sax he will favour for his first band The Konrads and which much later he cradles in the back cover photograph of his 1973 album *Pin Ups*.

Monday 5 February

Underwood celebrates his 15th birthday with a party at his family's home in Murray Avenue. David attends and according to Underwood is inebriated. Also present is a local girl, Carol Goldsmith, whom both David and Underwood are eager to date. This fierce competition will have dramatic consequences.

"Both David and I really fancied her," explained Underwood many years later. "During my birthday party I managed to get a date with her at the local youth club the following Friday, which I told David about."

Friday 9 February

In the early evening, as Underwood prepares for his

date, he receives a call from David, who informs him that Goldsmith wishes to back out of the date, but is too embarrassed to tell Underwood herself.

"David said Carol didn't want to go out with me after all, and asked if he could apologise for her," recalled Underwood.

"I was upset, wondering why she didn't want to speak to me directly. Anyway, I decided to go to the youth club, albeit later than originally intended. There, Carol's best friend told me that she had waited an hour for me and thought I had stood her up.

"I realised then what had happened; David had tricked me. I couldn't believe he would do that."

Monday 12 February

In the morning, a fight occurs in Bromley Tech playground after Underwood overhears David bragging to friends on the bus on the way to school that he was dating Goldsmith.

"By the time I got to the school I had had enough," said Underwood. "I saw a friend in the playground and I told him what David had done. He said, 'If that happened to me, I'd smack him one'.

"I'm afraid that's exactly what I did. David wasn't capable of fighting me so I thought that one short sharp punch would deliver the message. I wasn't wearing a ring or holding a battery – those stories are rubbish. I certainly never intended to cause him real damage.

"After I punched him, David went to have his eye bandaged by the school nurse, and, to his credit, he told the teachers he had fallen over, so as not to get me into trouble."[1]

David is attended by school secretary Sheila Cassidy before being taken to Farnborough Hospital, Orpington by headmaster Frederick French for treatment. He is given the all-clear and returns home to recuperate.

1. "David's family were really mad with me and for a time there was talk of me being prosecuted for assault," said Underwood. "I cried when I spoke to David's father about it. In the end nothing came of it, and we made up straight away, but I felt bad for a long time.

"The doctor asked me if I had been wearing a ring as he was surprised that the damage had just been caused by a fist.

"David and I have never spoken about the incident, but I don't really need to talk to him about it; he knew why I punched him."

Wednesday, 14 February

Complications set in and David is taken by his father to specialist treatment centre Moorfields Eye Hospital in the City of London. "I had a black eye and then a couple of days later the eye just exploded," David recalled. "My dad rushed me to the hospital and I had an emergency operation on it. The only other person I've seen with eyes like this is Little Richard."

David is kept in for treatment on his left pupil, which has remained permanently dilated. The medical term for pupils of unequal size is anisocoria. Both eyes are blue but the enlarged pupil gives a green effect.

David later spoke of the hospital's concern. "At first they thought I'd lose my eye," he said. "I was scared stiff, but in the end it turned out that one of the muscles which controls the pupil was damaged.

"For quite a while I was very embarrassed about it. Although I could see very well out of the eye, it made me self-conscious. But as I've grown older I've got to like it. It makes me feel different, distinctive!"

While David recovers in hospital, Underwood writes him a letter of atonement, though forgets to include the last – and most important – page before sealing the envelope.

"When I went to see him at the hospital he was puzzled," said Underwood. "David said something like, 'Funny letter that George, it just suddenly finished…'"

Spring

During a convalescence which lasts a couple of months, David starts to apply himself to learning to play the new saxophone bought in Tottenham Court Road. The family home already houses an upright piano, on which David has picked out his first basic chord sequences. Within a couple of years he is also learning acoustic guitar.

At the suggestion of jazz fanatic half-brother Terry, David arranges saxophone lessons with local legend Ronnie Ross,[1] who lives in neighbouring Orpington at 6 Irvine Way. These take place once a week over a two-month period.

"He was conservative, very shy and always on time," recalled Ross (who was born in Calcutta in 1932 and died in 1992). "I showed him how to blow, how to breathe and a little about how to read music. We talked about Charlie Parker and his records. I told him that, unless he really wanted to do it, not to come, but he stuck it out for that time and then disappeared. He did learn to read a little."

1. In a 1964 press release David (by then solo artist Davie Jones) is quoted as saying: "My idol on saxophone has always been Ronnie Ross. So I looked his name up in the phone book and asked him if he would give me lessons." Ross agreed, but after Davie played him a few bars Ross's comment was: "Right, now we can start working on you, that was bloody awful!" In 1972 David booked Ross for the recording session for Lou Reed's 'Walk On The Wild Side'. The saxophonist played the short, heartfelt tenor sax solo which ends the song.

Friday 6 April/Monday 9 April

As part of an effort to raise money for a sports pavilion at Bromley Tech, Owen Frampton organises a school pageant which takes place over two days.

One-off band George & The Dragons plays two performances, one on each day. The line-up is Underwood and schoolmates Peter Doughty, Ian Hosie and Del Taylor. It is likely that, had he not been nursing his wounded eye, David would have taken part.

Also on the bill are The Little Ravens, led by Peter Frampton and named after the school emblem (which was designed by Frampton senior). The show raises £50.

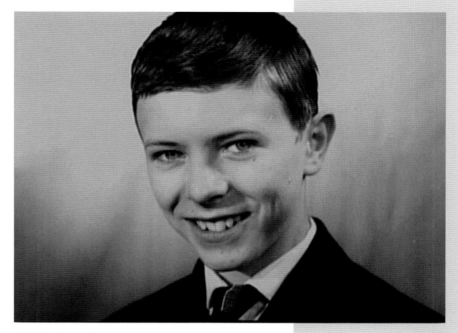

June

David begins rehearsals on saxophone with The Konrads; he'd been pressing vocalist George Underwood to become involved in the group for some time. "David was dying to get into the band," recalled Underwood, "he regularly asked if I could get him in." Once rehearsals are underway, David takes his last lesson with Ronnie Ross, excitedly telling his teacher about the group he has joined.

Saturday 16 June

▶ David is part of The Konrads' line-up for their performance at Bromley Tech's PTA fête, on the entrance steps of the main school building. Now a six-piece, they have been added to the bill as a result of David's request to music teacher Brian Lane.

Consisting in the main of songs by star instrumentalists The Shadows, the gig runs well over time and causes such a commotion among the gathered schoolboys that it is brought to an abrupt halt when Lane cuts the power.

David has since said of this, his first formal public performance: "I was incredibly nervous but it went OK."

Friday 22 June

The Kentish Times reports on the day with the headline 'Nearly 4,000 at School Fete': "In a continental style cafe one could sip soft drinks while

TOP: David at 14 years old, prior to his eye injury.

MIDDLE: A punch thrown during a playground fight is the cause of David's anisocoria (unequally sized pupils).

BOTTOM: David's sax teacher, Ronnie Ross.

1962

TOP: Bromley Tech stairs that inspired Owen Frampton's design for *The Raven's Wing* school periodical.

BOTTOM LEFT: David's art teacher Owen Frampton (photographed in 1972 by his son Clive at Bromley Tech) and Bromley Tech's school emblem designed by Frampton.

BOTTOM RIGHT: Entrance steps, Bromley Technical School (now Ravens Wood School), the setting for David's first live performance on 16 June 1962.

a group of young instrumentalists played music on guitars, saxophone and drums." The report misspells the group's name (as The Conrads).

Summer

▶ The Konrads pick up a small following and play local venues such as St David's College in West Wickham, Ye Olde Stationmaster on Old Hill near Chislehurst Caves, Farningham Country Club (a regular weekend gig) and the upstairs room of The Bell in Bromley.

A key booking is the large Beckenham Ballroom, at 2-4 High Street, next to Beckenham Junction railway station.

"The Konrads did cover songs of anything that was in the charts," said David many years later. "We were one of the best cover bands in the area and we worked a lot."

David also takes some tentative stabs at lyric-writing, initially on his own and later with guitarist Neville Wills. Occasionally The Konrads slip one of his compositions into their repertoire, but these slow the pace and subdue the audience eager to dance to familiar hits.

The Konrads' set ranges from covers of songs by Neville Wills' favourites The Shadows and Underwood's Elvis and Conway Twitty tunes to such rock'n'roll staples as Chuck Berry's 'Johnny B. Goode', Sam Cooke's 'Twisting The Night Away', Little Richard's 'Lucille', Bruce Channel's 'Hey Baby' and Frankie Laine's 'Jezebel'.

Initially, David is enlisted to play saxophone to expand The Konrads' sound. Soon he is also singing two recent hits at every gig: Curtis Lee's 'A Night At Daddy Gee's' and Joe Brown's 'A Picture Of You'.

The slot provides David with valuable experience and self-belief, as he later revealed in BBC TV's 1975 Omnibus documentary *Cracked Actor*:

"I was never very confident of my voice you see, and I couldn't decide whether I wanted to play jazz or rock'n'roll. And as I wasn't very good at jazz and I could fake it pretty well on rock'n'roll, I played rock'n'roll."

David also conjures up stage names for himself: Luther Jay, Alexis Jay and later Dave Jay, telling the other band members he found his surname "boring".

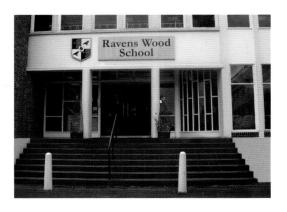

While cutting their teeth on the live music circuit, David and Underwood attend practice sessions for the junior team of the Blue Jays, a local baseball club which meets at Beckenham Place Park.[1] Underwood drops out after a few weeks but David practises a while longer with a new baseball glove bought for him by his father. However, he never makes the team.

During the summer, David and his parents invite school friend Brian Brough to join them for a holiday at a caravan site in Great Yarmouth.

Another Jones family holiday during this period is spent at Camber Sands on the East Sussex coast.

1. Beckenham Place Park abuts David's home in the early 70s, Haddon Hall. (▶8.69)

October

John Jones provides David with a weekly allowance of seven shillings and sixpence (the equivalent of 37.5p and a respectable sum for the time). Not unexpectedly, his son spends the bulk of the money on R&B records.

David's main source of vinyl is Medhurst's, a large local department store on Bromley High Street, whose record section (run by a gay couple called Jimmy and Charles), is as diverse as any he found in central London. The owners particularly like David, and give him a generous discount.

Another great enticement is counter girl Jane Greene, three or four years his senior. He regularly smooches with Greene in the listening-booth.

Among current purchases are Screamin' Jay Hawkins 'I Put A Spell On You'/'Little Demon' and The Alan Freed Rock'n'Roll Band's 'Right Now, Right Now'.

Freed's 1957 film *Mister Rock And Roll* has already made a great impression, particularly the performances by Little Richard and his band. "When I saw the sax line-up [in the film] that was it," David said in 1993. "I didn't want to do anything else in life but play the saxophone."

Saturday 13 October

David and Underwood witness a live performance by Little Richard at Woolwich Granada, topping a bill including Sam Cooke, Jet Harris & The Jet Blacks, Sounds Incorporated and Gene Vincent (who sings from the front row of the stalls due to work permit problems).

By this time US rock'n'roll is being rudely elbowed out of the art colleges and pubs of south-east England by the rise of British R&B.

David and Underwood regularly travel along the Thames to the clubs in Richmond, south-west of London, where the new music is being played. They visit the Crawdaddy Club at the Richmond Athletic Ground on Friday evenings to watch performances by the likes of Gary Farr & The T-Bones and The Tridents, the experimental four-piece featuring Jeff Beck before he joined The Yardbirds.

Over the coming months, David also witnesses

LEFT: 'Dave Jay' with The Konrads resplendent in their new stage uniforms, early 1963. David is cradling his original acrylic Grafton saxophone. The jackets were actually green (see overleaf), not blue – this photographic anomaly has been caused by the processing of the transparency at the time (the photos were not hand-coloured).

many early gigs at the legendary R&B club on Eel Pie Island, travelling back to Sundridge Park on the milk train.

Late October

▶ The Konrads' performance at Shirley Parish Hall near Croydon, south London, is the first to feature new drummer Dave Hadfield, who has recently left the Merchant Navy.

Lancashire-born Hadfield had placed an ad in Furlong's record shop looking for fellow musicians. This proclaimed he had drummed for Britain's biggest rock star of the period, Cliff Richard (they had attended the same school in Cheshunt, Herts, and played in a band together). His ad is answered by Neville Wills, and Hadfield is invited to meet David and Alan Dodds at the Wimpey bar opposite Furlong's on Bromley High Street.[1]

Hadfield meets the whole band for the first time at a rehearsal at Wills' parents' house in north Bromley. Underwood is particularly upset that Dave Crook has been abruptly dropped to make way for Hadfield and will only make a handful of appearances with the new line-up before leaving the band himself.

For his part, Hadfield isn't told about Crook and believes the band is just forming. "No one honestly mentioned a previous drummer to me, at all," said Hadfield in 2010, "I thought they had only just formed."

Hadfield is dating a fan of The Konrads,[2] Stella Patton (now Gall)[3] who has seen them perform at Beckenham's Top Ten Club. After a while, Hadfield persuades the group to take on Stella and her sister Christine as backing singers; for the next year The Konrads appear as an eight-piece at larger venues.

"Songs such as 'Bobby's Girl' and 'The Locomotion' were being released and female vocalists were becoming fashionable," said Stella Gall later,

adding, "There was always a spark about David. He was a real showman and quite a good-looking lad. He was also starting to write songs which he'd note down in an exercise book."

1. Around this time a local photographer, Peter Madge, offers to manage the band, but a lack of music business contacts isn't impressive and they turn him down.
2. David hyphenated the band's name when he designed and painted the logo onto Hadfield's bass drum. The hyphen is dropped after David leaves the band.
3. Stella Gall remained in the Bromley area and worked as a nurse. Her younger sister Christine, later Christine Gerety, died in 2007.

Saturday 17 November

▶ The Konrads perform at Cudham Village Hall, two miles south of Orpington, with a set list running to 58 songs. David sings eight numbers, including a cover of 'Let's Dance' by Chris Montez.

Upset over the dismissal of his friend Dave Crook, Underwood decides to leave the band. Wasting no time he begins to gig with the first of a number of bands, The Spitfires, with local guitarist Paul Bennett (who had been in a line-up of another band on the circuit, The Wranglers). The Spitfires take their name from popular venue the Hillsiders Youth Club, which is situated close to Biggin Hill airfield.

December

A small-scale publicity campaign is launched. The Konrads post a limited quantity of cheaply printed personalised Christmas cards to friends and those they hope will be interested in booking them.

The group are photographed on the front of the card in their stage gear with silver waistcoats, perched in a row on a stone balustrade in Church House Gardens, central Bromley. The sax player's name is signed 'Dave Jay'.[1]

1. David sometimes styles his autograph to use a saxophone motif for the 'J'.

In this year...

1962

June
RELEASE of Bob Dylan's eponymous debut album in the UK. The album featured 'Song To Woody', the title of which David parodied with his tribute 'Song For Bob Dylan' on his 1971 album *Hunky Dory*.
David has also said that Dylan's debut "became an integral part of what I wanted to eventually do".
FOUNDING of management and booking agency NEMS Enterprises by Brian Epstein, manager of The Beatles and many other acts. Epstein co-promoted David's first tour in December 1964, and in the late 60s and early 70s David was contracted to NEMS for live bookings.

Wednesday 24 October
CONCERT by James Brown at the Apollo Theatre on Harlem's 125th Street, New York. The performance was recorded and released the following year as *The Apollo Theatre Presents: In Person! The James Brown Show*. David was introduced to the record by Geoff MacCormack and it influenced some of his own recordings such as 'Rock 'n' Roll Suicide'. (▶ 6.6.72)

THIS PAGE

RIGHT: George Underwood's personal note of money still owed to him by The Konrads.

BOTTOM: Bromley Tech, 1963. From left: schoolmate Brian Brough, David (sporting dyed, 'Joe Brown' haircut) and Peter Doughty – who drummed in George Underwood's and Peter Frampton's school bands.

OPPOSITE PAGE

TOP: The Konrads' eight-piece line-up, 1963.

MIDDLE AND BOTTOM: The Konrads' Christmas card, 1962 (front and inside). From left: Rocky Shahan, Dave Jay, Neville Wills, Alan Dodds and Dave Hadfield.

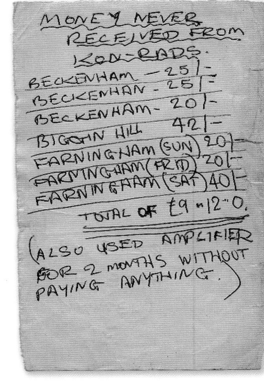

1963

January

The Konrads shift their rehearsals from a church hall on Bromley Common to another in Masons Hill, closer to the centre of town. Complaints about the volume from local residents soon prompt another move, to a scout hut in Prospect Place.

George Underwood's role as vocalist is taken by local lad Roger Ferris. Around this time Rocky Shahan[1] temporarily leaves the band and is replaced by a bassist, only remembered by his first name, John.

In Hadfield,[2] David has an ally in his quest for a more ambitious sound and stage performance. New outfits are brought in, comprising green corduroy jackets, brown mohair trousers, suede shoes, white shirts and striped ties.

1. Chaudhari (Rocky Shahan) resumes his place in The Konrads later in the year. He remained in touch with David for a number of years; future manager Ken Pitt met him once when visiting David and his then girlfriend Hermione Farthingale at their flat in Kensington in 1968.

2. Hadfield later founded a studio, Maximum Sounds, in south London where he produced acts including Manfred Mann (sometimes working as David Heath-Hadfield). In 2000, his instrumental 'Bert's Apple Crumble' featured on the soundtrack of film *Gangster Number One*. Recorded as a B-side in 1967 by The Quik at Hadfield's studio (and released on Deram), it became a dance-floor hit in the late 60s.

February

John Jones arranges a photo session of The Konrads' new line-up with the assistance of Dr Barnardo's in-house photographer Roy Ainsworth.

These are taken one Saturday afternoon on stage at Stepney Assembly Rooms, 18-26 Stepney Causeway in east London, which adjoins the charity's headquarters.

Most of the shots are of the core five members, though others include singers Roger Ferris and Stella and Christine Patton.

In the mid-90s, David purchased the archive of colour and black and white shots from Ainsworth, who recalled that David had also provided cover designs for the charity's magazine in the early 60s. "Unfortunately they were a bit too avant-garde for us," he said. "They were pretty way-out for the time."

John Jones' secretary Winifred Bunting remembered how proud he was of David: "He thought his son was absolutely marvellous. He always said he was going to do something great and talked about him all the time."

Spring

David is unsuccessful in persuading The Konrads to adopt a Wild West image. Similarly his proposal that the group change its name to Ghost Riders is rejected.

David's enduring fascination for American history is underlined when he announces he is considering changing his name to Jim Bowie. *The Adventures*

In this year...

1963

PUBLICATION by the Hogarth Press of *The Seed And The Sower* by Laurens Van Der Post. Nagisa Oshima's 1983 film *Merry Christmas Mr Lawrence*, starring David and Tom Conti, was based on this book.

FORMATION of new group Peter King & The Majestics in Hull, Yorkshire. In their ranks is a lead vocalist/ harmonica player Benny Marshall, who later formed The Rats (featuring Mick Ronson) and became a brief member of David's band Hype in 1970. (▶ 17.4.70)

Of Jim Bowie had been a popular TV show in the US between 1956 and 1958. Though not screened in the UK, the programme created international interest in the legend of this pioneer and soldier, whose story was covered in the 1960 John Wayne film *The Alamo*.

May

▶ When The Konrads play a regular Friday night at the Hillsiders Youth Club in the Women's Institute Hall, Lebanon Gardens, Biggin Hill, Kent, audience member Richard Ward takes photographs. It is only 12 years later, after David has achieved worldwide fame, that Ward realises he has some of the earliest images of the superstar in performance.

For a short period, David takes a Saturday job at Vic Furlong's record shop (where his father bought David his first saxophone).

"He was always a bit of a dreamer in that I'd give him a job to do, come back in about an hour and he was still chatting, the job unfinished, so he had to go," Furlong said in 1985.

Saturday 15 June

▶ Konrads drummer Dave Hadfield is married at St George's Parish Church in the centre of Beckenham. David and the band attend and then later The Konrads – with groom – perform in St George's Church Hall at the reception opposite the Church in Albermarle Road. They had also played at his engagement party in a house in the same road a few months earlier.

LEADING GUITAR — RHYTHM

DRUMS D.A. Hadfield

Dave Jay

Bowie

BASS

With Best Wishes for Christmas and the New Year from —

The Kon-rads
VOCAL & INSTRUMENTAL GROUP

DAVID HADFIELD (Manager)
61, OAKDENE ROAD
ORPINGTON, KENT

Tel. No. Orpington

LITTLE RICHARD

IN THE 50s, one artist above all others fired David's ambition to make music himself: Little Richard.

By the time David came by the 1957 release 'The Girl Can't Help It'/'She's Got It', he already owned a few 78s (although 45s had been in circulation for five years they were far from the dominant format), including his first purchase, Fats Domino's November 1956 hit 'Blueberry Hill'.[1]

Like many another teen of the time, David was also a fan of Elvis Presley. More unusually he liked the popular jazz clarinetist Acker Bilk: "The first person I ever really listened to was Acker Bilk," David recalled. "Acker Bilk was a jazzer when there was a boom in trad jazz. Acker Bilk led it all."

But the boisterous, sax-driven 'The Girl Can't Help It' and in particular 'She's Got It' captured his imagination.

David was given the 7in 45rpm single by his father; an American had donated his collection of records (some unavailable in the UK at that time) to Dr Barnardo's and John Jones picked out a batch for his son.

Since the family's record player was restricted to playing 78s, David was forced to develop a method of slowing the deck down by hand to hear the tracks at the correct speed.

Little Richard's flamboyant sound made such an impact that David was soon voraciously consuming rock'n'roll, ordering 78s at either Vic Furlong's record shop or Medhurst's on Bromley High Street.

The new music was already sweeping the nation's youth; the BBC had launched its dedicated pop programme *The Six-Five Special* in February 1957, and Teddy Boys were still a potent force, as David recalled in 1993: "It was exciting seeing them still on the streets. I remember two of them having a fight. I was on the other side of the road and it was really exciting. I was only about ten or 11 and couldn't take my eyes off them. And they had chains. Bicycle chains. I didn't run away, I wanted to watch them beating the shit out of each other."

Youth movie *Mister Rock And Roll* (which came out in the US in 1957 but is likely to have been seen by David in the early 60s) was to provide further revelation. Fronted by controversial American DJ Alan Freed, the man who had coined the term rock'n'roll and would later be jailed in a payola scandal, *Mister Rock And Roll* featured Little Richard and his band performing their raucous 'Lucille'.

"When I saw the sax line-up that was it," David said in 1993. "I didn't want to do anything else in life but play the saxophone."

It was this which prompted David to press his father to buy the Grafton saxophone (made from acrylic with ebonite reeds) which became his Christmas present in 1961.

David witnessed Little Richard perform twice in his formative years. On Saturday 13 October 1962, The Georgia Peach (as he was known) appeared at the Granada in Woolwich, south-east London with a teenage organ-player Billy Preston (later to work with The Rolling Stones and The Beatles).[2] Little Richard topped a bill which included Sam Cooke, former Shadow Jet Harris & The Jet Blacks, British instrumental act Sounds Incorporated[3] and rocker Gene Vincent.

A year later, on Thursday 31 October 1963, David and George Underwood were in the audience at the Lewisham Odeon[4] for another package tour headlined by Little Richard.

Rather than bring his own musicians from the US, the rock'n'roller was backed by Sounds Incorporated, who David rated highly, as he mentioned in a 1987 interview: "(Sounds Incorporated) were our only horn band, the only band that knew anything about saxophones. There was one other, Peter Jay and the Jaywalkers, but they weren't as good. Sounds Incorporated were the ones. I used to love all those sax players, 'cause that's what I wanted to do."

This concert was the first time David witnessed The Rolling Stones live, and he was particularly impressed with how Mick Jagger dealt with a heckler who told him to "get a haircut". Jagger retorted: "What? And look like you?"

In a 1987 interview, David mistakenly recalled the venue as the Brixton Odeon: "Little Richard – I saw him at Brixton Odeon. It must have been 1963, 'cause the Stones opened for him. And Little Richard was just unreal. Unreal man, we'd never seen anything like that. It was still mohair suits then – I mean, just great suits – baggy trousers and all that."

1. In 1975, during the filming of *The Man Who Fell To Earth*, David attended a Fats Domino concert in Albuquerque, New Mexico. A visit backstage to meet the artist after the show was unsuccessful; the dressing room door closed in his face.

2. The previous night The Beatles (whose first single was released that week) had supported Little Richard at the Tower Ballroom, Wallasey. This occasion was their introduction to Preston.

3. Later David became friendly with Sounds Incorporated saxophonist, Griff West.

4. David is unclear about the precise venue. Lewisham is the most likely since it was the closest to Bromley. Other possible venues are the New Victoria Cinema (where the package played on 29 September), Streatham Odeon (1 October) and the Hammersmith Odeon (11 October). Also featured on this tour of 11 acts were the Everly Brothers and singer Mickie Most, who would later produce a couple of David's songs. David played a sell-out concert at the Lewisham Odeon on his Aladdin Sane tour. (▶ 24.5.73)

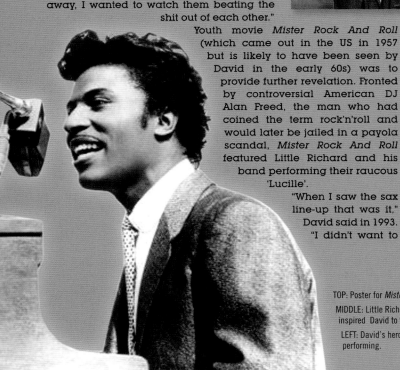

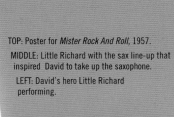

TOP: Poster for *Mister Rock And Roll*, 1957.

MIDDLE: Little Richard with the sax line-up that inspired David to take up the saxophone.

LEFT: David's hero Little Richard performing.

ANY DAY NOW | DAVID BOWIE | THE LONDON YEARS

July

David finishes school with a single exam pass: an art O-Level. Among others leaving Bromley Tech at this time is Michael Finnissy, who will go on to become an important classical composer under the patronage of West Coast acid-rockers the Grateful Dead.[1]

With the school's approval, David leaves a week before the end of term so that he can take up a post as a paste-up artist with the title Junior Visualiser at commercial art studio Nevundy-Hurst in Old Bond Street, close to Piccadilly in London's West End (though the school's records show that the company he joined is called the Design Group Ltd).

The job has been found for David by Owen Frampton. However, he is reluctant to make a go of it, believing it will be a hindrance to his musical ambitions.

"He only took the job for his father's sake," Peggy Jones said many years later. "His father thought that all this business with groups and music could well be a passing fad and that, at least if he spent a year or so at work, it would give him some stable grounding to fall back on. So David went to work there, though not without protest. I can remember him coming home and moaning about his 'blooming job'."

Luckily for David, his manager Ian is "a groovy modernist with Gerry Mulligan-style short crop haircut and Chelsea boots". Ian is just as passionate about music and cuts David some slack, sending him on enjoyable errands to buy records on his behalf.

These trips are often to Dobell's record store at 77 Charing Cross Road, where he buys for example, Bob Dylan's debut album (because he likes the look of Dylan), and two copies of the 1961 album *The Folk Lore Of John Lee Hooker*, one for himself.

1. Not all David's fellow students will pursue respectable careers. He later related how, during a US tour in 1972, one former class

member came to watch him perform and visited him backstage. "It was somebody I used to go to school with who ended up as a very big drugs dealer down in South America," he said in 1993. "He flew in to see one of the shows and reintroduced himself. He was the full bit, with the clothes and the piece and everything. I thought, 'My God, him!' This individual would inspire the line in his 1973 song 'Panic In Detroit', 'He looked a lot like Che Guevara...'

Another Bromley Tech alumnus is playwright and novelist Hanif Kureishi, who attended the school in the 70s and later forged an artistic association with David. Kureishi's book *The Buddha Of Suburbia* is set in the locale and includes references to the school. David supplied the soundtrack to BBC TV's dramatisation of the book in 1993.

June/July

After witnessing a performance by The Konrads at Orpington Civic Hall, Bob Knight, assistant to The Rolling Stones' manager Eric Easton, invites them to meet his boss.

During the meeting, David is greatly impressed when Mick Jagger drops in for a chat with Easton.[1]

The manager says he is interested in witnessing an audition, and tells the group to prepare over the coming weeks.

1. David's first substantial meeting with Mick Jagger will be in ten years' time, on 10 March 1973.

Thursday 29 August

The Konrads audition for Easton and Knight by recording an acetate of 'I Never Dreamed' (written by David and Alan Dodds) at Decca Records studios in Broadhurst Gardens, West Hampstead in north London.

Easton is basing his interest in signing the group on whether Decca thinks they have the potential for commercial release.

The song is chosen after much argument and deliberation; this is the only studio recording of The Konrads featuring David, who harmonises to Ferris's lead vocal.[1] In the event Decca isn't interested.[2]

FRIDAY, AUGUST 23, 1963

'Konrads to cut a disc'

ONE of the most popular local rock and roll groups, the Konrads, have been given a recording contract. The group will go into the Decca studios on Thursday to record four titles, including the popular, "I never dreamed," which was written by two of the boys, David Jones and Allan Dodds.

Leader of the group is 22-year-old drummer David Hadfield, of 61, Oakdene-road, Orpington. Also in the group are leading guitarist Neville Wills, of Lubbock-road, Chislehurst, rhythm guitarist Allan Dodds, of Shirley, "sax "-ist and singer David Jones, of Plaistow-road, Bromley, bass guitarist Rocky Shanan, of South America, and singer Roger Ferris, of 6, Winterborne-avenue, Orpington.

The group have played at many local clubs and dances since they formed last October, and have built up a quite a reputation.

A feature of their stage act is the special infra-blue lights which, when directed on their specially coated instruments, cause them to change colour—a big hit with the fans, and they already have a fan club in Bromley with more than 200 members.

TOP LEFT: The Konrads, 1963. David's plastic Grafton alto saxophone is resting on the stand to his right.

TOP RIGHT: Roger Ferris, Stella and Christine Patton and Dave Jay, 1963.

MIDDLE: Hillsiders Youth Club.

BOTTOM: *Bromley & Kentish Times* cutting, courtesy of Dave Hadfield.

David is despondent at the rejection, his lack of authority within the group, and the disagreements over which material to perform live.

1. In 2002 Dave Hadfield offered for auction at Christie's some of his Konrads archive, including a rehearsal tape of 'I Never Dreamed' recorded prior to the Decca sessions. The audition tape was discarded by Decca. An acetate exists of 'I Never Dreamed', but it is not thought to be the Decca version.

2. Easton keeps in touch with The Konrads and books them to support The Rolling Stones on tour in 1965, long after David has left the band.

Summer

While he considers how to make the final break with The Konrads, David teams up with Underwood for a couple of short-lived side projects with the assistance of a percussionist called Viv. (No one can remember his surname but, despite conjecture, this was not Viv Prince of The Pretty Things.)

Billed first as Dave's Reds & Blues and later as The Hooker Brothers, the blues trio make a few local appearances over the course of the summer, at a couple of private parties and also The Bromel Club at the Bromley Court Hotel.

The Hooker Brothers' name comes from David's purchase of *The Folk Lore Of John Lee Hooker* for his boss at Nevundy-Hurst, and the set is restricted to covers of favourite blues numbers. Hooker's 'Tupelo Blues' is performed, notably David and George add Viv's drums to enhance the traditional acoustic version of Bob Dylan's 'House Of The Risin' Sun', which had appeared on the singer-songwriter's debut LP the previous year, and Don & Bob's 'Good Morning Little Schoolgirl', a popular track in R&B circles, introduced to George by David.

David arranges The Hooker Brothers' first performance at The Bromel. With billing comprising a poster designed and drawn by Underwood and stuck on the hotel's front door, they appear as the intermission entertainment for the main act, The Mike Cotton Sound.[1]

Around this time, the restless David also rehearses for a couple of days with a group of musicians whose names cannot be traced for a soon-abandoned group called The Berries, inspired by The Hollies.

And he starts to seriously investigate home recording. "I borrowed somebody else's tape recorder," David said in 1991. "I was 15 or 16, and I'd just record a basic track on one tape machine, then play that back through the speaker, sing to it or play guitar parts over it onto the other tape recorder, backwards and forwards until there was nothing left but tape hiss, with the idea for a melody of a song way in the background. God, things haven't really changed very much now, except you don't get the tape hiss any more!"

Soon David creates an improvised home studio in his bedroom based around an Elizabethan model tape-recorder.

1. David tours with The Mike Cotton Sound in the following year.

Saturday 21 September

▶ The Konrads appear at the Civic Hall, Orpington. David later recalled: "I was originally the sax player, then our singer Roger Ferris got beaten up by some greasers at the Civic Orpington and I took over the vocals."

Autumn

The Konrads audition for a spot on UK network broadcaster Rediffusion's television talent competition *Ready, Steady, Win*. Appearing against stage scenery of cartoon musicians painted by David, they submit a one-track acetate of 'I Never Dreamed' but fail to make it past the first round so are not included in the series broadcast the following summer.

October

David presses for The Konrads to cover new release 'Can I Get A Witness' by Marvin Gaye. Written by Holland-Dozier-Holland, the song inspires many covers, including The Rolling Stones who will record their own version within three months. When the idea is rejected, David resolves to leave the group.

Thursday 24 October

▶ The Konrads top the bill at a day-long local pop talent show at Wickham Hall, Kent Road, West Wickham, Kent. David's hand-painted stage scenery is featured as the backdrop to their 11.30pm performance.

Also on the bill are The Trubeats featuring lead guitarist Peter Frampton. In contrast with the display of spirited teenage pop, interval music is provided by easy-listening pianist Hilda Holt.

Saturday 2 November

▶ The Konrads head the bill at Shirley Parish Hall, 81 Wickham Road, Croydon. Support is again supplied by The Trubeats.

OPPOSITE PAGE

TOP: The Konrads perform live at Wickham Hall, 24 October 1963. David painted the panels that formed their stage set. Rocky Shahan (far left) has returned after his departure at the beginning of the year.

MIDDLE: Original handbill for Konrads appearance at Lewisham Town Hall. One of David's final appearances with The Konrads.

BOTTOM: Adverts for gigs by The Konrads, 1963. Orpington Civic Hall and Shirley Parish Hall.

THIS PAGE

LEFT: The Konrads on stage at Stepney Assembly Rooms. Left to right: Neville Wills, Dave Hadfield (sitting), John, Alan Dodds and David.

TOP: A quiz featuring David in *Beat 64* magazine.

Sunday 24 November

▶ The Konrads appear at the South London Beat Show, an afternoon event at Lewisham Town Hall, 1 Catford Road, Catford, also featuring The Wranglers, The Vendettas, Dave Seaton and The Lyons, The Copains, The Cougars and Peter Budd & The Rebels.

Keen to join a new band, David arranges an audition with The Wranglers, while The Copains' keyboard player Tim Hinkley turns down an invitation to join The Konrads. His career as a professional musician later leads to him recording with The Rolling Stones, George Harrison, Humble Pie and Joan Armatrading.

Hailing from Bristol, Peter Budd & The Rebels are fronted by the future singer of folk/novelty act The Wurzels.

Saturday 14 December

▶ The Konrads play a Christmas dance at the Hillsiders Youth Club in Biggin Hill, Kent.

Tuesday 31 December

▶ David and Alan Dodds play their last gig with The Konrads[1] at a New Year's Eve party at Justin Hall, St David's College, Beckenham Road, West Wickham, supported by The Trubeats and The Couriers.

Even though two key members leave, the band resolves to continue and the line-up quickly adjusts. Ferris is replaced as lead singer by Rocky Shahan/ Chaudhari, and Tony Edwards is drafted in on keyboards and vibes.

As for David, he has his immediate future mapped out; teaming up again with trusted friend George Underwood, he is already planning his escape route from the humdrum routine of working life and membership of a covers band by adopting an earthier and altogether bluesier direction.

This way David will realise his ambitions to become a fully-fledged recording artist in his own right.

1. Alan Dodds went on to join the Salvation Army and is believed to have emigrated to Australia. Neville Wills died in 1981.

In this year...

1963

Friday 22 November

DEBUT by Mick Ronson as guitarist in new beat group The Mariners at Elloughton Village Hall in Hull. The band includes bassist Rick Kemp, who recalls: "I remember Mick joining The Mariners as it was the same day JFK got shot." Kemp later scored success in British folk/rock group Steeleye Span.

1964

FIRED by his live experiences with The Konrads and searching for an escape from his ad agency job, David resolves to make a go of music with George Underwood.

David is the focal point on vocals and saxophone when they form The King Bees with three older musicians, playing hard-edged R&B.

A cheeky appeal for financial backing to magnate John Bloom results in contact with agent/manager Leslie Conn, who also handles another unknown, Marc Bolan.

Conn signs a deal with Decca for a single, 'Liza Jane', with 'Louie, Louie Go Home' on the B-side. David leaves his day job and becomes a fully fledged professional musician.

Promotion for the single includes an appearance on *Ready Steady Go!* and BBC TV's *The Beat Room*, with David also playing saxophone.

The failure of 'Liza Jane' to chart leads to the disbandment of The King Bees. Conn has already hooked David up with The Manish Boys from Kent, though tensions arise over billing and David finds himself shuttling between Bromley and their base in Maidstone.

Davie Jones & The Manish Boys play R&B venues all over south-east England but struggle to make an impact. David makes his first appearance at Soho club the Marquee, which will become a significant venue in his life. He also meets girlfriend Dana Gillespie there.

In an attempt to create a stir, David forms The Society For The Prevention Of Cruelty To Long-Haired Men, again appearing on national TV.

The band secure a slot on the last six dates of a tour of northern England and Scotland with The Kinks, Marianne Faithfull and Gene Pitney. However, they do not receive billing, and the year ends with few gigs arranged and no recording deal.

PREVIOUS SPREAD: Davie Jones, comfortable in his first professional record company photo session.

THIS PAGE

ABOVE: David with The King Bees. Front row, left to right: Roger Bluck, Robert Allen, Dave Howard and George Underwood.

BELOW: Leslie Conn, David's first manager (photographed in 1986).

January – February

Aside from playing a couple of gigs with The Wranglers (for whom he'd tentatively auditioned a couple of months previously), one at Biggin Hill Hillsiders Youth Club, David concentrates on forming a new group, one in which he will be the focal point.

David finds a trio working together in Fulham, south-west London: drummer Robert Allen, guitarist Roger Bluck (born Roger Beresford Fluck) and bassist Dave Howard (born Francis David Howard).

It's likely that David has recruited them via a classified advert in music weekly *Melody Maker*, though in time David will claim that they met at a barber's shop.

Allen, Bluck and Howard form the backbone of new band The King Bees, after blues harp legend Slim Harpo's song 'I'm A King Bee'. This is the standard approach of the era – for example, The Pretty Things have taken their name from a Bo Diddley track while The Rolling Stones are named after Muddy Waters' 1950s song 'Rollin' Stone'.[1]

Taking the role of lead vocalist and tenor sax player, David decides on the stage name Davie Jones and recruits George Underwood as co-vocalist, guitarist and harmonica player. The other three musicians are around five and six years older than David and Underwood, and their approach is distinctly bluesier than that of The Konrads.

"At the time we really got into the blues," said Underwood in 2008. "That's what we wanted to do with The King Bees, but we could never actually achieve the sound we were looking for."

Rehearsing at Roger Bluck's home in Tournay Road, Fulham, there are occasional live excursions, either billed as The King Bees or with Davie Jones' name up front. Wearing jeans and T-shirts with a piratical flourish – David often sports fancy high-cut boots from London's fashionable theatrical shoe supplier Anello & Davide – The King Bees focus in their set on Muddy Waters' oeuvre, including 'Got My Mojo Working' and '(I'm Your) Hoochie Coochie Man', and supplement it with a couple of Chuck Berry covers as well as Harpo's 'I'm A King Bee' and a version of the traditional song 'Little Liza Jane' as performed by Huey 'Piano' Smith on his 1957 single of the same name.

There is also a residency at the Bricklayers' Arms[2] in south London's Old Kent Road, as David recalled in 1993: "We were a very typical Americanised London rhythm and blues outfit… quite influenced by [leading R&B act of the day] The Downliners Sect. We did a lot of pub work. We played the Bricklayers' Arms quite regularly but that's not there any more. I know, because I was showing Iman around David's London last year and half of it's bloody gone."

The regularity of the Bricklayers' bookings is a consequence of a smart policy operated by the landlord: he allows groups to play on 'talent nights', where there is the possibility of being spotted by A&R scouts, so doesn't pay performance fees. "The landlord there was a bit cunning," recalled George Underwood. "Every night was talent night and anyone could get up and play. But you weren't paid anything. It was on the pretext that record company scouts might see you, but that was rubbish. It was only the regular old drinkers you would play to."

David meanwhile maintains his job at Nevundy-Hurst. Local girl Rosemary Olive (now Mason), recalled in 2009 meeting David and George: "David and Georgie, they were so young and so cute, I can even remember the first day I met them at Bromley Fair [held on Bromley Common], as if it was yesterday." She also recalled meeting David on the London train: "David always wore very different clothes from the rest. In fact he looked so strange it used to embarrass me sometimes. I would see him get on the train to central London and would say to myself, 'Please don't sit with me!' But he would and it was fine really. He was very fashion conscious and a very talented commercial artist. I was very impressed with the work he showed me."

One evening Rosemary Olive bumps into David at a dance at the Orpington Civic. "I was with my girl friends and he walked up in his way-out clothes and dyed hair and said, 'Hello'," she later recalled. "He really looked so different it was a bit embarrassing."

1. The Stones feature a version of 'I'm A King Bee' on their self-titled debut released in April 1964.

2. Situated at the junction of the Old Kent Road and New Kent Road, the Bricklayers' Arms was close to Mason Street, where David's early exemplar and Britain's first pop star, Tommy Steele, was born.

March

Frustrated by the lack of income on the live R&B circuit – by now highly competitive – and eager to find a way out of his day job, David sends a letter to John Bloom, a high-profile media figure whose self-service laundry empire has made him millions. Bloom is a staple on Britain's celebrity circuit, which by now includes The Beatles.

Signing himself Davie Jones, David lobbies Bloom for financial help for The King Bees. The magnate, impressed by the youngster's pluck but unwilling to become directly involved, sends David a telegram containing the telephone number of a music business contact, Leslie Conn.

David calls Conn and a meeting is arranged at the home of an acquaintance of Conn's named Ronnie Pressman in Albion Street in London's Bayswater.

Conn said later he recognised David's natural charisma: "He was as broke as any of the kids in those days but he walked around like a star and was prepared to work very hard for success."

As a try-out, Conn engages The King Bees to perform at Bloom's wedding anniversary party,[1] held at Soho niterie Jack Of Clubs (owned by popular restaurateur Jack Isow).

The King Bees' appearance and loud brand of R&B aren't well received. "We were in jeans and rather shabby looking," said Underwood in 1993. "Even from the first number – 'Got My Mojo Working' – the crowd weren't quite sure what was going on. We didn't exactly get the bird but they just couldn't handle it."

Attended by such leading personalities as singer-turned-actor Adam Faith and comedian Lance Percival, the party is an opportunity to make an impression with a high-profile crowd, but David's hopes are dashed. Some audience members complain, holding their hands over their ears, and David is moved to tears (though the band do finish their set and receive a £100 performance fee).

After the show, Conn provides consolation: "Don't worry David, I liked it," he tells him.

1. Also on the bill are The Naturals, a London band whose set consists of covers of Beatles songs. Known as the 'Cockney Beatles', they score their only hit later in the year with their version of 'I Should Have Known Better'.

April

Conn decides to represent David and visits him and his parents in Bromley. Since he is under 21, David's parents sign the five-year management contract Conn has prepared. This contains an option for renewal for a further five years. Conn also agrees to manage the rest of The King Bees on a non-contractual basis, and arrange live bookings.

In this year...

January
AUDITION by David's former bandmates The Konrads for independent music producer Joe Meek at his famed studios in Holloway Road, north London.

Friday 13 March
PERFORMANCES by blues legend Sonny Boy Williamson, British singer Long John Baldry and west London outfit The Yardbirds open the Marquee in its new premises at 90 Wardour Street, Soho. Previously the club was situated nearby at 165 Oxford Street.

This was David's favourite venue for much of the 60s. He played his last concert there – a recording for US TV – in October 1973.

Thursday 26 March
RELEASE of 'Everything's Alright' by The Mojos. It was the group's only Top Ten hit; David included a version on his 1973 covers album *Pin Ups*. (▸ 19.10.73)

Davie Jones And The King Bees

LEFT: An original King Bees Decca promo photo.

RIGHT: An original Davie Jones Decca promo photo.

BELOW: Signed publicity shot for The King Bees.

Davie Jones

"Leslie was wonderful. He was so supportive but I think he really didn't know what to do with me," said David in 1993.

May

Conn negotiates a record deal for a single release with Decca, and sits in on a recording session at the company's studios in West Hampstead, scene of The Konrads' failed audition six months previously.

Here The King Bees record two tracks for a single to come out on Decca's Vocalion imprint. The A-side is their version of 'Liza Jane' and, in the style of the times, the manager claims sole credit as part of the financial arrangement he has reached with David for obtaining the Decca deal.

"David and I put that number together in my mum's kitchen," Underwood said in 2009.

Conn later claimed he had made some contribution to what was already the band's arrangement: "When the boys were jamming, they came up with a six-bar blues, which everyone uses. As they were doing that I came up with my own idea and we improvised and the song came together."

B-side 'Louie, Louie Go Home' is a cover of Paul Revere & The Raiders' 1963 track 'Louie, Go Home'. The King Bees' recording borrows from The Beatles' sound, especially David's Lennon-esque vocal intonation.

The music publishing for 'Liza Jane' is handled by Dick James, a friend of Conn's who also represents the songs written by Lennon & McCartney.

Thursday 4 June

With the heading 'Bloom Goes Into Pop', London's daily paper the *Evening News* claims that the tycoon has signed up 'Davy Jones and the King Bees from Bromley'. In the article, David relates the tale of the Jack Of Clubs gig: "We turned up in jeans and sweatshirts," grinned Davy. "It turned out to be a tie and tails do."

Friday 5 June

The release of 'Liza Jane'/'Louie, Louie Go Home' garners generally positive press: *New Musical Express* says the group 'lack melody, but compensate with a terrific beat' while David's local paper, the *Bromley Times,* claims he was 'introduced to show business at the age of 10'.

Writer Leslie Thomas[1] features the group in his *Evening News* column, having been tipped off by David's father, who regularly supplies him with news stories relating to Dr Barnardo's.

"One day he [John Jones] had something different to offer," recalled Thomas in 1984. "'My son David,' he said, 'is a pop singer. I think he sounds terrible but he must be some good because he's made a record. Do you think you could give it a mention?'"

The single is credited to Davie Jones & The King Bees, though right up until it went to press David had been contemplating the group name Tom Jones & The Jonahs. By the following January, fellow Decca artiste Tom Jones will score his first number one hit with 'It's Not Unusual'.

David wrote about this period in 2001: "I seriously wanted a name change. The first attempt of several. This one was adopted for about three weeks. I even did a photo session for it apparently. The name? Tom Jones."

1. Author best known for his comic army reminiscence *The Virgin Soldiers*, which became a successful film for which David appeared as an extra in 1968.

Saturday 6 June

David makes his television debut on BBC1's *Juke Box Jury*, first standing behind a screen while the panel – actresses Diana Dors and Jessie Matthews, comedian Charlie Drake and promoter/manager Bunny Lewis – listen to 'Liza Jane'.

They vote it a 'Miss' (as opposed to a 'Hit') and David makes his small-screen debut, appearing from behind the screen to shake the judges' hands. Underwood is in the audience and afterwards he and David meet popular crooner Matt Monro backstage. The show is broadcast from BBC's Wood Lane Studios in west London. David will come here often for TV recordings over the coming years.

Sunday 7 June

▶ The King Bees play at The Bedsitter, 120 Holland Park Avenue, in Notting Hill, London.

Wednesday 17 June

Brighton *Evening Argus* reporter (and later BBC Radio One DJ) Anne Nightingale sums up 'Liza Jane' as 'straight R&B with a strong Cockney inflection'.

Friday 19 June

The King Bees perform 'Liza Jane' (with David also playing saxophone) on *Ready Steady Go!*, recorded at Studio 9, Television House, Kingsway, in London's Holborn.[1] Broadcast by Rediffusion on 21 June.

Also on the bill is John Lee Hooker. David spies the blues legend in his dressing room and tells Underwood, "Go and look at his hands, they're amazing."

1. Autographs signed by David and two members of The King Bees at *Ready Steady Go!* were offered for sale in 2007 dated 19 June. *Record Mirror* incorrectly notes the name of the group in its TV listings as 'Daryl Quist and The King Bees' in its issue dated 20 June 1964.

July

David is fired from his job at Nevundy-Hurst after a blazing row with his employers; late-night gigging and full-time job evidently don't mix. David told journalist George Tremlett in 1967: "I was playing tenor sax with a group in the evenings, then I had a bust-up at work, and I decided to leave the job and become a musician."

His father agrees to provide financial support as

WHAT'S NEW

FROM THE PRESS ROOM OF THE DECCA RECORD COMPANY

01 439 9521

. . . . artist's news . . . . song news . . . . record news . .

INTRODUCING DAVIE JONES WITH THE KING-BEES . . . . . AND THEIR FIRST DISC "LIZA JANE"

Pop Music isn't all affluence. Just ask new seventeen year old recording star Davie Jones. Time was (two months ago, in fact) when he and his group were almost on their uppers. No money, bad equipment. Then Davie had a brainwave. "I had been reading a lot in the papers about John Bloom," says Davie. "So I put pen to paper and wrote him a letter." David told Bloom that he had the chance of backing one of the most talented and up-and-coming groups on the pop scene. All he had to do was advance the several hundred pounds it requires to outfit a pop group with the best equipment.

Davie didn't get the money, but he did get a telegram next day from John Bloom giving the phone number of Artist's Manager Leslie Conn. Davie got in touch, was rewarded with a booking at Bloom's Wedding Anniversary Party. "We were a dismal failure", recalls Davie. "It was a dinner dress affair and we turned up in jeans and sweat shirts and played our usual brand of rhythm and blues. It didn't go down too well. Still we'll know better next time "

However, all's well that ends well. Leslie Conn liked the earthy type of music the group played, arranged an audition with Decca Records which resulted in a contract and the first release by David Jones with the King-Bees, "Liza Jane", released by Decca on June 5th.

DAVIE JONES WITH THE KING-BEES

MET AT BARBERS

Davie Jones met up with his four member backing group the

LEFT: 'Liza Jane' press release.

LIZA JANE

Friday 5 June 1964

RELEASE of 'Liza Jane'/
'Louie, Louie Go Home',[1]
David's first single is released,
issued on Vocalion.

⊙ **Davie Jones and The King Bees**
A **'Liza Jane'** (Conn)
B **'Louie, Louie Go Home'**
(Revere/Lindsay)
Davie Jones (vocal, tenor sax)
George Underwood
(rhythm guitar,
harmonica, vocal)
Roger Bluck (lead guitar)
Dave Howard (bass)
Robert Allen (drums)
Produced by Leslie Conn
Engineered by Glyn Johns[2]
(Vocalion-Pop V.9221)

1. 'Liza Jane'/'Louie Louie Go Home' was
reissued as a single on the Decca label on
29 September 1978.

2. George Underwood believes that the young
engineer Glyn Johns – who would go on to work with
the likes of The Rolling Stones and The Who – was
responsible for producing 'Liza Jane' and 'Louie,
Louie Go Home'. Johns also worked on David's next
two singles as engineer. (▶ 5.3.65/20.8.65)

TOP RIGHT: The King Bees.
FAR RIGHT: Original 'Liza Jane' single.
BOTTOM RIGHT: 'Liza Jane' rare A4 Vocalion promotional leaflet.
ABOVE: 'Liza Jane' sheet music.

he dedicates all his time to making it in the music business.

"I just couldn't stand the pace – the advertising world was too much for me and I didn't have any interest in it," David said in 1993. "It was just so boring trying to compete with sketching out raincoats and things."

In 2000 David mentioned that, after losing the job, he applied for a post with agency J. Walter Thompson but was unsuccessful: "I failed and so did my enthusiasm for commercial art."

To provide David with ready cash, Conn arranges for the young musician to repaint his offices in Denmark Street (London's Tin Pan Alley) with another of his charges, Mark Feld (later to become Marc Bolan).

These are the inauspicious circumstances under which the pair (who will later become rivals and friends) first meet, though it appears neither is cut out for a career in interior decoration. Conn returns to find the paint-job half finished and his office deserted. He pays Underwood to complete the job.

Conn meets R&B outfit The Manish Boys at Soho's famed music industry rendezvous La Gioconda coffee bar in Denmark Street.

The group – horn player Paul Rodriguez, lead guitarist Johnny Edward Flux, Woolf Byrne on baritone sax, keyboard player Bob Solly, bassist John Watson and drummer Mick White (born John Whitehead) – are eager for success.

Having previously worked as The Band Seven, they have recently adopted their name from the title of Muddy Waters' 1955 single 'Mannish Boy'. Based in Maidstone, Kent, they have played unbilled support slots at such Soho clubs as the Marquee, The Scene and The Flamingo, also in Wardour Street, and built up a following at such regional venues as the Astor Theatre in Deal and Sellindge Village Hall, both in Kent.

"Those places were really good for us," said Woolf Byrne in 1993. "We travelled about in a battered Dormobile. I drove because I was the only one over 21 with a licence."

Bassist John Watson is currently taking vocal duties but when Conn suggests they audition David as a potential frontman, the group are receptive.

Sunday 19 July

Conn drives David to audition for The Manish Boys in the garage of Paul Rodriguez's home at 4 Heathside Avenue, Coxheath, near Maidstone in Kent.

Expecting a black American soul singer, they are initially unimpressed by "this thin guy with long blond hair", said Rodriguez in 1992.

Yet when he joins in with the rehearsals, David wins the group over. "You could clearly see he was incredibly talented, much more talented than any of us," said Rodriguez. "He was a better sax player than me. He was also doing a bit with guitar too, working up a good rhythm guitar style."

D. JONES AND CO.

ON their uppers, Stoney broke. Not only no money . . . but lousy equipment, too. Which for a beat group is worse than an empty wallet. Life, one might think, couldn't look worse for 17-year-old Davie Jones and the King Bees. . .

But Davie, like all the Joneses, knew WHO to keep up with in order to make progress. So he wrote to millionaire John Bloom and said, in effect: "Here's a chance for you to back one of the most talented up-and-coming groups in the country. Just a few hundred pounds and all will be well with us . . ."

I hate to spoil the fairy-story, but Davie DIDN'T get the money.

Now just a word or two about the high-buzzing King-Bees. There's Robert Allen on drums. Digs Jerry Lee Lewis, used to be a projec-tionist, photographic salesman, warehouseman and labourer. Rhythm guitar and harmonica is handled by George Underwood, whose dad is a greengrocer. He is studying at Ravensbourne College of Art.

Dave Howard, 22, married, plays bass. He makes picture frames for an antique dealer. Roger Bluck is on lead guitar. He learned cello when he was eleven, still plays this "square" instrument — and rate Dvorak's "Cello Concerto" as his favourite record. He has designed record sleeves and now works as a representative for a typewriter company.

David presents his fellow musicians with a copy of 'Liza Jane' and sings an *a cappella* version of a new song he has written, 'Don't Try To Stop Me'.

The Manish Boys like what they hear. It is agreed that David should join them as frontman but, for the time being, he also continues with The King Bees.

Saturday 25 July

❯ David makes his debut with The Manish Boys at Chicksands US Air Base Leisure Centre,[1] Shefford, Bedfordshire.

His and John Watson's long hair provokes homophobic remarks from a member of the US personnel.

1. From 1950 Chicksands was home to the American Servicemen of the 774th Air Base Group. The US Air Force remained at Chicksands until 1995. It is now the MOD's National Defence Intelligence and Security Centre (DISC). All of the air bases played by David in 1964/65 were for USAF.

Sunday 26 July

❯ The Manish Boys, Eel Pie Island Jazz Club, Twickenham, Middlesex.

This is David's first known appearance at the jazz and blues venue in the Eel Pie Island Hotel, the crucible for the British R&B scene. "The worst thing about playing on the island was getting the gear over the bridge, that was a real pain," recalled Bob Solly in 2008.

Monday 27 July

Davie Jones And The King Bees performance of 'Liza Jane' in front of an audience on *The Beat Room* is broadcast. When this fails to lift interest in 'Liza Jane', David leaves The King Bees and they disband.[1]

David throws his lot in full-time with The Manish Boys. Although he forges some strong friendships with band members, it is generally not a happy period. Their insistence on remaining in Maidstone proves a consistent problem.

"I didn't really like that band at all," David confessed in 1987. "It was rhythm and blues, but it

TOP: *Record Mirror*, 20 June.

ABOVE: George Underwood, school-friend, original Konrad and David's right-hand man in The King Bees.

In this year...

July
RECRUITMENT of Mick Ronson to The King Bees, not David's band but another combo inspired by The Rolling Stones and based in Hull, Yorkshire.

THIS AGREEMENT is made the   day of
One thousand nine hundred and sixty five BETWEEN the
within named ORBIT MUSIC COMPANY LIMITED (hereinafter
called "the Managers") of the first part the within
named DAVID ROBERT JONES   JOHN EDWARD FLUX   JOHN EDWARD
WATSON   FRANCIS PAUL   SYLVESTER RODRIGUES   WILFRED BYRNE
ROBERT LESLIE SOLLY and MICHAEL HENRY WHITEHEAD (hereinafter
called "the Artistes") of the second part and LESLIE CONN
of 6 Fairview Way Edgware Middlesex and ROBERT TERENCE
PETER RUSK of 10 Fairfax House Roehampton Lane London
S.W.15 (hereinafter called "the Further Managers") of
the third part _____
WHEREBY IT IS AGREED AND DECLARED as follows:

ABOVE: Draft copy of David Jones' and The Manish Boys' management contract, July 1964.

BOTTOM LEFT: Davie Jones And The King Bees on BBC TV's *The Beat Room*. David was also a member of The Manish Boys when he appeared on this programme.

BOTTOM RIGHT: *Radio Times* entry for *The Beat Room*.

wasn't very good. Nobody ever earned any money. The band was so huge it was dreadful. And I had to live in Maidstone."

The other members often play down David's input in local press reports, but this is the least of his problems. On one occasion he is subjected to a violent attack.

"Maidstone prison is one of the biggest in England," said David in 1987. "It's the only time in my life I've ever been beaten up, by some ex-prisoner I suppose. I don't know. This big herbert walking down the street just knocked me on the pavement and, when I fell, proceeded to kick the shit outta me. I haven't got many good memories of Maidstone."

Byrne has subsequently disputed this: "I am pretty sure we would have heard of such an incident," he

claimed in 2009. However, Bob Solly said in 2009: "Davie turned up with John Watson at my place one day and was all bruised from having been punched in the street for having long hair. I suppose he was very effeminate looking."

1. Ex-King Bees' Roger Bluck and Dave Howard teamed up with guitarist Colin Reece to form The Spectrum, which survived until 1968. Bluck and Reece later appeared in The Bully Wee Band, before departing to play in country and western groups. Drummer Bob Allen emigrated to the US and joined The Fabulous Minets. Les Conn introduced Underwood – then still studying at art college – to producer Mickie Most, for whom he recorded a single in 1965.

Saturday 1 August

▶ Davie Jones & The Manish Boys, Valley Hotel Assembly Room, 7 Station Avenue, Caterham, Surrey.

With David on board, the group's repertoire is reliant on tracks made famous by James Brown, David having already impressed his bandmates with his copy of Brown's 'Live At The Apollo'.

"It was absolutely amazing, just what we had been waiting for, fantastic," enthused Rodriguez in 1992. "We all enjoyed that music and featured it live. Davie and John Edward worked particularly well together on stage." David tries to steer The Manish Boys towards the sax-led music of Sounds Incorporated but they are happy to ape the commercial sound of Georgie Fame and James Brown. Mose Allison songs also creep into their repertoire, though the singer's material will appeal more to David in later years.

During August, the group make an open-air appearance in a field near Maidstone. "There was hay stacked up around the makeshift stage," said Solly in 2007. "It was a hot day but no one turned up to see us, so we decided to enjoy it as a paid practice session. I clearly remember David doing (The Kinks' hit of that summer) 'You Really Got Me'."

Monday 17 August

▶ Davie Jones & The Manish Boys, Astor Theatre, Stanhope Road, Deal, Kent.

Tuesday 18 August

The *Chatham Standard* reports that The Manish Boys 'are now backing Decca recording star Davie Jones, whose group, the King Bees, are no longer with him.'

Wednesday 19 August

▶ Davie Jones & The Manish Boys, Eel Pie Island Jazz Club, Twickenham.

They share the bill with Long John Baldry And His Hoochie Coochie Men (featuring Rod Stewart on vocals and harmonica).

Sunday 30 August

▶ Davie Jones & The Manish Boys, Savoy Ballroom (in the former Hippodrome Theatre), St Nicholas Street, Ipswich, Suffolk.

The group travel to the gig as usual in an unreliable second-hand 12-seater Commer van, driven and maintained by Byrne.

Wednesday 2 September

▶ Davie Jones & The Manish Boys, Eel Pie Island Jazz Club, Twickenham.

A diary item runs in the September edition of Kent-based magazine *Beat 64*: 'Decca Recording Artiste, Davey Jones, interested in Maidstone group to provide backing for recording and TV dates. Wonder who?'

Wednesday 9 September

▶ Davie Jones & The Manish Boys, RAF Wethersfield, near Braintree, Essex.

Like Chicksands, this base is occupied by the US Air Force.

Saturday 19 September

▶ Davie Jones & The Manish Boys, The Scene, Ham Yard, Soho, London.

David and the band are wary of the club's reputation for attracting pill-popping mods.

"We didn't even drink," said Bob Solly. "We all smoked cigarettes but none of us, including David, were interested in drugs in any way."

Pete Townshend later recalled its importance: "The Scene was really where it was at, but there were only about fifteen people down there every night. It was a focal point for the mod movement. I don't think anyone who was a mod outside Soho realised the fashions and dances all began there."

Monday 21 September

▶ Davie Jones & The Manish Boys, Invicta Ballroom, High Street, Chatham, Kent.

Wednesday 23 September

▶ Davie Jones & The Manish Boys, Medway County Youth Club, Maidstone Road, Chatham, Kent.

Friday 25 September

▶ Davie Jones & The Manish Boys, Willow Rooms,

Willow Street, Romford, Essex.

Earlier in the day the band meet with Decca A&R man Mike Smith and also audition for the Star Club.

Saturday 26 September

▶ Davie Jones & The Manish Boys, Acton Town Hall, Winchester Street, London W3.

Tuesday 28 September

▶ Davie Jones & The Manish Boys, The Jolly Gardeners, 266 Twickenham Road, Isleworth, south-west London.

Wednesday 30 September

A recording date for David and band with Richard Lloyd at Decca Studios, Broadhurst Gardens, West Hampstead is cancelled.

Thursday 1 October

Davie & The Manish Boys meet with Dick James at 2.30pm.

In 2009, Woolf Byrne recalled the meeting:

"James was keen to sign us and offered us a deal. But we really needed bookings and we weren't convinced that signing to him would get us more work. It was probably a mistake to pass on it because no doubt we would have made more records with his help."

Friday 2 October

▶ Davie Jones & The Manish Boys, Borehamwood, Herts.[1]

A booking at RAF Bentwaters, near Woodbridge, Suffolk, is cancelled for 3 October. (This would have again been for the USAF.)

1. The home of Elstree film and television studios. David would later return as a star to make numerous TV and film appearances there, including *Labyrinth* and a Christmas show with Bing Crosby in 1977.

ABOVE: Davie Jones & The Manish Boys photographed in Moat Park, Maidstone. From left to right: Davie Jones (vocals, sax), Woolf Byrne (sax), Mick White (drums), Bob Solly (keyboard), John Watson (guitar, vocals), Johnny Flux (guitar, vocals) and Paul Rodriguez (sax).

BELOW: Bob Solly's Manish Boys set list and notation.

Monday 5 October

David and The Manish Boys attend a meeting with leading independent record producer Mickie Most[1] at his office, 101 Dean Street, Soho, following an audition at Charlie Chester's Casino, 12 Archer Street, the previous week.

1. Most, working as an independent producer, signs acts to EMI, Decca and other major labels.

Tuesday 6 October

Following a meeting with producer Mike Smith the previous month, David and The Manish Boys record three tracks for Decca during an evening session at Regent Sounds[1] studio at 4 Denmark Street.[2] David and band are paid for the session. The recordings are not demos but are made for an actual single. Tracks recorded are Barbara Lewis' 'Hello Stranger', Gene Chandler's 'Duke Of Earl' and Mickey & Sylvia's 'Love Is Strange'.

Attempts by Smith[3] to harmonise David's and John Watson's voices via a single microphone prove unsuccessful and the deal is not forthcoming.[4]

1. Regent Sounds was a popular and inexpensive studio owned by Bill Farley, also its chief engineer. Regent was put on the map when The Rolling Stones recorded their debut LP there in 1963. Farley provided the lyric for the Pretty Things' hit 'Rosalyn', later covered by David on Pin Ups. (▶ 19.10.73)

2. In the mid-70s, The Sex Pistols lived and rehearsed at No. 6.

3. Mike Smith is notable for having witnessed a performance by The Beatles at The Cavern in Liverpool in December 1961 and recommended them to Decca, who famously rejected them.

4. Decca has not retained a copy of the master tape. Acetate recordings (if any exist) have yet to surface.

Wednesday 7 October

▶ Davie Jones & The Manish Boys, Eel Pie Island Jazz Club, Twickenham.

This is the second time they share the bill at the Eel Pie Island club with Long John Baldry And His Hoochie Coochie Men with featured vocalist Rod Stewart.

They also share the first-floor dressing room. Changing before the show, Stewart reveals he is wearing knickers. "We asked him why he wore girl's underwear and he said it was because they were more comfortable," said Solly in 2007.

Friday 9 October

▶ Davie Jones & The Manish Boys, Finchley, north London.

Saturday 10 October

▶ Davie Jones & The Manish Boys, Newmarket, Suffolk.

An advert lists the group at a dance evening at St Margaret's Hall, Orchard Street, Rainham, Kent. Solly later said that his diary notes state that they only played in Newmarket; it is likely the Rainham booking was not met.

Monday 12 October

The group return to Regent Sounds, Denmark Street, for an evening session, re-recording the three tracks attempted the previous week.

Tuesday 13 October

▶ Davie Jones & The Manish Boys, Putney, south-west London. This is likely to be the Putney Ballroom at St Mary's Hall, Putney High Street.

Earlier in the day, David and band have a 1.00pm appointment with TV producer Barry Langford (a friend of Les Conn's) at Regent Sounds studio. Davie & The Manish Boys will appear on his new BBC2 TV show early in the New Year.

Saturday 17 October

▶ Davie Jones & The Manish Boys, Tower Ballroom, Lee-on-the-Solent, Hampshire.

Wednesday 21 October

▶ Davie Jones & The Manish Boys, Medway County Youth Club, Maidstone Road, Chatham, Kent.

Earlier, David and the band audition for Arthur Howes. He is in need of a replacement act for the remaining dates of a UK group package tour headed by Gene Pitney, which is about to start.

Sunday 25 October

▶ Davie Jones & The Manish Boys, Tower Ballroom, Lee-on-the-Solent, Hampshire.

Saturday 31 October

▶ Davie Jones & The Manish Boys perform close to David's hometown at Justin Hall, West Wickham.

November

Beat 64 magazine confirms that David has joined forces with The Manish Boys and reports that their new single will be a version of Barbara Lewis' 'Hello Stranger' on Decca.

Monday 2 November

Headed 'For Those Beyond The Fringe', an article by Leslie Thomas in the Evening News covers David's founding of long-haired lobby group The International League For The Preservation Of Animal Filament.

David, who is named as the president of this body, tells Thomas:

"It's really for the protection of pop musicians and those who wear their hair long. Anyone who has the courage to wear hair down to his shoulders has to go through hell. It's time we united and stood up for our curls.

"Screaming Lord Sutch, P.J. Proby, The Pretty Things and, of course, The Stones and The Beatles – we want them all as members. You've no idea the indignities you suffer just because you've got long hair. Dozens of times I've been politely told to clear out of the lounge bar of public houses.

"Everybody makes jokes about you on a bus and if you go past navvies digging in the road it's murder!"

This is the beginning of a publicity campaign which, within a couple of weeks, results in David's first national television interview.

Friday 6 November

◗ Davie Jones & The Manish Boys, the Marquee Club, 90 Wardour Street, London.

Supporting Gary Farr & The T-Bones,[1] this is David's first appearance at the club and is something of a coup, since bookings at the Wardour Street venue are difficult to obtain.

With his long blond hair, David attracts the attention of 14-year-old audience member Dana Gillespie. The well-born Gillespie is music mad, attending clubs such as the Marquee nightly. She recalls: "One night there was Davie Jones and The Manish Boys. He came on stage with knee-length suede boots with fringes, a bit like the Robin Hood-Sherwood Forest look; long blond hair and a kind of loose pirate type shirt."

"I sat as usual in the front row with my mouth open, agog," she said in 1985. "I didn't particularly like the music and I wasn't particularly taken with his sax playing either. This was at the sound check, and during the break I was standing in front of the mirror, brushing my hair. David came up from behind and took the brush out of my hand. He started brushing my hair and asked me if he could walk me home that night."

The couple start to see each other regularly.

"He was my first boyfriend that wasn't upper class," said Gillespie, who is taken home to meet David's parents on one occasion. "We ate tuna fish sandwiches," she recalled. "This was the first time I had been in a house built on the proportions of the sort of houses in *Coronation Street*. I had never been in one of those before, nor seen a kitchen that was so tiny. I had never sat on chairs that had things that catch the grease on the back of them (lace antimacassars). Suddenly, I realised that I was in somebody's home where there was a big culture difference. But that's my own personal shake-up; it didn't affect David in the end."

1. This is the first of several occasions on which David will support Gary Farr & The T-Bones over the coming years. Led by the son of British champion heavyweight boxer Tommy Farr, the T-Bones included bassist Lee Jackson.

Saturday 7 November

◗ Davie Jones & The Manish Boys, Conservative Hall, Bedfordshire.

Sunday 8 November

◗ Davie Jones & The Manish Boys, Eel Pie Island Jazz Club, Twickenham.

Thursday 12 November

David has been busy seeking out publicity for The

HAIR ABOUNDS !

DAVIE JONES AND THE MANISH BOYS

Just over two months ago six musicians, disgruntled with their groups and the music they were playing, got together to form what will undoubtedly be The Kent Rhythm and Blues group, the Manish Boys.

With a line-up of organ, lead guitar, tenor and baritone saxes, bass guitar and drums they knew they could tackle almost any material.

Blond-haired John Watson is the lead vocalist and bass guitarist. Besides playing bass and singing John is also a very accomplished pianist. "But one day I could not take any more sonatas and concertos. I had always had a hankering for the bass guitar and took it up instead," said John. John is not the only one who joined the Manish Boys by a strange route. Paul Rodriguez, the tenor sax player, thought he had reached the end of his musical tether a couple of years ago when he was pumping out French horn concertos. Then he was offered a job as bass guitarist in a group and took it. One day the group's tenor saxist walked out without any notice. And Paul did the only thing a person could do in his position—he walked into Grimwoods in Maidstone and bought a saxaphone.

"Although I had never even thought of playing a sax before that day I am glad I took it up. The only snag was I had to play it at a booking rather less than two weeks after I had bought it."

Woolf Byrne, on the other hand, always liked saxes. "Not that it ever occurred to me to get one," admits Woolf freely. Then fate stepped in. "I was sort of road manager to a group and had taken them up to London. The gang of us were walking down Charing Cross road when the leader suddenly said, 'Ever thought of taking up the baritone sax?' Well, I hadn't. But I thought it was a good idea, ran to the nearest Post Office, drew out all my savings for the deposit and left London that evening with a baritone sax."

The organist is ex-Maidstone Art College student, Robert Solly. He guitared with a couple of groups before switching to the ivories with the Manish Boys.

Last, but not least, come the two ex-Cortinas, Mick White on drums and Johnny Flux, now the Manish Boys lead guitarist.

News of the rich sound the boys were producing quickly spread and reached the hair-covered ears of Decca recording artist, Davie Jones, who has asked them to be his backing group on disc and ballroom dates.

International League For The Preservation Of Animal Filament, which has been renamed The Society For The Prevention Of Cruelty To Long-Haired Men, and is featured on BBC2 news magazine show *Tonight*.

The segment centres on an interview with David conducted by *Tonight* presenter Cliff Michelmore at the BBC studios in Lime Grove, west London.

David is surrounded by fellow long-hairs including George Underwood and The Manish Boys' John Watson, Woolf Byrne and Paul Rodriguez, yet no mention is made of the group or their music.

Cliff Michelmore: "It's all got to stop, they've had enough. The worms are turning. The rebellion of the long hairs is getting underway. They're tired of losing their jobs. They're tired of being sent home from college. They're tired of being sent home from school,

ABOVE: David joins The Manish Boys, as reported in *Beat 64* magazine, October. The photograph was shot in Brenchley Gardens, Maidstone.

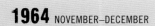

they're tired even of being refused the dole.

"So, with a nucleus of some of his friends, a 17-year-old, Davie Jones, has just founded The Society For The Prevention Of Cruelty To Long-Haired Men.

'Well, here we are. Long-haired men, you've got to have your hair, what, nine inches long before you can join?"

Davie Jones: "Well, I think we'll pass that over now."

CM: "Have you? Now, exactly who's been cruel to you?"

DJ: "Well, I think we're all fairly tolerant but for the last two years we've had comments like 'Darlin'' and 'Can I carry your handbag?' thrown at us. I think it's just had to stop now."

CM: "But does this surprise you, that you get this kind of comment? Because after all, you have got really, rather long hair, haven't you?"

DJ: "We have, yes. It's not too bad really. No, I like it and I think we all like long hair and we don't see why other people should persecute us because of this."

CM: "Did you get this off The Rolling Stones really?"

DJ: "No, that's stupid."

David follows up on his promise and invites a number of other musicians to join the 'society', including British shock rocker Screaming Lord Sutch.[1] "I was part of the Long Haired Society," recalled Sutch in 1993. "I was one of the few who really did have long hair. I had 18-inch hair when they said The Rolling Stones had long hair and it just touched their collars."

1. Born David Edward Sutch in November 1940, Sutch – who took his own life in 1999 – exhibited a flair for PR which reached its apotheosis with long-running spoof political group the Raving Monster Loony Party. Sutch worked with many of rock's luminaries including Jeff Beck, Jimmy Page, Ritchie Blackmore and Keith Moon. In 1984 David acknowledged Sutch in the Julien Temple-directed extended promo *Jazzin' For Blue Jean*, in which he played a rock star called Screaming Lord Byron.

Friday 13 November

▶ The Manish Boys (minus David), The Witch Doctor, Marine Court, St Leonards-on-Sea, East Sussex.

This is a popular venue which also houses The Cobweb Club; David will play here a few times over the coming years (we don't know the reason for him not appearing on this occasion).

Saturday 14 November

▶ Davie Jones & The Manish Boys, Royal Star, Pudding Lane, Maidstone. (Minus Paul Rodriguez.)

Around this time David tries out writing songs with Solly and Rodriguez (who are also writing their own material). The three come up with a song titled 'So Near To Loving You' which is not thought to have been recorded. "He had trouble working out chord sequences; although he could describe it, he couldn't actually play it," said Solly later.

Tuesday 17 November

The *Chatham Standard* reveals that the group has a deal for live bookings with the Arthur Howes Agency. A booking in Watford on 18 November is cancelled.

Friday 20 November

▶ Davie Jones & The Manish Boys, Justin Hall, West Wickham, near Bromley, Kent.

The group pose for promotional photos in Moat Park, Maidstone – taken by Solly using a timer.

Tuesday 24 November

Davie Jones & The Manish Boys rehearse a short set at the Saville Theatre (owned by Brian Epstein) for the forthcoming Epstein/Arthur Howes-promoted UK tour, which they will join the following week.

Monday 30 November

Rehearsal with Shel Talmy. (▶ 1.65)

Tuesday 1 December

▶ Davie Jones & The Manish Boys, ABC Cinema, Station Road, Wigan, Lancs. (Two shows)

This, David's first live booking outside southern England, comprises two shows as unbilled 'guest stars' on the last six dates of this UK package tour. The group are the opening act and replace Bobby Shafto with The Roofraisers.

Every night the musicians are required to play matinee and evening performances. A friend, Terry Rusk, acts as the band's road manager-cum-roadie.

Headliners are American singer Gene Pitney,[1] riding high in the UK charts with 'I'm Gonna Be Strong', and Gerry & The Pacemakers, who are about to release their career-defining hit 'Ferry Cross The Mersey'.

Initially the band were actually lined up to back Gene Pitney on the tour. This concerned David and the group who considered themselves not up to Pitney's standard. "I think that's how Les got us on that tour," Paul Rodriguez later said. "We were made out to be a competent backing band. But Leslie's gamble paid off." The band remonstrated with Conn that they were simply not up to backing someone of Pitney's calibre. "When he eventually told us we were going out as support we were all rather relieved to say the least," said Rodriguez in 1992.

Also on the bill are Marianne Faithfull[2] and The Kinks along with such acts as Mike Cotton Sound (who also backed Pitney), Kim Weston and The Earl Van Dyke Band (also unbilled). There is an ongoing joke among the tour company that David and Marianne Faithfull are sisters!

1. Pitney's single 'Twenty Four Hours From Tulsa' was a Top Five hit the previous December.
2. Faithfull and David became friendly in 1973 when she participated in US TV special *The Ninety Eighty Floor Show*. (▶ 18.10.73)

Wednesday 2 December

▶ Davie Jones & The Manish Boys, ABC Cinema,

Ferensway, Hull, Yorkshire. (Two shows)

Woolf Byrne misses the tour coach and has to make his own way to Edinburgh, arriving just in time for the afternoon sound check.

David will later claim to have been a supporting musician for Pitney on these dates. In 1971 David said: "I used to play sax with the Gene Pitney band. God, it was awful!"

Thursday 3 December

▶ Davie Jones & The Manish Boys, ABC Cinema, 120 Lothian Road, Edinburgh. (Two shows)

The group do not go down well with the 2,000-strong audience eager to see the stars of the tour.

Nevertheless, this is their first time north of the border, and all are impressed by the dramatic geography of the Scottish capital, despite being unprepared for the climate. "By the time we reached Edinburgh we were frozen stiff," recalled Solly. "We were only wearing light jackets."

Friday 4 December

▶ Davie Jones & The Manish Boys, ABC Cinema, Stockton-On-Tees, County Durham. (Two shows)

During the tour Faithfull and Pitney become close. "They took over the back seat of the coach, hardly coming up for air. They were all over each other," said Rodriguez in 1992.

Saturday 5 December

▶ Davie Jones & The Manish Boys, City Hall, Northumberland Road, Newcastle. (Two shows)

Over the course of the tour David strikes up a friendship with Ray Davies, frontman of The Kinks, who have recently scored their first number one hit with 'You Really Got Me' and a number two in October with 'All Day And All Of The Night'.

Sunday 6 December

▶ Davie Jones & The Manish Boys, Futurist Theatre, Foreshore Road, Scarborough, Yorks. (Two shows)

The final night of the tour and the worst reception for the group ("They hated us," recalled Solly many years later). The lasting impression left on David is the fact that he's been used as a gofer by 'a very well known rock star' on the tour, as he said in 1971:

"I used to run around the front and find these birds for him. I was really cheesed off because they never had friends."

Thursday 10 December

▶ Davie Jones & The Manish Boys (unbilled), the Marquee club, Wardour Street, London, supporting the Moody Blues (featuring Denny Laine).

This is the first of two occasions supporting the Moody Blues at this venue, as recalled by Woolf Byrne in 2009:

"What was funny about these shows was seeing how much the Moody Blues changed once they had a hit record ['Go Now']. The next time we supported

them at the Marquee they looked like a different band."

Sunday 13 December

▶ Davie Jones & The Manish Boys, Conservative Club, Bedfordshire.

Tuesday 15 December

Paul Rodriguez recounts the group's tour experiences in a report in the *Chatham Standard*: 'Having a fabulous tour, bigger success than we hoped for, especially as they have given us the job of opening the show. The audiences up North are great. However, entering theatres can be a dangerous task, not to mention leaving when the show is finished.'

Thursday 17 December

▶ Davie Jones & The Manish Boys, Brighton College, East Sussex.

David's first live appearance in the coastal town where he will rack up more than a dozen performances over the coming years.

Friday 18 December

▶ Davie Jones & The Manish Boys, Corn Exchange, Hertford, Hertfordshire.

Saturday 19 December

▶ Davie Jones & The Manish Boys, Corn Exchange, 6b Market Buildings, Maidstone, Kent.

Thursday 24 December

A Christmas Eve booking in Bude, Cornwall is cancelled.

Thursday 31 December

▶ Davie Jones & The Manish Boys, Finchley, north London.

The group drum up the majority of engagements themselves. But having been away on the Pitney tour, they haven't been able to promote themselves and miss out on lucrative work over the Christmas period save for this New Year's Eve appearance.

OPPOSITE PAGE
TOP: Gene Pitney/Kinks tour programme cover and advert for tour. This is David's first live booking outside of southern England. Davie Jones & The Manish Boys are unbilled and appear on the last six dates to replace Bobby Shafto.

BOTTOM: BBC2's *Tonight* show. David stands up for the rights for men with long hair.

THIS PAGE
ABOVE: The Manish Boys photographed in Maidstone.

In this year...

Tuesday 24 November
START of The Who's residency at the Marquee. Mod went mainstream as the quartet provided inspiration for many struggling musicians, including David the following April. (▶12.4.65)

December
RELEASE of The Yardbirds' debut album *Five Live Yardbirds* on Columbia. This contained the group's arrangement of Bo Diddley's song 'I'm A Man', later used as the basis for David's 1973 hit 'The Jean Genie'.

Thursday 24 December
PERFORMANCE by The Lower Third as part of a Christmas Eve all-nighter at La Discothèque, the venue where they auditioned David the following April. (▶12.4.65)

1965

IT'S all happening for David as his career steps up a few gears. Securing the interest of red-hot producer Shel Talmy, with The Manish Boys he records the single 'I Pity The Fool'. On the B-side is one of David's own songs, 'Take My Tip'.

This leads to a much-hyped TV appearance on BBC2's *Gadzooks! It's All Happening.*

Soon David has outgrown The Manish Boys and also parts company with manager Les Conn.

At Soho musician's hang-out La Gioconda, David hears about trio The Lower Third who are auditioning for a frontman. David wins them over and institutes a new set made up of his songs and a few covers performed in the bombastic style of The Who. These form the basis of their live set at venues such as the Marquee. Shortly after, he is taken under the wing of go-getter Ralph Horton.

A song of David's, 'You've Got A Habit Of Leaving', is produced by Talmy as the A-side of a new EMI single. The credit reads 'Davy Jones'.

Horton gains prestigious live bookings from pirate station Radio London as David & The Lower Third take to the road.

With the band's new mod image and songs reflecting the lifestyle of young Londoners, David is poised on the brink of a new beginning, and adopts a new name: David Bowie. He is featured in fashion spreads wearing the very latest gear.

The name change is suggested by experienced entertainment industry player Kenneth Pitt, who will loom large as the most important figure in David's career in the 60s.

Leading producer and A&R man Tony Hatch is bowled over by David's songs. Amid talk of working together on a musical, David is back in the studio, where he records an early version of one of the era's defining songs, 'The London Boys'.

HIS HAIR IS TOO LONG FOR TV!

THE Manish Boys of Maidstone, who had their first disc released in the shops over the week-end, have already run into trouble with their career.

The Boys were banned last week from their first television date. They were stopped from appearing on BBC-2's "Gadzooks" show because it was felt that singer Davy Jones' hair was too long. Davy is pictured above.

"I Pity The Fool," is the title of their record.

PREVIOUS SPREAD: Studio portrait taken at EMI House, Manchester Square, London.

THIS PAGE

TOP: David's long hair courts controversy.

BOTTOM LEFT: David's first professional producer, Shel Talmy.

BOTTOM RIGHT: Davie Jones with The Manish Boys drummer, Mick White, outside BBC TV Centre, Wood Lane, west London.

January

While David and The Manish Boys are on the road, Les Conn secures the interest of Shel Talmy, the hot 24-year-old American producer living in London who is behind the hits of The Kinks.[1]

Like many of the producers of the day Talmy is always on the lookout for new songs, and places one of David's, 'Take My Tip', with American actor Kenny Miller,[2] then trying to break into the UK pop scene.

'Take My Tip' appears as the B-side of Miller's single 'Restless', which is released in the UK by Stateside and becomes the first-ever cover version of one of David's songs.

Talmy also agrees to produce the first single by the group now that Conn has extricated David from his Decca deal and signed him to a fresh contract with EMI Parlophone.

1. Shelmond Talmy (born 1938) arrived in Britain in 1963. Produced hits for The Who and The Small Faces. In the 70s Talmy moved into book publishing and wrote the novel *The Ichabod Deception*. He returned to production for a Ralph McTell album in 1976. Failing eyesight has since restricted his musical output.

2. Kenny Miller (born 1931) appeared in TV series such as *The Cisco Kid* and *Flash Gordon* and the film *Custer Of The West*.

Friday 8 January

David's 18th birthday.

Saturday 9 January

❱ Davie Jones & The Manish Boys, Hermitage Ballroom, 1st Floor, 20 Hermitage Road, Hitchin, Herts.

The van breaks down en route.

Thursday 14 January

The group auditions for a company called Rocky River Promotions at the London Palladium, Argyle Street, central London, for bookings at the Star Club in Hamburg.

The promoter beckons David over after the audition and asks him whether his sexual preference is for girls or boys. David responds: "Boys, of course."

Paul Rodriguez said later: "He was just putting the guy on. We'd say anything to get a good gig." In the event, the booking doesn't materialise.

Friday 15 January

A 2.30pm run-through with Talmy at 2i's Coffee Bar, 56 Old Compton Street, Soho,[1] just around the corner from Talmy's production office in Greek Street.

At 7.00pm they visit IBC Studios at 35 Portland Place and under Talmy's direction record the A- and B-sides of a single for EMI's Parlophone label: 'I Pity The Fool'[2] and their own version of 'Take My Tip'. The session takes place in Studio A, where Talmy will produce the first four singles by The Who, starting with 'I Can't Explain' in February 1965.

Each song is recorded only twice since Talmy is not only keen to capture spontaneity but is also watching the clock. Such is the rush that, in one version of 'Take My Tip', David accidentally sings 'bider' instead of 'spider' and the mistake is left in.

The recording includes contributions from leading session musician Jimmy Page, who had listened in with Talmy on the band rehearsal at 2i's. Talmy wants to replace Johnny Flux on guitar with Page and John White on drums with another session musician but the band won't allow it. In the event, Page adds lead lines using a brand new fuzz-box effects pedal. Page says to Solly during the playback: "I don't think you're going to have a hit with this one."

Even though, the session is judged a success and the single is scheduled for release in early March. The Manish Boys pressurise Conn into omitting David's individual credit on the label, insisting that it reads only as The Manish Boys. David is furious and the omission effectively ends his interest in the band.

Talmy is impressed with David and will work with him over the next couple of years, supplanting Conn in the process. "I didn't think that what he was writing at the time had a snowball's chance in hell of making it, but I thought, 'He's so original and brash, let's take a flier'," Talmy said in 2003.

1. Scene of the birth of British rock'n'roll in the 50s, the 2i's performance area was in the basement, where David and the band rehearsed that day. The venue was active from 1950 to 1970 and has since become a restaurant, though a local authority plaque marks its significant place in popular music.

2. The song was popularised by the R&B singer Bobby 'Blue' Bland, who recorded it for Duke Records in 1961. The song-writing credit is Deadric Malone, a pseudonym of Duke Records' owner Don Robey.

Monday 18 January

❱ Davie Jones & The Manish Boys, Welwyn Garden City, Herts.

Transport problems – the van is playing up again – result in the group arriving too late to perform in their 9.45pm slot.

Saturday 23 January

❱ Davie Jones & The Manish Boys, Star Hotel, Maidstone, Kent.

They support John L. Watson/Hummelflugs, who hail from Swindon.

The show is in a room annexed to the hotel's ballroom, which had been a popular venue for dances in the 40s and 50s.

Saturday 30 January

▶ Davie Jones & The Manish Boys, Witch Doctor, Marine Court, St Leonards-on-Sea, East Sussex.

The club is on the first floor of the building so the band's gear has to be hauled into a rickety lift. After the show Solly and Flux are stuck in the lift for an hour in darkness when the power fails and it stops between floors.

Saturday 6 February

▶ Davie Jones & The Manish Boys, Bletchley, Buckinghamshire.

Monday 8 February

▶ Davie Jones & The Manish Boys, the Marquee club, London.

David and band support the Moody Blues for the second time.

Saturday 13 February

▶ Davie Jones & The Manish Boys, California Pool Ballroom, Whipsnade Road, Dunstable, Bedfordshire.

Also on the bill are Screaming Lord Sutch, The Cheetahs and The Five Just Men.

Monday 15 February

▶ Davie Jones & The Manish Boys, Welwyn Garden City, Herts.

This is a rebooking to fulfil the engagement they missed at the venue in January.

Wednesday 17 February

▶ Davie Jones & The Manish Boys, Medway County Youth Club, Maidstone Road, Chatham, Kent.

Bookings are usually made here by Flux, who lives close to the venue.

Saturday 20 February

▶ Davie Jones & The Manish Boys, Gliderdrome, Boston, Lincolnshire.

Friday 26 February

▶ Davie Jones & The Manish Boys, Portsmouth, Hants.

This gig supporting James Brown doesn't happen; again the unreliable van breaks down on the way, but they arrive in time to witness the great soul singer's show.

After the show they are stranded for the night. A local art student allows them to sleep on the floor of his digs.

Saturday 27 February

In the morning the group hitches home.

"I travelled with Paul and Davie," said Solly. "After a while it was clear we were never going to get a lift; once they saw our long hair they didn't want to know. So David called his father and we sat by the road for ages. Eventually he arrived to rescue us."

WHEN GUITARIST JOHNNY FLUX spotted a pair of shears in Brenchley Gardens, Maidstone, they certainly gave him ideas. He promptly lined up pop singer Davie Jones (pictured second from left) and Woolf Byrne and John Watson (pictured third from left) for a hair trim !

Wednesday 3 March

In advance of the release of 'I Pity The Fool', David reworks the 'long hair' publicity scam during an interview conducted earlier in the week with a journalist from the *Daily Mirror* at his family home in Bromley, where David lives most of the time (stays in Maidstone[1] are strictly for band rehearsals and gigs in the area).

He claims that he and The Manish Boys are encountering problems with a booking on a forthcoming edition of TV pop show *Gadzooks! It's All Happening*. In fact the brouhaha has been worked out in advance with the programme's producer, Barry Langford, who happily supplies quotes criticising David's choice of coiffure.

The *Daily Mirror's* story is headed 'Row Over Davie's Hair'.

'Davie, who comes from Bromley, Kent, says: "I've said that I have no intention of having my hair cut. Mr Langford has left the matter open till Friday in case I change my mind... but I won't." Mr Langford, thirty-nine, said: "Kids today just don't want this long hair business any more."'

Again there are references to David's organisation The Society For The Prevention Of Cruelty To Long Haired Men in the media. The *Mirror* puts forward the hirsute broadcaster and satirist William Rushton as a patron of the society.

David tells the *Mirror*: "I wouldn't have my hair cut for the Prime Minister, let alone the BBC. My girlfriend isn't keen on my hair either. Maybe it's because I get asked for more dates when we're out together."

ABOVE: David and The Manish Boys in Brenchley Gardens, Maidstone.

BELOW: David in the EMI boardroom, Manchester Square, London.

RIGHT: Davie Jones & The Manish Boys outside BBC TV Centre.

BELOW: The British Safety Council's letter to BBC producer Barry Langford regarding The Manish Boys' long hair.

BRITISH SAFETY COUNCIL
Registered with the Charity Commission under the Charities Act 1960   Registered Number 207826

MASON HOUSE · 163/173 PRAED STREET · LONDON W2
Telephone AMBassador 2415/9   Telegrams BRITSAFE LONDON W2   Cables BRITSAFE LONDON

JT/MK

4th March 1965

Barry Langford, Esq.,
BBC TV
TV Centre,
Wood Lane,
W.12.

Dear Mr. Longford,

We noted an item in this morning's press which states that you are insisting that "The Mannish Boys get their hair cut or else they do not appear on TV".

As an organisation concerned with the effects of accidents caused by unduly long and effeminate hair styles, we would like to congratulate you on your stand.

Yours sincerely,

James Tye, Controller,
British Safety Council.

BRITAIN'S LARGEST INDUSTRIAL SAFETY ORGANISATION

In the event the long-haired stunt does not lift interest in 'I Pity The Fool' but it does garner David his largest amount of publicity until 'Space Oddity' receives national media attention in four years' time.

> 1. David stayed over with most band members, but was generally put up at Rodriguez's house in Coxheath, Byrne's house in East Maidstone or at Solly's now-demolished home at 12 Carey Street, Maidstone.

Thursday 4 March

▶ Davie Jones & The Manish Boys, RAF Wyton, near St Ives, Cambridgeshire.

Friday 5 March

The single 'I Pity The Fool'/'Take My Tip' is released with the credit going to The Manish Boys.

Press coverage remains frothily concentrated on the publicity-seeking hair-length issue. According to the *Daily Mirror*, Langford has allowed David and group to perform on next Monday evening's live broadcast.[1]

There is a line-up rehearsal for the *Gadzooks! It's All Happening* BBC2 TV show at BBC Television Centre. After, David and The Manish Boys are photographed outside the BBC Centre's main gates by the *Daily Mirror*.

Between 4.00pm and 7.00pm, David and the band attend the recording of *Ready Steady Go!* at Rediffusion Studios, Kingsway.

A chance encounter with Donovan in Soho leads to an invitation to watch the folksinger record an

appearance on the programme. During the taping, David persuades presenter Cathy McGowan to interview him about 'I Pity The Fool'.

Also appearing on the show are solo singer Tom Jones, Lulu and pop act Dave Dee, Dozy, Beaky, Mick and Tich. The actress Diana Dors is in the audience.

Along with some other *RSG!* footage of this era, the recording is wiped. (▶ 25.3.66)

Also that evening David is interviewed, minus The Manish Boys, for *Ready Steady Go Radio!*, a Radio Luxembourg show hosted by Keith Fordyce and Dee Shenderry (broadcast the following week).

> 1. In 1992 Langford – who had previously encountered David in July 1964 when he was producer at *The Beat Room* and who went on to become a TV executive in Israel – explained he was behind the scam. "It has been credited to Leslie Conn, but it was me who thought up the idea of making a scene over the length of David's hair. There wasn't any question of David not appearing, it just made for a good story."

Saturday 6 March

▶ Davie Jones & The Manish Boys, Sevenoaks, Kent.

'I Pity The Fool' is described in *Record Mirror* as 'a bit of a raver after half-way but perhaps not catchy enough to make the charts'.

Monday 8 March

Davie Jones and The Manish Boys perform 'I Pity The Fool' live on *Gadzooks! It's All Happening*, after all-day rehearsals nearby at the BBC's Bush Theatre.[1] For the benefit of the press, Langford has said he has only let them play on the show on the basis that

Gadzooks! It's All Happening

 7.0

THE PRODUCER of *Gadzooks*, Barry Langford, is taking great care to keep his show up to date. 'I'm not booking far ahead,' he explains. 'I'm waiting to hear the releases before I engage the artists. The scene is changing so fast that some of the guests will come as a complete surprise.' **Davy Jones and the Mannish Boys**, who are appearing tonight, are likely to come into this category.

Little known outside the London clubs, they cut their first disc on March 5, and their main claim to fame at present is that they have produced another 'new sound.' It is the 'sax sound,' and the group contains two tenor saxophones (one played by Davy Jones himself), a baritone sax, a lead guitar, bass guitar, organ, and drums. All the boys come from Maidstone in Kent—except for eighteen-year-old Davy, who hails from Bromley.

complaints over their hair-length will lead to the fee being paid to entertainment charity The Variety Club Of Great Britain. Of course, this does not happen and the group receive their fee. The *Evening News & Star* features a photo of David having his hair set in preparation for the show. The recording is subsequently wiped.

Meanwhile, the lack of live work being drummed up by Conn is becoming an issue.

"We really thought we had made it," said Woolf Byrne in 2009. "I suppose we just sat back and waited for the phone to ring, and it never did. No one was hustling and following the thing up."

▶ After the TV taping, the group travel to the centre of London to perform as a favour for Shel Talmy at his wife Jenni's 21st birthday party. It is held at the Mayfair Hotel in Berkeley Street, near Berkeley Square, W1.[2]

1. In 2010 music venue the Shepherd's Bush Empire.
2. In 2010 the Radisson Edwardian Mayfair Hotel.

Tuesday 9 March

Milking the story for all it is worth, the *Mirror* carries a report claiming David will have to wait two weeks before he knows if he is to be paid for the *Gadzooks!* performance. As a result of the TV broadcast, David is recognised opposite Soho's Tin Pan Alley Club at 7 Denmark Street by Essex schoolgirl Linda Phillips, who takes a photograph of him (see page 53).

David's interview on *Ready Steady Go Radio!* is broadcast.

Wednesday 10 March

▶ Davie Jones & The Manish Boys, The Bromel Club, Bromley Court Hotel, Bromley Hill.

A short distance from his home, this venue has already witnessed performances by David as one of The Hooker Brothers. And the billing is indicative of the growing division between the frontman and the other musicians. On his home turf, David is able to ensure that his name is prominent; when other members of the group are responsible for bookings in venues closer to their Maidstone base, they exclude it from posters and promotion.

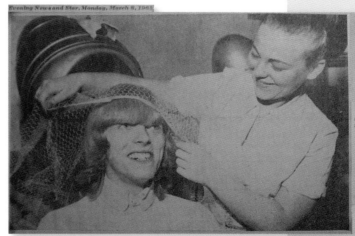

Evening News and Star, Monday, March 8, 1965

ALL SET! AS DAVY JONES HAS A TRIM AND A SET

Hairdresser Sylvia Halliday places a net over the head of singer Davy Jones for a set after trimming his long blond locks in readiness for to-night's television pop show "Gadzooks" on BBC-2. Davy, who sings with the Manish Boys pop group, was ordered to have his hair cut last week by producer Barry Langford. He said: "Kids to-day just don't want this long hair business any more." Davy and his group are launching their new disc "I Pity The Fool" on to-night's programme.

Indications of the growing dissent appear in an article published in a local Maidstone newspaper (highlighting one of the reasons why David will shortly leave the group): 'Although they are often misrepresented as "Davie Jones and The Manish Boys", this number will again be by The Manish Boys. Davie is a member of the group, and not, as many people think, the leader.'

Saturday 13 March

▶ Davie Jones & The Manish Boys, Royal British Legion Hall, Ancore Road, Coleford, Somerset.

When they arrive at the venue they are told that,

TOP LEFT: Barry Langford with Davie Jones, the day before taping *Gadzooks! It's All Happening*. Les Conn is on the far right; this is the only known photo of David and Conn together during the latter's tenure as David's manager.

TOP RIGHT: *Radio Times* entry for the bands appearance on *Gadzooks! It's All Happening*.

ABOVE: Getting his hair set for *Gadzooks!* performance, *Evening News & Star*, 8 March.

SINGLE RELEASES

Friday 5 March

RELEASE of 'I Pity The Fool'/'Take My Tip' on Parlophone.

⦿ **The Manish Boys**
A **'I Pity The Fool'** (Malone)
B **'Take My Tip'** (Jones)
Davie Jones (vocal, alto saxophone)
Paul Rodriguez (tenor saxophone, trumpet)
Woolf Byrne (baritone saxophone)
Johnny Flux (lead guitar)
Bob Solly (keyboards)
John Watson (bass)
Mick White (drums)
Jimmy Page (lead guitar on A-side, rhythm on B-side)
Produced by Shel Talmy
Engineered by Glyn Johns
(Parlophone R.5250)

Written by David, the B-side is the first record release of one of his songs. Additional guitar on both tracks was provided by Jimmy Page, a young college-leaver fast becoming a top-flight session musician often employed by Talmy. In 1966 he joined The Yardbirds.

The A-side, a well-known number by Bobby 'Blue' Bland, was written by Don Robey, writing under the name Deadric Malone, and introduced to David and The Manish Boys by Talmy. This would be David's last cover released as a single (as either Jones or Bowie) until his version of The Easybeats' 'Sorrow' in 1973.

David believed in the single enough to personally deliver a promo copy to Paul McCartney, handing it to the Beatle on the doorstep of his St John's Wood home.

Friday 20 August

RELEASE of 'You've Got A Habit Of Leaving'/'Baby Loves That Way', again on Parlophone.

⦿ **Davy Jones**
A **'You've Got A Habit Of Leaving'** (Jones)
B **'Baby Loves That Way'** (Jones)
Davy Jones[1] (vocal, harmonica)
Denis Taylor (guitar, vocal)
Graham Rivens (bass)
Phil Lancaster (drums)
Nicky Hopkins (piano)
Shel Talmy, Les Conn (backing vocal)
Glyn Johns (backing vocal)
Produced by Shel Talmy
Engineered by Glyn Johns
(Parlophone R.5315)

Recorded at IBC Studios, Portland Place, the tracks also featured Talmy and ex-manager Les Conn on backing vocals. The release also featured respected pianist Nicky Hopkins, who was hired for the session by Talmy. He had also sessioned for the producer on The Who's *My Generation* LP and single. This was the only Jones/Bowie release to feature Hopkins.

1. For this single, David's name was spelt Davy.

HOME GROWN

"I PITY the Fool" sings Manish Boy Davy Jones on the group's first release—issued last week on Parlophone. But he sings it again another 15 times before the record ends.

With this record, Medway's only group to find fame in the R and B boom is now on the verge of the national hit scene after less than a year playing in its present form.

Nobody can deny that this is a good disc—it opens with a low guitar introduction similar to the Stones' "Little Red Rooster," leading into a very prominent and melodic Davy Jones singing the melody line. The group's saxes and organ feature as one to build up the tension and then go off on their own lines as the vocal continues.

Apart from the repetition this is an extremely interesting disc—almost refreshing in fact—which stands a much-above-average chance of doing well. And if the dee-jays catch on then the Manish Boys are made.

The flip-side of the record, "Take My Tip," was written by Davy Jones himself—but it sounds rather like bass-guitarist John Watson singing it. Ironically this side may prove to be the better tune, although at first hearing it takes a little getting used to. It may grow on you, while "I Pity the Fool," so to speak, may grow off.

ABOVE: Singles by The Manish Boys and The Lower Third.
ABOVE LEFT: Single review from the *Chatham Standard*, March 1965.

despite the *Gadzooks!* media coverage, the gig has not been publicised locally so it is cancelled. Tired from the journey and with another long trek ahead of them to Norfolk, they are told by the caretaker they can sleep in the hall. They each make up temporary beds out of the Legion's uncomfortable chairs and spend a few restless hours in the cold.

Abandoning the hall in the early hours, they begin the long journey to their next gig in Cromer. If they aren't dispirited enough, shortly after setting off the van runs out of diesel.

"We stopped in the middle of nowhere, huddled together and slept the rest of the night in the freezing van," said Solly, speaking in 2007. "The following morning a couple of us set off and discovered there was an all-night petrol station just over the hill, five minutes away."

Sunday 14 March

▶ Davie Jones & The Manish Boys, Olympia Ballroom, Garden Street, Cromer, Norfolk.

Also on the bill are the Hudson Hi Four from Dundee, who generally worked as The Johnny Hudson Hi Four.

Flux's onstage moves cause controversy, it is claimed in another story fed to local paper the *Chatham Standard* by Rodriguez. This reports that the Olympia manager called the group a few days after the concert and said he would not book them again 'until Johnny Watson, Wolff [sic] Byrne and Davy Jones have their hair cut and Johnny Flux stops his dancing'.

Tuesday 16 March

▶ Davie Jones & The Manish Boys, Southsea Pier (near Portsmouth), Hampshire.

Saturday 20 March

▶ Davie Jones & The Manish Boys, Newmarket, Suffolk.

Thursday 25 March

During rehearsals at Maidstone's army barracks, the group receive a surprise visit from David's friend Steve Marriott.[1] Although he has his own R&B outfit (The Moments), Marriott has come along to try out for The Manish Boys at David's request. It is not made clear what his role will be. "We had enough money troubles so we didn't need another guy in the band," said Solly.[2] In the event, Marriott sits on the side of the stage and watches the rehearsal.

1. Born 30 January 1947, Marriott formed The Small Faces in June 1965, and Humble Pie with David's schoolmate Peter Frampton in 1969. After the demise of Humble Pie in the mid-70s he maintained a profile on the UK live circuit. Marriott died in April 1991 in a fire at his Essex home.

2. In 1999 David revealed he and Marriott considered forming an act around this time, using the name David & Goliath. It is possible David had hoped The Manish Boys would accept him and Marriott as co-frontmen.

Sunday 11 April

▶ Davie Jones & The Manish Boys, Trent Bridge, Nottingham.

Fed up with the lack of gigs, lack of money and continuing problems with the van, Woolf Byrne makes his last appearance with the band.

TOP LEFT: David photographed in Denmark Street by Linda Phillips, the day after his appearance on *Gadzooks! It's All Happening*, 9 March.

LEFT: Front page of Barry Langford's *Gadzooks!* script.

TOP RIGHT: Poster for appearance at Olympia Ballroom, Cromer, Norfolk.

MIDDLE: The Bromley Court Hotel, home of The Bromel Club, a venue played by David in the early- to mid-60s.

ABOVE: Advert for performance at Bromley's The Bromel Club; note David's name is flagged upfront.

ABOVE: Calvin James aka George Underwood.

RIGHT: Original painting by local art student Michael John, used to promote David's visit to Cardiff.

In this year...

Saturday 10 April
APPEARANCE by George Underwood under his stage name Calvin James on ITV's *Thank Your Lucky Stars* pop show, miming to new single 'Some Things You Never Get Used To'.

Sunday 9 May/ Monday 10 May
APPEARANCE by Bob Dylan at the Royal Albert Hall, Kensington, London. David was in attendance on one of the nights, while his manager from 1966–1970 was there on both in his capacity as publicist and consultant to Albert Grossman on the contractual aspects of Dylan's first UK tour.

Richard 'D.A.' Pennebaker filmed the concerts for inclusion in the documentary *Don't Look Back*. Kenneth Pitt – who briefly appears in a couple of scenes, including one shot in Dylan's dressing room at the Albert Hall – had previously worked with Grossman on Dylan's sell-out appearance at the Royal Festival Hall in 1964.

Pennebaker, meanwhile, directed *Ziggy Stardust & The Spiders From Mars The Motion Picture*, documenting the concert that concluded David's 1973 UK tour.

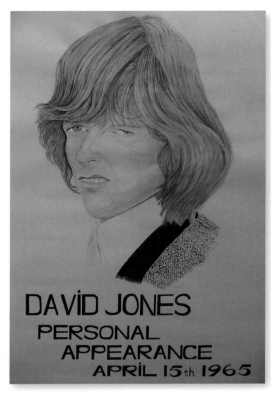

DAVID JONES
PERSONAL
APPEARANCE
APRIL 15th 1965

Monday 12 April

The group perform an unsuccessful audition for live bookings with a promoter at the Marquee. Such professional setbacks, the brewing disagreement over live billing and David's disappointment over the credit on 'I Pity The Fool' contribute to David's growing unease.

Thursday 15 April

As plans are now being laid to find a new band, David travels alone to Cardiff to plug 'I Pity The Fool' with a promotional appearance at a record shop in the Welsh capital.

On the same day George Underwood[1] (who is co-managed by Leslie Conn with Mickie Most's business partner and future Led Zeppelin manager Peter Grant) releases the single 'Some Things You Never Get Used To'/'Remember' under the stage name Calvin James, produced by Most and appearing on Columbia (Col DB7516).

1. This was Underwood's sole release. A follow-up single 'Ain't It Funny'/'She Wants To Be Loved' was recorded but never saw the light of day.

Saturday 24 April

▶ Davie Jones & The Manish Boys, Bletchley, Herts.
At the gig, which they fulfil without saxophonist Woolf Byrne, the band are invited to a local house party by two sisters. On the way home the van breaks down. The Manish Boys don't know it but the breakdown is symbolic – tonight is the last gig David will play with them and, indeed, is the last gig performed by The Manish Boys.

Wednesday 5 May

Having been invited to write songs by Talmy, Solly and Rodriguez visit the producer's office in Soho's Dean Street. Sitting in the reception area is David, whom they have not seen since the return journey from Bletchley. Unbeknown to them, David has also been contracted to contribute songs to Talmy. David tells them he is no longer interested in continuing with The Manish Boys.[1]

1. After the split was confirmed The Manish Boys went their separate ways. In various permutations Flux, Paul Rodriguez and Bob Solly also co-wrote songs for Shel Talmy. "That was probably the nicest six months of my life," said Rodriguez in 1992. "Shel paid us a weekly retainer. I don't think any of our work was recorded but it was a great time."

Johnny Flux became a DJ at offshore pirate radio stations Radio City and Radio London and remained friendly with David, who recorded jingles for him and also a general one for Radio City.

In 1982 Flux (as John Edward) wrote the number one hit single 'Save Your Love' for Renée & Renato. He also arranged, produced and released it on his Hollywood record label. In the mid-80s Edward created the children's TV character Metal Mickey, building the robot and performing the synthesised voice.

In the late 90s he returned to broadcasting again, this time for Medway FM, reverting to his birth name Johnny Flux.

Woolf Byrne also joined Radio City, broadcasting as the Big Bad Woolf. He also worked with Britain Radio, Radio 390 and the BBC World Service, and has acted in such TV programmes as BBC's *Silent Witness*.

Rodriguez became a song-plugger and later worked in music publishing. Solly writes about and deals in rare and collectable 1950s records. In 2005 *Record Collector* magazine published his book *100 Greatest Rock'n'Roll Records*.

Monday 17 May

▶ The Lower Third, Grand Hotel, Littlestone, Kent.
The Lower Third are a group of musicians from Margate, on the Kent coast.

Guitarist Denis 'Tea Cup' Taylor, bass player Graham Rivens and drummer Les Mighall have been billing themselves (together with Terry Bolton and Robin Wyatt) as Oliver Twist & The Lower Third, in reference to Charles Dickens' setting of his novel in Broadstairs, and giving a jokey nod to school. (The third year of secondary schools at the time was known as 'the lower third'.)

Shortening their name, they are gigging around the south of England and have scored a Saturday-night residency at Soho niterie La Discothèque.

They are also on the lookout for a frontman, spreading the word at music business hang-out La Gioconda.[1]

The coffee bar is situated at 9a Denmark Street in London's 'Tin Pan Alley', which houses music publishers, managers and agents in the buildings which line the narrow thoroughfare. David is a frequent visitor to La Gioconda,[2] mulling over ideas with Conn in the tiny, steamy, nondescript establishment where aspiring musicians gather to pass the time, talk shop and chase employment opportunities.[3]

On a visit to La Gioconda, David hears that The Lower Third are holding auditions at La Discothèque and heads across Charing Cross Road to the club's

premises at 17 Wardour Street.

There he finds his mate Steve Marriott also pitching for the gig. The try-out becomes a jam session that also includes ex-members of Georgie Fame's band, during which David impresses the Kent trio with his sax playing, taking the alto parts when Marriott performs Little Richard's 'Rip It Up'.

David also performs lead vocals on other songs, backed by Marriott and another vocalist.

"When I heard he was also a singer I said, 'We must have him!'," said Taylor in 1983. "He just looked so good." Back at La Gioconda[4] over egg and chips, David is offered and accepts the job.

Rehearsals with The Lower Third begin immediately, mainly at David's girlfriend's home in Bromley. The group develops a loud and gutsy live sound utilising feedback in the style of The Who. Among the numbers are those already performed with The Manish Boys such as 'Mars, The Bringer Of War' and 'I Pity The Fool' and two new compositions of David's: 'Born Of The Night' and 'You've Got A Habit Of Leaving'. Almost immediately they suffer a setback: the residency at La Discothèque abruptly ends. A general lack of live work will initially become an issue for the new group.

1. David's future musical collaborator Mick Ronson headed for La Gioconda when he arrived in London in 1966 looking for a band to join.

2. David and George Underwood had met singer/songwriter Johnnie Dee in the same cafe in 1964. Dee – best known for writing the hit 'Don't Bring Me Down' for The Pretty Things (which David covered on *Pin Ups* in 1973) – invited the pair to contribute to a recording of Barbara Lewis' 'Hello Stranger' at a nearby studio (most likely Embassy Sound). Underwood later said that Marc Bolan was also among those performing backing vocals that day. "We stood around listening to the playback," said Underwood in 1998. "He wanted to get a large chorus sound."

3. In 1966 Chris Farlowe scored a hit with the Jagger/Richards composition 'Out Of Time'. But in 1965 he was lead singer of The Thunderbirds. He later recalled David's presence at the cafe "hunched there, all emaciated, with hair dangling down on to the table".

4. La Gioconda changed hands in the mid-80s, and became the Barino Sandwich Bar. In 2008 it became French restaurant The Gioconda Dining Room.

Thursday 20 May

David & The Lower Third record commercial jingles at R.G. Jones' Oak Studios, London Road, Morden, Surrey.

In the evening David is featured as 'Teenager Of The Week' on BBC Radio Africa show *Turrie On The*

TOP LEFT: The original Lower Third line-up. From left to right, Terry Bolton, Les Mighall, Graham Rivens, Robin Wyatt and Denis Taylor. Ramsgate, 1964.

TOP RIGHT: Davie Jones & The Lower Third pre-mod styling. From left to right: Denis Taylor, David, Graham Rivens and Les Mighall. Bromley.

LEFT: Reunited at La Gioconda for the first time since disbanding, The Lower Third's Graham Rivens, Denis Taylor and Phil Lancaster in 1983.

BOTTOM: David's signed (as 'Davie Jones') portrait of Lower Third guitarist Denis Taylor.

Go! Despite the fact that his association with The Manish Boys is over, 'I Pity The Fool' is plugged. The Lower Third are in the audience for David's first known BBC radio interview.[1]

1. No archive recording remains of this previously undocumented appearance on BBC radio.

Friday 21 May

Paul Rodriguez is interviewed about The Manish Boys' split with David by the *Kent Messenger*, which reports: 'It is understood that 17-year-old Davey [sic] – who sported shoulder length blond hair – was upset when the record appeared without a personal credit on the label. "There was a furious row about this," said Paul.'

THIS PAGE

TOP: Stickers for The Lower Third featuring their first drummer Les Mighall, designed and drawn by David. Denis Taylor: "We used to stick these on the lamp-posts in Wardour Street."

MIDDLE: 'Bit Much' letter, written by David to *Melody Maker*, 3 July.

BOTTOM: Denis Taylor's scrapbook. Right photo: David, Mighall and Taylor.

OPPOSITE PAGE

TOP: David's 'Truth Shows' letter written to attract venues and promoters, May.

Bit much

AFTER playing a South Coast club we confidently anticipated a week's residency, if we reached the mark.

We soared above this mark. Then the promoter unblushingly told us we were "too good":—

As a four piece, we keep our price low. After our week the promoter was afraid that he would have to pay far higher to get a group of our standard.

Prestige is all very well, but must we spend hours rehearsing, just to be told to lower our standards? DAVIE JONES, The Lower Third, Bromley, Kent.

David draws up a press release to announce the formation of Davie Jones & The Lower Third. This mentions 'Born Of The Night', which they have recorded at Central Sound Studio in Denmark Street, next to La Gioconda. Though the song will be rejected by Talmy, David's hope is that the press release – which carries his home address and phone number – will stimulate interest elsewhere.

Tuesday 1 – Thursday 3 June

▶ Davie Jones & The Lower Third make their live debut at the Happy Towers Ballroom, Edgbaston, Birmingham.

The Happy Towers is on the lucrative Mecca circuit and, as such, an impressive early gig for a new group. Appearing on a revolving stage, they scrape by with a noisy set.

The following night they play in Tadcaster, Yorkshire. On the long journey home David encounters a familiar situation: The Lower Third's worn-out Atlas van breaks down. Once they are back in London it is replaced by a grey London County Council ambulance bought in Brixton for £145 by Rivens' parents.

The alarm bell is retained and word 'Ambulance' left on the side panel; both prove helpful in speeding the group to bookings, though they are frequently pulled over by the police.

The van itself provides a home for the band and their equipment, a place to sleep and a dressing room as they settle into a routine: In between London gigs, they overnight in the ambulance, sometimes parked in Denmark Street.[1]

On journeys, David and Lancaster are generally in the back with Taylor and Rivens upfront.

1. David talked about the ambulance in a 1993 BBC interview. "When I had the band The Lower Third we used to park up the ambulance outside the Gioconda. Two of us used to sleep in it because it was cheaper than getting a flat. That went on for about a month, night after night. Oh it was so cold! And Les [La Gioconda's proprietor] used to wake us up in the morning and bring us breakfast – he used to give us free breakfast. He was a good-hearted guy, old Les."

Friday 4 June

▶ Davie Jones & The Lower Third, Pavilion Ballroom, Westover Road, Bournemouth, Dorset.

Also on the bill are Jacqueline Rivers & The Boyfriends and Roger & The Rallies.

Friday 11 June

▶ Davie Jones & The Lower Third, Starlight Rooms, Montpelier Hotel, 2 Montpelier Road, Brighton.

Mighall quickly becomes homesick and particularly misses his girlfriend. After less than two weeks of rehearsals and around half-a-dozen gigs, he bails out from the group and returns home to Margate.[1]

The rest act quickly to find a replacement. Rivens spots an ad in music weekly *Melody Maker* placed by Phil Lancaster, a drummer based in Walthamstow, north-east London, who is seeking employment.

Lancaster is taken on after a meet, inevitably at La Gioconda.

"A couple of nights later we played together live for the first time, though we had never actually rehearsed together," said Lancaster in 1983.

During this period the group makes a Saturday-night appearance at the Hi-Fi Hop in Weybridge Hall, Church Street, Weybridge. David is billed as 'The Controversial Davy Jones'. They also perform at the Pilgrim Hotel in Haywards Heath, West Sussex, but live work dries up. It is becoming clear that Conn is losing interest.

1. After leaving The Lower Third, Les Mighall joined another Margate band, Spirits of Sound. Mighall died in March 2008, aged 65.

July

When David and Lancaster fail to obtain any bookings themselves after a day visiting Tin Pan Alley promoters, David pressurises Conn to strike another

recording deal with Talmy. Maybe a new single will raise the group's profile and attract the attention of promoters and agents.

The American producer is sufficiently taken with David's song 'You've Got A Habit Of Leaving' to agree to a new single for Parlophone.

During a session back at IBC Studios, Talmy produces 'Habit' and new song 'Baby Loves That Way'; Conn is among those on hand to supply backing vocals to the B-side. The engineer is Glyn Johns.[1] 'Habit' is not a new song; in fact it is the first track David demoed in the early 60s.[2] 'Baby Loves That Way' is a pastiche of the harmonies popularised by Herman's Hermits.[3] David presses for an attempt for the backing vocals to be sung in the manner of monks' chants, but the idea is dropped after a single attempt.

Working with Talmy isn't easy. There are frequent disagreements between him and David, which the rest of the group fear will damage their chances of success.

Worse is to come. After the recording there is a lull, with unexplained delays to the single's release. Seeking other ways to ignite interest on the live circuit, David visits agent Terry King's offices at 7 Denmark Street. Here he meets one of King's employees, Ralph Horton, an enthusiastic agent in his late 20s then handling Birmingham R&B group The Moody Blues. Featuring Denny Laine on guitar, The Moody Blues already have a massive worldwide hit under their belts with their cover of R&B standard 'Go Now'.[4]

Impressed with David's abilities and charisma, Horton arranges with promoter Kenny Bell for the group to make regular appearances at the Pavilion Ballroom in Bournemouth and the Ventnor Winter Gardens on the Isle of Wight over the coming weeks.

Horton also wins them warm-up slots in the intervals between Radio London's broadcasts of *The Inecto Show* from the Marquee (so called because it is sponsored by the Inecto shampoo brand). These short performances between those by more established acts are not broadcast or recorded.

1. Glyn Johns – who worked on The King Bees 'Liza Jane' recording the previous year – was the resident engineer at IBC Studios and was involved in sessions by many of the major acts of the period. A friend of Paul McCartney's, he later engineered The Beatles' 'Get Back' session and produced, among others, The Rolling Stones, The Who, and later The Eagles and Joan Armatrading.

2. David told photographer Mick Rock in 1972: "The first song I ever demoed was 'You've Got A Habit Of Leaving Me'. I'd saved up about £2 to hire a demo studio. Touted it around everywhere. Nobody wanted to know."

3. Herman's Hermits lead singer Peter Noone gave David's career a boost in 1971 when his cover of 'Oh! You Pretty Things', on which David played piano, reached number 12 in the UK chart.

4. The group had previously been Denny Laine & The Diplomats, co-managed by Horton and Denis Detheridge, editor of local music paper *Midland Beat*. Diplomats drummer Bev Bevan – later in The Move and ELO – recalled in 2008: "We were represented by Ralph Horton Enterprises, which occupied a first-floor office of a rambling, old Victorian building in Wake Green Road, Birmingham."

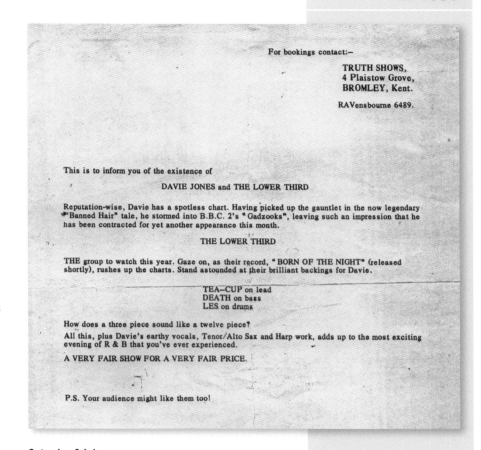

Saturday 3 July

During the wait for the single's release, the group try to jump-start interest with self-generated publicity. Denis Taylor's sister Jennifer[1] claims in a letter published in *Melody Maker*: 'The Who are only bordering on this new sound. If they want the real thing, listen to Davie Jones and the Lower Third from London.' The same paper will print a letter from David the following week.

The delayed release of 'Habit' forces David into action; he decides to part with Conn[2] and take up Ralph Horton's management interest by announcing that the group is to audition for him.

This takes place in an upstairs room of The Roebuck pub at 108A Tottenham Court Road, on the corner of Maple Street, in London's West End. Also in attendance are Kenny Bell and Neil Anderson.

It is agreed that Horton will represent the group, operating out of the two-bedroom basement flat in Warwick Square he shares with Bell.[3] Until recently this has been The Moody Blues' London base.

Also on the team is Horton's assistant Spike Palmer, who, it is said, has roadied for The Rolling Stones.

1. The letter was actually written by Graham Rivens who supplied her name to disguise his identity.

2. In 1984, David visited Les Conn's flat in the company of Mick Jagger, signing two books about Bowie in Conn's library with the line: 'From 1st Base To Home Run, Bo '84.' Conn – who died on 13 December 2008 – also attended David's first solo art exhibition in London in 1995.

In this year...

Tuesday 25 May
PROCLAMATION during a concert at La Locomotive in Paris by British rocker Vince Taylor that he is the Apostle St Matthew. This event, and David's encounters with Taylor, later informed David's creation of the Ziggy Stardust character.

Friday 2 July
APPEARANCE by George Underwood, again as Calvin James, at Orpington Civic Hall, co-headlining with The Alan Bown Set.

Sunday 4 July
APPEARANCE by David's ex bandmates The Konrads at the Pavilion Hall, Bournemouth, where comedian/singer Dickie Henderson topped the bill. The band have just returned to the UK from a series of live dates in Copenhagen, Denmark.

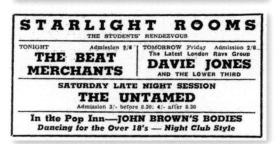

TOP LEFT: Davie Jones & The Lower Third, with their second drummer Phil Lancaster (far left). Pimlico, London.

ABOVE: The fading art deco splendour of St Leonard's seafront Marine Court, home of the Witch Doctor club (flyer pictured right) where David appeared with two different bands in the 60s.

MIDDLE: Advert for appearance at the Ballroom (in the Pavilion), Winter Gardens, Bournemouth, 4 June.

BOTTOM: Starlight Rooms, Brighton advert. Billed as "The Latest London Rave Group" for appearance on 11 June.

3. "Warwick Square was a great place to live," said Bell in 1992. "Interesting people would drop by all the time. There were a lot of parties."

Saturday 10 July

▶ Davie Jones & The Lower Third, Pavilion Ballroom, Bournemouth, Dorset.

The group begin a series of regular appearances at the venue.[1] These are booked by Horton's friend, local promoter Kenny Bell.[2] There is talk of a week-long summer booking but this doesn't happen.

Melody Maker publishes David's letter under the heading 'Bit Much'.

1. Ralph Horton shot 8mm footage of David and the band in Bournemouth over the summer. It has yet to emerge publicly.
2. Bell also booked dates on David's first run of Ziggy Stardust concerts in 1972.

Wednesday 14 July

▶ Davie Jones & The Lower Third, Bata Clan Club, off Regent Street, London W1.

Saturday 17 July

▶ Davie Jones & The Lower Third, The Witch Doctor, Marine Court, St Leonards-on-Sea, East Sussex.
Support act are The Sultans.

Friday 23 July

▶ Davie Jones & The Lower Third, Pavilion Ballroom, Bournemouth, Dorset.

The bill is headed by Cliff Bennett & The Rebel Rousers[1] and includes beat group Roger & The Rallies and compère Neil Anderson, who is managed by Ralph Horton and joins David and The Lower Third to share lead vocals on a couple of songs in their set.

1. The Rebel Rousers' line-up included keyboard player Roy Young, who played piano on David's 1977 album *Low*, and bassist Chas Hodges, half of hit 70s pop duo Chas & Dave.

Saturday 24 July

▶ Davie Jones & The Lower Third, Winter Gardens, Ventnor, Isle of Wight.[1]

Again headlined by Cliff Bennett & The Rebel Rousers, the bill includes Neil Anderson, who has a stint as weekly compère at the venue, and Patrick Kerr, who demonstrates dance moves and helps out with compèring duties.

1. David's first musical performance was on the Isle of Wight, during a cub scout trip there in 1958.

Sunday 25 July

▶ Davie Jones & The Lower Third, Moody Sunday Club, Pavilion Ballroom, Bournemouth.

With Anderson singing and Kerr MC-ing, the line-up is completed by Scottish group The Beatstalkers.[1]

David and the group fill in the days between gigs recording demos for other acts at R.G. Jones' Oak Studio in London Road, Morden, Surrey. David and Denis Taylor also write two jingles for Youthquake, a promotion of Swinging London fashions in New York. One of the songs is titled 'Puritan', named after the US manufacturer funding the campaign. This is written by Taylor's brother-in-law, Terry Bolton.[2]

1. From Glasgow, The Beatstalkers' bassist is Alan Mair, later in 70s group The Only Ones. Under David's future manager Ken Pitt's direction, The Beatstalkers covered three of David's compositions.

2. The Puritan jingle was based on Bolton's song 'It's A Lie'. None of these jingle recordings survive. Bolton, who married Denis Taylor's sister Jennifer, was a founder member of The Lower Third but had left before David joined the band.

Friday 30 July

▶ Davie Jones & The Lower Third, Pavilion Ballroom, Bournemouth, Dorset.

Though unlisted in the press, the group support Johnny Kidd & The Pirates.[1] During his act, much to the amusement of support acts, Kidd would dramatically wield his pirate cutlass around his head before launching it firmly into the stage floor. Kidd's band members would practically disappear into the wings to avoid his flying sword.

1. This wasn't the first time David had been on the same bill as Johnny Kidd & The Pirates. In early 63 The Konrads had supported them at a venue in Blackheath. David would also support Johnny Kidd with The Buzz. (▶ 3.4.66)

Saturday 31 July

▶ Davie Jones & The Lower Third, Winter Gardens, Ventnor, Isle of Wight.

Another date supporting Johnny Kidd & The Pirates with Neil Anderson also on the bill.

Sunday 1 August

▶ Davie Jones & The Lower Third, Pavilion Ballroom, Bournemouth, Dorset.

TOP: Waiting for the ferry back to Southampton. Fountain Pier, Cowes, Isle of Wight, 25 July. Left to right: Phil Lancaster, Moss Groves (Cliff Bennett band saxophonist), Cliff Bennett and David.

MIDDLE: Advert for Cliff Bennett Pavilion concert, 23 July.

BOTTOM: Advert for Cliff Bennett, Isle of Wight concert.

LEFT: Performance at the Marquee during interval of *The Inecto Show*, the Radio London programme sponsored by a shampoo brand. Photos taken by drummer Phil Lancaster's wife, Helene.

WINTER GARDENS
VENTNOR

Saturday, July 31st

JOHNNY KIDD
and the PIRATES

plus DAVY JONES and the LOWER THIRD
and NEIL ANDERSEN

Late Coaches to and from Cowes, Ryde, Newport

8—M-30   Fully Licensed   Admission 7/6

Next Saturday: THE PRETTY THINGS!!

Moody Sunday Club
PAVILION BALLROOM . BOURNEMOUTH
SUNDAY, 25th JULY

PATRICK KERR
(OF READY, STEADY, GO)
★
THE BEATSTALKERS
(FROM GLASGOW)
★
DAVY JONES and the Lower Third
★
NEIL ANDERSEN

7.30 p.m. - 11 p.m.   ONLY 5/-   ::   FREE MEMBERSHIP

Moody Sunday Club
PAVILION BALLROOM · BOURNEMOUTH
SUNDAY, 25th JULY

PATRICK KERR
(OF READY, STEADY, GO)
★
DAVIE JONES and the Lower Third
★
NEIL ANDERSEN
★
JUGS O'HENRY

7.30 p.m. - 11 p.m.   ONLY 5/-.   FREE MEMBERSHIP

JOHNNY KIDD   mono
I'LL NEVER GET OVER YOU
THEN I GOT EVERYTHING • HUNGRY FOR LOVE
A SHOT OF RHYTHM & BLUES

Johnny Kidd

TOP: Southampton. Waiting for the ferry to the Isle of Wight, Left to right: Phil Lancaster, David, Patrick Kerr and Johnny Kidd.

TOP RIGHT: Selection of Bournemouth and Isle of Wight adverts.

ABOVE: Johnny Kidd, whose biggest hit 'Shakin' All Over' was released in 1960. David supported Kidd and his group The Pirates several times during the mid-60s.

RIGHT: Southampton docks. Partly obscured by David is a bespectacled Ralph Horton. Left to right: Phil Lancaster, Neil Anderson, Patrick Kerr (bowing his head), Ralph Horton and David.

OPPOSITE PAGE:

TOP LEFT: Left to right: Graham Rivens, David, Pretty Things Phil May and Brian Pendleton, Unknown and Phil Lancaster.

TOP RIGHT: David, Phil Lancaster and *Ready Steady Go!* host Patrick Kerr on a Red Funnel steamer to Cowes.

MIDDLE: Winter Gardens, Ventnor, Isle of Wight.

BOTTOM: Singer Neil Anderson (left) with Ralph Horton's flatmate Kenny Bell on the Isle of Wight ferry. Anderson occasionally joined David and The Lower Third during their set.

Anderson and Kerr are joined on the bill by Birmingham act Jugs O'Henry (whose ranks include future Supertramp sax and keyboard player John Helliwell).

Around this time, and in preparation for the long-awaited release of 'You've Got A Habit Of Leaving', the group are photographed in and around Manchester Square, where their record company EMI is situated, as well as in the company building's in-house photographic studio.[1]

The group are wearing a set of clothes David has sourced from Carnaby Street retailer John Stephen. Just a couple of days earlier he had worn Stephen designs for a solo modelling shoot for teen magazine *Fabulous*.

The adoption of mod clothing is a sign of Ralph Horton's growing influence over David. He advises that London fashions will help propel the group, and David abandons his Keith Relf-like shoulder-length hair in favour of a neat side parting cut at upmarket hairdresser Charles of Queensway.

1. Cover of EMI's 1978 Davie Jones & The Lower Third/Manish Boys EP.

Friday 6 August

▸ Davie Jones & The Lower Third, Pavilion Ballroom, Bournemouth, Dorset.

The first of two appearances supporting The Pretty Things,[1] one of David's favourite groups of the period, who are noted for their frenetic stage shows and ultra-scruffy appearances. David strikes up a friendship with the group and this leads to him and The Lower Third demoing a set of other writers' songs for them. One track is re-recorded and appears on the R&B act's second album, *Get The Picture?*.

1. According to The Pretty Things' official website: 'The young David Bowie (then Jones) would slavishly follow them from gig to gig, intently watching (lead singer) Phil May's every androgynous, camp move win over both sexes in his outrageous and extreme stage performances. In the young Bowie's address book, Phil May's number was written underneath: 'God'! Listen to the early live takes of the hit 'Don't Bring Me Down' – May is singing 'I laid him on the ground' – waaaay out there in early '64.'

Saturday 7 August

▸ Davie Jones & The Lower Third, Winter Gardens, Ventnor, Isle of Wight.

Again supporting The Pretty Things,[1] with Neil Anderson, The Scapegoats and Tubs-In-Crowd on the bill.

This is David's last appearance on the Isle of Wight for many years[2] and by all accounts his time spent there over the summer is happy and fun-packed. He sees a lot of dancer and singer Susan Spurrier.[3]

1. In 1973 David paid homage to The Pretty Things by including covers of two of their hits on *Pin Ups*: 'Don't Bring Me Down' and 'Rosalyn'.

In the late 60s David had a chance encounter in Beckenham High Street with Pretty Things rhythm guitarist Brian Pendleton, who had left the group in 1966. Pendleton declined an offer to work with David, though in the 90s he led a group called Sam Therapy (the name taken from a lyric of David's 1977 song 'Sons Of The Silent Age'). Pendleton died of lung cancer aged 57 in 2001.

2. David did not return to the island until his headline appearance at the Isle of Wight Festival in 2004. According to festival veteran DJ Jeff Dexter, David was booked to appear on the last day of the 1970 event, but the promoter wasn't a fan of his work. Dexter ensured that David was booked to appear at the following year's Glastonbury Festival.

3. Susan Spurrier: "I first met him at a party in London. The Isle of Wight came up in conversation. I said, 'That's where I'm from.' The Lower Third used to travel around in a conventional ambulance, which was home from home. We used to walk along Ventnor front, along the cliff top. I was commuting from the island at the time and we used to meet in Bournemouth. He was very intelligent, always looking up at the stars."

Thursday 19 August

▸ Davie Jones & The Lower Third, The Radio Caroline Show, 100 Club, 100 Oxford Street, London W1.

Also featured on the bill are The Legends, The Strollers and Danny Williams.

Friday 20 August

❯ Davie Jones & The Lower Third, Pavilion Ballroom, Bournemouth, Dorset.

On the day that the group return to the Pavilion for David's only billing with The Who, the single 'You've Got A Habit Of Leaving'[1]/'Baby Loves That Way' is released on Parlophone.[2]

The accompanying press release features a short interview with David and a group bio by freelance journalist Roy S. Carson.

The release notes David's 'baby singing voice which "just stuck that way". Nevertheless, he's a very versatile singer, which will be seen in later records'.

Carson's release says that David plays tenor, alto and baritone saxophones, guitar, flute and clarinet. 'Insistently he claims the dubious honour of being Bromley's first "Mod" but has since changed his philosophy to become a "Rocker". He likes Spike Milligan, 18th-century architecture, Dutch School painting, Scandinavian "birds". Dislikes education, 9-5 jobs, long straight roads and "coppers" (in either sense – "cash" or the "law").'

The *Kentish Express* runs a feature on the group, noting David's new appearance with the heading 'Davie changes his hairstyle and his group'.

In the afternoon their sound-check at the Bournemouth Pavilion is interrupted by an appearance by Pete Townshend, songwriter and guitarist of the night's main attraction, The Who.[3]

"Pete came walking into the dance hall as we were going through Dave's songs," said Lancaster in 1983.[4] "He came to the stage and said, 'Whose stuff is that you're doing?' So David replied, 'It's mine,' to which Pete replied, 'That's a bit of a cheese-off, it sounds a lot like mine'. I sat down with Pete later and we had a natter about what we were earning. He wanted to know if we were getting as much as he was. We used to bump into them quite a lot after that."[5]

1. David re-recorded 'You've Got A Habit Of Leaving' in 2000 for his unreleased album *Toy*. This version was included as a bonus track on his 2002 single 'Slow Burn' on ISO/Columbia.

2. The credit spells David's first name as Davy, although most of the promotional material refers to him as 'Davie' Jones.

3. The Who achieved their first chart success in February and May 1965 with the singles 'I Can't Explain' and 'Anyway, Anyhow, Anywhere'. The latter was still in the charts when David and The Lower Third supported them in Bournemouth.

4. David mentioned this in an interview with *Q* magazine in 1993: "We had a thing about The Who. Townshend came into our sound-check and listened to a couple of things and said, 'You're trying to write like me!' I said: 'Yeah, what do you think?' He said: 'Mmm, well, there's a lot of bands around like you at the moment'. I don't think he was very impressed."

5. The pair developed a friendship over the ensuing years. Townshend contributed guitar to 'Because You're Young' on David's 1980 album *Scary Monsters*. David was also close to drummer Keith Moon, who died of a sedative overdose in 1978.

Thursday 26 August

❯ Davie Jones & The Lower Third, The Radio Caroline Show, 100 Club, London.

Also on the bill are Peter Jay and The Jaywalkers,[1] Gemini and Australian singer/actress Patsy Ann Noble (later known as Trisha Noble).

Music publisher Hal Shaper of Sparta Music – whose office is two minutes from the venue – attends the show.

"I wasn't invited," said Shaper in 1993. "I used

to go to gigs six nights a week and David was just another artist I encountered. I wasn't impressed with his singing but I could tell he was a great performer."

1. David meets and becomes friendly with The Jaywalkers' guitarist Terry Reid, later to become a leading light of the British blues scene. He was later asked by Jimmy Page if he would join him as singer in his new group Led Zeppelin (before Reid suggested Robert Plant).

Friday 27 August

Davie Jones & The Lower Third, Radio Luxembourg's *Friday Spectacular*, EMI Studios, Manchester Square, London W1.

This late-night show is sponsored by the group's record company, EMI, and co-hosted by Shaw Taylor (later to present British crime TV show *Police 5*). "I interviewed Bowie, amongst others (I was the first DJ to interview The Beatles), on a show called the *Friday Spectacular!* It was an hour-long show, between 10 and 11 on a Friday night and was produced in EMI Studios in Manchester Square," recalled Shaw in 2002. Even though this is a radio show the group perform a dance routine for the studio audience while 'You've Got A Habit Of Leaving Me' is played (they rehearsed the moves at Horton's flat).

Around this time an interview with David – recorded at the Marquee – is broadcast on Radio Luxembourg's *Kenny & Cash Show*.[1]

1. Kenny Everett (1944–1995). David's performance of 'Boys Keep Swinging' on *The Kenny Everett Show* in 1980 ended with a comedy routine performed with the popular British TV entertainer.

TOP: David and band at the gates of the Wallace Collection museum, Manchester Square, London.

MIDDLE: The Pavilion Ballroom, Bournemouth. The only venue where David and The Who appeared on the same bill, 20 August.

BOTTOM: Lower Third contact sheet photos from August.

Tuesday 31 August

With Horton now in control of their career, the group spend four hours on a recording session at R.G. Jones' Oak Studios. Around this time they use the studio to demo two new songs by David: 'Baby That's A Promise' and 'Silly Boy Blue'.[1]

1. David adjusted the lyrics to 'Silly Boy Blue' to reflect his interest in Buddhism when he re-recorded the track for his self-titled 1967 debut album.

Wednesday 1 September

Recording at R.G. Jones (two hours). A jokey song of David's from their set, 'Over The Wall We Go', is also demoed around this time.

Saturday 4 September

▶ Davie Jones & The Lower Third, Blue Moon, Cheltenham, Gloucestershire.

Horton also delivers more live work, though this means that the young musicians spend a lot of time in the ambulance, with Rivens handling driving duties. He is nicknamed 'Death', not because his driving skills are poor, but because he is constantly on the road.

"We'd go from London to Manchester, then back to London, then the following night up to Leeds," he said in 1983. "The rest of the group were all right, they had been sleeping all day. We used to arrive at the gigs at about four o'clock in the afternoon. I hadn't had any sleep because I had driven all night and then they would say, 'Come on, we've got to rehearse!'"

Sunday 5 September

▶ Davie Jones & The Lower Third, Moody Sunday Club, Pavilion, Bournemouth, Dorset.

Patrick Kerr is compère of this and the previous night's gigs. A former dancer on *Ready Steady Go!*, Kerr owns Hem & Fringe, a boutique and hairdressing salon in Pimlico, central London. David and The Lower Third are by now customers. Kerr's wife, Theresa Confrey, who had also danced on *RSG!*, would also cut David's hair.

Tuesday 7 September

▶ Davie Jones & The Lower Third, 100 Club, London.

This is the first of three weekly shows supporting Brit R&B/soul act The Artwoods,[1] and is later listed as a 'jazz show' by David in a BBC questionnaire for audition applicants.

David told comedian Ricky Gervais in an interview in the *Observer* in 2003. "He [Wood] was one of the first London musicians to popularise R&B. They [The Artwoods] were probably one of the most popular live bands in London.

"But there was no beating Red Hoffman[2] and the Measles. One of the great unsung R&B bands of the mid-60s. I was always finding myself on the same bill as 'Red'."

1. Led by Faces/Rolling Stones guitarist Ron Wood's elder brother

Davie (with an "ie" to differentiate between he and American singer Davy) Jones, who works with the lower third. First disc: "You've Got A Habit Of Leaving Me," out next week (Parlophone). Davie is 19, used to be an advertising artist, now plays tenor, alto, baritone saxes—and guitar. Group backing him comprises genuine characters . . . Graham Rivens, nicknamed "Death;" Dennis Taylor, alias "Teacup;" Phil Lancaster, drummer. They use a £170 1956 LCC Ambulance as their mobile workshop and hotel.
Pic by Roy Carson

TOP LEFT: Fully signed EMI promo photo. Davie Jones & The Lower Third in hipsters, flowery ties and white shirts from John Stephen, Carnaby Street.

TOP RIGHT: Davie Jones, *Record Mirror*, 14 August.

BELOW: *Kentish Times,* 20 August.

Arthur, The Artwoods featured Jon Lord (later of Deep Purple) on keyboards and drummer Keef Hartley, with whom David appeared in December 1968.

2. Red Hoffman's real name was Stan Dulson. The Measles were formed in Manchester in 1964.

Friday 10 September

Such is the group's association with Bournemouth that Horton is reported by the *Bournemouth Times* to be 'interested in opening a male fashion shop' in the coastal town.

Saturday 11 September

Record Mirror's review of 'You've Got A Habit Of Leaving' describes David as a 'highly talented singer. It's a curiously pitched vocal sound with powerful percussion and a slightly dirgy approach. Plenty happening: lots of wailing. Very off-beat'.

Tuesday 14 September

▶ Davie Jones & The Lower Third, 100 Club, 100 Oxford Street, London.

In the evening the group again support The Artwoods. During the day David signs a publishing deal with Hal Shaper's Sparta Music to represent his songwriting. The initial period is for a year.[1] The deal with Shaper[2] has been set up by Horton, who is unaware the publisher has witnessed David in performance at the 100 Club a couple of weeks previously.

The signing takes place at Sparta's offices at 155 Oxford Street, London.

"Ralph Horton was a very nice and persuasive fellow," said Shaper in 1993 (who died aged 72 in

2004, coincidentally on David's 57th birthday). "David looked amazing, but it never crossed my mind that he was a great singer. When he came into my office he was dressed in a half-military uniform, which was very impressive. He was like a peacock. He wasn't very assertive but Horton was really behind him. I liked the fact he was writing different songs from the rest and, with the onset of TV shows, a singer/songwriter with good looks was a good proposition."

1. The Sparta deal was renewed for another year in September 1966, but Shaper readily relinquished rights a few months later to enable David to reach a new arrangement with Essex Music. David recognised the gesture. In 1977, he asked Shaper to look after his

DAVIE CHANGES HIS HAIRSTYLE AND HIS GROUP

DAVIE Jones, who caused an uproar when he appeared on B.B.C. 2 in "Gadzooks, It's All Happening" when he was with a Maidstone group, has teamed up with a Thanet group on his next release.

The uproar came from the B.B.C. and Davie's fans. The B.B.C. said he couldn't appear with his hair so long, but his fans protested that he should go on and must NOT have his hair cut.

In the end, the programme director relented, and the show went on with Dave as the star, hair and all.

Davie's hair style now is a moderate "long back and sides," compared to his shoulder-length curls in the days of The Manish Boys.

His group, The Lower Third, wear the same "college boy" cut. Their only extrovert appearance seems to be in their silk ties—exotic in design and colour.

Ambition

Members of the group are: Dennis "Teacup" Taylor, born at Ramsgate 21 years ago. He plays lead guitar. Of his ambitions, he says his foremost

is to become a good musician.

Graham Rivens, bass guitarist—according to the boys, "the beanstick" of the group at 6ft. 1in.—was educated at Dane Court Boys' School, Broadstairs.

Phil Lancaster ("My ambition is to make loads of money and keep playing"), the drummer, is the "foreigner" of the group, being a Londoner.

Associated

And finally there is Davie himself. Although he wasn't born in Kent, he has been associated with groups in the county for three years since he was 17.

"It was either full-time singing or commercial art," said Davie this week. "I was doing both at the time and I thought singing was more creative."

While Davie was singing with these Kent groups, The Lower Third were in Thanet playing in their home area "looking for

some kind of foothold," said Graham.

In fact, they failed to find a foothold in Kent and moved to London for a few months to play at the Discotheque Club. Then they met Davie.

What does Davie and his new group think of the partnership? Davie feels it will be a success. "We have the same policies and fit rather well together," he said.

The disc that the group have recorded with E.M.I. is "You've Got A Habit Of Leaving"—and "Baby Loves That Way." Both were written by Davie.

The number is the first on wax for The Lower Third, but Davie had a disc out called "I Pity The Fool" when he was a Manish Boy.

• • •

TOP TEN IN KENT

1 (1) "Help!" The

Davie, with new hairstyle, and new group—The Lower Third

publishing for a three-year period. This was by then a lucrative deal and would normally have commanded a hefty advance. David asked for no advance and, when his lawyers requested an early termination so they could secure a broader deal elsewhere, Shaper immediately agreed as he had done in December 1966. "I'm a great admirer of David's. There's no doubt he is an absolute giant in the business," said Shaper.

2. Hal Shaper was an accomplished lyricist in his own right, with a catalogue of around 500 songs to his name. In 1964 Frank Sinatra recorded Shaper's 'Softly As I Leave You'; around 300 cover versions were subsequently recorded, the royalties enabling Shaper to set up Sparta in 1964. By 2008 the Sparta Florida group represented 20,000 songs.

Wednesday 15 September

In need of financial backing and a partner with an established track record, Ralph Horton visits manager and agent Kenneth Pitt[1] at his offices at 35 Curzon Street, Mayfair, to discuss whether Pitt is interested in becoming involved with The Lower Third, and David in particular.

Pitt, who has not heard of David, says that his client list is full, but agrees to attend a performance some time soon.

Pitt also advises Horton to persuade David to change his stage name. With a keen eye on British entertainment successes across the Atlantic, Pitt is aware that Manchester-born Davy Jones has created a stir as the Artful Dodger in the Broadway production of Lionel Bart's musical *Oliver!* at the Beck Theatre.

1. A leading British music business manager and publicist of the 60s, Pitt had on his client list at this time chart-toppers Manfred Mann and Crispian St Peters. (▶17.4.66)

Friday 17 September

David and Horton take little time to heed Pitt's advice. In a letter to Pitt, Horton announces: 'I have now changed Davie's name to David Bowie.'

Of course, the new surname is David's choice, made in homage to the US pioneer Jim Bowie,[1] and is one he toyed with when pressing The Konrads to adopt a Wild West image in emulation of his boyhood heroes three years previously.[2]

The name-change is symbolic. Happy that Horton is working on all fronts to further his career, David is able to hone his stagecraft through regular live appearances. Spurred on by a growing confidence in his songwriting abilities (as recognised by the Sparta deal), David now sets about the serious business of building a career in entertainment, one in which he is not reliant on other group members.

In addition, at 18, he is eager to live his life outside parental control. Around this time David moves into Horton's apartment, although this is a temporary arrangement and he soon returns home.

1. Jim Bowie's grandfather was a Welshman, John Jones (the same name as David's father). Jim Bowie's elder brother was christened John Jones Bowie, and another close relative was one David Bowie.
2. "I wasn't making any money as Davie Jones," David said in a January 1966 interview with Nigel Hunter for *Music Echo*. "I've read everything I can get hold of about the pioneering times in the States and I picked the name of Bowie after Jim Bowie, the bloke who invented that knife and died at the Alamo."

Tuesday 21 September

▶ David Bowie & The Lower Third, 100 Club, London.

The last gig of the stint supporting The Artwoods, this is the first performance by David billed under his new professional name.

Saturday 2 October

David is featured in two magazines. *Fabulous* runs the fashion shoot for which he modelled the previous month. David appears alongside 'Jeanette' (actually model Jan De Souza) and plugs John Stephen's clothes in the accompanying interview.

Meanwhile, *Boyfriend*[1] carries photographs of his new haircut and reports on David's abandonment of the long-haired look: '"I consider myself just to be fashion conscious, not a mod or anything," Davie said.'

1. David was photographed in Kingly Street, a popular Soho location of the 60s, by Fiona Adams, whose studio was nearby. Adams was part of The Beatles' circle, having taken the 'jumping' image for the sleeve of their 1963 'Twist & Shout' EP.

Friday 8 October

▶ David Bowie & The Lower Third, the Marquee, London.

This is a performance with Gary Farr & The T-Bones,[1] whom David had previously supported with The Manish Boys. Farr's band now includes Keith Emerson[2] on Hammond organ.

After this gig there is a lull in live engagements, during which time Horton prepares a contract formalising his management of David's career.

David and his father visit David's solicitors, Barfield & Barfield, at Danes Inn House in The Strand, Holborn, to review Horton's proposal.

1. Generally at the Marquee (and many other clubs in the UK), bands were contracted to perform twice during the evening. The support band would play first and the headline act would follow, both playing for 45 minutes. This would then be repeated, though each group generally performed a different set.

2. Emerson had joined the previous month. He went on to form The Nice in 1967 and 70s supergroup Emerson, Lake & Palmer.

Sunday 31 October

▶ David Bowie & The Lower Third, The Birdcage, Eastney, Portsmouth, Hants.

Tuesday 2 November

The BBC requires all groups to pass an audition before it will allow sessions to be broadcast on one of its pop programmes. David and The Lower Third audition,[1] performing James Brown's 'Out Of Sight', 'Baby That's A Promise' – the new song recently demoed at R.G. Jones – and surprise selection 'Chim Chim Cher-ee' (from film musical *Mary Poppins*).

The group are told they will have to wait two weeks to hear the decision of the selection panel.

1. The application form was filled in by David, who clearly started it before the name change; the surname update is clearly visible.

Friday 5 November

▶ David Bowie & The Lower Third, the Marquee, London.

As support for The Summer Set.

David's relationship with the venue is solid.[1] They sign up as 'Marquee Artists', which means that the club is now an additional booking agency for live engagements.

Within a month or so, however, only David's name will be billed in Marquee Artists' listings and adverts – a sign that Horton is grooming him for a future without The Lower Third.

Denis Taylor's sister Jennifer and her husband Tony attend one of David and The Lower Third's appearances at the Marquee. They have to leave midway through the evening when the crush and deafening music cause Jennifer to pass out.

1. "I got friendly with the [Marquee] owners; for me there were no rules at the door so I used to creep in and watch what was happening," David said. "The Marquee, The Scene, Eel Pie Island in Twickenham, they were all a circuit. At the time 16 years old, for me when I was frequently in those places it was during the era of the first batch of mods."

Saturday 13 November

▶ David Bowie & The Lower Third, The 'New' Barn, 75a West Street, Brighton, East Sussex.

Monday 15 November

While doing the rounds trying to drum up financial support, David and Horton have been introduced to industrial heating executive Raymond Cook, who is a director of a company called Petray.

A meeting at Horton's Warwick Square flat secures a loan of £1,500 from Cook on the basis that the money will be used to further David's career. The

OPPOSITE PAGE

TOP: The original Sparta Music agreement for 'And I Say To Myself'.

BOTTOM: Ralph Horton's historic letter to Ken Pitt announcing David's new stage name.

THIS PAGE

TOP LEFT: John Stephen advert.

TOP RIGHT: David and Jan De Souza, modelling assignment for *Fabulous* magazine, 2 October.

BOTTOM: Group photo, Pimlico, London.

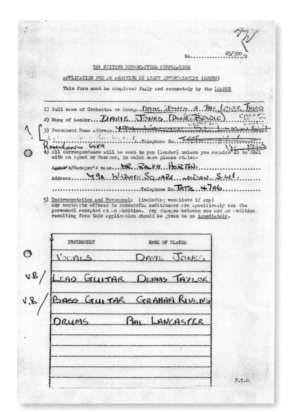

agreement does not give Cook any rights over management (and he will never see a return on his investment).

Around this time The Lower Third are afforded the luxury of their own road manager, Paul Williams, whose wages are occasionally paid by Cook.

Tuesday 16 November

The BBC Talent Selection Group returns a majority 'No' vote on the group's application for sessions.[1]

David and his singing style are described as 'a cockney type but not outstanding. A singer devoid of personality. Sings wrong notes and out of tune'.

1. David recorded the first of many BBC sessions in December 1967.

Friday 19 November

▶ David Bowie & The Lower Third, the Marquee, London.

Rather than supporting The Summer Set, the group shares billing.

David's friend Marc Bolan releases his debut single, 'The Wizard'/'Beyond The Rising Sun' on Decca.

Thursday 25 November

With the funding from Cook in place, David and Horton reach agreement on representation and sign a three-year management agreement endorsed by David's father.

Acting swiftly, Horton introduces David to leading songwriter/producer Tony Hatch at Pye Records' headquarters in Great Cumberland Place, central London. Horton has known Hatch for a couple of years, having first met him during his time with The Moody Blues in their incarnation as Denny & The Diplomats.

Impressed, Hatch signs David to Pye on the basis that he will produce the young songwriter's material himself.[1] Their first recording sessions are conducted at Pye Studios in ATV House, 40 Bryanston Street,[2] Marble Arch, the majority in Studio 2. The group record 'Now You've Met The London Boys' for potential single release.

Written earlier in the year as David familiarised himself with London's pill-popping nightlife, particularly the music scene in Soho, the song has already received positive audience reactions and is on its way to becoming a live performance highlight.

Despite a bravura vocal performance, Pye rejects the recording because of the lyric 'You tried a pill'.[3]

During a second session at Pye Studios, the group

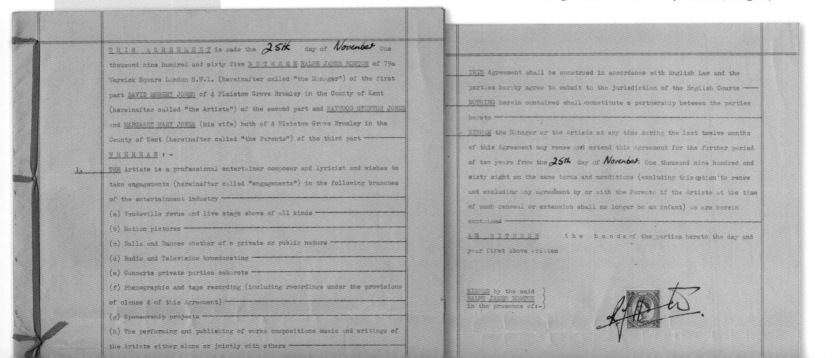

record two more new songs, 'Can't Help Thinking About Me' and 'And I Say To Myself'.

Attending the session are Horton and financial backer Ray Cook.

1. "[Bowie] and his manager came for an appointment and brought some good demo tapes," said Hatch in 1993. "I signed him on the strength of the tapes without a formal audition."

2. Pye Studios were in the basement of the building which later housed the Sportsman Casino.

3. The track was reworked with The Buzz and released as a David Bowie B-side a year later.

Friday 10 December

▶ David Bowie & The Lower Third, the Marquee, London.

The group return to live performance with another support for Gary Farr & The T-Bones.

Saturday 11 December

▶ David Bowie & The Lower Third, The Scene, Florida Ballroom, Brighton, East Sussex.

The group headline, with The Beat System supporting.[1]

1. The venue is featured in the 1978 film *Quadrophenia*. The Florida Ballroom became the Brighton Dolphinarium.

Thursday 23 December

David assigns 'Can't Help Thinking About Me' to publisher Sparta Florida.

Thursday 30 December

David and The Lower Third spend the night in the band's home town of Margate, prior to catching the

ferry from Ramsgate to France the following morning. David sleeps at Denis Taylor's home at 27 Kent Road.

Friday 31 December

▶ David Bowie & The Lower Third, Golf Drouot, 2 Rue Drouot, Montmartre, Paris, France.

The group's first concert date outside the UK is a New Year's Eve performance co-headlining singer Arthur Brown,[1] arranged by the Marquee's booking agency. Also on the bill are the club's regular acts Vigon And The Lemons, The New Turnips and The Sounders. "We were a little late arriving in Paris and the guy who had arranged to meet us was hopping up and down when we got there, but we managed to get on stage on time," recalled Phil Lancaster in 1983. With roadie Paul Williams helping to set up, the group performs matinee and evening sets on a small semi-circular stage. The audience goes wild.

"After we came off stage the girls were belting the door down to get to us," said Lancaster. David later recalled the Golf Drouot warmly. "It was the very first place I tried out something that was pretty much like a kind of punk thing," he said in 1977 when the club's owner, Henri Leproux, called a French radio phone-in featuring David. "His club was very inspirational for me, it really was, because we were trying out, at that time, what we considered was fairly exciting music. We had a chance to play somewhere, and he let us work with it."

1. Arthur Brown (born 24 June 1942) developed a theatrical performance style and charted the number one UK hit 'Fire' in 1968.

Late 1965

Pye's European licensees Columbia/EMI feature the B-side 'Baby Loves That Way' on the rare early compilation titled *Beat '66*. Issued in Germany, this is the first album to feature material by David, who was recording as Davy Jones at the time.

In this year...

Thursday 11 November

LIVE debut of The Velvet Underground at a high-school dance in Summit, New Jersey. Introduced to the group's music by manager Ken Pitt in the mid-60s, David regularly included versions of the Velvets' 'I'm Waiting For The Man' and 'White Light/White Heat' and formed an association with vocalist/songwriter Lou Reed in the early-70s which resulted in him co-producing Reed's solo album *Transformer*.

Friday 19 November

RELEASE by Pye Records of 'Till The End Of The Day'/'Where Have All The Good Times Gone' by The Kinks. David covered the B-side on his 1973 album *Pin Ups*. (▶ 19.10.73)

Thursday 25 November

ENTRY at number 17 in the US charts of The Yardbird's 'I'm A Man'. The song was later used as the basis for David's 'The Jean Genie'. (▶ 24.11.72)

1966

DAVID'S songwriting matures under Tony Hatch's guidance, and he moves on from The Lower Third in favour of a new set of backing musicians, The Buzz.

Although new single 'Can't Help Thinking About Me' barely troubles the charts, Pye renews David's contract and he and The Buzz log up an impressive number of live dates, adopting the latest Carnaby Street styles.

Follow-up 'Do Anything You Say' flops but David and Ralph Horton launch a showcase residency The Bowie Showboat at London's Marquee. Music bigwig Ken Pitt joins forces with Horton to steer David's career.

'I Dig Everything' is recorded with leading session musicians and, although this paean to Swinging London is not a hit, it points the way to a new musical direction.

Dropped by Pye, David and The Buzz demo ambitious new songs including 'Rubber Band', which is snapped up by Decca for release as a single on its progressive Deram label. Horton's lack of financial acumen is becoming evident but Pitt engineers a deal with Deram that will enable David to record and release an album.

The Buzz subsequently disband, though the members remain loyal to David and are among the backing musicians during the recording of the album with producer Mike Vernon and assistant Gus Dudgeon.

The sessions reveal Anthony Newley's influence on David and David's interest in Buddhism on the song 'Silly Boy Blue'.

David's recordings are released in other countries, including the US. 'David Bowie' makes his first solo appearance and Pitt returns from the US with a test pressing of a new group's debut album. *The Velvet Underground & Nico* will have a profound effect on David's creativity for years to come.

PREVIOUS SPREAD: Modernist David in early 66.

THIS PAGE

TOP: Horton encouraged David to wear suits for many of his mid-60s photo sessions, Clapham Common, London.

TOP RIGHT: Gaiety Bar record launch invitation.

Saturday 1 January

▶ David Bowie & The Lower Third, Bus Palladium, 6 Rue Fontaine, Montmartre, Paris 9e.

The group's stint in the French capital[1] continues with a matinee at the Golf Drouot and an evening show at Le Bus Palladium, a venue which has only been open a few months in Paris' red-light district, Pigalle.[2]

1. The performances were covered in a short report in French pop magazine *Salut Les Copains* in February 1966.

2. Described in local guides as 'a rock & roll temple', Le Bus Palladium was still open as a music venue in 2010.

Sunday 2 January

▶ David Bowie & The Lower Third, Golf Drouot, Paris.

The success of these shows points to David's growing confidence. His fellow musicians are

You are invited to meet
DAVID BOWIE
with
The Lower Third
in
The Gaiety Bar
from 12 noon to 2.30 p.m. on
THURSDAY, JANUARY 6th. 1966.
at the
VICTORIA TAVERN 10a STRATHEARN PLACE.
HYDE PARK. LONDON. W.2.

encouraged to improvise on songs.[1] Many climax in high-volume soloing and shrieking feedback (in the style of The Who) and David also performs two or three ballads on his acoustic guitar before the set is brought to a close with a chaotic version of Holst's 'Mars The Bringer Of War' from *The Planets Suite*.[2]

"We got louder as we progressed," said Taylor in 1994. "'Mars' had lots of feedback – fantastic and very noisy."

1. Including covers of the Kinks' song 'You Really Got Me'.

2. The music was used as the theme for one of David's favourite 50s TV series *Quatermass*.

Monday 3 January

Having arrived the night before, Ralph Horton announces that David is accompanying him home on a plane (David's first flight) while The Lower Third are forced to suffer the discomfort of a journey back in the ambulance.

This aggravates growing dissent among David's fellow group members, who are already upset that Marquee Artists have been advertising his name alone. The realisation that they are now little more than backing musicians is capped by Horton's revelation that David must return to London swiftly for a meeting with the powerful *Ready Steady Go!* producer Vicki Wickham (who had intended to attend the final Golf Drouot show). Their presence isn't required.

Thursday 6 January

With just over a week to go before its release, new single 'Can't Help Thinking About Me' is launched at The Gaiety Bar, the Victoria Tavern, 10a Strathearn Place, Bayswater, London WC2.[1]

Among those attending is John Lennon's father, Freddie, who has controversially signed a recording deal with Pye against the wishes of his son.

David and The Lower Third pose together for many photographs[2] before David is shepherded away by Horton to meet and greet the guests, further inflaming the sense of disunity.[3]

In its reviews column, *Record Retailer* describes the single as 'an original song about teenage trouble'.

1. The launch party costs backer Ray Cook £95.

2. None of these photographs have surfaced in the intervening years.

3. "It was very much about David Bowie, not about David Bowie and the band," said Phil Lancaster in 1994.

Friday 7 January

▶ David Bowie & The Lower Third, the Marquee, London.

Another gig supporting Gary Farr & The T-Bones coincides with the publication of an interview with Phil Lancaster in local paper the *Walthamstow Independent's* Teen And Around column.

He tells journalist Adella Lithman: "On the Saturday we played at the 'Golf Drouot' and the following night at the latest in-most club in Paris, The Palladium. We went down like a bomb."

Saturday 8 January

▶ David Bowie & The Lower Third, Radio London Saturday Show, the Marquee, London.

This is an afternoon show as David celebrates his 19th birthday. Also on this day Ken Pitt – yet to meet David or see him perform – is visited by Mike Pruskin, who is hoping Pitt will be interested in replacing the departed Leslie Conn as co-manager of David's friend Marc Bolan.

At the time Bolan is living at Pruskin's basement flat, 22a Manchester Street, on the opposite side of the road to Pitt's apartment.

1. Members of The Lower Third remember seeing Stevie Wonder rehearse in a back room at the Marquee. Just 15, Wonder made a guest appearance at the club during this time to promote 'Uptight (Everything's Alright)', which became a top 20 hit in early February 1966.

Friday 14 January

Pye Records release 'Can't Help Thinking About Me'/'And I Say To Myself' single.[1]

⊙ **David Bowie with The Lower Third**
A **'Can't Help Thinking About Me'** (Bowie)
B **'And I Say To Myself'** (Bowie)
David Bowie (vocal, tambourine)
Denis 'T-cup' Taylor (guitar)
Graham Rivens (bass guitar)
Phil Lancaster (drums)
Tony Hatch (piano on A-side)
The whole group (backing vocal)

Produced by Tony Hatch
(Pye 7N 1702)

As in many of David's songs from this period, the lyrical content is confessional and reflective, evoking his life in Bromley: tensions with his mother, Sundridge Park Station, the recreation ground at the end of his street, St Mary's Church and a girlfriend.[2]

There is no doubt that David is benefiting from the sure hand of Tony Hatch, who has considerable success under his belt producing the likes of Petula Clark (for whom he wrote the hit 'Downtown').

David is also moving away from the noisy R&B he has played with The Lower Third towards an MoR sound. He adopts a less affected singing style for the duration of his association with Hatch, and roots for London with lyrics and storylines set in the capital at a time when The Beatles and Merseybeat have powered a movement towards the provinces.

"At first he had this big thing about writing and singing about London as if he had to put the metropolis on the map against Liverpool, Manchester and Birmingham, whose bands and cities were getting all the media attention," said Hatch in 1990. "I distinctly recall one title called – or about – Hackney Marshes.[3]

"He was young, very easy to communicate with and ready to try all my ideas just as I was ready to try all his. He was the epitome of courtesy and even came to the recording sessions in a suit."

The press release accompanying the single quotes David: "If the record is a hit, that's alright, but I really want to become established." The *NME* describes the single thus: 'Absorbing melody, weakish tune'.

David's local paper, the *Bromley & Kentish Times*, covers the single's release with a report headed 'Pop Singer Changes His Image'. This quotes a claim from David that he and the band "use ballet steps in our performance".

1. This became the first US David Bowie release, on Warner Bros in May 1966.
2. David performed the song often in the late 90s, sometimes

Sunday 9 January
NAMED after bluesmen Pink Anderson and Floyd Council, The Pink Floyd play their first gig of the year at the The Goings On Club, Archer Street, Soho, London.

Formed in 1965, bassist Roger Waters (born 1944), drummer Nick Mason (born 1945), keyboard player Rick Wright (1945–2008) and guitarist/singer Roger 'Syd' Barrett (1946–2007) are soon to become the pioneers of British psychedelia, counting David among their early fans.

LEFT: David's first music paper front cover (the *NME*), albeit a half-page advertisement.

BELOW: Tony Hatch, David's producer at Pye.

Davie Jones is back in his locker .....

at the bottom of the sea. And instead we have DAVID BOWIE, a 19 year old singer discovered by Tony Hatch. Why David Bowie? "There are too many Davie Jones's" David explains. "David Jones is my real name and when I first turned professional two years ago and my pirate-like character was just right at that time, and the name fitted in with the image I wanted to give myself."

Looking at DAVID BOWIE it would be difficult to recognise under that smart exterior the somewhat controversial and angry young singer who styled himself after his famous namesake. Gone are the outlandish clothes, the long hair and the "wild" appearance and instead we find a quiet, talented vocalist and song writer – DAVID BOWIE.

His debut disc has been written by himself and tells the story of a young man leaving home. Most of David's lyrics are taken from his own experiences of city life – a theme about which he is well qualified to write since he has attempted 'to make his own way' since he was sixteen.

CAN'T HELP THINKIN' ABOUT ME
c/w And I Say to Myself   Pye 7N 17020

is released on January 14th and will no doubt give a lot of pleasure to the already numerous Davie Jones fans. But more important, DAVID BOWIE has already established a tremendous fan following after his six Radio London appearances at the Marquee Club, London, and numerous appearances in clubs and ballrooms all over England. This record should help to establish a bright new talent for 1966 and bring him the hit parade honours he so justly deserves.

David's first interest in all forms of art comes from his Art School days where he studied to become a graphic designer "but although I was very interested in design I found that I could not express myself satisfactorily designing graphically. When I first wrote songs I started by changing the words of nursery rhymes and then graduated to a more serious form of song writing." David has since written hundreds of songs and explains that "writing is a recreation for me, it helps me to relax and is an outlet." Tony Hatch, his Recording Manager, and himself an internationally known song writer, is enormously impressed with David's fresh young talent and already has plans for an LP and EP of David's own songs.

David's writing is always done at home and very often after a performance and a long drive. His lyrics are neatly written into an exercise book and put into a drawer in his desk. Consequently he has found more than once that when he arrived at the studio he had left his exercise book at home. This happened when recording 'Can't help thinkin' about me', but what could easily have become a problem was no more than a challenge to David's quick mind. He sat down quietly in the studio and re-wrote the lyrics.

Amongst many ambitions, the two most important are "to act in a musical and dance in a film" explains David. And since he is in the process of writing a musical, the day when he can realise at least one of his ambitions may not be so far off.

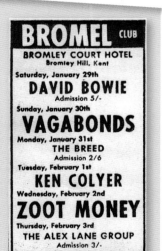

TOP AND OPPOSITE PAGE: 'Davie Jones is back in his locker' press release (front and back).

TOP RIGHT: 'Can't Help Thinking About Me' alternative newspaper advert.

MIDDLE RIGHT: Radio London and Radio Caroline adverts for 'Can't Help Thinking About Me'.

ABOVE: The writing was already on the wall for The Lower Third. The advert for their Bromel Club appearance listed David alone. Unbeknown to the band, Horton had already placed audition ads for their replacements.

admitting embarrassment at the lines he had penned more than 30 years earlier.

3. A large area of parkland and recreation space to the east of the city.

Wednesday 19 January

▶ David Bowie & The Lower Third, The Cedar Club, Constitution Hill, Birmingham.

After the show, David meets local bass player Chris 'Ace' Kefford, who is in a group called The Vikings, and guitarist Trevor Burton, of The Mayfair Set. Impressed that David is writing and performing his own songs, they act on his advice that they should do the same.

Over the coming months they join forces with guitarist/songwriter Roy Wood from Mike Sheridan & The Nightriders, then recruit Carl Wayne on vocals and former Denny & The Diplomats drummer Bev Bevan to form The Move (whose first three singles become Top Ten hits).

Around this time David & The Lower Third play three more bookings to promote the single release, in Harrow, north London, Newmarket, Suffolk, and Carlisle, near the Scottish border.

Saturday 22 January

Music Echo publishes a feature headed 'Hey presto – there's a new name from Davie Jones's locker', in which David reveals the influence of early British rocker Joe Brown.[1]

"I was a sort of Joe Brown then, bouncing about like he does and doing all the Cockney bit," he says. "I sang all his songs, sounded very like him, and I thought he was marvellous. I still do."

1. Born 31 May 1941, Brown was among the first wave of British rock'n'rollers, surfing the skiffle fad with a cheeky cockney persona. Managed by impresario Larry Parnes, Brown had hits in the early 60s with 'A Picture Of You' (performed by David in The Konrads), 'It Only Took A Minute' and the novelty 'I'm Henry The Eighth', among others.

Friday 28 January

▶ David Bowie & The Lower Third, Stevenage Town Hall, Stevenage, Herts.

A *Bromley & Kentish Times* report claims that Horton has insured David for £50,000, though quite how this is calculated is not revealed. "David is worth much more than £50,000 to me - financially," says Horton. "I am sure it represents only a small proportion of his potential earning."

Horton and David are already colluding on moving his career forward without The Lower Third. An advert seeking replacement musicians has been placed in *Melody Maker* and Taylor, Rivens and Lancaster are about to find out for certain they are surplus to requirements.

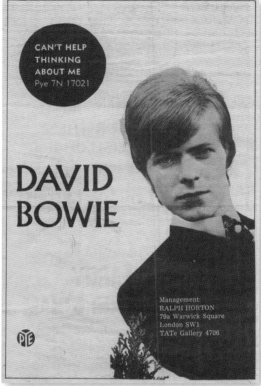

Management:
RALPH HORTON
79a Warwick Square
London SW1
TATe Gallery 4706

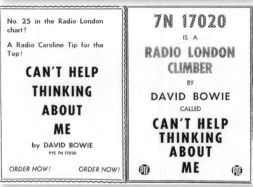

No. 25 in the Radio London chart!

A Radio Caroline Tip for the Top!

CAN'T HELP THINKING ABOUT ME
by DAVID BOWIE
PYE 7N 17020

ORDER NOW!   ORDER NOW!

7N 17020
IS A
RADIO LONDON CLIMBER
BY
DAVID BOWIE
CALLED
CAN'T HELP THINKING ABOUT ME

Saturday 29 January

▶ David Bowie & The Lower Third, the Marquee, London.

This is an afternoon show before the group travel south to perform at David's local venue, The Bromel Club, in the evening for a fundraiser he has organised for alma mater Bromley Tech.

The atmosphere is such that even Phil Lancaster's father – who is in the audience – recognises that there is little point in the musicians continuing with David because of his stand-offish on-stage attitude to them.

This is confirmed not only by the billing for The Bromel appearance – credited to just David Bowie – but also when Horton informs them that there will be no wages since the money is needed to cover travel expenses.

The trio journey to Bromley and confront Horton in

TOP: John Eager's audition diary entry for 3 February.

BOTTOM: David in Ralph Horton's lounge at 79A Warwick Square.

an attempt to wrestle payment from him before the performance. He is adamant they must play for free.

David avoids the confrontation, pacing the low wall outside the hotel and listening in while the band remonstrate with Horton.

"It was a real choker," said Lancaster in 1986. "We realised that Dave wasn't backing us up. I walked over and said, 'Ta-ta, Dave,' because I couldn't just walk away. But he wouldn't answer me… that hurt. Then off we went. That was the end of David Bowie & The Lower Third."[1]

The gig is cancelled, and David is never to play The Bromel again.

1. The Lower Third continued to perform as a three-piece but went their separate ways in the late summer of 1966.

Thursday 3 February

Auditions are held for new backing musicians at the Marquee. Among those who respond to the *Melody Maker* ad is drummer John Eager.

"The guy previous to me at the audition was a real heavy rock drummer and I thought crikey, there's no way I'm going to get this job," said Eager in 1991.

Bass player Derek 'Dek' Fearnley meets David at Horton's apartment in Warwick Square. "He looked really thin and weak; I wasn't immediately impressed," said Fearnley in 1991. "Then he played me some of his songs and I thought 'Wow, this is different.' It was really good stuff. I played along with him on bass."

Sunday 6 February

With Fearnley on board, Eager is offered the job as drummer. They join David and Horton's assistant Spike Palmer back at the Marquee for an audition by guitarist John 'Hutch' Hutchinson, who has been given David's number by the club's assistant director, Jack Barrie.

Hutchinson has just returned to the UK after a year in Goteborg, Sweden, with a local R&B group called The Apaches. After being offered a place in the band, Hutchinson recommends a friend from his native Scarborough, Yorks: keyboard player Derek Boyes, who also impresses David.

With the line-up complete, David's friend, Radio London DJ Earl Richmond,[1] suggests the group's new name, The Buzz,[2] at one of the station's promotional gigs.

1. John Dienn (1926–2001), broadcaster and hotelier.
2. Coincidentally, Scottish act The Buzz released a single 'You're Holding Me Down'/'I've Gotta Buzz' shortly after David's new group was formed.

Monday 7 – Wednesday 9 February

Rehearsals take place in the ground-floor flat above Horton's in Warwick Square, which is occupied by a couple of nurses. Derek Boyes moves into this apartment shortly afterwards. The members of The Buzz retain their day jobs (most of them in offices); David is the only professional musician.

Band nicknames are established: Eager is dubbed 'Ego' by Derek Boyes, who in turn becomes 'Chow'.

Eager becomes intrigued by David's personality. "He was always an interesting person to talk to; I often found that you may not always get the answer you were expecting," said Eager in 1991. "David would generally go off at a tangent. You could tell he was different and thought about things and expressed himself in a different way."

The members of The Buzz are taken with Horton's dry sense of humour, with lines delivered in his sing-song Midlands accent. "Ralph could be very funny," said Fearnley in 1991. "He amused me, the way he took people off and minced around."

Horton also makes it clear, with this new line-up, that David will not play any instruments during live performances. "Ralph would never let David play the guitar on stage, or the sax," said Fearnley. "In fact, I never ever heard him play the sax."

David's new backing musicians are impressed with Horton's conviction that he can make David a star, despite operating in somewhat reduced circumstances.

"There were terrible situations at the flat in Warwick Square," said Eager. "He [Horton] would never answer the door because it was likely to be a bailiff trying to collect money. He did well to keep it all together."

David has recently demoed songs such as 'Love You Till Tuesday' and the musicians understand that he is the focal point rather than a band member.

There is a deliberate shift from The Lower Third's heavy rock style (which had started to gain a small following on the live circuit) towards a more moderately paced and lighter presentation.

Thursday 10 February

▶ David Bowie & The Buzz, Mecca Ballroom, Leicester.

The group make their debut performance supporting The Graham Bond Organisation,[1] whose line-up includes the wild, jazz-influenced drummer Ginger Baker.[2]

Also on the bill are Brit-soul act Jimmy James & The Vagabonds. At David and Horton's insistence The Buzz are decked out in green trousers and matching checked shirts. They also have freshly cut mod hairstyles (Fearnley particularly dislikes his).

The new look serves only to confuse the audience of mods, who expect recognisable R&B numbers so are unresponsive to the set as it mainly comprises David's own songs, which suffer from a lack of rehearsal.

"It wasn't a very enjoyable experience," said Eager. "We didn't really get a very good crowd response, perhaps some polite applause at best. We certainly weren't a part of the mod scene."

However, Horton's faith in David is evident when he takes over as driver of the group's touring bus, another converted ambulance.

When it is not on the road, the ambulance – even more basic than that used for The Lower Third's live forays – is parked outside Fearnley's brother's house in Worcester Park, Surrey (where the guitarist lives).

"It stank of diesel fumes and was very uncomfortable," said Eager. There are no fitted bunk-beds, just a second-hand couch which seats three, and the vehicle frequently runs out of diesel and has an unpredictable steering alignment.

It is soon decorated with graffiti but, unlike with other groups, this is all self-generated; the young females who adorn vans belonging to rival acts with lipsticked messages are remarkable by their absence apart from one who tries to communicate with Fearnley by leaving her phone number and the message: 'Call me on Fridays 'cos my mum's out.'

1. Led by organist/saxophonist Graham Bond (1937–1974), the pioneering R&B artist who suffered mental health problems and committed suicide at a north London underground railway station. Bond made a cameo appearance in the 1973 rock film *That'll Be The Day* playing sax in a seedy show band led by singer Billy Fury.

2. Born 19 August 1939, Baker has an interest in fusion music which has led him into collaborations with a wide variety of musicians, from Eric Clapton in Cream, Afrobeat superstar Fela Kuti, John Lydon in Public Image and British rock band Hawkwind.

Friday 11 February

▶ David Bowie & The Buzz, Radio London Show, the Marquee, London.

The group appear with Boz and The Sidewinders[1] to fulfil an engagement made for David & The Lower Third; this is stated in the contract and the billing.

In fact, all three Lower Third members are in the audience. Still smarting from the split, they pronounce themselves unimpressed with the new backing band and the change of style.

This is the least of The Buzz's problems. They are not only under-rehearsed but also daunted by this debut at the important venue (which also hosts gigs by Rod Stewart and David's old saxophone teacher Ronnie Ross this month).

"This is the show I remember best because I was terrified as it was the Marquee," said Fearnley. "We hardly had time to rehearse – I can remember reading the chord changes off of the floor."

Also in attendance are *Fabulous* journalist and occasional *Ready Steady Go!* presenter Michael Aldred, who brings two guests, singer Kiki Dee[2] and performer/entrepreneur Jonathan King.[3]

"What a knockout he is too!" Aldred raves about David in the magazine. "Mr King wouldn't stop enthusing about David's lyrics and he said something to the effect that he thought Mr Bowie would emerge as one of the names of 66."

1. Boz Burrell (1946–2006). Later a member of King Crimson and Bad Company.

2. Born Pauline Matthews, 6 March 1947, British singer-songwriter notable for her association with Elton John, with whom she topped the British charts with duet 'Don't Go Breaking My Heart' in 1976.

3. Born Kenneth George King, 6 December 1944, British music business performer/entrepreneur.

Saturday 12 February

▶ David Bowie & The Buzz, Bowes Lyon House Youth Club, St George's Way, Stevenage, Herts.

This is an evening show; in the afternoon David & The Buzz play another Radio London Show at the Marquee.

Earl Richmond
RADIO LONDON

TOP: The Ambulance. This is the only known photo of David (with keyboard player Derek Boyes) with one of his legendary mid-60s group vehicles. Note the lipstick messages written on the side, which David highlights with mock indignation. The photo was taken by John Eager's sister Angela.

BOTTOM: Earl Richmond (real name John Dienn), was often referred to on Radio London as 'The Earl of Richmond'. A keen early supporter of David and his music.

In this year...

Tuesday 1 February

DEATH of comic American actor, Buster Keaton, aged 70. An admirer of the actor, David would reference Keaton in his 1977 video of the song 'Be My Wife' by wearing similar pancake make-up and giving a Keaton-esque performance.

ABOVE: Gerald Fearnley (photographed in 2010), elder brother of Buzz bassist Derek and the photographer of David's first album sleeve. David and band would often stay and rehearse at Gerald's home and central London studio during this period.

RIGHT: David performing 'Can't Help Thinking About Me' at a *Ready Steady Go!* rehearsal in Wembley, Middx, 3 March.

Sunday 13 February

'Can't Help Thinking About Me' enters the *Melody Maker* chart at number 45, and will rise another nine places over the coming fortnight.

However, the music paper's chart is not the national one, on which radio airplay and appearances on national TV show *Top Of The Pops* are based. It is likely Horton bought the record into the chart.[1]

In his *Music Echo* column, Jonathan King champions the single under the heading 'Bowie's Record Does Not Deserve To Die'.

1. Though illegitimate, this was a common music business practice at the time.

Tuesday 15 February

◗ David Bowie & The Buzz, The Pavilion, Bournemouth, Dorset.

The gig is notable for an approach made to David backstage. "This guy asked if he could record one of David's songs," recalled Eager. "Maybe it was 'London Boys'. I don't think anything came of it, but it amazed me at the time."

The song has been given a lyrical makeover by David since he and The Lower Third recorded it a few months ago, tracking the experience of a comedown as dawn breaks after a speed-fuelled night on the town.

Friday 18 February

David Bowie & The Buzz are listed as Marquee Artists in an *NME* advertisement.

Saturday 19 February

◗ David Bowie & The Buzz, The Boy's Club, Crawley, West Sussex.

David's Pye recording contract is extended for another year.

Apart from journeys to and from engagements, David's interaction with his fellow musicians is limited. "He did the work and then went home again," said Eager in 1991. "I felt he wanted to keep his personal life separate, so there wasn't a great deal of socialising."

In *Boyfriend* magazine, David shows off clothes he has designed for himself: 'A head swivelling grey suit with an imperial cut about it. It has a row of crowned brass buttons down the front, and a high black suede collar. This style is going into John Stephen's boutiques.'[1]

1. David wore this military-style jacket on the front cover of his first album. (▶ 1.6.67).

Monday 21 February

At rehearsals, Horton reveals that David and The Buzz have been booked to appear on *Ready Steady Go!*

Tuesday 22 February

During a session at Regent Sounds studio in central London, a demo of new song 'Do Anything You Say' is recorded. Tony Hatch attends and agrees that it should be the next single.

Friday 25 February

◗ David Bowie & The Buzz, The Kasbah Club, London Road, Southampton, Hants.

At a basement venue with a cramped and crowded performance area, this is the first of many shows in Southampton this year, including an extended run at the city's Adam & Eve club, whose owner, Mrs Bicknell, has taken a shine to the group.

Saturday 26 February

◗ David Bowie & The Buzz, Saturday Scene, The Corn Exchange, Chelmsford, Essex.

The support is local group Coltrane Union. David collapses on stage during the performance, which is cut short. Eager's diary attributes it to 'worry and nervous exhaustion' while a local paper puts it down to 'flu, bordering on pneumonia'.

Headed 'A Message To London From Dave', the first of many interviews with David over the coming years is carried by *Melody Maker*.

David mentions that his new song 'Now You've Met The London Boys' is going down well live, but that Hatch is not prepared to record it with the current drug-related lyrics.

Since it has been recorded a couple of months earlier, it is likely that David means that his A&R man is not happy for the song to receive commercial release.

LEFT: *Ready Steady Go!* rehearsal, Wembley with The Buzz; Dek Fearnley (bass), John Eager (drums), David and John Hutchinson (guitar) (keyboard player Derek Boyes is concealed behind Hutch). John Eager's kit was loaned for this run-through from Dave Dee, Dozy, Beaky, Mick and Tich.

BELOW: Star of *Ready Steady Go!* (broadcast the previous evening), David signs copies of his new single at Cranes in Birmingham. He is pictured with Cranes staff members' Pauline Williams and Mary McGuckin.

Monday 28 February

◗ David Bowie & The Buzz, Club Continental, 123 Terminus Road, Eastbourne, East Sussex.

The group make the first of three visits this year to this popular coastal resort, with advertising claiming support by a 'celebrity disc jockey'.

Thursday 3 March

The Buzz tape the backing track to 'Can't Help Thinking About Me' at Rediffusion's TV studios in Wembley, ahead of their *Ready Steady Go!* performance the following day. During the rehearsal for cameras, David casually runs through the vocal rather than performing it, even though his friend Steve Marriott, now of The Small Faces, is watching from behind the cameras, dancing and shouting, "Leap about, you're on TV!"

"David would never put on the show for technicians," recalls Fearnley later.

Photographer Cyrus Andrews, who also captures David at Horton's Warwick Square home around this time, is taking shots during the rehearsal.

Friday 4 March

◗ David Bowie & The Buzz, Chislehurst Caves, Bromley, Kent.

In the early evening, the group perform 'Can't Help Thinking About Me' on *Ready Steady Go!* [1] Only David's vocals are live. He insists on wearing a white suit provided to him by John Stephen.

This causes a kerfuffle: the unsophisticated television cameras produce a 'dazzle' effect when broadcasting pure white objects, and David is told he must wear something else. Eventually producer Francis Hitching relents when adjustments are made to the lighting.

During the show, host Cathy McGowan interviews Stephen about the suit and his Carnaby Street empire. Also appearing are The Yardbirds,[2] Manfred Mann, The Small Faces and Dave Dee, Dozy, Beaky, Mick & Tich.

After the broadcast, David and The Buzz head for Chislehurst Caves, carved out over 8,000 years, forming miles of labyrinthine underground tunnels.

"We never felt safe performing there," said Eager in 1991. "There was water running off the walls, all around the speakers and guitar leads. It was a wonder no one was electrocuted."

Also appearing on the bill is David's schoolmate Peter Frampton, in his group The Train.

1. *Ready Steady Go!* was broadcast from Television House, Kingsway, London, from 1963, moving to Wembley in 1965 where it remained until the last show in December 1966. None of the recordings of David's appearances on the show have survived.

2. The Yardbirds' single 'Shapes Of Things' had just entered the UK charts. David included a cover on 1973 album *Pin Ups*.

Saturday 5 March

◗ David Bowie & The Buzz, Rowing Club, Trent Side, Trent Bridge, Nottingham.

During the day David makes a personal appearance at Cranes & Sons record store in Birmingham city centre,[1] signing copies of 'Can't Help Thinking About Me' and posing for photographs.

The Nottingham and Union Rowing Club upstairs room was

SINGER David Bowie has been touring the country visiting leading record stores to meet the staff and distribute publicity material for his first record, "Can't Help Thinkin' About Me." Here he is seen autographing a copy of his disc for Pauline Williams and Mary McGuckin at the record department of Cranes in Coimore Circus, Priory Ringway, Birmingham.

CLUB ONE-O-ONE

(Formerly The New Barn)   75a WEST ST., BRIGHTON (opp. Odeon)

TONIGHT, FRIDAY, MARCH 11th, 8.30 p.m. till 12 Mid   Admission 2/6

ONE OF YOUR FAVOURITE LOCAL GROUPS

SATURDAY, 12th MARCH
THIS IS AN ALL NITE RAVE
FEATURING
DAVE BOWIE & THE LOWER 3rd
(This Group really gives a great performance)

SUNDAY, 13th MARCH   Good Value for only 2/6
NON-STOP from 2 p.m. till 11.30 p.m., PLUS A GROUP
_____

**Only One Month to go before our Great Untouchable
Non-stop Easter Rave**

TOP: Advert for Cub One-O-One gig, Brighton.

RIGHT: Marquee Artist announcement.

BOTTOM: David's brief meetings with Barrett in 1966 were not successful but his admiration for the artist remained undiminished.

marquee   artists

GERrard 6601   18 CARLISLE STREET, LONDON, W.1

EARL RICHMOND   TAT 4706

DAVID BOWIE   GER 6601
AND THE BUZZ   TAT 4706

a popular 60s and 70s music venue; the club still remains. David and the Buzz played there twice.

1. Cranes, which also sold musical instruments, was at 35-36 Colmore Circus, Ringway, Birmingham.

Monday 7 March

The group gather at Pye Studios in Marble Arch, central London, and record 'Do Anything You Say' and 'Good Morning Girl', both sides of a forthcoming single. The Buzz trio are paid £10 each for the session and Hatch tells them: "I've never heard you guys swing like that before."

Eager later attributed this to the material: "Out-and-out jazz is what Dek and I played before we were with Bowie."

'Good Morning Girl' is replete with jazz influences; David even scats throughout. The title is taken from The Yardbirds' version of Sonny Boy Williamson track 'Good Morning Little Schoolgirl'[1] (also covered by Rod Stewart), but the two songs bear no other resemblance.

1. David lifted the vocal intro from The Yardbirds' hit for his 1976 composition 'TVC15'.

Thursday 10 March

▶ David Bowie & The Buzz, unknown venue, Peterborough.

Friday 11 March

With planned dates in Scotland for 11-13 March cancelled, the *RSG!* broadcast provokes a response from The Lower Third's Phil Lancaster. In an article in local paper the *Walthamstow Independent* headed 'Pop Groups Hopes Dashed', Lancaster blames Horton for the split. 'Phil said the trouble started when their manager concentrated all his efforts on

making Mr Bowie the "leading light".'

Saturday 12 March

▶ David Bowie & The Buzz, Club One-O-One, 75a West Street, Brighton, East Sussex.

Billed in the local press for this 'all-night rave' as Davie Jones & The Lower Third, the group are paid £30.

Eager's diary also confirms a performance in Newmarket earlier in the evening, most likely at the Drill Hall in the Suffolk town.

Sunday 13 March

The Pink Floyd inaugurate a series of weekly hosted Sunday evenings at the Marquee under the banner Spontaneous Underground. Moving away from their blues origins in favour of extended psychedelic rock workouts, the band incorporate back projections and light shows at these gigs.

David is there and will use a similar format to launch a showcase for his own talents soon.

David was a great admirer of the group – including a cover of their hit 'See Emily Play' on his 1973 album *Pin Ups* – and in particular Syd Barrett (1946–2006).

"Barrett was a huge influence on me, absolutely," he said on Barrett's death. "I thought Syd could do no wrong… he was a massive talent. He was the first I had seen in the middle 60s who could decorate a stage. He had this strange mystical look to him, with painted black fingernails and his eyes fully made up. He weaved around the microphone and I thought, 'This guy is totally entrancing'. He was like some figure out of an Indonesian play or something and wasn't altogether of this world. It's so sad that he couldn't continue with the fever that he started with.

"The few times I saw him perform in London at UFO and the Marquee clubs during the 60s will forever be etched in my mind. He was so charismatic and such a startlingly original songwriter. Along with Anthony Newley, he was the first guy I'd heard sing pop or rock with a British accent. His impact on my thinking was enormous. A major regret is that I never got to know him."

Tuesday 15 – Thursday 17 March

David and the band occupy the Marquee during the day for rehearsals but run the risk of triggering a 'decibel meter', which automatically cuts the power if volume levels are exceeded. This stops acts disturbing office workers above the venue and in the area.

Friday 18 March

▶ David Bowie & The Buzz, the Marquee, London.

During the afternoon Ralph Horton and John Eager accompany David to a personal appearance at the Target Club in the Co-op Memorial Hall, Paul's Row, High Wycombe, Bucks, to promote 'Do Anything You Say'.

David is interviewed by Earl Richmond as part of

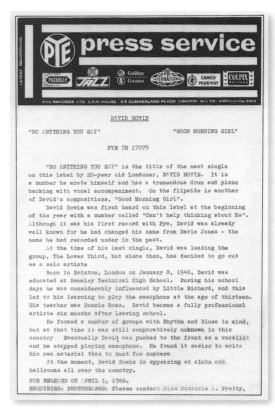

THE TWO R's
THE RAILWAY HOTEL
WEALDSTONE BRIDGE
FRIDAY AND SUNDAY

SUNDAY MARCH 13th
The group with the most
TARGET 66

FRIDAY MARCH 18th
A sound to be heard
SIDEWINDERS

SUNDAY MARCH 20th
The return of
*GARY FARR
& THE T- BONES*

FRIDAY MARCH 25th
This fantastic group
DAVID BOWIE
& THE BUZZ

SUNDAY MARCH 27th
A group you may have heard
BLUE SYNDICATE

EVERY FRIDAY & SUNDAY 8 - 11p.m.
BUSES 158, 114 & 18 PASS THE DOOR

The Buzz are unhappy with the sound, feeling that Tony Hatch has put a dampener on the session.

Saturday 2 April

The group and Ralph Horton travel in a hired six-wheel Transit van to Scotland for a couple of dates to promote the new single north of the border.

The first booking, close to the Scottish border in Carlisle, is cancelled, though it is claimed the band are greeted by exuberant fans outside their hotel.

On the same day, Dusty Springfield's review of 'Do Anything You Say' appears in *Melody Maker*. Springfield writes: 'I haven't got a clue who this is either but I can see the effort that has gone into this record. It's nice. The sound is a bit messy.'

Sunday 3 April

▶ David Bowie & The Buzz, Top 10 Club, Dundee, Tayside.

Top of the bill is Johnny Kidd & The Pirates, while The Premiers[1] are co-support act. Eager records in his diary that 'screaming Scots girls are wild'.

1. The Premiers were a three-piece from Fauldhouse, near Dundee, who adopted the new name 1-2-3 on moving in the late summer of 1966 to London, where they met David again.

Monday 4 April

▶ David Bowie & The Buzz, unknown venue, Hawick, Roxburghshire.

Immediately after the performance, the group – unable to afford hotel accommodation – leave for the overnight drive to London, with Horton at the wheel.

Tuesday 5 April

After driving through the night, Horton delivers the

a Radio London 'Big L' promotion, along with singer David Ballantyne, who is plugging his single 'Love Around The World'.

Monday 21 March

▶ David Bowie & The Buzz and the Earl Richmond Show, The Galaxy Club, St Joseph's Hall, Western Way, Basingstoke, Hampshire.

Friday 25 March

▶ David Bowie & The Buzz, The Railway Hotel, Bridge Rail Approach, Wealdstone.

Famous for being the site where The Who were discovered, this is also a local haunt of John Eager's.

Friday 1 April

'Do Anything You Say'/'Good Morning Girl' is issued (in the UK) just ten weeks after David's first Pye single, and is notable for being his first solo release which also carries his first sole writing credit:

⊙ **David Bowie**
A **'Do Anything You Say'** (Bowie)
B **'Good Morning Girl'** (Bowie)
David Bowie (vocal)
John 'Hutch' Hutchinson (guitar)
Dek Fearnley (bass)
John Eager (drums)
Tony Hatch (piano – A-side)
Derek Boyes (keyboards – B-side)
The whole group (backing vocal)
Produced by Tony Hatch
(Pye 7N 17079)

LEFT: Pye Press release for 'Do Anything You Say'.

MIDDLE: Advert for performance at The Galaxy Club, Basingstoke, 21 March.

RIGHT: The Two R's, Railway Hotel promo flyer, 25 March.

band to their homes and then visits Ken Pitt at his offices in Curzon Street, Mayfair.

Still working hard to secure Pitt's interest in a co-management arrangement, Horton[1] outlines his and David's plans for a regular Sunday showcase starting at the Marquee at the weekend. This is to be called The Bowie Showboat, along the lines of a multimedia residency created recently at the venue on the same day by The Pink Floyd.

Horton is hoping to tap into the attention Pink Floyd are enjoying, as well as attracting the hip young tourists flooding into Soho. Pitt agrees to attend The Bowie Showboat on 17 April.

London is now in full swing, though The Buzz feel no affinity with the mod movement and are already uncomfortable with David's new material.

"As far as the mod thing went, I never felt we were ever a part of that," said Fearnley in 1991. "We weren't performing the kind of material all the other bands were. When we got to the line 'Bright lights, Soho, Wardour Street' in 'The London Boys', the audience would cheer. I felt that at least with 'The London Boys' our audience could relate to it."

1. Horton also approached The Yardbirds' manager Simon Napier-Bell, inviting him to meet David at Warwick Square. Napier-Bell declined to co-manage him, but took Marc Bolan under his wing later in 1966 and drafted the singer-songwriter into the line-up of one of his other groups, John's Children.

Thursday 7 and Friday 8 April

▶ David Bowie & The Buzz, unknown venues.

The group are booked for three separate engagements by agency Galaxy Entertainments of Oxford Street, central London.[1]

1. It has not been established which venues were played on these dates as only payment details from the promoter were retained.

Saturday 9 April

▶ David Bowie & The Buzz, the Marquee, London.

This a Saturday afternoon show which acts as a try-out for the first in the season of Showboat showcases the next day.

Sunday 10 April

▶ The Bowie Showboat, the Marquee, London.

Booked by Marquee manager Jack Barrie from 3 to 6pm every Sunday for the next nine weeks, The Bowie Showboat includes two sets by David Bowie & The Buzz as well as DJ slots by Ray Peterson, who is instructed by David to play the latest hits and songs relevant to the audience.

Radio London's Earl Richmond also DJs from time to time, as does David himself.

Wednesday 13 April

David & The Buzz rehearse new material, though nothing is recorded.

Thursday 14 April

▶ David Bowie & The Buzz, the Marquee, London.

The group fill in at the last moment for The Mark Leeman Five – who are managed by Ken Pitt – as a goodwill gesture following the meeting a few days earlier.

Friday 15 April

▶ David Bowie & The Buzz, Starlight Ballroom, Greenford, Middx.

They support Pitt-managed beat combo Dave Antony's Moods.

Saturday 16 April

Fabulous magazine tips David as 'the biggest thing to happen in 1966'.

Sunday 17 April

▶ The Bowie Showboat, the Marquee, London.

Pitt witnesses David in performance for the first time and is captivated. Noting that David is wearing 'a biscuit-coloured, hand-knitted sweater, round-necked and buttoned at one shoulder, its skin-tightness accentuating his slim frame', Pitt takes in the set leaning against the wall at the back of the club.

The group's show comprises David's two Pye singles, some R&B covers and several new songs delivered 'with intense conviction, as if each song was his ultimate masterpiece', according to Pitt, speaking in 1983.

"He oozed confidence and was in total command of himself, his band and his audience. His burgeoning charisma was undeniable, but I was particularly struck by the artistry with which he used his body as if it were an accompanying instrument, essential to the singer and the song."

Pitt also notes David's grasp of stage theatrics, particularly leading up to the climactic version of 'You'll Never Walk Alone', the show tune popularised by Gerry & The Pacemakers a couple of years earlier.

"At the close of the performance he waited for the applause to die down then, after pausing a moment or two longer, he slowly walked a few paces forward, the group fell into darkness, a spot focused on David and with his head held high he sang the Judy Garland classic," Pitt wrote in 1983. "It was daring and delightful."

After the show Pitt joins Horton and David at Warwick Square, where he agrees to become Horton's partner in managing David.

Saturday 23 April

▶ David Bowie & The Buzz, California Ballroom, Whipsnade Road, Dunstable, Bedfordshire.

Headliners are novelty rockers Frankenstein & The Monsters (who perform in monster outfits), The Flashbakks and Kent quartet the Avengers.[1] This venue is to become a regular for David and The Buzz over the coming months.

1. In 1968 the Avengers changed their name to Vanity Fare. Three of the original line-up was still playing live dates in the UK in 2010.

Sunday 24 April

▶ The Bowie Showboat, the Marquee, London.

As well as the residency performance, the group provide music for a pilot radio show sponsored by men's clothing outfitters Harry Fenton.

David is interviewed by Earl Richmond, and a performance by the group is recorded. David reveals that he is working on a musical with Tony Hatch and that he has ambitions to become a cabaret performer. David and Horton listen to a playback after the show.

Monday 25 April

▶ David Bowie & The Buzz, The Wallaby Club, Chester, Cheshire.

After just one week, Pitt receives a letter from Horton enclosing a court order raised by Pye, which is pursuing £22/2/6 (£22.12p) for unpaid copies of 'Can't Help Thinking About Me'. Horton asks Pitt to forward the sum to Westminster County Court the following morning.

Ignoring Horton's request, Pitt concentrates on furthering David's career by writing to the producer of ATV's children's programme *Five O'Clock Club* requesting an audition for David as the show's compère.

Saturday 30 April

▶ David Bowie & The Buzz, Drill Hall, Newmarket, Suffolk.

During the afternoon, David is guest of honour in his home town, crowning Bromley's May Queens in the annual event at Bromley Football Club's ground in Hayes Lane. The previous year, this ceremony had been carried out by David's friend from school and fellow member of The Konrads, George Underwood (using the Calvin James stage name).

On the journey to Newmarket, David and Horton occupy their usual seats together, talking business.

THE ROY TEMPEST ORGANISATION LTD.

Representing Britain's Leading
BANDS, CABARET, & VARIETY ARTISTS

Mr. Ralph Horton

13-14, Dean Street, London, W.1.
Telephones : GERrard 1633 - 6

REMITTANCE ADVICE / INVOICE / STATEMENT ......5th May, 196 6

DATE	BAND	VENUE	FEE	£ s. d.	£ s. d.
12th March	DAVID BOWIE	Newmarket	£30	Less 5% com.	1 10 0
30th April	DAVID BOWIE	Newmarket	£40	Less 10% com.	4 0 0
					5 10 0

Please let us have your cheque for £5. 10s. -d. by return. If we have to send you any more Invoices for commissions, we will have to obviously, in future, make sure that DAVID BOWIE does not pick up any cash on the night, as we are not having this difficulty in collecting such small amounts.

MRS. A. DOYLE (Accountant)

Licensed Annually by the L.C.C.

"When we were on the road it became a bit 'them and us'," Fearnley later recalled. "This was Ralph's way of trying to project David to stardom."

However, some of David's ideas for the live show are considered too outrageous by Horton. "David always had a lot of ideas which he would constantly bounce off us, but Ralph wouldn't let him do them," said Fearnley. "If he'd been given more freedom to develop some of these ideas and incorporate them into the act he would have created a lot more interest. Personally I wasn't at all surprised with his stage act later on. That was in David, trying to get out, when we were with him."

May

'Can't Help Thinking About Me'/'And I Say To Myself' is released in the US on Pye's American licensee label Warner Bros.

The press release focuses on David's songwriting abilities: "'I compose all the time," he said. "Sometimes I just sit down and think out a song and other times they just come to me."'

It also mentions the Showboat residency and his DJ stints at the Marquee as well as his ambition to visit Tibet and is described as an 'expert in astrology and a believer in reincarnation'.

Sunday 1 May

▶ The Bowie Showboat, the Marquee, London.

Admission for the afternoon is three shillings (15p) and the event is occasionally billed as 'three hours of music and mime'.

In this year...

Sunday 10 April
DEATH of novelist Evelyn Waugh, author of *Decline And Fall* and *Brideshead Revisited*. His 1930 satire *Vile Bodies* proved to be a prime inspiration for David's album *Aladdin Sane*. (▶ 13.4.73)

Saturday 30 April
ENTRY of 'Sorrow' by The Merseys into the UK charts. David covered this on his 1973 album *Pin Ups* and reached number three in the single charts with the track in October that year.

FRIDAY, MAY 6, 1966

Registered at General Post Office as a newspaper.

CROWNING MOMENT

In glorious sunshine on Saturday eight Bromley May queens were crowned by local pop singer David Bowie, at Bromley Football Club ground in Hayes-lane.

They were (left to right) Anne Button (Bickley), Christine Baker (Hayes Common), Carol Sharp (Pickhurst Park), Linda Dutton (Sundridge Park), Rosemary Reynolds (Bromley), Jacqueline Mann (Shortlands), Yvonne Lomax (Bromley Common), and Sandra Cousins (Southborough). About 500 people watched the event, at the end of the day's football match.

Before the ceremony the May queens and their attendants walked in procession down Bromley High-street, starting from Queens Garden, on their way to the football ground, accompanied by the 13th Company, Bromley Boys Brigade band, and that of the 1st St. Mary Cray Girls Life Brigade.

The queens and their contingents will take part in the crowning of the London May queen on Hayes Common on May 14.

ABOVE: David Bowie with the Bromley May Queens for 1966. The event was held at Bromley Football Club on 30 April.

Saturday 7 May

▶ David Bowie & The Buzz, University of Leeds, Woodhouse Lane, Leeds, Yorkshire.

Sunday 8 May

▶ The Bowie Showboat, the Marquee, London.

Shirley Wilson, who runs the David Bowie Fan Club[1] is in attendance at many of the Showboat performances ('Caroline', who is described in promotional material as one of the club secretaries and answers mail and sends messages to fans, is, in fact, Ralph Horton).

Wilson and her friends keep in touch with David, calling him at Plaistow Grove for updates on live bookings and record releases. They often photograph him and his fellow musicians for their personal collections. "It was easy to walk up to him then," Wilson said in 1983. "He'd sit and talk to you and was always very friendly."

1. Shirley Wilson, from Bromley, started the first David Bowie fan club with her friends Sandra Gibling and Violet Neal in 1966. She had witnessed David's performances in Bromley with The King Bees and often encountered him on the London train. The fan club issued cheaply printed newsletters and supplied signed photos, for the price of a postage stamp: 6d. David and his fellow musicians signed photos and ephemera for the club.

Saturday 14 May

▶ David Bowie & The Buzz, private party, Ingram Avenue, London NW11.

This 21st birthday celebration in a private residence on the borders of upmarket Hampstead arrives via a regular attendee at the group's Marquee bookings. "I remember the guy said to David, 'I booked you because I saw a great quality in you'," said Eager in 1991. "That was something we could all see. But it was great coming from a punter. And it was a very posh house."[1]

1. In this period there was at least one other private party booking, to celebrate a female fan's birthday.

Sunday 15 May

▶ The Bowie Showboat, the Marquee, London.

There is still little sign that the series of showcases is fulfilling Horton's dreams of attracting greater attention to David's talents; gigs are only ever around half-full.

Monday 16 May

A replacement ambulance – painted blue and white – is purchased from Middlesex Council for £125. The first has irrevocably broken down and remains parked outside Horton's flat.

Friday 20 May

▶ David Bowie & The Buzz, Birmingham College of Education, Birmingham.

This is a support for the Liverpool act The Escorts; The Buzz's keyboard player Derek Boyes had been a member at one point.

Sunday 22 May

▶ The Bowie Showboat, the Marquee, London.

The Mamas & The Papas' hit 'Monday Monday'[1] is incorporated into the group's set.

1. This went to number three in the UK chart in May 1966. The score for David's first feature film, *The Man Who Fell To Earth* (1976), included music selected by The Mamas & The Papas' founder John Phillips.

Monday 23 May

▶ David Bowie & The Buzz, California Pool Ballroom,[1] Dunstable, Bedfordshire.

The group appears as part of the Earl Richmond Show. This is a regular Monday evening gig for the DJ.

1. "There were usually three bands on at the Cali Ballroom," said Eager in 1991. "I think we played there with The Crazy World Of Arthur Brown who were incredibly funny to watch."

It is possible that Brown was the 'croaking man' who 'raved' on stage referred to in David's lyrics for his 1966 song 'Join The Gang'.

Parts of the balcony hung over the stage, enabling disgruntled audience members to shower beer over the heads of performers they didn't like. David and The Buzz played the venue at least six times, and avoided a soaking every time. The venue was demolished in the late 70s and was replaced by housing.

Sunday 29 May

▶ David Bowie & The Buzz, Blackpool South Pier, Blackpool Pleasure Beach, Lancashire.[1]

This is a Pitt package; the rest of the bill consists of acts he also manages: singer Crispian St Peters[2] and groups Dave Antony's Moods and The Mark Leeman Five.[3]

David watches from the wings as St Peters misses his curtain call and audience applause, and walks on stage to silence.

After the show Ken Pitt travels back to London with David, Horton and The Buzz in the ambulance.

1. There appears to have been a double booking on this date. Music press adverts listed David Bowie & The Buzz performing at the Marquee, supported by The Soul System. It is certain, however, that the Blackpool performance took place and such is the distance from London that it is impossible both could have been fulfilled.

2. Born Robin Smith 5 April 1939. Best known for March 1966 hit 'The Pied Piper'.

3. The Mark Leeman Five continued after lead singer Leeman (real name John Ardey) was killed in a car crash on 27 June 1965. Roger Peacock took over as frontman and later became the lead vocalist in Dave Antony's Moods. The pianist in The Mark Leeman Five was Tom Parker, who will work with David in 1971. (▶ 25.9.71)

Tuesday 31 May

Bailiffs call at Horton's home and threaten to remove property, since he has failed to maintain the remaining payments on the money owed to Pye. Horton brings in Pitt, who strikes a deal with Pye to pay the outstanding amount, thus ending the court action.

Friday 3 June

◗ David Bowie & The Buzz, Pleasurama, The Boulevard, Ramsgate, Kent.
This late evening booking follows afternoon rehearsals in London.

Saturday 4 June

◗ David Bowie & The Buzz, Dorothy Ballroom, Sussex Street, Cambridge.

Sunday 5 June

◗ The Bowie Showboat, the Marquee, London.
The Showboat picks up passing trade, mainly tourists. David's parents are in the audience for a couple of shows and the Marquee operators are happy since it generates business at a time of the week when the club is usually closed.
"There were a lot of clubs to go to in the Soho scene in the 60s but the Marquee was top of the list, because musicians did hang out there, pretending to talk business and picking up gigs – but picking up girls mostly," said David in 2001. "One of my keenest memories of the Marquee in the 60s was having a permanent erection because there were so many fantastic looking girls in there. It was all tourists, especially in summer, all flocking to London to get an R&B star."

Monday 6 June

◗ David Bowie & The Buzz, California Pool Ballroom, Dunstable, Bedfordshire.
This booking follows a fraught day at Pye Studios in Marble Arch, where the group attempt to record David's jaunty new song 'I Dig Everything' with a brass section – including Dave Antony's Moods trumpeter Andy Kirk – and Dusty Springfield's backing singers Madeline Bell,[1] Kiki Dee and Lesley Duncan.[2]
David and Fearnley provide an arrangement but there has been no prior rehearsal with the horn players or singers. Tony Hatch isn't happy and calls a halt to the session.
"I frequently tried sessions with musicians recommended by singer/songwriters, often their own bands," said Hatch in 1990. "Sometimes it worked

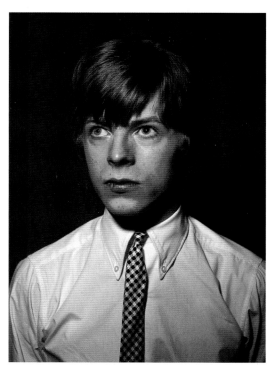

and you could capture a natural raw quality."
It is clear, however, this is not one of those occasions.
"The arrangement wasn't up to it," later recalled Eager. "The horn section were OK at playing soul music, but not what we wanted."

1. Born Madeline Bell Brodus on 23 July 1942 in New Jersey, USA. A prolific backing singer, most notably with Dusty Springfield, she joined group Blue Mink in 1969 with whom she recorded a string of top twenty hits including 'Melting Pot' and 'Banner Man'.

2. Born Lesley Cox in Stockton-on-Tees (1943–2010), singer/songwriter Duncan is best remembered for her work during the 70s. She introduced David to a UFO observation/meditation group in Hampstead in 1969. He demoed a version of her most famous composition 'Love Song' the same year.

Thursday 9 June

Fearnley books The Buzz – listed as The David Jones Trio – into R.G. Jones' Oak Studio in Morden, Surrey, for a two-day recording session. It is felt that they need to sharpen up since Fearnley and David are encountering problems presenting their ideas to session musicians.

Friday 10 June

◗ David Bowie & The Buzz, Co-op Hall, Catford, London SE6.
During the day, David's backing musicians cancel the second day of the R.G. Jones recording session, while the Catford booking arrives as a last-minute replacement for Dave Antony's Moods.

Saturday 11 June

◗ David Bowie & The Buzz, California Pool Ballroom, Dunstable, Bedfordshire.
The group top the bill at the venue for the first time.

City of Birmingham College of Education
! A HOP !
THE ESCORTS
(from LIVERPOOL)
&
DAVE BOWIE
& THE BUZZ
MAY 20th J.C.R.
8 - 11 pm.   TICKETS 5 Shillings
A.B.D. PRINTERS

ABOVE: Advert for a Birmingham College gig, 20 May.
LEFT: Early promotional shot.

In this year...

Thursday 26 May/ Friday 27 May
PERFORMANCES by Bob Dylan at London's Royal Albert Hall during the controversial 'Judas' tour on which he adopted an electric backing band. Ken Pitt was employed as the publicist for Dylan's manager Albert Grossman. David did not attend either of the concerts; he had witnessed Dylan perform live at the same venue the previous year.

KENNETH PITT

KEN Pitt's acumen, considerable experience and range of contacts across the international entertainment industry were to provide a secure home for David's talents for nearly five years, from his late mod phase through to the folk/hippy leanings of the late 60s.

Unlike the largely disinterested Les Conn and the maverick Ralph Horton, Pitt managed to pull off a series of career-boosting coups on behalf of his client, winning him his first album deal, encouraging and promoting David's first hit single and funding his first film, *Love You Till Tuesday*.

Alongside these business achievements, Pitt provided David with arguably his most significant musical influence by introducing him to the songwriting of Lou Reed and the music of The Velvet Underground before the release of their first album. He also encouraged David to investigate fin-de-siécle literature, art deco antiques and contemporary theatre and musicals.

It should also be noted that David adopted the new surname Bowie on the basis of Pitt's advice.

Kenneth Pitt was born on 10 November 1922 in Southall, west London. From an early age he was a keen artist and earned a place at London's renowned Slade School of Art.

On leaving college in the early 40s he joined the design department of the monolithic J Arthur Rank film company, where he transferred to its publicity department.

Here Pitt was granted his first taste of showbiz, and came into contact with the company's impressive roster of film stars.

Pitt's direct involvement in the music industry started in 1947, when he acted as compère and publicist in his own 12-piece dance orchestra, The Modernaires, from south-west London.

In 1949, he broke away from full-time employment at Rank's and launched his own PR company, based at 116 Shaftesbury Avenue in London's theatre district. He shared an office with Harold Davison, one of the country's top big-band agents and later Frank Sinatra's manager.

In 1950 Pitt handled Frank Sinatra's UK publicity which consolidated his reputation. The following year he made his first trip to America, with British singer Alan Dean (who had just topped the *Melody Maker* poll for most popular male singer).

During this visit Pitt made the acquaintance of many of his future clients, including Billy Eckstine and Louis Armstrong. He also visited Hollywood where he met leading film publicist Henry Rogers of Rogers & Cowan and heard early rock'n'roll and rhythm-and-blues for the first time.

During the mid-50s Pitt was featured with Elvis Presley in a New York radio broadcast. After the show, Presley recommended Pitt look up his friends Freddie Bell & The Bellboys while in Las Vegas.

Pitt did so, and became the act's UK publicist, helping them get to number four in the UK charts in September 1956 with single 'Giddy-Up-A-Ding-Dong' and handling their 1957 UK tour.

By this time, Pitt's client roster represented a Who's Who of popular 50s entertainment figures, including singers Georgia Brown, Vic Damone, Frankie Laine and Mel Torme, band-leaders Johnny Dankworth, Ted Heath, Lionel Hampton and Count Basie, and rock'n'roller Jerry Lee Lewis.

In 1963, Pitt met The Mann-Hugg Blues Brothers after a performance at the Hamborough Tavern in his home neighbourhood of Southall. Soon after, he became manager of the renamed Manfred Mann, and promoted their first three singles, which included '5-4-3-2-1' and their first number one, 'Do Wah Diddy Diddy'.[1]

This association lasted until 1966, by which time Pitt had also forged a strong relationship with Bob Dylan and his manager Albert Grossman, having publicised Dylan's first UK visit in 1964 and helping to set up the path to his first UK hit, 'The Times They Are A-Changing', in 1965. Grossman openly credited Ken with maximising UK media interest in his artist. (▶ 26.5.66)

By the time Ralph Horton approached Pitt to become involved in David's career, in 1966, Pitt was managing Crispian St Peters (for whom he promoted three hits: 'You Were On My Mind', 'Pied Piper' and 'Changes').

The agreement reached with Horton in April 1966 was on the basis of Pitt handling David's business commitments while Horton assisted David in reaching artistic and creative decisions.

On assuming the role of sole manager in February 1967, Pitt quickly became a significant figure in David's personal life, encouraging him to visit theatrical productions to fire his imagination with ideas for performance, lighting, stage and costume design.

"Before he met me, he'd rarely been to the theatre; I introduced him to that," said Pitt in 1983. "Theatre was always a big part of my life."

An admirer of late Victorian literature, Pitt owned an impressive collection, including works by Ernest Dowson and Lord Alfred Douglas as well as many Oscar Wilde first editions. David devoured these when he moved into Pitt's central London apartment in the spring of 1967 as the pair entered an intense period of personal collaboration centring on the release of David's debut album.

1. In 2001, Pitt appeared on *This Is Your Life* as a contributor to the TV show's examination of the life and career of Manfred Mann's first lead singer, Paul Jones.

ABOVE: Kenneth Pitt on his travels, 1968.

FAR LEFT: Frank Sinatra with Pitt at the Palladium, London, 1950.

LEFT: Robert Zimmerman and Pitt at London Airport, 26 April 1965, on the eve of his first UK tour.

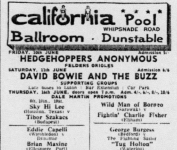

Sunday 12 June

▶ The Bowie Showboat, the Marquee, London.
This is the last Showboat. In the evening The Pink Floyd conclude their weekly Spontaneous Underground performances.

Wednesday 15 June

Suffering from the lack of a regular salary, John Hutchinson leaves The Buzz and returns with his family to Yorkshire. It will be more than two years before he sees or works with David again. (▶ 17.11.68)

Thursday 16 June

Rehearsals and auditions for Hutchinson's replacement are held in the basement of the Church of the Annunciation in Bryanston Street, central London. This is near Pye's offices in Marble Arch and next door to the photographic studio run by Dek Fearnley's brother Gerard.

Among the applicants is Dave Loveland, who has been recommended by John Eager but doesn't get the job. "David didn't think that his style was suitable," said Eager in 1991. "He said his playing was 'a bit too flowery'."

Fearnley puts forward his friend Pete Hampshire, who rehearses with them for a day but fails the audition.[1]

1. Hampshire returned to David's life in 1967, playing guitar on the single 'The Laughing Gnome'. (▶ 26.1.67)

Friday 17 June

In a letter to Pitt, Horton writes: 'David and self have been interviewing guitarists over the past three days and we have another to view at 3.00pm today.'

Saturday 18 June

▶ David Bowie & The Buzz, Thetford, Norfolk.
The musicians work as a four-piece.

Sunday 19 June

▶ David Bowie & The Buzz, Brands Hatch motor racing track, Longfield, Kent.
This Radio London-hosted awards event features the Walker Brothers, The Kinks, The Small Faces, Paul & Barry Ryan, Chris Farlowe and David Garrick.

On arrival at the racing circuit their ambulance is mobbed by screaming girls who believe it contains the chart-topping Walker Brothers.

After the race meeting, the quartet perform in front of an audience of around 5,000, on a stage set up on the race track, along with Episode Six,[1] John McCoy's Crawdaddies and Tom Jones' former backing band The Squires.

1. Episode Six's line-up included Deep Purple founder members Roger Glover and Ian Gillan.

Monday 20 June

▶ David Bowie & The Buzz, California Pool Ballroom, Dunstable, Bedfordshire.

Saturday 25 June

▶ David Bowie & The Buzz, unknown venue, Lowestoft, Suffolk.
This is the group's fourth gig without a lead guitarist, but subsequently David is introduced to young musician Billy Gray by agent and Horton's friend Kenny Bell. From Kilmarnock, Scotland, Gray is just 16 years old and has previously been in R&B group The Anteeks. He passes the audition and becomes The Buzz's new lead guitarist.

Monday 27 June

▶ David Bowie & The Buzz, California Pool Ballroom, Dunstable, Bedfordshire.
The group is back to a five-piece for an evening fronted by DJ Earl Richmond and billed as 'The Pop Scene'.

Saturday 2 July

▶ David Bowie & The Buzz, Lion Hotel, 65 Bridge Street, Warrington, Cheshire.
While David and Horton are satisfied with Billy Gray's musicianship, his exuberance and onstage showmanship don't go down so well and, after a couple of shows, Horton asks him to tone down his performance because he is distracting the audience from David.

Sunday 3 July

▶ David Bowie & The Buzz, the Marquee, London.

Tuesday 5 July

A month after the abandoned attempt at recording new single 'I Dig Everything' with The Buzz, David is summoned to Pye Studios for another attempt, but with session musicians booked by Hatch.

Also recorded is David's composition for the B-side, 'I'm Not Losing Sleep'.

The musicians who took part in the recording have not been documented. Hatch said in 1990:

TOP: Advert for California Ballroom gig, 11 June.

ABOVE: John Eager in 1966.

LEFT: Dek, David and Hutch pose outside the back doors of the Marquee in Richmond Mews, photographed by Shirley Wilson, who ran David's first fan club.

BOTTOM: Map drawn by David for Ken Pitt's first visit to Plaistow Grove, Bromley.

Tuesday 12 July

LETTER from David's early 70s collaborator, guitarist Mick Ronson, to his girlfriend Sandra Nelson. 'I have been to the Marquee club tonight to see The Action. They were very good.'[1]

1. David appeared at the Marquee just a few days earlier. David also witnessed west London mod act The Action live around this time. In 2005 he likened them to British rock band *Arctic Monkeys*, whom he had just seen live in New York.

Saturday 30 July

ENTRY of The Beach Boys' 'God Only Knows' at number two in the UK chart. A favourite song of David's, he released it as a track on his 1984 album *Tonight* and produced a version by his backing singers The Astronettes for an unreleased project in 1973.

"I couldn't tell you for certain who played on the re-recording but in those days, for 'rock' sessions I always hired great musicians like Jimmy Page, John McLaughlin, Jim Sullivan, Herbie Flowers, Clem Cattini, Tony from Sounds Incorporated, Roger Coulam and Alan Hawkshaw, the 'hooligans' of their time. Come to think of it – most of these people also featured on the Petula Clark sessions too."

The session is judged a success and the single scheduled for release within a month or so.

Saturday 9 July

▶ David Bowie & The Buzz, Blue Moon,[1] High Street, Cheltenham, Glos. This is a popular mod venue and discotheque.

1. Renamed The Night Owl, as of 2010 this was the UK's longest-running independent rock venue.

Friday 15 July

▶ David Bowie & The Buzz, Loughton Youth Centre, 106 Borders Lane, Essex.

This gig was attended by Shirley Wilson and other members of David's Bromley-based fan club.

Saturday 16 July

▶ David Bowie & The Buzz, Club One-O-One, West Street, Brighton, East Sussex.

Sunday 17 July

▶ David Bowie & The Buzz, The Playboy Club, 45 Park Lane, London W1.

Hugh Hefner's London establishment is just a short walk from Ken Pitt's Curzon Street office; he often places acts here.

Billy Gray is unable to make the show, so The Buzz is a three-piece again for the night. John Eager remembered it in 2010 as 'a really fantastic show'. Gray's absence provokes the thought that maybe the group can survive without their latest recruit. "We realised after the show that we could manage as a three-piece," said Eager.

Monday 18 July

Pitt sends *Ready Steady Go!* driving force Vicki Wickham an advance copy of 'I Dig Everything'. It is posted back by return with a note: 'Very many thanks for the David Bowie disc. I am sorry, but yet again I really do not think it is a hit. One day I am going to surprise you!'

Saturday 23 July

▶ David Bowie & The Buzz, unknown venue, Chepstow, Monmouthshire, Wales.

Sunday 24 July

▶ David Bowie & The Buzz, Downs Hotel, Hassocks, West Sussex.

This popular venue is just off the London to Brighton road. Its 'Ultra Club' evenings attract the likes of The Yardbirds and The Who.

Friday 29 July

Music weekly *NME* announces the Big L Dance Tour', a Radio London tour featuring David and The Buzz. The MC at these shows is the station's promotions manager Gordon Sheppard, who recalled David as "a bright young lad, a great singer and performer. Big L didn't believe in paying big performance fees; instead it promoted them on air. David used to play for £15 a gig."

Saturday 30 July

▶ David Bowie & The Buzz, the Marquee, London.

There is another show this evening, at The Rhodes Centre in Bishops Stortford, Hertfordshire, supported by The U-No-Who.[1]

During the afternoon, England play West Germany in the World Cup (football) final at Wembley, which England win. It's an interesting thought that, as Geoff Hurst fires home England's legendary fourth goal, just a few miles away David is probably singing 'You'll Never Walk Alone' (which features regularly in his set and is later adopted as a football terrace anthem).

1. Members of this Birmingham group formed prog rock trio Bachdenkel and appeared on the same bill as David in 1970.

Sunday 31 July

▶ David Bowie & The Buzz, Rowing Club, Trent Bridge, West Bridgford, Nottingham.

Wednesday 3 August

David and Ralph Horton visit Pitt at his Manchester Street home to obtain funding for their idea of including backing tapes during performances.

Pitt provides the cash for Horton to build and design a box of effects to play pre-recorded tapes on cue. This is an early investigation by David into the use of effects and vocal distortion which will manifest itself in recordings within a year.

Thursday 4 August

▶ David Bowie & The Buzz, Adam & Eve Discotheque, Spa Road, Southampton, Hants.

The first of a series of appearances at this popular Southampton venue. The club's Africa-themed decor features tiger-striped wallpaper, tribal drums and shields, while the staff sport animal-print outfits.

Tuesday 9 August – Wednesday 10 August

The group rehearse intensively to co-ordinate their music and stage show with the backing tapes and effects created by Horton's 'black box'.

Friday 12 August

▶ David Bowie & The Buzz, Latin Quarter, Leicester.

An advert in *NME* announces David Bowie as a Robert Stigwood Agency artist. Most of David's bookings during this period are co-ordinated by RSA's Robert Masters. This adds another agency to the roster for booking live performances.

Saturday 13 August

▶ David Bowie & The Buzz, Coventry Air Display, Baginton, Warwickshire.

During this open-air concert David's fellow musicians are increasingly impressed with David's stage craft. "He didn't just stand there and sing," said Dek Fearnley in 1991. "David's movements were always interesting, totally original for the time."

John Eager commented recently: "When I watched the later performances, such as Ziggy, I realised he was doing that back then."

Thursday 18 August

▶ David Bowie & The Buzz, Adam & Eve Discotheque, Southampton, Hants.

Friday 19 August

Pye Records release 'I Dig Everything'/'I'm Not Losing Sleep'[1] single in the UK. The single does not include the Buzz:

⊙ **David Bowie**
A **'I Dig Everything'** (Bowie)
B **'I'm Not Losing Sleep'** (Bowie)
David Bowie (vocals)
Session musicians unknown
Produced by Tony Hatch
(Pye 7N.17157)

The *NME* describes it as 'another disc that's perfect for dancing' and *Disc & Music Echo* comments that David 'wrote it himself and sings it, with his voice moving very well against the backing'.

The single receives a poor sales response, though there is some airplay. On hearing 'I Dig Everything', The Premiers – who supported David and The Buzz at their date in Dundee in April and have by now changed their name to 1-2-3 – incorporate it into their set.

1. David's publisher Sparta registered 'I'm Not Losing Sleep' with the title 'Too Bad'.

Sunday 21 August

▶ David Bowie & The Buzz, the Marquee, London.

By now it is clear that Pitt is grooming David for expansion into the entertainment business beyond the routine of playing sweaty R&B clubs.

Pitt is accompanied to the Marquee by two acquaintances looking for a group to feature in a short film musical: producer Maurice Hatton of independent production company Mithras Films, and composer Carl Davis.[1]

Pitt introduces David to the pair, and over the coming weeks he and Davis work together, producing songs for the project.

1. Born in New York in 1936. Davis composed for TV programmes including *The World At War* theme and *The Naked Civil Servant* and film scores including *The French Lieutenant's Woman*.

Friday 26 August

▶ David Bowie & The Buzz, Coronation Ballroom, Pleasurama, The Boulevard, Ramsgate, Kent.

Ahead of this appearance at another of Radio London's Big L Disc Nights, local paper the *Kent Messenger* reports that David and The Buzz have developed 'a completely new act' by using the pre-recorded tapes in their live set: 'The group has been spending as much as eight hours a day rehearsing.'

However, during the performance at the Coronation Ballroom, the tapes do not synchronise with the songs, causing on-stage problems.

Saturday 27 August

▶ David Bowie & The Buzz, Starlite Ballroom, Wembley, Middx.

The group are pleased that members of the fan club have again come to see them, but Horton's 'black box' is abandoned after another evening of missed cues and technical difficulties.

Sunday 28 August

▶ David Bowie & The Buzz, the Marquee, London.

Saturday 3 September

▶ David Bowie & The Buzz, Witch Doctor, St Leonards-on-Sea, East Sussex.

Sunday 4 September

▶ David Bowie & The Buzz, Britannia Pier Theatre, Marine Parade, Great Yarmouth, Norfolk.

The group give two performances of around 15-20 minutes each. Freddie & The Dreamers are on the same bill, though the other acts listed in promotional material do not appear.

Tuesday 6 September

▶ David Bowie & The Buzz, The Civic Hall, Blackshots Lane, Grays, Essex.

During the day, David visits Ken Pitt alone before heading off with the group to Essex to perform two hour-long sets.

Pitt then conducts a separate meeting with Ralph Horton about the disappointing response to David's singles, now that it is clear that 'I Dig Everything' has flopped. They decide David should leave Pye Records.

David has consistently resisted Tony Hatch's demands that he record some of the A&R manager/producer's songs instead of his own.

Hatch later said he wanted to continue their working relationship, but that he was 'talked out of it' by his Pye colleagues. "We'll never know whether a second year with Pye would have produced the break-through," Hatch said in 1990. "But it's highly likely that the loss of his record contract inspired Bowie to new levels rather than dampened his enthusiasm."

David later told Buzz organist Derek Boyes his version of why he parted with Hatch: "One of the main reasons David split with Tony Hatch was because Hatch wanted him to record some of his material too, but David had made a decision and just wanted to record his own stuff."

Coincidentally, on this day Sparta takes up the option to continue handling David's song publishing.

Saturday 10 September

▶ David Bowie & The Buzz, Jazz Cellar, The Orford Arms, Orford Place, Norwich, Norfolk.

This popular venue is always crammed and has an intimate feel due to the low ceiling (which drips with sweat on busy nights). David has fond memories of The Orford Arms of all the places he plays in the 60s.

Sunday 11 September

▶ David Bowie & The Buzz, The Central Hotel, Gillingham, Kent.

David and the group also appear in the afternoon at the Marquee, booked by the agency run by Soho mover and shaker Rik Gunnell, who owns the Flamingo in Wardour Street.

Monday 12 September

▶ David Bowie & The Buzz, Woodhall Community Centre, Cole Green Lane, Welwyn Garden City, Herts.

Wednesday 15 September

▶ David Bowie & The Buzz, Adam & Eve Discotheque, Southampton, Hants.

The group perform two 45-minute sets.

Friday 16 September

▶ David Bowie & The Buzz, The Place, Bryan

DAVID

BOWIE

Street, Hanley, Stoke-on-Trent, Staffs.

The group perform two one-hour sets.

Saturday 17 September

▶ David Bowie & The Buzz, The Ballroom, Lyme Regis, Dorset.

Thursday 22 September

▶ David Bowie & The Buzz, Adam & Eve Discotheque, Southampton, Hants.

Friday 23 September

▶ David Bowie & The Buzz, the Marquee, London.

Another support slot for Gary Farr & The T-Bones is followed by a late evening performance at the Coronation Ballroom in the Kent coastal town of Ramsgate, for which they are paid £30.

Saturday 24 September

▶ David Bowie & The Buzz, 2B's Club, 2B Bank Street, Ashford, Kent.

The group receive £40 for two 45-minute sets.

Sunday 25 September

▶ David Bowie & The Buzz, the Marquee, London.

This is another in the post-Showboat run of Sunday afternoon gigs at the Soho venue.

Monday 26 September

In the evening David visits Pitt at his Manchester Street apartment to discuss film and recording opportunities. David updates Pitt on his work with Carl Davis.

Tuesday 27 September

▶ David Bowie & The Buzz, Adam & Eve Discotheque, Southampton, Hants.

They receive a £30 performance fee.

Wednesday 28 September

In a letter to film producer Maurice Hatton, Pitt reports on progress on the musical project: '(David) has spent some time with Carl Davis and has been hard at work writing numbers. He wrote about seven in four days. Doing one-night-stands, preparing his new cabaret act and working on these songs has exhausted him and I think it essential that he cut down on his activities for a while.

Friday 30 September

▶ David Bowie & The Buzz, Southlands Teacher Training College, Athlone Hall, Wimbledon, London SW19.

This replaces a cancelled appearance at Parkside Hall in Ampthill, Bedfordshire, and the group receive a fee of £20.

Ralph Horton receives a letter from Madeline Hawkyard, contracts manager at Pye Records, formalising David's departure from the label: 'I have been advised by Mr Tony Hatch that he has agreed to release David Bowie from his recording contract with this company and I therefore enclose herewith the necessary formal termination in duplicate.'

Saturday 1 October

▶ David Bowie & The Buzz, Starlite Ballroom, Wembley, Middx.

Thursday 6 October

▶ David Bowie & The Buzz, Adam & Eve Discotheque, Southampton, Hants.

Friday 7 October

In a letter to Horton, Hawkyard confirms that David may re-record 'The London Boys' but points out that the label retains its rights in the recording made the previous year.

Saturday 8 October

▶ David Bowie & The Buzz, Witch Doctor Club, The Savoy Ballroom, Catford, London SE6.

The group perform two 45-minute sets but are docked £2 from their £40 fee because of their late arrival.

Monday 10 October

With a date the following day at Aberystwyth University, the group is driven to Wales by Horton in the ambulance, staying en route with his elderly relatives in Forge, near Machynlleth, Powys.

The musicians take a walk over the hills and return to a warming fire and a heaving table. "It was really something, a great evening, one of those occasions which develop the really strong bonds you make within bands," said John Eager in 2010.

The house has a piano, on which David and Fearnley work out musical arrangements, including a new one for the song they are about to re-record, 'The London Boys'.

Tuesday 11 October

▶ David Bowie & The Buzz, Kings Hall, Aberystwyth University,[1] Penglais, Dyfed.

The group play two 45-minute sets for which they receive £50. Headlining are Unit Four Plus Two, whose single 'Concrete And Clay' had been a UK number one hit the previous year.

1. David returned to the university in 1972 with The Spiders From Mars, during the first Ziggy Stardust tour.

Tuesday 18 October

David Bowie & The Buzz, plus two session musicians, one of whom is trumpeter Chick Norton (who was in The Tommy Sampson Orchestra in the late 40s), are booked into R.G. Jones' Oak Studio. The session is organised and paid for by Pitt at a cost of £70.

He needs new material to play to the record labels he is approaching, and wants to offer enough

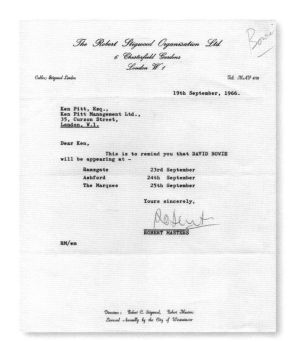

tracks for an EP. Over the course of the afternoon they re-record 'The London Boys' and two new songs of David's: 'Rubber Band' and 'The Gravedigger' (which is later retitled 'Please Mr Gravedigger').

Just as they had failed to deliver for the first attempt at recording 'I Dig Everything', David and Fearnley's inexperience in song arrangement remains evident. Fortunately the more experienced session players come to their aid.

"We'd worked out what kind of sound we wanted and had painstakingly written out the notation, but all the timings were wrong," said Fearnley in 1991. "Luckily the musicians interpreted what we had written, and we got through it."

Thursday 20 October

▶ David Bowie & The Buzz, Adam & Eve Discotheque, Southampton, Hants.

During this, their last visit to this venue, the group

TOP LEFT: Letter to Ken Pitt, dated 19 September, from The Robert Stigwood Organisation.

BOTTOM: Promo flyer for an appearance at the Place, Stoke-on-Trent, 16 September.

FAR RIGHT: R.G. Jones budget.

RIGHT: Pye Records letter regarding 'The London Boys', to Ralph Horton, 7 October.

MIDDLE: David's first album contract with Decca, endorsed by his father.

BOTTOM: Marquee club contract, 26 October.

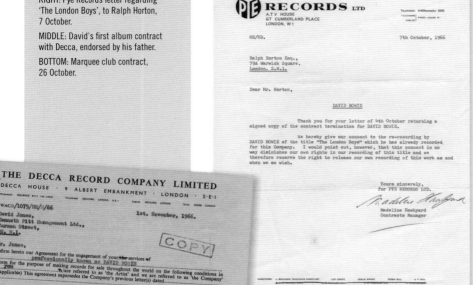

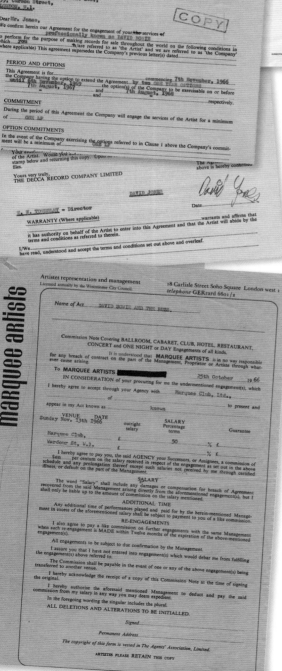

play three 40-minute sets for which they are paid £30.

During the day Pitt visits Tony Hall, head of promotion at Decca, whose signings include The Rolling Stones. Pitt plays Hall an acetate of 'Rubber Band', which is David's favourite from the session conducted two days earlier.

Hall is impressed (saying in 1983, "I must say I did flip. This guy had such a different sound, such a different approach.") and in turn plays the recording to Decca's albums artist manager Hugh Mendl.

Mendl had previously worked with Pitt on an album by one of his clients, Alan Klein.

Mendl likes 'Rubber Band' and arranges another meeting with Pitt to hear more of David's material.

Friday 21 October

▶ David Bowie & The Buzz, Drill Hall, Newmarket, Suffolk.

The group are paid £25 for two 45-minute sets.

Saturday 22 October

▶ David Bowie & The Buzz, Falmer House, University of Sussex, Falmer, East Sussex.

For this student union evening David and The Buzz again receive £25 for two 45-minute sets.

Also appearing are Gary Farr & The T-Bones.[1] This is the sixth time David has supported them in the last two years.

1. Gary Farr & The T-Bones disbanded at the end of the 1966. Bassist Lee Jackson and keyboard player Keith Emerson formed The Nice and drummer Andy Steele joined Peter Frampton's The Herd.

Monday 24 October

Pitt meets Hugh Mendl again with one of Decca's in-house producers, Mike Vernon. On the strength of the R.G. Jones recordings of 'The London Boys' and 'The Gravedigger' – as well as the previously heard 'Rubber Band' – Mendl offers a recording contract for David with Decca's progressive pop label, Deram.

Pitt has secured David an album deal, a rare opportunity in the mid-60s for an unproven signing. It is agreed that Vernon will produce already this year he has overseen albums by John Mayall's Bluesbreakers (featuring Eric Clapton) and The Artwoods.

Thursday 27 October

During the day David signs the Decca contract, returning to the company which put out his first single in 1964. He is encouraged by the fact that Mike Vernon has worked with Anthony Newley as engineer on various Decca recordings. David is paid an advance of £100 and £150 for the master tapes of 'Rubber Band' and 'The London Boys', which will be released as his first single with the label.

"When Ken Pitt brought David Bowie to my office he brought a marvel – I thought David Bowie was incredible," said Mendl[1] in 2002.

As well as David's father, Decca director W.W. Townsley endorses the contract on their behalf, which is dated 7 November.

1. Hugh Mendl (1920–2008) retired from Decca when the company was sold to Polygram in 1980.

Friday 28 October

▶ David Bowie & The Buzz, The Catacomb, Seaside Road, Eastbourne, East Sussex.

The group are paid £35 for two 45-minute sets.

Saturday 29 October

▶ David Bowie, The Shoreline, Esplanade, Bognor Regis, West Sussex.

The Buzz, Starlite Ballroom, Wembley, Middx.

With the recording contract secured, Horton, Pitt

and David set about rethinking his career. For a start, The Buzz's days are numbered.

They fulfil the Starlite engagement (with Fearnley handling vocal duties), and are paid £30, while David undertakes his first solo appearance on a packed bill for the opening of a new club which proclaims itself 'The Marquee at Bognor Regis'.

Backing himself on acoustic guitar, David performs his own songs, including his Pye singles.

The other performers are London mod-pop group The Action, R&B singer Long John Baldry and Bluesology, featuring Reginald Dwight (soon to become Elton John) on keyboards.

Saturday 5 November

An appearance by David Bowie & The Buzz at the Manor House in Haringey, London, is cancelled; the focus is now on readying David for the release of the new single.

Sunday 6 November

David is the subject of a photo shoot at south London park Clapham Common.

At one point he is posed on the park's Victorian bandstand; this had appeared in the first episode of one of David's favourite programmes from the early 60s, *The Strange World of Gurney Slade*, which was written by and starred his hero Anthony Newley.

David takes a short break and over a cup of coffee outside the park's cafe he writes a new song, 'Join The Gang', as recorded in the press release issued with the photos:

'It was twelve o'clock and he had just got up. "I can't do anything until I've had a cup of coffee!" he groaned and we dashed off to an open-air cafe on Clapham Common. It was completely deserted.

'"I feel a tune coming on," said David, so we left him to compose it in peace. Half an hour later when we got back, he was still there surrounded by a pile of cups and plates. "What did I have? Um, six coffees, baked beans, spaghetti and eggs and two doughnuts. Oh! And I finished the song. It's called 'Join The Gang' – about some kids, like most of my songs."'

Tuesday 8 November

David and Mike Vernon meet at Pitt's Mayfair office to discuss the forthcoming recording schedule (Pitt is accompanying his artist Crispian St Peters on a tour of the US and the Far East).

David also signs a one-off publishing agreement with Cooper Music to handle 'Rubber Band'.

Wednesday 9 November

David features in another photo session, this time shot by Decca's David Wedgbury on and around the Thames embankment.[1] Wedgbury has met David before, when he was with The King Bees, and introduces fellow Decca artists Love Affair[2] to one of David's songs, 'Cobbled Streets and Baggy Trousers'.

They rehearse but never record this track.

1. One of the photos appears on the back cover of David's first album.
2. Love Affair hit the number one spot in the UK in 1968 with the song 'Everlasting Love'.

Thursday 10 November

During a trip to New York, Ken Pitt visits Walt Maguire at Decca's US sister label, London Records, and plays him 'Rubber Band'.

Maguire agrees to release it in the US,[1] choosing a song of David's called 'There Is A Happy Land' as the B-side in preference to 'The London Boys' because of the drug reference.

1. The single was issued in June 1967 as a promotional only release, so sent to radio stations and not released commercially.

Saturday 12 November

▶ David Bowie & The Buzz, Le Disc A Go Go Club,[1] 9 Holdenhurst Road, Landsdowne, Bournemouth, Dorset.

1. Le Disc A Go Go is notable as the venue where The Who's drummer Keith Moon met his wife-to-be Kim Kerrigan when his group played there in January 1965.

Sunday 13 November

▶ David Bowie & The Buzz, the Marquee, London.

Advertised as another in The Bowie Showboat series to bolster attendance, this is poorly attended and antipathy among the musicians is growing; John Eager records in his diary that the show was 'pathetic'.

The Marquee contract stipulates that David has to supply and pay the support act, but the name of the additional group is not noted.

ABOVE: The Shoreline club in Bognor Regis was the scene of David's first solo performance, 29 October.

LEFT: David photographed at Clapham Common's open-air cafe writing 'Join The Gang' on 6 November.

In this year...

Monday 3 October
There is a misleading note in the diary of the R.G. Jones recording studio in south London: 'Lower Third LP all numbers with Davy Jones. American ad. Denis Taylor. Harman 8619.' David was not in fact involved in this session, but was at the studio the following week.

Friday 7 October
DEATH of singer Johnny Kidd, whom David supported with The King Bees, The Lower Third and The Buzz, in a head-on collision on the A58 near Radcliffe in Lancashire.

Wednesday 12 October
FORMATION of the line-up of The Jimi Hendrix Experience in London, with Noel Redding on bass and drummer Mitch Mitchell, previously of The Riot Squad. David formed a temporary association with The Riot Squad in the spring of 1967, when he also witnessed Hendrix and his bandmates in concert.

Saturday 29 October
ENTRY of The Easybeats' 'Friday On My Mind' into the UK charts. David included his version of the song on *Pin Ups* in 1973.

TOP: David's first promotional photo session for Deram, 9 November.

ABOVE: Decca's Broadhurst Gardens studio. The building at 165 is now used as the rehearsal and administration base of the English National Opera.

ANY DAY NOW I DAVID BOWIE I THE LONDON YEARS

Monday 14 November

David and The Buzz make their first visit to Decca's studios in West Hampstead[1] to begin recording David's debut album. The group are paid as session musicians, with Fearnley credited as arranger.

With Vernon overseeing production, the engineering is handled by Gus Dudgeon.[2]

David has been here before – in 1963 as a member of The Konrads when that group unsuccessfully auditioned for Rolling Stones co-manager Eric Easton.

Keyboard player Derek Boyes can't make it because of suspected appendicitis, but two new tracks are taped: 'Uncle Arthur' and 'She's Got Medals'. The retinue varies as the session progresses; at one stage members of the London Philharmonic Orchestra contribute.

Arrangements and musical direction are handled by Fearnley, who feels under pressure.

"When it came to the recording sessions I was on my own," he said in 1991. "Because a lot of what David and I wrote was technically incorrect, some of the musicians would throw the score back at me and I'd have to redo it there and then. That was really quite frightening. David was OK. He was up in the control box out of the way with the producer."

1. Decca's recording studios were at 165 Broadhurst Gardens, near the junction with West End Lane, the road that directly links into Abbey Road and that thoroughfare's famous studios. The building still stands, though in 2010 was in urgent need of renovation.
2. Gus Dudgeon (1942–2002) went on to become a top-flight producer, recognised for his work with Elton John.

Tuesday 15 November

With the musicians rehearsing or ensconced in the studio, Ralph Horton has time to evaluate his and the group's financial position, and realises it is far from healthy.

He writes to Pitt (who is by now in Australia): 'Ken, we are broke with a capital B. It looks now as though I will have to go bankrupt. I wish you were here so we could discuss it.'

Saturday 19 November

 David Bowie & The Buzz, Royal Links Ballroom, Cromer, Norfolk.

Eventually the group plays two 45-minute sets, but the realities of on-the-road life are never more apparent than on this eventful trip to the Norfolk coast.

The ambulance breaks down three miles from the venue, and they only just make it on stage in time. After the show they leave the ambulance to be repaired and all return to London by taxi, taking a big chunk of the £40 performance fee.

The events prove to be the final straw for young guitarist Billy Gray, who quits The Buzz.

Gray quickly takes up an offer of work in Italy, where he becomes a founding member of new band The Trip, whose ranks include future Deep Purple guitarist Ritchie Blackmore.

According to Pitt, Gray – who died of a brain haemorrhage in 1984 – had found David difficult to get to know. "But as a person I could not fault him," Gray told Pitt in 1983. "I would have been very surprised if David had not become a star. He was single-minded, dedicated and worked very hard."

Monday 21 November

'The London Boys' is registered by publisher Sparta.

Thursday 24 November

Live bookings are cancelled – including dates in Croydon, Lowestoft and Baldock. Not only is this to make way for recording; The Buzz are about to find out they no longer play a part as a group in Pitt and Horton's plans to make David a solo star.

For the time being this is not made clear, and Boyes, Eager and Fearnley take part in another session at Decca, where four more tracks are completed: 'There Is A Happy Land', 'We Are Hungry Men',[1] 'Join The Gang' and 'Did You Ever Have A Dream'.

Among outside contributors is session-player Big

Jim Sullivan,[2] who plays sitar and acoustic guitar on 'Join The Gang'.

"We decided on that during the take," said Fearnley in 1991. "After he had played the sitar section, I was supposed to lift the sitar off his lap and give him the guitar. But Big Jim wasn't having this – evidently the sitar had cost him a small fortune and he was the only one who could touch it. So that plan didn't work."

1. 'We Are Hungry Men' was listed as 'We Are Not Your Friends' by Sparta Florida.

2. Born James George Thompkins, 14 February 1941, Sullivan was the leading session guitarist of the 60s and 70s, reputedly playing on a thousand charted singles.

Friday 25 November

During a meeting at Pitt's office, David and Horton inform The Buzz that he no longer requires their services beyond fulfilment of a handful of live commitments.

They are offered work with Pitt's other artists: John Eager with Crispian St Peters and Derek Boyes with The Truth.

When the group tell David they are prepared to continue without pay, he breaks down in tears and leaves the room.

As in the case of the split from The Lower Third, The Buzz have been dropped just as a new single is being readied for release. Again, Horton has been on hand to enable the break, though the timing is curious, to say the least. As a unit, the musicians are midway through recording an album. Later it is felt that David and Horton were confident that the trio, in particular Fearnley, would stick around to see the project through.

"As much as I had faith in Dave and believed in his eventual stardom, when the singles and the records started to dry up I knew we just weren't going to make it," he later said. "The financial situation was deteriorating rapidly; we were all virtually working for nothing, so I wasn't really surprised when it all actually happened. It seemed inevitable to me."

Saturday 26 November

▶ David Bowie & The Buzz, The Community Centre, Bury Road, Gosport, Hants.

The first of three engagements as a quartet involves two 45-minute sets.

Horton writes to Pitt in Australia 'from the so-called dressing room at Gosport to Ken in the warm'.

In it he outlines the reasons for the dissolution of The Buzz. 'Yesterday David and myself decided to finish the ballroom scene for the following reasons (1) no work (2) wage bill mounting (3) David far too busy with writing (4) because of pressures his health will be impaired. So we gave the boys one week's notice and they are all accommodated with jobs already.'

Horton also reveals that the incessant touring and the fans have become an issue for David: 'This has been what David has wanted for some time because he hates the ballrooms and the kids.'

Meanwhile Horton is upbeat about the album's progress and says that the next single has been selected: 'The LP is working out fine and everybody happy. Completely knocked out with Bowie's arrangements… We have chosen the next single, called "Sell Me A Coat".'

Sunday 27 November

▶ David Bowie & The Buzz, The Maid's Head, Tuesday Market Place, King's Lynn, Norfolk.

Friday 2 December

'Rubber Band'/'The London Boys' single released in the UK, David's first for Deram and his fourth single of the year. Both tracks are from the 18 October R.G. Jones session:

⊙ **David Bowie**
A **'Rubber Band'** (Bowie)
B **'The London Boys'** (Bowie)
David Bowie (vocal, guitar, saxophone)
Dek Fearnley (bass)
John Eager (drums)
Derek Boyes (organ)
Chick Norton (trumpet)
Additional session musician unknown
A-side
Produced by David Bowie and Dek Fearnley
B-side
Produced by Dek Fearnley and David Bowie
Arranged by Dek Fearnley and David Bowie
(Deram DM107) (mono)

The A-side of the new single marks the introduction of a new writing style which informs David's work during this period, while the B-side has been a live favourite, particularly among the group's modest-sized Marquee audience.

However, David's Anthony Newley-style delivery on this release does not play well with everybody at his new record company.

At Decca weekly meetings – which Hugh Mendl dubs 'Geniusville' – company executives hear the latest recordings.

"It all went wrong for David at the first Decca A&R meeting. I was personally very excited about David's first single, but when it was played at Geniusville, someone said, 'Sounds like Tony Newley to me'," recalled Mendl in 2002. "From the start, that sealed David's fate at Decca."

▶ David Bowie & The Buzz, The Severn Club, Wyle Cop, Shrewsbury, Shropshire.

On the day the new single is released, David and the Buzz make their final appearance together, having totted up around 100 performances in 11 months.

At the gig, the musicians decide to enjoy the night, and the tensions of the previous weeks are lifted. "This was really just a fun show for all of us, not as tense as the others," said Fearnley in 1991. "As this was the last gig we just let go, we didn't have to worry about the future of the band."

ABOVE: David, central London. "I still get that same feeling walking down Wardour Street." David Bowie talking about 'The London Boys' in 1973.

In this year...

Friday 11 November
MEETING between Ken Pitt, Andy Warhol and Lou Reed at The Factory in New York. Pitt was given a test pressing of The Velvet Underground's debut album which he passed on to David – with profound effects (▶ 5.4.67). David visited Warhol at the second Factory five years later. (▶ 10.9.71)

Saturday 12 November
LETTER from Ken Pitt to Andy Warhol regarding plans to bring The Velvet Underground to the Roundhouse for a week 0of concerts, along with a concurrent Warhol exhibition at the Whitechapel Gallery. Pitt also obtained Warhol's approval to use the artist's films during their trip. In the event, promoter Michael White pulled out of the project, which would have occurred five years before Lou Reed's actual London debut.

BIOGRAPHY
DECCA GROUP RECORDS

DAVID BOWIE	DERAM

D for December, D for David, D for Deram — December 2nd is D-day all round, for that's when Deram launches its exciting new contract star DAVID BOWIE singing his own outstanding song "RUBBER BAND".

David not only wrote the song, he scored the arrangement and produced the master recording.

"RUBBER BAND" is probably as near as David will ever get to moon and June. A love story without a happy ending, it is pathos set to tubas. A happening song.

On the 'B' side is "THE LONDON BOYS", David Bowie's partly autobiographical cameo of the brave and defiant little mod racing up-hill along Wardour Street to an empty Paradise.

ABOVE: 'Rubber Band' press release.

Saturday 3 December

▶ David Bowie, Starlite Ballroom, Wembley, Middx.

David makes another solo appearance, for which he receives a £30 fee.

Record Mirror points out that singer Neil Christian[1] is wearing David's military-style jacket in a TV documentary called *A Tale Of Two Streets*. Directed by Ken Aston, the film compared the contemporary male fashion of Carnaby Street with Savile Row. A shot of David in the jacket will become the cover of his Deram album.

1. Christopher Tidmarsh (1943–2010) reached the Top 20 in the UK in 1966 with the single 'That's Nice' backed by his group The Crusaders, whose line-up included at different times Jimmy Page and Ritchie Blackmore. David gave Christian demos of some of his songs to consider recording himself.

Wednesday 7 December

Publishing contract agreed with David Platz and Essex Music International,[1] negotiated by Ralph Horton in Ken Pitt's absence. Horton is advanced £500, exactly half of what Ken Pitt had earlier discussed with Essex (though Ken had since negotiated a $30,000 deal with publisher Koppleman & Rubin, which he expected would be confirmed on his return). Hal Shaper of Sparta Music waived his contract with David to allow him to sign the Essex deal. A show pencilled in for Eel Pie Island[2] is cancelled (as would be one with David and the Hype in May 1970).

1. Platz deliberately named his company Essex Music International so that it shared initials with the world's most famous label, EMI. The company was based at Dumbarton House, 68 Oxford Street, London W1. David was a regular visitor there for the remainder of the 60s. In time Essex Music was renamed Westminster Music Ltd.

2. The only known dates for any David Jones (or Bowie) performances at this venue were with The Manish Boys in 1964, though it was one of his early haunts.

Thursday 8 December – Friday 9 December

Recording of four more songs is completed: 'Sell Me A Coat', 'Little Bombardier', 'Silly Boy Blue' and 'Maid Of Bond Street'.

David has reworked the lyrics of 'Silly Boy Blue' to reflect his interest in Buddhism, transforming what was a mod anthem into a far more sophisticated track. While the recording sessions are proving productive, the prospects for the new single do not look good.

In another letter to Pitt, Horton says there are difficulties in achieving airplay: 'Radio London have turned down "Rubber Band" because it's not commercial and too "in". So to hell with them, who needs them anyway? I'll get the record off the ground even if it kills me.'

Saturday 10 December

▶ David Bowie, Espresso Club, Eastbourne.

This solo appearance is a booking rescheduled for David and The Buzz from the previous month.

Monday 12 December

Another new track, 'Come And Buy My Toys', is recorded at Decca with John Renbourn[1] providing accompaniment on acoustic guitar.

Renbourn also works with David on a track called 'Bunny Thing' intended for inclusion on the new album.

1. Born 1944, Renbourn became noted for his work with fellow guitarist Bert Jansch and in 1967 formed pioneering folk group The Pentangle, the line-up of which included drummer Terry Cox, who played on David's hit 'Space Oddity' in 1969.

Tuesday 13 December

A new version of 'Please Mr Gravedigger' is recorded

during what is planned to be the final album session at Decca, though David and his fellow musicians will return in the New Year to record additional tracks.

Wednesday 14 December

An acetate[1] is created from the finished masters of the tracks recorded in West Hampstead.

1. An acetate is cut for artist and producer to evaluate their work.

Friday 16 December

Ken Pitt returns from his overseas trip. Among his presents for David is a test-pressing of the album *The Velvet Underground & Nico*, given to him by Andy Warhol during a visit to the pop artist's New York studio The Factory in November.

With the name 'Warhol' scrawled on the label, this becomes one of David's most treasured possessions.

"The first track glided by innocuously enough and didn't register. However, from that point on, with the opening, throbbing, sarcastic bass and guitar of 'I'm Waiting For The Man', the linchpin, the keystone of my ambition was driven home," said David in 2002.

"Actually, though only 19, I had seen rather a lot but had accepted it quite enthusiastically as all a bit of a laugh. Apparently, the laughing was now over. I was hearing a degree of cool that I had no idea was humanly sustainable. Ravishing. One after another, tracks squirmed and slid their tentacles around my mind. Evil and sexual, the violin [viola] of 'Venus in Furs', like some pre-Christian pagan-revival music.

"By the time 'European Son' was done, I was so excited I couldn't move. It was late in the evening and I couldn't think of anyone to call, so I played it again and again and again."

Another live booking – this time in Edmonton, north London – is cancelled.

Saturday 17 December

▶ David Bowie, Lewes Town Hall, Lewes, East Sussex.
According to Pitt's diary, David is paid £45 for two 45-minute sets – commensurate with the fees David received with The Buzz.

Sunday 18 December

David and Ralph Horton visit Pitt at his home in Manchester Street to discuss plans for 1967.

It is time to take stock: in 1966 David and his band earned £2,204, but this doesn't take into account the £3,000 in advances from private backer Ray Cook (which will remain outstanding).

During 1966 David has registered a number of songs with publisher Sparta, but there are several more which have yet to be registered including 'Take It With Soul', 'It's Getting Back To Me', 'Your Funny Smile', 'Send You Money', 'The Fairground', 'The Girl From Minnesota' and 'You Better Tell Her'.[1]

1. As of 2010, none of these titles have been released, officially or otherwise.

Friday 23 December

A booking at the Witch Doctor in Catford, south east London, is cancelled.

Saturday 31 December

Disc & Music Echo poses the question 'Are These The '67 Chartbusters?'

Among those selected are The Pink Floyd, Jimi Hendrix… and David Bowie.

Late 1966

The inclusion of David & The Lower Third's single 'Can't Help Thinking About Me', on Pye's *Hitmakers Vol. 4* compilation marks the first appearance of a track by David Bowie on an album. Also included are songs by The Kinks, Sandie Shaw, The Searchers and Donovan (Pye NPL 18144).

The Shel Talmy Demos

In 1991, Rhino Records issued a 17-track mid-60s Bowie retrospective CD entitled *Early On 1964–1966* featuring a collection of early singles from 64 to 66, with the addition of five previously undocumented demos, made with Shel Talmy.

Featuring some of David's earliest surviving demos, tracks: 5, 6, 7, 10 and 11 were issued for the first time (plus two tracks with alternative vocals):

3. 'I Pity The Fool': Features an alternative vocal take.
4. 'Take My Tip': Features an alternative vocal take.
5. 'That's Where My Heart Is': David accompanies himself solo on acoustic guitar.
6. 'I Want My Baby Back': Accompanied by a lead guitarist (probably Denis Taylor) David double-tracks his vocals.
7. 'Bars Of The County Jail': David accompanies himself solo on acoustic guitar. The song's main verse is very similar to Roger Whittaker's 1969 hit single 'Durham Town (The Leavin')'.
10. 'I'll Follow You': Recorded at IBC, David is accompanied by The Lower Third.
11. 'Glad I've Got Nobody': David is accompanied by The Lower Third.

On release Talmy said of the previously unreleased tracks:

"David and I went straight to monaural tape on those demos. Certainly they weren't multitrack, we did it specifically to do demos. They were things we were talking about recording at a future date."

1. 'Liza Jane' 2. 'Louie Louie Go Home' 3. 'I Pity The Fool' 4. 'Take My Tip' 5. 'That's Where My Heart Is' 6. 'I Want My Baby Back' 7. 'Bars Of The County Jail' 8. 'You've Got A Habit Of Leaving' 9. 'Baby Loves That Way' 10. 'I'll Follow You' 11. 'Glad I've Got Nobody' 12. 'Can't Help Thinking About Me' 13. 'And I Say To Myself' 14. 'Do Anything You Say' 15. 'Good Morning Girl' 16. 'I Dig Everything' 17. 'I'm Not Losing Sleep'.
(Rhino R2 70526)

TOP: Decca promo postcard.

ABOVE: *Hitmakers Vol. 4*, the first album to feature a David Bowie song.

In this year…

Friday 23 December
OPENING of Britain's first psychedelic club, UFO, in the basement of a pub at 31 Tottenham Court Road, London. The Pink Floyd played the first night and returned there regularly. UFO quickly became a popular venue and was a meeting place for the in-crowd until its demise in October 1967. Marc Bolan was discovered by David's producer Tony Visconti at UFO.

LAST edition of leading pop show *Ready Steady Go!* broadcast in the UK, re-titled *Ready Steady Goes!*.

1967

DAVID severs his management ties with Ralph Horton, and Ken Pitt takes sole control of the young musician's career as he continues to record his compositions as well as offer them to other artistes.

Heavily influenced by the album *The Velvet Underground & Nico*, he rehearses with quintet The Riot Squad, who are reeling from the death of mentor Joe Meek. David's media profile is growing as he continues his low-key experiments with the band before bidding them farewell.

'The Laughing Gnome', featuring an Anthony Newley-esque vocal delivery, is released as a single to a muted critical reception, but the fruits of David's album labours for Deram see the light of day on 1 June – the same day as The Beatles' masterpiece, *Sgt Pepper's Lonely Hearts Club Band*.

David Bowie, which features famed session musicians as well as his old friends from The Buzz, confirms his blossoming reputation as a teller of short stories in song form.

Despite gaining overseas releases, the album makes no commercial impression, but it helps to found a relationship with bohemian dancer and mime artist Lindsay Kemp, a confirmed fan.

David moves into Pitt's London flat as he immerses himself in plans to diversify his art and furthers his interest in Buddhism.

Meetings with American producer Tony Visconti prove highly promising and they soon begin recording together.

David's newly taken out membership of the Equity union confirms his interest in acting and scriptwriting, and as the year draws to a close he is involved in a Lindsay Kemp musical stage play. His first brush with costume brings him into contact with designer Natasha Kornilof.

1. Oscar Beuselinck Jr, born Peterborough 1945, the son of a notable showbiz lawyer and a former pianist with Screaming Lord Sutch's backing band The Savages. Later changed his name to Paul Nicholas and found fame as a member of the London cast of *Hair*. He scored a series of pop hits in the mid-70s and moved into acting, appearing in The Who film *Tommy* and becoming a British sitcom star in the 80s. Nicholas recalled in 1997 that David played him the demo: "He wrote the song about a series of prison breakouts which had occurred around that time. On the demo, David joined in on the choruses and shouted the prison-style 'roll call'," said Nicholas. "He also spoke the dialogue in the middle section."

Saturday 14 January

David takes part in a production meeting at Decca Studios. Like all Deram albums there will be a stereo version of his new album as well as the standard release in mono.

Tuesday 17 January

Impressed by Pitt's firm control and experience, David is now keen to break from Ralph Horton, having tired of the seat-of-the-pants approach to finances and lack of progress until Pitt stepped into the picture.

David visits Pitt at his Manchester Street apartment and asks his advice on how this can be achieved. Later he attends a meeting with his publisher David Platz at the offices of Essex Music[1] in Oxford Street.

Pitt applies for David to join the Performing Right Society, the organisation which pays out income to songwriters for radio play. This lists 29 of his songs, 26 of which have been recorded.

1. From time to time, David bumps into another Essex Music-signed songwriter at Platz's office: Pete Townshend. "I used to meet him very, very occasionally, because we had the same music publisher, and he was always complimenting me on odd songs he'd heard at the publishers which hadn't been released," said Townshend in 1975. "I'd heard quite a lot of his work, a fantastic amount of which just piled up. I think that, when he finally launched himself in the business, he used up all that experience and, although you've got this tremendously spacey, glittery and unreal figure, the incredible thing about it was that it was a very, very real thing as well."

Thursday 19 January

Horton visits Pitt to tell him he is willing to give up his management interests in David, not least because he has incurred considerable debt trying to establish David as a star.

Horton drops in on Pitt's Curzon Street offices over the next few months but soon disappears from view, doubtless in an attempt to shake off the creditors who continue to pursue him.[1]

1. Horton is an enigmatic figure in David's early professional life. Having expended considerable energy on his young artist over a period of a year-and-a-half, Horton was forced to yield to the more experienced Pitt within a few months of bringing him on board.

The whereabouts of the rarely photographed Horton after the early spring of 1967 remain unknown. It is established that he moved on to a job at the Royal Automobile Club at the organisation's central London offices, but soon cut off communication with Pitt and all his other music business contacts.

Friday 20 January

Witnessed by his friend and business partner Kenny Bell, Horton signs documents cancelling the management contract.

Tuesday 3 January

Ken Pitt visits fellow manager and agent Robert Stigwood at his offices in Chesterfield Gardens, W1, and plays him a demo of David's composition 'Over The Wall We Go'. Stigwood deems the song suitable for release on his label Reaction by young singer Oscar.[1] At a meeting with Oscar, David agrees to help out on the recording sessions (providing backing vocals).

PREVIOUS SPREAD: Gerald Fearnley captures one of David's earliest make-up experiments at his Bryanston Street studio.

THIS PAGE

ABOVE: David photographed on the roof of 39 Manchester Street by Pitt.

RIGHT: Ralph Horton's agreement, cancelling his management contract with David.

Saturday 21 January

David spends an evening at The Bricklayers Arms,[1] Old Kent Road, south-east London, with John Eager and Dek Fearnley, who is performing there with his new group. "David and I sat in with them for quite a few numbers," said Eager in 2010. "David performed some blues things. It was completely unrehearsed and, I'm sure, not that great."

1. The pub was demolished to make way for a flyover within a few months.

Monday 23 January

Pitt and Horton meet to exchange the documents formally ending Horton's eighteen-month tenure as David's manager.

Tuesday 24 January

David and John Eager are in the audience of a student orchestral concert at the Guildhall School of Music & Drama in the City of London.

The following day Eager notes in his diary: 'Arrange record in evening with Bowie.'[1]

1. In 1991 Eager couldn't remember to what this alluded.

Thursday 26 January

David and fellow musicians reconvene at Decca Studios to record the backing tracks for new songs 'The Laughing Gnome' and 'The Gospel According To Tony Day' with producer Mike Vernon. It's been decided that these should be the A and B-sides of David's next single.

Bob Michaels of Dave Antony's Moods plays organ on the latter track, while guitar on both is provided by Pete Hampshire, the former RAF colleague of arranger Fearnley, who tried out for The Buzz the previous year.

B-side out-takes reveal that there is a lot of light-hearted studio banter between David and engineer Gus Dudgeon, with jokes occasionally made at the expense of the label's senior staff.

Also in attendance for his first recording session with David is Pitt.

Monday 30 January

Oscar's single 'Over The Wall We Go'/'Everyday Of My Life' is released on Reaction. The A-side is Bowie's composition, while the B-side is written by Beuselinck.

'Over The Wall We Go' receives radio play and is performed shortly after its release on comedian Ken Dodd's TV show,[1] with David's spoken-word section being done by DJ/announcer David Hamilton. The single fails to chart.

David takes a white label copy to DJ Jeff Dexter, whose central London nightclub Tiles is a major mod hangout. "I played the record all the time, for years afterwards," said Dexter in 1995.

1. *Doddy's Music Box*, broadcast by independent network ATV on Saturday evenings from 7 January to 11 March 1967. Dodd joined Oscar in performing the song.

Friday 3 February

David asks Pitt to formally become his manager since no official arrangement is in place in the wake of Horton's departure.

Tuesday 7 February

David works on the vocal track for 'The Laughing Gnome' at Decca's Studio 2 through the afternoon and into the evening.

A light-hearted children's novelty song, 'The Laughing Gnome' will later prove something of a burden.[1]

The voices are provided by David and Gus Dudgeon, and treated by Vernon using the vari-speed effect popularised by the children's TV puppet show *Pinky & Perky*.[2]

Trainee engineer Barry Johnston, who also assists Dudgeon, notes session details, collating writer and publishing information and issuing matrix numbers.

"David was very keen on sound effects; working on his album in particular was a lot of fun," said Johnston (son of the late British cricket commentator Brian Johnston) in 2002. "Since we were about the same age, we got on very well. Recording 'The Laughing Gnome' was actually quite tricky."[3]

1. When Decca re-released 'The Laughing Gnome' as a single at the height of Ziggymania in 1973 it reached number six in the UK charts and threatened to undercut David's status as a serious artist.
2. The same vocal effect was used on novelty hit 'Ragtime Cowboy Joe' by Dave Seville & The Chipmunks in 1959.
3. The Decca archive contains a number of rejected versions, some with 'gnome' voices recorded at different speeds and others with different jokes and dialogue.

Thursday 9 February

David accompanies Pitt – who is taking his Australian cousins (who are visiting for the first time) – to the Prince of Wales Theatre for musical revue *Way Out In Piccadilly* starring singer Cilla Black and comedian Frankie Howerd.

Friday 10 February

David continues to work on 'The Laughing Gnome' vocals in the studio. Pitt writes to John Jones: 'David has confirmed to me that he, your wife and you would like me to manage his business affairs and I shall therefore have a mutually suitable contract drawn up.'

Sunday 12 February

With John Eager, David is at a Stravinsky concert performed by the Guildhall youth orchestra at the Royal Festival Hall. He is already a fan; in a press release the previous year promoting his single 'Rubber Band', David included Stravinsky among his favourite composers.

Tuesday 14 February

A lyric by David, titled 'You Gotta Know', is assigned by Essex Music. It is set to an existing foreign-

DAILY RECORDING INFORMATION

This information is intended only as a guide. It is not necessarily accurate or complete.

To :- DISTRIBUTION   c (See over) From :- STUDIOS   Date 2nd March 1967

ARTIST:- DAVID BOWIE
Prod. Mike Vernon
Mus Arr. David Bowie & Arthur Greenslade (for * only)
M.D. DEK TEARNLEY

Rec date. 14th & 24th Nov
8th & 9th Dec.
25th Feb 67

Mat. No.	Time	Title	Composer	Publisher
SIDE 1.				
ZDR 59651	2.07	1. UNCLE ARTHUR	BOWIE	ESSEX
ZDR 59652	3.50	2. SELL ME A COAT	"	ESSEX
ZDR 59957	2.15	3. RUBBER BAND *	"	COOPER MUSIC
ZDR 59958	3.07	4. LOVE YOU TILL TUESDAY	"	ESSEX
ZDR 59655	3.11	5. THERE IS A HAPPY LAND	"	SPARTA
ZDR 59657	2.58	6. WE ARE HUNGRY MEN	"	ESSEX
SIDE 2				
zdr 59658	3.24	1. LITTLE BOMBADIER	"	ESSEX
ZDR 59659	3.57	2. SILLY BOY BLUE	"	SPARTA
ZDR 59660	2.07	3. COME AND BUY ME TOYS	"	ESSEX
ZDR 59661	2.16	4. JOIN THE GANG	"	ESSEX
ZDR 59662	2.26	5. SHE'S GOT MEDALS	"	ESSEX
ZDR 59663	1.44	6. MAIDS OF BOND STREET	"	SPARTA
ZDR 59760	2.34	7. PLEASE MR GRAVEDIGGER	"	ESSEX.

TOP: Decca Daily Recording Information sheet, featuring tracks on the *David Bowie* album, 2 March.

ABOVE: Mike Vernon and Gus Dudgeon in the Studio 2 control room at Decca's Broadhurst Gardens, the studio where David recorded most of his first album.

language track, but it isn't clear which song this translation is for.

Wednesday 22 February

David and his half-brother Terry attend a performance by Cream at Bromley venue The Bromel Club. David revealed to Radio One in 1993:

"I did in fact take him to a Cream concert at the Bromel Club, which would have been, I guess, 1967, something like that, and I was very disturbed because the music was affecting him adversely. His particular illness was somewhere between schizophrenia and manic depressiveness and I know that he was getting to a pretty tranced-out state watching Cream, because I don't think he had ever been to something as loud as that in his life. I remember having to take him home because it was really affecting him."

Saturday 25 February

Back at Decca's Studio 2, 'Rubber Band' is re-recorded in stereo (the single version was in mono) and two more tracks are completed for inclusion on the album: 'Love You Till Tuesday',[1] and 'When I Live My Dream'.[2]

Produced by Mike Vernon with uncredited arrangements by leading orchestrator Arthur Greenslade, the trio of tracks is taped and mixed in stereo between 10am and 6pm.

Pitt instructs his lawyers to draw up a new management contract for David.

1. There is a demo of 'Love You Till Tuesday' dating from 1965. This home recording features a basic acoustic guitar refrain and an impressive vocal echo, including a double-tracked chorus.

2. The original plan was to record a new stereo version of 'The London Boys' at this session, referred to in a letter from Pitt to David on 17 February.

Tuesday 28 February

'Say Goodbye To Mr Mind' is registered at Essex Music.

Wednesday 1 March

During the day, the final touches are made to David's

debut album, following initial work on 29 February. Both the mono and stereo versions of *David Bowie* are compiled and the release date is set for June.

In the evening David again joins Pitt and his cousins at the theatre, this time to see singer Cliff Richard in an extended run of pantomime *Cinderella* at the London Palladium. This also features The Shadows and comedians Jack Douglas, Terry Scott and Hugh Lloyd. Afterwards they all dine in the revolving restaurant at the top of the new Post Office Tower.

Wednesday 8 March

David is at Decca Studios for the creation of the final version of 'The Laughing Gnome' which, as the tape box is inscribed, has 'less gnome voices'.

In the evening David probably records a cover of 'Pussy Cat', a song popularised by MoR singer Jess Conrad.[1]

1. This recording is included in an undated reel of tape though not corroborated by Decca documentation (no date or matrix is assigned).

Monday 13 March

David's application to become a member of the Performing Right Society is accepted.

In the afternoon David rehearses with quintet The Riot Squad[1] at The Swan public house, High Road, Tottenham, north London.

Heavily influenced by *The Velvet Underground & Nico* album Pitt had brought him from the US a few months previously, David is keen to investigate new avenues of performance which draw on pop-art and a tougher musicality.

He has joined the group in an unofficial capacity, but has not informed either Pitt or his friends who had been in The Buzz.

David is using the period between the departure of Horton – who would never have allowed him to experiment in this way – and his formal signing with Pitt to test out ideas often discussed with previous band colleagues.

The Riot Squad is a ready-made unit. As such, David has no responsibility for wages and no long-term commitments to consider. For their part, the band members are aware that David is pursuing a solo career and that this liaison will be short-lived.

Like David, The Riot Squad are also at a cross-roads, not least because they are still reeling from the impact of the violent death of their champion Joe Meek[2] just six weeks previously.

Thus David's arrival in their midst, full of ideas for presentation and propelled by the new music being created across the Atlantic by The Velvet Underground, brings a new direction and purpose.

Despite this association with a new set of musicians, David spends the evening with former member of The Buzz John Eager at The Cockney Pride, a large subterranean pub in Piccadilly Circus. There they bump into producer Mike Vernon, with whom David discusses a number of ideas he has for future projects.

1. Formed in London in 1964, The Riot Squad were initially managed and produced by British pop impresario Larry Page and were stable-mates of David's at Pye Records, to whom they were signed between 1965 and 1967. The group's first three singles featured Jimi Hendrix Experience drummer Mitch Mitchell. Deep Purple keyboard player Jon Lord was also fleetingly a member. By the time they met David the line-up consisted of Bob Evans (sax, flute), Brian Croke Prebble (bass, vocals), Rod Davies (guitar), Derek Roll (drums) and George Butcher (keyboards).

2. Meek produced The Riot Squad's final single for Pye, 'Gotta Be A First Time', which was released just after his death on 3 February 1967.

Saturday 18 March

Scottish three-piece group 1-2-3[1] begin a weekend residency at the Marquee, with a set featuring distinctive song covers led by organist Billy Ritchie.

1-2-3's set includes a version of David's recent single 'I Dig Everything' which bassist Ian Ellis has taped from the radio.

David visits the Soho club after hearing on the grapevine about their take on his song. "I was taken aback, it was so radically altered but retained its heart and soul," he said in 1994. "The audience reaction was interesting: they didn't know what to make of it. I suppose that Billy was yet another unrecognised genius. I used to talk to him at the Chasse club,[2] but we lost touch."

Ritchie and David become friendly for a period. "We'd go to the Fox & Hounds in Wardour Street and talk," said Ritchie in 2006. "It was an exciting time for us both; we had so many ideas. No one else could get a look-in when we got together. David was great, but I thought I was the one who was going to be the star. I didn't have any doubts about it."

1. As The Premiers, the group had supported David and The Lower Third on a Scottish date the previous year. Ellis and 1-2-3 drummer Harry Hughes later played on demos for tracks which appeared on David's early 70s albums *Hunky Dory* and *Ziggy Stardust*.

2. La Chasse was a small musicians' retreat/drinking club in Wardour Street, yards from the Marquee (also in Wardour Street) and Trident Studios in St Anne's Court. One of the bartenders was Yes frontman Jon Anderson. David would later be introduced to Mick Ronson there. (▶ 3.2.70)

Monday 20 March

Totally unaware of David's involvement with The Riot Squad, Pitt remains on the case of the Mithras Films film musical project mooted six months previously. He sends producer Maurice Hatton a demo tape containing seven of David's songs, along with a lyric sheet. These are likely to be the new Deram recordings.[1]

1. Pitt never received a response. Hatton had by this time started work on another film, *Praise Marx And Pass The Ammunition*, starring popular British actor John Thaw. He died in 1997.

Tuesday 28 March

▶ David appears on stage with The Riot Squad at Kodak's Social Club, Eastman Hall, Kodak Sports Ground, in north London suburb Harrow.

Augmenting their flashing blue police light, at David's suggestion, the group add hand-painted props, extravagant make-up and bright clothing to their stage show.

The set includes an instrumental take on 'Silly Boy Blue', a version of Lou Reed's 'I'm Waiting For The Man', and a new song called 'Little Toy Soldier'.

David invites John Eager to meet him at the venue but he is unable to attend.

Wednesday 5 April

David connives with engineer Gus Dudgeon to make use of downtime at Decca Studios, and with The Riot Squad records the key three tracks from their new stage show: 'Little Toy Soldier', 'Silly Boy Blue' (this is the third version he has recorded) and 'I'm Waiting For The Man'.[1]

Pitt, Vernon and the former members of The Buzz are not informed. "That session with David was all done on the quiet; it was a bit hush-hush," confirmed Dudgeon in 1991.

On the Velvet Underground cover, David's harmonica is reversed on tape and the sax is played by The Riot Squad's Bob Evans. Dudgeon supplies laughter and vocal sound effects.

'Silly Boy Blue' is an instrumental recorded for a routine David and The Riot Squad are preparing for their live set.

'Little Toy Soldier' has the same musical arrangement as The Velvet Underground's 'Venus In Furs' and some of Reed's original lyrics. "When we recorded it, the song originally finished on the line 'And he beat her to death'," said Dudgeon in 1991. "One day I was playing around with the vast selection of sound effects at Decca and added a final section."

1. The surviving quarter-inch master tape of this session contains seven takes of 'Silly Boy Blue', four of 'Little Toy Soldier' and three of 'I'm Waiting For The Man'. In the early 80s Dudgeon gave copies of 'Little Toy Soldier' and 'I'm Waiting For The Man' to a friend. These were later bootlegged without his consent.

Sunday 9 April

Ken Pitt visits David's father in Bromley to go through a new management contract.

Thursday 13 April

▶ David appears at Tiles Club at 79-89 Oxford Street as a member of The Riot Squad.

As will be the format for David's appearances with the group over the coming weeks, his name is not mentioned. In fact he is listed as 'Toy Soldier' when the line-up is featured in *Jackie* magazine's 8 July issue.

For the Tiles show David recycles a green corduroy jacket, last worn in December 1963 in his final days with The Konrads, by adding blue lines himself using cartridge ink.[1]

The shows with The Riot Squad allow David to investigate a number of exaggerated make-up techniques, mimes and image manipulation he has not had the opportunity to try out in a live context.

The end result, as the promotional leaflet reveals, owes as much to the pantomime characters David had seen at The Palladium the previous month as to the rock-oriented likes of Syd Barrett on stage with

TOP: From Scotland, 1-2-3. Left to right: Ian Ellis, Harry Hughes and Billy Ritchie. Ellis and Hughes later helped David record *Hunky Dory* and *Ziggy Stardust* demos.

BOTTOM: Advert for Riot Squad appearance at Tiles night club, 13 April. David appeared as part of Riot Squad.

In this year...

Sunday 26 February
PERFORMANCE by David's musician colleagues John Eager and Derek Boyes with The Truth at London's Saville Theatre.

Saturday 1 April
ENTRY of The Pink Floyd's single 'Arnold Layne' at number 20 in the UK charts. David paid part tribute by naming a musical project *The Arnold Corns* in 1971, and also performed a version at the Royal Albert Hall on 29 May 2006.

Gnome'[1] is heavily influenced by the delivery of his hero Anthony Newley, whose trademark was to end his recordings with a laugh. This may have prompted the theme of this song.[2] In fact the track's basic rhythm comes from a surprising source: The Velvet Underground's 'I'm Waiting For The Man'.[3]

The B-side (originally titled 'The Gospel According To Tony Day Blues') features David and Dek Fearnley on Velvets-style backing vocals. This song/monologue is an odd choice for coupling with a children's song when David's nursery tale 'Come And Buy My Toys' might have been more suitable. Delivered in a droll, jaded style similar to the cynical tones of British comedian Tony Hancock, the track lists in throwaway fashion a number of fictional characters and their shortcomings.

1. This single was never deleted from the Deram catalogue. With some minor repromotion Decca rode in the wake of David's early 70s popularity by remarketing it. Subsequently, it reached number six in the UK charts in 1973.

2. David and Gus Dudgeon cut a version of the A-side featuring only gnome vocals, as 'The Rolling Gnomes'.

3. In 1990, David conducted a phone poll for songs to perform on that year's Sound + Vision tour. The *NME* campaigned for 'The Laughing Gnome'. Due to this campaign the song came top, to which David commented: "I was wondering how to do it, maybe in the style of the Velvets or something, until I found out the poll was a scam."

Saturday 15 April

The *NME* gives 'The Laughing Gnome' a positive review: 'A novelty number chock full of appeal. This boy sounds remarkably like Tony Newley, and he wrote this song himself. An amusing lyric, with David Bowie interchanging lines with a chipmunk-like creature.'

Tuesday 25 April

Ken Pitt and David formalise the arrangements for Pitt to become manager by signing a one-year contract with four options to renew, creating a potential five-year duration.

Friday 5 May

Pitt sends a demo tape to EMI producer John Burgess (who has overseen hits by Manfred Mann), containing three new compositions by David: 'Going Down', 'Summer Kind Of Love' (later reworked as 'Social Kind Of Girl') and 'Everything Is You'.

Sunday 7 May

David, Dek Fearnley, John Eager and their girlfriends are at London's Saville Theatre for a performance by The Jimi Hendrix Experience. Of the party, only David and Eager enjoy the show. Among the support acts are David's friends 1-2-3 and Denny Laine's Electric String Band, led by the guitarist who had been a member of The Moody Blues and was associated with David's ex-manager Ralph Horton.

"I'm pretty sure David came backstage to see us that night like he always did," said 1-2-3 organist Billy Ritchie in 2006. "We shared our dressing room with Hendrix so they may have met. I went for a drink with David afterwards. He was with Jane, who he had

The Pink Floyd at the Marquee.

The Riot Squad are more than happy to follow David's lead and will continue with this flamboyant image when David moves on after a few weeks and a handful of appearances with them.[2] One show with The Riot Squad is at a regular Radio London-sponsored event, at the Down Beat Club, The Swan Hotel Ballroom, 73 High Street, Maldon, in Essex. The DJ/compere was Dave Cash.

1. He later gave the jacket away and in 2005 Bromley Museum bought it at auction. The following year it featured in an exhibition of local history.

2. The new stage presentation did little to lift long-term interest. Sax player/vocalist Bob Evans left the group for a new life in Venezuela at the end of 1967 and the group broke up the following year.

Friday 14 April

Deram release 'The Laughing Gnome'/'The Gospel According To Tony Day' single.

⊙ **David Bowie**
A **'The Laughing Gnome'** (Bowie)
B **'The Gospel According To Tony Day'** (Bowie)
David Bowie (vocal, gnome voices)
Gus Dudgeon (gnome voices)
Pete Hampshire (guitar)
Dek Fearnley (bass, vocal on B-side)
Derek Boyes (keyboards)
Bob Michaels (keyboards)
John Eager (drums)
Additional session musicians unknown
Produced by Mike Vernon
Arranged by David Bowie and Dek Fearnley
(Deram DM123)

David's part-spoken performance on 'The Laughing

TOP: David outside St Giles Church at the end of Denmark Street, London W1, April.

TOP RIGHT: An original handbill designed by Bob Evans (pictured bottom left), given out by David and friends on Oxford Street to promote an appearance at Tiles Club. It features the earliest known photograph of David in full make-up (pictured top left).

ABOVE: 'The Laughing Gnome' provided David with his first picture sleeve single, issued in Belgium.

chatted up at our agents, NEMS.[1] David always had attractive women with him."

1. NEMS was the artist agency operated by Beatles manager Brian Epstein, who had bought The Saville Theatre in 1965. In this period David was a regular visitor to the NEMS offices at Sutherland House, next door to The Palladium in Argyle Street.

Saturday 13 May

David and Pitt see *Oliver!* – the hit musical by Lionel Bart[1] – at the Piccadilly Theatre, London.

1. Lionel Begleiter (1930–1999), writer/composer responsible for such pop hits as Cliff Richard's 'Livin' Doll' and Anthony Newley's 'Do You Mind?' as well as the musicals *Fings Ain't Wot They Used T'Be*, *Oliver!*, *Maggie May* and *Blitz*.

Friday 19 May

David meets Lewis Rudd, head of children's programmes at broadcaster Rediffusion TV, at their offices in Kingsway, Holborn, London, to pitch for the job as compère of new ITV children's programme *Playtime*.

He gives Rudd a tape of his song 'There Is A Happy Land' but the meeting comes to nothing.

Meanwhile, Pitt sends a copy of David's debut album to Polly Devlin, journalist at London's *Evening Standard*, with a note: 'You may remember our meeting a few years ago when I brought Bob Dylan to your office at *Vogue* to be photographed.

'I would like to introduce you to another interesting writer/singer, namely David Bowie. David has a most unusual talent and I am sure has a tremendous future ahead of him. This album, containing fourteen of David's own compositions, is released on June 1st, the same day as The Beatles album.'[1]

1. *Sgt Pepper's Lonely Hearts Club Band*.

Monday 22 May

Ken Pitt sends promotional copies of *David Bowie* to around 30 recipients, including journalist Nik Cohn at *Queen* magazine, producer Mike Smith, Beatles manager Brian Epstein and their producer George Martin.

Saturday 27 May

London Records issues 'Rubber Band'/'There Is A Happy Land' as a promo single in the US, with limited numbers circulated to media, radio stations and record retailers to gauge their reaction ahead of a proper release.

'There Is A Happy Land' is considered a safer bet than 'The London Boys' – the narrative of an unhappy, pill-popping mod – but the surprise is that the US label has even considered 'Rubber Band', which had flopped in Britain six months earlier.

Monday 29 May

Music critic William Mann reviews The Beatles' *Sergeant Pepper* in *The Times* and mentions David's recent single release in passing, referring to it as 'a heavy-handed facetious number about a laughing gnome which was ecstatically plugged for several

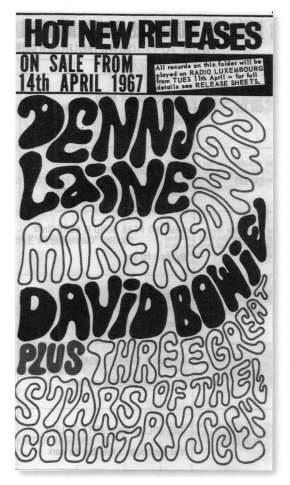

weeks by the pirate radio stations but steadfastly remained the flop it deserved to be.'

Wednesday 31 May

David is interviewed by Peter Jones for *Record Mirror*, meeting him at the music paper's offices at 116 Shaftesbury Avenue, central London.

Thursday 1 June

On the day *David Bowie* is released by Deram, David meets film director Franco Zeffirelli and assistant Mike Lovell at 65 Dean Street, Soho. They are looking for a score for Zeffirelli's new film, *Romeo & Juliet*.

Pitt receives a letter from Mike Vernon: 'I think you know how I feel about Bowie. He is one of the greatest talents we have seen at Decca for many years, and I am very proud even to be associated with his recordings.'

TOP: Decca promotional leaflet featuring 'The Laughing Gnome'.

BOTTOM: 'The Laughing Gnome' Deram singles newspaper advert.

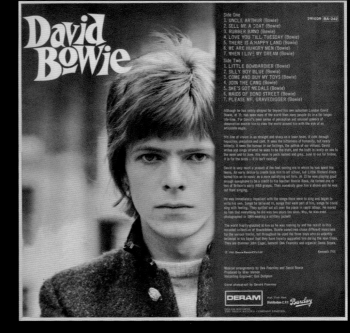

ABOVE: *David Bowie*, David's first album release.

DAVID BOWIE Released Thursday 1 June

Side One
1. UNCLE ARTHUR (Bowie) (2.07)
David Bowie (vocal)
Dek Fearnley (bass)
Derek Boyes (piano)
John Renbourn (guitar)
John Eager (drums)
Orchestral session musicians

2. SELL ME A COAT (Bowie) (2.58)
David Bowie (vocal)
Dek Fearnley (bass)
John Renbourn (guitar)
John Eager (drums)
Orchestral session musicians

3. RUBBER BAND (Bowie) (2.17)
David Bowie (vocal)
Dek Fearnley (bass)
Derek Boyes (piano)
John Eager (drums)
Orchestral session musicians

4. LOVE YOU TILL TUESDAY (Bowie) (3.09)
David Bowie (vocal)
Dek Fearnley (bass)

BELOW: Mike Vernon, producer of David's first album.

Derek Boyes (piano)
John Renbourn (guitar)
John Eager (drums)
Orchestral session musicians

5. THERE IS A HAPPY LAND (Bowie) (3.11)
David Bowie (vocal)
Dek Fearnley (bass)
Derek Boyes (piano)
John Renbourn (guitar)
John Eager (drums)
Orchestral session musicians

6. WE ARE HUNGRY MEN (Bowie) (2.58)
David Bowie (vocal)
Dek Fearnley (bass)
Derek Boyes (organ)
John Renbourn (guitar)
John Eager (drums)
Gus Dudgeon (Newscaster)
Mike Vernon (Nazi voices)
Orchestral session musicians

7. WHEN I LIVE MY DREAM (Bowie) (3.22)
David Bowie (vocal)
Dek Fearnley (bass)
John Renbourn (guitar)
John Eager (drums)
Orchestral session musicians

Side Two
1. LITTLE BOMBARDIER (Bowie) (3.24)
David Bowie (vocal)
Dek Fearnley (bass)
Derek Boyes (piano)
John Eager (drums)
Orchestral session musicians

2. SILLY BOY BLUE (Bowie) (3.48)
David Bowie (vocal)
Dek Fearnley (bass, backing vocal)
Derek Boyes (piano)
John Eager (drums, backing vocal)
Marion Constable (backing vocal)
Orchestral session musicians

3. COME AND BUY MY TOYS (Bowie) (2.07)
David Bowie (vocal)
John Renbourn (guitar)
Dek Fearnley (bass)

4. JOIN THE GANG (Bowie) (2.17)
David Bowie (vocal)
Dek Fearnley (bass)
Derek Boyes (piano, organ)
John Eager (drums)
Big Jim Sullivan (sitar, acoustic guitar)
Orchestral session musicians

5. SHE'S GOT MEDALS (Bowie) (2.23)
David Bowie (vocal)
Dek Fearnley (bass)
Derek Boyes (piano)
John Renbourn (guitar)
John Eager (drums)
Orchestral session musicians

6. MAID OF BOND STREET (Bowie) (1.43)
David Bowie (vocal)
Dek Fearnley (bass)
Derek Boyes (piano)
John Eager (drums)
Big Jim Sullivan (guitar)
Orchestral session musicians

7. PLEASE MR GRAVEDIGGER (Bowie) (2.35)
David Bowie (monologue)
Gus Dudgeon, David Bowie (sound effects)

Musical arrangements by Dek Fearnley, David Bowie
Tracks 3, 4, 7 arranged by Arthur Greenslade
Produced by Mike Vernon
Engineered by Gus Dudgeon
Cover photography by Gerald Fearnley
Sleeve notes by Kenneth Pitt
(Deram DML 1007) Mono
(Deram SML 1007) Stereo

ABOVE: Rare out-take from Gerald Fearnley's album cover session.

a first LP that is different

DAVID BOWIE

SML 1007   DML 1007   12" stereo or mono LP record

another great new sound on **DERAM**

Deram Records Decca House Albert Embankment London SE1

David Bowie, David's first album, is a collection of 14 disparate tales with no apparent overarching theme, offering little clue to what had been or what was to come for this singular young talent.

The songs lacked lead guitar lines (though a jazz riff appears on the track which takes the listener to the thoroughfare where David once worked at an advertising agency, 'Maid Of Bond Street'), and their story-telling, word-play and theatricality would have appeared comfortably within the confines of a mid-60s West End stage.

After all, David had been much taken with the idea of writing for the theatre ever since he witnessed Anthony Newley's musical *Stop The World – I Want To Get Off* in 1961.

And here is another unique aspect to *David Bowie*: just as his Newley-esque vocalising marked him out from the rest of the class of Britrock 1967, it also served to distance the listener not attuned to such stylised delivery.

David summed up his debut thus in 1976: "It got some airplay, as we say in the biz. But I didn't get people buying me and I wasn't asked to perform, so I suppose in that respect it was a bit of a failure. But the idea of writing sort of short stories, I thought was quite novel at the time – excuse the pun!"

In this way *David Bowie* may be viewed as an experiment in short-story writing; the observational technique, use of detail and much of the material is rooted in the London and its suburbs of the time.

It is worth bearing in mind that David was a teenager when he wrote most of the songs ('Maid Of Bond Street' and 'Silly Boy Blue' were almost certainly written shortly after leaving school).

As Ken Pitt wrote in the sleeve notes to the original release, 'Although he has rarely strayed far beyond his own suburban London, David Bowie at 19 has seen more of the world than many people do in a far longer lifetime.'

In part, David's songs follow the style of traditional folk stories, in which bizarre little worlds are created. The nursery-rhyme characteristics of some of the album relate directly back to David's fascination with Frank Loesser's composition 'Inchworm', sung by Danny Kaye in 1952.

They also bring to mind another favourite of David's at the time, Randolph Caldecott's colourful illustrations of children's stories: in particular 'Sell Me A Coat', 'When I Live My Dream' and 'Come And Buy My Toys' bring to mind such pastel-coloured evocations of

David's album co-arranger and bass player Dek Fearnley, circa 1968.

childhood innocence.

By contrast three tracks – 'Rubber Band', 'Little Bombardier' and 'She's Got Medals' – evoke the brass-buttoned militarism of the Edwardian era, much in vogue in the year of recording. These three songs dominate the album, though none of David's characters created for them emerges covered in glory. The grey military-style jacket David designed and wore for the cover-shoot adds to the final effect.

Of the three, 'Little Bombardier' has the most interesting provenance. The waltz-like arrangement initially alludes to a pleasant Sunday afternoon in the park, but the subject matter reveals a darker tale hinting at loneliness, child molestation and the threat of arrest.

In fact, the name of the little bombardier Frankie Mere was taken from the three-year-old son of an acquaintance of David's, The Beatstalkers' bass player Alan Mair.

When rehearsing the song at Pitt's Manchester Street apartment, David attempted Alan Mair's broad Scottish accent and took advice from him on pronunciation. In the end, he decided not to pursue this direction.

Meanwhile, 'Join The Gang', written during an autumnal afternoon photo session on Clapham Common, brings together a group of strange and disparate characters (in a similar manner to 1967s 'The Gospel According To Tony Day'). 'Join The Gang' is also the only track to openly allude to drug-taking, with references to 'acid trips' and 'joints'. But, as he had previously done with 'The London Boys', the message is delivered in mock tones rather than with praise.

David Bowie is also notable for presenting the singles which mark his rapid creative progress at the time, with the inclusion of the stereo re-recording of a song he had performed with The Buzz, 'Rubber Band', and an early version of its successor, the jaunty, near-MoR pop of 'Love You Till Tuesday'.

The album's radio-friendly veneer contrasts with the willingness to experiment with instrumentation, vocals and effects: 'Silly Boy Blue' starts with drummer John Eager crashing a giant Chinese cymbal, one which David would borrow for mime appearances. Dek Fearnley's friend Marion Constable was visiting the studio the day they recorded the track, and features with David and arranger/bassist Fearnley on backing vocals (on the multi-track master tape David can be heard openly flirting with Constable between takes).

Session player Big Jim Sullivan added a sitar intro to 'Join The Gang' in a tongue-in-cheek allusion to contemporary pop's embracing of the Indian classical stringed instrument. The end result is more akin to Peter Sellers in film comedy *The Party*

LEFT: Gus Dudgeon (1942–2002). "I've always thought David was very nice and easy to get on with."

than George Harrison's 'Within You Without You'.

Engineer Gus Dudgeon produced a number of sound effects for 'Join The Gang' and pulled out all the stops, creating horror-movie thunder and dripping rain, for the macabre Poe-like final track 'Please Mr Gravedigger'.

For this unusual sung-through monologue, David recorded his stumbling footsteps in a gravel tray and dramatically acted out the gravedigger's actions in the studio, pretending to be cold, hunched and dishevelled, throwing the dirt over his shoulder as he 'dug' the grave.

Some of the writing for *David Bowie* took place at Fearnley's brother Gerald's house in Worcester Park, south-west London, and the material was largely rehearsed at Eager's home in Pinner, Middx; one reason was that he possessed an upright piano.

Many of the arrangements were scored on the piano using a recently purchased copy of *The Observer Book Of Music* which David and Dek Fearnley scoured for practical advice (neither having been trained to read or write music).

"We didn't realise how ludicrous (the scores) must have looked," said David in 1993. "I guess it was just the audacity of it that none of the guys laughed us out of the studio. They actually tried to play our parts and they made sense of them. They're quite nice little string parts – we were writing for bassoon and everything. If Stravinsky can do it, then we can do it!"

On release, *David Bowie* failed to register commercially. The album was neither youth-orientated nor marketed towards an older demographic, and its failure was blamed at the time by Pitt on lack of belief and foresight at Decca's London HQ.

However, it was released in many other countries, including Belgium, Holland, Germany, Switzerland, Australia and South Africa, but suffered a similar fate even though these regions did their best with promotion.

Similarly, in the US, Decca really put its weight behind David's Deram output, heavily canvassing radio stations and press with promotional copies of the album and its singles, though again it failed to break through.

But all was not lost. *David Bowie* was successful in helping to forge two significant if diverse relationships: first with Lindsay Kemp, who fell so much in love with the record he used it as interval music for his shows, which in turn drew David into his troupe ("I played it until it had no grooves left," said Kemp in 1992); and second with the BBC, who recognised that its quality confirmed him as an artist worthy of broadcast.

Mike Vernon was selected by Decca's Hugh Mendl as producer. His background was heavily weighted towards the blues, having established the groundbreaking label Blue Horizon, recently worked with the likes of R&B legend Eddie Boyd and overseen in 1966 the recording of the epochal British blues album *John Mayall's Blues Breakers With Eric Clapton*.

Yet Vernon had served at Decca since November 1962 (initially as assistant to producer Frank Lee) and worked with a wide range of artists and composers.

"I wouldn't say that we struggled, but it was an adventure," said Vernon in 2009. "I wasn't sure what to make of it at the time or if it was even commercial, but as usual I just put all my likes and dislikes aside and got on with it. It was a very, very quirky, one-off record and ideal for Deram."

Vernon had not witnessed a performance by David and they were never to meet again after 1968. "I think I did see that this guy had an enormous talent. There was a definite charisma about him," he added. "It was really just a matter of time."

Another crucial aspect to the mix was Vernon's simpatico working relationship with engineer Gus Dudgeon, who was given the space to contribute his own ideas during sessions.

"It's difficult to say who was responsible for the direction of the album," said Dudgeon. "There's no question that David had a

unique way of approaching anything. I think Mike and myself would have to admit that David basically led in the direction he wanted to go. He could sound like Anthony Newley, to the point that we would comment on it, and then David would just say, 'I can't sing any other way.'"

Dudgeon voices the role of the Goonish newscaster who opens the apocalyptic 'We Are Hungry Men'. Replete with cartoon German exclamations of 'Achtung!' by Vernon, this song is a light-hearted precursor to the darker themes explored and developed on *The Man Who Sold The World*.

A recently discovered two-sided acetate (these are usually one-sided lacquered discs used by artists, producers and engineers to check on how well music transfers to vinyl) reveals that at one time there were two extra tracks being seriously considered for inclusion on *David Bowie*.

Neither yet issued, these were an R&B track in the style of The Buzz, 'Your Funny Smile', and a laid-back beat poem entitled 'Bunny Thing'.

These appeared on an ultra-rare acetate of the initial LP running order prepared in mid December 1966 for David and Mike Vernon to consider over the Christmas and New Year break. Revealing that 'Did You Ever Have A Dream' was initially included on the LP, it runs:

Side One	Side Two
1. **'Uncle Arthur'** (Bowie)	1. **'Little Bombardier'** (Bowie)
2. **'Sell Me A Coat'** (Bowie)	2. **'Silly Boy Blue'** (Bowie)
3. **'Your Funny Smile'** (Bowie)	3. **'Come And Buy My Toys'** (Bowie)
4. **'Did You Ever Have A Dream'** (Bowie)	4. **'Join The Gang'** (Bowie)
5. **'There Is A Happy Land'** (Bowie)	5. **'She's Got Medals'** (Bowie)
6. **'Bunny Thing'** (Bowie)	6. **'Maid Of Bond Street'** (Bowie)
	7. **'Please Mr Gravedigger'** (Bowie)

'Your Funny Smile' featured the line-up of Fearnley, Boyes, Eager and David on vocals, but fittingly sounds like an unpolished recording from David's spell with Pye Records in 1966. As such it would have been quite out of place on *David Bowie*, as would 'Bunny Thing', featuring David on spoken vocal, accompanied by leading acoustic folk guitarist John Renbourn.

Fearnley's original choice of guitarist was too busy to work on the session. Recorded the same days as 'Come And Buy My Toys', 'Bunny Thing' is delivered in the style of a beat poet at a live event, complete with an improvised musical section. In jokey beat lingo ('He was a drag, dad… he'd lost his bag of groove…') David tells the tale of a group of delinquent rabbits smuggling 'bunny drugs' past an ageing (and dying) customs official (named 'Br'er Hans Hitler'). David even attempts a broad Germanic accent.[1]

"'Bunny Thing' was one of my favourites," said Fearnley in 1991. "I was really disappointed that it didn't make the LP; I thought it was a great track and I was very pleased John Renbourn did it in the end."

These two tracks were then forgotten and left in the Decca archive, along with another called 'Pussy Cat'. This track simply wasn't up to the quality of the other material and so was never considered for release.

Written by US duo Kal Mann and Dave Appell (whose biggest hit was Chubby Checker's 'Let's Twist Again' in 1961), 'Pussy Cat' as performed by David is a true oddity. The recording features the same session players as other contemporary Deram recordings by David, but is rougher in quality and execution (as well as being an untypical song to cover because of its MoR qualities). Towards the end, David's vocal deteriorates as he appears to tire of the song, so that the track sounds little more than a demo. In 1970 Jess Conrad also covered the song on his single 'Crystal Ball Dream'/'Pussy Cat', released by President Records.

On the album acetate, during 'Come And Buy My Toys', parts of the vocal were 'dropped-in' (i.e. elements were added after the main vocal had been recorded) and, throughout the cutting, the sound levels and mix were adjusted, often mid-song.

The acetate makes clear that the earlier decision not to include 'Rubber Band' was reversed in February when a new version was recorded to replace 'Your Funny Smile'.[2]

The front cover photograph of *David Bowie* was taken by Gerald Fearnley in his basement studio in a church in Bryanston

Street, central London. The back photo was taken by the late David Wedgbury near Decca's offices on the Thames embankment. BBC producer Bernie Andrews was so taken by the sleeve that he propped it up on the mantelpiece of his Mayfair flat, which was visited at the time by the likes of The Beatles and Billy Fury, who remarked on it and listened to tracks.

"It was never off my record player," said Andrews in 2000. "I played it to everyone who came by and I had a lot of visitors."

Ken Pitt's authoritative sleeve notes did an effective job of introducing this unconventional talent to the world, though he reserves his conclusion for the former members of The Buzz who had played an integral part in making the record:

'Bowie sometimes chose different musicians for the various tracks, but throughout he used the three boys who so ardently believed in his talent that they have loyally supported him during the lean times. They are drummer John Eager, bassist Dek Fearnley and organist Derek Boyes.'

If there is a single over-riding influence on *David Bowie* – supplying stylistic cohesion to the entire package – it is that of Anthony Newley,[3] though this is to the fore on just three tracks. The singer, actor, dramatist and performer provided far more than a vocal model for David; he introduced theatre, stagecraft, choreography, grotesque characterisation, winsome narrative, make-up and mime to David at a crucial stage in his development. Newley's voice was an unadorned representation of the accent of his Cockney Jewish roots.

"I always made fun of it, in a sense," said Newley in 1992. "Most of my records ended in a stupid giggle, trying to tell people that I wasn't being serious. I think Bowie liked that irreverent thing, and his delivery was very similar to mine, that Cockney thing. But then he went on to become madly elegant and very, very original."

David acknowledged Newley's influence in 1976: "I hadn't found any voice style. I was very much in the Tony Newley thing, mainly because I came from London and it seemed more natural."

And he has also openly tipped his hat to Newley's 1960 TV series *The Strange World Of Gurney Slade*.

"It was quite the most bizarre piece of work I'd ever seen on television," he said in 2004. "(Newley) developed it on surrealist lines: it didn't have a literal story line; he made association games that he would play with adverts on the buses and he would go into little monologues and soliloquies in his head. It was just the most bizarre programme. He could have done the ordinary thing and just made pop songs and been an actor but he really took chances, until he went to the States and then frankly it was all over."

The white-faced clown Littlechap played by Newley in his 1961 production *Stop The World – I Want To Get Off* also clearly left its mark on David, who said in 1972: "It was the first time I'd seen theatre with no props. Just this white face of his. That's where the mime came in. And I loved the lyrics. He sang really ordinary words that I could understand, and it wasn't all gooey."

For his part, Newley only became aware of David's interest in him many years after the release of *David Bowie*.

"The first I knew of his respect for my work was in an article, I believe in *Time* magazine, in which he mentioned how much my early work as a rock'n'roll singer had been an influence. It's strange because I was a really uninspired singer. I mean, I didn't write my own material in those days. Bowie, of course, I understand, very quickly began writing his own. He was most gracious in the *Time* article and I was very touched and wrote him a letter to which I didn't receive an answer, but I presumed he was very busy."

Newley's use of orchestration on releases such as his 1960 album *Tony* and single version of 'Strawberry Fair' of the same year represented part of the sound and style David sought as he

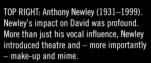

TOP RIGHT: Anthony Newley (1931–1999). Newley's impact on David was profound. More than just his vocal influence, Newley introduced theatre and – more importantly – make-up and mime.

ABOVE: *Stop The World – I Want To Get Off*, Newley in the guise of Littlechap.

RIGHT: *The Strange World Of Gurney Slade*.

avoided the more straightforward rock line-up of instrumentation for his debut (which was coincidentally recorded at the same studios as *Tony*).

It should be noted that, in line with the majority of David's early creative interests, his absorption of Newley's Cockney vaudeville was a passing fad which reached its height in the six-month period in which *David Bowie* was conceived and delivered. Nevertheless, a trace of Newley still remains to this day as part of David's performance make-up.

Sad to say, the two entertainers never met, although they did acknowledge one another's presence across a Parisian restaurant in the mid-90s.

Newley, who died in 1999, recalled a close call in 1983. "I was subsequently told that, when he played Los Angeles, where I was living, he had invited me to come to his show. I didn't get the invitation for some reason, or hear about it until it was over and I was very sad that I hadn't gone. It's extraordinary that we have never met."

1. David is believed to have performed the 'Bunny Thing' monologue at north London arts/music venue The Roundhouse in 1970 in a similar style.

2. 'Love You Till Tuesday' doesn't feature on this acetate either because it wasn't recorded until February 1967, even though David wrote the track a couple of years earlier.

3. Anthony George Newley (1931–1999), became a child actor, with a notable appearance playing the Artful Dodger in David Lean's 1948 film *Oliver Twist*. A contract player in many Rank Organisation movies, from 1959 Newley appeared in the charts with a number of rock'n'roll singles and went on to write hits for Sammy Davis Jr, Tony Bennett and Shirley Bassey (the title tune for Bond movie *Goldfinger*). Many of these were composed with Leslie Bricusse, with whom he also wrote stage shows, including *Stop The World – I Want To Get Off* and *Willy Wonka & The Chocolate Factory*.

LEFT: Decca Records *David Bowie* press release.

TOP: Photographed during the summer.

ABOVE: On a central London rooftop in front of the recently built Centre Point in New Oxford Street, September.

RIGHT: David photographed by Dezo Hoffman in his Soho studio.

In this year...

Saturday 17 June
PUBLICATION of Small Faces frontman Steve Marriott's review of single 'At The Third Stroke' by The Piccadilly Line in *Melody Maker*:
'It's got a nice vocal sound. Is this David Bowie? It sounds the sort of thing that David Bowie writes.'

Saturday 24 June
ENTRY of The Pink Floyd's 'See Emily Play' in the UK charts. David covered the Syd Barrett composition on his 1973 album *Pin Ups*.

Friday 7 July
RELEASE of 'The Laughing Gnome'/'If I Were A Rich Man' by popular singer Ronnie Hilton, best known for his 1965 hit 'Windmill In Old Amsterdam'.

Saturday 3 June

On the basis that 'Love You Till Tuesday' and 'When I Live My Dream' are contenders for future singles, they are re-recorded at Decca's No. 3 studio. Each track is provided with MoR string arrangements by Ivor Raymonde,[1] who also adds the tongue-in-cheek segment on the end of 'Love You Till Tuesday' which quotes the romantic song 'Hearts & Flowers'.

1. Born Ivor Pomerance (1926–1990), Raymonde provided string arrangements for Dusty Springfield, The Walker Brothers and others. His son Simon was a member of 80s/90s group The Cocteau Twins.

Wednesday 7 June

David and Pitt view Franco Zeffirelli's new film, *The Taming Of The Shrew*. The film stars Natasha Pyne, an actress friend of David and Pitt's whose TV work includes a role in popular sitcom *Father Dear Father*.

Thursday 8 June

David appears in mime-style make-up in an advert in *Record Retailer*.

Saturday 10 June

Disc & Music Echo reviews the album under the heading, 'Hear David Bowie – he's something new'. The music paper hails the release as 'a remarkable, creative debut by a 19-year-old Londoner'.

Sunday 11 June

David moves into Pitt's apartment at 39 Manchester Street; the pair are now close personally, and promotional and recording commitments make it necessary for David to be in London permanently.

Another reason cited is that his nocturnal lifestyle in the family home in Bromley disturbs his father's routine; John Jones has to rise early to commute to his job at Dr Barnardo's in central London.

David occupies the bedroom on the top floor which has a window overlooking the street. The apartment, including the roof-space and the shuttered windows in the sitting room on the first floor, will be featured in many photo sessions.

"He was a great lodger, never a problem, except for the joss sticks!" said Pitt in 1980. "I came home one day for a serious business meeting and walked into this smell. It was part of his Buddhist phase."

David regularly dines at the local Italian restaurant Ristoranti Anacapri.[1]

Encouraged by Pitt, David seeks out collectables from Martins-Forrest Antiques, in nearby Barrett Street. This establishment specialises in Art Nouveau and Art Deco.

1. Now Anacapri, this was still open at 10 Dorset Street, London W1, in late 2010.

Monday 12 June

Pitt sends Franco Zeffirelli a batch of David's demo tapes containing musical ideas for the *Romeo & Juliet* soundtrack and promises that there are three more pieces to come.

In the afternoon David is the subject of a photo session with freelance photographer Nicholas Wright, which carries on the following day.

Friday 16 June

David and Pitt attend a late afternoon meeting with Graham Churchill at Essex Music. In the evening David meets film director Michael Armstrong to talk about a future project.

Sunday 18 June

▶ Accompanied by his parents, David returns to Radio London's Motor Racing and Pop Festival at Brands Hatch racing circuit, Kent, for another promotional visit; having appeared the previous year with The Buzz.

Plugging new single 'Love You Till Tuesday' and his debut album, David appears on stage along with such acts as Chris Farlowe & The Thunderbirds, Shell Shock, Episode Six, The Moody Blues, Dave Dee, Dozy, Beaky, Mick and Tich, David Garrick and finally The New Vaudeville Band.[1] Hosted by DJs Ed Stewart, Mike Lennox and Mark Roman.

1. Riding high on the success of single 'Winchester Cathedral'.

Saturday 24 June

The *NME* publishes a short review of *David Bowie*

saying, 'Here's a Cockney singer who reminds me of Anthony Newley and Tommy Steele, which can't be bad. He sings songs with a mild beat about ordinary things like a Rubber Band, an Uncle Arthur and about a romance which started on Sunday and he promised to Love You Till Tuesday… A very promising talent.' But a letter David has written to *Record Mirror* defending his friends 1-2-3 causes more of a stir.

He has been upset about journalist Derek Boltwood's unfair comparison between the Scottish group and The Jimi Hendrix Experience in a review of the previous month's Saville Theatre show.

Headed 'Bowie The 19-yr-old Epistle Writer', the story quotes David's letter to Boltwood.

"The letter he wrote to *Record Mirror* was typical; he has a great generosity," said Billy Ritchie in 2006.

Tuesday 27 June

Walt Maguire of American label London Records writes to Pitt, despondent at the US reaction to the 'Rubber Band' promo single: 'I'm not happy with the results.'

Following their meeting of 16 June, David meets actor/director Michael Armstrong at the Manchester Street apartment to discuss involvement in *A Floral Tale*, a film comedy in pre-production.[1]

Armstrong, an acquaintance of David and Pitt's friend BBC producer Bernie Andrews, discovered David's LP in a central London record shop. He tells Ken Pitt, "I loved the wicked humour."

Armstrong is keen for David to play the part of the mythological Orpheus and also to act as musical director. A new composition of David's, 'Flower Song', is also considered for inclusion.[2]

In the evening David and Pitt attend a reception at Chappell's music shop[3] in Bond Street to celebrate the opening of its recording studio. Making the most of the free drink, David is intoxicated. (▶ 12.7.68)

1. *A Floral Tale* doesn't make it into production though David worked on Armstrong's film *The Image*. (▶ 13.9.67)

2. This song has not surfaced since.

3. Chappell's supported David's career with in-store promotions of his records. Another London record store also keen to advertise David's early work was One Stop in Mayfair thoroughfare South Molton Street. This became a virtual shrine to David, as they displayed his debut album and subsequent releases in the window. In the mid-70s the shop's staff included *NME* writer and broadcaster Danny Baker.

Wednesday 28 June

David is interviewed by *Melody Maker* editor Bob Dawbarn.

David's father writes to Ken Pitt: 'My wife and I are very grateful to you for sending us a copy of the album – this was indeed a kind thought.'

Friday 30 June

Pitt writes to David's father: 'I think David is having a little difficulty with the work he is doing, speculatively, for Franco Zeffirelli. It is probably a little too soon for him to attempt writing of this kind, but he is having a very brave try and I am submitting the results to Rome.'[1]

Pitt also mentions that David is intending 'to concentrate on cabaret rehearsals'.

1. In the event Zeffirelli chooses Donovan to provide songs and Nino Rota to provide the orchestral score. His version of *Romeo & Juliet* achieved critical acclaim and won two Oscars (for cinematography and costume design).

Saturday 1 July

David visits the Midlands town of Northampton for regional promotion of the new album.

Wednesday 5 July

A meeting is held at 39 Manchester Street between David, John Eager and Dek Fearnley to pool ideas regarding David's plans to launch himself as a cabaret act.

Monday 10 July

David is interviewed by Christine Osbourne for *Fabulous 208* magazine.

Tuesday 11 July

At 5pm David is the subject of another photo session at Decca.

ABOVE: Photographed by Robin Bean.

BOTTOM: David's letter to a *Record Mirror* journalist is turned into a feature.

BOWIE THE 19-YR-OLD EPISTLE WRITER

DAVID BOWIE — his new LP is out on Deram — all self-penned numbers (Dezo Hoffman RM Pic).

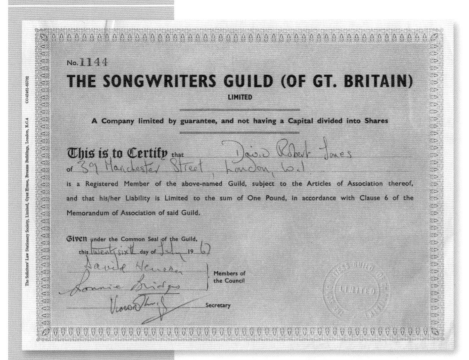

No. 1144

THE SONGWRITERS GUILD (OF GT. BRITAIN)
LIMITED

A Company limited by guarantee, and not having a Capital divided into Shares

This is to Certify that *David Robert Jones*
of *39 Manchester Street, London, W.1*
is a Registered Member of the above-named Guild, subject to the Articles of Association thereof,
and that his/her Liability is Limited to the sum of One Pound, in accordance with Clause 6 of the
Memorandum of Association of said Guild.

Given under the Common Seal of the Guild,
this *twenty-six* day of *July* 19 *67*

Members of
the Council

Secretary

Wednesday 12 July

David meets with production assistant, Doreen
Kelson, to talk about his involvement in *A Floral Tale*.

Thursday 13 July

David's school-friend and bandmate from The
Konrads and The King Bees, George Undwerwood,
re-enters David's musical life; he takes part in
rehearsals with David and Fearnley of some song
ideas at Manchester Street.

Friday 14 July

Deram release 'Love You Till Tuesday'/'Did You Ever
Have A Dream' single in the UK.
  ⊙ **David Bowie**
  A **'Love You Till Tuesday'** (Bowie)
  Orchestral session musicians
  Produced by Mike Vernon
  Musical Director: Ivor Raymonde
  Engineer: Bill Price
  Tape Op: Dave Grinsted
  B **'Did You Ever Have A Dream'** (Bowie)
  David Bowie (vocal)
  Dek Fearnley (bass)
  Derek Boyes (organ)
  John Eager (drums)
  Big Jim Sullivan (banjo)
  Unknown session musicians
  Produced by Mike Vernon
  Musical Director: Dek Fearnley
  Engineer: Gus Dudgeon
  Tape Op: Dave Grinsted
  (Deram DM135)
The A-side is the re-recorded version of the album
track.[1] The B-side features former member of The

Buzz Derek Boyes playing a honky tonk piano,
conveniently kept at Decca Studios, augmented by
banjo from sessioneer Big Jim Sullivan.

Delivered in a light-hearted manner, the subject
matter of 'Did You Ever Have A Dream' is astral
projection of the body achieved by meditation,
something David has encountered as part of his
growing fascination with Buddhism.[2]

This has been ignited by his reading of Jack
Kerouac's books in the early 60s, and rekindled
by a spontaneous visit to the Buddhist Society's
British headquarters at 58 Eccleston Square in
central London, just yards from the Warwick Square
apartment where he lived temporarily with former
manager Ralph Horton.

"It was empty," David recalled in 2001. "I went
down the stairs and saw a man in saffron robes. He
said, in very broken English, 'You are looking for me.'
I realised years later that it was a question, but took
it as a statement: 'You are looking for me.' The man
in the saffron robes, Chime Youngdong Rinpoche,[3]
became my guru."

David and Pitt visit Holland Park Studios for a
lunchtime meeting with producer John Bryan and
director Robert Freeman, who are casting a soft-porn
romp, *The Touchables*.

David auditions for the part of an abducted pop
star, David Copperfield.[4]

1. This version was used as the theme for the 1969 film of the
same name.
2. "I was studying Mahayana Buddhism, which is very deeply involved
with astral projection," David said in 1993. "With his [Youngdong
Rinpoche] meditation methods I often felt that I got three or four feet,
maybe even further, outside my body and I was absolutely and totally
aware of it."
3. Lama Chime Youngdong Rinpoche, born eastern Tibet in 1941 and
raised in Benchen Monastery. One of a small group of monks who fled
Tibet in 1959 to escape invading Chinese forces and arrived in the
UK in 1965.
4. This role was renamed Christian and played by actor David
Anthony when the film went into production. Christian's manager
was played by John Ronane, who adapted and starred in a BBC play
featuring David in 1968.

Saturday 15 July

Record Mirror is encouraging about the new single,
announcing 'this boy really is something different'.

Tuesday 18 July

David and Ken Pitt attend a meeting at Essex Music
with David Platz.

Friday 21 July

Pitt receives a letter from Teldec Telefunken (Decca
Hamburg) confirming that David's 'Love You Till
Tuesday' single 'is already in production'.

The Riot Squad appear at The Electric Garden,
43 King Street, Covent Garden. It's not clear if David
joins them that night.

Saturday 22 July

In *Melody Maker*, staff writer Chris Welch champions

David as a rare talent: 'Dave Bowie is one of the few really original solo singers operating in the theatre of British pop.' But the same paper carries a less favourable response to the new single from one of David's heroes, Syd Barrett of The Pink Floyd: 'Yes it's a joke number. Everybody likes jokes. The Pink Floyd like jokes. It's very casual. If you play it a second time it might be even more of a joke. Jokes are good. The Pink Floyd like jokes. I think that was a funny joke. I think people will like the bit about it being Monday, when in fact it was Tuesday. Very chirpy, but I don't think my toes were tapping at all.'

A small news item in *Jackie* is David's first mention (under his own name) in the popular girl's magazine.[1]

1. David saw *Jackie* as an important media outlet. He personally kept in touch with journalists there into the early 70s, supplying news stories and posing for photo sessions.

Monday 24 July

David Platz contacts Pitt to inform him of a new American producer that Denny Cordell has recently employed. Tony Visconti,[1] has just arrived from New York and is eager to make his mark.

Pitt arranges a meeting with Visconti to discuss the possibility of him working with David. Pitt said in 2010: "As I was leaving the flat David was excited and said, 'ring me as soon as you can, I'll be sitting by the phone'."

Pitt is impressed and an appointment is then set-up for David and Visconti to meet to discuss the American's involvement in recording sessions due to start in September.

"We were supposed to talk about working together, but we ended up talking about Buddhism, obscure recordings and foreign films," said Visconti in 2007. "We ended our first interview by going to the cinema to see *A Knife In The Water* by Roman Polanski."

In 1977 Visconti recalled that it was David's record label which suggested that he and David should work together.

"At the time I was on Deram," said Visconti. "One day the Deram man called me into his office and said, 'We've got this young man David Bowie and no one quite knows what to do with him. You seem to be the expert on weird people. I'd like you to meet him.' I remember the first time we met, he was, and still is, the complete Englishman."

David said in 1976: "We became friends first, we didn't talk much about music. I was still wondering if I found God as a Buddhist or whether I wanted to be a rock'n'roll star, so we had a lot to talk about – East and West – and Tony was well into the Tibetan thing. We used to spend crazy evenings alone, and with (British orchestrator) Paul Buckmaster as well."

1. Born Tony Edward Visconti in Brooklyn, New York, in 1944, he entered the music business in the late 50s as guitarist in local group Mike Dee & The Dukes, covering songs by Buddy Holly and Duane Eddy.

In 1963, Visconti formed folk duo Tony and Siegrid with his first wife. They recorded for RCA, achieving a minor hit with single 'Long Hair', and Visconti moved into session-playing, arranging and demo production.

Impressing British producer Denny Cordell during a New York session for British R&B star Georgie Fame, Visconti moved to London to work as assistant to Cordell (David Platz's partner in Essex Productions).

Within three days of arriving, Visconti had met Jimi Hendrix backstage at the Saville Theatre, as well as Donovan and Brian Jones, who walked in on a session in which he was involved.

Visconti was set on remaining in England, but his first wife returned to New York. After their divorce he married British singer Mary Hopkin.

Visconti was David's producer on many of his classic albums, including *David Bowie* (1969), *The Man Who Sold The World* and *Young Americans*. Simultaneously he formed a crucial creative partnership with Marc Bolan and was responsible for many T.Rex hits. As recently as 2003 he produced David's album *Reality*.

He subsequently produced for a range of acts, including Thin Lizzy, The Boomtown Rats, The Stranglers, Adam Ant and Morrissey, the last writing the foreword to Visconti's 2007 autobiography *Bowie, Bolan And The Brooklyn Boy*.

Saturday 29 July

David appears in *Fabulous 208*. Under the heading 'On Our Wavelength', Christine Osbourne reports that David still lives at home with his parents: '"I'd never leave them; we've got a good thing going," he said frankly.'[1]

1. Although he was living with Pitt Monday to Friday, unless he had any work assignments, he would go to Bromley for weekends. This is why he would sometimes say he was still living with his parents.

Friday 4 August

Accompanied by Michael Garrett[1] on piano, mime artist Lindsay Kemp[2] begins a two-week run of his new show *Clowns Hour* at the Little Theatre, Garrick

RIGHT: Wearing Ken Pitt's leather jacket on the roof at Manchester Street.

MIDDLE: Lindsay Kemp, whose unique presentations are difficult to categorise but delve into the traditions of music hall, mime and dance.

BOTTOM LEFT: David's teacher, Chime Youngdong Rinpoche, photographed in 1970.

BOTTOM RIGHT: The home of Tibetan culture in exile, Samye Ling's new temple was opened in 1988. The original lodge and retreat where David slept and studied still remains in the grounds.

Yard, St Martin's Lane, Covent Garden.

During the interval David's album is played, as he is informed by his girlfriend Jan,[3] Pitt's secretary, who persuades him to attend a lunchtime performance.

"She knew my liking for both theatre and the unusual and had prodded me to go with her and see this mime," said David in 2002. "A mime, what could be less interesting? Then she told me he was using my one album as his interval music. A mime, how interesting."

After the show David and Jan visit Kemp in his dressing room; the singer and the mime artist are bowled over by each other's personalities. Not long after, David joins Kemp's movement classes at the Covent Garden Dance Centre.[4] They soon conspire to work together.

In 1991 Kemp said that David was already talking about becoming a Buddhist monk and preparing to live in a monastery in Scotland:

"He was very into Buddhism at the time and had these beautiful Tibetan boots.[5] I told him you can give yourself to God, and to me, and to the public at one and the same time, which is what he did for a bit."

Kemp recalled an early meeting with David after

their first encounter: "It was at my home in Bateman Buildings, Bateman Street, in Soho. I don't know how he found me, I just remember him being there. I felt a bit like the Virgin Mary confronted by this vision of the Archangel Gabriel, glowing, shining, incredibly beautiful and immediately inspiring."

The Bateman Street flat was directly above a striptease club, which added to the Bohemian decadence of Kemp's non-conformist lifestyle. In 1972 David recalled strippers popping in to borrow "cups of sugar from downstairs. It was just this circus. I had joined the circus.

"Dear old Lindsay, Lindsay was a trip-and-a-half, I've never known anybody commit suicide so many times. He lived on his emotions, he was a wonderful influence. His day-to-day life was the most theatrical thing I'd ever seen, ever. Everything I thought Bohemia probably was, he was living."

In 1971, David expanded on Kemp's larger-than-life persona: "Lindsay Kemp was a living Pierrot. He lived and talked Pierrot. He was tragic and dramatic and everything in his life was theatrical. And so the stage thing for him was just an extension of himself. There's a lot of material from his private life that would beat any script."

1. Michael Garrett started providing musical accompaniment for Kemp in 1962, when they met at the Guildhall School of Music & Drama. He also worked with David and Kemp on their collaborative project *Pierrot In Turquoise*.

2. Born in 1938, Kemp's passion for dancing particularly concerned his parents, who sent him to naval college to be toughened up. Unharmed by the experience, Lindsay began dancing professionally in northern working men's clubs, where his feminine gestures received less than universal admiration.

In the 70s Kemp became known for such flamboyant productions as *Salome*, and also appeared in director Derek Jarman's films *Sebastiane* and *Jubilee*.

In 1991 Kemp toured the Kabuki-influenced *Ornagata* and in 1995 staged his version of *Cinderella*.

Kemp's last documented meeting with David was in 1 May 1978 in Canada, after a concert by David in Maple Leaf Gardens, Toronto.

3. Pitt cannot recall Jan. "We had people come and go all the time," he said in 2002. "We also took on a lot of temps when we had a particularly busy period. But David was always in the office and would often date the girls working there."

4. In 1975 then unknown singer/songwriter Kate Bush joined Kemp's movement classes in Covent Garden, inspired by David's connections. In 1993 Kemp appeared in Bush's short film adaptation of *The Red Shoes*.

5. David later loaned these decorated leather boots to his friend Johnnie Dee and they were not returned. David covered 'Don't Bring Me Down', a song of Dee's, in 1973.

Wednesday 9 August

David meets photographer Robin Bean and an M. Runsbourg, who is an associate of young writer/director Michael Armstrong, at 39 Manchester Street to discuss his involvement in Armstrong's forthcoming short film *The Image*.

Friday 11 August

In the afternoon David takes part in another photo session conducted by Nicholas Wright.

David Bowie is released in the US without two tracks on the UK version – 'We Are Hungry Men' and

'Maid Of Bond Street' – which are both removed for copyright payment reasons. There is also a different back cover photo.

Monday 14 August

Pitt's diary notes: 'David wrote English lyrics to Israeli songs.' No further details are known.

In the afternoon there is another photo session, this time for *Fabulous 208*. David borrows Pitt's brown paisley shirt for the shoot with Peter Freeman.

Friday 18 August

Pitt meets Platz to discuss renewing David's publishing contract and takes a tape of a new song, 'Karma Man'.

This is David's homage to Buddhism as he draws on his visits to his guru Chime Youngdong Rinpoche at the Buddhist Society and at the monk's home in leafy north London suburb Hampstead.

Tuesday 22 August

David is interviewed by Sally Cork for the *Fabulous 208* piece to accompany the photos from last week's shoot.

Thursday 24 August

David and Ken Pitt are in the audience for *Loot*, by Joe Orton,[1] at the Criterion Theatre, Piccadilly Circus. The play features Michael Bates, Sheila Ballentine and Simon Ward.

1. Two weeks earlier Orton (1933–1967) was murdered by his lover Kenneth Halliwell, who then took his own life.

Friday 25 August

Manfred Mann guitarist Tom McGuinness visits Pitt, who gives him a demo of 'Karma Man' as a potential cover for the group.

Monday 28 August

David's single 'Love You Till Tuesday'/'Did You Ever Have A Dream' is released in America on Deram.

September

Applies for Equity membership.

The full extent of David's fascination with Buddhism is revealed during an interview with journalist George Tremlett. David is regularly spending afternoons at the Buddhist Society with Lama monks Vidyadhara (which means 'the venerable') and Chögyam Trungpa Rinpoche and Chime Youngdong Rinpoche (Rinpoche means 'precious one').

"I just sit there asking questions, and he [Chime] usually answers them with another question," David tells Tremlett. "In fact, he's teaching me to find my own solution, to meditate. You can't show people what Buddhism is, you can only show them the way towards it. It's really a process of self-discovery, of discovering truth."

David also talks to Tremlett about Buddhism's

influence on his attitude to wealth: "Material things just don't interest me. I have one good suit in case I have to go anywhere important, but I don't want a car and I live with my parents. I'm not interested in clothes at all, really."

Chime visits David and his manager at Pitt's office in Curzon Street.

"There was Chime perfectly turned out, immaculately dressed in his orange robes, with David at the height of his scruffiness," said Pitt in 2002. "Quite a contrast!"

Buddhist paraphernalia is acquired from a specialist shop in Monmouth Street in Covent Garden, where David also buys early-19th century French lithographs, one of which he pins up in his Manchester Street bedroom.

David has also discovered controversial Buddhist text *The Rampa Story* by T. Lobsang Rampa[1] and is considering joining a group establishing a monastery and temple at a disused shooting lodge, in Eskdalemuir, Dumfriesshire, in Scotland.[2]

TOP LEFT AND RIGHT: In a 'bolero' jacket purchased by Ken Pitt in Jerusalem.

LEFT: Kenneth Pitt Management/David Bowie *Billboard* magazine advert.

MIDDLE RIGHT: US promotion for 'Love You Till Tuesday'.

BOTTOM: Advert for US single release of 'Love You Till Tuesday'.

In this year...

Sunday 27 August
DEATH of Beatles manager and Ken Pitt's friend Brian Epstein after an overdose of sleeping pills.

TOP RIGHT: One of the French lithographs purchased by David at Martins-Forrest Antiques of Barrett Street.

TOP LEFT: Dee Dee sheet music – rarer than the actual record.

ABOVE: Dee Dee single sleeve.

In this year...

September

RELEASE of 'Love Is Always'/'Pancho' single in Belgium, recorded by Dee Dee (a pseudonym for Andrée Giroud). The English lyrics for both songs are supplied by David, with music by Willy Albimoor and Andree Giroud. David also supplies the publisher with a demo tape containing the correct pronunciations. This commission is arranged by Essex Music for Editions Belmusic of Brussels and is released in Belgium only on the Palette (Color in Music) label.

Chime has told him all about the project, which is headed by fellow monks Chöje Akong Rinpoche and Chögyam Trungpa Rinpoche.

When he travels to the lodge[3] David attends meditation classes given by Chögyam and seriously considers moving in permanently and submerging himself in the religion. He later tells close friends that his change of heart about staying came during transcendental meditation, when he was directed to continue with his career. (▶3.1.70)

After a few months acting as David's guru, Chime advises him to stick to songwriting "because I wasn't going to make a great monk," said David in 1993. "I thought, oh well, that's another thing blown out of the window! All right then, I won't be a monk."[4]

The Richmond Organisation distributes 600 copies of a promotional 32-page music and lyric booklet in America. Titled *Songs By David Bowie* and intended to boost David's profile Stateside, it contains 20 of David's songs published by Essex.

1. Cyril Hoskin (1910–1981), who claimed he was Tibetan Lama Tuesday Lobsang Rampa, was one of the most notable literary fraudsters of the post-war period. His best-selling book *The Third Eye* was exposed as a fiction by the national media in 1958, though David did not discover the truth about Rampa until 1968 when employed at London printing company Legastat (▶6.68).

2. The Friends of the Western Buddhist Order was founded in the basement of this store in 1967.

3. The property, donated to the Buddhist Society by the Johnstone Trust, was later renamed Kagyu Samye Ling and today it is the largest Buddhist temple in the West. The temple was officially opened in 1988 and the adjacent lodge where David stayed is still a hostel and admin building.

4. During a 1968 recording session for BBC Radio One David included Chime's name in a performance of 'Silly Boy Blue'.

Friday 1 September

David informs Pitt that he is going to record some 'pop rubbish'. In fact, he and Tony Visconti work together for the first time as the latter produces two songs at Advision Sound Studios, 83 New Bond Street, central London;[1] 'Let Me Sleep Beside You' and 'Karma Man'.

These songs take six hours to complete and among the session musicians are guitarist John McLaughlin, Visconti's wife Siegrid on backing vocals, Big Jim Sullivan on second guitar and drummer Andy White. Visconti plays bass and there is an orchestral backing.

In 1977 Visconti described the finished tracks as 'terrible' though this does not diminish the growing friendship between him and David.

One evening David is introduced to Visconti's parents, who are visiting from New York. David is accompanied by a girl called Kitty and he tells them that he has known her since schooldays.

Also present at this gathering are Stan Bronstein and Myron Yules of New York band Elephant's Memory.[2] They discuss recording one of David's songs.

Soon after this get-together, David brings his parents and half-brother Terry to meet Visconti at Elgin Avenue,[3] cementing their newly established friendship.

After Visconti moves to Earls Court (at 108 Lexham Gardens), David is a regular visitor. Here he again meets Marc Bolan, who is also working with Visconti (and is keen on regularly utilising the American's record player and bath since his own accommodation lacks both). The three spend many hours talking and listening to records.

1. Resident engineer at Advision was Gerald Chevin, who worked on David's 1970 album *The Man Who Sold the World*. In March 1968 Visconti produced *My People Were Fair And Had Sky In Their Hair, But Now They're Content To Wear Stars On Their Brows*, the debut album by Bolan's Tyrannosaurus Rex, over the course of two days at Advision.

2. Elephant's Memory recorded two albums with John Lennon and Yoko Ono, including 1972 release *Some Time In New York City*. Pitt later recalled reading in early 1968 that Elephant's Memory had recorded David's 'Silly Boy Blue'.

3. Visconti's first flat was in Elgin Avenue, Maida Vale, where he lived with Siegrid; when she returned to the US he moved to Lexham Gardens, Earls Court.

Saturday 2 September

US magazine *Cashbox* gives the thumbs-up to 'Love You Till Tuesday': 'Vivacity and wide-open wit delivered with a wink-of-an-eye snap certainty make this the most delightful deck to bow in a long while. Brilliant coupler too.'

Tuesday 5 September

David spends the morning being interviewed by journalist David Rider for BBC Radio's European English Service programme *Let's Go* at Rider's flat, 13 Tiverton Mansions, 140 Gray's Inn Road, near Holborn.

'He arrived just before eleven and proved to be utterly charming and quite different from the picture I had formed,' wrote Rider in his diary. 'We dispensed with the interview quite quickly and spent a most agreeable hour or so talking generally. He was quite taken with my tramcar lithographs and I showed him the entire collection plus some of the black and white photographs. We seem to share an enthusiasm here and I recommended a homage at Clapham.'[1]

In the afternoon David is interviewed by journalist Vicki Hibbert.

1. This is a reference to the Museum of British Transport in the south London suburb.

Wednesday 6 September

David is back in the studio.

Saturday 9 September

David receives his first American fan letter from Sandra Adams of Española, New Mexico, which Ken Pitt retains on file. She writes: 'I have your album and it's groovy.'

Monday 11 September

Having applied for membership of actors' union Equity, David signs a contract with Border Film Productions to appear in Michael Armstrong's silent horror film *The Image*. Photographer Robin Bean (who also works for *Films & Filming* magazine) takes preliminary stills of David so that artist William Mason can render a portrait of David's ghost-like 'image' which is central to the plot.[1] The photo session takes place on the roof of 39 Manchester Street and around the corner at Paddington Street Recreation Ground.

1. Armstrong gave the painting to Pitt after the film was made. He hung it in the hallway of the Manchester Street apartment, where it remained until he vacated the building in 1983. It was later sold at auction.

Wednesday 13 – Thursday 14 September

The Image is filmed in a derelict house near west London's Harrow Road. The parts are taken by David and Michael Byrne.[1]

Based on a screenplay written by Armstrong[2] in 1964, *The Image* is shot in black and white with a minimal storyline, no dialogue and an oppressive drum soundtrack (by Noel Janus).[3] It is only half-complete when the shoot comes to a close.[4] Armstrong also films some exteriors of David running over a hill, but this sequence is scrapped.

1. Born 7 November 1943, Michael Byrne has appeared in such films as *Braveheart*, *The Saint*, *Tomorrow Never Dies* and notably as the evil Nazi officer in 1989's *Indiana Jones & The Last Crusade*.

2. Born 24 July 1944, Michael Armstrong directed such horror-genre movies as *Haunted House Of Horror* and *Mark Of The Devil*. He also wrote and starred in the bawdy *Eskimo Nell* and directed episodes of such TV series as *The Professionals* and *Return Of The Saint*.

3. Noel Janus (1939–2009) father of actress/singer Samantha Janus (now Womack). He starred in Armstrong's 1969 film *The Hunt*.

4. Production company Border subsequently ordered Armstrong to extend an edit it had made in his absence so that its length exceeded 14 minutes. That would have made it eligible for a subsidy under the government's Eady Levy subsidy scheme. Since there was no more footage Armstrong had no choice but to repeat segments. The film received a limited release in 1968 when it appeared as a filler in cinema programmes, mainly for sex films.

Friday 15 September

New single 'Silver Tree Top School For Boys'/'I've Lost A Friend And Found A Lover' is released by The Slender Plenty.[1]

The A-side is one of David's compositions. He

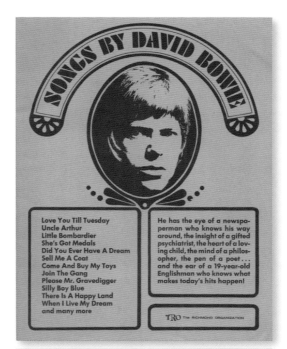

wrote it after reading about a pot-smoking scandal at public school Lancing College. The intro and rhythm owe a lot to Jeff Beck's hit of earlier in the year, 'Hi Ho Silver Lining'.

Local paper *Chelsea News* publishes an interview with David headed, 'Today I feel so happy...'.

Interviewer Barbara Marylin Deane writes:

'David assures me, "My only ambition is to be in the position to get out before I am thirty." His first love seemed to be given to the classical music wave. He loved the work of The Beatles and Dylan and gave praise to the Fugs, an involved sounding group from Greenwich Village who perform "weird" sounds, something on the lines of the Mothers of Invention.

'"Ray Davies is terribly under-rated. People have failed to recognise his trends. About three years ago he used the sitar on 'See My Friends'. He is terrific. I class Dylan in much the same category."

'Favoured along different lines are the songs of Glenn Miller, Stan Kenton and Gary MacFarland, who, David informed me, is an American vibes player.

'David lives at home with his parents in Bromley, Kent. "We have an understanding relationship and find it easy to get on together. I have no deep passion for the countryside and must admit that I hated London at one time."'

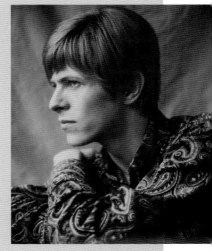

LEFT: *Songs By David Bowie*, a limited edition music and lyric booklet, published (in the US only) by the Richmond Organisation. It is the first publication to bear David's name.

TOP RIGHT: Photographed for a *Fabulous 208* feature, wearing Pitt's paisley shirt.

MIDDLE: Photographed for a *Fabulous 208* feature.

BOTTOM: Producer and bass player Tony Visconti.

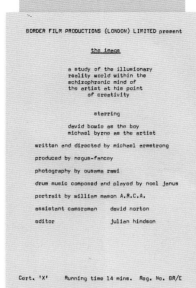

BORDER FILM PRODUCTIONS (LONDON) LIMITED present

the image

a study of the illusionary
reality world within the
schizophrenic mind of
the artist at his point
of creativity

starring

david bowie as the boy
michael byrne as the artist

written and directed by michael armstrong

produced by negus-fancey

photography by ousama rawi

drum music composed and played by noel janus

portrait by william mason A.R.C.A.

assistant cameraman   david norton

editor   julian hindson

Cert. 'X'   Running time 14 mins.   Reg. No. BR/E

TOP LEFT: Promotional leaflet for
The Image.

TOP RIGHT: The original William Mason
painting as featured in *The Image.*

ABOVE: Contact sheet for *The Image.*
Artist William Mason used a still (top, far
right) as the basis for the painting used
in the film.

'What was the most notable point in David's life? "Meeting a person called the venerable Saiku Chin Magden who is in England translating Tibetan into English for Buddhists. I have never known a man with more compassion." There was a short pause. "And Donovan is one of the nicest guys whom I have ever met."'

1. The Slender Plenty is made up of session musicians brought together by Andy Black, an A&R man at Polydor, specifically to record the single.

Monday 18 September

Decca executives meeting at their weekly selection committee (at which decisions are made about forthcoming releases) decide against a proposal to issue 'Let Me Sleep Beside You' as a single. The problem lies with the sexual connotations of the title; it is suggested that this is changed to 'Let Me Be Beside You'.

In South Africa, 'Love You Till Tuesday'/'Did You Ever Have A Dream' is released as a single by Deram.

Saturday 30 September

Fabulous 208's feature on David is headed 'Bowie Bows To Age'.

'David Bowie is no longer a teenager,' writes Sally Cork. 'He has reached the grand age of twenty, but he does know all about being a teenage success – and he doesn't believe in Teen Power.

'"The people who are the powerful ones are about twenty-five," he told us. "Teenagers are the consumers. These people turn out what the young want. The teenagers buy what is in the shop but they don't put it there and they don't get the money and it's money that is power!"

'Asked what he wanted to be doing when he was

twenty-five he replied: "I hope to be in Tibet studying Eastern philosophy. I don't expect that I will have enough money to retire exactly, but money doesn't mean all that much to me."'

Illustrating the piece are Peter Freeman's shots of David in a white polo neck sweater and in Pitt's paisley shirt.

Monday 2 October

David has a working lunch with BBC radio producer Bernie Andrews, who proves an important ally. Andrews is keen for David to audition again for the corporation so that he can perform sessions for broadcast (David failed to pass this audition with The Lower Third in November 1965).

Andrews sees opportunities for sessions by David for new pop station Radio One, which has been launched just two days previously. David's recording of a trial broadcast is delayed by his work on *The Image*, otherwise he might have been one of the very first artists to appear in-session on the new station.

Tuesday 3 October

Pitt sends copies of a new demo by David, 'C'est La Vie', to a number of contacts: US publisher Howie Richmond in New York, David's UK publisher David Platz in London and American singer Chris Montez.[1]

The 'C'est La Vie' quarter-inch master tape provides a unique insight into David's song construction, containing as it does around eight versions of the song, each reworked until the sound and content are polished.

Pitt also writes a strongly worded letter to Decca about its lack of promotional effort and suggests to the label's A&R manager (and head of singles)

LEFT: Trial shot for *The Image*, Ken Pitt stands in for actor Michael Byrne, 11 September.

ABOVE: David's first big screen appearance – Michael Armstrong's *The Image*.

BELOW LEFT: Section of 'Silver Tree Top School For Boys' unpublished sheet music.

Dick Rowe[2] that 'When I Live My Dream' should be backed by 'Karma Man' as the next single.[3]

1. Born Ezekiel Montanez 17 January 1943 in California, Montez scored a number two UK hit with 'Let's Dance' in 1962. His other 60s hits included 'Call Me' and 'The More I See You'. Pitt received no response to the 'C'est la Vie' approach.

2. Rowe is notorious for rejecting The Beatles in favour of Brian Poole & The Tremeloes in 1962. He later signed a number of prominent acts, including The Rolling Stones. Early in 1967 David made a disparaging reference to Rowe in an out-take recording of 'The Gospel According To Tony Day'.

3. In the event, Decca's selection panel rejects this option.

Monday 9 October

Decca representatives Hugh Mendl, Mike Vernon and US executive Walt Maguire visit Pitt's Curzon Street offices for a pow-wow. David is also in attendance.

Derek Ingrey of the BBC Television Script Unit rejects a script for a short television play called *The Champion Flower Grower*, written speculatively by David, who had written it in long-hand before it was typed up by Pitt.

David added by hand suggestions for the actors to take part: Hywel Bennett,[1] Gay Shingleton[2] and Philip Locke.[3] David has the part of a 'Sammy Slap'.

Ingrey offers constructive criticism and concludes his letter: 'With regret I return his manuscript and what, my secretary assures me, is a splendid LP.'

Pitt also sends a script and a copy of the album to BBC TV head of drama Sydney Newman.[4]

1. Born 8 April 1944, Bennett acted in films such as *The Virgin Soldiers*, in which David features as an extra.

2. Shingleton had been a dancer on *Ready Steady Go!* and recorded a 1965 single 'In My Time Of Sorrow', produced by Jimmy Page.

3. Locke (1928–2004) played roles such as Vargas in 1965 Bond movie *Thunderball*.

4. Newman was the executive responsible for creating TV series *The Avengers* for ATV in 1961.

Friday 13 October

David visits impresario and broadcaster Ned Sherrin[1] at his home in Bywater Street, Chelsea, regarding *The Virgin Soldiers*, a film project in pre-production based on the popular comic novel of the same name by Leslie Thomas (who reported on David's Society For The Prevention Of Cruelty To Long Haired Men escapade in 1964).

1. Sherrin (1931–2007) was responsible for early 60s satirical TV show *That Was The Week That Was*, theatre productions *Side By Side By Sondheim* and *Jeffrey Bernard Is Unwell*, and presented BBC Radio 4 magazine series *Loose Ends*.

Tuesday 17 October

David attends a meeting at Decca's Embankment offices.

Ken Pitt receives a response from BBC TV light entertainment head Tom Sloan to his speculative letter and album seeking television exposure for David.

Sloan tells Pitt he has forwarded the package to TV

In this year...

Saturday 16 September
RELEASE of *Scott*, the first solo album by former member of The Walker Brothers Scott Walker.[1] The album proved a great influence on David, who also covered the two Jacques Brel tracks it featured: 'My Death', which was performed on the Ziggy Stardust live dates of 1973 (and captured in D.A. Pennebaker's film); and 'Amsterdam' which appeared as the B-side to 'Sorrow', also in 1973.

In April 1992, David asked Walker to sing at his wedding to Iman. Walker was unable to attend. The two met in 1995, when Walker attended a date on David's Outside tour.

1. Born Noel Scott Engel on 9 January 1943 in Ohio.

BOWIE BOWS TO AGE

DAVID BOWIE is no longer a teenager. He has reached the grand age of twenty, but he does know all about being a teenage success—and he doesn't believe in Teen Power.

David left school at sixteen after having passed his O levels and three A levels (keep going you lot!) He worked as a commercial artist for six months but then gave it up to write songs.

Since David started composing he has penned between sixty and seventy numbers though he only thinks ten of them are any good. Modesty! He has also recorded a few himself: *The Laughing Gnome* and *Love You Till Tuesday* among them. But alas none have made any chart impression. Not that that worries him, he makes enough money by his song writing and admits that he hardly makes a *thing* by his voice. (Very honest is our David.)

Maybe that is why he is so ready to admit that there is no such thing as Teen Power, to his mind.

"The people who are the powerful ones are about twenty-five," he told us. "Teenagers are the consumers. These people turn out what the young want. The teenagers buy what is in the shop, but they don't put it there and they don't get the money if it's *money* that is power!"

Asked what he wanted to be doing when he was twenty-five, he said:

"I hope to be in Tibet studying Eastern philosophy. I don't expect that I will have enough money to retire exactly, but money doesn't mean all that much to me."

One thing's for sure, David may not be rich or at the top of the charts, but in one sense, he has Teen Power. He thinks for himself. And that is what all swinging teenagers are doing.

Fab 208 David Bowie

DERAM DM 135
DAVID BOWIE
LOVE YOU TILL TUESDAY

THROUGH MY WINDOW I CAN SEE
IF THE WORLD IS THERE FOR ME
WILL BE MY SHADOW ON THE FLOOR
THINK OF LET ME GO
AND TOMORROW CALLS MY NAME
BUT I DON'T WANT TO GO
THROUGH THE BURNING FLAMES OF TIME
C'EST LA VIE
C'EST LA VIE

THIS PAGE

TOP LEFT: David's first colour magazine feature, in *Fabulous 2008*.

TOP RIGHT: David on the set of *Fan Club* on Dutch TV (and opposite page).

MIDDLE RIGHT: Part of David's original lyric for 'C'est La Vie'. The song never made it past demo stage.

FAR RIGHT: David's Equity card.

ABOVE: The Dutch sleeve for 'Love You Till Tuesday'.

OPPOSITE PAGE

TOP & BOTTOM: David on the roof of Manchester Street, around the time he wrote *The Champion Flower Grower*.

director Stanley Dorfman,[1] who is selecting guests for *The Julie Felix Show*.

1. Pitt heard no more from Dorfman, though singer Felix recalled in 1991 that she and the director did consider David for the show. In 1977 Dorfman directed videos for David and his record label RCA, including promos for singles "Heroes" and 'Be My Wife'.

Saturday 28 October

David is confirmed as an Equity member (the actors' union). His number is 57135.

Tuesday 7 November

Accompanied by Pitt, David flies to Amsterdam to record his first TV appearance outside the UK on teen show *Fan Club*. They overnight at a motel in Naarden.

"It was working on these shows that gave us the idea to do our own special featuring David," said Pitt in 1983. "Colour TV had only just arrived and European pop programmes seemed to use every colour under the sun in their backdrops – not at all tasteful. We thought we could do a lot better."

B 6747

BRITISH ACTORS' EQUITY ASSOCIATION
MEMBERSHIP CARD

Wednesday 8 November

David is filmed performing 'Love You Till Tuesday' for *Fan Club*,[1] which is broadcast at the end of the week. The single had been released in Holland and Germany in October. Also on the show is John Walker,[2] who has launched a solo career following The Walker Brothers' split a few months earlier. He arranges to meet David the following week in London to listen to more of his material.

1. *Fan Club* director Ralph Inbar booked David to perform 'Space Oddity' on Dutch TV show *Doebidoe* in 1969.

2. John Maus, born 12 November 1943 in New York. After The Walker Brothers went their separate ways in May 1967, John Walker was the first of the trio to hit the charts as a solo performer with the August 1967 top 30 song 'Annabella'. He and the other two members – Gary Leeds and Scott Engel – were reunited for three years in the mid-70s.

Monday 13 November

Pitt sends David's script *The Champion Flower Grower* to independent network ABC Television.

Tuesday 14 November

David meets John Walker at 39 Manchester Street about the possibility of supplying him with songs. Pitt has circulated demos of songs as potential covers to a number of performers, including Johnny Gustafson, the former bassist in The Merseybeats.

Wednesday 15 November

After a morning meeting with publisher David Platz, David spends the afternoon going through dance moves with choreographer John Linden.

Thursday 16 November

David and Pitt shop for stage outfits for an

appearance David is making at the weekend.

Sunday 19 November

▶ David makes his first appearance on stage in nearly six months at a charity show called *The Stage Ball* [1] at the Dorchester Hotel, Park Lane.

He has been invited to participate by Barry Linnane, a friend of director Michael Armstrong. For his 10-minute performance David is accompanied by the hotel's resident musicians, Bill Saville & His Orchestra.

This is a showbiz affair; in the audience is popular British drag star Danny La Rue and seated at David's table is TV actor Frazer Hines.

TV executive Marilyn Fox, who works on BBC One children's show *Jackanory*, is impressed and invites David to BBC Television Centre a number of times over the coming months to discuss his appearance in a children's TV project.

1. *The Stage Ball* was an evening in aid of charities the Catholic Stage Guild and the British Heart Foundation.

Saturday 25 November

Fabulous 208 follows up on its colour feature with a smaller piece which refers to *The Image*: 'Bowie – The lean and dreamy David. At 20 he's song-writing, singing and filming.'

Friday 1 December

Pitt sends John Walker an acetate of David's 'Something I Would Like To Be', one of the songs played during their Manchester Street meeting the previous month.

Pitt-managed Scottish band The Beatstalkers[1] release a version of 'Silver Tree Top School For Boys' as the A-side of their new CBS single (which is backed by a track written by bass player Alan Mair, 'Sugar Chocolate Machine').

The track has been engineered by Gus Dudgeon and produced by Mike Smith.

At one point David is enlisted as a voice coach for The Beatstalkers' lead singer Dave Lennox to help him sound less Scottish, though the idea is quickly abandoned as his brogue is too broad.

1. The Beatstalkers were David Lennox (vocals), Alan Mair (bass),

Jeff Allan (drums), Eddie Campbell (keyboards) and Ronnie Smith (rhythm guitar). They first crossed paths with David in 1965 when they shared the bill with him and The Lower Third in Bournemouth and at the Marquee.

That year The Beatstalkers signed to Decca, for whom they recorded three singles: 'Everybody's Talking 'bout My Baby', 'Left Right Left' and 'A Love Like Yours'. In 1967 the group was signed by CBS and joined Pitt's roster.

"Denny Cordell was our producer; when we came to London he said we should get a good manager," said Mair in 1992. "That's when we got in touch with Ken Pitt, who was really trying to push David at the time as a songwriter. David came along to some of our rehearsals and it went from there."

The Beatstalkers failed to find chart success and split up in 1969 after the release of final single 'Little Girl'. In 1976 Mair joined The Only Ones, who achieved success during the punk and post-punk period, most notably with single 'Another Girl, Another Planet'.

THIS PAGE

TOP: David's Christmas gift to his manager, Ken Pitt. A signed facsimile of Randolph Caldecott's *The Farmer's Boy*, originally published in 1881.

TOP RIGHT: Summer 1967.

ABOVE: BBC Producer Bernie Andrews (pictured right) asks musician and arranger Arthur Greenslade how much his organ is worth. Greenslade had also worked earlier in the year with David on some Decca recordings.

BOTTOM RIGHT: The Beatstalkers, who covered three of David's songs. Left to right: Ronnie Smith (rhythm guitar), David Lennox (vocals), Alan Mair (bass), Jeff Allan (drums) and, crouching, Eddie Campbell (keyboards). Alan's son Frank Mair helped supply the name for David's 'Little Bombardier'. (▶ 1.6.67)

OPPOSITE PAGE

TOP: Natasha and David's *Pierrot In Turquoise* stage curtain design makes its debut while The Great Orlando takes a bow.

MIDDLE: Natasha Kornilof, designer extraordinaire (pictured in 1991).

BOTTOM: Manchester Street, 1967.

Monday 4 December

David meets film producer Barry Krost[1] to discuss a potential project, though he is more occupied rehearsing for a part in a new Lindsay Kemp production, *Pierrot In Turquoise*,[2] which is due to open in Oxford at the end of the month.

This is a musical play coupled with dramatic, non-verbal vignettes, based around the character of the Pierrot daydreaming at the end of a pier. Some of these humourous ideas have been culled from earlier Kemp productions, including *The Tinsel People* and *The Strange World of Pierrot Flour*.

David is introduced to costume designer Natasha Kornilof,[3] who creates a bespoke costume for his character, Cloud.

"I remember Lindsay Kemp telling me about this boy, this singer. He said, 'He's a bit stiff but I think we can do something with him'," said Kornilof in 1992. "It was the very first time he had ever been in costume. He'd dressed himself up in the manner of The Beatles, because it was the fashion of the time for these groups to wear the suits with the nice hair cut, but he'd never been in costume before."

1. Krost was also agent and advisor to Cat Stevens.

2. A 1970 Kemp TV production, also called *Pierrot In Turquoise*, bore little resemblance to the original stage production.

3. Born in India of Russian extraction, Kornilof was raised in Rhodesia before coming to London in the 60s. She began her association with Kemp after meeting him during an Oxford Playhouse production of Ben Jonson's play *Volpone* in 1965.

Kornilof worked with David on a number of projects, from early 70s extravaganzas to his 1978 world tour, for which she created 30 costume changes.

One of her most noted designs was the Pierrot costume David wears in the 1980 video for 'Ashes To Ashes'. In her later years she was a popular figure in south-east London, acting as a guide at Southwark Cathedral. Natasha Kornilof died in London on 4 November 2008.

Thursday 7 December

Renewing David's publishing contract for another year (with a further six-month option), Essex Music advances David £1,500. Among songs registered by Essex in 1967 are the unreleased 'Mother Grey', 'April's Tooth Of Gold' and 'C'est La Vie'.

'Something I Would Like To Be', although demoed, remains unregistered, as does the previously undocumented 'Now That You Want Me'.[1] Other previously undocumented songs written by David by 1967 are 'Silver Sunday', 'A Picture Of You', 'Lincoln House' and 'Home By Six'.

1. Both have yet to be released.

Monday 18 December

David is at the BBC studios at 201 Piccadilly[1] to record a performance for BBC radio's progressive pop show *Top Gear* (for broadcast on Christmas Eve).

With Tony Visconti on backing vocals, David performs 'Love You Till Tuesday', 'Silly Boy Blue', 'When I Live My Dream',[2] and 'Little Bombardier', a favourite of producer Bernie Andrews, with whom it has been agreed that this will serve as David's second audition for recording sessions for the BBC.

David's plan is to include 'Something I Would Like To Be', but this is replaced with another new song, 'In The Heat Of The Morning'.[3]

David is backed by Arthur Greenslade's 16-piece orchestra (Greenslade arranged tracks for David earlier in the year).

1. 201 Piccadilly is next to Simpsons. In 2010 it was home to Boots the Chemist.
2. This version varies lyrically from the Decca recording of the following year. (▶12.3.68)
3. In 2010, the session was released, for the first time, on a compilation CD *David Bowie Deram Deluxe*.

Thursday 21 December

David's local paper in his hometown, the *Bromley Advertiser*, carries a short front-page news item headed 'On the Air and on the Boards'.

'Bromley's versatile 19 year old pop star, David Bowie, who plays several instruments, sings, mimes and acts, and is now learning dancing, has two engagements at the end of the year, one with the BBC and one on stage.

'David went to Bromley Technical High School, where he studied graphic art, and was a noted runner and athlete.'

Sunday 24 December

The *Top Gear* session is broadcast,[1] providing David with his largest single audience to date.

1. It was repeated in January 1968.

Tuesday 26 December

John Jones writes to Pitt: 'Let us hope that one of his numbers, sung either by him or some other artiste, will make number one then prospects will really look bright.'

David and Natasha Kornilof spend Boxing Day at her home in Greenwich, painting the front curtain for *Pierrot In Turquoise*. Kornilof draws the outlines of the play's characters, who are caricatured in the style of a Victorian poster, and she and David colour them in. As part of the performance David is to hoist the curtain by hand.

In the evening they watch the first airing of The Beatles' *Magical Mystery Tour*, but the television set is faulty.

"The picture gradually shrank in front of our eyes," Kornilof said in 1984. "It eventually went down to a two-inch circle. We got closer and closer to the TV – it was hilarious."

Thursday 28 December

In the evening, *Pierrot In Turquoise* premières at the New Theatre, George Street, Oxford. It is listed as 'an experimental show' for the theatre's Young Playhouse Association.

The title for *Pierrot In Turquoise* has been inspired by David's interest in Buddhism (in which turquoise is the colour of everlastingness).[1] With Kemp as the Pierrot and Jack Birkett[2] as the Harlequin, David sings his songs, including 'When I Live My Dream',

'Sell Me A Coat' and 'Come And Buy My Toys', to augment the stories, accompanied by Michael Garrett on piano.

"He did the bit that you could hear and I did the bit that you could see," said Kemp in 1995.

1. In 1969, Kemp performed a piece called *Turquoise Pantomime* without David's involvement.
2. Jack Birkett (1934–2010), born in Leeds. Birkett, who began losing his sight in 1966, was Kemp's friend and collaborator who often performed as the Great Orlando. He also appeared in Derek Jarman's 1978 'punk' film *Jubilee*.

Friday 29 December

There is faint praise for *Pierrot In Turqoise* in the *Financial Times*, where B.A. Young describes David as 'a young pop-singer whose songs tend to follow ambition beyond the boundaries of his talent. I am on his side, because (among other reasons) he sings without a microphone'.

In the *Oxford Mail*, Don Chapman is more effusive: 'Natasha Kornilof has designed a beautiful backdrop and some gorgeous costumes. And David Bowie has composed some beautiful songs, which he sings in a superb, dreamlike voice.'

In the New Year the production is to move to Rosehill Theatre, an events performance space in Whitehaven, Cumbria, where there is to be as much drama off stage as on as David becomes entangled with both Kemp and Kornilof.

1968

AS he turns 21, David is becoming more involved with Lindsay Kemp who is, however, jealous of his young friend's relationship with Natasha Kornilof.

Kemp's *Pierrot In Turquoise* moves to London and David also performs in an adaptation of a Pushkin drama, *The Pistol Shot*, for BBC TV. There he meets beautiful dancer Hermione Farthingale, and the couple embark on a close relationship that will bear artistic fruit but ultimately heartbreak for David.

David is still working on musical projects, but it's his mime and acting career that is in the ascendancy. He splits from the Deram label and the search is on for a new record deal.

There are radio sessions and benefit appearances for 'underground' causes, at which David showcases his mime talents, and he is also developing a cabaret act. He takes part-time jobs to help pay the bills.

His path once again crosses that of Marc Bolan as he appears at the Royal Festival Hall, and his acting career seems set to develop as he reads for a role in the film *The Virgin Soldiers*.

His crack at a cabaret career is a non-starter, but David is now living with Farthingale and playing with her and songwriter/guitarist Tony Hill in a short-lived trio called Turquoise.

The group appear at a benefit concert at London's Roundhouse, where among the audience is young American Mary Angela Barnett – the future Angie Bowie.

David's appearance in *The Virgin Soldiers* turns out to be a tiny cameo, but Turquoise are by now recording and evolving. Hill leaves and is replaced by John 'Hutch' Hutchinson and the group is renamed Feathers.

There are a few gigs for the group, but a year of transition ends with David having released no records.

'Pierrot in Turquoise'

PRESENTED as the centre-piece attraction of the Oxford Young Playhouse Association's recent Christmas programme, "Pierrot in Turquoise" gave Lindsay Kemp, whose work as the dwarf in Frank Hauser's production of "Volpone" is still vividly remembered in Oxford, ample opportunities to display his impressive mimetic skill.

As Pierrot pursuing an invisible Columbine whose presence is, however, subtly and often strongly suggested, entranced by his acquisition of a new and resplendent coat; wrongly and viciously accused of theft, in trouble with authority and in many other moods and situations, Mr. Kemp gives versatile proof of the flexible power of the wordless theatre.

In more broadly comic vein his impression of a strip-tease performer is informed with the same disciplined bodily plasticity and, as it were, silent wit.

INVENTIVE

David Bowie, the show's inventive composer, makes several striking appearances as Cloud, a multi-purposed and multi-guised character, and Jack Birkett is a compelling Harlequin.

The décor and costumes of Natasha Kornilof, already much-admired in Oxford as a designer for several recent Playhouse productions, bring much visual delight, in terms of colour, to the simple curtain setting, and her masks give keen dramatic point to the action.

In these days of mass-media entertainment it is heartening to sense the successful impact which this, one of the oldest forms of living theatre, is having upon a predominantly young audience, many of whom are making their first acquaintance with the ageless art of mime.

The Oxford Young Playhouse Association are to be congratulated on their enterprise in presenting Mr. Kemp's entertainment, which is shortly to be seen in London.

PREVIOUS SPREAD: At Manchester Street with *Yellow Submarine* cut-out Beatles figures, painted by David and Ken Pitt for a proposed cabaret project.

THIS PAGE

ABOVE: *Pierrot In Turquoise* review from *The Stage*, 1 January.

RIGHT: David posing during a drawing session at Tony Visconti's Lexham Gardens flat. Photo by Ray Stevenson.

Tuesday 2 January

David travels with Lindsay Kemp's troupe for a three-night run of *Pierrot In Turquoise* at the Rosehill Theatre in the remote northern England village of Moresby, near Whitehaven in Cumbria.

David is quietly huddled in a corner suffering from a cold for most of the 270-mile journey from London in a rented Transit van with the other passengers – Kemp, pianist Michael Garrett and stage director Craig San Roque and his wife. The driver is the only licence-holder, costume designer Natasha Kornilof.

Wednesday 3 January

Lindsay Kemp becomes jealous of the relationship between David and Kornilof.

Just before the performance is to open, Kemp is whisked to Whitehaven Hospital for attendance to superficial cuts, having symbolically taken a sharp blade to his wrists.

Kemp is well enough to return and the show goes on with his wrist bandages slowly staining red with blood in full view of the bemused audience. Kemp recalled with anguish in 1991: "Much of the time I spent with David Bowie was bloody painful."

Pierrot In Turquoise has been booked by patron Sir Nicholas 'Miki' Sekers, a flamboyant silk manufacturer much interested in the arts. He staged the Kemp company's *The Strange World Of Pierrot Flour* the previous spring, and donates 30 yards of luxurious cloth to the current production.

David is out of favour with both Kemp and Kornilof. "We were both beastly to him for a long time afterwards," she said in 1986. "He looked cold and tired and we were shouting at him, 'Go on! Do that! Get that!'"

The Rosehill Theatre,[1] with the interior wall coverings in Sekers' trademark silk, has a seating capacity of less than 100. Unpaid and at the mercy of the older drama queens, David is miserable and is consigned to sleep on a couch in the ice-cold hallway of the Sekers' farmhouse.

1. Designed in the late 50s by leading theatrical designer Oliver Messel, the Rosehill Theatre still thrives in 2010, regularly staging concerts and plays.

Saturday 6 January

Kemp's company makes the return journey to London in the freezing Transit. *Pierrot In Turquoise* has proved itself a viable piece of theatre, and there are plans to stage it in London. However, the Cumbrian expedition has failed to improve the company's material well-being. "Of course it wasn't a financial success; nothing Lindsay did then ever was," said Kornilof in 1986.

Monday 8 January

David celebrates his 21st birthday. He is no longer based full time at Pitt's Manchester Square apartment but often back with his parents in Bromley. Despite the events in Whitehaven, David is also spending a lot of time with Kemp, who has been invited to take part in forthcoming BBC TV Russian drama *The Pistol Shot*.[1] Kemp encourages David to join him in a sequence in the play which takes place at a dance.

1. Adapted by Nicholas Bethell from Alexander Pushkin's 1831 short story *Vystrel*, which is about an honour duel. Ironically, Pushkin himself died from a single pistol shot wound in a duel in 1837.

Monday 15 January

David has a meeting with Liberty Records A&R controller Ray Williams[1] and plays him potential tracks for surreal comedy act the Bonzo Dog Doo-Dah Band.[2]

1. Williams was interested enough for David to make a number of return visits but nothing came of this unlikely association with Viv Stanshall's Dada-inspired ensemble. The previous year an advert placed by Williams in *Melody Maker* was answered separately and simultaneously by struggling piano session player Reg Dwight and lyricist Bernie Taupin. When Dwight became Elton John, Williams initially managed him. Much later, in 1986, Williams was the music supervisor for the soundtrack to movie *Absolute Beginners*, which featured an appearance by David and two of his songs.
2. Formed in 1962, The Bonzo Dog Doo-Dah Band began life as a trad jazz combo headed by tuba player and later lead vocalist Vivian Stanshall with fellow art student and saxophonist Rodney Slater. By

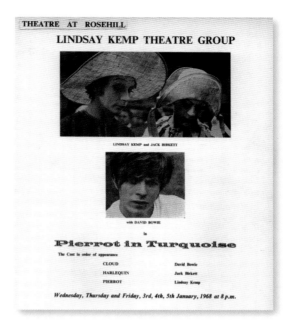

THEATRE AT ROSEHILL

LINDSAY KEMP THEATRE GROUP

LINDSAY KEMP and JACK BIRKETT

with DAVID BOWIE

is

Pierrot in Turquoise

The Cast in order of appearance

CLOUD .... David Bowie

HARLEQUIN .... Jack Birkett

PIERROT .... Lindsay Kemp

Wednesday, Thursday and Friday, 3rd, 4th, 5th January, 1968 at 8 p.m.

1967 they had adopted a rock sound whilst maintaining their highly eccentric comic writing and performances, signing to Liberty Records around the same time. Their 1968 hit 'I'm The Urban Spaceman' was produced by Paul McCartney and Gus Dudgeon. Vivien Stanshall died in a fire at home in north London in 1995.

Friday 26 January

Pitt writes to David expressing his concern at 'this sudden lack of communication between us... Fortunately, Lindsay telephoned me and was able to acquaint me with some of your activities'.[1] Among these are rehearsals for *Pierrot In Turquoise*, which is set to open at London's Mercury Theatre in six weeks.

1. Pitt wrote in his 1983 memoir: 'It was about this time that I first experienced what was to become known in the office as "David walkabouts", when he would disappear for a few days at a time and defy all attempts at finding him.'

Monday 29 January

As part of his near-daily routine of writing to David, Pitt sends a letter about BBC TV's children's storytelling programme *Jackanory*; David met the producer Marilyn Fox just a month before.[1] Pitt says there may be an opportunity for David, since there are plans to add music and movement to the show, which is based on the static premise of a single person – usually a celebrity – reading a story from an armchair.

The day before, David's Christmas Eve appearance on Radio One's *Top Gear* is repeated.

1. As a result of this a meeting took place with Fox and BBC TV head of children's programmes Monica Sims at the broadcaster's west London headquarters Television Centre in the spring of 1968, but nothing came of the talks.

Wednesday 31 January

In satin breeches and powdered wig, David takes part in the recording of the dance scene in *The Pistol Shot*[1] at BBC studios in west London. In a brief appearance, Kemp leads a group performing a minuet. Among them is David and beautiful young

LEFT: *Pierrot In Turquoise* programme, Rosehill Theatre, Moresby, Cumbria.

In this year...

Tuesday 30 January
RELEASE in the US of The Velvet Underground's second album *White Light/ White Heat*. The title track was a firm favourite of David's, who performed it many times live, at least once with its composer, Lou Reed, at the Royal Festival Hall. (>8.7.72)

Monday 22 January
PREMIERE of musical revue *Jacques Brel Is Alive And Well And Living In Paris* at the Village Gate Theatre, New York. The production, a celebration of the songs of the Belgian singer-songwriter, ran for nearly 2,000 performances and included translated versions of two songs David covered in the early 70s: 'Amsterdam' and 'My Death'. (▶12.7.68)

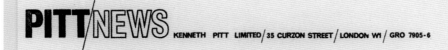

KENNETH PITT LIMITED / 35 CURZON STREET / LONDON W1 / GRO 7905-6

28th., February 1968

DAVID BOWIE, successfully bridging the gap between pop and showbiz, opens at the Mercury Theatre on Wednesday 6th March in the Linsay Kemp Theatre Group production "Pierrot In Turquoise". David has been studying Mime under Lindsay Kemp and has become his star pupil.

This week David Bowie is in Hamburg appearing in the "Musik fur Junge Leute" television programme.

ABOVE: Pitt News Bowie press release, 28 February.

dancer Hermione Farthingale (who has been booked by the BBC, not Kemp).

Once again Kemp feels wounded as he watches David and Farthingale walk together towards Shepherds Bush tube station, their mutual attraction evident. This is the beginning of David's first mature relationship.[2]

1. Broadcast on 20 May 1968, *The Pistol Shot* was a Theatre 625 presentation by Nicholas Bethell and John Ronane. Repeated on 24 December 1968, the tape was subsequently wiped.

2. Farthingale's real name is Hermione Dennis. A doctor's daughter raised in the pleasant rural surroundings of Edenbridge in Kent, Farthingale went on to become David's musical collaborator as well as lover, and appeared in a number of film musicals, mainly as a dancer: *Oh! What A Lovely War* (1968), *Dancing Shoes* (1969), *The Song Of Norway* (1970) and *Tales Of Hoffman* (1971). In 1972's MGM production *The Last Waltz*, Farthingale played a character called Louise.

Saturday 3 February

Gerald Fearnley's photograph of David taken six months earlier in full mime make-up appears in a *Jackie* magazine article headed 'Eye Spy!': 'David is a mime addict and used the make-up when doing a special cabaret show in London. He even went to a famous Mayfair beauty salon to learn the correct technique, and once a week David takes a mime lesson from the famous exponent Lindsay Kemp.'

Monday 5 February

David is on the lookout for work. He visits Hungarian-born voice coach Florence Wiese Norberg at her studio at 59 George Street, in central London.[1]

Around this time David also meets up with choreographer and agent Michael Summerton at his office in Duke Street, Mayfair, to investigate opportunities in the dance world.

1. In 1974 David recommended Norberg to his friend Amanda Lear.

Wednesday 7 February

Music publisher Geoffrey Heath, whose company Good Music shares office space with David's publisher David Platz, returns from Paris with a demo disc of a new song by French singer Claude François.

Written by François with Gilles Thibault and Jacques Revaux, this is entitled 'Comme D'Habitude' ('As Usual')[1] and Heath is in search of an English-language lyric.

Platz suggests David, who is enthusiastic and comes up with a set of lyrics he calls 'Even A Fool Learns To Love':

'There was a time, the laughing time,
I took my heart to every party,
They'd point my way,
How are you today?
Will you make us laugh? Chase our blues away?'

Pitt confirms by letter to Platz that David is working on the new lyric and is interested in recording the outcome himself.

The letter gives Pitt an opportunity to vent his frustration at what he perceives as Tony Visconti's tardiness: 'We are anxious to get to work on the next LP, but I am not sure if anything was finalised with Tony Visconti, or in fact if he is in the slightest bit interested in the project. I have tried speaking to him on the telephone a number of times during recent weeks and I am not encouraged by his refusal to return the calls.'

Pitt's frustration stems from the fact that he and David have already worked on a rough outline for the second album, with a tracklisting including a number of songs which have reached demo stage: 'C'est La Vie', 'Silver Tree Top School For Boys', 'When I'm Five',[2] 'Everything Is You', 'Tiny Tim', 'Angel Angel Grubby Face', 'Threepenny Joe' and 'The Reverend Raymond Brown (Attends The Garden Fete On Thatchwick Green)'.[3]

David has also been working on the music and lyrics for a four-page playlet entitled *Ernie Johnson*. This takes the form of a rock opera for film or TV. The surreal nature of the narrative has been inspired by Anthony Newley's *Gurney Slade* TV series, with some ideas drafted in from a play called *Peacocks Farm* David tinkered with in 1966.

The home-made multitrack is created in the lounge at Manchester Street, featuring David on acoustic and electric guitars and multi-dubbed vocals.[4]

David's first entry in stage directory *Spotlight* is also published.

1. With a lyric written by US singer Paul Anka, this became 'My Way', the signature tune released by Frank Sinatra in 1970. According to Pitt, David called him at the time, exclaiming: "Frank Sinatra's recorded that French song, I've just heard it on the radio."

2. 'When I'm Five' was inspired by the Velvet Underground's 'Sunday Morning', the opening track on their first album.

3. These are still in Ken Pitt's possession or the original quarter-inch tape.

4. A copy of the *Ernie Johnson* tape came up at auction at Christie's in 1996 along with copies of typed lyrics and suggestions for camera positions. The tape featured 14 tracks, 11 of which were written specifically for the play and were previously undocumented. David's original typewritten script and lyrics remain in Pitt's possession, while David retains the master tape and its copyright.

The *Ernie Johnson* tracklisting was:

1. **'Tiny Tim'** (You're Smart, You're Pretty Tiny Tim)
2. **'Where's The Loo'**
3. **'Season Folk'**
4. **'Just One Moment Sir'**
5. **'Various Times Of Day'**
6. **'Early Morning'**
7. **'Noon, Lunch-time'**
8. **'Evening'**
9. **'Ernie Boy'** (Ernie Boy – when you look in the mirror whose face you see)
10. **'This Is My Day'** (A song of the morning. The big morning in Ernie's life)
11. **Untitled track** (situated in a Carnaby Street boutique)
    Also on the tape were other compositions of David's: **'Going Down'**, **'Love You Till Tuesday'** and **'Over The Wall We Go'**.

Friday 9 February

Pitt visits Essex Music with a recording of David's English lyric for 'Comme D'Habitude'. This has been created by David singing his version over the top of the original demo disc on to quarter-inch tape.[1]

Pitt also has a meeting with executives at Decca, who express interest. These plans are scuppered when the song's French publisher raises strong objections to David recording it, because he is an unknown.

"Their attitude was that they wanted a star to record the song, not this yobbo from Bromley," said Geoffrey Heath in 1983.

In 1993 David recalled being told Frank Sinatra was keen on recording the song: "They said, 'Look, Frank Sinatra wants to do it'. I said, 'That's great!' 'And he hates your lyric.' 'That's not great!' 'So we've given it to Paul Anka to do.'"

1. On the demo, still in Pitt's possession, David can be heard cueing the French disc on a turntable around 10 times before he is satisfied enough to start his vocal. In 2005, David declared it to be 'so awful, really embarrassingly bad'.

Tuesday 13 February

At the weekly meeting of the BBC's selection committee, David's *Top Gear* recording is used as an audition tape. David is approved as an artist suitable for further BBC broadcasts. On 22 February David Dore, assistant to the BBC Radio light entertainment booking manager, confirms in writing to Pitt that David is deemed acceptable for broadcast.

Monday 19 February

Keen on securing the 'Comme D'Habitude' commission, Pitt writes to David Platz: 'I do hope that we can all take it for granted that David has an "exclusive" on "Even A Fool Learns To Love".'

Wednesday 21 February

Lionel Bart is positive about the copy of David's album Pitt has sent him. 'He's certainly on my list of faces to watch,' Bart writes to Pitt.

Monday 26 February

David travels to Hamburg to make his first TV appearance on German television for the ZDF network's *4-3-2-1 Musik Für Junge Leute* (4-3-2-1

Music For Young People).

Accompanied by Joan Barclay, secretary to top Decca executive Marcel Stellman, he has been booked by producer Dr Gunther Schneider.[1]

1. Schneider became a champion of David's talents, booking him three times on German TV shows.

Tuesday 27 February

On the German show (which is to be broadcast in a couple of weeks), David sings two songs to backing tapes: 'Love You Till Tuesday' and 'Did You Ever Have A Dream'. He also performs a mime to 'Please Mr Gravedigger'.

Wednesday 28 February

David returns to the UK.

Thursday 29 February

As David fails to check in with Pitt on his return, Pitt assumes he is on another 'walkabout' with Farthingale, so cancels David's potentially important meeting with major Broadway producer Harold Prince[1] at the Mayfair Hotel.

1. Born New York City, 30 January 1928, Harold Prince has won 21 Tony Awards and is notable for his association with Stephen Sondheim (*West Side Story*, *A Little Night Music*, *Sweeney Todd*), and direction of the Broadway productions of Andrew Lloyd Webber's *Evita* and *Phantom Of The Opera*.

Monday 4 March

A final dress rehearsal for *Pierrot In Turquoise* takes place at the Mercury Theatre,[1] Ladbroke Road, Notting Hill Gate, west London.

The director of this production is Jean-Pierre Voos and the music is arranged by Gordon Rose, who also provides original compositions to complement seven of David's: 'When I Live My Dream', 'Sell Me A Coat', 'Silly Boy Blue', 'Love You Till Tuesday', 'There Is A Happy Land', 'Come And Buy My Toys' and 'Maid Of Bond Street'.

This dress rehearsal is photographed by Jak Kilby.

1. Mercury Theatre was where Lindsay Kemp first met Jack Birkett in 1956, while both were studying under Marie Rambert.

Tuesday 5 March

Pierrot In Turquoise begins an 11-day run at the Mercury Theatre.

With Pitt, David's parents attend the opening night, and, after the show, David introduces Pitt to Hermione Farthingale for the first time.

David's colleague from The Buzz, Dek Fearnley, is in the audience with his wife Judith for one of the performances. "David should have seriously continued mime – he was really very good at it," said Judith Fearnley in 1991. "I was amazed."

Other visitors to the show include David's ex Dana Gillespie and producer Gus Dudgeon, who enjoys the performance but is surprised to hear David sing.

"I thought the whole point of mime was not to make any noise," said Dudgeon in 1991. "There was David singing his songs!"

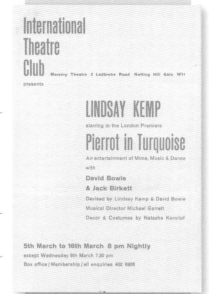

International Theatre Club
Mercury Theatre 2 Ladbroke Road Notting Hill Gate W11
presents

LINDSAY KEMP
starring in the London Premiere

Pierrot in Turquoise

An entertainment of Mime, Music & Dance
with

David Bowie
& Jack Birkett

Devised by Lindsay Kemp & David Bowie
Musical Director Michael Garrett
Decor & Costumes by Natasha Kornilof

5th March to 16th March 8 pm Nightly
except Wednesday 6th March 7.30 pm
Box office / Membership / all enquiries 402 6926

TOP: International Theatre Club programme for Kemp's Mercury Theatre run of *Pierrot In Turquoise*.

ABOVE: A favourite early venue for David, the Mercury Theatre, Notting Hill Gate; now a private residence.

In this year...

Thursday 8 February
RECORDING by The Beatles of 'Across The Universe' completed at Abbey Road Studios. David performed a duet with its composer, John Lennon, on his cover of the song on 1975 album *Young Americans*.

In this year...

Tuesday 2 April
PREMIERE of Stanley Kubrick's *2001: A Space Odyssey* at the Uptown Theatre, Washington DC. The film, which opened in London the following month, provided the primary inspiration for David's first hit single, 'Space Oddity'. (▸ 20.6.69)

Wednesday 3 April
DEPARTURE of founder member Syd Barrett from The Pink Floyd because of his increasingly erratic behaviour. For David, Barrett's exit from the group marked the end of an era, and of his interest in Floyd, as he later said. "Syd will always be Pink Floyd for some of us older fans." (▸ 19.10.73)

DAILY RECORDING INFORMATION				
This information is intended only as a guide. It is not necessarily accurate or complete.				
To :- DISTRIBUTION	(See over) From :- STUDIOS		Date 14th March 1968	
Mat. No.	Time	Title	Composer	Publisher
		David Bowie Arranger & Prod: Tony Visconti Engr Gus Dudgeon		
DR 42239	N/A	London, Bye, Ta Ta	Bowie	Essex Music
DR 42240	N/A	In the Heat of the Morning	Bowie	Essex Music

Wednesday 6 March

Pitt brings friend Arlene Fischer, the ex-wife of US jazz singer Mel Tormé, to the second night of *Pierrot In Turquoise* at the Mercury.

Friday 8 March

David is described as 'a fair swain with shining eyes' in London daily the *Evening Standard*'s review of the production by Annabel Farjeon, while his local paper, the *Bromley Times*, notes in its coverage (headed 'Bromley 21-year-old Songwriter goes on Stage'):

'David plays the secondary characters and in one sketch is a flower seller. Furthermore, David wrote the score and music which Lindsay Kemp produces, and sings seven of his own songs, recently featured on his LP *David Bowie* and issued under the Deram label.'

Tuesday 12 March

Work begins on recording two new songs, 'London Bye Ta-Ta' and 'In The Heat Of The Morning', for potential release as a single. The sessions take place at Decca Studios in West Hampstead, with Tony Visconti handling arrangement and production and Gus Dudgeon engineering.

Guitarist is Mick Wayne, who has just formed his own group, Junior's Eyes, which will feature prominently in David's future plans. Andy White is on drums.

Thursday 14 March

In the morning David meets film producer James Clarke at the offices of Vic Films, 33 Bruton Street, London W1, regarding a role in a film being developed entitled *Alain*.[1]

In *Stage and Television Today*'s review of *Pierrot In Turquoise*, David is picked out not only for his 'mind-bendingly off-beat songs' but also his 'effective mime'.

1. David auditioned for *Alain* – although no information can be found of the film – and also for Richard Attenborough's film version for the satirical *Oh! What A Lovely War,* which went into production later in 1968, but failed to gain a role in either. Hermione Farthingale, however, appeared as a dancer in the latter.

Saturday 16 March

Tonight is the final performance of the mime at the Mercury. *Pierrot In Turquoise* is to transfer to another small London venue and there is talk of it representing the UK at the International Mime Festival in Prague in June.[1]

Also tonight, David's performance on TV show *4-3-2-1 Musik Für Junge Leute* is broadcast in Germany by ZDF.

1. In the event this does not transpire.

Sunday 17 March

In the running as a possible compère, David is at the recording of a pilot for a new ABC Television pop show called *68 Style* at Teddington Studios in south west London.[1]

1. The pilot – which didn't feature David – was screened but the programme was not commissioned.

Friday 22 March

Billy Fury[1] single 'One Minute Woman'/'Silly Boy Blue' is released on Parlophone, featuring David's composition as the B-side.

Fury has been introduced to David's work by BBC producer Bernie Andrews, who took a copy of the debut album to the 60s star's home in Ockley, Surrey, and it has been anticipated that David's song would be the A-side (as indicated on the demo discs prepared just before release).

However, at the last minute Parlophone has switched the sides without informing Fury or his manager, pop impresario Larry Parnes.[2]

Parnes writes to Pitt: 'I'm sorry to say that EMI decided to flip this record to the "B" side in my absence on vacation. Both Billy and I are most upset about this.'

Nevertheless, David is extremely pleased that Fury had even considered recording one of his songs.

"David Bowie once told me he modelled himself on Billy Fury," said Parnes in 1988. "He said his brother used to take him to the shows and he thought Billy was wonderful. I think that's a great compliment. As far as pre-60s British rock'n'roll is concerned, Billy should be credited as the most important figure this country ever produced."

1. Billy Fury, born Ronald William Wycherley (1940–1983). He released his first hit single for Decca, 'Maybe Tomorrow', in 1959. In the early 60s he had numerous top ten singles including 'Halfway To Paradise' and 'Jealousy' in 1961. Among Fury's film roles were *Play It Cool* (1962) and *That'll Be The Day* (1973).

2. Larry Parnes (1930–1989). One of Britain's first pop impresarios, Parnes played a major role in developing Britain's late 50s/early 60s music industry and managed many UK pop singers. He built a reputation by cultivating striking new images, commissioning recording material and choosing expressive new surnames such as (Dickie) Pride, (Marty) Wilde, (Billy) Fury and (Georgie) Fame.

Monday 25 March

A final dress rehearsal takes place for *Pierrot In Turquoise* at the Intimate Theatre, which is in St Monica's Hall, at 521 Green Lanes in Palmers Green, north-east London. Kemp later recalled David's physical vulnerability: "I don't know how he got through the shows," he said in 1991. "He always had a cold or a cough and he always needed looking after."

Tuesday 26 March

Pierrot In Turquoise opens for a five-day run at the Intimate Theatre.

The production features drummer John Eager's prized Chinese cymbal, which is later returned by David at a brief meeting at Harrow-on-the-Hill's Metropolitan Line tube station.

Wednesday 27 March

David sings backing vocals on 'Everything Is You' and 'When I'm Five', two of his songs The Beatstalkers are recording at CBS Studios, Whitfield Street, London.

Friday 29 March

At the request of Decca's selection panel – which decides on whether tracks are worthy of release – David is back at Decca Studios in West Hampstead in the afternoon and evening with Tony Visconti, adding voice overdubs to 'London Bye Ta-Ta' and 'In The Heat Of The Morning'.

Saturday 30 March

The final night of *Pierrot In Turquoise* at the Intimate Theatre. David is never to appear as part of Kemp's mime company again, though he will work with the mime maestro on a couple more projects in the years to come. (▸ 19.8.72)

Friday 5 April

On a visit to London, TV producer Gunther Schneider takes David to a performance of Fred Ebb and John Kander's musical *Cabaret*, which has recently transferred from Broadway to the Palace Theatre, Cambridge Circus, central London.

"The stage lighting was phenomenal," said David

in 1993. "What I didn't know is that it was Brechtian lighting. It was just stark white light. I'd never seen that before in my life, and that became a central image for me of what a stage should look like. I'd never seen it in a rock'n'roll stage. That was lighting to die for."[1]

1. This approach to stage lighting was adopted by David for early Ziggy Stardust shows (▸ 25.8.72) and the Station To Station tour of 1976.

Wednesday 10 April

More work is undertaken on tweaking 'London Bye Ta-Ta' and 'In The Heat Of The Morning' at Decca's studios.

Thursday 18 April

In another letter to David, Pitt informs him that a planned BBC children's TV show in collaboration with broadcaster Adrian Love has been scheduled for 23 December at 5.25pm.[1]

David and Tony Head of Dave Antony's Moods record backing vocals for The Beatstalkers at CBS Studios in central London. They receive a session fee of £9 each. This is further work for the group's forthcoming single, which is to feature David's song 'Everything Is You' on its B-side.

In the evening, David is back at Decca Studios with Tony Visconti and Gus Dudgeon for final adjustments to 'London Bye Ta-Ta' and 'In The Heat Of The Morning'.

But the powers that be at Decca are not satisfied and announce that they are not prepared to release either track, even though Pitt has already put the wheels in motion behind 'In The Heat Of The Morning' as the next single.

'I had arranged for David to perform the work on another *Top Gear* broadcast when the news came through that the Decca selection panel had found that song and 'London Bye Ta-Ta' unsuitable for release,' wrote Pitt in 1983. 'I immediately telephoned Hugh Mendl, whom I found to be sympathetic and now even more embarrassed by the action of his colleagues. He said, "I cannot blame you if you wish to leave us".'

The master tape of 'London Bye Ta-Ta' disappears, but at least two different acetates are cut, one featuring a tail-off of the sounds of horses' hooves on a cobbled street.[2]

1. This production never reached the screens.

2. The other alternative mix, minus the horses' hooves, was released for the first time in 2010 on the *David Bowie Deram Deluxe* package.

Monday 22 April

David's departure from Deram Records is confirmed after 18 months with the label.

Tuesday 23 April

Wasting no time, Pitt visits Terry Doran at Apple Music, in search of a new record deal for David. (▸ 15.7.68)

OPPOSITE PAGE

TOP LEFT: Rehearsals for *Pierrot In Turquoise*. Photos by Jak Kilby.

TOP RIGHT: Lindsay Kemp and David performing in *Pierrot In Turquoise*, Mercury Theatre, London.

MIDDLE LEFT: Natasha Kornilof costume design for *Pierrot In Turquoise*.

MIDDLE RIGHT: Detail from Decca Daily Recording information sheet for 'London Bye Ta-Ta'.

BOTTOM: The Intimate Theatre, Palmers Green, London. David's last performance of *Pierrot In Turquoise* was staged here.

THIS PAGE

TOP: Ronald Wycherley, better known as Billy Fury, 1968.

ABOVE: Bill Fury 'Silly Boy Blue' single label.

BELOW: David's *Cabaret* programme, left at Manchester Street after he moved out in 1969.

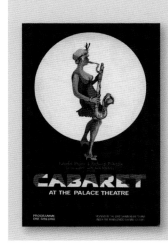

THIS PAGE

ABOVE: Photographer Ray Stevenson with girlfriend and his younger brother, Nils Stevenson, 1968.

TOP, MIDDLE, BOTTOM: Using Ken Pitt's large home-made green coffee table as a dais, David poses in full make-up in two different mime costumes for a simple but effective photo session. Pitt is also the photographer.

TOP RIGHT: David in action at Gandalf's Garden, Covent Garden, the night he met photographer Ray Stevenson.

OPPOSITE PAGE

TOP: Mime contact sheet from 7 May Manchester Street session.

BOTTOM: David with Ken Pitt's teddy, 'Bobby'.

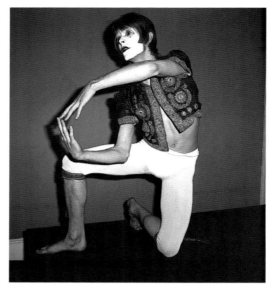

Thursday 25 April

David renews his contract with Kenneth Pitt Ltd for another four years.

Tuesday 30 April

❯ David makes his first appearance of the year in the upstairs room of the Nags Head in York Road in south London neighbourhood Battersea. David appears as a favour to Mike Vernon's wife, Judy, who promotes the evening as a blues club called Kilroys, which has been popularised by British blues band Savoy Brown.

The bill includes her husband and John Peel – as well as blues singer Duster Bennett and John Steven.

Tuesday 7 May

Ken Pitt conducts an evening photo session with David in the front room of 39 Manchester Street to promote forthcoming mime performances – and in particular his performance at the Royal Festival Hall in June. David poses in various mime positions and costumes on Pitt's sturdy coffee table for Pitt's camera. (❯3.6.68)

Monday 13 May

David records his second slot on Radio One's *Top Gear* at the BBC's Piccadilly 1 studio in The Strand in London's West End. As musical director, Tony Visconti hires the musicians, including guitarist John McLaughlin, drummer Barry Morgan (co-owner of Morgan recording studios and a member of psych-pop band Gulliver's People), keyboard player Alan Hawkshaw and Steve Peregrin Took of Tyrannosaurus Rex,[1] who adds backing vocals with Visconti and David on two tracks, 'Silly Boy Blue' and 'Karma Man'. Took[2] slept at Visconti's apartment the night before and accompanies him to the studio on the spur of the moment.

Also recorded for the BBC session are 'In The Heat Of The Morning', 'London Bye Ta-Ta' and 'When I'm Five'.

1. The previous week Marc Bolan's group achieved its first success; single 'Deborah' entered the UK charts at number 34.

2. Stephen Ross Porter (1949–1980). His stage name was taken from Tolkien's *Lord Of The Rings* character Peregrine Took. In 1967 Marc Bolan and Took formed Tyrannosaurus Rex, with Bolan on lead vocals and guitar and Took on bongos. He was replaced by Mickey Finn in

1969. Thereafter he worked with various artists including the Pink Fairies and Syd Barrett, as well as producing solo work. He died at his home in Notting Hill, London, after choking on a cherry stone.

Sunday 19 May

▶ David Bowie, Middle Earth, Basement, 43 King Street,[1] Covent Garden, London.

David performs a mime set[2] during an eight-hour festival benefit to raise funds for the King's Road hippy café and hangout Gandalf's Garden, whose owner Muz Murray operates an underground magazine with the same name.

Compère for the evening is John Peel. Also appearing on the packed bill are David's friends Tyrannosaurus Rex and Junior's Eyes as well as Ginger Johnson, Hapshash & The Coloured Coat, Edgar Broughton Blues Band, Tibetan Mind, poet Christopher Logue, Exploding Galaxy, Mandala Jazz Group, Third Ear Band, Flame, Tyres and Tales of Justine.

For David, tonight is a trial run for a forthcoming mime showcase at the Royal Festival Hall. Included in his backing music is the recent recording of 'Silly Boy Blue'.

In the audience is promoter/DJ Jeff Dexter.[3] "His mime was about the flight of the Tibetans from East to West," said Dexter in 1995. "It consisted of a pre-edited tape played on a reel-to-reel tape machine through a PA. His soundtrack featured ritualistic Tibetan music; gongs, cymbals, drums, taped voices/dialogue."

Another audience member is young photographer Ray Stevenson,[4] who is just a year into his career. "My friends Flame were playing," said Stevenson in 1983. "They were sharing the dressing room with David, and with a room that size you have to make friends.

"I met David before he went on stage and I thought, 'Oh he's a nice man, I'll take some pictures of him.' I took several pictures of him because I liked him as a person."

Around this time David also performs a short acoustic set at Middle Earth. He is booked by the club's box office girl Jenny Fabian,[5] after visiting her accompanied by Farthingale.

"They were hustling for a gig," said Fabian in 1990. "Finally he was told he could play at the end of the evening for a fiver. He sat on the stage and played, but nobody took any notice."

Jeff Dexter also remembered this performance as 'not terribly good... very disappointing'.

1. Situated close to Covent Garden Opera House, in the 19th century 43 King Street had been a popular music hall. Previously known as the Electric Garden, Middle Earth was housed in a series of connecting rooms in the basement, each featuring performance areas. Weekend all-night happenings were particularly popular. Middle Earth closed in 1969 after a police raid, which was followed by a violent attack from the local market porters, who saw the club as a den of iniquity. It moved on to a series of venues, including The Roundhouse.

2. "It's very easy to be a mime," said David in 1976. "There wasn't much competition. I was only reasonably good. My technique was quite poor, actually, but nobody really knew. I've got a very good body and it does things I want it to do, but I'm still not disciplined enough to ever compete with a Marcel Marceau. Mime helped me learn a lot about body language. That's all."

3. Born London, August 1946, Dexter began his career as a dancer and singer before establishing himself as one of London's top club DJs. He subsequently became a record producer, band manager, promoter and events organiser, involved in many of the major UK festivals in the late 60s, including some of the free festivals in London's Hyde Park. In 1971 he managed the group America and co-produced their first album, including the number one US hit 'Horse With No Name'.

4. Ray Stevenson chronicled the UK folk music scene and photographed David often until 1970. In 1976 Stevenson was drafted in by Sex Pistols manager Malcolm McLaren as group photographer and went on to depict the burgeoning mid-70s UK punk scene. Among his books is the photo-journal *The Sex Pistols File*. Stevenson's late brother Nils managed another leading punk act, Siouxsie & The Banshees.

5. Jenny Fabian achieved notoriety with her thinly veiled fiction *Groupie*, which revealed the seedy side of London's late 60s music scene.

Monday 20 May

David, Farthingale and Lindsay Kemp are seen briefly in the BBC2 broadcast of *The Pistol Shot*.

MARC BOLAN

By the time David and elfin rocker Marc Bolan appeared on the same bill together in May 1968 at the Royal Festival Hall, they had known each other for four years, a period in which their careers had developed along parallel lines.

David had first encountered Bolan in 1964 when he was still using his birth-name Mark Feld and, like David, looking to manager Les Conn for guidance.

The two teenagers had bonded during a spell picking up pin-money by painting and decorating Conn's Denmark Street offices (as Conn himself reflected, "I wonder how much it would have cost for the same work in the early 70s!") and like many of their generation journeyed along a similar route – from smart-suited mod to flower power, and the ethereal and spiritual concerns it embraced.

Bolan's street-smart outlook has been recalled with affection by David.

"It was Marc who introduced me to the idea of running around Carnaby Street and King's Road after the shops had closed to go through the dustbins," he said in 1993. "Because at that time they had shop-soiled shirts and things and the buttons were missing and whatever, they would just throw them away. By the end of the night you could have quite a good wardrobe together for free. Marc was full of these tricks, he was a real survivor."

Just as David had investigated proto-glam/garage in his brief association with The Riot Squad in 1967, that same year Bolan had been drafted by new manager Simon Napier-Bell into mod/pop-art group John's Children.

Bolan's retreat, with musical partner Steve Peregrin Took, later that year from this abrasive ensemble style into acoustic folk-rock duo Tyrannosaurus Rex was mirrored to some extent by David's reaction to the failure of his debut album: his engagement with mime and Buddhism found expression in the gentler approach of first Turquoise and then Feathers.

Producer Tony Visconti provided the glue which reactivated their relationship, producing Tyrannosaurus Rex's debut album, *My People Were Fair And Had Sky In Their Hair But Now They're Content To Wear Stars On Their Brows*, as he simultaneously started to build the foundations of arguably the most important musical association of David's career.

And David brought his visual sensibilities to Bolan, introducing him to his artist friend from the days of Bromley Tech and The Konrads and The King Bees, George Underwood, who provided the illustration that adorns Tyrannosaurus Rex's debut.

David and Bolan were at their closest in 1968 and 1969. An important factor was that David's friend's wife, June Bolan (who had at one stage worked with his hero Syd Barrett), was one of the few people in their circle who owned a car, in this case a battered and rather old Mini estate. During David's relationship with Hermione Farthingale, the two couples would occasionally escape London and stay at her parents' home in Sussex.

Bolan was also significant in providing David with live performance opportunities at a time when he had withdrawn from the gig circuit: twice as support, once in June 1968 at the Royal Festival Hall; and once in a short UK tour in February/March 69 as an outlet for his mime interests. By this time, their popularity had been boosted by constant championing by DJ John Peel on his late-night BBC Radio One show.

That year Peel was a visitor to David's Beckenham Arts Lab in the company of Took, while Bolan also performed a solo set there.

When Took was replaced in the summer of 1969 by Mickey Finn, the stage was set for Bolan's rise as one of the first stars of the post-hippy period. Featuring electric guitar and issued under the band's new, shortened name T.Rex, single 'Ride A White Swan' was a great success, setting the scene for glam.

Visconti's wall-of-sound production and the addition of drummer Bill Legend and bassist Steve Currie propelled T.Rex's 'Hot Love' to the top of the charts in 1971, and this was followed by a slew of hits, including chart-toppers 'Get It On', 'Telegram Sam' and 'Metal Guru'.

By 1973, however, Bolan and T.Rex's fortunes were failing as public interest moved in favour of David, whose media profile all but overshadowed his friend and rival.

Bolan largely disappeared from the scene in the ensuing years as a series of disappointing releases put paid to his commercial viability.

However, recognition of Bolan as a major influence by the punk generation of 1977 re-elevated him and, at the time of the car-crash in Barnes, south London that took his life in September that year, he had toured successfully and completed a new television series.

In the final episode, recorded a week before his death, David appeared, performing his single "Heroes" and jamming with Bolan and his band over the final credits.

TOP: Tyrannosaurus Rex, Marc Bolan and Steve Peregrin Took, photographed by Stevenson in Hermione Farthingale's back garden, summer 1968.

ABOVE: Bowie and Bolan jamming on Bolan's TV show, *Marc*, recorded at Granada TV's studios in Manchester, September 1977.

Sunday 26 May

David's recording for BBC Radio One's *Top Gear* is broadcast, though 'Silly Boy Blue' is held back until the session is repeated in June.

Produced by Bernie Andrews, the show is hosted by John Peel, who later confessed he was not struck by David's talents at this stage in his career.

"This was during the Anthony Newley period of his career, which I didn't care for a great deal," said Peel in 1988. "I played bits and pieces on the pirate ships and on *Top Gear*. The sessions he'd done for *Top Gear* by and large had been because Bernie Andrews was keen on his work. I wasn't, but I had no influence on who did sessions."

Thursday 30 May

David follows up on his meeting with impresario Ned Sherrin from last October to discuss the possibility of a role in the film version of *The Virgin Soldiers*.[1] Also present at Sherrin's apartment in Bywater Street off the King's Road is director John Dexter.[2]

The three dine at top Chelsea restaurant Alvaro's. It is agreed that David will test for the film. Sherrin wrote in his 2005 autobiography that he and Dexter agreed that David's 'strange quality was too elusive to capture on screen. Bowie weaved a fascinating story about his apparently glass eye. He insisted he had lost it in a fight with another man over a girl'.[3] After the meal, David heads to the BBC's Broadcasting House for an interview on radio magazine programme *Late Night Extra* with Barry Alldis.

1. Sherrin and Dexter also met Mick Jagger regarding a part in the film. 'There was talk of an important cameo,' wrote Sherrin in 2005. 'Mick didn't think it was "the right career move". John and I felt some relief.'

2. David met Dexter again in 1974 regarding the development of *Diamond Dogs* as a theatrical stage production. (▶ 25.3.74)

3. David often made up stories about his mismatched pupils. In 1969 he told friend Mary Finnigan that he had been born with the condition.

Monday 3 June

▶ David Bowie, Royal Festival Hall, South Bank, Waterloo, London.

Today is Whit Monday, a British holiday, and David is invited by Marc Bolan to perform a mime as the opening act for Tyrannosaurus Rex.

Also on the bill for this so-called Babylonian Mouthpiece Show are Roy Harper, Stefan Grossman and Vytas Serelis. Host is the omnipresent John Peel.

David performs 'Jetsun And The Eagle', the 12-minute piece debuted at Middle Earth a few weeks back about China's invasion of Tibet, set to a full-volume soundtrack which includes 'Silly Boy Blue'.

Watching from the wings are David's spiritual advisers, the Buddhist monks Trungpa Rinpoche and Chime Rinpoche, but the performance provokes at least one agitated audience member to stand up and shout: "No politics!"

David appears unconcerned, as Ken Pitt recalled

in 1981: "He was quite pleased, actually. David was glad to get any crowd reaction at the time."

However, David wrote in 2002: 'Word had got around that I would be doing this spot of propaganda and all the Maoists turned up and heckled me, waving their little red books in the air. Marc Bolan was delighted and thought it an unmitigated success. I was trembling with anger and went home sulking.'

Tuesday 4 – Wednesday 5 June

David continues to develop his cabaret act, which he has been developing to placate his father, who is becoming concerned about his financial circumstances.

The act is to consist of David performing a selection of his own songs and covers, complete with theatrical props. Pitt also provides input.

With a less than full engagement diary, around this time David starts occasional employment at a printers called Legastat at 57 Carey Street, in Holborn, close to the legal chambers of Lincoln's Inn.

He has been offered the job by a friend, John Eddowes, the son of the owner, and averages £6 per week operating the Rank Xerox copier in the basement with another young guy, Steven Pataky.

During downtime both play their guitars, in a country & western style according to colleagues.

This ad-hoc work suits David, enabling him to come and go between rehearsals and auditions.

It is during his time at Legastat that David makes a discovery about one of the Buddhist texts he has been studying – *The Rampa Story* by T. Lobsang Rampa (in reality British-born Cyril Hoskin).

While copying legal documents, David discovers papers revealing the truth. "That really brought me down," David said in 1992. "I thought, oh, he's a

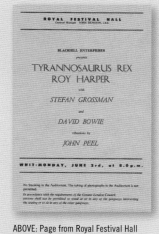

ABOVE: Page from Royal Festival Hall programme, 3 June.

LEFT: Kenneth Pitt Management promotion for David's upcoming mime performances.

In this year...

Sunday 26 May
BOOKING of The Rats as support for The Jeff Beck Group at the Cat-Balou Club, Grantham, Lincs. The Rats' guitarist Mick Ronson met his hero Beck backstage and was shown how to play the signature tune 'Jeff's Boogie'. Ronson asked Beck to slow his playing down so that he could follow the action. Beck replied: "I can't do it any slower – that's how it is!"

In 1973, Beck joined David, Ronson and the other Spiders From Mars on stage at the Hammersmith Odeon for a performance of a 'The Jean Genie'/'Love Me Do' medley and 'Round And Round'. Unhappy with his performance, Beck refused permission for the sequence he features in to be included in the Pennebaker film *Ziggy Stardust – The Motion Picture*. (▶ 3.7.73)

Tuesday 4 June
SHOOTING of Andy Warhol by radical feminist Valerie Solanas at his studio, The Factory.

TOP: Using the cut-out figures pictured with The Beatles (far right) David traced and copied them to create his own set for his proposed cabaret.

BOTTOM: In his bedroom at Manchester Street, the night before his haircut for *The Virgin Soliders*.

fake. Little did I know, creating characters would become a big part of my life too!"

As well as working at Legastat, David takes on agency work cleaning houses. "There was this endless period where I was scrubbing out people's kitchens," David said in 1993.

Friday 7 June

On another visit to London, German producer Gunther Schneider takes David to see the West End production of the Cy Coleman, Dorothy Fields and Neil Simon musical *Sweet Charity*.

Friday 14 June

Underground newspaper *International Times* reports on the Royal Festival Hall mime: 'David Bowie, although one or two drags were heckling

him, received the longest and loudest applause of all the performers, and he deserved it. It was a pity that he didn't have a longer set.'

Monday 17 June

David auditions for the musical *Hair*, which is due to transfer from Broadway to London's Shaftesbury Theatre in the autumn.[1]

1. *Hair* opened at the Shaftesbury Theatre on 27 September 1968 and ran until July 1973. The original London cast included David's friend Oscar Beuselinck, using his new stage name Paul Nicholas, as well as *Rocky Horror Show* creator Richard O'Brien and performer Tim Curry, along with singers Elaine Paige and Marsha Hunt.

Thursday 20 June

David's *Top Gear* recording is broadcast again by Radio One, this time with 'Silly Boy Blue', complete with his repeated interjection of the refrain 'Chime, Chime, Chime' during the chorus, as a tribute to friend Chime Youngdong Rinpoche.

Friday 21 June

The new single by Ken Pitt-managed The Beatstalkers is released. 'Rain Coloured Roses' features David's song 'Everything Is You' on the B-side.

Around this time David also writes and demos an unreleased song, 'A Social Kind Of Girl',[1] which is registered with publisher Essex Music.

1. 'A Social Kind Of Girl' was a rewrite of 'Summer Kind Of Love', which David had demoed at Manchester Street in early 67.

Friday 5 July

David undertakes a script reading for *The Virgin Soldiers* at Ned Sherrin's office in 53 Kensington Park Gardens, near Ladbroke Grove in west London.

BELOW: *Jacques Brel Is Alive And Well And Living In Paris*; the double album that turned David on to Jacques Brel.

BOTTOM: First and only draft of David's *Cabaret* script.

Friday 12 July

A film-test for a speaking role in *The Virgin Soldiers* is confirmed, so David attends a costume fitting at theatrical costumiers Bermans.

Musical *Jacques Brel Is Alive And Well And Living In Paris* opens at the Duchess Theatre in London's Covent Garden. During the five-week run David is in the audience in the company of Farthingale and an American friend, Calvin Mark Lee.[1]

"I went to see this show and was absolutely floored," David said in 2002. "And the subject matter – there were songs about venereal disease. I mean, (Brel) touched on subjects that you wouldn't hear in the English language, and it just blew me away."[2]

After the show Lee introduces David to Mort Shuman, the American songwriter who has translated Brel's songs for the musical.[3]

1. David first met Lee – a leading socialite of 60s London – in 1967 at Chappell's music shop in Bond Street. Known as 'The Doctor' – in reference to the three-year post-doctoral fellowship he had undertaken at Chelsea College of Science & Technology – Lee was born in 1936 in San Francisco of Chinese-American parentage.

Lee was among the signatories of the celebrity-led petition for the legalisation of cannabis published in *The Times* in July 1967, and worked at leading King's Road fashion outlet Dandie Fashions, where he supplemented his income by selling rare West Coast posters and artwork.

David occasionally visited him there, though contact was initially infrequent; they kept in touch by post for several months.

2. David's interest in Brel was sparked by Scott Walker's 1967 debut solo album *Scott*, which included the Belgian songwriter's 'Amsterdam' and 'My Death'.

Shortly after seeing the musical, David acquired the cast LP of the New York production, which included Shuman's translations of both of these songs. David regularly performed the latter on his farewell concert tour of 1973. His version of 'Amsterdam' was released as the B-side of 'Sorrow' in October 1973.

3. In 1973 Shuman invited David to perform 'Sorrow' on a French TV special. He did not take up the offer. (▶ 29.10.73)

Monday 15 July

While David takes part in rehearsals for *The Virgin Soldiers* at the Mayfair Gymnasium, in Paddington, west London, Pitt has been endeavouring to find him a new record label.

Pitt receives a letter from Peter Asher,[1] head of A&R at Apple Records: 'As we told you on the phone, Apple Records is not interested in signing David Bowie. The reason is that we don't feel he is what we're looking for at the moment.'

1. Born London 1944, brother of actress Jane and one half of singing duo Peter & Gordon, Asher went on to produce hit albums by such artists as James Taylor, Linda Ronstadt and Bonnie Raitt.

Tuesday 16 July

David attends a film test for *The Virgin Soldiers* at Twickenham Film Studios in south-west London.

Wednesday 17 July

Cartoon cut-outs of The Beatles,[1] used as a special foyer display for tonight's premiere of *Yellow Submarine* at London's Pavilion Theatre, are stored in the film's production offices below Ken Pitt's at 37 Curzon Street. With permission, Pitt borrows them so that he and David can trace copies as props for use in David's proposed cabaret act.[2]

1. In January 1975 David co-wrote and recorded 'Fame' with John Lennon. The only time he is known to have socialised with all three remaining Beatles is at Eric Clapton's wedding to Patti Boyd on 27 March 1979, at Bethel Temple in Tuscon, Arizona.

2. These were sold at auction for £1,300 in 1988. Pitt and David's copies were discarded many years before.

Thursday 1 August

▶ David Bowie, the Marquee Club, Wardour Street, London.

David makes his first appearance (since late 1966) at his old haunt as support for The Beatstalkers and Australian band The Groop[1] in a show booked by Ken Pitt.[2]

1. From Melbourne, The Groop's roadie was Ian 'Molly' Meldrum, who also worked as a journalist. He interviewed David in 1969 for a feature in Australian music paper *Go-Set*. In 1974 Meldrum became the presenter of ABC's enduring music TV show *Countdown*, on which David appeared a number of times.

2. On the same evening, just 100 yards from the Marquee, The Beatles recorded 'Hey Jude' at Trident Studios in St Anne's Court. The session from 5pm to 3am was a rare departure for the group from Abbey Road Studios; Trident was chosen for its state-of-the-art eight-track facilities. This session put the studio on the map and David became a frequent client, starting just a few months later.

The main studio was situated down a flight of stairs directly in front of the main entrance, with the mixing desk and tape decks two floors up. Trident closed in the late 80s; at this point it still housed the 100-year-old Bechstein grand piano which appeared on many important recordings, including several of David's. In the early 90s the building reverted from office usage back to being a studio.

David returned to have a nostalgic look around with journalist David Sinclair for a *Rolling Stone* article in 1993.

Thursday 15 August

David auditions his cabaret act for influential promoters. Using backing tapes, he performs a 27-minute set consisting of his own songs, 'Love You Till Tuesday', 'The Laughing Gnome' (with a gnome glove puppet), 'When I'm Five', 'When I Live My Dream', and his English-language version of 'Comme D'Habitude', 'Even A Fool Learns To Love'.

COLUMBIA BROADWAY MASTERWORKS

"...IMPASSIONED AND POWERFUL, CAPABLE OF STIRRING AN AUDIENCE ALMOST TO A FRENZY... SPLENDID ACTOR-SINGERS... I RECOMMEND 'JACQUES BREL' WHOLEHEARTEDLY."
—Clive Barnes, N.Y. Times/WQXR

JACQUES BREL IS ALIVE AND WELL AND LIVING IN PARIS

Production Conception, English Lyrics, Additional Material by ERIC BLAU and MORT SHUMAN
Based on Brel's Lyrics and Commentary
Music by JACQUES BREL

with
ELLY STONE
MORT SHUMAN
SHAWN ELLIOTT
ALICE WHITFIELD

Directed by MONI YAKIM
Musical Direction by MORT SHUMAN
Consultant to the Producers NAT SHAPIRO

PRODUCTION SUPERVISED BY ERIC BLAU

```
avid Bowie cabaret script. First draft.

Hand mic, straight in to

                    LOVE YOU TILL TUESDAY

Place mic on stand during "Well, I might stretch it till Wednesday"

Seg into        WHEN THE CIRCUS LEFT TOWN

Various lights to suit mime, moods, tempi etc


Spot opens up on top half of DB, he sings
                    WHEN I'M FIVE
Spot opens wider on action such as mime bits and other movements. Suggest flickering
light on fluttering butterfly wings mime. Spot closes to pencil on DB face as the
song ends and fades out slowly as he yawns. Total blackout - pause- then all
lights up for applause.
Take hand mic

Announcement: "That was a little boy of four just longing to grow up - but here's
```

ABOVE: Turquoise on stage at the Wigmore Hall, London, 16 September.

TOP: David's first true love, Hermione Farthingale (nee Dennis).

MIDDLE: David and Hermione as Turquoise, photographed at the Country Club, Hampstead, London, 20 October.

BOTTOM: Turquoise: Hermione, David and Tony Hill, photographed by Ray Stevenson at Clareville Grove. David and Hermione painted their room turquoise to align with their Buddhist philosophy.

There are also covers of The Beatles' 'When I'm Sixty-Four', 'Yellow Submarine' (featuring the copies of the life-size cut-out cartoon figures of The Beatles) and 'All You Need Is Love', as well as 'At Lunchtime – A Story Of Love' (by Liverpool poet Roger McGough)[1] and 'The Day The Circus Left Town'.[2]

First, in the afternoon, David showcases for Sydney Rose[3] at Pitt's Mayfair office.

In the evening, in mime make-up, he gives a second run-through for booking agents Harry Dawson and Michael Black at the Astor Club,[4] in Lansdowne Row, off Mayfair's Berkeley Square.

Dawson isn't keen. "I turned around to Ken and said, 'Let him have a good day job – he's never going to get anywhere'," Dawson recalled in 1988. "Ken said, 'You're out of your mind. I'm going to make him an international star.' Bowie basically did impressions at the time. I couldn't see it."

1. This Roger McGough poem was taken from the book *The Mersey Sound*, an anthology by three Liverpool poets, first published in 1967. 'At Lunchtime – A Story of Love' finds the poet, anticipating

an invented nuclear holocaust, trying to persuade a passenger on a bus to make love with him before the world ends at lunchtime. Coincidentally, the following month David appeared on the same bill as McGough's group, The Scaffold. (▸ 14.9.68)

2. Written by Carolyn Leigh and E.D. Thomas and recorded by Eartha Kitt for her 1955 RCA album *Down To Eartha*. David incorrectly titled the song 'When The Circus Left Town' in his script.

3. Sydney Rose (1939–2007). His career in the entertainment industry spanned over four decades – as a producer, writer, personal manager and agent, working with the likes of Judy Garland, Bob Hope, The Beatles and Frank Sinatra.

4. A basement hostess club owned by entrepreneur Bertie Green, the Astor was an occasional meeting place for underworld figures. In 1965 east London's notorious gang led by the Kray brothers used the Astor as the venue to settle differences with rival gang the Richardsons from south London. The talks broke down, but not before Richardsons' associate George Cornell unwisely insulted Ronnie Kray by calling him 'a big fat poof'. Three months later, Kray shot Cornell dead at the Blind Beggar pub in Whitechapel, east London, in one of the defining incidents of 60s British crime.

Friday 16 August

Dawson writes to Pitt: 'Just a line to let you know how much I enjoyed David Bowie's act last night. I will put my thinking cap on to see the best angle to approach for David regarding cabaret or review.'

This comes to nothing. "I never wanted David to go into cabaret at all," said Pitt in 2006. "It was simply a way of trying to help him to make some quick money to appease his father, which is why it didn't go further than the auditions we did that day."

Having been seen to at least try to explore his father's suggested route to bring in some much needed extra income, David comes under less pressure and the cabaret idea is dropped in favour of a new direction which coincides with a fresh phase in David's life; around this time he moves from Bromley into a small attic room with his girlfriend Hermione Farthingale at 22 Clareville Grove, near the busy Brompton Road in South Kensington, west London.

The room, which has been vacated by an acquaintance, becomes the base for short-lived new group Turquoise, a trio consisting of David, Farthingale and Tony Hill, a songwriter/guitarist who has recently been a member of British-based US group The Misunderstood (work permit issues have forced the others to return to America).

Hill has been introduced to the couple at the apartment of promoter/manager Wayne Bardell[1] in Abbey Road, St John's Wood, and has taken to them immediately. "It was funny listening to David and Hermione arguing about the merits of British music against West Coast," said Hill in 1992. "Dave really liked Hermione; she was a lovely girl."

The trio begin working up a set with all three harmonising on vocals and contributing guitar. They work on a number of new compositions of David's including a chiming track entitled 'Ching-A-Ling', the melody for which he has created by running the tape of an older song backwards through his reel-to-reel. Turquoise also work on a cover of Brel's 'Amsterdam'.

Among visitors to 22 Clareville Grove are photographer friends Ray Stevenson and Vernon Dewhurst,[2] who both take shots of the couple and Hill.

1. Bardell had worked at The Beatles' Apple Corp before forming west London-based Clearwater Promotions with partner Doug Smith. Clearwater handled bookings for such bands as Hawkwind, and Bardell went on to manage a number of acts, including Tony Hill's High Tide (▶ 16.10.69) and The Sutherland Brothers.

2. Dewhurst's photographs of David and Farthingale in the attic room were lost after the negatives, along with much of his archive, were stolen when he lived in Paris in the 70s.

Friday 30 August

In his first letter to David at Clareville Grove, Ken Pitt confirms he has been selected as an extra for *The Virgin Soldiers*. The Columbia Productions contract refers to his part as 'Soldier in recreation hall'.

Saturday 14 September

▶ Turquoise, The Roundhouse, Chalk Farm Road, Camden, London NW1.

Headlined by The Scaffold[1] and Pete Brown & His Battered Ornaments, this is an all-night benefit for community body The Neighbourhood Service organised by Blackhill Enterprises.[2]

Also on the bill are Ron Geesin, Terry Reid's Fantasia, David's friends Junior's Eyes, Principal Edwards Magic Theatre, Spider & The Stable, Gethsemane, Moonlight & Sun and DJ Pete Drummond.

Turquoise perform for 30 minutes at midnight. This is a significant evening; not only is this David's first performance at the major London rock venue but in the audience,[3] accompanying his friend Calvin Mark Lee, is young American Mary Angela Barnett, the woman who will become David's wife and accompany him on his stratospheric rise through the early 70s.

'Seeing David for the first time on stage at London's Roundhouse, my sympathies spilled over for Calvin,' she wrote in 1981. 'Who could not lose their heart to someone with so much charisma?

'A lean, blonde, enigmatic figure in a pastel-striped sweater and mustard-coloured sailor's flares and a voice as compelling that no one could turn a head, David captivated every single member of the audience. The exhilaration of that night left me reeling. It was my first rock'n'roll concert.'

In the early hours after the concert, David is introduced to Barnett in the crowded dressing room by Mark Lee. The meeting is brief, and it is more than six months before they meet again.

Ken Pitt is in the company of Marty Kristian, a young singer he met while on tour with Crispian St Peters in Australia.

Kristian is on a visit to the UK and occupying the top-floor bedroom at 39 Manchester Street vacated by David who only days earlier had removed his remaining property.

"I met David a few times at the flat," said Kristian in 1989. "I thought he was very nice but he seemed to have a bit of a chip on his shoulder, very angry that he hadn't made it. I remember jamming with him in the kitchen on acoustic guitars on a few numbers."

1. David and The Scaffold appeared on the same bill again in 1972. (▶ 18.2.72)

2. Run by Peter Jenner and Andrew King, Blackhill booked David a

number of times between 1968 and 1970. King, who also managed Syd Barrett, was introduced to David by Marc Bolan. Encouraged by Bolan, at some point in 1968 David auditioned for King, who decided against representing him.

3. David hinted that he once met Jim Morrison at The Roundhouse. The Doors and Jefferson Airplane appeared at the venue the previous week on 7 September. This was filmed by British broadcaster Granada TV for a documentary entitled *The Doors Are Open*.

Monday 16 September

▶ Turquoise, Wigmore Hall, 36 Wigmore Street, London W1.

The trio support The Strawbs in what is the second of the three documented appearances by Turquoise.

Thursday 19 September

David travels with Ken Pitt to Hamburg to record another appearance on TV show *4-3-2-1 Musik Für Junge Leute*.

TOP: David drawing at Tony Visconti's flat, summer 68.

ABOVE: David's sketch of Tony Hill (right) with friend.

ABOVE: David with John Hutchinson and son Christian at Clareville Grove.

RIGHT: In army fatigues for his role in *The Virgin Soldiers.*

Friday 20 September

David records a second appearance for the German pop show. During his stay, Pitt is approached by musician Gibson Kemp, the drummer who replaced Ringo Starr in Rory Storm & The Hurricanes in the early 60s and was a member of The Beatles-endorsed Paddy, Klaus & Gibson.

Pitt proposes to Kemp that he works with David to record one of his songs as a one-off single. Interested, Kemp says he will look into setting up a studio session in Hamburg soon. (▶7.11.68)

Saturday 21 September

David and Pitt return to London from Germany.

Monday 30 September

Pitt receives a reply to a letter he has sent to Jim Haynes, a leading figure in the British Underground whose Arts Lab venue in Drury Lane has set the tone for the convergence of creativity in London. 'Thank you for your letter regarding David Bowie,' writes

Haynes. 'As far as I am concerned, this is what the Arts Laboratory is all about, that is to be able to help people with new ideas.'

Tuesday 8 October

David and Pitt meet Pitt's former assistant Malcolm J. Thomson, now a film producer with his own company, Thomasso Films,[1] at Manchester Street to discuss ideas for a feature based on David.

1. *Love You Till Tuesday* was the only known production of Thomasso Films.

Sunday 20 October

▶ Turquoise, The Country Club, Haverstock Hill, Hampstead, London NW3.

At the invitation of Bob Harris,[1] co-founder of a new London listings magazine called *Time Out*, Turquoise appear at a benefit.

Also on the bill are the Third Ear Band, Doris Henderson, George 'Harmonica' Smith & Mike Vernon, Pegasus Blues, Mimi & Mouse and DJs Simon Stable and Pete Drummond.

1. Born Northampton, April 1946, Bob Harris (affectionately known as 'Whispering Bob' due to his understated delivery) became a Radio One DJ in 1970. From 1972 to 1978 he presented BBC2's TV rock programme *The Old Grey Whistle Test*. As of 2010 he was still hosting his own Radio Two music show.

Thursday 24 October

Produced by Tony Visconti, Turquoise record two songs at Trident Studios, Trident House, 17 St Anne's Court, Soho.[1] One is 'Ching-A-Ling'[2] and the other is a Tony Hill composition 'Back To Where You've Never Been'. Hill leaves amicably to form new group High Tide.[3] (▸ 28.2.70)

Meanwhile, David's guitarist from The Buzz, John 'Hutch' Hutchinson, has returned to the UK from Canada and written to David at his parents' Bromley home expressing a desire to collaborate musically.

"I dropped into Tony Hill's job," said Hutchinson in 1992. "I was a completely different guitar player into playing acoustic and listening to Leonard Cohen and Joni Mitchell and a lot of good Canadian songwriters." This interest in acoustic music slots neatly into David's evolving musical vision and, with Hutchinson on board, a new name for the trio is instituted: Feathers.

1. St Anne's Court is a passage linking Wardour Street to Dean Street in London's Soho district. In front of the studio is another narrow passage leading directly into Richmond Mews and the rear of the building which housed the Marquee Club and Marquee Recording Studio.

2. Tony Visconti did not clear these sessions with his bosses at New Breed Productions, Denny Cordell and David Platz. When they were billed for the studio time he came close to losing his job.

3. High Tide's line-up included violinist/keyboard player Simon House, who played in David's band for his 1978 tour and contributed to 1979 album *Lodger*.

Tuesday 29 October

Sporting a severe short-back-and-sides haircut and army fatigues, David starts a week as an extra without a speaking role on the set of *The Virgin Soldiers* at Twickenham Film Studios in St Margaret's Road, south-west London. Pitt photographs David wearing the fatigues the following day at 22 Clareville Grove.

Monday 4 November

David completes his stint on *The Virgin Soldiers* which will result in a split-second appearance in the film, being hoisted behind the NAAFI bar during a rowdy sequence. He receives £40 for his work.

Thursday 7 November – Friday 8 November

Gibson Kemp's session to record a new single for Phonogram/Philips in Munich with David is cancelled at the last minute by the German record company, despite the fact that contracts have been drawn up.

Sunday 10 November

David flies via Paris to Munich with Pitt for an appearance on another German pop show organised by his friend Gunther Schneider.

Monday 11 November

With his unfashionably short haircut, David performs a 'pantomime' routine and one song, thought to be 'When I Live My Dream' for the recording of ZDF TV's *Für Jeden Etwas Musik* (Music For Everyone).[1]

1. There is no known archive of this appearance. In earlier correspondence (18 September 1968) Pitt recorded that the Munich trip was for David to mime to Stravinsky's 'The Circus Polka'.

Tuesday 12 November

David and Pitt return to London for immediate talks with Malcolm Thomson about the proposed film. Meanwhile Feathers' rehearsals continue at 22 Clareville Grove.

Sunday 17 November

▸ Feathers, The Country Club, Hampstead, London.

Mis-billed as Turquoise, this is the first live manifestation of the collaboration between David, Farthingale and Hutchinson as Feathers, supporting jazz drummer Jon Hiseman's Colosseum.

Also on the same bill are the Third Ear Band and Doris Henderson. Feathers' set, which earns them £6, denotes a progression from Turquoise and bears the influence of Lindsay Kemp.

There are occasional dance sequences performed by Farthingale, as well as a 'mixed-media' presentation, with backing tapes handled by Hutchinson, and poetry and mime, including David's piece 'The Mask'. As in Turquoise, the three Feathers members all contribute vocals and play guitars.

Wednesday 20 November

The three members of Feathers meet Pitt at his Manchester Street apartment to discuss contractual terms and conditions for future bookings and recordings.

Wednesday 27 November

Overseen by Tony Visconti, Feathers re-record the backing vocals for 'Ching-A-Ling', though there is tension. Visconti demands that Hutchinson sing in a much higher register than he is used to. David, who feels that Hutchinson has been unnecessarily embarrassed, becomes annoyed. As a result Visconti mixes Hutchinson's vocals with those recorded by Hill a few weeks earlier.[1]

True to form, 'Ching-A-Ling' had been presented in final form to Hutchinson before they arrived at the studio. "David would always have a song completed before he played it," said Hutchinson in 1992. "They kept appearing like that, with a very basic guitar style and chords."

In attendance are Bob Harris and photographer Ray Stevenson, by this time a contributor at *Time Out*. Stevenson shoots images of the group at work and at rest; these are the only known photos of David recording in the studio where he will record his most notable work.

TOP: The original Buddhist block print design which David and Hermione kept framed above their fireplace at Clareville Grove (pictured opposite).

ABOVE: David as an extra in *The Virgin Soldiers*.

THIS PAGE

ABOVE: Waiting for recording time. Hermione Farthingale, David, Tony Visconti and John Hutchinson sit in the rest room at Trident prior to re-recording vocals on 'Ching-A-Ling', 27 November.

RIGHT: David at work for the second time in the studio. Here he will record his most famous recordings including 'Space Oddity' and LPs *Hunky Dory* and *Ziggy Stardust*. At this session, there was no need for instruments as only vocals were re-recorded. Left to right: Hutch, Hermione and David.

1. 'Ching-A-Ling' failed to stoke interest when canvassed around the music industry by publisher David Platz. It appeared in the 1969 film *Love You Till Tuesday* and was released in 1983, when the film was finally distributed. Elements of the song were absorbed into the much darker 'Saviour Machine', a track on 1970's *The Man Who Sold The World*.

Friday 6 December

▶ Feathers, The Arts Lab, Drury Lane, London WC2.
Arts Lab figurehead Jim Haynes delivers on the interest in David he recently expressed to Ken Pitt and books Feathers for his central London venue.

Feathers' performance includes a cover of 'Strawberry Fields', which segues into 'The Princes'

Parties', an unrecorded composition of David's.

The trio also perform 'Life Is A Circus', a song by four-piece vocal harmony group Djin, who have been recommended to David by Visconti.

Djin are led by songwriter and political activist Roger Bunn, who wrote 'Life Is A Circus' with lyricist John Mackie during a visit to Afghanistan.[1]

"I remember we passed the hat around," said Hutchinson in 1992. "We had a tape recorder; my job was to switch it on for the mime pieces. David did 'The Mask' alone and, for a couple of others, Hermione danced.

"During the mime pieces I played guitar along with the tape, making avant-garde noises, scraping the strings and tapping the guitar, things like that. I also had to learn some bits of poetry.

"David did (Roger McGough's) 'At Lunchtime – A Story of Love' and I did a couple of real short ones because I was quite embarrassed having to read poems out, sitting on a stool. It was a bit arty for me."

The Arts Lab is the springboard for many artists, including Yoko Ono and actor/writer Steven Berkoff – who, for a while, shares rooms with Lindsay Kemp and directs his first production there.

Even though he is later to describe it as 'pretentious', David will use the format for an arts project of his own within a year.

1. David recorded a demo version of the song in 1969. After recording the track with Djin at Visconti's Lexham Gardens flat, Bunn left the group and moved from London. David was offered the opportunity to replace Bunn, but was rejected after an audition since the other musicians didn't rate him.
When Bunn returned to London he became upset that David hadn't been accepted and visited 22 Clareville Grove to make amends.
"I went with John Mackie to see David at his tiny flat, which he was sharing with his girlfriend," said Bunn in 2003. "I was very embarrassed that the other group members had treated him so badly and I apologised to him. John Mackie had seen David perform 'Life Is A Circus' with his mixed-media group. I had no idea until now that he had recorded the song. What a great surprise."
In 1971, Bunn was in the first line-up of Roxy (soon to be Roxy Music), with Bryan Ferry, Brian Eno, Andy Mackay and Dexter Lloyd.

Saturday 7 December

▶ Feathers, University of Sussex, Falmer, East Sussex.
The group play an end-of-term concert for students, booked by a friend of Farthingale's.

David's Essex Music contract is extended a further six months by David Platz under an option allowing collection of unrecouped royalty payments.

Wednesday 11 December

An article by Sheila More in *The Times* newspaper features David, Feathers and Dana Gillespie under the heading 'The Restless Generation: 2'.

'David Bowie, 21, and Hermione Farthingale, 19, write and perform their own rather high-class brand of poetry, mime, folk-song and dance,' writes More. 'He is interested in Buddhism, she was trained as a classical ballet dancer. "My father tries so hard," said David. "But his upbringing was so different that we can't communicate. He and all his friends were in the army during the war – an experience I can't imagine

– and he takes naturally to iron discipline."'

The photograph accompanying the piece is by Clive Arrowsmith.[1]

1. Arrowsmith was responsible for the cover photograph for Mick Ronson's 1975 album *Play Don't Worry*.

Monday 16 December

As executive producer and financier, Malcolm Thomson prepares a memo regarding the new film with the working title *The David Bowie Show* (later retitled *Love You Till Tuesday*). Filming is to begin in January.

Friday 20 December

A booking for Feathers at the Birmingham Arts Lab in the Moseley & Balsall Heath Institute in the West Midlands city is cancelled by the promoter because of financial problems.

Tuesday 24 December

▶ David Bowie, The Magicians' Workshop, Falmouth, Cornwall.[1]

David has been booked, by friend Gerry Gill, to perform on Christmas Eve with The Steve Miller Band.[2]

David has connections to the coastal town; five years earlier his half-brother Terry had lived and worked in Falmouth for a year.

The Pistol Shot TV production featuring David, Farthingale and Kemp is repeated by BBC2.

1. In January 2007, the BBC News website invited people to email their memories of David to coincide with his 60th birthday celebrations. This recollection was posted by 'Timothy': 'An unknown David Bowie was appearing at the local hall in Falmouth, Cornwall.

I was one of a dozen people there. He sang Brel. I dragged five other people from the bar to see him. In the interval I went backstage and there he was crouched over a suitcase applying make-up. I asked questions and he was charming, humble. Later he joined us in the bar and did a duet with my chum Terry. He could not have been more friendly. He was well spoken, almost shy and conservatively dressed. A few months later 'Space Oddity' hit the charts.'

2. The US band formed in San Francisco in 1967 and at one time featured guitarist Boz Scaggs. After his departure and under Miller's stewardship the group scored hits in the 70s and 80s with such songs as 'Fly Like An Eagle' and 'Abracadabra'.

Wednesday 25 December

David spends Christmas Day with Gill and friends at his home, The Coach House in Pool near Redruth, Cornwall.

Thursday 26 December

▶ David Bowie, The Magicians' Workshop, Falmouth, Cornwall.

For this second performance at the venue, David is backed by drummer/percussionist Keef Hartley.[1]

After the show David makes his way back to London to celebrate the New Year with Farthingale. There is much to ponder: 1968 is the first year of his career as a professional musician in which he has not released any records. This will not happen again for nearly a decade-and-a-half.

1. Born Keith Hartley, 8 April 1944, in Preston, Lancs. His drumming career began as one of the successors of Ringo Starr in Rory Storm & the Hurricanes. He played and recorded with The Artwoods – and met David on the R&B circuit in 1965 – then became John Mayall's drummer before forming The Keef Hartley (Big) Band, playing Woodstock Festival in 1969. He left the music business to set up a joinery and cabinet-making business. Hartley is now retired and in 2010 was living in Preston.

1969

KEN Pitt urges David to create a special piece of music for the TV film *Love You Till Tuesday*. David composes what turns out to be 'Space Oddity', inspired by a viewing of *2001: A Space Odyssey*.

Filming and soundtrack recording go well, although TV networks will show no interest in the film. Friction between David and Hermione Farthingale reveals that their relationship is over.

Surreptitious recording of an album demo meets with an intrigued response from record company executives; meanwhile, the heartbroken David is moving in with Mary Finnigan in Beckenham.

Just as the couple are hatching plans to open a folk club, David's life is transformed when he meets Angie Barnett. She is to have a profound influence on him in the coming years.

David and Finnigan's Beckenham Arts Lab opens its doors, developing out of the folk club, and it spawns a fondly remembered free festival.

Mercury offers a one-album deal and are keen to release 'Space Oddity' to coincide with the Apollo moon landings.

The single is released to critical acclaim but initially to little response from music fans. Meanwhile, recording of David's second album starts at London's Trident Studios.

David's grief over the death of his father does not stop his work on the album or the free festival. He and Angie move into Victorian villa Haddon Hall.

At last, 'Space Oddity' starts to sell. David's first *Top Of The Pops* appearance provides the impetus for the record to peak at number five.

The album – like the 1967 offering titled *David Bowie* – has been recorded with Tony Visconti, Gus Dudgeon and musicians from Junior's Eyes. It receives a mixed critical response.

Friday 10 January

The Beatstalkers release 'Little Boy'/'When I'm Five', the second single by the Scottish group to feature a composition of David's on the B-side.

"They met David in my office and heard his demonstration tapes being played," said manager Ken Pitt in 1983.

Produced by Tony Reeves and issued by CBS, the single is not a success and the members of The Beatstalkers go their separate ways soon after its release.

Guitarist Alan Mair, who has fashion ambitions and designed the group's outfits, remains in London, working out of a spare room in Pitt's Curzon Street office.

"Ken was a really nice man," said Mair[1] in 1992. "When the band folded, he said I could work out of his office making clothes if I answered his phone. I got to know David well, as he was always in and out of there. No matter who was there and whatever the circumstance, if he felt like singing he would just do it. He was never inhibited, he would just sing. I always found that very impressive."

Mair is also privy to some of the creative tensions between artist and manager. "I know that David became a bit of a handful for Ken," he said. "David began to ignore the ideas Ken was putting forward, trying to encourage him to be more daring on stage, that kind of thing."

1. After working from Pitt's office, Mair opened a clothing stall in fashionable Kensington Market at 49 Kensington High Street. He established a reputation for his footwear and was often visited by David, who received a pair of boots as a gift even after the late 1969 success of 'Space Oddity'.

The stall opposite Mair's was run by Farrokh Bulsara, better known as Freddie Mercury of Queen. "It's amazing to think how famous those guys would become, both chatting on my stall," said Mair in 1992. Over a two-year period in the early 70s, Mair employed Mercury as a sales assistant.

Monday 13 January

David meets dance instructor Timothy Hest at the Covent Garden Dance Centre, and undertakes a short course in 'free movement' in preparation for the filming of the Ken Pitt-funded project, now titled *Love You Till Tuesday*.

By this time David has completed a new song in response to Pitt's urging for 'a very special piece of material' for the film. This is 'Space Oddity', inspired by a viewing of Stanley Kubrick's new film *2001: A Space Odyssey* while stoned.

Saturday 18 January

David's November appearance on German TV show *Für Jeden Etwas Musik* is repeated by broadcaster ZDF.

Wednesday 22 January

David is featured in the filming of a TV commercial for Lyons Maid's Luv ice lolly. The actors convene at 7 Eccleston Square in Victoria, central London, and the advert is shot in monochrome on a London double-decker bus and at a mocked-up live concert; David appears holding the product while climbing the stairs of the bus, and also as a singer/guitarist in the 'band'.

Friday 24 January

Recording begins at Trident on the soundtrack for the TV film (no broadcaster has yet committed itself to screening it, although there s some interest in a German-language version from David's TV producer friend Gunther Schneider). Using backing tracks from the debut album, David begins to record his German vocals for 'Love You Till Tuesday' and 'When I Live My Dream'. Overseeing the session is Jonathan Weston,[1] who is working on the film's soundtrack.

Although he continues to be close to David and is his intended producer should a new record deal materialise, Tony Visconti is neither involved in the film nor keen on 'Space Oddity'.

1. Weston was a partner with Denny Cordell in New Breed Management, which employed Tony Visconti. Weston also managed Procol Harum for a period and produced the promo film for their 1967 worldwide hit 'A Whiter Shade Of Pale'.

Saturday 25 January

Soundtrack recording at Trident continues. Between 5pm and 10pm, David, John Hutchinson and Hermione Farthingale record a new vocal track for 'Sell Me A Coat'.

Sunday 26 January

Filming of *Love You Till Tuesday* begins in north London parkland Hampstead Heath with director Malcolm J. Thomson and his small crew. As executive producer, Pitt has agreed a budget of £6,977 with Thomson's production house Thomasso Films, and seven days are set aside for shooting. The plan is to present the completed project to a TV network for broadcast.

David wears hair extensions to disguise his military cut from *The Virgin Soldiers* for a sequence sound-tracked by his song 'When I Live My Dream'.

Farthingale and Hutchinson also appear as figures

PREVIOUS SPREAD: In Paddington Street Gardens, photographed by Kenneth Pitt.

THIS PAGE

ABOVE: David and Hermione Farthingale filming *Love You Till Tuesday* on Hampstead Heath, 26 January.

in the Heath's woodland.

"It was a bitterly cold day and, when they were not needed for filming, Hermione and David remained huddled up in the back of the car," said Pitt in 1983.

Tuesday 28 January

David receives instruction in German pronunciation from Gunther Schneider's secretary Lisa Busch in preparation for the re-recording of vocals for translations of 'When I Live My Dream' (Mit In Deinem Traum) and 'Love You Till Tuesday' (Liebe Dich Bis Dienstag), as well as for the voiceover for the mime 'The Mask'.

The following day (between 2pm and 4pm) he records both German-language songs and 'The Mask' monologue[1] at Trident Studios.

1. The German-language version of 'The Mask' monologue has never been issued. A German version of 'Let Me Sleep Beside You' was planned but not recorded.

Saturday 1 February

Love You Till Tuesday filming moves to Clarence Studios at 7 College Approach, Greenwich.

David, Farthingale and Hutchinson are filmed performing 'Sell Me A Coat' and 'Ching-A-Ling'. David and Hutchinson wear flamboyant large-collared, puff-sleeved shirts with matching white shoes and trousers and Farthingale is in a filmy patterned dress.

In the resulting film, Malcolm J. Thomson intercuts images of such hip London boutiques as Mr Fish[1] at the beginning of 'Sell Me A Coat', while the trio are filmed seated on the shop's cushions for 'Ching-A-Ling', in which Farthingale and Hutchinson trade verses on lead vocals.

In the morning there is an argument in the dressing room between David and Farthingale; it transpires that, after a year, she has put an end to their relationship.[2] The reasons for the breakdown are not revealed. "I was madly in love last year," said David in 1970. "But the gigs got in the way."

1. Avant-garde tailor Michael Fish was responsible for the resurgence of the wide 'kipper tie' in the 60s and such outfits as the so-called 'man-dress' worn by David on the UK cover of *The Man Who Sold the World*. He also designed the white frock-coated outfit worn by Mick Jagger for The Rolling Stones' free concert in London's Hyde Park in July 1969.

2. Ken Pitt believes the relationship was over before filming of *Love You Till Tuesday* began, and that Farthingale had agreed to appear in the film as a gesture to David.

For a period, David attempted to keep open the lines of communication in the hope of a reunion, openly sending her messages in such songs as 1969's 'Letter To Hermione'.

David subsequently said that, after filming of *Love You Till Tuesday* ended, Farthingale fell in love with dancer Stephen Reinhardt while appearing as an extra on location for the 1970's film adaptation of musical *Song Of Norway*.

David has since encountered Farthingale just once, in 1972 or 1973. At that time she was working as a cartographer, assisting her anthropologist boyfriend in mapping out previously uncharted rivers in South America.

Sunday 2 February

'Space Oddity' is recorded at Morgan Studios, High Road, Willesden, London.

This version is for the TV film soundtrack;[1] David and Hutchinson contribute vocals and guitars, backed by Dave Clague (bass), Tat Meager (drums) and Colin Wood (Hammond organ, Mellotron, flute).[2] Jonathan Weston is again handling production.

1. Issued for the first time in 1984 on the hotch-potch *Love You Till Tuesday* album accompanying the film's eventual release that year. With this early version of 'Space Oddity' as its centrepiece, the album is compiled of songs from the film, the Turquoise/Feathers period and earlier.

These include the second version of 'Love You Till Tuesday' from 1967, which was remixed for the film and omitted the 'Hearts And Flowers' ending; 'Ching-A-Ling' from the November 1968 sessions (also abridged for the film); and David's original 'Sell Me A Coat' backing track to which Feathers added a new set of vocals. 'When I'm Five' stems from David's second BBC Radio session of May 1968 (the only studio version he made of this song) and 'Rubber Band' is a remix of the version he re-recorded for his first album *David Bowie*.

'Let Me Sleep Beside You' is one of two tracks (the other being 'Karma Man') of David's to be produced by Tony Visconti (and was first issued on *The World Of David Bowie* of March 1970), while 'When I Live My Dream' saw first light on this compilation. This was David's second recording of the song from February 1967 and, as with 'Love You Till Tuesday', it featured a new arrangement by Ivor Raymonde.

1992 saw the release of another compilation titled *Love You Till Tuesday* by Pickwick Music. This also featured the film version of 'Space Oddity', including the extended ending. This album also contained the full version of 'Ching-A-Ling', with an extra verse sung by David released for the first time.

2. Clague, Meager and Wood joined singer-songwriter Kevin Coyne in the band Siren in 1969. Clague was in The Bonzo Dog Doo-Dah Band between 1967 and 1968, and he and Meager later became members of the Bonzos' Roger Ruskin Spear & His Giant Orchestral Wardrobe. This ensemble appeared on the same bill as David at The Roundhouse in July 1970.

Monday 3 February

Filming resumes at Clarence Studios with David performing 'Rubber Band' and the film's title piece 'Love You Till Tuesday'.

Tuesday 4 February

David is filmed performing *Love Me Till Tuesday* highlight 'Let Me Sleep Beside You' as well as scenes

BELOW: 'In 1910 I was so handsome and so strong...' David filming 'Rubber Band' in Greenwich, London.

for 'When I Live My Dream'. He wears the same blue floral shirt[1] as in 'Sell Me A Coat' and 'Ching-A-Ling'. This will become a staple of TV and live appearances over the coming months.

1. Pitt subsequently gave the shirt to another of his clients, Marty Kristian. It was in the singer's possession until the early 80s when his wife, unaware of the garment's history, donated it to a charity shop.

Wednesday 5 February

In white ruffled shirt over white leotard and full make-up, David spends the entire day filming the mime 'The Mask'.

Thursday 6 February

The 'Space Oddity' sequence is filmed at Clarence Studios. David plays two parts – the T-shirted 'ground control' figure in round Lennon-esque spectacles and 'Major Tom' in a silver suit, blue visor and breast plate.[1]

Inflatable clear plastic furniture and camera effects simulate take-off, and the segment in which the character loses contact and floats through space features actress Samantha Bond and the film's production assistant Suzanne Mercer as celestial sirens in curly blonde wigs and diaphanous gowns.[2]

1. Ken Pitt later auctioned the multi-coloured space boots worn by David in the shoot for charity. The rest of the production clothing was sold.

2. The 'Space Oddity' segment became the best-known element of *Love You Till Tuesday* when it was released to broadcasters as a promo film for RCA's reissue of the single, which reached number one in the UK charts in November 1975.

Friday 7 February

Final touches to the 'Space Oddity' segment are shot as *Love Me Till Tuesday* wraps with a final day of filming, which includes David emulating a child's expressions for 'When I'm Five', the scene completed by a birthday cake and giant prop candles.

Tuesday 11 February

❱ David Bowie & Hutch, Sussex University, Falmer, East Sussex.

With Farthingale no longer in David's life, David and Hutchinson make the first of a few appearances as a duo, performing songs from the Turquoise and Feathers repertoire as well as new compositions such as 'Space Oddity', 'Janine', 'Love Song' and 'Lover

To The Dawn',[1] the last two with Hutchinson on lead vocals.

1. Some of the lyrics and melody of this song were folded into 'Cygnet Committee', another track on 1969's *David Bowie*.

Friday 14 February

Featuring a large photo of David, Samantha Bond and Suzanne Mercer in costume on the *Love You Till Tuesday* set, the London *Evening News* runs a story anticipating distribution deals for the film: 'Malcolm Thomson, who is producing it, says: "The sale to Germany is just the start. We estimate the total from abroad will be in the region of £50,000."'

Saturday 15 February

❱ David Bowie, Birmingham Town Hall, Birmingham.

David travels with Ken Pitt to the city in the heart of England for tonight's solo mime appearance as one of the support acts on the five-date 'Tyrannosaurus Rex & Friends' UK tour.

Also on the bill are sitar player Vytas Serelis; compère is once again DJ John Peel.

David performs a 15-minute mime backed by high volume sound-effect tapes, some of which have been prepared with Tony Visconti.

"When Marc started cracking it as Tyrannosaurus Rex, he had the good grace to let me take the support spot on quite a few shows," David later said.

Sunday 16 February

❱ David Bowie, Fairfield Halls, Croydon, Surrey.

Thursday 20 February

At 10.30am David auditions again for the musical *Hair* at London's Shaftesbury Theatre. In the evening he attends a performance of the show accompanied by Pitt (with whom he is again residing, having moved from 22 Clareville Grove after the split with Farthingale).

David is unimpressed with the production, but receives a call-back for another audition.

Saturday 22 February

❱ David Bowie, Manchester Free Trade Hall, Peter Street, Manchester.

David travels between dates on the Tyrannosaurus Rex tour with John Peel, who dislikes the mime act and encourages him to give it up and concentrate on music.

Sunday 23 February

❱ David Bowie, Colston Hall, 13 Colston Street, Bristol, Avon.

Although billed, David does not appear at this Bristol concert as one of Tyrannosaurus Rex's 'friends'. Instead, Fairport Convention are support.

Friday 28 February

David auditions unsuccessfully yet again for a part in *Hair*.

Saturday 1 March

▶ David Bowie, Philharmonic Hall, Hope Street, Liverpool.

David is back on the bill performing his mime for the Tyrannosaurus Rex tour.

Monday 3 March

David and Pitt visit London's Criterion Theatre to witness *Brief Lives*, a one-man show by all-round performer Roy Dotrice.[1] After the show David tells Pitt, "Now that's what I call theatre."

1. Born 26 May 1923. A British actor working mainly in the theatre. In 2008 he toured in a revival of *Brief Lives*. In 1974 David shared billing with Dotrice on US prime-time TV show *The Dick Cavett Show*.

Saturday 8 March

▶ David Bowie, Brighton Dome, 29 New Road, Brighton, East Sussex.

This is the last night of the Tyrannosaurus Rex tour.

David's friend Calvin Mark Lee is keen to champion the new music David is writing, and is in a position to act, having become assistant European director under head honcho Lou Reizner[1] at the London office of Mercury Records.

Working out of Mercury's UK HQ at 7 Albert Gate Court, 124 Knightsbridge, Lee starts a campaign for his label to sign David (though Ken Pitt is initially unaware of Lee's association with Mercury).

In an attempt to circumvent his boss Reizner's antipathy to David's music, Lee arranges for David and Hutchinson to surreptitiously record a 10-track demo for Mercury executives in the US.

The songs are taped in Reizner's office. "It was the only place we knew with good recording equipment we could use for free," said Lee in 2009.

The songs are picked from the set the duo have been performing together: 'Space Oddity', 'Janine', 'An Occasional Dream', 'Conversation Piece', 'Ching-A-Ling', 'I'm Not Quite',[2] 'Love Song' (with the lead vocal taken by Hutchinson),[3] 'When I'm Five', 'Lover To The Dawn' and 'Life Is A Circus'. (▶ 6.12.68)

There is much levity. The pair chat between tracks, pretending to spot passing celebrities and, at one stage, David tells Hutch, "Hey, we're starting an Arts Lab, isn't that a gas!"

Subsequently Lee sends the 10-track demo tape to Mercury's Chicago head office. Here he finds two allies, English-born head of product Simon Hayes and publicity director Ron Oberman. (▶ 23.1.71)

All the songs on the demo are David's compositions apart from 'Love Song',[4] which has been written by David's singer-songwriter friend Lesley Duncan, who has introduced him to a UFO-watch-cum-meditation group based in Redington Road, Hampstead. David is attending the group's Tuesday evening meetings, where he reacquaints himself with DJ/promoter Jeff Dexter.

After evenings of discussion and meditation, the group usually walk to the top of Hampstead Heath and watch the sky for unusual celestial activity.

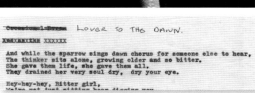

Initially sceptical, Tony Visconti joins David in attending the group meetings.

1. Lou Reizner (1934–1977) also signed Rod Stewart to Mercury and was executive producer of his first three solo albums before going on to oversee orchestral productions including The Who's *Tommy* and an all-star version of *Sgt Pepper's Lonely Hearts Club Band*. It has been claimed that Reizner was not a fan of David's because he had also, at one time, been the boyfriend of Angela Barnett (Angie Bowie).

2. 'I'm Not Quite' was soon retitled 'Letter To Hermione'.

3. On this recording, David only sang half of the lyrics he wrote for 'Lover To The Dawn'. This version reveals traces of Paul Simon's 'Mrs Robinson'.

4. Lesley Duncan recorded 'Love Song' as the B-side on her 1969 RCA single 'A Road To Nowhere'. Elton John duetted with her for his cover of the song on his 1970 album *Tumbleweed Connection*. In 1969 David worked on an unrecorded song of his own, titled 'Love Song'.

OPPOSITE PAGE

TOP: One of *Love You Till Tuesday*'s highlights, David performing in the style of Elvis.

BOTTOM: Cover of Malcolm J. Thomson's production notes for David's first promotional film, *Love You Till Tuesday*.

BOTTOM RIGHT: Performing 'The Mask'.

THIS PAGE

TOP LEFT: Filming 'Space Oddity'.

TOP RIGHT: *Evening News* article from 14 February.

MIDDLE LEFT: David as a visored Major Tom.

BOTTOM LEFT: 'Lover To The Dawn' lyric with David's hand-written note changing the title from 'Occasional Dream'.

ABOVE: Small note referring to a Michael Armstrong stage revue.

RIGHT: In the front room of 39 Manchester Street.

BELOW: Extract from David's letter to Ken Pitt, dated 9 April.

```
                                              24, Foxgrove Road
                                              Beckenham
                                              Kent.
650 3432
                                      Wed. April 9th 1969
Dear Ken,
         That ( foxgrove) is the new address from Monday 14th. I better
point out, just to be safe, that the phone is ex-directory so maybe
personal messages should be passed on via you or my folks.
         How do you dig the new communication-media. I thought it could be
a new angle on our "getting it together" path. It also gives me a good
platform on which to collocate the various bits of thought that collect,
or rather, drift through my mind. I believe it's called a letter.
```

Saturday 22 March
ENTRY of The Who's 'Pinball Wizard' into the UK singles chart. This was a key track on their May 1969 concept album *Tommy*, which was performed for the first time live at the Royal Albert Hall in the summer of 1969; David was in the audience. (▸ 5.7.69)

April
RELEASE of Ohio Players single titled 'Here Today And Gone Tomorrow'/'Bad Bargain' in the UK, which was performed by David on his 1974 Diamond Dogs tour and appeared as a bonus track (retitled 'Here Today, Gone Tomorrow') on the 1990 and 2005 reissues of the 1975 album *David Live*.

Thursday 10 April
RECORDING starts on Syd Barrett's album *The Madcap Laughs* at Abbey Road. The cover photo was taken by Mick Rock as his first music business commission; Rock later worked with David as his personal photographer. (▸ 17.3.72)

Monday 10 March

David is at Impel Productions at 119-125 Wardour Street in Soho as post-production continues on *Love You Till Tuesday*.

Tuesday 11 March

▶ David Bowie & Hutch, University of Surrey, Battersea Park Road, London SW11.

The duo give a 35-minute performance as part of the Guildford Arts Festival.[1] Ken Pitt attends and, of all the performances by David he is to see, this is one of the most memorable, since David's self-assured performance displays a clear advance in his stage technique (possibly inspired by Roy Dotrice's one-man show he witnessed the previous week).

For the first time, David uses Hutchinson as the straight man for an impromptu comedy routine: "This is Hutch. He's my friend. I found him in the classified ads in *Time Out* — under macrobiotics."

1. The reason this festival was named after a town 30 miles to the south west of London is because the venue – previously the Battersea Polytechnic Institute – was in the process of moving to a new campus in Guildford. Among those working on publicity for David and Hutchinson's appearance at this festival was photographer Adrian Boot, who went on to take classic shots of such artists as Bob Marley and The Sex Pistols.

Saturday 15 March

▶ David Bowie & Hutch, Guildford, Surrey.

This performance is not connected with the Guildford Arts Festival in Battersea.

David appears on Bromley's electoral register for the first time, registered as David R. Jones, along with his mother and father at 4 Plaistow Grove.

David has moved on from Pitt's Manchester Street abode, initially back to his family home in Bromley and then to poet Barrie Jackson and his artist wife Christina's apartment at 24 Foxgrove Road in nearby Beckenham. He has known Barrie since they were childhood neighbours in Plaistow Grove.[1]

This retreat back to his roots has been spurred by David's jaded experiences of living in London as well as his broken heart over the collapse of the relationship with Farthingale.

1. Jackson had also been a member of the 18th Bromley Cub Scouts with David and George Underwood when they were children, and appeared with both of them in 1964 on the *Tonight* TV show's coverage of The Society For The Prevention Of Cruelty To Long-Haired Men.

Tuesday 18 March

Atlantic Records founder Ahmet Ertegun[1] responds with interest to an approach by Ken Pitt about David and Hutchinson's songs.

1. Ertegun (1923–2006) co-founded Atlantic Records with his brother Nesuhi in 1947. Having achieved great success with rock, soul and R&B acts, he changed direction to rock and in 1968 famously signed the newly formed Led Zeppelin and three years later the more established Rolling Stones. After his death aged 83, the three remaining Led Zeppelin members reformed to perform a one-off tribute concert in his memory at London's O2 Arena.

Friday 21 March

▶ David Bowie & Hutch, Bishop Grosseteste College, Newport Road, Newport, Lincoln.

In the afternoon David has a meeting with young director Stephen Frears[1] of Yorkshire TV at 7 Portman Place, in central London, before heading off to Lincoln to perform two 35-minute sets.

Feathers had been booked to appear so, expecting a mixed-media presentation, the promoter asks David to include 'as much mime as possible'.[2]

1. Stephen Frears (born 20 June 1941), British television and film director; films include *Prick Up Your Ears* (1987), *Dangerous Liaisons* (1988), *High Fidelity* (2000) and *Dirty Pretty Things* (2003).
2. This is the last documented performance by the duo. However, David personally booked a few more gigs for them over the next couple of weeks. For one, in north London, the two travelled to the venue by underground. In 1990 Hutchinson recalled David wearing soccer boots – 'studs and all' – during the journey and throughout the gig. At another London date they were visited by singer Robert Palmer, a friend of Hutchinson's from his hometown, Scarborough. Palmer (1949–2003) later fronted rock-blues outfit Vinegar Joe before achieving solo success with such hits as 1986's 'Addicted To Love'.

Tuesday 25 March

David attends a stage revue script meeting with producer/director Michael Armstrong (who had featured him in the 1967 short *The Image*).

David is disappointed with what is on offer and writes to Pitt: 'So here is the script (?) I think you

will agree that we should think very carefully about the pro's and con's of going into this venture. As it stands, this revue can do nobody in the cast anything but harm. It stinks.' Concluding, 'Remember that I have a photo session tonight. So I won't have time to cook'.

Monday 31 March

Ken Pitt follows up on the correspondence with Atlantic's Ahmet Ertegun with a meeting at the label's London offices. He plays UK managing director Frank Fenter[1] the demo tape recorded at Reizner's office.

1. Pitt related in 1983 that Fenter later told him the music was "not my cup of tea".

Wednesday 9 April

In a letter to Pitt informing him of his new address, David tells him of recent record company interest: 'I can't walk into Mercury without some guy piping up with "Hey, America have instructed us to get you signed up. Like Pronto" (Simon Hayes – London rep).'[1]

The letter also discusses a potential residency for David and Hutchinson at the Tuesday folk evenings held at the Sir Christopher Wren pub near St Paul's Cathedral in the City of London. These, David writes, 'will provide a great bandbox/fan-maker (LPs for the buying of) for "David Bowie and Hutch".'[2]

David's choice of address at the top of the letter is significant: Flat 1, 24 Foxgrove Road, Beckenham.

This is the home of Mary Finnigan, a freelance writer and underground press journalist who is a neighbour of David's friends the Jacksons. She lives on the ground floor of the property with her two children.

"I was sitting in the garden one sunny afternoon when I heard someone playing guitar from the upstairs window," said Finnigan in 1986. "I shouted up to find out who it was, and David appeared."

He and Finnigan become lovers, and he moves into her flat, exerting a profound influence over her, in particular encouraging her interest in Buddhism.

Another person who is lodging at Finnigan's apartment in this period is David's friend Spud Murphy, who also attends the Buddhist centre at Samye-Ling on David's suggestion.

Soon David and Finnigan hatch a plan to open a folk club in the back room of local pub The Three Tuns. The intention is that this will attract performers from London and stimulate local creativity, in line with the arts labs which have sprung up around the country inspired by the original operated in Covent Garden by underground figure Jim Haynes. It will also help pay the rent on the Foxgrove Road flat.

In the evening David, Calvin Mark Lee and his date Angela Barnett are at music biz haunt The Speakeasy in Margaret Street in London's West End for the invitation-only debut concert performance by King Crimson, the progressive rock group led by guitarist Robert Fripp.[3]

David is drawn to the confident and attractive 19-year-old Barnett: "David asked me if I could jive, so I replied, 'Certainly'," recalled the woman who would become Angie Bowie in 1970. "So we got up and started to dance. It was a fantastic night."

Such is the attraction between the two they spend the night together at Tony Visconti's flat in Lexham Gardens.

1. A reference to the Chicago-based Mercury executive who was immediately impressed with the demo tape.

2. The Sir Christopher Wren booking didn't materialise. Lack of live work soon conspired with family commitments to force Hutchinson to leave the music business and return to Scarborough in the spring of 1968 and pick up his trade as a draughtsman. (▸19.1.73)

3. Robert Fripp, born 16 May 1946 in Wimborne Minster, Dorset, had set up The Speakeasy date to attract interest from record companies; Lee was among those keen on signing the act. In the event King Crimson was snapped up by management/publishing company EG, which released the group's groundbreaking 1969 debut *In The Court Of The Crimson King* via Island Records. Fripp led the group as the only constant in its shifting membership, and collaborated with Brian Eno on such explorations as 1973's *No Pussyfooting*. In 1977, during the recording sessions for David's album *"Heroes"*, Fripp played guitar on the hit single title track. Fripp also contributed to David's 1980 album *Scary Monsters*.

Thursday 10 April

This evening David and Angie go on their first date. Soon he is inviting her back to Finnigan's Beckenham apartment.

Finnigan is quick to recognise that someone else has entered his life. Accustomed to David's untidiness, she returns home one day to find the flat clean and neat and guesses correctly that another woman has been there.

Although Finnigan[1] is unhappy at this development, she is soon won over and becomes a close friend of Angie's, as well as remaining on good terms with David as they prepare for the opening of their folk

TOP LEFT: David and Hutch go Simon & Garfunkel, approx March 69. Velvet and Edwardian ruff, a particular favourite for David in the 60s. This is the new image the duo debuted at the University of Surrey on 11 March.

TOP RIGHT: The Three Tuns – a public house in 1969, a restaurant in 2010.

ABOVE: Basic 'Folk Lab' advert from an early Arts Lab newsletter.

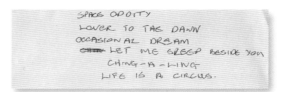

TOP RIGHT: A short set list, written by David.

TOP LEFT: David performing at the Beckenham Arts Lab.

ABOVE: Appearing on BBC2's *Colour Me Pop*, recorded 10 May and broadcast 14 June.

club at The Three Tuns.

1. Finnigan wrote the script for Stage Broadcast's 1986 radio documentary *The David Bowie Story*, produced by Kerry Juby and narrated by Angie.

Monday 14 April

Ken Pitt meets Mercury's Simon Hayes to discuss a deal for David. With Calvin Mark Lee, they view a private screening of *Love You Till Tuesday*. "It was really due to Simon Hayes that David got the deal with Mercury," said Lee in 2009.

Tuesday 29 April

▶ David Bowie, Ealing College, London.

David is paid £12 for a lunchtime acoustic set. In the evening he meets Pitt to discuss Mercury's interest.

Sunday 4 May

▶ Folk Club, The Three Tuns,[1] 157 High Street, Beckenham.

This is the birth of the Beckenham Arts Lab in the backroom of this mock-Tudor pub, inaugurated by David with an acoustic set of the songs he has developed this year, many of which are destined to appear on his next album. David has also designed the poster, which is displayed in the pub.

Singer/guitarist Tim Hollier, a friend from the folk scene, is featured, and acquaintance Barry Low provides a psychedelic liquid light show.

Along with David and Finnigan, the founder members of the Arts Lab include neighbours Barrie and Christina Jackson. Tonight there is an audience of around 50 people, including local musician Roger Wootton and the other members of his group Skin. They will feature in forthcoming Arts Lab evenings and change their name to Comus.[2]

The club is off to a good start; the ticket money provides the organisers with a respectable £10 profit.

The intention is that the club will be multimedia rather than focused purely on presenting music. "The way we organised it was that David was the anchorman, he was a sort of resident musician, and every week we would have one paid performer who would be highlighted as the 'performer of the week'," said Finnigan in 1986.

Among those invited to give talks and make presentations are David's one-time spiritual teacher, the Buddhist monk Chime Youngdong Rinpoche, and *Oliver!* composer Lionel Bart, who gives a series of comic monologues.

On a couple of occasions Marc Bolan performs solo as well as with David, and The Strawbs also play there.

At one stage a surreal puppet theatre operated by local student and illustrator Brian Moore and his friend Barbara Cole becomes a major draw, and for one event David rents a print of Salvador Dali and Luis Bunuel's silent movie classic *Un Chien Andalou*.[3]

1. On 6 December 2001, Finnigan and Christina Ostrom (formerly Jackson) unveiled a plaque on the exterior of the pub (then called The Rat & Parrot), commemorating the Beckenham Arts Lab and David's links to the site. Steve Harley (whose glam band Cockney Rebel had played the venue in 1973) marked the occasion by playing a short lunchtime set. This event was the first official acknowledgement of David's creative and cultural impact on the area. In 2003, after 300 years as a public house, the premises were sold and part of the main building rebuilt as flats. In 2004 the former pub became a branch of Italian restaurant chain Zizzi; the listed frontage has been preserved.

2. In 1993 David described Comus as 'really quite interesting… kind of these really moody 19-year-old bands that were going to change the world. They were very po-faced, very serious. You didn't talk through their songs, I'm telling you. They would just stop playing and wait for it to get quiet and then start again. It was so studenty! It was fun though'.

3. *Un Chien Andalou* was screened before David's gigs at London's Rainbow Theatre in August 1972 and also before dates on his Station To Station tour of 1976.

Tuesday 6 May

▶ David Bowie, The Three Horseshoes,[1] 28 Heath Street, Hampstead, London NW3.

David plays another lunchtime gig at this popular north London venue.

1. Renamed The Horseshoe, in 2010 this was home to the Pentameters Theatre.

Thursday 8 May

David views the completed *Love You Till Tuesday* for the first time at the Crown viewing theatre in Soho's Wardour Street.

In the evening he's at the Royal Albert Hall in Kensington for a gig headlined by blues boogie merchants Ten Years After, supported by prog-rockers Jethro Tull and Clouds (David's Scottish friends who have, until recently, been the 1-2-3).

Friday 9 May

David auditions for casting agent Allan Foenander at offices at 61 Kinnerton Street, Belgravia, for a part in a TV commercial for chocolate bar Kit Kat.

Saturday 10 May

David is invited to the BBC's Television Centre in west London by folk-rock band The Strawbs as a guest on their recording for music show *Colour Me Pop*.

Introduced to The Strawbs by Tony Visconti, David had supported them in September 1968, and performs a mime for their song 'Poor Jimmy Wilson' from their eponymous debut album released this month (produced by Gus Dudgeon with assistance from Visconti).

Sunday 11 May

▶ The Three Tuns Folk Club, Beckenham.

David's artist school-friend and former member of The King Bees George Underwood has designed the poster to advertise tonight's event; he will occasionally perform here as well.

As spring turns to summer the audience increases to around 200, often spilling out into the beer garden.

Monday 12 May

David's music publisher David Platz views the final cut of *Love You Till Tuesday* with Ken Pitt. Problems with the 'When I'm Five' sequence are solved by extending the introductory shot of the birthday cake.

Pitt's £7,000 budget has been exceeded and interest from broadcasters is lukewarm. In particular, acquaintance Gunther Schneider decides not to commission it for screening in Germany. Nevertheless, the film is significant since it captures David during a period of transition, with the three performances by Feathers (who do not receive a group credit) demonstrating his particularly ornate take on acoustic folk-pop.

In addition 'The Mask' mime preserves a performance typical of those given by David at underground club Middle Earth (though his teacher Lindsay Kemp is not impressed when he views it).

Other high points include the bleached-out rendition of 'Let Me Sleep Beside You'. With his dummy guitar and parodic Elvis moves, this predates David's glam presentation by a few years.

In 'Sell Me A Coat', David's sadness at the collapse of his relationship with Farthingale is evident, particularly when he sings the lyric 'And when she smiles, the ice forgets to melt away. Not like before, her smile was warm in yesterday.'

Further work on the 29-minute film is abandoned; the original intention had been for it to be an hour long, with the songs interspersed with chat, at least one special guest and another mime titled 'Graffiti'.[1]

1. Early production notes listed 'Graffiti' as requiring a 'new session' for a 'sound collage of special effects, not normal music'.

Wednesday 14 May

David visits ad agency J. Walter Thompson regarding his potential appearance in the Kit Kat commercial.

Friday 16 May

From New York, Simon Hayes confirms in a telephone conversation with Ken Pitt that Mercury Records is interested in signing David for an album and single deal. The term of the contract is one year.

Sunday 18 May

◗ Folk Club, The Three Tuns, Beckenham.

David performs again; his set varies on every occasion but consists in the main of the songs featured on the Mercury demo. Also appearing are Mike Absalom,[1] who plays the 'phono-fiddle', The Gas Works[2] and Skin (soon to be Comus).

1. By day a journalist, Absalom interviewed David earlier in the year with Farthingale and Hutchinson for the *Notting Hill Herald* at his home at 17 Hornton Street in Kensington, west London. The newspaper folded before the feature could be published.

2. "I was as knocked out when I heard Gas Works as I was when I first heard Dylan on his first trip to Britain," said David in 1969.

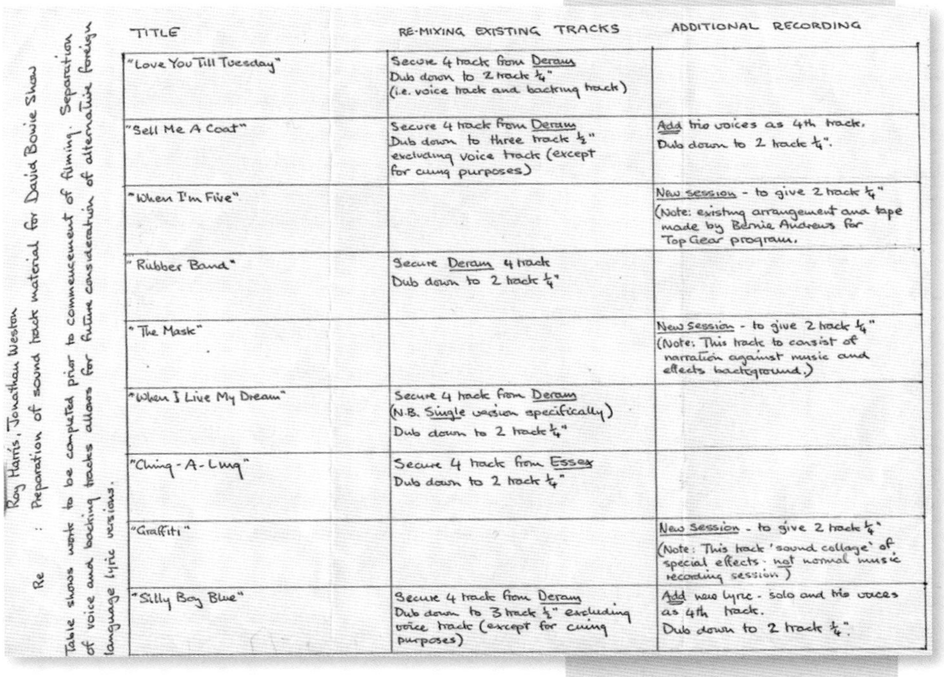

Roy Harris, Jonathan Weston

Re : Preparation of sound track material for David Bowie Show

Table shows work to be completed prior to commencement of filming. Separation of voice and backing tracks allows for future consideration of alternative foreign language lyric versions.

TITLE	RE-MIXING EXISTING TRACKS	ADDITIONAL RECORDING
"Love You Till Tuesday"	Secure 4 track from Deram Dub down to 2 track 1/4" (i.e. voice track and backing track)	
"Sell Me A Coat"	Secure 4 track from Deram Dub down to three track 1/2" excluding voice track (except for cuing purposes)	Add trio voices as 4th track. Dub down to 2 track 1/4".
"When I'm Five"		New session – to give 2 track 1/4" (Note: existing arrangement and tape made by Bernie Andrews for Top Gear program.
"Rubber Band"	Secure Deram 4 track Dub down to 2 track 1/4"	
"The Mask"		New Session – to give 2 track 1/4" (Note: This track to consist of narration against music and effects background.)
"When I Live My Dream"	Secure 4 track from Deram (N.B. Single version specifically) Dub down to 2 track 1/4"	
"Ching-A-Ling"	Secure 4 track from Essex Dub down to 2 track 1/4"	
"Graffiti"		New Session – to give 2 track 1/4" (Note: This track 'sound collage' of special effects – not normal music recording session)
"Silly Boy Blue"	Secure 4 track from Deram Dub down to 3 track 1/2" excluding voice track (except for cuing purposes)	Add new lyric – solo and trio voices as 4th track. Dub down to 2 track 1/4".

ABOVE: Production note memo for *Love You Till Tuesday*, listing 'Silly Boy Blue' and the mysterious sound collage called 'Graffiti'.

Monday 19 May

Pitt conveys Mercury's offer to David by letter: 'He (Hayes) is confirming this to me in writing, but meanwhile I believe he requires (you) to quickly produce a single version of 'Space Oddity'.'

Initially cool about the track, Mercury has stepped up its interest now that news has broken that the crew of space mission Apollo 11 are to land on the moon on 20 July. Soon afterwards, the label's publicity director, Ron Oberman, meets up with David during a trip to London.

Thursday 22 May

◗ David Bowie, Wigmore Hall, 36 Wigmore Street, London W1.

Lyons Maid withdraws the Luv ice lolly film commercial featuring David because of poor sales and the product itself is taken off the market.

In the evening he dances and mimes during 'Evolution',[1] the closing number of a show led by singer Tim Hollier and featuring US singer-songwriter Amory Kane, Canadian singer/guitarist Rick Cuff and drummer Clem Cattini.

As the musicians launch into 'Evolution', David joins them on stage for a performance art piece, dressed in a sculptured space-suit costume. By the song's climax he has stripped down to a jock strap.

1. Written by Amory Kane, 'Evolution' appeared on Hollier's eponymous 1970 Fontana album.

Friday 23 May

Underground magazine *International Times* features an announcement from Mary Finnigan on its information page: 'We are starting an Arts Lab in home suburb, Beckenham, and getting things moving with Contemporary Folk on Sunday

In this year...

May

FORMATION of Mott The Hoople in Herefordshire. The name was given to them by producer Guy Stevens, who took it from a Willard Manus novel of the same name. When Mott were on the verge of breaking up in 1972, David provided them with top ten hit 'All the Young Dudes'. (▸ 8.9.72)

RIGHT: David holding court at the Arts Lab.

BELOW: Front page of Arts Lab progress report from 9 June.

Mary Finnigan works the door. "It caught on just like wild fire," said Finnigan in 1986. "It was as if we had fulfilled a need amongst people – we just hit it at the right moment."

The pub's landlord isn't used to the crowds now regularly teeming into the backroom, yet his worries are tempered by the sizeable increase in bar takings.

Sunday 8 June

▶ Beckenham Arts Lab, The Three Tuns, Beckenham.
David's performances are becoming a major attraction. Conversing with the audience between numbers, he makes announcements about forthcoming events and bookings, reads poetry and unloads his thoughts about matters personal and general.

"There were times on those Sunday nights when he just transcended everything, when the person hired as the 'featured artist' looked extremely silly against David's brilliance," said Finnigan in 1986.

"He'd play for two-and-a-half hours, maybe with a 10-minute tape break. He was thoroughly professional, deciding what he was going to do each week and working on it for a couple of days.

"David would record backing tapes at home so he could multi-layer his music. He'd know exactly where he wanted to play and when. There were times when he played to that audience which were just unbelievably brilliant, I mean just exquisite. And there were times in my flat when it was just out of this world," she recalled.

Monday 9 June

The Beckenham Arts Lab committee – comprising David, Finnigan and Barrie and Christina Jackson – compiles a progress report.

This seven-page 'manifesto' outlines the achievements so far and future goals, including:

'(Item) 5. Travelling entertainers for parties – we plan for this winter, charging fees like £15 for an evening from David Bowie, going up to £25 for Bowie plus a group and light show.'

The report also refers to the planned use of the Lab's large van which will be 'for David Bowie's own use to take his proposed "electric circus"[1] around the country'.

Also today Calvin Mark Lee receives a session budget from Gus Dudgeon for the re-recording of 'Space Oddity': 'Drums, bass, electric guitar, Mellotron, total £256.00'. Dudgeon is producing this song since Tony Visconti – who has agreed to produce David's new album – does not like it.

"I played (Visconti) 'Space Oddity' and he said, 'No, I'm not doing that, that's terrible'," said David in 1976. "So I said, 'Do you mind if I go and ask someone else to do it?' and he said, 'Sure'."

Visconti personally recommends Dudgeon, who has been keen to produce David since engineering his debut album in 1967 and is impressed with the track. "It blew my socks off, I just couldn't believe it," said Dudgeon in 1991. "I rang Tony and said, 'You

evenings at the local boozer… The people involved are musician/composer David Bowie, artist Christina Jackson, her poet husband Barrie and myself. We'd welcome support from interested parties and suggestions for premises, money, etc. For further information contact Mary Finnigan or David Bowie, 01-650-3432.'

David's father, John Jones, is enthusiastic about David's current activities in a letter to Pitt: 'David is keeping very cheerful and seems to be keeping himself fully occupied with the folk club and various other things.'

Sunday 25 May

▶ Folk Club, The Three Tuns, Beckenham.
Special guest is Tucker Zimmerman, a friend of Tony Visconti whose recently released debut album *Ten Songs By Tucker Zimmerman* is already a favourite of David's.

As well as music, the club encourages a variety of creative endeavours. A mini-market develops in the pub's conservatory, with stall-holders showing and selling paintings, jewellery, posters, candles and clothing.

A friend of Finnigan's lends her a liquid-light machine, which she often works. This and the burning joss sticks set the mood.

Sunday 1 June

▶ Beckenham Arts Lab, The Three Tuns, Beckenham.
After a month or so it becomes obvious to David and Finnigan that the folk club has grown into a multimedia event. At one gathering David asks the audience whether they would like the club to be known as an Arts Lab, and the answer is a resounding 'Yes'. With that the Three Tuns Folk Club was no more and the weekly night is given the full title 'Growth – The Beckenham Arts Lab'.

In between acts David plays specially prepared tapes and encourages newcomers to participate while

really can't be serious about not wanting to record this song,' and he said, 'I just don't like it.'"

1. David was still considering this 'electric circus' idea for himself and friends in 1971.

Wednesday 11 June

▶ David Bowie, Cambridge Midsummer Pop Festival, Midsummer Common, Cambridge.

David performs a 15-minute acoustic set in the afternoon of this open-air free concert organised by the university city's arts lab.[1] Also on the bill are Pretty Things, The Strawbs, Audience and Family.

1. In the summer of 1969, David made a number of undocumented solo appearances, including one at the famous folk cellar in Bunjies Coffee House at 27 Litchfield Street near Charing Cross Road in central London.

Saturday 14 June

The mime performance with The Strawbs on *Colour Me Pop* is broadcast on BBC2.

International Times carries an advert placed by David seeking 'a good singing/speaking acoustic guitarist for exciting project – must be alive'.

Sunday 15 June

▶ David Bowie, the Marquee, Wardour Street, London W1.

David returns to familiar surroundings for 'An Evening with The Strawbs and Their Friends' which features the first UK appearance by singer-songwriter James Taylor,[1] who is signed to The Beatles' label Apple but is in the process of breaking away; his producer/manager Peter Asher is unhappy with the introduction of Allen Klein as Apple's business manager. Each of the three acts is paid a £4 share of the takings. The Marquee booking means that David does not appear at the Beckenham Arts Lab this evening.

1. James Taylor, born Boston, Massachusetts, 12 March 1948, became a major recording artist in his own right, scoring a US number three hit with 'Fire And Rain' in 1970 and a number one in 1971 with 'You've Got A Friend'.

Tuesday 17 June

Following a decision to add orchestration to the forthcoming 'Space Oddity' session, Gus Dudgeon revises the total budget to £493.18 on the basis of extra musicians listed to Lee: '8 violins, 2 violas, 2 celli, 2 arco basses, 2 flutes and hire of organ'.

Friday 20 June

David is at Trident for the re-recording of 'Space Oddity', and at 4.30pm signs the recording deal with Mercury Records, overseen by Lou Reizner. Calvin Mark Lee is also present.

The contract – which is initially for one album and three singles starting with 'Space Oddity' – has been drawn up at Mercury's Chicago headquarters and provides for the company's European affiliate Philips to release David's records in the UK and continental Europe.

With a record deal in place for the first time in 14 months, David cracks on with the creation of what will become his first major hit and arguably the most significant release of his career.

The team are under the gun; Mercury insists that the track (backed by the dramatic 'Wild Eyed Boy From Freecloud') is released as a single ahead of the Apollo 11 moon-landing in exactly a month's time. Angie and Nita Bowles (a friend from the Arts Lab) are at Trident to lend support.

Since neither he nor David can read music, Dudgeon draws a large notational chart for them both, marking individual instrumentation with symbols and shapes colour-coded above the lyrics. Orchestrator Paul Buckmaster[1] is on hand to translate this into a regular musical score for the musicians.

"The minute I heard it I thought this thing has got to be a big sound for it to work," said Dudgeon in 1991. "Bowie, without my knowledge, called Paul Buckmaster to write string parts. I must admit I didn't hear strings and flutes on it at the beginning, but once the track was done it was obvious that it would work very well."

At this time Buckmaster becomes an important person in the development of David's songwriting, advising him to move on from narrative-based output and instead focus on creating an overall sound for each track.

"We had some wonderful, intellectual discussions," said Buckmaster in 2007. "The first ones we had had a lot to do with a pop science-fiction mysticism, mixed with a lot of metaphysics and spiritualism. We were talking about aliens and UFOs a lot when we first met. It seemed to be a primary topic of debate."

This is also the first time David works with bassist Herbie Flowers[2] and keyboard player Rick Wakeman. The latter was booked by Dudgeon to play Mellotron on Visconti's recommendation.

As with Flowers, this is one of the 20-year-old Wakeman's first studio sessions. Paid £7 10s (£7.50), he records his contribution on his second run-through having heard the demo just once.

Drummer on the session is Terry Cox, a member of Alexis Korner's Blues Incorporated and The Pentangle, who have just entered the UK chart with their single 'Once I Had A Sweetheart'.

The distinctive guitar solo is supplied by Mick Wayne, main man of rock group Junior's Eyes, who is initially unhappy with his contribution (even though it will be the most notable recording of his career).

"I had been away and all of my equipment was stuck at Gatwick airport, so I had to borrow a guitar to do the session," said Wayne in 1992. "I just couldn't keep it in tune so I really wasn't happy. David

TOP: David's passport, 1969, with a photograph taken by Ray Stevenson.

BOTTOM: Gus Dudgeon's budget for 'Space Oddity' (on Tuesday Productions letterhead).

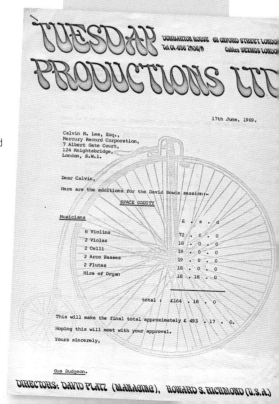

ABOVE: David at work at Trident, 1969.

RIGHT: Calvin Mark Lee's 'Space Oddity' internal record company memo, 27 June.

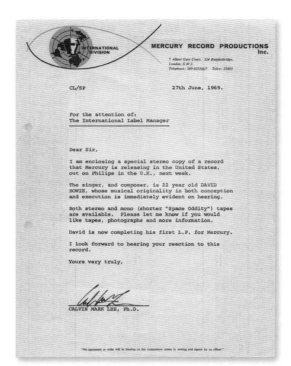

had asked me to do my Wes Montgomery bit, which meant to play octaves. Both he and Gus Dudgeon really liked the first thing I did."

Dudgeon is impressed with the efforts of Calvin Mark Lee, who draws on his contacts to speed the process up and personally ferries tapes to Apple's disc-cutting studio at 3 Savile Row.

1. Buckmaster was a member of Sounds Nice and The Third Ear Band. On the recommendation of Gus Dudgeon, David and Elton John worked with Buckmaster on their first hit singles – respectively 'Space Oddity' and March 1970's 'Your Song'. Other early successes included string arrangements for Harry Nilsson's 'Without You' (1971) and Carly Simon's 'You're So Vain' (1972). Buckmaster was still Elton John's orchestrator and arranger in 2010 and has worked with The Rolling Stones, Miles Davis, Leonard Cohen, the Grateful Dead and Ben Folds. In 1975, David invited Buckmaster to Hollywood's Cherokee Studios to work on instrumental soundtrack material he was preparing for Nicolas Roeg's The Man Who Fell To Earth. Buckmaster was accompanied by classically trained keyboard player J. Peter Robinson and Herbie Flowers.

2. Brian Keith Flowers, born 1938, came to prominence as co-founder of such groups as Blue Mink and CCS before performing sessions for David, Lou Reed (playing bass on hit 'Walk On The Wild Side'), Elton John and many other 70s stars. A member of David's initial touring band of 1974 and T.Rex in 1977, in 1970 Flowers wrote the novelty hit 'Grandad' for Clive Dunn and became a popular figure on UK children's TV, playing the tuba as well as the bass.

Saturday 21 June

A session to complete the work on 'Space Oddity' is postponed; David has fallen ill with conjunctivitis and glandular fever. It is completed a few days later along with the B-side – a new song called 'Wild Eyed Boy From Freecloud', which features David on acoustic guitar and Paul Buckmaster playing cello.

The song has been written at Mary Finnigan's flat in Beckenham, and David later tells her that her young son Richard helped inspire the song. The title and some lyrical influence have also come from the

1805 book The Wild Boy Of Aveyron.[1]

Gus Dudgeon is paid a one-off fee of £100 for his production work on these two songs.[2]

David isn't well enough to attend the Arts Lab the following day.

1. Written by Jean-Marc-Gaspard Itard, this documents the true story of a feral boy running wild with wolves in the forests of central southern France. François Truffaut based his 1970 film L'Enfant Sauvage (The Wild Child) on this tale.

2. Shortly before his death in 2002 Dudgeon instituted a legal action against David, pursuing £1m in production royalties from 'Space Oddity'.

Friday 27 June

Due to rent rises, Ken Pitt closes his office in Curzon Street, Mayfair, and shifts his Kenneth Pitt Ltd business to his home address at 39 Manchester Street.

Sunday 29 June

▶ Beckenham Arts Lab, The Three Tuns, Beckenham.

A street theatre group becomes part of the Arts Lab's activities around this time, encouraged by David and Angie. "They used to practise in the local park," said Finnigan in 1986. "This was with a view to doing some theatrical happening in Beckenham High Street on a Saturday morning when all the shoppers were out and about."

Local guitarist Bill Liesegang, who forms group Appendix To Part One, was an early attendee at The Three Tuns along with his friends.

"Bowie used to get people up on stage to play or do mime, or do their own thing," said Liesegang in 2007. "One day he gathered a bunch of us 16-year-old hippies and took us into Beckenham Place Park where we re-enacted various scenes from The Lord Of The Rings."

Saturday 5 July

During The Rolling Stones' free concert in London's Hyde Park, David's freshly completed 'Space Oddity' single is played over the PA, making its public debut – an important contributory factor in its subsequent success believes Ken Pitt, given that there are upwards of 200,000 people there.

David isn't at Hyde Park, but with Calvin Mark Lee to see The Who perform less than a mile away at the Royal Albert Hall; they are premiering the live rendition of their concept album Tommy, and Mercury artist Chuck Berry is supporting.

"David and I sat right at the front, in the orchestra pit area, looking straight up at the stage," said Lee in 2009. "We went backstage afterwards and hung out."

David gives The Who leader Pete Townshend an advance copy of 'Space Oddity'. "He had the goodness to write me a little note afterwards, saying that he liked the song very much," said David in 1999. "I thought, 'If I ever get really big, I'll try to be as nice as that to people'."

Sunday 6 July

▶ Beckenham Arts Lab, The Three Tuns, Beckenham.
This evening John Peel plays 'Space Oddity' on his Radio One show *Top Gear*, commenting that he doesn't believe it is bound for the charts.

David writes to Peel asking for a financial contribution to the Arts Lab, and includes sketches showing how he wants to change the room's layout. Although Peel helps similar projects, this time he doesn't respond.

Friday 11 July

Philips[1] release 'Space Oddity'/'Wild Eyed Boy From Freecloud' single in the UK.

⊙ **David Bowie**
A **'Space Oddity'** (Bowie)
David Bowie (vocal, guitar, Stylophone)
Mick Wayne (guitar)
Herbie Flowers (bass)
Rick Wakeman (Mellotron)
Terry Cox (drums)
Session orchestra
B **'Wild Eyed Boy From Freecloud'** (Bowie)
David Bowie (vocal, guitar)
Paul Buckmaster (arco bass)
Produced by Gus Dudgeon
Arranged by David Bowie and Paul Buckmaster
(Philips BF 1801)

Promotional copies sent to the media and radio stations are in stereo, while those stocked by retailers are standard mono.

The B-side of the promos features a spoken introduction by David: "This is 'The Wild Eyed Boy From Freecloud' with Paul Buckmaster on arco bass."

The following day 'Space Oddity' receives positive reviews in the music press.

'This Bee Geeian piece of music and poetry is beautifully written, sung and performed. Strangely, it could be a hit and escalate Bowie to the top,' writes Chris Welch in *Melody Maker*.

Penny Valentine also picks up on the Bee Gees reference in *Disc & Music Echo*, but adds: 'I have a bet on in the office that this is going to be a huge hit – and knock everyone senseless.'

1. The Philips Group of companies owned Mercury Records, having bought the company in 1962. Some releases, like this single, were issued by the parent company, some (like the album *The Man Who Sold The World*) were issued by Mercury.

Sunday 13 July

▶ Beckenham Arts Lab, The Three Tuns, Beckenham.
Plans for an Arts Lab-organised free festival to be held in a local park – along the lines of the Stones in Hyde Park and other live events which have taken place over recent months – are beginning to crystallise.

Tuesday 15 July

▶ David Bowie, Hounslow Arts Lab, The White Bear, 198 Kingsley Road, Hounslow, Middx.
Backed by Tony Visconti on bass and Junior's Eyes drummer John Cambridge, David plays a set at the club run by Dave Cousins of The Strawbs to reciprocate for the folk group's appearance at his own Arts Lab a few weeks earlier.

This is a sign of things to come; even though he again mimes during The Strawbs' set, David is performing with a line-up approaching that of a rock band.

Meanwhile, on the eve of recording sessions for David's new album, Calvin Mark Lee announces he is leaving Mercury.

Lee receives a letter from publicity chief Ron Oberman: 'Just got your note... am really shocked. What happened? I can't think of anyone who's more together than you. Losing you will be an irreplaceable loss for Mercury.... About David's record, let me say this: never in my two and a half years at Mercury have I been so flipped out about a single record. Simon Hayes played it to me about two weeks ago in New York and it really made my day (and entire week for that matter). One listen and I knew it was a smash.'

Wednesday 16 July

Recording of David's new album begins at Trident with starts made on three tracks between 2pm and 5pm and then 7pm to 12pm: 'Janine', 'An Occasional Dream' and 'Letter To Hermione'.

Tony Visconti is back in the producer's seat, working with engineer Malcolm Toft, and has determined that Junior's Eyes[1] will form the core of musicians on the sessions. Minus vocalist Graham 'Grom' Kelly they are: drummer John Cambridge, bassist John 'Honk' Lodge, rhythm guitarist Tim Renwick and lead guitarist Mick Wayne.

1. Junior's Eyes' roots are in Mick Wayne's mid-60s Hull-based R&B band The Hullaballoos. Cambridge replaced drummer Harry Dunn in 1966, though did not join the other members when they moved to London eight months later. Led by Wayne, the group went through various permutations, as The Bunch of Fives (with Pretty Things drummer Viv Prince in the line-up) and then The Tickle. Wayne invited John Cambridge, then with Hull's The Rats alongside guitarist Mick Ronson, to rejoin the line-up. On the same day in 1968, guitarist Tim Renwick was also recruited.
Junior's Eyes released the Tony Visconti-produced album *Battersea Power Station* in 1969 and broke up in 1970. Renwick formed Quiver which merged with The Sutherland Brothers before moving into session and touring work with such artists as Eric Clapton and Pink Floyd. Wayne spent some time in Los Angeles before returning to the UK in 1972. He became a painter and also performed session work for Joe Cocker, Sandy Denny, Steve Winwood and Ringo Starr. In June 1994 Wayne died in a fire after returning to the US to record.

Thursday 17 July

Recording of 'Janine' and 'An Occasional Dream' continues, with two mixes of the latter produced by Visconti.

Sunday 20 July

▶ Beckenham Arts Lab, The Three Tuns, Beckenham.
David performs at the Arts Lab, where guest artist

TOP: Junior's Eyes, left to right: Graham Kelly (vocals), John Cambridge, Mick Wayne, Tim Renwick and John Lodge.

ABOVE: 'Space Oddity' UK label, the single released on 11 July.

ABOVE: David at Foxgrove Road, 21 July.

RIGHT: David's note to his manager attached to his Malta song festival lyric 'No-One Someone'.

BELOW: Programme for the Oscar 1969 Malta International Song Festival.

Ken,
Here is the lyric for the malta song. Could you advise what song I should do as the second of my own compositions. Also , what news if any on the clothes bit... or any news really? However I hope to hear from you soon.

Bowie

P.S. The arrangements for the two new songs are being done by ?

is avant-garde composer Ron Geesin.

At 9.18pm GMT the US lunar module Eagle lands on the moon. Six and a half hours later, in the early hours of Monday morning, Neil Armstrong becomes the first man on the moon.

Despite a temporary ban on records with space themes, the BBC plays 'Space Oddity' during its special *Man On The Moon* broadcast, much to the delight of Angela, Finnigan and their friends, who are gathered around the TV at 24 Foxgrove Road.

David watches the broadcast at a girlfriend's place and is elated, though amazed his song has been used.

Thursday 24 July

David embarks on a 10-day trip to the continent with Ken Pitt to appear at two music festival competitions.

'He was made aware of the festivals' shortcomings and what would be required of him in return,' wrote Pitt in 1983. 'He accepted all this and entered into the spirit of the thing.'

Saturday 26 July

◗ David Bowie, Oscar 1969 Malta International Song Festival, Hilton Hotel, Portomaso, St Julian's, Malta.

On the first night of the festival David performs 'When I Live My Dream' next to the hotel's swimming pool, wearing the blue suit as seen

in *Love You Till Tuesday*.[1]

At the event, organised by local university lecturer John B. Cassar, all 17 competitors[2] perform with an orchestra which is conducted by 'guest of honour', orchestrator and arranger Norrie Paramor, whose successes include many Cliff Richard hits.

David invites Austria's representative Peter Horton to join the bill of the forthcoming Beckenham free festival.

1. The suit was bought from Just Men by Nikki of Tryon St, London SW3. David removed some of the jacket's white trim for these appearances.

2. Among them was Pat McGeegan (actually McGuigan) who had come fourth the previous year in the Eurovision Song Contest, two places behind Cliff Richard. Son Barry became world featherweight champion boxer in the 1980s.

Sunday 27 July

◗ On this, the second evening of the Malta Song Festival, he and the other contestants perform their own rendition of a local song, singing words they have already prepared. David titles his version 'No-One Someone':

'She loved to walk by the neon-lit fountain
T'catch the foam, t'catch the morning rays
To pass the shops in their humourless offerings
From the hands of the men who could sell you
better days...'

As David is away, Ken Simmons deputises for him at the Arts Lab.

Monday 28 July

Tonight at the Malta Song Festival award ceremony David comes second to Spanish entrant Christina and collects a Silver Oscar. The evening is rounded off with a performance by the Lilian Attard Ballet School. The following day, David joins other song festival delegates to visit giant aircraft carrier the USS *Saratoga*, which is on her ninth Mediterranean deployment. They put on an impromptu performance for the crew, with David on acoustic guitar.

Wednesday 30 July

David, Pitt and the other contestants leave Malta for Italy and another song competition organised by John Cassar, the regional Festival Internazionale del Disco in Tuscany.

After a flight to Rome, they take a six-hour coach journey to the Hotel Reale, which is at 7 Via Palestro in Monsummano Terme near Pistoia, for a repeat performance.

David sends Angie a telegram: 'Town Monsummano Terme 30th. Small town. Two Hotels. Love Bowie.'

Angie is in Monsummano Terme to meet David on his arrival; she stopped off en route to visit her parents in Cyprus.

Friday 1 August

◗ David Bowie, Festival Internazionale del Disco, Hotel Reale, Monsummano Terme.

The competitors sing to backing tapes they have been advised to bring. Tonight David is dressed more casually in a new outfit Angie has brought with her from London. Again he sings 'When I Live My Dream', this time utilising his backing tape.

Saturday 2 August

▶ At the closing awards ceremony David receives a special award for best-produced record.

Sunday 3 August

▶ Beckenham Arts Lab, The Three Tuns, Beckenham.
Returning to the UK via Rome, David makes it back to the Beckenham Arts Lab in time to share the bill with Drama Band.

After his set Mary Finnigan informs him that his father is unwell. Angry that he hasn't been told earlier, David hastily leaves the pub with photographer Ray Stevenson, who drives him to 4 Plaistow Grove. Here David discovers his father semi-conscious, suffering from pneumonia.

The following day David calls his manager to let him know that his father is seriously ill.

Tuesday 5 August

John Jones dies of pneumonia at home in Bromley, aged 57.

David is recording at Trident, and receives the news over the phone. He openly weeps during the subsequent session, though his fellow musicians are at a loss as to why. "I didn't know his father had died," said Tim Renwick in 1998.

In 1993, David spoke to writer and fellow one-time Bromley resident Hanif Kureishi about the loss of his father:[1]

"It was at a point where I was just beginning to grow up a little bit and appreciate that I would have to stretch out my hand a little for us ever to get to know each other. He just died at the wrong damn time, because there were so many things I would have loved to have said to him and asked him about – all those stereotypical regrets when your father dies and you haven't completed your relationship. I felt so... Damn! Wrong time! Not now, not now!"

1. David still wears the gold crucifix his father gave him.

Wednesday 6 August

Ken Pitt travels to Bromley to help David arrange his father's documents.

Sunday 10 August

▶ Beckenham Arts Lab, The Three Tuns, Beckenham.
The Arts Lab committee puts the final touches to the free festival, to take place in six days' time.

Monday 11 August

David father's funeral takes place at Elmers End Cemetery in Bromley. His ashes are scattered in the memorial gardens behind the chapel. A small reception is held at 4 Plaistow Grove where David

and friends (including Angie and Calvin Lee) take to his bedroom.

Half-brother Terry Burns is there; in the last few years his relationship with John Jones had been repaired since his step-father had become remorseful over his treatment of Burns when he was young.

In the immediate aftermath of his father's death, David and Angie move to the grand-sounding Haddon Hall, at 42 Southend Road, Beckenham.[1]

Neighbour Mark Pritchett recalled the occasion in 1994: "It was chaos. They were organising the free festival and moving at the same time. He was also dealing with his father's death; it was a difficult time."

The imposing red-brick, detached Victorian villa takes its name from a historic 12th-century stone building near Chesterfield, Derbyshire.

David and Angie rent the entire ground floor from the owner, a Mr Hoy, and invite Tony Visconti and his girlfriend Liz Hartley to move in with them ('We were all there for the purpose of making David Bowie a star,' Visconti later wrote in 2007).[2] The rooms border a large central hall and a dark oak staircase leads to a gallery which circles above the hall. The upper-floor rooms are let to other tenants and are accessed via side entrances.

Gothic windows at the top of the stairs give the interior a musty, museum-like atmosphere. A room at the rear houses a battered grand piano, a gift from a friendly neighbour, which David often uses when writing songs. This overlooks a veranda and the large back garden where the elderly Mr Hoy can often be seen working.

In the basement live Sue and Tony Frost, who become not only very friendly with David and Angie but also involved in David's career.

Visconti later converts the basement wine cellar into a small rehearsal studio and Sue Frost regularly retreats upstairs to join Angie away from the loud music, though rehearsals are restricted because Tony Frost works nights.

David's newly widowed mother takes advantage of his proximity, regularly preparing Sunday lunches, her King Charles spaniel following closely at her heels. The dog stays on at Haddon Hall when Mrs Jones moves from Bromley to a flat in Beckenham.

The large house is perfect for entertaining, and David and Angie sometimes stage late-night parties, often waking Visconti and Hartley as they return from London with guests in the early hours.

There is also a resident ghost, a Mrs Grey, who is blamed when items fail to work or go missing. Visconti says he sees her gliding around the garden dressed in a white shroud, though not all the residents are convinced.

There are the usual tensions of a group of young people living together, mainly due to a lack of collective funds. "There was very little love'n'peace at Haddon Hall," Tony Visconti later said.

1. The house was reputedly built in 1851 for one of the founders

TOP: Haddon Hall, Beckenham. David's home from 1969 to 1973. Photo taken from the garden of Mark Pritchett's house.

MIDDLE: Ken Pitt wearing the paisley shirt David often borrowed. Hilton Hotel, Malta. Photo taken by David.

BOTTOM: John Jones (1912–1969). He worked at Dr Barnardo's for 34 years.

In this year...

Wednesday 6 August
EUROPEAN concert debut of Mott The Hoople at the Bat Caverna Club, Riccione, Italy. Ian Hunter had joined the band after attending an audition at Denmark Street's Regent Sounds Studio in May.

THIS PAGE

TOP LEFT AND RIGHT: David performing at the Beckenham Free Festival on 16 August, just five days after his father's funeral.

MIDDLE LEFT: Front cover of Growth (Beckenham Arts Lab) 'Festival issue' newsletter.

MIDDLE RIGHT: Dave Cousins (far right) and The Strawbs, preparing to go on stage at the Beckenham Free Festival. David is at the back waiting to introduce them. Left to right: cellist Claire Deniz, Tony Hooper, David, Dave Cousins and bassist Ron Chesterman.

BOTTOM: David roadies for Comus at the Beckenham Free Festival.

OPPOSITE PAGE

TOP LEFT AND RIGHT: On the set of Doebidoe in Hilversum.

BOTTOM: Scruffy in Amsterdam, David photographed at the home of Dutch reporter Jojanneke Claassen for Het Parool. David's guitar is a Hagstrom 12 string, a present from Ken Pitt. He later gave the guitar to Mark Pritchett.

of Price's Candles, a huge and profitable London-based business established in 1830 by partners William Wilson and Benjamin Lancaster.

Demolished in 1981, Haddon Hall stood on what is now an apartment block and Shannon Way. The small residents' car park leads to the place where Haddon Hall's woodshed (where David was often photographed) once stood. The centre of what was the large back garden has since been redeveloped and an additional apartment block added.

2. Visconti and Hartley moved in later in the year.

Saturday 16 August

▶ Growth Presents The Beckenham Free Festival, Croydon Road Recreation Ground, Beckenham.

Held from noon to 8pm, David compères and performs a set, occasionally with backing from musicians including Tony Visconti.

Other performers include folksinger Bridget St John, composer Lionel Bart, singer-songwriter Amory Kane, Sun, Kamirah & Giles & Abdul, guitarist-singer Keith Christmas, Oswald K, Comus, Gun Hill, The Gas Works, Nita Bowes and Dave Jones, sitar musician

Clem Alford[1] and blues band Appendix To Part One.[2] Peter Horton (who performs Bach's 'Jesu, Joy Of Man's Desiring' on acoustic guitar) has accepted the invitation extended to him by David in Malta, and The Strawbs also play; the DJ is Tim Goffe, who lived with Angie and Bob Harris at a shared rented house in Charlton earlier in the year.

The festival is a great success, with an estimated 3,000 in attendance over the day, though David is clearly suffering from his recent bereavement.

David said of the aftermath of his father's death in 1970: "When he died, I was in one of my terrible moods. I have these terrible moods, and when I'm in one I don't feel anything concerning other people. When my father died I hardly felt anything for weeks, then it suddenly hit me..."

John Peel, although listed, doesn't attend and nor do Junior's Eyes; they are in Hamburg, for a short residency at the city's legendary Star Club.

There are numerous side events, including Brian Moore and Barbara Cole's Puppet Theatre, street theatre demonstrations, an exotic tea stall, a Tibetan shop, jewellery and ceramics stalls, the Culpepper Herb & Food stall and an 'assault course' for kids.

To raise funds for the Arts Lab, Angie has a hamburger stand (cooking in a new wheelbarrow) and Calvin Mark Lee sells rare psychedelic posters from his collection.

An Arts Lab 'Festival issue' newsletter (Vol.1 No.7) is distributed at the event.

1. Alford joined short-lived progressive folk-rock group Magic Carpet, formed in 1971 by singer/songwriter Alisha Sufit.

2. Based in neighbouring Penge, Appendix To Part One singer Neil Holmes became friendly with David, often visiting him at Haddon Hall. Shortly after the event, the band's guitarist Bill Leisagang was invited to join a new group project being developed by David and Visconti. He declined but would later meet David in Bristol. (▶ 13.10.69)

Sunday 17 August

▶ Beckenham Arts Lab, The Three Tuns, Beckenham.

In the aftermath of the festival the Arts Lab is becoming increasingly sophisticated; Mary Finnigan's light machine has been superseded by half a dozen 'very professional light shows'.

Tuesday 19 August

David and Finnigan head up a Growth general meeting in the Three Tuns' garden. David derives the title of a new song – 'Cygnet Committee' – from these gatherings.

Friday 22 August

▶ David Bowie, Catacombs Club, Temple Street, Wolverhampton.

David and Angie travel to the Midlands town where he performs two 30-minute mime sets for a fee of £40. With them is Ray Stevenson, who photographs David in action.

Around this time Bob Harris invites David to appear as a guest at a disco he is organising at London's Imperial College. An unbilled David performs 'Space

Oddity', but receives a hostile reception.

At the end of David's set, Harris jumps to the stage and tells the hecklers: "Mark my words, this guy is going to be a big star. Believe me."

Sunday 24 August

▶ Beckenham Arts Lab, The Three Tuns, Beckenham.
Singer/songwriter Keith Christmas is a regular performer at the Arts Lab. Dr Sam Hutt, later mock-country performer Hank Wangford, gives a talk about alternative medicine.

Monday 25 August

David flies to Amsterdam with Ken Pitt and records a performance of 'Space Oddity' on Hilversum's TV pop show *Doebidoe* shortly after their arrival.

At the studio, Pitt is in the control room as David is about to sing when the producer notices someone walk across the studio and approach the stage. Highly irritated, the producer shouts into his mic: "Who's that?" Pitt looks down from the control room to see Mark Lee holding up the whole show.

Even though it is at least a month since Lee left Mercury, Pitt still doesn't know, and is not enlightened by David.

In the afternoon David is interviewed by photo-journalist Jojanneke Claassen[1] at her flat for the newspaper *Het Parool*.

Later she accompanies David and Pitt to a nightclub, Napoleon's, in Keizersgracht, close to their hotel, the Ardina.

1. Jojanneke Claassen went on to become an established author and photographer in Europe. She died in September 2008.

Tuesday 26 August

David is interviewed on Radio Hilversum and Radio Veronica.

After lunch with Phonogram executive Herman Katz, Pitt returns to London, leaving David with Lee. They return the following day.

Thursday 28 August

David travels to south coast venue Leas Cliff Hall in The Leas, Folkestone, where the BBC's Radio One Club is hosting an event. He is interviewed about 'Space Oddity' by DJ Dave Cash.

Saturday 30 August

David's performance on *Doebidoe* is broadcast in the Netherlands and *Het Parool* publishes Jojanneke Claassen's feature with the heading 'David Bowie's grote liefele is zijn Arts Lab' (David Bowie's great love is his Arts Lab).

Sunday 31 August

▶ Beckenham Arts Lab, The Three Tuns, Beckenham.

Tuesday 2 September

David, Lee and Pitt meet to discuss plans for a concert at London's Purcell Room entitled 'An

Evening With David Bowie'.

Friday 5 September

David and Pitt visit Philips Records in Stanhope Place near Marble Arch for a meeting with a sales manager, a Mr Voyder.

'Space Oddity' has not sold as expected, and there are mutterings at the weekly sales meetings that it should be withdrawn. But the record is being stoutly defended by Philips' A&R scout Dick Leahy.[1]

"He put 'Space Oddity' on the release and plug list (promotional priorities for radio stations)," said the ex-Philips executive Ralph Mace in 2010. "After a couple of weeks there was barely a single sale and no airplay. Sales managers started saying that they thought it wouldn't do anything. Dick said, 'No, it stays on the plug list.' This went on for several weeks and the general consensus was that it was a no-hoper.

"At a later marketing meeting, Dick met all the opposition by saying that, as far as he was concerned, it was far too good a single to be ditched and that it would stay on the plug list until something did happen. I have often thought that, had Dick not stuck with it as he did, David's might have been a different story."

1. Prominent British A&R executive and music publisher who has worked with such acts as Mary Hopkin, 10cc, Wham! and subsequently closely with George Michael.

Saturday 6 September

'Space Oddity' makes its first appearance in the charts at number 48, eight weeks after its release.

Sunday 7 September

▶ Beckenham Arts Lab, The Three Tuns, Beckenham.

Monday 8 September

David, the members of Junior's Eyes, Visconti and engineer Malcolm Toft work a double session at Trident on his new song about the events at Croydon Road Recreation Ground a few weeks previously, 'Memory Of A Free Festival'.

In this year...

Thursday 21– Sunday 24 August
STAGING of the Woodstock Festival in New York state. David's guitarist Mick Ronson acquired property in the town and lived there for many years in the 80s.

ANGELA BARNETT

The woman who became inextricably intertwined with David's rise to fame was born Angela Barnett in Xeros, Cyprus, in 1950, the daughter of George and Helene Barnett. Her father was an American mining engineer of English parentage, her mother of Polish descent. She has one sibling, a brother 16 years her senior.

Schooled in Europe and America, Angela completed her education in London at Kingston Polytechnic, taking an HND course in business studies.

In 1968 she dated Mercury Records director Lou Reizner and also his colleague, David's friend, Calvin Mark Lee.

By 1969 she was employed as a telephonist in a live-in job at the Nomad Travel Club in Sussex Gardens, Paddington, west London, where David sometimes stayed.

Shortly after their relationship began in April that year, David introduced her to DJ Bob Harris (at that time one of the founders of listings magazine *Time Out*) and she rented a room in the same house as him in Charlton, south-east London. She lived there until moving to Haddon Hall with David in August.

Throughout their time together, she and David conducted a celebrated polyamorous relationship which allowed them separate and shared partners. This open accord made them notorious (and ideal media copy).

Their marriage on 19 March 1970 was often claimed by others (and sometimes David himself) to be a marriage of convenience, enabling Angie to remain resident in the UK and David to have better access to the US at an important time in his career.

This gainsays the undeniably close nature of their relationship in the early years. At times – particularly during the recording of 1970's *The Man Who Sold The World* – producer Tony Visconti found working with David difficult because he was so distracted by her presence at the studio. (▶ 11.4.71)

The May 1971 birth of their only child Zowie was followed by bouts of post-natal depression; as a result Angie would often spend time away from both David and the baby.

This fierce independence set a pattern, and frequent trips became a passion, continuing throughout Zowie's childhood and stoked by the 'open' lifestyle which permitted exploration of relationships with other people.

There is no doubt that Angie played an invaluable role in David's breakthrough. Although her own memoirs have somewhat clouded her significance, markedly in the vitriol directed towards Pitt and the down-playing of her own role, she was a powerful and inventive force in David's life at a pivotal moment, with a boundless energy and huge belief in his abilities.

Her appreciation of fashion and visual style was the key. As a bisexual woman she occasionally dressed up and role-played as a man, all the while subtly encouraging David to wear her clothes, which she began to buy with him in mind.

David had never been shy about experimenting with his appearance, yet Angie

ABOVE: David and Angie on their wedding day, 19 March 1970.

pushed him further, both off and on stage, helping to create the look of what is now recognised as the first glam rock gig: David Bowie & Hype at north London's Roundhouse in February 1970.

"It was Angela who encouraged David and the rest of the band to dress up for the first time," said drummer John Cambridge in 1991. "She was the outrageous one back then. It was Angela who got all of that together. She was amazing."

She remained on good terms with David's guitar cohort Mick Ronson right up until his death in 1993.

In 1991 he pinpointed her talents and importance to David's career: "Angela was responsible for a lot of the things that went on and she was responsible for getting the clothing together. She was always into the way things looked. She put all of her effort into David. She was 100% David all of the time."

Since the breakdown of their marriage in 1977, her musical achievements have failed to match David's. In the early 80s she performed her own poems backed by bassist Mick Karn (formerly of post-punk group Japan), appearing on BBC TV's rock show *The Old Grey Whistle Test* (which was presented for many years by her former housemate Bob Harris).

In 1985 she released the single 'Crying In The Dark', produced and written by New York guitarist Chico Rey, and also made a number of one-off appearances with her own band; Ronson made an appearance with them at London's Hippodrome nightclub on Valentine's Day in 1986.

Writing and lecturing (particularly on the subject of bisexuality) has been Angie's most consistent activity. She has appeared in a couple of films and also featured in a 1992 musical revue called *Straight From The Heart* in Atlanta, Georgia.

"I love Angie," said Ronson in 1991. "She gets a little crazy. She's almost too enthusiastic about everything, but she's got a very good heart."

David and Angie were formally divorced on 8 February 1980. They had been married just a month short of 10 years. Her daughter Stasha was born to her and punk singer Drew Blood (real name Michael Lipka) later that year.

In 2002 Angie released the album *Moon Goddess* on a British independent label and more recently has been working on a follow-up as well as preparing a book on sexuality, fashion and music. These days she is based in the US.

"Her energy was fearsome, and her ideas ranged from the brilliant to crazy," said former MainMan Vice President Tony Zanetta in 1987. "It was apparent that she was pushing David, pushing him further than she had dared go before. She wanted him to be brilliant and dazzling. It was the only way she seemed to have to display her own brilliance."

LEFT: Angela and Mary Finnigan at the Beckenham Free Festival.

Work on the single concludes at Trident the following day. At this stage 'Conversation Piece', the song David has been performing since he and John Hutchinson became a duo, is still a contender for inclusion on the new album.

Thursday 11 September

Recording moves to Pye Studios in Marble Arch.

With guitarist Keith Christmas, an attempt is made to tape David's song 'God Knows I'm Good'. But the session is cut short because of problems with the studio equipment.

John Cambridge has brought a friend of his from Hull, Benny Marshall, along to the session.

"The sound was terrible," said Marshall in 1991. "It always had been. David said, 'That was horrible, scrap that one', and decided to re-record it at Trident."

Saturday 13 September

▶ David Bowie, Library Gardens (aka Church House Gardens), Bromley, Kent.

David compères and performs a solo acoustic set at this open-air concert inspired by the recent Beckenham Free Festival and organised by Geoffrey Bradbury, a student from nearby Ravensbourne College of Art.

For his own set, David follows another local young band led by vocalist/guitarist John Aldington, who remembered the day in 2009:

"My band Maya was playing on the same bill as local pop star David Bowie, who was the headlining act. I was only 16 and still at school but the band already had an enthusiastic local following. We were just finishing when David Bowie appeared on the stage with some friends in tow, and turned to us and shouted: 'Do you guys know 'I'm So Glad' by Cream?' We nodded nervously and before we knew it we were accompanying him. That was the start of a 30-year journey down a long road of performing, recording and writing."

Held at the amphitheatre in the Gardens (just off the High Street, behind Churchill Theatre) this all-dayer also features Comus and Gun Hill from the festival, as well as Aslan and Puckles Blend. The free concert attracts around 1,000 people.

Today 'Space Oddity' drops out of the UK Top 50 after just one week at number 48.

Sunday 14 September

▶ Beckenham Arts Lab, The Three Tuns, Beckenham.

Tuesday 16 September

'God Knows I'm Good' is re-recorded at Trident.

Keith Christmas is featured prominently on the track; he is just about to release his own album, *Stimulus*, on RCA. "I was convinced mine was going to be a huge success, but I didn't think David's stood much of a chance," said Christmas in 2001. "It seemed such a shame. I thought David Bowie was a

really nice guy and deserved to be famous – just as much as me!"

Saturday 20 September

'Space Oddity' re-enters the charts at number 39 as the result of increased exposure; the BBC had lifted its ban on the broadcast of any space-related material the previous month.

Sunday 21 September

▶ Beckenham Arts Lab, The Three Tuns, Beckenham.

Media interest in 'Space Oddity' is beginning to gather momentum; David is interviewed by journalist Frances Donnelly for the BBC World Service.

Monday 22 September

Lou Reizner writes to Ken Pitt and informs him that Calvin Mark Lee no longer works for Mercury Records. Reizner's concern is that studio time is being booked without the label's sanction: 'We now find that we have many studio bills to approve which we knew nothing about.'

Tuesday 23 September

▶ David Bowie, Three Horseshoes Folk Club, Heath Street, Hampstead, London NW3.

David returns to the venue for an evening hosted by folk group The Exiles.

Wednesday 24 September

More press for 'Space Oddity': David is interviewed by Valerie Mabbs for *Record Mirror* and during the

LEFT AND ABOVE: David poses on electrical sculpture by artist Dante Leonelli for a photo session with David Bebbington. The jacket was a gift from Calvin Mark Lee.

DAVID BOWIE

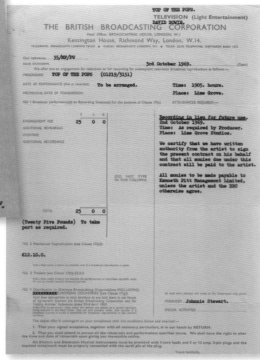

TOP: 'Space Oddity' sheet music, printed after the single had charted.

RIGHT: *Top Of The Pops* contract for 2 October recording.

MIDDLE: Trading card featuring David.

ABOVE: 'Space Oddity' newspaper advert.

In this year...

Sunday 5 October
BROADCAST of *Monty Python's Flying Circus* for the first time on BBC TV. The series was a firm favourite of David's and the other Haddon Hall residents. He witnessed the comic troupe's live show and became friendly with member Eric Idle (who is his son Duncan's godfather). (▶ 19.5.73)

afternoon a session takes place at Pitt's Manchester Street apartment with photographer Chris Walter.

In the evening there is an Arts Lab meeting at The Three Tuns.

Thursday 25 September

David is interviewed again for BBC's Radio One Club, this time by DJ Keith Skues, while Pitt follows up on an approach he made in March by contacting the Institute of Contemporary Arts again, proposing a performance by David at its London multimedia arts venue Nash House in The Mall.[1]

During the evening, David presents a meeting about the dangers of drug-taking at Bromley Centre Of Music & Arts in Sundridge Avenue, not far from the house where he was brought up.[2] He also heads a similar discussion about the dangers of LSD with members of the Arts Lab around this time.

1. An offer was not forthcoming. David's first work to appear at the ICA was his 'coffin' art installation in the Institute's Nash Room as part of the 1996 events held marking the 10th anniversary of the death of French writer Jean Genet.
2. This is now the Ripley Arts Centre.

Saturday 27 September

'Space Oddity' has risen to number 25 in the charts. This prompts a booking on the BBC's chart show *Top Of The Pops*.

Around this time David performs solo to a sell-out audience at the London Hospital Medical College,[1] in Whitechapel in London's East End, arranged by Beckenham Arts Lab member Tim Goffe, who DJed at the festival.

1. David visited the hospital's private museum in 1980 to view the skeleton and artifacts of The Elephant Man Joseph Merrick, as part of his research for his stage performance as the benighted figure in

Bernard Pomerance's play of the same name in Chicago, Denver and New York between July 1980 and January 1981.

Sunday 28 September

▶ Beckenham Arts Lab, The Three Tuns, Beckenham.

Monday 29 September

Hoping to capitalise on the interest in 'Space Oddity', Pitt takes a copy of film *Love You Till Tuesday* to the BBC's headquarters in Lime Grove, west London, to show TV executive Gordon Smith.[1]

1. The BBC was not interested in screening the film. Smith later told Pitt he should make a film about Tom Jones instead.

Wednesday 1 October

▶ David Bowie, The Downham Folk Club, The Bal Tabarin, Downham Way, near Bromley, Kent.

During the day, David is interviewed by Julie Webb for *Fabulous 208* magazine before making his way to this local folk club for a solo appearance. Around this time, with fellow Arts Lab member Ken Simmons also on acoustic guitar, David appeared at the Orpington Folk Club, at the town's Royal Oak pub.

However, he is about to step up a level in terms of concert bookings, having been selected to support heavy rockers Humble Pie on their forthcoming UK tour.

Thursday 2 October

In a car owned by his late father, David – who has just passed his driving test after instruction from friends Barrie Jackson and Tony Frost – drives in the afternoon to the BBC's Lime Grove studios for the recording of his first appearance on *Top Of The Pops*. He is accompanied by his mother and Pitt.

Dressed in a silver jacket and belt given to him by Calvin Mark Lee, David plays the Stylophone and guitar during his performance of 'Space Oddity' to backing tapes prepared by Gus Dudgeon. One of Dudgeon's jobs is to synchronise the accompaniment from the BBC Orchestra, which includes Barry Morgan (who played with David in May on BBC Radio's *Top Gear* show) on drums.

David is filmed in a small side studio so his image may be mixed with Nasa space footage. These elements marry perfectly on the first take, but Dudgeon is unhappy with the orchestra's timing and asks for the song to be recorded again. Although time has over-run, a second take is allowed, and the orchestration is much tighter. However, the visual mix of space footage with David's performance is less successful, but there is no time left to improve on it.

"It was a nightmare," said Dudgeon in 1991. "I did three different mixes of the backing tape and we had to experiment in the studio on the night. If we had had the chance of a third take it would have been brilliant."

The recording[1] is to be broadcast on the following week's edition of the show.

During the afternoon, *Disc & Music Echo* journalist

Penny Valentine interviews David at the studio.
1. This was subsequently wiped by the BBC.

Friday 3 October

Visconti oversees an edit of David's new album to establish the running order.

Following the lecture David arranged on 25 September, under the heading 'Drugs – The Peril Victims Face', the *Kentish Times* reveals: 'David Bowie, Bromley's own pop singer, who admits he smoked pot at one time, presented the meeting to improve communications between the generations.'

The following day 'Space Oddity' continues its climb up the singles chart to number 20.

Sunday 5 October

▶ Beckenham Arts Lab, The Three Tuns, Beckenham.

Monday 6 October

With recording of the new album complete, preparation of the running order continues.

Wednesday 8 October

▶ David Bowie, Coventry Theatre, Coventry.

David drives Pitt to the Midlands city for the opening night of Changes '69, a package tour showcasing Humble Pie, the group recently formed by David's friend, the ex-Small Faces frontman Steve Marriott, with his school friend from Bromley Tech, Peter Frampton.[1] Also on the bill are rock acts Samson, Griffin, as well as Love Sculpture led by singer/guitarist Dave Edmunds.

David has been booked by Humble Pie manager and former Rolling Stones impresario Andrew Loog Oldham to perform mime pieces, but tellingly jettisons that act in favour of a short set of songs with acoustic guitar for accompaniment.

Among the songs are 'Space Oddity' and a selection of others intended for the new album, including one which will never see commercial release in its current form: 'Lover To The Dawn'.

This tour is a first for David – he can afford hotel accommodation. Up until this point he has always had to make do with sleeping in, or travelling back to London in uncomfortable ambulances and vans.
1. Also in Humble Pie were Greg Ridley (former Spooky Tooth bassist) and 17-year-old Jerry Shirley on drums.

Thursday 9 October

▶ David Bowie, Leeds Town Hall, The Headrow, Leeds, Yorkshire.

At 7pm, David's 'Space Oddity' performance on *Top Of The Pops* is broadcast. The show also features The Temptations, Esther Ofarim, The Hollies, Lou Christie and Bobby Gentry and is hosted by Pete Murray. Meanwhile, the Changes '69 tour is suffering organisational problems, with much chaos behind the scenes. Nevertheless, David's 20-minute set is generally well received by audiences, particularly 'Space Oddity'.

However, certain crowd members are less sympathetic in the quieter spells of his set. David later claimed that, on some dates, 'gum-chewing skinheads' threw lit cigarettes at him.

Friday 10 October

▶ David Bowie, Birmingham Town Hall, Victoria Street, Birmingham.

Ken Pitt writes to David: 'Reaction to *Top Of The Pops* is E-N-O-R-M-O-U-S.'

The *Kentish Times* reports positively on his recent gig at the Downham Folk Club: 'The large audience, including many new faces, were quickly won over by David's unassuming personality and boyish charm.'

Saturday 11 October

▶ David Bowie, Brighton Dome, 29 New Road, Brighton, East Sussex.

The involvement of Oldham's friend, the celebrated theatrical designer Sean Kenny, in Changes '69 proves instructive.

Kenny (whose credits include the stage sets for two productions David admires, Lionel Bart's *Oliver!* and Anthony Newley's *Stop The World, I Want To Get Off*) has designed a large prop in the shape of a performing elephant which acts as a screen for stage projections and also belches smoke and emits flashing lights.

During the tour, David discusses stage lighting techniques with Kenny, and picks up ideas which will emerge in his own shows in a few years.

Meanwhile, David is beginning to reap

CHANGES '69
HUMBLE PIE
LOVE SCULPTURE
DAVID BOWIE
SAMSON
Changes designed by Sean Kenny

Wed Oct 8 Coventry Theatre
Thurs Oct 9 Town Hall Leeds
Fri Oct 10 Town Hall Birmingham
Sat Oct 11 The Dome Brighton
Mon Oct 13 Bristol Colston Hall

Tues Oct 21 Queen Elizabeth Hall London
Thurs Oct 23 The Usher Hall Edinburgh
Sat Oct 25 Odeon Manchester
Sun Oct 26 Empire Liverpool
One Performance Nightly 7.30.

LEFT: Steve Marriott, David and Peter Frampton backstage at the Brighton Dome on the Changes '69 tour, 11 October.

ABOVE: Changes '69 advertisement.

BELOW: Photographed by Ken Pitt in Paddington Street Gardens, which is a short distance from Pitt's Manchester Street apartment. The shoulder bag was designed by ex-Beatstalker Alan Mair.

1969 OCTOBER

RIGHT: *Disc & Music Echo*, 11 October.
BELOW: Swiss magazine article with pics taken at Rebecca's club, Birmingham, on 19 October, photographed by Alan Johnson.
BOTTOM: Small article from *NME*.

DISC and MUSIC ECHO 1s
OCTOBER 11, 1969 · EVERY THURSDAY

Amen Corner funeral rave-up SEE BACK PAGE

Beach Boys coming soon! SEE PAGE 6

Paxton, folk's gentle giant SEE PAGE 7

Skinheads launched on record!

MEET DAVID BOWIE, THE 'HUMAN ODDITY' — INTERVIEW ON PAGE 3

POP SÄNGER

Weil niemand seine Lieder singen wollte, musste der 22jährige David Bowie selber ins Aufnahmestudio. Nach zwei unkommerziellen Langspielplatten traf er mit seiner Supersingle «Space Oddity» den Nagel auf den Kopf. Und seit seiner «Hits a Gogo» Sendung im November kriegt er täglich Fanbriefe aus der Schweiz. Doch er bleibt mit Popsänger under Wellen.

the charts

DAVID WAITED FIVE YEARS

"SPACE Oddity," the strangely appealing, highly contemporary disc, inspired by Kubrick's "2001 A Space Oddysey," has given David Bowie the chart break he has waited five years for.

Major Tom, the astronaut, who simply chooses to remain in deep space rather than return home, is a space-age drop out.

"Home for Bowie and Major Tom," says David, "is the world we inhabit, where we eagerly subscribe our taxes to finance the space programme and where all we want in return is to know what our helmeted heroes eat for breakfast."

It was not written originally with a hit single in mind, but for David's own one-man colour TV show last winter.

Impressed

Everyone in the studio was so impressed that David decided to get it released as a single. He's now very surprised and pleased to find it in the charts.

Five years ago David formed one of Britain's earliest R&B groups, the Buzz, who some of you may remember from the Marquee on Saturday afternoons. In 1967 he made an LP before having issued a single, a rare occurrence in those days.

He has performed his songs throughout Britain and in almost every European country. This summer he won trophies at Maltese and Italian song festivals.

David has already made a follow-up release and a new LP is on the way. So those of you who like David's highly individual singing style should be well satisfied.

JAN NESBIT

DAVID BOWIE

---

the rewards of his first successful record, experiencing more media interest and quality music press coverage than at any time in his career thus far.

Today *Record Mirror* carries a quarter-page interview with Valerie Mabbs while *Melody Maker* refers to him as 'David Space Oddity Bowie'.

In *Disc & Music Echo* Penny Valentine gushes: 'His charm is so overpowering that it has given him more freedom to achieve his ideals than you would have thought possible in this day and age. "Space Oddity" is the first tenuous link in a long chain that will make David Bowie one of the biggest artists, and one of the most important people, British music has produced in a long time.'

Valentine's feature is trailed by a front-cover colour photo taken in Paddington Street Gardens, around the corner from Pitt's Manchester Street base.

In the afternoon David is interviewed by Ward Bogaert at the BBC's Broadcasting House in central London for the Belgian Radio Service. Bogaert had met David at the Malta Song Festival in the summer while accompanying Belgium's entrant Ann Soetaert.

In the evening David is interviewed in Brighton by Anne Nightingale for national newspaper the *Daily Sketch*.

Sunday 12 October

◗ Beckenham Arts Lab, The Three Tuns, Beckenham.

David performs at the Arts Lab. In the audience is Bogaert, who records some of the evening's performance, including a poetry reading by an individual billed as 'The Erotic

Roger Kany'.

During the day David is interviewed by Alastair Clarke for the *Kentish Times*.

Monday 13 October

◗ David Bowie, Bristol Colston Hall, Colston Street, Bristol, Avon.

Last date on the Changes '69 tour before an eight-day break.

David's friend from the Arts Lab Bill Liesegang (who performed at the festival as a member of Appendix To Part One) is in the audience and visits David backstage before the show. David is keen to play Steve Marriott 'Space Oddity' and he and Leisagang dash across the city to pick up a Dansette record player from a flatmate.

When he returns backstage to retrieve the deck, Liesegang discovers everyone, including David, has left, and the temperamental Marriott has smashed the Dansette, leaving the pieces scattered across the dressing-room floor.

Tuesday 14 October

David is photographed for another *Fabulous 208* feature and in today's issue he reveals: "I didn't want ('Space Oddity') released as a single at all. It was meant to be the tour de force of an album of space music I have worked on for a year."

And in the *Daily Sketch* interview with Anne Nightingale, David bangs the drum for the Arts Lab: "We are trying to encourage people to brighten up the streets where they live. We think they should pull up their paving stones and put down pink and blue ones instead. If I make enough bread from the record, I'm going to buy up a whole street, just to show what really can be done."

Thursday 16 October

David is photographed for the *NME* by Stuart Richman in and around Pitt's Manchester Street apartment. Shots are also taken outside the Lincoln Inn – the pub on the corner of Manchester Street and Blandford Street – as well as Varners coffee shop in George Street, near Marylebone High Street. He also poses on the steps of Catholic Church Spanish Place.[1] David conducts a phone interview with Sandie Robbie for *Mirabelle* and in the evening makes a guest appearance at counterculture community venue All Saints Hall[2] in Powis Gardens, Notting Hill, supporting underground bands The Entire Sioux Nation (ESN) and Annan.

David has been booked by his friend Wayne Bardell's company Clearwater. ESN is the brainchild of future Pink Fairies guitarist Larry Wallis,[3] while Powis Gardens has been used for exterior shots of the bohemian home of the character Turner (played by Mick Jagger) in Nicolas Roeg and Donald Cammell's film *Performance*.[4]

1. Renamed St James's Roman Catholic Church.
2. In 2010, The Tabernacle arts centre.

3. Pink Fairies' 1973 album *Kings Of Oblivion* takes its title from a lyric in David's 1971 song 'Bewlay Brothers'. Mick Wayne of Junior's Eyes joined the Pink Fairies line-up for a spell in 1975.

4. Filmed in 1968, contractual difficulties held up the release of *Performance* until 1970. David took the lead role in Roeg's 1976 film *The Man Who Fell To Earth*.

Friday 17 October

▶ David Bowie, Tiffany's, Commercial Road, Exeter, Devon.

David performs two solo acoustic sets each lasting 45 minutes.

A review by Andy Gray in the following day's *NME* describes David's recent appearance at the Brighton Dome: 'At about 9.23, David Bowie, a tall sensitive looking lad with curls started his act, singing among other things his "Space Oddity". He got the biggest applause of the night for it.'

Sunday 19 October

▶ David Bowie, Rebecca's Club, 7 Severn Street, Birmingham.

David plays a 45-minute solo set.

Monday 20 October

David receives a £100 cheque from Dübreq, the manufacturers of the Stylophone, the tiny hand-held electronic synthesizer featured on 'Space Oddity'.

With the song a hit, Dübreq's Bert Coleman offers David £500 to mention in interviews that he wrote the track on the keyboard.

Ken Pitt reaches a deal whereby David receives £100 every time he plays it on TV; today's cheque stems from his recent *TOTP* appearance.

In the afternoon David takes *NME* photographer Stuart Richman to a screening of *Love You Till Tuesday* and later, backed by Junior's Eyes, he records three tracks for Radio One's *Dave Lee Travis Show* at the Aeolian Hall, in London's New Bond Street.

Producer Paul Williams has requested David play 'four commercial numbers' to go with the show's broadcast of the 'Space Oddity' single, so the musicians perform 'Unwashed And Somewhat Slightly Dazed', 'Let Me Sleep Beside You' and 'Janine'.

After the session, David is interviewed by DJ Brian Matthew for his *Top Of The Pops*[1] International transcription disc series and talks about the success of 'Space Oddity' and the unreleased 'Let Me Sleep Beside You'.

1. A transcription series for radio not connected with the BBC TV show of the same name.

Tuesday 21 October

▶ David Bowie, Queen Elizabeth Hall, South Bank Centre, Belvedere Road, London SE1.

The Changes '69 tour resumes and George Underwood is in the audience to see his former school mates David and Peter Frampton perform.

Wednesday 22 October

David is interviewed at Manchester Street for Australian radio station 3XY Melbourne by journalist Bill Gates.

Thursday 23 October

▶ David Bowie, Usher Hall, Lothian Road, Edinburgh.

This date on the Changes '69 tour is David's first in the Scottish city since he played here with The Manish Boys in 1964.

Saturday 25 October

▶ David Bowie, Manchester Odeon, Oxford Street, Manchester.

On the day Changes '69 reaches this northern city, David's UK music publisher David Platz receives a letter from his US counterpart, Marvin Cane of the Richmond Organisation:

'After several discussions with Irwin Steinberg, the new President of Mercury Records, and John Sippel, his A&R Chief in Chicago, they have now agreed to go along with the re-release of the David Bowie single "Space Oddity".'

Cane says that there will also be a budget for adverts in American trade publications: 'The essence of the ads and renewed efforts will be based on the spectacular success of this recording in England, and now in Holland.'

Meanwhile, in *Disc & Music Echo* David provides a track-by-track summary of his new album for Penny Valentine.

David Bowie

TOP: Outside the Lincoln Inn pub (now the Tudor Rose), on the corner of Manchester Street and Blandford Street.

BOTTOM: German trading card late 69/early 70.

In this year...

Tuesday 21 October
DEATH of beat writer Jack Kerouac. David later said he was "genuinely upset" at the news, and in 1972 announced: "I wanted to be Jack Kerouac, I wanted to be a rebel."

TOP: Ron Oberman's 'Space Oddity' press release, Mercury/Fontana.

RIGHT: Billboard advertisement for 'Space Oddity'.

ABOVE: Computers single, released November. It was this single that encouraged David to record his own Italian version of 'Space Oddity'.

In this year...

Saturday 15 November
ENTRY of Blue Mink's single 'Melting Pot' into the UK singles chart, where it peaked at number three. Three members of the band – bassist Herbie Flowers, guitarist Alan Parker and drummer Barry Morgan – worked with David, on different projects and collectively on the single 'Holy Holy'. (▸ 17.1.71)

Sunday 26 October

❱ David Bowie, Empire Theatre, Lime Street, Liverpool.

Tonight is the final night of the Changes '69 tour so David is not at the Arts Lab this evening.

In the morning Radio One broadcasts the *Dave Lee Travis Show* radio session, featuring two songs and some of the Brian Matthew interview. The following day David is interviewed by Gordon Reid for the Glaswegian press.

Tuesday 28 October

With Pitt, David travels to Berlin for another appearance on TV show *Musik Für Junge Leute*. Staying at the Plaza Hotel, Kurfürstendamm, they dine with show's producer Gunther Schneider and visit a couple of nightclubs.

Wednesday 29 October

David visits the Berlin Wall for the first time.[1] Later in the day he performs 'Space Oddity' to backing tapes for the ZDF show before returning to London.

1. David returned to Berlin briefly in 1973 en route from Moscow to Paris by train and then to live there in 1976. The following year he recorded "*Heroes*" in the city's Hansa Tonstudios, which is in full view of the Berlin Wall. Here he was partly inspired by the structure to write the album's title track and hit single.

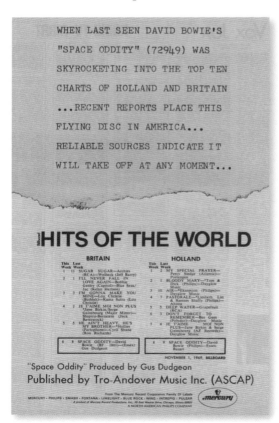

WHEN LAST SEEN DAVID BOWIE'S "SPACE ODDITY" (72949) WAS SKYROCKETING INTO THE TOP TEN CHARTS OF HOLLAND AND BRITAIN ...RECENT REPORTS PLACE THIS FLYING DISC IN AMERICA... RELIABLE SOURCES INDICATE IT WILL TAKE OFF AT ANY MOMENT...

Thursday 30 October

David is interviewed by Rosemary Lord for teen girls' magazine *Jackie*.

Friday 31 October

❱ David Bowie, General Gordon, Cedar Avenue, Gravesend, and Aurora Hotel, Brompton Road, Gillingham, both in Kent.

Performing at two Thames-side venues, David experiences an eventful Halloween.

The appearances have been arranged by a friend of David's at bookings company London City Agency (the General Gordon pub[1] and the Aurora Hotel[2] are relatively close to each other). He is supported at the latter booking by rock groups Fortes Mentum and Magna.

The Gravesend gig is one of David's least pleasurable performances to date; the impatient and inebriated audience throw beer cans and lit cigarette ends at him. Angie, who has accompanied David, becomes involved in scuffles with some of the offenders during David's set. This evening in particular serves to put David off future solo performances (unless they take place in the respectful atmosphere of the Arts Lab).

1. The General Gordon burnt down in 1992.
2. The Aurora Hotel was renamed the King Charles Hotel in 1980.

Saturday 1 November

'Space Oddity' peaks at number five in the chart, acting as a perfect trailer for the release of the new album in mid-November.

Meanwhile, he receives more favourable press from the Changes '69 tour. 'David Bowie (in our opinion) was the best,' says *Fabulous 208*.

In the Netherlands, David's reviews of eight newly released singles are published in *Muziek Express*.

Sunday 2 November

David flies to Zurich in Switzerland to record a TV appearance on his first visit to the country where he will live for nearly 20 years.[1]

'Space Oddity' had made the top 10 in the country. David and Ken Pitt stay at the Hotel Excelsior in Dufourstrasse.

In his absence the Arts Lab is compèred by Ken Simmons. Black Snake, Sempervivum and a composer friend of David's, Stephen Roberts, perform.

1. Having initially lived in Blonay, near Montreux, in 1982 David bought a large house in Upper Lausanne, Switzerland. He moved from the property, named Château du Signal, in 1997. The house was used extensively for Claude Chabrol's 2000 film *Merci Pour Le Chocolat*.

Monday 3 November

David lip-syncs to 'Space Oddity' on TV programme *Hits A GoGo*,[1] which is broadcast live from Zurich. Since the show has a haunted-house theme to coincide with the recent Halloween David wades through copious amounts of dry ice.

Also featured are The Nice,[2] Ayshea,[3] Julian Clerc, Mitwirkende, Les Charlots and Die Minstrels.

1. This edition of *Hits A GoGo* has survived, making it the only known pre-1972 continental European performance by David on tape.

2. The Nice line-up included Keith Emerson and drummer Brian Davison, both of whom had played alongside David in 1966 as members of the Ken Pitt-managed Mark Leeman Five. David had witnessed The Nice live at the Marquee earlier in 1969.

3. Ayshea Brough (originally Ayshea Hague) had been releasing singles since 1965. She also fronted Granada TV's 1969 show *Discotheque*, then *Lift Off* (which began in November 1969 and became *Lift Off With Ayshea*). (▶ 21.6.72)

Tuesday 4 November

David returns to the UK. This is the last flight he and Ken Pitt will take together.

Friday 7 November

▶ David Bowie, Blue Web Club, Salutation Hotel, 34 South St, Perth, Scotland.

Ahead of the release of his new album, David embarks on his first headlining tour; a week-long Scottish excursion which starts tonight. As well as backing David, Junior's Eyes perform a set of their own.

"It was very low-budget, no-tour manager," said Junior's Eyes guitarist Tim Renwick in 1998. "We jumped into a Transit and headed north. The venues were not particularly suitable. David mostly played his 12-string guitar, but I don't think the audiences really knew how to respond, it was all a bit much for them."

The band and equipment travel in the van driven by Roger Fry, an Australian who lives with David and Angie at Haddon Hall (and is inevitably nicknamed 'Roger The Lodger'). David is driven by Barrie Jackson in a second-hand Rover he has recently bought, sometimes sitting cross-legged on the back seat of the car, strumming his guitar.

Saturday 8 November

▶ David Bowie, Community Centre, Well Road, Auchinleck, and Grand Hall, London Road, Kilmarnock.

On the day *Disc & Music Echo* publishes a piece by journalist Phil Symes about David's use of the Stylophone for composing, particularly on 'Space Oddity', David and Junior's Eyes play an afternoon and an evening show at two different venues.

Sunday 9 November

▶ David Bowie, Kinema Ballroom, Dunfermline.

The Kinema's resident support band The Shadettes[1] kick off the evening.

The following morning drummer John Cambridge is left sitting on the toilet, stranded in Dunfermline when the band leaves for Glasgow without him. He rushes to the local bus garage and arrives ahead of the band, who are amazed to see him waiting for them since no one has even noticed he is missing.

As Junior's Eyes now have to fulfill some pre-booked gigs of their own, David has to complete

his tour alone. Over half of the remaining dates are cancelled as they have been booked on the understanding that David would have a backing group with him.[2]

With time to kill, David spends the next few days exploring Edinburgh. He will return to the city often over the next five years.

At the Beckenham Arts Lab, David's MC role is again filled by the capable Ken Simmons.

1. In February 1970 The Shadettes changed their name to Nazareth and subsequently hit the charts in 1973 via 'Broken Down Angel' and 'Bad Bad Boy' and 'My White Bicycle' in 1975.

2. Cancelled dates are Glasgow's Electric Garden (10 November), Stirling Albert Hall (11), Aberdeen Music Hall (12) and Hamilton Town Hall (13).

Friday 14 November

▶ David Bowie (solo), Adam Smith Hall, Bennochy Road, Kirkcaldy, Fife, and a midnight performance at Frisco's Club, Caley Picture House, 31 Lothian Road, at the foot of Edinburgh Castle.

Today Mercury/Philips releases David's new album, titled, like its predecessor, *David Bowie*. During the day, David – who is staying with friends at their apartment near Edinburgh Castle – is interviewed by Ben Lyon for BBC Glasgow and by DJ Dave Lee Travis, who is in Scotland for a Radio One Club booking at Glasgow's Electric Garden (the venue David was supposed to play on 10 November).

If you've ben wondering how those weird astral effects were obtained in the DAVID BOWIE hit " Space Oddity " — he used a Stylophone. This is the pocket-sized electronic organ first introduced to TV last year by Rolf Harris. David does all his composing on this battery-operated instrument, which is now growing in popularity with many record fans who are using it to play along with groups on disc.

TOP LEFT: Photo session to promote the Stylophone by Dübreq, as featured on 'Space Oddity'.

MIDDLE LEFT: Lee Jackson, bass player with The Nice, jams with David at the end of *Hits A GoGo* in Zurich, 3 November.

BOTTOM LEFT: Telegram to Ken Pitt from promoter Derek Nicol regarding tour of Scotland, 25 September.

TOP RIGHT: Performing 'Space Oddity' on *Hits A GoGo*.

BOTTOM RIGHT: Stylophone press article, October.

LEFT: The *David Bowie* album cover was designed by David and Calvin Mark Lee with photography and technical assistance by Vernon Dewhurst. The Vasarely design is titled CTA 25 Neg. RIGHT: Back cover 'Width Of A Circle' (the correct title) painting by George Underwood.

DAVID BOWIE Released Friday 14 November

Side One

1. SPACE ODDITY (Bowie) (5.14)
David Bowie (vocal, acoustic guitar, Stylophone)
Terry Cox (drums)
Rick Wakeman (Mellotron)
Mick Wayne (guitar)
Herbie Flowers (bass)
Session orchestra
This track only produced by Gus Dudgeon
Arranged by David Bowie, Paul Buckmaster

2. UNWASHED AND SOMEWHAT SLIGHTLY DAZED
(Bowie) (6.10)
David Bowie (vocal, acoustic guitar)
John Cambridge (drums)
Mick Wayne (guitar)
Tim Renwick (guitar)
John Lodge (bass)
Benny Marshall (harmonica)
Unknown brass and sax musicians

3. (DON'T SIT DOWN) (Bowie) (0.39)
David Bowie (vocal, acoustic guitar)
John Cambridge (drums)
Mick Wayne (guitar)
Tim Renwick (guitar)
John Lodge (bass)

4. LETTER TO HERMIONE (Bowie) (2.30)
David Bowie (vocal, acoustic guitar)
Keith Christmas (acoustic guitar)

5. CYGNET COMMITTEE (Bowie) (9.30)
David Bowie (vocal, acoustic guitar)
John Cambridge (drums)
Mick Wayne (guitar)
Tim Renwick (guitar)
John Lodge (bass)

Side Two

1. JANINE (Bowie) (3.19)
David Bowie (vocal, acoustic guitar, kalimba)
John Cambridge (drums)
Mick Wayne (guitar)
Tim Renwick (guitar)
John Lodge (bass)
Keith Christmas (acoustic guitar)

2. AN OCCASIONAL DREAM (Bowie) (2.56)
David Bowie (vocal, acoustic guitar)
John Cambridge (drums)
Mick Wayne (guitar)
Tim Renwick (guitar, flute, recorder)
John Lodge (bass)
Keith Christmas (acoustic guitar)
Tony Visconti (flute, recorders)

3. WILD EYED BOY FROM FREECLOUD (Bowie) (4.47)
David Bowie (vocal, acoustic guitar)
Paul Buckmaster (arco bass)
John Lodge (bass)
Session orchestra

4. GOD KNOWS I'M GOOD (Bowie) (3.16)
David Bowie (vocal, acoustic guitar)

Mick Wayne (guitar)
Tim Renwick (guitar)
John Lodge (bass)
Keith Christmas (acoustic guitar)
John Cambridge (drums)

5. MEMORY OF A FREE FESTIVAL (Bowie) (7.07)
David Bowie (vocal, acoustic guitar, Rosedale electric chord organ)
Keith Christmas (acoustic guitar)
Tim Renwick (guitar)
Mick Wayne (guitar)
John Cambridge (drums)
John Lodge (bass)
David Bowie, Marc Bolan, Bob Harris, Sue Harris, Tony Woollcott, Girl (backing vocals)

Produced by Tony Visconti
Arranged by David Bowie, Tony Visconti
Engineered by Ken Scott, Malcolm Toft,
Barry Sheffield
Photograph by Vernon Dewhurst
Painting by George Underwood
Design by David Bowie/CML33
(Philips SBL7912) – UK

BELOW LEFT TO RIGHT: David at the studio of Vasarely by Christian Simonpietri in 1977, Victor Vasarely, Calvin Mark Lee in 2009, George Underwood in 2010, Ken Pitt in 1969. FAR RIGHT: The concept was based on a sleeve George had painted for Tyrannosaurus Rex in 1968.

My people were fair and had sky in their hair...
But now they're content to wear stars on their brows

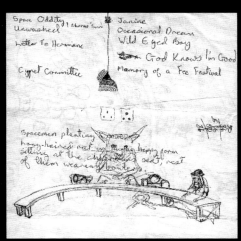

TOP LEFT AND MIDDLE: David's sketched ideas for George which also include a drawing of Ken Pitt and Calvin Mark Lee, though they didn't make the final design due to a lack of space. TOP RIGHT: George Underwood's original final artwork. ABOVE LEFT AND MIDDLE: Album press adverts. RIGHT: David miming with The Strawbs to their song 'Poor Jimmy Wilson' at the White Bear pub in Hounslow, west London.

RECORDING of David's second album started on 16 July 1969 at Trident Studios in central London; in the afternoon time was set aside at the studio for him to sign his new record deal with Mercury.

The night before, David had signalled the musical ground which would be covered on the record – a fusion of his acoustic folk leanings with a growing interest in electric rock – by playing an impromptu gig at the arts lab held by his friends The Strawbs at a pub in the nondescript outer-west London suburb of Hounslow.

Here, rather than the arch folk-pop excursions of the recent Turquoise and Feathers period, David ran through some of the tracks written for the new album, backed by his producer Tony Visconti on bass and John Cambridge of Junior's Eyes on drums.

The album sessions coincided with a series of key events in David's life: as well as his heart-breaking split with Hermione Farthingale, the recently released Gus Dudgeon-produced single 'Space Oddity', which undertook its slow rise to the top five in the UK singles chart, and The Beckenham Arts Lab, which went from strength to strength, drawing ever-larger crowds and increasingly distinctive performers (though its success was predicated on his own growing public profile).

David's tirelessness was evident professionally in his role as the driving force in the organisation of August's impressive Beckenham Free Festival, while on the personal front his move with Angie into Haddon Hall represented the establishment of his first home of adulthood.

But these activities were eclipsed less than three weeks into recording with the sudden death of his father, who succumbed to a bout of pneumonia at the age of 57. So, the album's transitory nature may be attributed to the seismic occurrences of that summer.

'This album seems to serve as an intimate discussion between old friends. This is more than a record. It is an experience'
Music Now!

In his approach to the album, David was unwavering in one regard: despite the sterling job carried out by Dudgeon (who would soon assist Elton John's career), he retained Visconti as producer of all the remaining tracks.

"I did the rest of the album with Tony, which I think hurt Gus at the time," David said in 1976. "Sorry Gus, I didn't mean to do that to you! I was friends with Tony you see, and I didn't know you very well. You were petit bourgeois, you had an apartment!

"If things had gone another way I guess I would have stayed with Gus. I might have been Elton John, mum!"

By the time David entered Trident, a number of the songs had been honed, not only in regular performances at the Arts Lab and on London's busy folk scene but also in the recording of the so-called 'Mercury demos' with John Hutchinson in the spring of 1969.

Hutchinson's retreat from London put paid to the hope that they would record an album as a duo, though it was always in the plan that the songs would have the broader palette supplied by a number of backing musicians.

Visconti's recommendation of Junior's Eyes paid dividends; they were a coherent unit able to interpret David's ambitions. And drummer John Cambridge became such a good friend that he moved into Haddon Hall in 1970, by which time he was a member of David's next backing group, Hype.

Cambridge's importance to David's story is sealed by the fact that he introduced him to Mick Ronson early in 1970, setting the scene for David's key musical collaboration of the first part of the next decade.

In a certain regard, Hutchinson's role as sensitive foil was filled by the inclusion of singer-songwriter Keith Christmas, a gifted 12-string guitarist who appeared regularly at the Arts Lab and also performed a memorable set at the Free Festival. His dexterity on the lovelorn 'Letter To Hermione' and 'An Occasional Dream' in particular provides a taste of what might have been had David Bowie & Hutch become a viable entity.

With a settled vocal technique, lyrically the 1969 *David Bowie* album – which became known as *Space Oddity* after its 1972 reissue – demonstrates clear advances on David's debut (recorded two-and-a-half years previously, when he was just 19).

The failure of the relationship with Hermione Farthingale is a preoccupation, as evinced by 'Letter To Hermione', 'Occasional Dream' and 'Unwashed And Somewhat Slightly Dazed'. The latter song was also informed by the phase during which David adopted an uncharacteristically scruffy appearance, which grated with his manager, Ken Pitt.

And the suitably ragged harmonica playing was spontaneously contributed by Benny Marshall, who had been brought along by his friend John Cambridge.

During the session David invited Marshall to play on Cambridge's enthusiastic recommendation.

"I did it in one take," said Marshall in 1990. "They gave me a standing ovation in the control room when I finished. Tony Visconti said to Calvin Mark Lee, 'You've got to pay the man something for that'.

"David bought the harmonica especially for the session and whenever I saw him performing he would call me up on stage to join them on that number. For a time he always had that harmonica with him."

It's clear that the song's subject – David's own unkempt appearance – reflected his inner malaise particularly over Farthingale. He told *Disc & Music Echo's* Penny Valentine, "The lyrics are what you hear – about a boy whose girlfriend thinks he is socially inferior."

Although he sent Farthingale a copy of the record, David said in 1972, "Didn't do any good – I never saw her again."

There are concerns aside from those of the heart; 'Cygnet Committee' even extends to an expression of socio-political rage.

This track had started life as another song with the title 'Occasional Dream' but with a different lyric. David then called it 'Lover To The Dawn' and performed and recorded it with Hutch in demo form. (▸ 11.3.69)

During the album's recording sessions – which took place over a seven-week period between mid-July and the end of September – David expanded it into the nine-and-a-half-minute summation of political disenchantment which appears on the finished album.

'Cygnet Committee' was in part inspired by his frustration with the Arts Lab, which he felt lost sight of the objective of becoming an artistic community project when crowds arrived simply to watch him perform rather than contributing their own creative ideas.

As such, this collection marked a turning point; David was now drawing on life rather than composing winsome stories.

Yet the most famous track, 'Space Oddity', stands apart. "I never thought that the album had anything to do with 'Space Oddity' at all," said Dudgeon in 1991. "To me it was 'Space Oddity' and a collection of other songs – not surprising, as there were two different producers.

"It was understood from the word go that

it was a long-term relationship as far as Bowie and Visconti were concerned. I wasn't upset when David finished the LP with Tony because I knew that from the outset."

The recording of the album coincided with the waning of David's allegiance to Pitt, the music business sophisticate who had rescued him from the scuffling mid-60s R&B circuit and nurtured both his interest in the arts and the expansion of his creative horizons.

When his manager attended sessions he was uncomfortable with the new cabal surrounding David: Calvin Mark Lee, Angie and other friends from Beckenham. And so tension built and matters came to a head within a few months of the album's release. (▸ 24.4.70)

The album is textured by the lighter touches and throwaway elements which became a trademark (particularly on 1971's *Hunky Dory* with its spoken intro to 'Andy Warhol').

At just 40 seconds, 'Don't Sit Down' is a jam, taking its title from David's sparse, spontaneous lyric. Not even accorded a reference in the track-listing.

"David always had a lot of ideas, a lot of energy," said Tim Renwick – who played lead guitar on 'Don't Sit Down' – in 1998. "I was struck by how sensitive he was during the recording of the album. I felt you had to be careful what you said to him, though we always got on very well and I enjoyed working with him."

Meanwhile, 'Janine' was penned by David about a Mauritian girlfriend of album-sleeve artist and close friend George Underwood.

"I couldn't figure out what David was trying to say with the song," confessed Underwood in 1995. "He told me, 'I'm doing it like Elvis Presley'. I think he was trying to tell me something but I still don't know what. He never came out and said he didn't like my girlfriend or anything, he was always nice to her and she never upset him as far as I knew."

The album's version of 'Wild Eyed Boy From Freecloud' expands on that produced by Dudgeon for the B-side of 'Space Oddity'. Paul Buckmaster's arco bass was replaced by Visconti's dramatic orchestration. Describing the earlier recording as 'throwaway', Visconti spent five days working on the arrangement.

'I heard a Wagnerian orchestra in my head,' he wrote in his memoir. 'I set up the studio of 50 musicians with David sitting right in the middle playing his 12-string. I was standing in front of him conducting the orchestra. We were both very nervous.'

This trepidation was compounded by technical problems with Trident's 16-track deck, which rendered most of the three-hour session unusable. Against the odds and with time running out, the very last take was recorded successfully.

While the dual inspirations for 'Wild Eyed Boy From Freecloud' were his landlady Mary Finnigan's young son Richard and 19th-century French book *The Wild Boy Of Aveyron*, 'God Knows I'm Good' was David's take on a newspaper item about an elderly lady accused of shoplifting. This was according to photographer friend Ray Stevenson, who visited David while he was writing it and even offered suggestions for lyrics.

As a narrative piece, this song bears similarities with some of those on his debut album. 'Memory Of A Free Festival', on the other hand, is a purely personal attempt at evoking the good-natured atmosphere of the Arts Lab-organised event at Croydon Road Recreation Ground on 16 August 1969 (even though David himself was, by all accounts, in the darkest mood that day, wracked by grief over the recent loss of his father).

Set against the drone of a Rosedale electric chord organ – a cheap children's reed instrument purchased from Woolworth's which he sometimes used in live performance – David conjures up this hippy idyll before seguing into the choral climax which takes up the final third as layered voices repeat the line 'The sun machine is coming down.

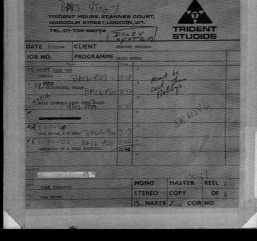

ABOVE: Master tape box for *David Bowie*, with deletion of conversation piece evident

ABOVE: Album session promotional shot. RIGHT: The US release on Mercury was titled *David Bowie* (see footnote).

we're gonna have a party, ha-ha-ha' against squealing electric guitars.

The 'crowd' was in fact David, DJ/journalist Bob Harris and his wife Sue, their friend Tony Woollcott (who became a bigwig at record label Sony in the 80s), Marc Bolan and an American performer known only as Girl.

The Harrises and Wollcott recorded their contributions first. "Tony built up this huge crowd from the four of us chanting into a microphone," said Bob Harris in 1991. "He kept over-dubbing until it sounded full enough."

Bolan added his voice to the mix at another session. "We were all gathered around a microphone and Bolan was standing opposite me," said Cambridge in 2009. "As we were singing, for a laugh I encouraged Marc to copy some Temptations-style dance moves, like pointing at the sky and then the floor, along to the music."

David invited Girl along after meeting her at hippy clothing haven Kensington Market. "David recognised me from an appearance I had made at the Roundhouse and he invited me to Beckenham, where he was living with Angie," said Girl (who declined to reveal her real name) in 2001. "I had no idea who he was, but was pleased that he liked my music. I hung out with David and Angie for about a month, jamming until dawn most nights. He then invited me to sing on 'Memory Of A Free Festival'." Girl can be heard enthusiastically shouting the odd 'yippee!'.

The song was re-recorded in 1970 by David and Visconti for potential release as a single. (▸ 26.6.70)

The album sessions also marked the entry of Ken Scott, one of London's top recording engineers, into David's life. Scott (who co-engineered with Trident co-owner Barry Sheffield) was hired by Visconti, who used him again on 1970's *The Man Who Sold The World*. After that Scott co-produced with David his next four albums. (▸ 17.12.71)

Ken Pitt's exclusion from the album was underlined by the fact that his counsel was not sought over the gatefold sleeve.

The front superimposed a portrait photograph of David by Vernon Dewhurst on a geometric design by Victor Vasarely, a Hungarian artist whose work was collected by Calvin Mark Lee.

Lee (credited as CML33) and David came up with the concept; this artwork, titled CTA 25 Neg, dated from the mid-60s and was one of the many Vasarely prints which decorated Lee's apartment.

Pitt thought the front cover crude and unflattering to Vasarely, whose work he also enjoyed. David opted not to allow use of the image again until a reissue as part of his back catalogue series by EMI in 1999.

The back cover comprised an illustration in pen and Indian ink by George Underwood. This depiction of characters and themes from the album's songs was executed in the style of his cover for Tyrannosaurus Rex's 1968 album *My People Were Fair And Had Sky In Their Hair... But Now They're Content To Wear Stars On Their Brows*.

Underwood's drawing (which is still in David's possession) was a faithful rendition of a sketched proposal roughed out in biro by David (though his original included separate small portraits of Pitt and Lee, which never made it to Underwood's version).

The album sleeve calls Underwood's illustration Depth Of A Circle; David had meant this to read Width Of A Circle and was annoyed at the record company error. The unused title appeared as the name of a song on his next album, *The Man Who Sold The World*.

The blue with white text inner gatefold featured the album's song lyrics.

None of the musicians, apart from David, were credited on the 1969 pressing, as most were under contract to other labels in the UK.

However, their roles were mentioned on the sleeve of the US release, which was also titled *David Bowie*, though is commonly known as *Man Of Words/ Man Of Music*.[1]

In the US, Mercury decided against Vasarely's artwork on the cover, which instead featured a similar Dewhurst photograph. However, this suffered from sloppy technical application and the image appeared washed out as a result of poor duplication of the transparency.

As with the UK release, the song lyrics were printed on the inner gatefold.

Drummer John Cambridge still treasures his copy of the American release.

"David showed me a copy; I was really pleased to see I was credited inside," said Cambridge in 1991. "I kept on to David to let me have it and he kept saying 'It's my only copy.' Eventually he gave in and gave it to me. I've still got it."

1. The US album was actually called *David Bowie* like its UK counterpart. Man Of Words/Man Of Music was added as a description of the artist and was not intended to be the main title (this is why the actual album labels say David Bowie only). All Philips/Mercury paperwork refers to the release only as *David Bowie*. An unreleased stock copy of single 'All The Madmen'/'Janine' also confirms this title on the label. However, it is now commonly known as *Man Of Words/Man Of Music* which, to save confusion, is how it is listed in this book.

TOP: Promotional flyer for appearance at the Purcell Room, Southbank, London, 20 November.

BOTTOM: Poster designed by Peter Chasseaud for an Egg Workshop Arts Lab performance, Croydon, Surrey, 18 November.

In this year...

Saturday 6 December
PERFORMANCE by The Rolling Stones at the Altamont Speedway, near San Francisco. At the gig audience member 18-year-old Meredith Hunter was killed by Hell's Angels hired as security. The gig continued to the end as the band were unaware of the death.
Hunter had approached the stage brandishing a revolver and was overpowered and mortally wounded. In 1972, David, in a paranoid state, believed that he would be shot on stage, just as he was about to become successful.

Saturday 15 November

▶ David Bowie (solo), Caird Hall, City Square, Dundee.

Mercury have been planning to issue the upbeat 'Janine' as the follow-up single to 'Space Oddity' today but are unconvinced about its commercial appeal and shelve it.

In an interview with Gordon Coxhill published in *NME*, David confesses to feeling amazed at the success of 'Space Oddity': "I've been the male equivalent of a dumb blonde for a few years, and I was beginning to despair of people accepting me for my music. It may be fine for a male model to be told he's a great looking guy but that doesn't help a singer much, especially now that the pretty boy cult seems to be on the way out."

Monday 17 November

On his return from Scotland, David and Angie take part in their first professional photo session together: a mocked-up Christmas feast at Rules Restaurant in London's Covent Garden for the Yuletide cover of *Fabulous 208*. The photographer is Roger Brown.

David conducts interviews for two other magazines at 39 Manchester Street: with George Tremlett[1] for *Jackie* and in the evening with Tim Hughes for gay title *Jeremy*. It is agreed that Hughes will shadow David for a period of nearly two months as part of his research for an article with fellow associate editor Trevor Richardson.

1. George Tremlett interviewed David a number of times in the 60s and early 70s and was the first person to write a book about him, 1974's *The David Bowie Story*.

Tuesday 18 November

▶ David Bowie, Egg Workshop Arts Lab, The Gun Tavern, Crown Hill, Croydon, Surrey.

David performs a solo set at this sister arts lab and also joins the other band on the bill, Medicine Hat.

Wednesday 19 November

▶ David Bowie, Brighton Dome, 29 New Road, Brighton, East Sussex.

David returns to this venue for the third time this year to give a 20-minute performance on the same bill as The Edgar Broughton Band,[1] The Strawbs, Heaven, Steamhammer, Clouds, Success and Fox. The evening is compèred by his friend Jeff Dexter.

David performs three songs, including 'Space Oddity', but the audience – who are there for the rock acts – are unmoved. Viewing David's evident discomfort from the wings is Clouds singer and keyboard player Billy Ritchie, who has known David since he was in 1-2-3 and covered 'I Dig Everything' in 1966.

"As he came off stage he walked our way and I said 'Hi David' but he hardly acknowledged me and walked away," said Ritchie in 2007. "It really upset me so I told him to 'fuck off'. In retrospect he had just had a bad experience on stage and probably

was in no mood to talk to anyone, but I didn't see it like that at the time. It was the last time I saw David. It was very sad, after all the time we had spent together talking." The other two members of Clouds, Ian Ellis and Harry Hughes, believe David is stoned and don't take the response as a slight.

1. David's first known encounter with underground act The Edgar Broughton Band. He occasionally appeared live with them in 1970, performing a mime to one of their songs. They reciprocated by appearing at the Arts Lab.

Thursday 20 November

▶ An Evening With David Bowie, Purcell Room, South Bank, Belvedere Road, London SE1.

Support is provided again by Junior's Eyes, along with Arts Lab favourites, the six-piece progressive rock group Comus.

In the audience are many friends and supporters: David's mother is there with Ken Pitt, and Gus Dudgeon and Lionel Bart[1] are also present.

"David was very, very nervous," said Tim Renwick in 1998. "There were a lot of friends and music business people there and it got to him a bit. I know he didn't enjoy that show even though it did go very well."

Dudgeon is disappointed when David dismisses other musicians from the stage for a solo rendition of 'Space Oddity'. "I was amazed," said Dudgeon in 1991. "He had the chance of a full backing band and it rather spoilt it for me."

After the show, David remains on stage and greets well-wishers but becomes irate when informed by Pitt that no national daily paper journalists have attended. Apparently there has been a mix-up over press invitations, and Calvin Mark Lee – as the driving force behind the booking – bears the brunt of David's disappointment. In the event, David receives a glowing review in national Sunday newspaper the *Observer* as well as in several magazines.

Philips' large display of *David Bowie* album sleeves in the foyer is stripped bare as the audience exits for the night.

1. Bart became a regular visitor to Haddon Hall over the next four years.

Friday 21 November

▶ David Bowie, Poperama, Devizes, Wiltshire.

Local promoter Mel Bush[1] books David. The contract for this gig states that David's fee of £125 will rise to £150 if 'Space Oddity' has reached at least number five in the UK charts. Since the single has just made the grade, David receives the bigger payment.

The following evening, David's performance of 'Space Oddity' on *Musik Für Junge Leute* is broadcast in Germany.

1. Bush also promoted David's extensive 1973 UK tour. (▶12.5.73)

Sunday 23 November

▶ Beckenham Arts Lab, The Three Tuns, Beckenham.

Monday 24 November

There is a daytime photo session and interview at *Mirabelle*'s offices at 22 Long Acre in Covent Garden.

Pitt writes to Decca's Hugh Mendl the following day with David's selection and running order for *The World Of David Bowie*. Decca is cashing in on David's new-found success by issuing a compilation of tracks from 1966–1968. (▶6.3.70)

Wednesday 26 November

▶ Growth (formerly the Beckenham Arts Lab), Ripley Arts Centre, Sundridge Avenue, Bromley. David arranges another event at his local Arts Centre, in the building's music room. This time the evening is focussed on all things Buddhist.

David and Comus supply the music whilst Trungpa Chogyam Rinpoche (one of the founders of Samye Lyng) instructs on Sadhana ritual and meditation and Chime Youngdong Rinpoche 'talks about Buddhism'.

Thursday 27 November

▶ Beckenham Arts Lab, The Three Tuns, Beckenham.

During the day he meets producer Marion Brinkman in Half Moon Street, near Curzon Street, Mayfair, regarding a role in John Schlesinger's new film, *Sunday Bloody Sunday*. Schlesinger has caused a storm in the summer with his controversial movie *Midnight Cowboy*. Impressed, Brinkman arranges for David to meet the director the following day.

Pitt receives a Mercury/Philips statement showing that 134,000 copies of 'Space Oddity' have been sold in the UK.

In the evening David contributes a set to the first Thursday gathering of the Arts Lab.

Friday 28 November

David meets Schlesinger[1] at Vic Films, 33 Bruton Street.[2] He auditions for the role of the young bisexual designer who wreaks havoc on a marriage.[3]

During the morning, David attends a band call rehearsal at the Victoria Palace Theatre in Victoria Street for an appearance at the Save Rave charity concert at leading West End venue the London Palladium.

1. John Schlesinger (1926–2003), achieved prominence in 1966 with his film *Darling*. He won the Oscar for best director in 1970 for *Midnight Cowboy* and in 1973 unsuccessfully tried to interest David in another film role. In 1985 David contributed the title song to Schlesinger's *The Falcon And The Snowman*.

2. In 1994 David contributed artwork to an exhibition called Minotaurs, Myths & Legends at the Berkeley Square Gallery at 23A Bruton Street.

3. The role was taken by another singer, Murray Head. In 1970 David claimed that he wasn't offered it because he looked too young.

Sunday 30 November

▶ David Bowie, London Palladium,[1] Argyll Street, London W1.

David performs 'Space Oddity' and 'Wild Eyed Boy From Freecloud' at the Save Rave evening to raise money for the Invalid Children Aid Association.

The guest of honour is Princess Margaret, who is presented to the performers after the show.[2] His appearance at Save Rave precludes David from joining in at the Arts Lab.

1. This is David's first appearance at the Palladium. He rehearsed at the venue with The Manish Boys in 1965.

2. Also on the bill are Grapefruit, Karen Young, Magna Carta, Marmalade, Settlers, Clodagh Rodgers, Graham Bond Initiation, Tiny Tim, Lou Christie, The Equals, Dusty Springfield and dance troupe the Gojos.

Monday 1 December

David is interviewed at 39 Manchester Street by Tim Hughes and Trevor Richardson for *Jeremy*.

Also this month 'Space Oddity' is among the tracks released on compilation *Philips Revolutionaries* in New Zealand.

Thursday 4 December

▶ The Beckenham Arts Lab, The Three Tuns, Beckenham.

ABOVE: *Fabulous 208* magazine feature, 29 November. David's waistcoat was designed and made by Alan Mair.

BOTTOM LEFT: Waiting in line to meet Princess Margaret at the Palladium, London, 30 November. Left to right: David, Lou Christie, The Equals, Tiny Tim and Dusty Springfield. Tim made US TV history the following month when he married his partner on the *Johnny Carson Show*

BELOW: David performing at the Save Rave evening at the Palladium, 30 November.

ABOVE: *Music Now!* interview and feature by Kate Simpson, 20 December.

Week ending December 20, 1969   MUSIC NOW!   7

DAVID BOWIE

HIS THOUGHTS AND IDEAS REVEALED IN CONVERSATION WITH MUSIC NOW'S

KATE SIMPSON

SEVERAL people I know see David Bowie as a one-hit-wonder. Until recently I shared their doubts as to his future beyond the song-that-made-him-famous, 'Space Oddity.' Then there was his recent concert at London's Purcell Room. I changed my mind.

    His performance was astounding. He had the audience bewitched with his words, his music, his voice, and his professionalism. With simplicity and sincerity he sang his songs. He has his own style, but also great imagination and versatility.

    There are strains of 'Major Tom' in most of his compositions but not noticeable enough to be boring after the third song. You can hear every word he sings, which is nice as the words are in fact very worthwhile. He sings of things he's seen, he's dreamed, he's felt. Songs about old ladies who steal from supermarkets; space-men, and a girl he never really got to know and didn't really like very much.

    Several months ago Tony Norman interviewed David Bowie. His record was a hit, and he was full of beautiful ideas. With the success of his first album, I went to talk to him again, and find out just how much success had altered his ideas and views.

    Our conversation covered many topics from pop to politics. Having seen the audience's reaction at the Purcell Room, I was interested to see how much it meant to him . . .

    When you're playing are you always involved with the audience. Do they mean anything to you—the people out there?

    "Oh yeah, because its the very reason I write and work. But not as a kind of 'I love you' audience. They are a reception for me."

    Their reactions?

    "Their reactions are important—of course they are. I don't write with the idea of teaching, because I don't think what I've got to say is very important. I don't like the artists who come on with this 'this is how you save the world' stuff".

    So when you say you write for your audiences—in what way do you write if you're not teaching them?

    "I write about pretty average things, most of them are everyday occurrences."

own lives up for themselves. You can't do anything for anybody. They have to do it themselves. You have to do your own 'thing,' and if you haven't got that awareness you are not the kind of person who is going to be able to run your life. Unless of course you are in a certain state where you are happy to be able to follow other people. You can't analyse it. We've been trying for two thousand years.

DAVID BOWIE: David Bowie (Philips SBL 7912).

The 'Space Oddity' chart smasher is included in this collection of self-penned offerings by talented young David Bowie. Some of the other tracks bear similarities to the initial hit but a couple of spins soon dispel this feeling as you begin to get into the lyrics. And these lyrics are not heavy. Deep, thoughtful, pivoting, exposing, gossiping at your innards. David Bowie I've yet to meet, though we are in fact suburban near neighbours, yet this album seems to serve as an intimate discussion between old friends.

This is more than a record. It is an experience. An expression of life as others see it. The lyrics are full of the grandeur of yesterday, the immediacy of today and the funky of tomorrow. This is well worth your attention. This is David Bowie!

---

1. Patrick Procktor RA (1936–2003). Procktor's painting *The Guardian Readers* was used as the cover artwork for Elton John's 1976 double album *Blue Moves*.

Friday 5 December

David travels to Dublin to record a performance of 'Space Oddity' on Irish TV show *Like Now*.

Saturday 6 December

David and his new album receive a mixed response in the press. According to trade paper *Music Business Weekly*, 'He is far better at folk – both writing and singing – and should have concentrated on developing this talent.'

    In an interview with Sandie Robbie, David tells *Mirabelle*: "I moved around a lot when I was a kid but I originally came from Brixton. That's my home all right. My mother didn't have any real ambition for me and wasn't at all put out that I wanted to be a pop star. I doubt if she could have discouraged me. My mind was set on getting somewhere with my music."

Sunday 7 December

Again, David does not appear at tonight's Arts Lab, but *The Observer* carries a flattering review by Tony Palmer of the Purcell Room gig: 'On stage he is quite devastatingly beautiful. With his loofah hair and blue eyes, he pads around like every schoolgirl's wonder movie-star. He smiles; you melt. He winks; you disintegrate.'

Tuesday 9 December

With Ken Pitt and *Jeremy*'s Tim Hughes and Trevor Richardson, David attends The Pierrot Players at Queen Elizabeth Hall on the South Bank. This includes a performance of Peter Maxwell-Davies's *Vesalii Icones*. Painter Patrick Procktor[1] – who is a neighbour of Pitt's – is also in the party. David hates the show.

Thursday 11 December

▶ The Beckenham Arts Lab, The Three Tuns, Beckenham.

Sunday 14 December

▶ The Beckenham Arts Lab, The Three Tuns, Beckenham.

Wednesday 17 December

David has a lunchtime meeting with music producer Claudio Fabi, who has been hired to teach David to sing the Italian lyrics to 'Space Oddity' ahead of the recording of the translated version 'Ragazzo Solo, Ragazza Sola' for release in Italy. This has been requested by Philips due to the release of another Italian version by the Computers on the Numero Uno label, with lyrics written by Ivan Mogul.

Thursday 18 December

▶ The Beckenham Arts Lab, The Three Tuns, Beckenham.

    David and Claudio Fabi rehearse the pronunciation for the recording of the Italian-language 'Space Oddity'.

Friday 19 December

David signs with live booking agency NEMS Enterprises for a probationary period of 26 weeks.

Saturday 20 December

Records the vocal for 'Ragazzo Solo, Ragazza Sola' at Morgan Studios, Willesden, north-west London, with Fabi, who produces the session. Gus Dudgeon is on hand to proffer advice.

    In *Music Now!*, journalist Kate Simpson reflects on the Purcell Room show: 'Several people I know see David Bowie as a one-hit wonder. Until recently I shared their doubts. Then there was his recent concert at London's Purcell Room. I changed my mind. His performance was astounding. He had the audience bewitched with his words, his music, his voice, his professionalism.'

    In the same article, some of David's quotes pre-empt radical comments made in the mid-70s: 'This country is crying out for a leader. God knows what it is looking for, but if it's not careful it's going to end up with a Hitler.'

    Today's release of 'Space Oddity' in Japan marks David's first release in the country.

Sunday 21 December

▶ Beckenham Arts Lab, The Three Tuns, Beckenham.
    The Arts Lab holds its Christmas party in the evening.

Monday 22 December

In the morning Pitt and music publisher David Platz visit Bush House in London's Aldwych to finalise the probate of David's father's estate.

Later Pitt and David meet Tony Palmer at 8 Albert Gate Court, Knightsbridge. Palmer's interest in David, as expressed in his recent review in the *Observer*, has sparked an invitation to contribute music to his B-movie *Groupie Girl*.[1] David's producer from 1964, Shel Talmy, is also at the meeting.

David and Pitt spend the evening in Chelsea with Nina van Pallandt, one half of singing duo Nina & Frederik (who had recently separated from Frederik, her husband).

1. David did not pursue *Groupie Girl*, which was released in June 1970 with a screenplay co-written by Suzanne Mercer, who had worked on *Love You Till Tuesday*. Palmer featured David in his late 70s rock documentary *All You Need Is Love: The Story of Popular Music*.

Thursday 25 December

Angie is at her parents' home in Xeros, Cyprus, David with his mother in Beckenham. During one of their frequent telephone conversations, he plays Angie a new song he has written about her: 'The Prettiest Star'. In a letter, David proposes marriage.

Saturday 27 December

David and Angie appear on the cover of *Fabulous 208*.

In *Disc & Music Echo* Penny Valentine elects 'Space Oddity' her record of the year: 'It stood head and shoulders above the bunch. And it gritted its teeth and fought three months to prove it.' Meanwhile, in the year-end issue of *Music Now!*, David is voted 'number one British Male Newcomer'.

Sunday 28 December

▶ Beckenham Arts Lab, The Three Tuns, Beckenham.

Monday 29 December

Brian Howard, artistic director of Harrogate Theatre, contacts Ken Pitt and proposes David as narrator and actor in a forthcoming adaptation of Sir Walter Scott's 1828 novel *The Fair Maid Of Perth*. Recently David has also been offered a part in a D.H. Lawrence play, but the production hasn't made any progress.

Around this time David and George Underwood record potential single 'Hole In The Ground' at Trident. With Visconti producing, Underwood is on lead vocals with David backing, Tim Renwick plays guitar, Terry Cox drums and Herbie Flowers bass.

An instrumental jam is recorded as the B-side. This, an extended version of the A-side's backing track, is given the working title 'Bump On The Hill'.[1]

1. These recordings remain unreleased tracks. David retains the master (which is undated).

Wednesday 31 December

As the 60s come to a close, David has a chance to reflect on the influences discovered during the decade rather than the disappointments he faced. "I was open to any kind of possibilities that would come along during the middle to late 60s. I was learning about how to play rhythm and blues. Learning how to write,

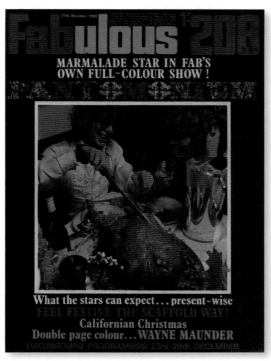

finding everything that I read, every film that I saw, any bit of theatre, everything went into my mind as being an influence.

"One door always opened up into many, many others. I really took advantage of every possible influence and experience that I could have. It all got mixed into this stew that became all the elements of what I could use when it became my turn. In a way, if anything had happened for me in the mid-60s, I might well have been cut off from an awful lot of influences."

LEFT: Some festive cheer at Rules Restaurant (reputedly the oldest restaurant in London). Four years later David would be the honoured guest at a special end-of-year lunch presentation at Rules, held by RCA Records. (▶ 31.12.73)

ABOVE: David in Haddon Hall, autumn. Photograph by David Bebbington.

BELOW: *The Spotlight* actor's directory, late 1969.

THE SPOTLIGHT   Juvenile and Juvenile-Character Men

Height 5 feet 10½ inches   1969   *From The Virgin Soldiers*

DAVID BOWIE

Films: THE VIRGIN SOLDIERS—*Columbia.* THE IMAGE—*Border Television:* MUSIC FOR YOUNG PEOPLE—*Hamburg.* MUSIC FOR EVERYONE—*Munich.* THE PISTOL SHOT—*BBC.* TOP OF THE POPS—*BBC.* COLOUR ME POP—*BBC.* LOVE YOU TILL TUESDAY—*Solo Colour Spectacular.* DOEBIDOE—*Holland*

KENNETH PITT MANAGEMENT LTD., 35, Curzon Street, W.1   01-486 4293

1970

RECORDING of what will turn out to be the next single ('The Prettiest Star') features Marc Bolan – himself about to make it big – on guitar. David starts to put together another line-up of backing musicians.

He works again with Lindsay Kemp and, back on the musical front, plays for the first time with guitarist Mick Ronson.

Meanwhile, work is proceeding on giving the stage act a much more theatrical feel, with extravagant costumery. The birth of glam rock can be traced to a Roundhouse concert at which stage characters are created for band members David, Ronson, Tony Visconti and John Cambridge.

Settling on the name of Hype for his backing band, David embarks on more gigs as 'The Prettiest Star' is released, with little impact.

David's mother makes an uninvited appearance as he and Angie are married in a low-key ceremony at Bromley's Register Office. There's no time for a honeymoon...

Cambridge is replaced as drummer by Mick Woodmansey, while manager Ken Pitt looks set to make way for music business lawyer Tony Defries.

Recording of a new album proceeds as David receives an Ivor Novello Award for 'Space Oddity', but Visconti is disillusioned by David's input into recording and his choice of new management, and quits.

The other musicians are disgruntled too, and Ronson and Woodmansey abruptly return to Hull without warning.

The US release of the album, titled *The Man Who Sold The World*, follows the signing of a publishing agreement with Chrysalis.

The split from Pitt is completed, although Defries is not distinguishing himself in his early management of a man about to hit a creative peak that will change the face of popular music.

MY PHILOSOPHY

" I'm not a well-adjusted person. I've spent too long philosophising. Sometimes I feel I was never a teenager – just an old man. I've already had most of the experiences that I'm likely to go through in the next forty years. " *DAVID BOWIE*

PREVIOUS SPREAD: Haddon Hall, summer 1970, photo by Keith MacMillan.

THIS PAGE

TOP: Feature in *Rave* magazine titled; 'David Bowie – My Philosophy', 3 January.

BOTTOM: Mercury Records executive Robin McBride, photographed in 2010.

Thursday 1 January

Belgian radio station BRT broadcasts Ward Bogaert's interview with David about the Beckenham Arts Lab.

During the programme Bogaert describes David as "the symbol of the youth and the England and the world of tomorrow. With his fanatical following he reminds one of a prophet."

Saturday 3 January

David discusses the importance of Buddhism in a *Rave* interview headlined 'My Philosophy'. He tells journalist Julie Webb about the impression made by T. Lobsang Rampa's later discredited text *The Rampa Story*: "It was a book I read that first changed my ideas. I was about fourteen at the time and very impressionable. The book outlined what would now be described as a hippy way of life."

Sunday 4 January

❱ Beckenham Arts Lab, The Three Tuns, Beckenham.

Wednesday 7 January

At midnight David sets off to the studio at Trident in Soho where a session has been booked between 1am and 4am for a recording of a new single, comprising a reworking of 'London Bye Ta-Ta' and a new composition, 'The Prettiest Star'.

Tony Visconti is producing and playing bass, with Rick Wakeman on piano, funk drummer Godfrey McLean[1] (who is also on congas) and David's singer-songwriter friend Lesley Duncan lending support on backing vocals with session singers Sue and Sunny.[2]

Marc Bolan makes his only significant appearance on a record of David's, contributing guitar to 'The Prettiest Star' at the request of Visconti. However, the atmosphere is fraught since Bolan is jealous about the success of 'Space Oddity'. His wife-to-be June Child[3] is not impressed with the song or David, who said in 1994: "I think it was Visconti trying to get us

back together again as pals and not have us quite so wary of each other. Which was fairly petty of me because I really think that Marc was a wonderful guitar player."

"Marc came to the session for an hour, played his solo and left promptly," said Visconti in 1983. "The atmosphere was very heavy. The only other time they played together was on that television programme of Marc's."[4]

1. McLean was a member of The Gass, who had been produced by Visconti. He described their sound as 'a funky black early disco sound' in 1990.

2. Susan Glover (real name Yvonne Wheatman) and her sister Heather Wheatman made their recording debut together in 1963 as The Myrtelles before becoming The Stockingtops. As Sue and Sunny they were in-demand session singers in the 60s and 70s.

3. Bolan married Child at Kensington Registry Office in the King's Road three weeks later, on 30 January 1970.

4. *Marc*, broadcast 28 September 1977 just after Bolan's death.

Thursday 8 January

❱ David Bowie, The Speakeasy,[1] 48 Margaret Street, London W1.

During the day – David's 23rd birthday – his music publisher Essex Music forwards the French lyrics for 'Space Oddity'[2] to Ken Pitt.

In the evening a performance at London club The Speakeasy marks a new phase in David's career, one which will last nearly two years, as he tests out new songs and fresh cover versions on stage and in the studio with a variety of sometimes short-lived musical line-ups.

At 'The Speak' he is backed by Tony Visconti on bass, guitarist Tim Renwick and drummer John Cambridge.

The set includes a cover of singer-songwriter Biff Rose's 'Fill Your Heart'[3] and a reading from a bawdy poem by US singer/guitarist Mason Williams.[4]

Pitt is at the club in the company of Tim Hughes and Trevor Richardson, the two *Jeremy* magazine journalists shadowing David in preparation for their forthcoming profile.

After the show, David invites Cambridge to join a new backing band he is putting together.

1. The Speakeasy became Bootleggers nightclub and is now called Match bar.

2. 'Un Homme A Disparu Dans Le Ciel' (A Man Has Disappeared From The Sky). Recorded by French singer Gérard Palaprat in 1971.

3. 'Fill Your Heart' appeared on David's 1971 album *Hunky Dory*.

4. From Williams' 1964 poetry collection *Bicyclists Dismount*. David sometimes read from this at the Beckenham Arts Lab. Williams' single 'Classical Gas' had been a top 20 UK hit in August 1968.

Friday 9 January

Disinterested and tired from The Speakeasy gig, David is photographed by Johnnie Clamp for *Jeremy* at Haddon Hall.

Sunday 11 January

❱ Beckenham Arts Lab, The Three Tuns, Beckenham.

Tuesday 13 January

Recording continues at Trident on 'The Prettiest Star'

as well as 'London Bye Ta-Ta'.[1] Pitt writes to Mercury Record's Robin McBride about the Italian-language 'Space Oddity' and adds: 'We are now going for a Spanish version.'[2]

1. This version of 'London Bye Ta-Ta' was eventually released on the *Sound + Vision* compilation in 1989.
2. This was not recorded.

Thursday 15 January

▶ Beckenham Arts Lab, The Three Tuns, Beckenham.
On the completion of the single recording sessions, David and Angie meet Pitt, Visconti and Philips A&R man Ralph Mace and agree that 'London Bye Ta-Ta' should be the A-side.

Sunday 18 January

▶ Beckenham Arts Lab, The Three Tuns, Beckenham.
Ken Pitt spends the evening with David and Angie at the Arts Lab.

Thursday 22 January

▶ Beckenham Arts Lab, The Three Tuns, Beckenham.

Saturday 24 January

David comes in at number 11 in the best British male singer category in the *NME*'s annual poll, collecting 362 votes. Tom Jones is the winner with 5,332 votes.

Sunday 25 January

▶ Beckenham Arts Lab, The Three Tuns, Beckenham.
Ken Pitt meets with Irwin Steinberg and Robin McBride of David's US label Mercury at London's Hilton Hotel in Park Lane, Mayfair. During discussions McBride announces that he favours a reworked, shortened version of album track 'Memory Of A Free Festival' as David's third single for the label.

In the US, Mercury has released David's second album as *David Bowie – Man Of Words/Man Of Music* and included 'Space Oddity' on its compilation, *Zig-Zag Festival*.

Thursday 29 January

David makes a solo appearance on the Scottish TV show *Cairngorm Ski Night*. He is accompanied on the trip north by Angie, Tony Visconti and percussionist Tex Johnson[1] and is driven by former neighbour and occasional assistant Barrie Jackson. (They had broken their journey to Aberdeen the previous day with an overnight stop in Glasgow.)

Staying in cheap boarding houses (so low are the temperatures that they are forced to sleep fully clothed), David uses the Grampian TV and Aberdeen University bookings as an opportunity to reconnect with Lindsay Kemp, whose troupe is in Edinburgh to perform and film a new interpretation of *Pierrot In Turquoise*, also for Scottish TV.

On *Cairngorm Ski Night*, recorded at Queens Cross in Aberdeen and hosted by presenter Jimmy Spankie, David performs 'London Bye Ta-Ta', playing acoustic guitar with backing from the show's resident musicians The Alex Sutherland Band.

mirabelle 31st JANUARY 1970 EIGHTPENCE

EXCLUSIVE! Twiggy & Justin on love

SUPER 2 PAGE FASHION FUN SPECIAL
THE REAL PAUL McCARTNEY – BY HIS FRIENDS
WHY BEING A BEDSIT GIRL IS A GAS
THE TREMS IN LUVLY COLOUR

1. Johnson had toured the previous year with Delaney & Bonnie And Friends (whose line-up included Eric Clapton). In the early 70s he played on recording sessions for Clapton as well as Joe Cocker.

ABOVE: David featuring as an uncredited model on teen mag *Mirabelle*, 31 January.

Friday 30 January

▶ David Bowie, Johnston Halls, College Bounds, Aberdeen University.
David is accompanied by Visconti on bass and Johnson on congas. The line-up has been put together because Junior's Eyes have live commitments again in Germany.

Johnson has been brought in by Visconti. "Tex was a session musician introduced to me by Denny Cordell," said Visconti in 1994. "He was South American and wore ethnic African clothes with a big hat. He was older than us, in his 40s, and we were a couple of spunky young guys, so it was a bit of a strange mix."

The evening is a formal annual ball, and David has been asked to perform 'appropriate' material.

In this year...

January
PRODUCTION of Elton John's eponymous second album at Trident by 'Space Oddity' producer Gus Dudgeon. This includes breakthrough hit 'Your Song'.

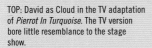

TOP: David as Cloud in the TV adaptation of *Pierrot In Turquoise*. The TV version bore little resemblance to the stage show.

ABOVE: The Gateway Theatre, Leith Walk, Edinburgh. The venue, which became Scotland's first colour TV studio in 1969, closed in 2005 and has since been redeveloped.

TOP RIGHT: In rehearsals for *Pierrot In Turquoise Or The Looking Glass Murders* at Gateway Theatre, Edinburgh, 31 January.

MIDDLE: David and Lindsay Kemp share a joke during rehearsals.

BOTTOM RIGHT: David and Lindsay Kemp recording the show at the Gateway Theatre, 1 February.

Saturday 31 January

Today *Mirabelle* features David and a female model on its front cover, in a shot from a modelling assignment conducted two months earlier.

Meanwhile, David joins friend and former mentor Lindsay Kemp and his company in rehearsals for *Pierrot In Turquoise* at the Gateway Theatre, Leith Walk, Edinburgh.

The production now has 'Or The Looking Glass Murders' appended to the title. David – who again assumes the role of the muse Cloud – is reunited with Kemp's foil Jack Birkett and pianist Michael Garrett.[1]

In this production, Columbine is played by actress Annie Stainer.

During rehearsals David writes two new tracks – 'Harlequin' and 'Columbine' – and also provides a new lyric for a third song called 'Threepenny Pierrot' (Kemp asked David to rewrite lyrics from 'London Bye Ta-Ta' especially for this production).

These are recorded as backing tracks, along with Kemp's favourite, 'When I Live My Dream', with David singing and Garrett playing organ, beginning and ending the performance.

David and Angie stay with Kemp at 34 Drummond Street, Edinburgh, sleeping on the floor. This is the first time Angie has met Kemp; on return to London she will visit his dance and movement classes.

1 In 1969, Ken Russell commissioned Michael Garrett to compose music for his film *Women In Love*, in which Garrett also appeared.

Sunday 1 February

Director Brian Mahoney films *Pierrot In Turquoise Or The Looking Glass Murders* for an episode in a Scottish TV arts strand which shows the work of a variety of avant-garde performers.

The series is to be called *Another World*, but this title will be dropped in favour of *Gateway* (after the theatre where it is shot).

This 'pantomime' (as Kemp dubs it) presents a series of tableaux in which both the Pierrot and the Harlequin fall in love with Columbine, the climax being the Pierrot's murder of both. As such, it bears little resemblance to the production in which David appeared a couple of years previously.

At the end of the opening rendition of 'When I Live My Dream', Garrett can be seen clambering underneath a grand piano.

The set is littered with mannequins, as well as antique dolls and toy automata loaned by the Museum of Childhood in Holyrood, Edinburgh. Kemp is bare-chested throughout and Birkett is similarly semi-naked, with black body paint, ripped yellow tights revealing his bottom, gold glitter make-up and a heavy gold earring. In the opening scene he sits knitting on the unmade bed which is central to the piece.

Like other members of the cast, David's hair is teased into a bird's-nest bouffant, and for much of the performance he sits atop a step-ladder in a puff-sleeved gown. He leaves it once – to sing 'Threepenny Pierrot' from the bed.

Filming complete, David, Angie and their friends head back to London.

Tuesday 3 February

▶ David Bowie, the Marquee, Wardour Street, London W1.

Erroneously listed in *Time Out* as 60s singer Dave Berry, David shares the bill with Junior's Eyes, whose members John Cambridge and Tim Renwick are in his backing band with Visconti.

Also on the bill are progressive mod act Timebox[1]

and in the audience is guitarist Mick Ronson, invited by his friend and one-time colleague in The Rats, Cambridge, who has driven them both to London from Hull in his Hillman Minx.

After the show the musicians gather at La Chasse,[2] a one-room drinking club above a betting shop at 100 Wardour Street. David is introduced to Ronson at the club, and the party heads back to Haddon Hall. The pair hit it off and agree to work together. Ronson is available since his tenure with The Rats has come to an end.

1. Hailing from Southport, Lancs, Timebox featured impassioned vocalist Mike Patto and guitarist Ollie Halsall. Among the recordings they made for David's former label Deram between 1967 and 1969 was the single 'Beggin', which became a UK club hit on reissue after use in TV advertising in 2005.

2. La Chasse was run by Marquee co-manager Jack Barrie, who had introduced David to John Hutchinson in 1966. La Chasse closed in the spring of 1970 when the Marquee gained its own drinks licence.

Wednesday 4 February

David invites Ronson to join him as lead guitarist on a BBC Radio One session to be recorded tomorrow afternoon. There is little time for rehearsal since David has a meeting with film executive Rex Sheldon, who is interested in hiring David to supply music for a film about car manufacturers Charles Rolls and Frederick Royce to be called *Silver Lady*.[1]

During the meeting at 4 Denbigh Place in Victoria, David accepts Sheldon's invitation to perform at a charity concert for mental health charity Mencap.

Later in the afternoon, David is interviewed by Penny Valentine at Pitt's Manchester Street apartment for *Disc & Music Echo* ahead of the magazine's readers' poll awards ceremony.

1. The film did not make it to production.

Thursday 5 February

In the morning Ronson joins David, Visconti and Cambridge in ad hoc rehearsals, jamming on a few of David's songs at Haddon Hall.

They also use the afternoon sound check at BBC Paris Studio,[1] Lower Regent Street, central London, as an opportunity for him to become better acquainted with the songs.

This, David's fourth BBC radio session, is for broadcast on *The Sunday Show* with John Peel, and is something of a baptism of fire for Ronson.

"We rehearsed in the morning and did the show very badly," was David's summary in 2000.

The four musicians perform 'Amsterdam' (which Peel announces as a composition by 'Jack Brel'), a shortened version of 'Memory Of A Free Festival' and the ambitious new 'Width Of A Circle', which is already benefiting from Ronson's input ahead of its inclusion on David's next album.

"I didn't know any of the material – I was really nervous," said Ronson in 1984 "I just followed David, watched his fingers on the guitar. I guess it worked OK because he wanted to work with me again."

Peel interviews David on a number of topics,

including the Beckenham Arts Lab. "It's impossible to call it an Arts Lab because of the simple fact that most people won't participate, they prefer to have things fashioned for them," says David, expressing disgruntlement with the way the club-night has settled around his performances. "We're still involved with putting on things but it's futile calling it an Arts Laboratory because it's much more like a scout patrol or something unless everybody else joins in."

Peel asks him: "Are you going to be doing gigs with this band?"

"Well, looking at them, no!" laughs David. "Yes, we're going to do some gigs. Are we Michael? Michael doesn't really know. He's just come down from Hull and I met him for the first time about two days ago through John the drummer, who's worked with me once."

In attendance are Ken Pitt (who meets Ronson for the first time) and his friend, journalist George Tremlett, who grabs an interview with David before the show starts.

After the radio show, Mick returns to Hull; he has to work out his notice in the northern city's parks department.

1. In a lower ground floor of Rex House, 12 Lower Regent Street, Paris Studio had been a cinema. Shortly after the Second World War it became a BBC radio studio, during which time it retained the original cinema seating and decor. To access the theatre, audiences descended two floors. It closed when the BBC left the building in 1994. Until 2009 it was the home to St Alban restaurant.

Sunday 8 February

▶ Beckenham Arts Lab, The Three Tuns, Beckenham.
In the evening, David and Hype's John Peel *Sunday Show* session is broadcast on Radio One. In Hull, Ronson's family proudly tune in, cheered by this upturn in his fortunes.

Monday 9 February

At 8pm, David has a meeting with film producer John Sherrard of Le Treport Productions, 34d Upper Montague Street in Belgravia, about involvement in *Perspective*, a feature in pre-production.[1]

During the day David and Ken Pitt each receive a copy of 'Ragazzo Solo, Ragazza Sola', the Italian-language version of 'Space Oddity', from producer Claudio Fabi in Milan. This has recently been released by Phonogram[2] in Italy.

Backed by the original English version of 'Wild Eyed Boy From Freecloud', this single is not a translation of David's lyric, but a version penned by songwriter Ivan Mogul[3] for a cover by the Italian group Computers (who released their version in late 1969).

1. It is not known if this was made.

2. 'Ragazzo Solo, Ragazza Sola' was included on two Phonogram Italy promotional EPs featuring new releases by various artists in early spring 1970.

3. Mogul wrote another Italian version of the song for popular Milanese group I Giganti (The Giants). Entitled 'Corri Uomo Corri' (Run Man Run), this was released on the Miyra label and was more faithful to the sound of David's original.

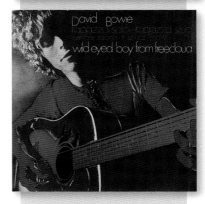

TOP: Ad for Marquee appearance, 3 February.

ABOVE: 'Ragazzo Solo, Regazza Sola', the Italian version of 'Space Oddity'.

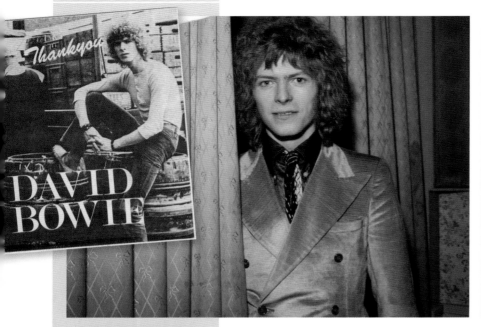

Thursday 12 February

▶ Beckenham Arts Lab, The Three Tuns, Beckenham.

Friday 13 February

At a lunchtime award ceremony in The Dubarry Room at the Café Royal in Regent Street, Piccadilly, David is presented with an award as Brightest Hope in the 1970 *Disc & Music Echo* readers' poll from another poll-winner, Radio One DJ Tony Blackburn.

David poses with Blackburn for photographs and with other award recipients including enduring British pop stars Cilla Black, Lulu[1] and Cliff Richard.

"I wasn't particularly pleased to meet Cliff," said David. "I was never a great fan of his."

A couple of hundred miles north east of London, Mick Ronson resigns his post as gardener and groundsman with Hull council's municipal parks department.

Local paper the *Hull Times* is excited that one of the city's musicians is hitting the big time with a Top Ten star. When interviewed, Ronson reveals: "At the moment I'm re-laying some school football pitches."

Within a few days David, Angie, Tony Visconti and his girlfriend Liz Hartley visit Hull for a short break; David also takes the opportunity for his grey Rover to be cheaply serviced by friends of John Cambridge.

With Visconti and Hartley put up at Cambridge's house in nearby Beverley, David and Angie stay at Cambridge's father's home in west Hull, where David uses the phone to call promoters to book gigs around the UK.

Ronson visits David in the evening to work on musical ideas. David also visits the Ronson family home in the city's Bexhill Estate, and tells him the principle purpose of his trip is to seek out antiques.

The party from London is introduced to The Gondolier cafe in the city centre. Hull's equivalent to London's La Gioconda.

During this trip David meets Ronson's friend Stuart George, who had assisted The Rats. Known as Stuey, he will in time become a familiar sight by David's side as his personal bodyguard.

1. In 1993 Lulu said: "I can't remember meeting David at those awards. Isn't that terrible?"

Sunday 15 February

▶ Beckenham Arts Lab, The Three Tuns, Beckenham.

Monday 16 February

The *Disc & Music Echo* award stokes national media interest. In newspaper the *Daily Sketch* Anne

A new star shoots upwards, and one STILL shines

BIG WEEK FOR BOWIE

'EL' KEEPS HIS CROWN

Nightingale reports: 'Judging from the mail I receive about this romantic singer and songwriter, he could be the giant heart-throb that Scott Walker was… all of which leaves David Bowie quite detached. "I don't relish the idea of that kind of stardom much".'

Nightingale, who reviewed David's first single, 'Liza Jane', back in 1964 and fails to make the connection in her piece, also reports that David's new single is to be 'The Prettiest Star', not, as expected, 'London Bye Ta-Ta'.

Wednesday 18 February

David drives Ken Pitt to Haddon Hall then on to The Three Tuns, where they meet Angie. This is the trio's second meeting in a month.

Together David and Angie have been cooking up a new, more theatrical presentation for David's live act.

Inspired by David's recently renewed contact with the flamboyant Lindsay Kemp, they have talked Cambridge, Ronson and Visconti into joining David in wearing extravagant costumes on stage.

Ronson has moved into Haddon Hall, which has now been vacated by Visconti and Liz Hartley. Having been brought up in a small terraced house in east Hull, he is impressed with the grandness of his new surroundings. "The rooms were huge," he said in 1984. "That's the main thing I remember about that place, the size of the rooms."

Thursday 19 February

❱ Beckenham Arts Lab, The Three Tuns, Beckenham.

Saturday 21 February

David features in *Disc & Music Echo*'s awards photo-spread. The issue also runs a Penny Valentine story about David headed 'A new star shoots upwards'.

Sunday 22 February

❱ David Bowie, Implosion, the Roundhouse, Chalk Farm Road, London NW1.

David and his band – which is not yet billed as Hype – have been booked for the Camden venue's regular Sunday-night Implosion, which is promoted by friend and DJ Jeff Dexter with a colleague from underground club Middle Earth, Paul Waldman.

Also on the bill are progressive soft-rockers Caravan, blues band The Groundhogs[1] and prog-rock outfit Bachdenkel.[2] There is also a light show courtesy of a Vince Dunn.

This gig marks a turning point in David's career – and, arguably, the development of popular music in the early 70s – since it inaugurates the glam rock era's focus on sartorial flamboyance, though the stage drama and theatricality have yet to come (and the promoters have stipulated by contract that David provide a mime).

Angie and Visconti's girlfriend Liz Hartley have dressed the group in a range of colourful creations.

Each member takes on a character: David is Spaceman; Visconti, Hyperman; Ronson, Gangsterman; and Cambridge, Cowboyman.

In the audience is guitarist Tim Renwick.[3] With Cambridge joining forces with David, Visconti and Ronson, Junior's Eyes have disbanded and an invitation to join the new group is being dangled.

"I realised it wasn't for me," said Renwick in 1998. "It didn't feel right. It may have been the worst mistake I've made in my career, but there you go!"

Pitt is another attendee. Feeling edged out by the pace with which David is ringing the changes, he is also uncomfortable with the vibe tonight.

"There wasn't a nice feeling there, something was wrong," he said in 1983. "It could have been an argument between David and Angela or something, but the atmosphere wasn't good."

The evolution which is taking place in David's artistic life is underlined by the fact that across town there is another Beckenham Arts Lab evening without David. This is headlined by folk-rock act Sempervivum.

1. On their 1972 UK tour, David and The Spiders From Mars played one of their only support gigs for The Groundhogs. (❱14.2.72)
2. Bachdenkel were a popular live draw in France.
3. Within a few months Renwick became a founding member of soft rock group Quiver, who appeared on the same bill as David at another Roundhouse event. (❱5.7.70)

Thursday 26 February

Beckenham Arts Lab, The Three Tuns, Beckenham.
Again David is absent from the Arts Lab.

OPPOSITE PAGE

TOP LEFT: *Disc & Music Echo* Valentine Awards issue with David's thank you message for readers who voted him 'Brightest Hope for 1970'.

TOP RIGHT: *Disc* awards ceremony, Dubarry Room, Café Royal, London, held on 13 February.

FAR RIGHT: David with Cliff Richard at the Café Royal.

MIDDLE LEFT: Live at the Roundhouse, 11 March.

BOTTOM: *Disc* Valentine Awards issue, 14 February.

THIS PAGE

TOP LEFT: Ray Stevenson attended and photographed both Roundhouse Hype gigs. The first was on 22 February and the second on 11 March, when David added a necklace and blue cape to his costume.

TOP RIGHT: Roundhouse *Implosion* promotional ads.

BOTTOM: Mick Ronson in the suit David had often worn for 'Space Oddity' TV promotion work. the Roundhouse, London, 22 February.

TUESDAY

HOUNSLOW ARTS Lab

DAVID BOWIE

AND HIS NEW ELECTRIC
BAND
SEASONING
WITH MAGGIE NICHOLS

White Bear, Kingsley Road,
Hounslow.

8.30
Cairngorm Ski Night

SYLVIA McNEILL
DAVE McINTOSH
THE LORNE GIBSON TRIO
HAMISH IMLACH
DAVID BOWIE
The Alex Sutherland Band

Join the party of skiers as they relax
to the best of Scottish apres-ski entertainment provided by the resident
team. Introduced by James Spankie.
DESIGNER ERIC MOLLART: DIRECTOR
TONY HARRISON
Grampian Television Production

the TEEN scene

HE LIKES OUR FISH 'N CHIPS!

LAST WEEK we
mentioned that two
Hull lads, Michael
Ronson and John
Cambridge, were now
working with David
Bowie, whose record,
"Space Oddity," rock-
eted up the charts last
year.

David was in Hull last
weekend. What did he
think of the city on his
first visit?

"It's OK," he said, "and
with two Hull lads in the
group I may make it a
second home." He was par-
ticularly impressed with a
local fish-and-chip res-
taurant.

David stressed that the
group containing Michael
and John, to be called Hype,
and which is not a backing
group but that both he and
the group would retain
their separate identities.

Hype are to start work
next month on their own

LP, and David will pre-
bably start on one himself
same time.

David Bowie. His hunt for antiques proved unsuccessful.

Friday 27 February

David's appearance on *Cairngorm Ski Night* is
broadcast by Scottish TV.

Saturday 28 February

▶ David Bowie, Basildon Arts Lab, Basildon Arts
Centre,[1] St Martin's Square, Basildon, Essex.

The gig at this 'experimental music club' has been
trailed in *Melody Maker* advertising as 'David Bowie's
New Electric Band' though David has now settled on
the name Hype for his backing musicians.

David's friends The Strawbs have been double-
booked so David and his band co-headline with High
Tide, featuring David's colleague from Turquoise,
Tony Hill, and violinist/keyboard player Simon
House.[2] Support acts for the evening are Iron Maiden[3]
and Overson.

"As a favour, David kindly booked High Tide into a
couple of venues and sort of introduced us," said Hill
in 1992.

"I think High Tide had some really dynamic
ideas," said David later. "Excellent band – they were
really quite strong competitors for the same area as
The Doors as far as I was concerned, in terms of
British bands."

By now David has purchased a Transit van to
transport his fellow musicians, instruments and
amplifiers to and from gigs. Haddon Hall neighbour
Tony Frost[4] is in charge of the vehicle and acts as
road manager, often with roadie Roger Fry.

1. As of 2010 this venue had become the Towngate Theatre.

2. House later joined the Third Ear band. He joined Hawkwind in
1974 and played live with David in 1978.

3. Not the internationally successful heavy metal band formed
in 1975.

4. Frost later worked with Stuey George as one of David's bodyguards,
and travelled with his former neighbour in that capacity on David's
first US tour in 1972.

Sunday 1 March

▶ David Bowie & Hype, Beckenham Arts Lab,
The Three Tuns, Beckenham.

David showcases his new band on home turf.

A typical set with Hype includes a version of the
Velvet Underground's 'I'm Waiting For The Man',

TOP LEFT: Advert for Hounslow
appearance, 3 March.

TOP RIGHT: David's social visit to Hull
is reported in the *Hull Times*.

MIDDLE LEFT: *Cairngorm Ski Night*, *TV
Times* entry for appearance on
27 February.

BOTTOM LEFT: Advert for Basildon Art
Centre, 28 February.

BOTTOM RIGHT: *Jeremy* magazine (Vol
1, No. 6) interview and feature. David is
posing in the listed woodshed at Haddon
Hall that later burnt down.

Bowie for a song

It's a bitterly cold December afternoon. David is
rehearsing a "Save The Children" charity show
at the Palladium. He is going solo with acoustic
guitar – wisely dispensing with the pit orchestra
hastily assembled for the Royal Occasion.
Princess Margaret and Peter Sellers will be there.
There's a hassle over the sound equipment.
The management seem unable to produce a
supplementary mike for his guitar. Justifiably he's
upset with having to make do with one.
The gigantic white safety curtain drops in.
Isolated in a single spot, against mammoth
projections of the Apollo Space Shot, David
performs *Space Oddity*. It's spectacularly
effective and contrasts strongly with the tatty
presentation of the rest of the show.
Afterwards David sits quietly with us in the stalls.
A strapping Radio 1 D.J. introduces a stunningly
bad parade of groups and soloists. He cracks a
stream of excruciating gags and occasionally
opens his dress shirt to reveal an expanse of
rotating stomach flesh. Dusty arrives to rehearse
in a trim suede trouser suit. She assumes control
of the rehearsal. Out go the pit orchestra. In come
her own sixteen session men, sound balancers,
backing girls and extra amplifiers. All of us,
including David, are suitably impressed by her
dazzling professionalism.
Another scene, another place. The concrete halls
of the South Bank are filling up as the electronic A
summons the cultured to an evening's serious
entertainment. Half-an hour later the serried
ranks of the sober-suited may be seen on the
Queen Elizabeth Hall monitor gravely grooving
to the refined sonorities of a Haydn string
quartet. Who would imagine that next door in
the Purcell Room *Junior's Eyes* are belting out
the big sound, warming up a very different
audience for the appearance of David Bowie.

The concert is to launch his new L.P. released by
Philips. The publicity says simply that it is given
by 'David Bowie and Friends'. It is clear that this
refers as much to the audience as to the
performers. For David is not a pop star in the
conventional sense. He is a very switched-on,
creative young man, rightly admired by the
discerning for his talent and known only to the
masses for his guaranteed-success single
Space Oddity.
In the interval the two audiences surge together
for drinks and two cultures mingle strangely, the
orthodox and the freaked-out. They view each
other's appearance, whether bizarre or
commonplace, with mixed feelings ranging from
amused tolerance to confused mistrust.
But all are curiously united by the same artistic
experience, whose expression alters with the
vagaries of time and taste, but whose roots are
constant. Oddly enough the Bowie band looks
more baroque than the Haydn mob.
After the interval David at last appears. Perched
on a stool he begins with some quiet reflective
songs, accompanying himself with acoustic
guitar. Some 'friends' join him and the sounds
become more involved. Finally *Junior's Eyes*
plugs in and suddenly there's a really hard
sound and one can scarcely believe that its
centre is the slight pre-Raphaelite figure who
first appeared. The range is incredible. But he
says of himself, "I've been grown up for too long."
He could never do a whole programme of
unrelenting rock and roll, as many groups do.
His creativity needs more than one outlet and he
has too much to express for one medium. His
background is unusually varied – art school,
tenor sax with Ronnie Ross's modern jazz group,
poetry, mime with Lindsay Kempe, films. And
even now he feels that he hasn't really begun

From Purcell Room to Palladium, from
Zen Buddhism to Art Nouveau.
Tim Hughes and Trevor Richardson
track down the prismatic personality of
Britain's Pop phenomenon, David Bowie.
Photographs by Johnnie Clamp.

25

'Unwashed And Somewhat Slightly Dazed' and 'Janine', from David's recently released album, and new song 'The Width Of A Circle'. 'London Bye Ta-Ta' is also performed,[1] though this will now not be David's new single; 'The Prettiest Star' has been flipped to the A-side and 'Conversation Piece' from the recent album sessions has been chosen to back it.

1. These tracks were recorded during an early rehearsal by Visconti and are still in his possession.

Tuesday 3 March

▶ David Bowie & Hype, Hounslow Arts Lab, The White Bear, Hounslow, Middx.

The quartet are invited to showcase their new sound by the Hounslow club's organiser, Dave Cousins of The Strawbs. Also performing is Scottish free jazz and improvisational vocalist Maggie Nichols. Nichols – with drummer John Stevens – is also a member of the experimental group The Spontaneous Music Ensemble.

Thursday 5 March

▶ David Bowie & Hype, Beckenham Arts Lab, The Three Tuns, Beckenham.

On the day of David's final participation in an Arts Lab event (just under a year after he helped establish the club) the feature on him by Tim Hughes and Trevor Richardson appears in *Jeremy*.

Ken Pitt has been the driving force behind the article, which he believes will bolster David's androgynous profile in Britain's gay community, now emerging from the shadows following the partial decriminalisation of homosexuality in Britain in 1967.

Hughes and Richardson provide insight into David's working practices and creative development over a three-month period, having attended a number of performances and spent time with him at Pitt's Manchester Street residence and at Haddon Hall. Despite the nature of the publication, David is not yet prepared to discuss his sexuality beyond stating: "I don't feel the need for conventional relationships."

In *Zig Zag* Marc Bolan is equally circumspect. When asked if he is bisexual he says: "Eric Clapton and George Harrison have been working together, because they get on well, and I've been playing on David Bowie's new record, because I really dig David – I like his songs and we have a very good head thing... but we don't make love. To make love wouldn't be repulsive to me."

David's coolness to the *Jeremy* feature concerns Pitt, who was particularly disappointed by his all-too-evident disinterest in the photo session.

Meanwhile, the organisers of the Arts Lab hold a meeting to finalise the switch-over to a new folk club night.

Friday 6 March

▶ David Bowie & Hype, University of Hull West Refectory, Cottingham Road, Hull, Yorks.

Mercury release David's new single, 'The Prettiest Star'/'Conversation Piece'.

⊙ **David Bowie**
A **'The Prettiest Star'** (Bowie)
B **'Conversation Piece'** (Bowie)
David Bowie (vocal, guitar)
Marc Bolan (guitar on A-side)
Tony Visconti (bass on A-side)
Godfrey McLean (drums on A-side)
Unknown (organ on A-side)
Mick Wayne (guitar on B-side)
John Cambridge (drums on B-side)
John Lodge (bass on B-side)
Session orchestra (A- and B-side)
Produced by Tony Visconti
(Mercury MF 1135)

Visconti also remixes the A-side for consideration as an American single, following a request by Robin McBride at Mercury, while David circumvents Pitt and his publisher Essex Music and personally organises for a promo copy to be passed to Sacha Distel, in the hope that the French crooner might be interested in recording a cover version.

"I mentioned to David I was a friend of Distel's manager Claude Deffes," said photographer Vernon Dewhurst in 1999. "He asked me to give a copy of 'The Prettiest Star'[1] to Deffes but Sacha didn't like it."

Since it didn't make the cut of his second album, but has been mixed down in mono, 'Conversation Piece'[2] is ready-made to appear as the B-side.

Also today, Decca act on the post-'Space Oddity' interest in David by releasing compilation *The World Of David Bowie*.[3]

The cover photograph has been supplied by Arts Lab friend David Bebbington, and the track-listing has been approved by David, who has also come up with the running order.

The core of the collection is his 1967 debut album, with the removal of four tracks; 'Please Mr Gravedigger', 'Join The Gang', 'Maid Of Bond Street' and 'We Are Hungry Men'. Replacements are three previously unreleased recordings, 'In The Heat Of The Morning', 'Let Me Sleep Beside You' and 'Karma Man', along with 1966 B-side 'The London Boys'.

In 1968 David described the three unreleased tracks to Pitt as 'pop rubbish', while Visconti later disowned them. "I think these tracks were the reason David was thrown off Deram," he said in 1977. "They really were terrible."

Still, David is interested enough to purchase his own copy from a record shop in Beckenham High Street, formerly managed by ex-Konrad Dave Hadfield.

Shortly after the album's release, Pitt receives a letter from a Birmingham fan called Christine, who praises the compilation and declares: "I'd love to meet him. Does he have anything against fattish girls?"

The release of David's new single and this early career retrospective coincides with something

TOP: *The World Of David Bowie* compilation album, Decca, 1970, with cover photograph by David Bebbington.

ABOVE: 'Prettiest Star' review, *NME*, 7 March.

In this year...

Friday 6 March
RELEASE of Michael Chapman album *Fully Qualified Survivor* featuring Mick Ronson on guitar. This was also produced by Gus Dudgeon.

LAST Beatles' single 'Let It Be', released on the same day as 'The Prettiest Star'.

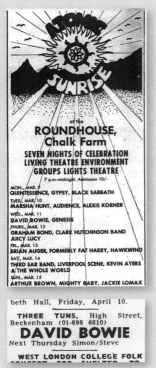

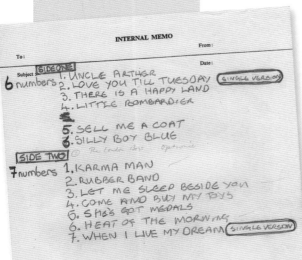

TOP LEFT: Atomic Sunrise Roundhouse advert including David's appearance on 11 March.

TOP RIGHT: A rare find; a ticket from David & Hype's visit to Hull on 6 March.

ABOVE: Advert for appearance at the Three Tuns, Beckenham.

BOTTOM: Part of David's original running order notes for *The World Of David Bowie*. David had wanted both 'Love You Till Tuesday' and 'When I Live My Dream' to be the single versions, but in the end the original album tracks were used.

of a homecoming for Mick Ronson and John Cambridge. The Hull University gig is also enhanced by an appearance by former member of The Rats Benny Marshall, who repeats the harmonica accompaniment he provided to the album sessions on a rousing version of 'Unwashed And Somewhat Slightly Dazed'.

1. Shortly after release, the master tape of 'The Prettiest Star' disappeared. David reworked the A-side for *Aladdin Sane* a few years later. (▶ 13.4.73)

2. David re-recorded 'Conversation Piece' during the sessions for his 2001 album *Toy* (produced by Visconti), and included this version as a bonus track on limited edition CD sets.

3. Decca's Hugh Mendl had proposed a straight reissue. At Pitt's suggestion it was included on the label's *World Of...* series.

Saturday 7 March

▶ David Bowie & Hype, Regent Street Polytechnic, Little Titchfield Street, London, W1.

With support from folk singer Bridget St John (who had appeared at the Free Festival)[1] and jazzers The Alan Skidmore Quintet, tonight's one-hour set at Angie's alma mater is a disaster. Mick Ronson's guitar volume all but obliterates David's voice and even Cambridge's drums, clearing the seats directly in front of his amps.

In *Melody Maker* Chris Welch greets 'The Prettiest Star' as 'not such an original composition as his "Space" hit, but a pleasant

performance, and quite likely to twinkle from the top of the hit parade', while *Disc & Music Echo*'s loyal Penny Valentine enthuses that the track has 'the most compact, catchy melody I've ever heard'.

1. In 1972 Bridget St John appeared as an unlikely support at an early Ziggy Stardust concert. (▶ 4.3.72)

Monday 9 March

In the afternoon David meets writer/director John Gorrie at ATV House in Great Cumberland Place near Marble Arch, to discuss playing a part in forthcoming television play *Private Lillywhite Is Dead*.[1]

1. Screened by ATV later in 1970, the play received a BAFTA award. David did not appear in it.

Wednesday 11 March

▶ David Bowie & Hype, the Roundhouse, London NW1.

In the afternoon David is interviewed at *Melody Maker*'s offices at 161 Fleet Street by Ray Telford before heading across town to the Roundhouse for an appearance during week-long festival Atomic Sunrise,[1] which also features Quintessence, Graham Bond (with Jack Bruce on bass), Hawkwind, Third Ear Band, Kevin Ayers & The Whole World (with Mike Oldfield on guitar), David's friend Peter Straker and The Hair Band (the musicians from the hit musical featuring singer Alex Harvey).

Tonight's gig, billing of which is shared with Genesis,[2] shows how much effort David and Angie have put into developing stage presentation and costume. David's silver jacket and metallic belt (both gifts from Calvin Mark Lee) and sparkly silver tights have been retained from 'Space Oddity' filming. These are matched with a purpose-made satin cape attached at each wrist and a pair of second-hand buccaneer-style, thigh-length leather boots.

The show is witnessed by Marc Bolan, wearing a plastic Roman soldier's breastplate, and his friend Pete Sanders, who takes colour photographs.[3]

Three songs are filmed: 'Memory Of A Free Festival', 'The Supermen' and 'I'm Waiting For The Man'[4] while a version of John Lennon's 'Instant Karma!' (released in February) is added to the set.

At one of the Hype Roundhouse gigs, David is introduced to singer-songwriter Caetano Veloso[5] by Mercury's Ralph Mace (who has recently secured a recording and publishing deal with Paramount for Veloso and his fellow Brazilian exile Gilberto Gil).

During the encounter, Veloso interests David in an idea he has for a stage musical about the outrageous 30s Latino star Carmen Miranda.

A theft backstage results in the band's everyday clothes being stolen; all but John Cambridge are forced to make the chilly journey back to Haddon Hall in their stagewear. Cambridge had arrived in his outfit. "They were pretty much the only clothes I had then," he said in 2010.

1. This festival was a 'Living Theatre Environment' production, the bands booked by Stuart Lions, who also booked artists into the nearby Country Club.

2. Featuring Peter Gabriel and Mike Rutherford, drummer Phil Collins joined Genesis in late 1970, replacing John Mayhew.

3. Sanders subsequently lost the photographs.

4. The soundtrack for this 16mm colour film was lost when the film's owner failed to keep paying the film's storage fee. Footage of the three songs listed were saved, each filmed from three different camera positions.

5. Brazilian composer, singer, writer and political activist. Together with Gilberto Gil, Veloso had been exiled following a three-month spell in prison. Both had upset officials of the Brazilian military dictatorship due to an involvement with the country's controversial musical movement Tropicalismo, but were allowed to return home in 1972.

Thursday 12 March

▌David Bowie, Royal Albert Hall, Kensington Gore, London SW7.

With the venue listed incorrectly in *Disc & Music Echo* as the Royal Festival Hall, David delivers on his promise to film producer Rex Sheldon and performs a 20-minute solo set as part of a night in aid of Mencap.

The show's mixed-bag line-up includes The Faces and tenor singer Josef Locke. David is accompanied by Angie and Ken Pitt; as they walk together to the nearest underground station, David informs Pitt of his and Angie's decision to marry, but not when. It is to be a low-key affair; they have not even told David's mother.

Friday 13 March

▌David Bowie & Hype, Locarno Ballroom, Fillmore North, Sunderland.

Dressed in the costumes worn at the Roundhouse, the band deliver a one-hour set, supported by Principal Edwards Magic Theatre, Circus and Man.

Promoter Geoff Docherty later recalled David's on-stage performance and off-stage courteousness in his 2002 book *A Promoter's Tale: Rock At The Sharp End*.

Saturday 14 March

▌David Bowie, University of Surrey, Stag Hill, Guildford.

Continuing to alternate between all-out rock with Hype and more sedate acoustic styles, David performs a single 45-minute solo set.

Tuesday 17 March

Less than two weeks after its release and already it is apparent that 'The Prettiest Star' is not destined to emulate the success of 'Space Oddity'. Sales have reached just 798 copies, though it has stimulated interest in David's second album – its sales have crept up to 5,025 copies.

Thursday 19 March

Angie and David spend the afternoon at London's hippy fashion emporium Kensington Market. She chooses an ankle length floral patterned design as her wedding dress and David selects a pair of black satin trousers.

At his Manchester Street flat, Ken Pitt receives a call from David's mother. She is anxious for more

information about the wedding, but Pitt hasn't been told and is unable to help.

▌In the evening, David celebrates his stag night with a solo performance at The Three Tuns' new folk club run by Ian Shaw and Ken Simmons. David's well-received set includes Arts Lab favourite 'Wild Eyed Boy From Freecloud'. His friend, artist and actress Clare Shenstone,[1] also plays a solo acoustic

TOP: Just days after David's second Roundhouse glam debut, David and Angela Barnett tie the knot at Bromley Register Office. David is wearing a silver Andre Courrèges belt given to him by Calvin Mark Lee.

LEFT: Husband and wife, with the groom's mother, pose on the steps of the glamorous Bromley Register Office. The local celebrity marriage made the front page of the *Bromley & Kentish Times*. David's mother had alerted the press to the event. (▶ 27.3.70)

ABOVE: Mark Pritchett (left) and Tim Broadbent of Rungk.

RIGHT: Advert for David Bowie & Hype at the Star Hotel, 23 March.

In this year...

Tuesday 24 March

RECORDING of tracks 'Oh Baby' and 'Universal Love' by Marc Bolan with John Cambridge, Tim Renwick and Tony Visconti at London Weekend TV's four-track studios. Mick Ronson was present but didn't contribute, and in 1981 Tony Visconti quashed speculation that David was involved. "This was a period when Marc became very jealous of David and David stayed away from him. There was always a lot of talk about their recording this together, but I can assure you it never happened."

Around this time Visconti cut another single at the LWT studio with a line-up which included Ronson. The songs recorded were 'Dee Dah Shuka Shuka Dooah' and 'Skinny Rose', the latter released for the first time as a bonus on Visconti's 1998 CD reissue *Inventory*.

Monday 11 April

LAUNCH of Apollo 13 space craft, led by commander James A. Lovell. Two days after the launch the spacecraft was crippled by an explosion and was lucky to make it home. The event was dramatised in the 1995 movie *Apollo 13* starring Tom Hanks, who played Lovell. In 1975, Lovell made a cameo appearance with David in the film *The Man Who Fell To Earth.*

THE happy STAR HOTEL ★ W. CROYDON
296 London Road, Broad Green
MON., MARCH 23rd
LIGHTS
SOUNDS **CARAVAN & EASY LEAF**
NEXT MONDAY: **DAVID BOWIE HYPE + UGLY ROOM**

set. This is to be David's last known performance at the Three Tuns.

Later, Shenstone, David, Angie, her brother and other friends continue the celebrations back at Haddon Hall.

1. Shenstone was prominently featured in designer Alan Aldridge's poster for Andy Warhol's 1966 film *Chelsea Girls*. After completing her MA at the Royal College of Art in the late 70s, Shenstone became friendly with revered artist Francis Bacon, whom she painted and sketched many times.

Friday 20 March

David and Angie and witnesses Clare Shenstone and John Cambridge are greeted on the steps of Bromley Register Office[1] in the town's Beckenham Lane by David's uninvited mother.

During the 15-minute ceremony, when Cambridge makes a move to sign the register, he is intercepted by Mrs Jones, who signs in his place, David acknowledges his drummer with a shrug of the shoulders.

Taking the place of wedding rings are a set of Peruvian bangles[2] (a gift from Angie's brother). Guests include roadie Roger Fry and Tony Visconti's girlfriend Liz Hartley (asked to be David's best man, Visconti is unable to attend due to recording commitments with The Strawbs).

After posing for photographs for local press and friends, the party crosses the road to the Swan & Mitre pub for a drink. Later in the afternoon the couple hold a celebratory party at Haddon Hall, where they intend to spend their honeymoon.

1. The register office has since been demolished.

2. These became a trademark accessory for David; he wore Peruvian bangles until 1976 when his marriage irrevocably broke down.

Saturday 21 March

With 'The Prettiest Star' dead in the water commercially, recording commences at Trident Studios on a follow-up – a new version of 'Memory Of A Free Festival' as requested by David's US label. This is to be split over both the A- and B-side.

David and Angie are still celebrating their marriage and stop by to tell Ralph Mace, who has left Philips and is by now working for music publisher Famous Music in Soho's Wardour Street.

Sunday 22 March

David, Visconti and the other members of Hype continue recording at Trident.

Monday 23 March

As well as recording 'Memory Of A Free Festival', work starts at 11pm on a new song, 'The Supermen'. The session lasts until 3am and proves to be the

last in the studio with John Cambridge as drummer; there is friction over his inability to master the track's doom-laden rhythm.

"I had a bit of trouble and things got a bit heated," said Cambridge in 1991. "It didn't help when Mick Ronson got angry and told me it was easy."

Wednesday 25 March

David and Hype record an appearance for Radio One's *Sounds Of The 70s* at the Playhouse Theatre in Northumberland Avenue, off Trafalgar Square.

First they have to wait because of a rehearsal over-run by Keith Emerson's group The Nice. Also on the bill are Clouds – David knows them from their previous incarnation as 1-2-3, but they record at different times and don't meet.

Ken Pitt drops by but realises all is not well. "It was Mick Ronson who gave the whole game away by the look on his face. He smiled knowingly as if he knew something that I didn't. But at that moment I did know. Something was afoot."

Friday 27 March

With the headline 'The Bridegroom Wore Satin...', the *Bromley Times* carries a front-page report on the recent nuptials: 'But there will be no honeymoon for David and Angela, who met just one year ago in a London club where they had both gone to see the underground group King Crimson. "Unfortunately, I'm far too busy working," said David over a pint in the Swan & Mitre.'

Saturday 28 March

Publication of David's interview with Ray Telford in *Melody Maker* confirms his intention to maintain his solo career as a priority over considerations for Hype: "Although we're all happy with the set-up, I can't see it becoming a permanent thing. I want to retain Hype and myself as two separate working units whereby we can retain our own identities."

Monday 30 March

▶ David Bowie & Hype, Star Hotel, London Road, Croydon, Surrey.

Support is by local group Ugly Room.[1] Tonight's gig is David's final on-stage appearance with John Cambridge.

For a while, gigs with Hype are cancelled as David focuses not only on recording and songwriting but also resolution of his growing unease over Ken Pitt's management strategy.

1. Vocalist of Ugly Room was Tony De Meur, who later became a member of mid-70s new-wave novelty act The Fabulous Poodles, before he adopted the persona of comedian Ronnie Golden.

Tuesday 31 March

David visits Ken Pitt at Manchester Street and informs him he wishes to manage his own affairs. 'I thought he was not being perfectly frank with me and that somebody was already waiting in the wings,' Pitt wrote of the meeting in 1983.

David is unclear as to why he wants to break away but when prompted voices concerns over too many gigs and not enough time set aside for recording. A solution is suggested and agreed upon and the meeting ends amicably when David asks Pitt for a £200 advance.

Wednesday 1 April

Pitt meets Visconti to work out a schedule for the recording of David's next album. It is even being mooted that this new collection should be titled *Memory Of A Free Festival* as a tie-in with the new single, even though this appeared as a track on the 1969 *David Bowie* album.

The budget for the new record is tight and sessions are going to have to be booked largely in studio dead-time – late at night and at weekends.

A gig the following day at The Penthouse, Scarborough, Yorks, is cancelled in favour of another session at Trident between 6pm and midnight. This has been booked by Visconti, who has not informed Pitt.

Friday 3 April

Recording of the new version of 'Memory Of A Free Festival' concludes at Advision Sound Studios, next door to BBC Broadcasting House, at 23 Gosfield Street in London's West End.[1] A Moog synthesiser hired from George Martin's Air Studios and accompanied by young technician Chris Thomas[2] is played by Ralph Mace, since Ronson has been unable to get to grips with the instrument.

Meanwhile, Mace has arranged a separate record deal for Hype with Philips. This contract has been nurtured by Angie, who is a friend of the label's newly promoted general manager, Olav Wyper.[3]

On the domestic front, David's mother and half-brother Terry Burns are leaving the family home in Plaistow Grove, as reported in the *Bromley & Kentish Times*:

'"The move will just be a change for us," said Mrs Jones. "And I can become Mrs Jones again! At the moment, a lot of people call me Mrs Bowie."'

The story, headed 'Star's mother leaving town... to get her own identity back', says they are shifting base to Finchley, north-west London.

In fact they are moving to Albermarle Road, Beckenham; Finchley has been fed as a location to the press so that they can retain privacy in the wake of the success of 'Space Oddity'.

1. Still studios, the premises were being occupied by The Sound Company in 2010.
2. Thomas is a prominent record producer, having worked with Roxy Music, John Cale, The Sex Pistols, The Pretenders and, more recently, U2, Pulp and Razorlight.
3. Later became commercial director at RCA Records, London.

Saturday 4 April

David and Visconti at Trident preparing a 16-track mix of 'Memory Of A Free Festival'.

Monday 6 April

The incident during the recording of 'The Supermen' was a portent; David tells John Cambridge that his services are no longer required. "I was painting the ceiling when I heard Angie saying to David 'You've got to tell him, you've got to tell him now,'" said Cambridge in 2010. "So David came in and reluctantly told me that they were looking for a new drummer. Not, he said, because there was anything wrong with my drumming, but they wanted someone who could help them with arrangements."

In the evening some of the songs from the recent *Sounds Of The 70s* session are broadcast on Radio One's *Andy Ferris Show*.

Tuesday 7 April

At the crack of dawn Cambridge rises, loads his drums into his Hillman Minx, borrows £5 from David for petrol and heads back to Hull. Cambridge's departure prompts Mick Ronson to suggest a replacement: 20-year-old Mick Woodmansey, another drummer from the north-eastern city who has served time in The Rats.

"Bowie phoned me up and said, 'Mick says you're a good drummer, do you want to come and join me?'" said Woodmansey in 1994. "So I said, 'Yes', and came down to London."

Woodmansey passes an audition at Haddon Hall and, like Ronson before him, quits his day job (as an assistant foreman at an optical company) and moves into the large house in Beckenham.

Woodmansey's flexibility appeals to David. "He was quite open to direction and in a way sort of carried out what I wanted done much more than most of the other drummers I have worked with," David said in 1994.

For a brief spell after his arrival, Woodmansey and David emulate Marc Bolan's Tyrannosaurus Rex formula with percussionist Mickey Finn by playing a handful of performances as a duo.

"David asked me to get a rug for both of us to sit on just like Tyrannosaurus Rex," said Woodmansey. "So I picked up one of the rugs at Haddon Hall and David said, 'Yeah, that'll do'. Some nights we did two or three gigs, going from one place to another. One night we arrived without the rug. David asked where it was, and I said that I'd forgotten it. So that finished that idea."

Soon after Woodmansey's arrival at Haddon Hall, Pete Sanders takes photos of him, Ronson and Visconti at the house and in the back garden for promotional purposes for Hype.

Hype members Ronson, Visconti and Woodmansey sign the Philips contract (pre-dated 3 April), which is witnessed by David. The £4,000 advance is used to buy a new PA system for the band, who intend

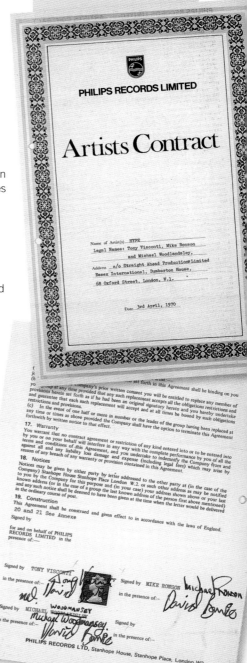

BELOW: The original Philips/Hype contract, endorsed by David, 3 April.

RIGHT: Early promo pics for Hype. Mick Ronson and Woody Woodmansey are pictured in the grounds of Haddon Hall and Tony Visconti in the basement where he was sound-proofing the small rehearsal space. All taken the same day in March or April by Pete Sanders.

to go out live without David on occasion.

The trio will form the core of Hype, augmented live occasionally by neighbour Mark Pritchett on guitar and vocalist/harmonica player Benny Marshall.

Sunday 12 April

▶ David Bowie, Harrogate Theatre, Oxford Street, Harrogate, Yorks.

David's performance of two half-hour solo sets at 4.30pm and 7.30pm (on the same bill as The Keef Hartley Band) affords an opportunity to hook up with Brian Howard, the theatre producer keen to include him in a staging of *The Fair Maid Of Perth* at the venue.

In the audience at the Harrogate Theatre is Hull-based bass player Trevor Bolder. His friend Mick Ronson has tipped him off about David.

Tuesday 14 April

Howard travels to London to lunch with David and continue discussions about the play. He leaves with the impression that David is keen to appear in *The Fair Maid Of Perth*.

In the afternoon David is at Elstree Film Studios[1] in Borehamwood, Herts, for a meeting with writer/

director Frank Nesbit[2] about a part in a film entitled *Dulcima*.[3]

A five-hour session starting at 7pm at Advision finds David and the remaining musicians – since Cambridge's drum track has already been taped[4] – working again on the single version of 'Memory Of A Free Festival'.

1. In 1977, David filmed his appearance in *Bing Crosby's Merrie Olde Christmas* TV show at Elstree's ATV Studios and, in 1985, he appeared in *Labyrinth*, director Jim Hensor's children's feature film shot at Elstree Film Studios.

2. Nesbit requested copies of David's albums from Pitt, but no role was offered.

3. Released in 1971, *Dulcima* starred John Mills and Carol White.

4. Ironically, Cambridge's drum track was eventually preferred, even though problems recording it cost him his pace in the band.

Wednesday 15 April

Back at Advision for another stint between 7pm and midnight, the single is completed.

Friday 17 April

Work begins on David's next album with a session at Advision starting at the inauspicious – and relatively inexpensive – hour of 1am.

Over the course of four hours the musicians work on tracks including 'All The Madmen'.

This is the start of five weeks of recording which will stretch the limits of the relationship between David and producer Visconti, who also plays bass.

Saturday 18 April

Preoccupied with his new marriage, David is also taking the breakdown of his relationship with Pitt very much to heart, and most days he doesn't rise before 3pm. Visconti later recalled David doing "an awful lot of tincture of cannabis". In 1986 David said: "At the time I was generally asleep."

Following his contribution to 'Memory Of A Free Festival', Ralph Mace has been brought on board to play Moog on a number of other album tracks, and Benny Marshall is present at some of the recordings, having been invited by Ronson after visiting him at Haddon Hall in the company of future Spider From Mars Trevor Bolder.[1]

1. It was over a year before Bolder was invited to work with David. (▶ 17.5.71)

Tuesday 21 April

Another late-hour recording session is held at Trident between 11pm and 5am.

Wednesday 22 April

11pm to 5am recording session at Trident.

A letter from Visconti to recently departed drummer John Cambridge reveals some of the tensions – not least financial – which lurk beneath the surface of David's current activities:

'Down here it's still up in the air. Angela's working from 9-5 in an office so I guess the other guys have some peace during the day. David and Mick have got a lot closer. In fact we're all a lot closer, but still starving. Woody cut his finger on a knife and had three stitches from the hospital. He can't play for two weeks now. We've had to cancel two sessions and a gig in Cheshire. David is pretty uptight for bread at the moment. So could you send him what you owe him from this cheque.'[1]

At this time Angie encourages David to express his concerns about his contract with Pitt to Olav Wyper at Philips.

Wyper suggests David meet his lawyer Tony Defries,[2] who has worked for producer Mickie Most.

1. A reference to £5 owed to David by Cambridge. When they met again in 1989 backstage at a Tin Machine gig in Bradford, John told David he had dropped in to settle the debt.

2. Wyper suggested three people that David could see and it was Defries who he chose to meet.

Friday 24 April

In a letter drafted with Angie, David terminates his agreement with Kenneth Pitt Management Ltd.

'In effect, the letter said he no longer considered me to be his personal manager and that he required my confirmation, within seven days, that I would no longer act as such,' wrote Pitt in 1983.

David has already had his first meeting with Tony Defries who is an employee of solicitors Godfrey Davis & Batt in Cavendish Square, central London.

"He said, I can get you out of that," said David of Defries' view on his management contract with Pitt. "I just sat there and openly wept. I was so relieved that somebody was so strong about things."

Pitt receives the letter on 27 April.

Saturday 25 April

Starting at 3pm, the musicians embark on a seven-hour recording session at Trident.

Sunday 26 April

Another extended recording session takes place at Trident between 2pm and 10pm.

Monday 27 April

▶ David Bowie, POW Club, Stockport Sixth Form Union, Poco a Poco, Manchester Road, Heaton Chapel, Stockport, Cheshire.

The injury to Woodmansey's finger, to which Visconti referred in his recent letter, forces this to be an acoustic solo gig on a bill with Barclay James Harvest, former Feathers bandmate Tony Hill's High Tide and The Purple Gang.

David asks The Purple Gang – best known for their 1967 jug-band track *Granny Takes A Trip* – to back him.

The group's founder, Joe Beard, recalled in 2002 that he and his fellow musicians "bottled out". David took the stage "all in denim – he was bloody brilliant, of course."

Wednesday 29 April

In a long and detailed written response, Pitt rejects David's claims of mismanagement, but offers him the opportunity to discuss ways 'by which we might end our professional relationship.'

David forwards Pitt's letter to Defries with a short hand-written note:

'Dear Tony,

I had to prepare for a recording session so I could not make it over. Anyway, here's the letter that I received.

Can we make sure monies are paid to me, you, or held, by Decca Records Mercury/Philips P.R.S. etc.

Mercury (Robin McBride) owe me a min £120 expenses for the LP I am currently making. Can we claim this.

Can I enter, at this stage, into a publishing deal with Essex. Bowie'

Thursday 30 April

Work continues on the new record with another eight-hour session at Trident starting at 2pm.

Friday 1 May

A five-hour Trident session commences at 9pm. An undated master tape from these sessions lists three recordings: 'Suck;[1] Suck (edit section); Door.'

1. 'Suck' was the basis for *The Man Who Sold The World* track 'She Shook Me Cold'.

Monday 4 May

With another club engagement for David and Hype postponed today, two tracks – 'Running Gun Blues' and 'Saviour Machine' – are recorded at Trident

ABOVE: Photographed by Rolf Adlercreutz at Trident, during sessions for *The Man Who Sold The World*.

1970 MAY

THIS PAGE

TOP LEFT: Ivor Novello Awards leaflet.

TOP RIGHT: Photographed in one of the top-floor offices at Trident, David is interviewed by Swedish journalist Bosse Hansson, 4 May.

ABOVE: At the Ivor Novello Awards singing 'Space Oddity', 10 May.

OPPOSITE PAGE

TOP: *Melody Maker* advert for 'Memory Of A Free Festival'.

MIDDLE: German single release of 'Memory Of A Free Festival Part I & II'.

BOTTOM: Detail from single press release, confirming correct release date of 26 June.

between 6pm and 10pm. Ralph Mace adds Moog overdubs.[1]

David's original name for 'Saviour Machine' is 'The Man Who Sold The World', but the completed version does not contain the phrase. He works it into another melody and comes up with the song which will eventually grant the album its title.

Before the session begins, David is interviewed at the studio by Swedish journalist Bosse Hansson and photographed by London-based freelance Rolf Adlercreutz, who have arrived unannounced.

Impressed with David's 1969 album, Hansson has tracked him down via his record label's London HQ in Stanhope Place.

"A young man at the office didn't know who David Bowie was but he checked in the register and told me that David was recording at a studio in St Anne's Court, Soho," said Hansson in 1998.

"We went there, Rolf, my wife Bodil and I, and entered a dark studio. I spotted two men sitting on the floor: David and Tony Visconti. I introduced myself and said I came from Sweden. David replied 'Oh, the land of Carl Larsson'."[2]

Visconti escorted Bodil Hansson to a local pub while David was interviewed.

"The studio was in working order, but the office part was not yet furnished so we all sat on the floor," recalled Adlercreutz in 1998.

"Bosse Hansson was quite worked up during the interview and kept saying to David, 'You are going to be the Bob Dylan of the 70s'. At this time, David was more or less a one-hit-wonder with 'Space Oddity'. But Mr Hansson turned out to be correct and lived high on his prediction among other rock journalists in Sweden."

However, David is unhappy with the comparison, complaining to Hansson, "Dylan is a poor guitarist, his songs are boring and he has a bad voice. Let's drop the subject."

David also claims he can "take or leave success". He adds: "All I do is record for myself, I don't care if anyone buys the record or if people like it or not. Making the charts is of no importance to me, I don't even care if I earn enough money."

The interview complete, David, the photographer and journalist join Visconti and Bodil Hansson in The Salisbury in St Martin's Lane. "David told me it was wonderful to do just that, without screaming fans around," said Hansson.[3] Here David tells them he is due to tour Sweden in the summer.[4]

1. The multi-track box from this date lists the contents as 'Cyclops' and 'Invader', likely to be the working titles for 'Running Gun Blues' and 'Saviour Machine'. An eight-track master features out-takes of 'Cyclops' and 'The Invader'. The latter track was later incorrectly annotated as having come from sessions for David's 1971 album *Hunky Dory*.

2. Carl Larsson (1853–1915), Swedish illustrator and artist.

3. David and the Hanssons maintained contact for a while, exchanging Christmas cards. "Then fame took over and we lost touch," said Hansson in 1998.

4. Earlier in the spring, Ken Pitt had endeavoured to set up a tour of Sweden between 28 May and 14 June with the Scandinavian Booking Agency. This did not materialise.

Tuesday 5 May

A six-hour recording session takes place at Trident followed by a four-hour recording session there the following day.

Thursday 7 May

David and his new legal advisor Tony Defries meet Ken Pitt at his Manchester Street apartment for a discussion.

Pitt later said of the meeting: "I said that there was no point in David and me continuing our professional relationship if he was unhappy with it, but I had spent a great deal of money on him and required to be compensated for loss of future earnings. Defries nodded and said that as he did not have any figures to hand he would need time to consider the matter, but he thought that compensation should be based on my earnings to date. Had he then asked me if I had a sum in mind I would have said £2,000, a modest sum that would have satisfied me, but he did not ask and the meeting ended, along with my management of David Bowie."

'After they had gone I stood at the window watching them walk up the road,' wrote Pitt in 1983. 'I experienced a feeling of great relief that a heavy and often frustrating responsibility had been taken from me. I wondered what David would be thinking. What now were his expectations?'

Later that evening David has another three-hour recording session at Trident.

Saturday 9 May

David has been nominated for an Ivor Novello Award and asked to perform at the ceremony for the presentation of these music business songwriting accolades, so takes part in rehearsals at CTS Studios, 49 Kensington Gardens Square, in Bayswater.

Sunday 10 May

▶ David is presented with the award for most original song for 'Space Oddity' at the Ivor Novellos at The Talk of the Town[1] in 1 Cranbourn Street, Leicester Square.

Sharing the award with Peter Sarstedt's 'Where Do You Go To (My Lovely)?', David performs 'Space Oddity' on acoustic guitar, backed by a large orchestra conducted by Les Reed (who has been instructed in recreating the sound of the single by David's arranger/orchestrator Paul Buckmaster).[2]

The 90-minute show is televised live in Australia and to parts of the US and Europe. It is also broadcast live on BBC radio.

Other award recipients include the recently split Beatles and also Tom Jones. Tony Macaulay is awarded British Songwriter of the Year for 'Love Grows (Where My Rosemary Goes)'. After the show, produced by Jack Lynn, David and Angie attend the celebration dinner.

1. In the 80s The Talk of the Town became Peter Stringfellow's Hippodrome nightclub and was subsequently renamed The Cirque At The Hippodrome by new owners. It closed as a public venue in 2005.
2. Also performing were Blue Mink, Frankie Vaughan, Ginger Baker's Airforce, Marmalade, Peter Sarstedt, Sandie Shaw and Dusty Springfield. Sir Noel Coward also received an award for Oustanding Services to British Music.

Monday 11 May

'The Width Of A Circle' and 'Wild Eyed Boy From Freecloud' (recorded in March) are broadcast on Radio One's *David Symonds Show*.

Tuesday 12 May

Recording and mixing of the new album switches to Advision (which has moved from New Bond Street to Gosfield Street) for a 10-hour session ending at midnight.

Wednesday 13 May

Another 10-hour booking at Advision includes Ralph Mace adding Moog to some of the new album tracks.

Sunday 17 May

More recording and mixing at Advision during an eight-hour session.

Thursday 21 May

▶ David Bowie & Hype, The Penthouse, 35 St Nicholas Street, Scarborough, Yorks.

With album recording nearing completion, David and Hype make their first appearance in nearly two months, fulfilling the booking originally scheduled for 3 April.

Just before the show – Woodmansey's first live appearance in the group – David's former musical collaborator John Hutchinson drops by for a catch-up. Mark Pritchett is making one of his occasional appearances in Hype on guitar. The group stay in nearby Whitby.

Friday 22 May

David and his fellow musicians head back to Advision in London for final mixing[1] of the new album, which he now intends to call *Metrobolist* (a play on Fritz Lang's 1923 film *Metropolis*).

Visconti is not impressed when David chooses this last-minute opportunity to record the vocal for 'The Man Who Sold The World'. "This was the beginning of David's new style of writing – 'I can't be bothered until I have to'," said Visconti in 1977. "When it was finished, on the last day of the last mix, I remember telling David, 'I've had it, I can't work like this any

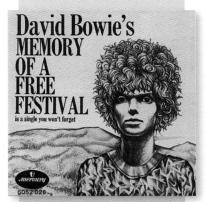

News From The Philips Group London

DAVID BOWIE CONTINUES HIS THEME OF "MAN VERSUS MACHINE"

"Memory Of A Free Festival" released on June 26

Ever since his astounding record "Space Oddity", David Bowie has been hailed as one of the biggest assets British music has.

He won a special Ivor Novello Award For Originality from the Song Writers Guild Of Great Britain for "Space Oddity" last year, at which time his first Philips album was released.

Recently, David has been working with lead guitarist Mick Ronson, drummer Michael Woodmansey and record producer/bass

TONY DEFRIES

BORN 3 September 1943 in Rickmansworth, Herts, Anthony Defries suffered from fragile health as a child, plagued by severe asthma attacks and spending many months in hospital.

Brought up close to David in south London's Croydon, he attended Heath Clark School and, on leaving, followed his brother Nicholas into the legal profession, taking his articles and working for 10 years at central London practice Martin Boston as a litigation clerk.

In the mid-60s he met the practice's client, producer and manager Mickie Most. Defries and colleague Laurence Myers advised Most on a dispute with the British Invasion band The Animals and, during his time working with Most, Defries had occasional dealings with Allen Klein, the infamous New York-based businessman who represented The Rolling Stones and The Beatles. Klein's tough-minded approach to contracts and business in general rubbed off on Defries.

In 1968 Defries was working as a solicitors' clerk at Godfrey Davis & Batt at their offices in Cavendish Square. Here his representation of the Association of Fashion & Advertising Photographers led to an introduction to leading photographer Brian Duffy (often considered as the third part of the triumvirate of Swinging London photographers made up by David Bailey and Terence Donovan).

By the spring of 1970 Defries and Myers were contemplating going into showbiz management. Enter David Bowie planning a fresh strategy for a new decade, a plan that required new management and a new direction. Although David had been worried that his contract with Ken Pitt was unbreakable, he hadn't factored in Pitt's generosity. Realising that David earnestly wanted to end their working relationship, Pitt – though bitterly disappointed – stood to one side. In the end the break that had so concerned David was conducted in a gentlemanly fashion and without legal recourse. Pitt requested only that his percentage of David's earnings be honoured for the remainder of their contract, which in the fall of 1970 he estimated at just £2,000.[1]

David with Tony Defries in Memphis, 24 September 1972.

In particular, David felt restricted by a contract that was not due to expire until April 1972, so Philips general manager Olaf Wyper's recommendation of Defries and Myers was quickly followed up.

Wyper recalled in 1986: "David said that the friendship was getting in the way of a career, and that Ken wasn't the person to take him on to that next stage."

David's first meeting with Tony Defries took place at Godfrey Davis & Batt in Cavendish Square. David was bowled over by Defries' implacable approach to his contractual concerns.

"He said, 'I can get you out of that'," David said in 1972. "I just sat there and openly wept. I was so relieved that somebody was so strong about things."

On his advice, David wrote to Pitt terminating their agreement exactly two years before the term was due. Despite Pitt's initial resistance, and within two weeks of that notice being served, Defries had freed David from the agreement.

Payment was never settled, however, and was complicated further when Defries requested a full audit of David's Kenneth Pitt Ltd account, only to find that, far from fleecing David, Pitt had actually undercharged him.

Strong as his legal and business acumen were, Defries' inexperience in handling talent was exposed in the first year of his nominal stewardship of David's career. So disinterested was he in his artist that David's publisher Bob Grace was often forced to fulfil the managerial role de facto at David's insistence.

Notably, Defries did not accompany David on an important promotional tour of the US at the beginning of 1971. For much of that period Defries instead focused on pitching hard to become Stevie Wonder's manager once the Motown star reached 21 years of age in May 1971, an attempt which ultimately failed.

Meanwhile, David was finally proving himself as a songwriter of commercial worth by supplying ex-Herman's Hermit Peter Noone with his top 20 hit 'Oh You Pretty Thing'.

With a renewed buoyancy surrounding David's career, Defries re-entered the fray, drawing again on his shrewd deal-making and -breaking skills.

Warning off Grace and David's personally hired PR, the veteran Bill Harry, Defries set about extricating David from the limited horizons offered by his deal with Mercury US.

Defries flatly refused Mercury's offer of an extension to the existing deal and persuaded the label's top execs to part with the rights to the two albums David had recorded for them, in return for a one-off payment of just under £20,000.

With David entering the first golden phase of his recording career, Defries was able to present *Hunky Dory* to potential labels as a finished project. The feeding frenzy he created among US record companies resulted in David's triumphant return to New York in September 1971 to sign the deal with RCA, which would see him release his era-defining and career-making music of the 70s.

Defries was the perfect foil for David; not only was he fearless in the boardroom but he was also prepared to fulfil his charge's creative ambitions to be the figurehead of a musical firmament which included talented friends George Underwood and Dana Gillespie and long-admired heroes such as Iggy Pop and Lou Reed.

But the MainMan edifice constructed by Defries was bound to topple, and, when it did, so did David's business and personal contact with Defries. Following the severing of their relationship in 1975, Defries retained a stake in David's work from 1969 to 1983, when David signed with EMI. Defries finally relinquished this interest – for a hefty price – in 1997.

By this time he was based in the US. He had long invested in new technologies and, in 2010, was the CEO of a solar technology company, though still retains MainMan as a going concern which occasionally releases music.

1. Ken Pitt was never recompensed during Tony Defries' tenure as David's manager. In 1975 a settlement was finally reached with David after he had broken away from MainMan. Instead of the £2,000 that Pitt had originally asked for as a final settlement in 1970, the High Court eventually awarded him £15,000 plus his legal costs.

David's counsel told the judge in conclusion:

"This is not one of those cases where management and artist had fallen out. Both sides hoped for a settlement of this kind."

ABOVE: David's publicist Anya Wilson. Her first work with David was to promote 'Memory Of A Free Festival'.

LEFT: David and Tony Visconti rocking at the Roundhouse, during the last known Hype performance. It was a live shot from this period that David wanted to include in a collage on the back cover of *The Man Who Sold The World*.

BELOW: On the set of *Ready, Eddy Go!* TV show in the Netherlands, prior to his performance of 'Memory Of A Free Festival'. The booking arranged by Anya Wilson.

more – I'm through. I've got Marc Bolan who wants to record night and day and is keen to go, and I might as well put my energies into him because you really don't want to work very hard.' David was very disappointed."

In 1993, David described Visconti's views regarding his input on *The Man Who Sold The World* as "exaggerated" adding, "I think they – the songs – are largely there."

1. A reference tape made to check progress on the album in May 1970 contains unfinished mixes of 'The Width Of A Circle', 'After All', 'All The Madmen' (with a gap waiting for the insertion of the spoken line "He followed me home Mum. Can I keep him?"), 'Black Country Rock' (which features extended Marc Bolan-style vocals) and 'The Man Who Sold The World' (minus the fade).

A Trident acetate of the album, offered for sale in 2009, had 'The Man Who Sold The World' opening side one and 'Width Of A Circle' opening side two, but excluded 'Running Gun Blues'.

A song demoed by David on vocals and acoustic guitar but not recorded for the album was 'Tired Of My Life', which was subsequently bootlegged. In 1980 David updated the lyrics and it became a new song, 'It's No Game', two versions of which, with different tempos, appeared on the 1980 album *Scary Monsters*.

Saturday 23 May

A booking for an appearance by David Bowie & Hype at Eel Pie Island in south-west London is cancelled.

With the album complete, David and Angie decide to take a break and write a short note to Defries saying: 'We're leaving for Scotland in a few hours and now we are getting very excited.'[1]

1. On one visit to Scotland in 1970 David saw Lindsay Kemp's production of Jean Genet's *Our Lady Of The Flowers* at the Traverse Theatre at 15 James Court, Lawnmarket in Edinburgh.

Tuesday 16 June

▶ David Bowie & Hype, Cambridge University May Ball, Jesus College, Jesus Lane, Cambridge, Cambs.[1]

Although *Melody Maker* has mistakenly listed this gig as taking place five days earlier, David and Hype

are on the bill with Deep Purple, Black Widow and The Move (with whom they share a dressing room).

"It was a rather haphazard performance, nothing went terribly well," said occasional guitarist Mark Pritchett in 1994. "We went on between 4am and 5am, just after Deep Purple. It was more of an acoustic set. Woody played bongos."

By this time David has formally signed as Tony Defries' first act at Gem Management,[2] a company owned by partner Laurence Myers and based at 252-260 Regent Street in central London.

1. Although historically called May Balls, these events are always held in mid-June, at the end of the academic year. They are traditionally formal affairs and stipulate evening dress. Promoter Rufus Manning Associates tried to book David for an appearance there the following year but was unsuccessful.

2. Gem Management became part of GTO, Laurence Myers' Gem Toby Organisation, whose companies later included budget record label K-Tel and GTO Films.

In this year...

6 June
PERFORMANCE of first and only solo gig by former Pink Floyd founder member Syd Barrett. He was backed at London's Olympia exhibition centre by David Gilmour and Jerry Shirley. During the fourth song, Barrett abruptly ended the show by removing his guitar and walking off the stage.

Thursday 18 June

In a letter to Benny Marshall in Hull, Mick Ronson expresses his growing disenchantment: "Things are a bit boring down here and I want to reform The Rats one day soon. Keep it all quiet though, won't you?"

This is one of three letters to Marshall this month in which Ronson talks about getting The Rats back together. However, Woodmansey is of a more positive frame of mind.

"I have only good memories of the days at Haddon Hall," he said in 1994. "We knew David had something but we didn't know quite what. It was an adventure and we used what talent we had to help him. After we did a few tracks we thought, 'Shit! This is good stuff'."

Friday 26 June

Mercury release 'Memory Of A Free Festival Pt 1'/ 'Memory Of A Free Festival Pt 2' single.

⊙ **David Bowie**
A **'Memory Of A Free Festival Pt 1'** (Bowie)
B **'Memory Of A Free Festival Pt 2'** (Bowie)
David Bowie (guitar, keyboard, vocal)
Mick Ronson (guitar, solo backing singer)
Tony Visconti (bass)
John Cambridge (drums)
Ralph Mace (Moog synthesiser)
Produced by Tony Visconti
(Mercury 6052 026)

This version of the song commemorating the August 1969 Beckenham Free Festival begins with the various instruments stuttering into life. "We didn't plan it that way," said John Cambridge in 2009. "We all started playing at different times and Tony [Visconti] liked it."

The single – also released in America this month – was originally scheduled for UK issue on 12 June.

David appears on Granada TV performing his new single. This is the first booking achieved by Gem's plugger Anya Wilson,[1] who accompanies him to the studios. "It was nice we were supported by Granada," she said in 2001. "We certainly weren't at BBC TV!"

1. Wilson joined Gem in January 1970 after helping to secure a number one hit for the Edison Lighthouse song 'Love Grows (Where My Rosemary Goes)', written and produced by her boyfriend, Tony Macaulay, who had an office at Gem. She went on to play a part in the success of T.Rex's October 1970 hit 'Ride A White Swan'.
Working as the Acme Plug Company, Wilson's vivacity ensured her popularity among radio and television programmers, producers and journalists.
She continued working for David and Defries up to the 1975 release of *Young Americans*. These days Wilson heads a successful promotions agency in Toronto.

Saturday 4 July

◗ David Bowie, Open Air Concert, Queen's Mead Recreation Ground, Queen's Mead Road, Shortlands, Bromley, Kent.

It is clear now from the billing that Hype are no more; from now on David appears with backing musicians but under his own name whether he is performing a solo acoustic set or not.[1]

As the *Bromley Times* reported the previous week, 'David Bowie will be backed by his own group, previously known as Hype.'

The concert has been organised by guitar virtuoso and former leader of Fleetwood Mac Peter Green, who appears on the bill. Held over the course of seven-and-a-half hours, it also features Clark Hutchinson,[2] Skin Alley,[3] Rungk,[4] Bubastis, Aslan and High Tide.

"David made a point of picking out Mick Ronson for me to watch," said High Tide's Tony Hill in 1995.

1. In early 70 David mentioned in an interview that he sometimes called his backing band Harry The Butcher. John Cambridge confirms that he never heard David mention the name.
2. Andy Clark and Mick Hutchinson; Clark joined post-glam act Be Bop Deluxe in 1975 and played synthesiser on David's 1980 album *Scary Monsters*.
3. From August 1970 Skin Alley's line-up included keyboard player Nicky Graham, who was the first piano player to work with David and The Spiders From Mars. (▶ 10.2.72)
4. Rungk guitarist Mark Pritchett also played in Hype and David's post-Hype backing groups, including The Arnold Corns. (▶ 25.2.71)

Sunday 5 July

◗ David Bowie, Implosion, the Roundhouse, London, NW1.

David heads the bill with Ronson, Visconti and Woodmansey, supported by Country Joe McDonald, Idle Race,[1] Roger Ruskin Spear & His Giant Kinetic Wardrobe, Quiver, James Litherland's Brotherhood, Medicine Head and Jeff Dexter as DJ/compère. Each of the groups receives a performance fee of £20.

Among the audience members are 16-year-old future Adam Ant Stuart Goddard and young journalist Charles Shaar Murray, who notes the excessive volume, Ronson's 'black-dyed hair' and David's impressive performance of 'Space Oddity'.

Photographer Byron Newman's shots from this evening will be included in a feature in British rock monthly *Cream*. "I met David through a mutual friend, Calvin Lee, who was a real believer in the early days and worked tirelessly to put Bowie on the map," said Newman in 2007.

1. Jeff Lynne had been a member of Idle Race until January 1970, when he left to form The Electric Light Orchestra with Roy Wood.

Wednesday 8 July

Pierrot In Turquoise Or The Looking Glass Murders is broadcast late in the evening on Scottish TV's series *Gateway*.

Saturday 18 July

◗ David Bowie, Fickle Pickle Club, The Cricketers Inn, 228 London Road, Southend-on-Sea, Essex.

Again supported by his trio of backing musicians, David shares this bill with an act called Aquila. At the venue, David is invited to perform at a charity gig in the town the following month.

Meanwhile in the Netherlands, his TV appearance performing 'Memory Of A Free Festival' alone at a keyboard is broadcast on *Ready, Eddy Go!*

Saturday 1 August

▶ David Bowie, Rock With Shelter, Eastwoodbury Lane, Southend-on-Sea, Essex.

David, with Mick Ronson on bass, performs at this open-air event as one of the support acts on a bill raising funds for housing charity Shelter. Headliners are The Edgar Broughton Band, for whom David performs a mime, just as he has done at some of their other live appearances. Also performing are May Blitz,[1] Formerly Fat Harry, Roger Ruskin Spear & His Giant Kinetic Wardrobe, Surly Bird and the Mike Chapman Band – Ronson knows Chapman of old and contributed to his debut album.

"I was quite surprised at David because he treated it like a theatrical event and did some mime, that kind of thing," said Michael Chapman in 1991. "Mick was good at playing bass of course, but he was such a great guitarist. It all seemed a bit strange for an audience that had come out for live music and the sunshine."

1. May Blitz drummer Tony Newman played on David's 1974 album *Diamond Dogs*.

Tuesday 4 August

Without David, Hype record four tracks for a proposed Phonogram album with working titles: 'Only One Paper Left', 'It's 12 O'Clock', 'Invisible Long Hair' and 'Will You Sleep Beside Me' (aka 'Sleep Beside You').

With Tony Visconti producing, the songs are recorded on to eight track, but not mixed down and are left unfinished without the addition of vocals.

By this time, Visconti's disillusionment over David's input into *The Man Who Sold The World* sessions has been compounded by his dislike of Defries. Also the frustration he experienced recording the new album and its delayed release compounded Visconti's opinion. The New Yorker announces his decision to part ways with David outside Gem's offices in Regent Street.

"I said goodbye to him right then and there," said Visconti in 1977 "He looked at me very quizzically. He was in pain. 'But why?' he said.

"'I told you, I can't deal with this any more,' I replied, 'and I don't like Tony Defries.'

"It's funny, I never really did like him and Ken Pitt thought I always wanted them to be together. It was clearly David's choice and that was it. That was the last time I saw David for about four years."

Mick Ronson and Woody Woodmansey are also disgruntled with David and in particular the lack of money (they have never been offered a wage). Travelling from London to Birmingham in the West Midlands for a gig (unidentified), crammed into a taxi with their equipment while David is driven in his Rover, they take action. As they approach the M1 Birmingham turn-off, the pair direct the driver to continue onwards and take them home to Hull.

David is forced not only to complete the

engagement solo but also to start looking for other musicians.

Monday 21 September

The absence of Ronson, Visconti and Woodmansey coincides with a realisation that Defries is not providing the promised managerial direction.

Angie has already tried to take matters into her own hands; as early as June she had attempted to book the Brighton Dome for a performance by David on 3 August. This hadn't come off, so she turns her energies to David reappearing at the Purcell Room, where he had successfully showcased his act the previous year.

Calvin Mark Lee is asked by Angie to oversee arrangements. Although these come to nothing, Lee, Angie and David embark on developing concepts for David's next project, which Angie types up into a quasi-manifesto.

This proposes the next band should be called 'Imagination' (becoming 'David Bowie's Imagination' when backing him) and states: 'Angela doesn't like the guitarist', doubtless a reference to the fall-out with Ronson.

Around this time David is photographed by Keith MacMillan[1] in Haddon Hall for the cover of his new

OPPOSITE PAGE

TOP: David still found time to visit his local pub, the Three Tuns Folk and Blues Club, taking a break from recording demos at Haddon Hall. From right to left: David, Mick Ronson (obscured), Mark Pritchett, Woody Woodmansey and Angie Bowie.

THIS PAGE

ABOVE: Alternative 'dress shot' out-take from album session by Keith MacMillan.

BOTTOM: Rock With Shelter advert for an appearance on 1 August.

In this year...

September

DEPARTURE of Lou Reed from The Velvet Underground line-up. Reed moved to his parents' home in Long Island. NAME change for Marc Bolan's band from Tyrannosaurus Rex to T.Rex.

Friday 18 September

DEATH of Jimi Hendrix in London, aged 27.

November

RELEASE of the eponymous album *Kraftwerk*. The new German electronic band was formed by Ralf Hütter and Florian Schneider. Together with Can's *Future Days*, Kraftwerk's early albums proved a great influence on David's output from the mid- to late-70s.
   David titled an instrumental on his 1977 *"Heroes"* album 'V-2 Schneider' after the Kraftwerk member.
RELEASE in the UK of Mercury Record's *Dimension Of Miracles*, a double album compilation which includes David's 'The Width Of A Circle'.

BELOW: David's letter to Bob Grace with mini biography, 17 November.

November 17th, 1970
Haddon Hall

Mr. Bob Grace
Chrysalis Music Ltd
368/396 Oxford Street
London W1

Dear Bob

I was born in Brixton and went to some Schools thereabout and studied Art. Then I went into an Advertising Agency which I didn't like very much. Then I left and joined some Rock 'n' Roll Bands playing Saxophone and I sang some which nobody liked very much.

As I was already a Beatnik, I had to be a Hippie and I was very heavy and wrote a lot of songs on some beaches and some people liked them. Then I recorded 'Space Oddity' and made some money and spent it which everybody liked.

Now I am 24 and I am married and I am not at all heavy and I'm still writing and my wife is pregnant which I like very much. (Roger still lives with us).

David

LOVE DAVID

---

album, at this stage still called *Metrobolist*.

1. Keith MacMillan moved into directing music videos (including those for Paul McCartney's 'Pipes Of Peace' and Michael Jackson duet 'Ebony And Ivory') and created the format for ITV's 90s programme *The Chart Show*.

Sunday 4 October

David and Defries meet at Gem to discuss David's next single, 'Holy Holy', which is to be recorded in November. They are joined by 'Space Oddity' bassist Herbie Flowers, who has been chosen by Defries as producer partly due to his recently achieved success with his group Blue Mink,[1] as well as the promotion teams from Gem and Blue Mink.

1. Blue Mink reached the UK top ten with 'Melting Pot' in November 1969 and 'Good Morning Freedom' in March 1970. The group's biggest hit was 'The Banner Man' which reached number three in May 1971.

Tuesday 6 October

David's friend from Bromley Tech, the artist George Underwood, has also been picked up by Gem Management, which engineers a recording deal for him. Today he signs with New York-based Bell Records.

Friday 23 October

On the expiration of his deal with Essex Music, David signs a music publishing agreement with the recently founded Chrysalis Music.[1] The new company's stated aim is to work with less mainstream artists. Already they have snapped up blues band Ten Years After and folk/prog rockers Jethro Tull.

At a meeting attended by Defries, David is signed by manager Bob Grace for £5,000 (20 per cent of which goes to Gem).

Grace has been alerted to the completion of David's Essex term by Laurence Myers, who also points out that the new album is recorded and ready for release. As such, David is a ready-made proposition for a new company eager to acquire rights.

"This man with shoulder-length hair, in a long blue coat which touched the floor, looking very much like Lauren Bacall, played me a cassette [a demo] of 'Holy Holy' which I liked a lot," said Grace in 1985. "I liked him. I could tell he was very intelligent and incredibly ambitious. I wanted to sign him straight away. David treated the meeting just like an interview. I mean: he was interviewing me."

At the signing, Chrysalis partner Chris Wright reluctantly draws up cheques for Bowie and Gem and signs them.

"His hand was visibly shaking," recalled Grace. "Chris said to me, 'Are you sure about this?' But I was totally sure. I had absolutely no doubt that we should sign him."[2]

Almost as soon as the new contract is signed, David is keen to begin demoing new material.

Grace books him time in Radio Luxembourg's London studio at 38 Hertford Street in central London (this is a cheap facility since it is plagued by radio interference from a local taxi company).

But David's need for attention soon becomes a problem for Grace.

"He basically wore out his welcome, he just wouldn't leave me alone," said Grace. "It got to the point where David would always be around. He even got the keys from the porter of my flat and was waiting for me there.

"He wanted me to manage him and even acted like I was his manager. At that point, Defries and Myers really weren't terribly interested in David. I'm sure they hadn't seen the real potential. Defries wasn't around."

1. Chrysalis was founded in 1969 by Chris Wright and Terry Ellis (hence the name Chris-Ellis). Ellis appears in Pennebaker's documentary about Bob Dylan's 1965 UK tour, *Don't Look Back,* in a scene where he is lambasted by the American folk star. Ken Pitt was publicist for this tour. Earlier in 1970 Chrysalis failed to send a representative to a gig of David's. He told Benny Marshall that night: "There is no way I'm going to sign with them."

2. Chrysalis' representative in the contract negotiations was the extremely capable US entertainment business lawyer Normand Kurtz, who obtained a solid and binding contract on its behalf. As David's career took off in the early 70s, Defries repeatedly attempted to have the deal dissolved, to no avail.

Saturday 24 October

T.Rex's 'Ride A White Swan' reaches number two in the UK singles chart, an out-of-the-blue success for Bolan which causes David much private dismay since the production is courtesy of former friend and housemate Tony Visconti. "He thinks he can do anything now," David says of the producer to Marshall.[1]

Yet Bolan's new-found popularity is just what is needed to shake David out of the doldrums.

"It was like treading water all through the 60s, and when 1970 kicked in, I thought (snaps fingers) 'We're here. Right. God, this is exciting. I'm going to go for it now'," said David in 1993. "I really felt it was my time. Then Marc Bolan fucking did it first (laughs). That really pissed me off."

1. Benny Marshall's membership of Hype was confirmed by a letter from Philips dated 22 December, 1970.

Wednesday 4 November

David is fuming over Mercury's release of his new album in the US. His explicit instructions for the sleeve design have been ignored and proposed title *Metrobolist* has been replaced by *The Man Who Sold The World*. (▶10.4.71)

On the basis that the British unknown does not qualify for the more expensive gatefold format, Mercury's executives have reduced the package to a single sleeve, and significantly have removed all of the photos David supplied, including the MacMillan shots of him in the Mr Fish gown.

The sleeve debacle and the continuing delays to the album's UK release are sowing the seeds of discontent deep within David. Meanwhile, his former cohorts Mick Ronson, Woody Woodmansey and Tony Visconti have recorded two more songs as Hype at Advision: the completed 'Come On Down To My House' and backing track 'Clorissa'.[1]

With Visconti again producing, they add to the four tracks recorded at Advision on 4 August but at the end of the sessions the bulk of these are unfinished.

1. 'Clorissa' appeared as a bonus track on the CD version of Tony Visconti's 1998 album *Inventory* – originally released on vinyl in 1977.

Monday 9 November

Recording begins on new single 'Holy Holy' at Island Studios in Notting Hill's Basing Street with producer Herbie Flowers.

Flowers is involved at Defries' suggestion (a rare example of Defries making a creative contribution) and has brought along his cohorts from session group Blue Mink, Alan Parker and Barry Morgan.

"It was a weird one," said Flowers in 1992. "I didn't like the song very much and asked David to add another section which I played to him. He later dropped this and it was a much better song."

Tuesday 10 November

A copy-master of David's new album is made in London. Despite the fact that the US version has settled on the title of its most outstanding track, the tape box still lists the contents as *Metrobolist*.

However, David and his manager are already favouring an alternative. In a letter to Mercury US executive Robin McBride, Tony Defries stresses David's wish that the release should have a different title in the UK: 'The new single has almost been completed and I understand that David spoke to you yesterday and that you do not want to call the album *Holy Holy*, which is the title of the single, although it is generally thought that if the single is a success then it will generally assist the album sales to have the same title, notwithstanding that the title track is not on the album. There are other instances where this has been done with great success, and I would ask you to consider the matter again."

Friday 13 November

David, Flowers and their fellow musicians are back at Island's Basing Street studios for further work on the new single.

Monday 16 November

The recording of 'Holy Holy' concludes at Island. David creates a minor dispute with Mercury by promising each musician a fee of £35. When presented with the bill, the label is only prepared to pay the standard £12 session fee. Defries has to clear the extra cash with a reluctant McBride, who then caps future 'special musician' fees at double scale.

The following day David sends a mini biography to Bob Grace at Chrysalis.[1]

1. This letter was reproduced in a promotional folder for the 1971 release of *The Man Who Sold The World*.

Tuesday 1 December

In the US, Mercury releases 'All The Madmen' as a double-sided promo single[1] to promote *The Man Who Sold The World*. A limited number of copies are pressed with 'Janine' on the B-side, but are withdrawn prior to release.

1. A number of stock copies were also produced, featuring the regular red Mercury label, but were not officially distributed.

Friday 4 December

David takes part in a 'Holy Holy' promotion meeting at Nikki and Jo's Productions' offices[1] in Knightsbridge, SW1 with Herbie Flowers, Defries and Gem plugger Anya Wilson.

1. Friends of Flowers, they had previously promoted Blue Mink.

Tuesday 8 December

Ken Pitt pays a visit to Defries at Gem's offices since no financial settlement has been reached over David's breaking of the management contract. 'I sat in the reception area idly looking through magazines until suddenly a soft voice said, "Hullo Ken,"' wrote Pitt in 1983. 'I looked up and at first did not recognise the person addressing me. The only other time I had seen Defries he had looked very different, but now he had metamorphosed into the last of the 60s swingers, complete with roll-top sweater, neck chains, hanging medallions and Afro hairstyle.'

NIKKI AND JO PRODUCTIONS LTD

8 Albert Gate Court,
124 Knightsbridge,
London, S.W.1

Tel: 589-6293/4

TO: Tony Defries

'The first haunted song' ....
'HOLY HOLY' by DAVID BOWIE
(release date: 15/1/71)

David Bowie's latest release, a follow up to 'Space Oddity', the smash hit of October, 1969, is a sure winner. Entitled 'HOLY HOLY', this great disc was written and compiled by David Bowie, together with Herbie Flowers of BLUE MINK.

It is a haunting melody - wicked, sad, mysterious and fascinating. Its unusual production gives it the same quality as 'Space Oddity'.

HOLY HOLY is one of Blue Minks first big productions outside their own material. Bowie and Flowers intend to continue working and writing together because with their combined talent they make an amazing team.

HOLY HOLY is on the Mercury label and the publishers are Titanic Music Ltd. and Chrysalis Music Ltd. It was produced by Blue Mink.

JO KEMP..

JO KEMP

ABOVE: Nikki & Jo Productions letter to Tony Defries.

In this year...

December
PERFORMANCE by composer Philip Glass and his ensemble at the Royal College of Art. In the audience were David and Brian Eno.

In 1993 Glass released his orchestral interpretation of three tracks from David's album *Low*.

Eno later said of the RCA performance: "This was one of the most extraordinary musical experiences of my life – sound made completely physical and as dense as concrete by sheer volume and repetition. Though he was at that time described as a minimalist, this was actually one of the most detailed musics I'd ever heard."

DAVID is giving regular airings to his Mr Fish gowns as the single 'Holy Holy' is released and he embarks on a month-long US tour to promote *The Man Who Sold The World*.

He returns to London fired by his first American experiences – his first live viewing of The Velvet Underground among them – and with a fistful of new songs.

Recording of new material gets under way as *The Man Who Sold The World* finally makes its UK bow and David's 'Oh! You Pretty Things' is released as a single by Peter Noone, gaining the songwriter valuable exposure in the charts.

Mercury's stint as David's label comes to an end as Tony Defries finally gets to grips with his artist's potential.

Mick Ronson accedes to David's request that he rejoin him, and the pair form a tight unit with Mick Woodmansey and newcomer bass player Trevor Bolder.

David and Angie's son, Duncan Zowie, is born and inspires the song 'Kooks'.

Recording for the next album gathers pace and David makes a dawn appearance at the Glastonbury Fayre.

Press coverage is being ramped up and David is also being promoted, with ex-girlfriend Dana Gillespie, via a privately pressed album.

Ronson's studio influence is growing as recording progresses, and David signs a three-album deal with RCA.

He and Ronson absorb further American influences on a New York trip notable for David's first meeting with Andy Warhol – a meeting that proves inspirational to him.

Recording for the follow-up album is already taking place as *Hunky Dory* is released in the UK and US. Produced by Ken Scott, it pulls together American and British influences in a truly original mix that startles critics and listeners alike.

PREVIOUS SPREAD: At the Gem office in Regent Street, London, summer.

THIS PAGE

TOP LEFT: Blue Mink, 1970. Three members of the band appeared on 'Holy Holy'. Left to right: Barry Morgan, Roger Cook, Herbie Flowers, Madeline Bell (who sang on 'I Dig Everything' in 1966), and Alan Parker.

TOP RIGHT: Front cover of German single issue of 'Holy Holy', January.

ABOVE LEFT: 'Holy Holy' producer Herbie Flowers.

ABOVE RIGHT: *Melody Maker* ad for 'Philips group' singles, January.

OPPOSITE PAGE

TOP RIGHT: David's first visit to America; with Ron Oberman on his arrival at Dulles International in Washington, 23 January.

TOP LEFT: Photographed by Jeff Mayer at the Holiday Inn during his first visit to New York. David later said about the city: "It was the first time I realised how important environment was for writing."

MIDDLE: David with Ron Oberman (centre) and his brother, at the Oberman family home in Silver Spring, Maryland, 23 January.

BOTTOM: In New York. Pictured below with Mercury Records' Paul Nelson.

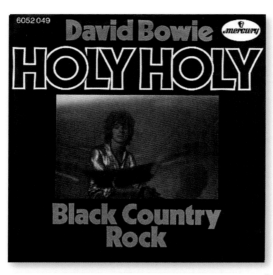

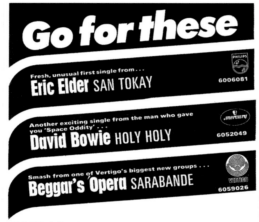

Monday 4 January

Gem's Laurence Myers writes to showbiz manager Gordon Mills at his company MAM: 'I am enclosing herewith a David Bowie composition "How Lucky You Are" for your consideration for Tom Jones.'

Wednesday 6 January

David's presence is required in the US for promotion of *The Man Who Sold The World*, though work permit restrictions (as stipulated by the American Federation of Musicians) rule out live appearances.

Tony Defries receives instructions from Mercury's US publicist Ron Oberman: 'Arrive no later than Sunday morning 24 January. This will allow him to get some rest prior to departing on a gruelling schedule. Because this tour will entail "rapping" only to press and radio people, a normal visitor's visa for David is all that is required.'

David tells underground paper *Friends*: "I'm taking my box and if I get the chance I'll play whether I'm asked to or not."

Saturday 9 January

A week ahead of its release, new single 'Holy Holy'

receives mixed previews in the music press. Chris Welch writes in *Melody Maker*: 'Dave sounds a bit like Syd Barrett here on this strangely attractive sound', while *NME*'s Derek Johnson describes it as 'a strange little piece… oddly fascinating' and *Music Now*'s review by Karen de Groot draws comparisons with Marc Bolan – 'Bowie – A Funky T.Rex'.

Friday 15 January

Mercury release 'Holy Holy'/'Black Country Rock' single in the UK.

⊙ **David Bowie**
A **'Holy Holy'** (Bowie)
B **'Black Country Rock'** (Bowie)
David Bowie (vocal, guitar)
Alan Parker (guitar on A-side)
Herbie Flowers (bass on A-side)
Barry Morgan (drums on A-side)
Mick Ronson (guitar, keyboard, vocal on B-side)
Tony Visconti (bass, piano on B-side)
Mick Woodmansey (drums on B-side)
**A-side Produced by Herbie Flowers
(A Blue Mink Production)
B-side Produced by Tony Visconti**
(Mercury 6052 049)

The single is accompanied by a press release from publicists Nikki & Jo Productions which describes the A-side as 'wicked, sad, mysterious and fascinating'.

Monday 18 January

In one of his Mr Fish gowns and accompanying himself on acoustic guitar, David promotes 'Holy Holy' with a return appearance on Granada TV's magazine programme *Six-O-One: Newsday*.

David is driven in his Rover to the TV studios in Manchester by roadie Roger Fry in the company of publicist/journalist Dai Davies.

When asked by the programme producer to explain the significance of his outfit, David shrugs: "It's just a nice dress."

During recording, a chance meeting helps spark an interesting chain of events. David is introduced to producer/writer Roger Damon Price, later to create children's sci-fi series *The Tomorrow People*, which will feature a master-race known as Homo Superior.

In 2006 Price acknowledged that he discussed his ideas for the programme with David on the set of the show, and 24 hours later David incorporated some of them in the new song called 'Oh! You Pretty Things' he demos at Radio Luxembourg's central London studio.

David has southern singer Leon Russell in mind to cover it, and gives a tape of the track – which features the line 'Got to make way for the Homo Superior' – to publisher Bob Grace.[1] The following day Grace plays this to producer Mickie Most during a meeting at annual music biz gathering Midem in the south of France.

In turn, Most plays it to former Herman's Hermits singer Peter Noone,[2] who is on the lookout for a single to launch his solo career.

1. The song also includes a reference to Edward Bulwer-Lytton's 1871 cult science fiction novel *The Coming Race*. The book is considered one of the first of its genre and can still be found in print today.
2. Peter Blair Denis Bernard Noone, born on 5 November 1947. English singer, songwriter and actor, best known for fronting popular 60s band Herman's Hermits.

Tuesday 19 January

Ken Pitt receives a letter from Tony Defries informing him that David's management company has moved a short distance to Roxburghe House, 273/287 Regent Street, London W1.

Saturday 23 January

In his Universal Witness blue fur coat, David leaves alone for his first visit to the US on a month-long trip to promote *The Man Who Sold The World*. Tony Defries has opted not to accompany him on the trip, which is financed by Mercury Records.

David is met at Washington's Dulles International Airport by Mercury's Ron Oberman, who has brought his parents with him. There is a delay when David is detained at customs for 45 minutes for questioning, caused, apparently, by his unusual outfit.

Spending his first night in America at the Obermans' family home in Silver Spring, Maryland, David is taken to dinner at the town's Hofberg's Deli. "When we walked in you wouldn't believe all the stares he got," said Ron Oberman in 2009.

Monday 25 January

Sending David's busy schedule to Bob Grace, Defries informs him he is not on the trip but that Oberman is overseeing the itinerary.

While in Washington, David gives interviews to a local underground newspaper and a radio station before travelling to Philadelphia with Oberman on the evening train from Pennsylvania Station, Baltimore.

Tuesday 26 January

David is interviewed on Philadelphia's 94 WYSP radio. The interviewer informs David that Elton John's real name is Reg Dwight, to which David replies: "Really? I didn't know that. Stone me."

Wednesday 27 January

In the late morning, David and Oberman arrive in New York for a four-day stay.

"The record company arranged for him to have a room in the most American of hostelries, the Holiday Inn," said journalist Ed Kelleher[1] in 1977. "Within hours of arriving in Manhattan, David had found his way to Nat Sherman's, the connoisseurs' tobacco shop, for some thin cigars; was browsing in Times Square record shops for discs unavailable in England (a clerk in King Karol's recognised him and David was genuinely astounded); spent an afternoon studying the paintings at the Metropolitan Museum of Art; and was scouring the East Side antique stores for objets d'art."

Tonight there is a storm-like icy wind but David

ventures out with Mercury publicity chief Paul Nelson[2] to a Greenwich Village coffee-house to catch a performance by folksinger Tim Hardin.

He fails in an attempt to make contact with Hardin backstage after the show, but is impressed with the venue.

"I'd like to play a club like this," David tells Nelson. "I know I don't have a work permit, but maybe I could do a guest set later in the week."

Soon after his arrival, Ed Kelleher plays David the recently released Velvet Underground album *Loaded*.

David is determined to catch the band live, since they are playing a residency at the Electric Circus in Manhattan. But this is the reconstituted line-up, with main-man Lou Reed replaced by Doug Yule, and viola player John Cale long gone.

David doesn't realise it is the new line-up. "Afterwards I waited at the back-stage door, and I was banging on it, and Lou comes and I went on and on about how great I thought it was and at the end of the conversation he says: 'Look, actually buddy, my name's Doug Yule!'[3] I thought: 'Oh no!' I was so embarrassed because I thought I'd been talking to Lou Reed for about 15 minutes."

David also reconnects with his cousin Kristina Paulsen for the first time since 1957, when they were rock'n'roll-mad kids together, taken by David's father to see Tommy Steele perform live and swapping Elvis Presley 78s. Paulsen lives close to Central Park.

Another New York resident makes for an intriguing encounter: the street performer Moondog.[4]

'The earliest graphic image I have (of New York) is of Louis Hardin, better known as Moondog, the legendary boho and musical outsider,' wrote David in 2003.

In this year...

Saturday 9 January
RECRUITMENT of Brian Eno as member of Roxy Music.
(▸ 25.6.72)

'One of the guys who worked at Mercury Records, with whom I was under contract at the time, took me over to 54th Street, and there, dressed as a sort of Viking, Moondog stood. Usually he would be playing his strange compositions accompanied on a keyboard or some kind of homemade drums, but not this day.

'I went for sandwiches and coffee, which we consumed as we sat on the sidewalk. He told me something about his life, and it came home to me only after a while that he was completely blind.'

1. Ed Kelleher (1944–2005) became a screenwriter, playwright and film critic, writing cult horror movies such as *Invasion of the Blood Farmers* (1972), *Shriek of the Mutilated* (1974) and *Prime Evil* (1988).

2. Paul Nelson (1937–2006) was hired by Ron Oberman in 1970 to head Mercury Records' US publicity. An influential rock journalist since the early 60s, Nelson was educated at the University of Minnesota, where he met and became friendly with Bob Dylan. Nelson was interviewed in Martin Scorsese's celebrated 2005 Dylan documentary *No Direction Home*.

3. John Cale exited The Velvet Underground in 1968. David believed he briefly met Cale after the show too. Yule replaced Cale and appeared on studio recordings *The Velvet Underground* (1969) and *Loaded* (1970) as well as *Live 1969* and *Live At Max's Kansas City*.

4. Louis Thomas Hardin (1916–1999), American musician and composer who lived on the streets of New York for approximately 20 years, where he performed his compositions. His appearance was an interpretation of the Norse god Thor, for which he earned the moniker The Viking of 6th Avenue.

TOP: David relaxing in Detroit, photographed by Charlie Auringer for *Creem*, 2 February.

ABOVE: Music journalist Penny Valentine (1943–2003). A great admirer and loyal supporter of David's work in the early years.

Thursday 28 January

Without notice, David's half-brother Terry Burns moves into Haddon Hall. David mentions this during an interview with Patrick Salvo for *Circus*.

"I just phoned up my wife and it seems he's [Terry] staying with us now," says David. "She wouldn't tell me on the phone because he was in the room. I'm not sure whether he's kinda run away or what. The majority of the people in my family have been in some kind of mental institution. As for my brother, he doesn't want to leave. He likes it very much.

"He's just been changed to a new one [psychiatric hospital], which he doesn't like. but the old one, Cane Hill, he really liked. He'd be happy to spend the rest of his life there, mainly because most of the people are on the same wavelength as him. And he's not a freak, he's a very straight person."

Monday 1 February

David and Oberman take an evening flight to Detroit's Metropolitan Wayne County Airport.

At a Holiday Inn hotel on Grand Boulevard, the following day, David is interviewed by Dave Marsh for the Detroit-based rock magazine *Creem,* and Charlie Auringer takes photographs.

"I was impressed by the virtually unknown artist at the time. Bowie was amazingly articulate and expressive," said Auringer in 2008. The following morning they fly to Minneapolis St Paul for more interviews.

Thursday 4 February

David flies to Chicago for a two-day stay. Oberman takes him to the Quiet Night club for a performance by an act he is representing, Wilderness Road. The following day David meets Mercury's head of A&R Robin McBride at the company's 35 East Wacker Drive HQ.

Saturday 6 February

David returns to Detroit. In the UK a Penny Valentine feature, 'Bowie, music and life', is published by new music weekly *Sounds*.

Monday 8 February

In the morning David is taken by car with Oberman to Milwaukee for more promotional duties. In the evening, he flies from General Mitchell International Airport to Atlanta, Texas.

Wednesday 10 February

After a flight to Houston, David spends the morning visiting radio stations but his attire prompts a violent reaction. An individual pulls a gun on him and calls him a 'fag'.

In the afternoon, he heads for a three-day stay in the more accommodating city of San Francisco, where he is met and accompanied by Mercury's West Coast publicist Lewis Siegel, who has organised for

Rolling Stone journalist John Mendelssohn to cover David's trip and review *The Man Who Sold The World.*

David is in buoyant mood, telling a KSAN-FM DJ: "My last LP was, very simply, a collection of reminiscences about my experience as a shaven-headed transvestite."

He is also guest DJ at a San José radio station and is encouraged by Mendelssohn to play records by The Stooges and, interest piqued by the band's singer Iggy Pop, he acquires one of their albums, *Fun House.*

Saturday 13 February

With David on the morning flight to Los Angeles is Mendelssohn, who notices David is becoming agitated by the frequent air travel.

Meeting them at LAX International is Rodney Bingenheimer, LA DJ and scenester in his official capacity as Mercury's California publicist.[1]

Almost immediately upon arrival, David informs his hosts of a new album concept based on a character called Ziggy Stardust. This has been sparked by his acquisition of The Stooges album after the guest DJ slot with Mendelssohn. (▶1.72)

David's first night in LA is eventful. Wearing a Mr Fish gown, he is refused entry to a restaurant on the grounds that he is a transvestite. He stays with the well-connected RCA Records staff producer Tom Ayres, who manages the Sir Douglas Quintet.

Ayres' house in 8233 Roxbury Road, off West Sunset Boulevard, was once owned by actress sisters Dorothy and Lillian Gish, and has recording facilities.

Recently returned from a UK tour with Screaming Lord Sutch, Gene Vincent is there recording demos, and David takes the opportunity to also demo material, in particular a new song, 'Hang Onto Yourself'.

Double-tracking his vocals and playing all the instruments, David includes the title from the yet-to-be-released T.Rex single 'Get It On', he even sings these words at the start of each chorus.[2]

"David gave me 'Hang Onto Yourself' for Gene to record but he died before he could cut it," said Ayres in 1996.[3]

"Gene liked David, they got on very well. David respected Gene for what he was and Gene was very impressed with him. That was quite amazing when you think that David was virtually nobody then. I think in some oblique way, 'Hang Onto Yourself' could have been written about Gene Vincent. You know, kind of get a grip on yourself, on your life..."

Ayres introduces David to The Boneshakers, a Texan bluegrass quartet dexterously using 17 acoustic instruments. The unlikely combination record more demos together.

"David was living very much in his own world," said Ayres. "He had about four albums of his own stuff that he had recently written. At my house he worked with a tape-op called Ronnie; I clearly

LEFT: David in San Francisco.
RIGHT: David outside the Holiday Inn, San Francisco, photographed by John Mendelssohn.

remember a few times when David jumped out of bed at about three in the morning, woke us up and said 'I've got an idea' and if we were sober enough we would record it straight away."

During his stay, Ayres encourages David to consider signing with RCA since he continues to fume over Mercury's intervention into his design for *The Man Who Sold The World* and is disenchanted with Mercury's delays to the release in the UK.

Ayres informs David he would become a priority since RCA's roster is slim and top-heavy: "The only thing they've got is Elvis, and Elvis can't last forever."

To this end, Ayres introduces David to RCA's West Coast publicity head Grelun Landon, who declares: "He's very bizarre, but I think he's going to be the Bob Dylan of the 70s."

1. Born 15 December 1946, Bingenheimer was the subject of 2003 documentary *Mayor Of The Sunset Strip*, which included a contribution from David. The host of the enduring *Rodney On The ROQ* late-night show on LA station K-ROQ, Bingenheimer broadcasts a 'Bowie Salute' on David's birthday every year.
2. Bolan himself recorded 'Get It On' in Los Angeles in April 1971. The tape of this demo session at Ayres' home includes an unreleased snippet of David thumping away at a piano and bellowing at the top of his voice.
3. On his return from the US, David mentioned to a reporter that Vincent was set to record one of his songs and as late as August 1971 told *Jackie* magazine: "Gene Vincent is going to record 'Hang Onto Yourself'." Claims that Vincent contributed vocals to the demo recorded at Ayres' home are incorrect. Vincent died from a ruptured stomach ulcer aged 36 in October 1971. Tom Ayres died in 2000.

Sunday 14 February

David is invited by John Mendelssohn to jam with his band Christopher Milk[1] during rehearsals at A&M studios on La Brea in Hollywood.[2]

Since there is no transport available, David

THIS PAGE

TOP: Tom Ayres, the man who helped introduce David to RCA.

MIDDLE: David and Rodney Bingenheimer reunited at an LA party in the early 90s.

BOTTOM: John Rechy's impressionable 1963 novel *City of Night*, a firm favourite of David's during this period.

OPPOSITE PAGE

TOP: David making his US performance debut at a private party at the LA home of Paul Feigen.

MIDDLE: Freddie Burretti, striking a familiar pose for a model agency photo session and *The Man Who Sold The World*, 1972 reissue.

BOTTOM: Freddie Burretti, Capri, 1971. Burretti wears one of his suits and designed a near identical version for David in 1974.

astounds his LA hosts by insisting on walking with his guitar case the two miles along Sunset Boulevard in his gold brocade coat and floppy hat.

"For the most part, he just watched our rehearsal, which must have been fairly excruciating for him, but he's a Brit and didn't grumble," said Mendelssohn in 2001. "By-and-by he joined us and we played 'Waiting For The Man' together. We later added it to our live repertoire."[3]

In LA, David feels more comfortable in his Mr Fish gowns, and wears a different one to each Valentine's Day party.

▶ The first has been arranged for him at the home of attorney Paul Feigen. Here David gives his first US performance, sitting cross-legged on a waterbed playing his acoustic guitar and singing 'All The Madmen', 'Space Oddity', 'Amsterdam' and the just-written 'Hang Onto Yourself'. However, there are just a few people paying attention, so he gives up and socialises.[4]

David is then taken to another gathering, hosted by Hollywood socialite Dianne Bennett, where Warhol 'superstar' Ultra Violet[5] is the guest of honour. Also recording demos at Ayres' home studio, she poses for photographs with David and Bingenheimer. While hanging out in LA, David also comes into contact with struggling actor Don Johnson[6] and, via Rodney Bingenheimer, United Artists A&R man Eli Bird. Bingenheimer ferries David to a number of radio stations in a convertible Cadillac lent by Ayres.

"He enjoyed every minute," said Bingenheimer in 1992.

They visit KMAC in Long Beach, and CIMS and KYMS both based in Santa Ana, where David is accompanied by a girl called Kaji he met the previous evening at the Topanga Canyon Corral club.

David spends most of the interview passing compliments to Kaji, who is sitting next to him in the studio.

While in town, David takes in a performance by pianist/composer Biff Rose (whose 'Fill Your Heart'[7] and 'Buzz The Fuzz' he has performed live).

Rose is very late on stage and impresses David by devoting much of his set to a long and amusing story about his journey to the venue.

1. Christopher Milk's debut album *Some People Will Drink Anything* was released by Warners in 1972.

2. A&M was based on the site of the Charlie Chaplin Studios lot at 1416 North La Brea. In 2010 was home to Jim Henson's company.

3. Mendelssohn related how his fellow rock critic Lester Bangs sent him a postcard in 1972 having seen David perform the song with the Spiders From Mars. "He said he thought our version of WFTM was far superior to theirs," said Mendelssohn in 2001. "Ours was very much less an homage to the Velvets."

4. Bingenheimer broadcast a tape of part of this rendition of 'All The Madmen' on his radio show in the early 90s.

5. Born Isabelle Collin Dufresne in France in 1935, Ultra Violet had brightly dyed, lilac-coloured hair – thus her pseudonym, which Warhol suggested.

6. Johnson made his name in the 80s as one of the stars of TV series *Miami Vice*.

7. 'Fill Your Heart' was co-written by Rose and US songwriter Paul

Williams. Oddball singer Tiny Tim's cover version appeared on the B-side of his 1968 hit 'Tiptoe Through The Tulips'.

Thursday 18 February

Taking a direct flight overnight from LA to London, David's imagination has been fired by the experiences of the American excursion.

Armed with a number of new songs, he is also weighed down with a suitcase full of records (including new albums by Kim Fowley – whom David had met in LA – and Leo Kottke). He is already well over his baggage allowance, and Mercury forwards a further batch of records he has left behind.

During his absence, on 15 February, UK coinage has been decimalised. On his return he discovers it is now 'two new pence to have a go'.[1]

Of more import, 'Holy Holy' has failed to sell in the five weeks since release, though David quickly disregarded the single and wasn't in the country to promote it anyway.

Back in the US, John Mendelssohn reviews *The Man Who Sold The World* in *Rolling Stone*: 'Bowie's music offers an experience that is as intriguing as it is chilling, but only to the listener sufficiently together to withstand its schizophrenia.'

1. A line from the soon-to-be recorded *Hunky Dory* track 'Andy Warhol'.

Monday 22 February

Friends also reflects on the duality of David's music, describing it as 'a combination of Bowie's da-da-esque lyrics and fantasy machinations and the heavy sound of the band he formed last year to back him on gigs, called Harry the Butcher'.

Noting that Hype are no more, following such debacles as the out-of-control volume at a Roundhouse gig, David tells *Friends*: '"It was frightening. We all knew we were too loud but there wasn't one of us capable of taking four steps back and turning the bloody volume down."' The piece continued: 'After what might be described as a disastrous set, Bowie went home to Beckenham, thought about things and went back the following week, alone.'

Thursday 25 February

Eager to ride the impetus of his US trip, David is back at Radio Luxembourg's studios in Hertford Street, central London, to record new songs, 'Moonage Daydream' and 'Hang Onto Yourself' for a new project he has been cooking up, The Arnold Corns.

As a means of testing new material without Mercury's knowledge, the session has been arranged by publisher Bob Grace.[1]

David produces and provides lead vocals and rhythm guitar, backed by the musicians who make up another band, Rungk: guitarist and occasional member of Hype, Mark Pritchett;[2] bass player Pete De Somogyl;[3] and drummer Tim Broadbent.

Partly to try to protect David's anonymity, The

Arnold Corns is fronted by young designer Fred Burrett,[4] whom David is grooming for stardom, having met him at Kensington gay bar The Sombrero[5] with his friends Daniella Parmar, Micky King, Wendy Kirby and hairdresser Antonello Parqualli.

Encouraged by John Rechy's novel *City Of Night* and the bizarre gay-themed film *The Queen*, David and Angie are aware that their association with Burrett and his friends will enhance the ambivalent appeal David is already fostering with his Greta Garbo hairstyle and Mr Fish gowns.

David has written 'Moonage Daydream' specifically for Burrett, now christened Freddie Burretti (and occasionally to be known as Rudy Valentino). However, Burretti does not sing a note on these sessions.[6]

The members of Rungk – formed in 1967 while they were schoolmates at south London public school Dulwich College – are also granted new monikers: Pritchett becomes 'Mark Carr-Pritchard', Broadbent is now 'Timothy James Ralph St Laurent Broadbent' and Somogyl is 'Polak De Somogyl'.

Burretti's Continental flair – he is fluent in three languages – and design talents will stand David in good stead, particularly when he works in conjunction with his exotic friend Daniella Parmar, who is of Indian extraction and has an accent identical to that of *Performance* actress Michèle Breton.

1. The 25 February 1971 acetate packaging stated this was 'A Butterfly Record Productions Session'. Butterfly was a Chrysalis label overseen by Bob Grace.

2. A Beckenham Arts Lab regular, Pritchett's mother was a neighbour of David and Angie's and often babysat for them. Like Broadbent, Pritchett gave up music in favour of advertising.

3. Swedish De Somogyl – who died in a light-aircraft accident – took the band's name from native slang for 'wank'.

4. Frederick Robert Burrett (born 1951, died 11 May 2001), raised in Hackney, east London. At the age of 14 he moved with his family to Bletchley, Buckinghamshire, returned to London four years later, initially living with his grandmother before finding his own apartment in Holland Park, west London. Burrett studied fashion and in 1971 was employed by Andreas, a west London tailor.

5. Basement nightclub Yours And Mine, named after Mexican restaurant El Sombrero on the ground floor. The club boasted a small, underlit, translucent tiled dance-floor, similar to the one featured in *Saturday Night Fever*. David frequented The Sombrero from the late 60s when it was an Espresso bar. In 1998 Ken Pitt recalled a visit there in 1968: "While at our table we noticed the singer David Garrick (who fronted heavy rock band Uriah Heep in the 70s as David Byron) walking down the stairs. This was particularly memorable because David was very fond of Garrick's work at the time and rated him highly."

6. At one point an Arnold Corns album was discussed with the proposed title *Looking For Rudi*. It is near impossible to be exact about the circumstances and musicians who worked with David in this period, and not just on The Arnold Corns. Recordings were sometimes discreetly carried out so that Mercury did not become aware of new material. David also experimented with different combinations of musicians, though quickly began to miss ex-members of Hype, and in particular Mick Ronson.

Saturday 27 February

Having just recorded with David as The Arnold Corns Rungk are at Beckenham Public Hall, supporting Ugly Room (who supported David and Hype in Croydon in March 1970).

Tuesday 9 – Wednesday 10 March

David records demos of new songs 'Lady Stardust'[1] and 'Right On Mother' at Radio Luxembourg's studio.

Work on demoing the two songs is completed the following day. 'Right On Mother' is David's account of Mrs Jones' acceptance of his relationship with and marriage to Angie. For percussion, David rattles the bangles which formed part of his marriage ceremony, just as he did on his demo for 'Oh! You Pretty Things' earlier in the year.

1. This version was included on Rykodisc/EMI's 1990 reissue of *Ziggy Stardust*.

Tuesday 16 March

In a letter to Ken Pitt regarding the payment of outstanding funds for his final settlement, Tony

THIS PAGE

TOP LEFT: David and Freddie Burretti.

BOTTOM: Burretti with snake.

TOP RIGHT: Bob Grace, Freddie Burretti and David in May.

OPPOSITE PAGE

TOP: Rungk (who became David's Arnold Corns), Beckenham Public Hall, February. From left: Mark Pritchett, Tim Broadbent and Pete De Somogyl.

MIDDLE: Daniella Parmar. Daniella's 'synthetic hair colouring' later partly inspired David to die his hair shocking red.

BOTTOM: Ron Oberman's letter to David.

Defries explains he has not received 'substantial' income from David's career to make this possible.

Saturday 20 March

Marc Bolan celebrates his first Number One single with T.Rex's 'Hot Love'.

A feature in *Disc & Music Echo* highlights the changes in David's life and career since winning the publication's Brightest Hope award more than a year previously: "'It's funny how I seem to have taken off as a songwriter. But this is what living down here has done for me. I'm wrapped up in my friends and include them in my songs. One of my songs, 'Rupert The Riley', is about the car.'"

Friday 26 March

David plays piano on the recording of Peter Noone's version of 'Oh! You Pretty Things' at Kingsway Studios, 129 Kingsway, Holborn, London.

Mickie Most is producing. On bass is 'Holy Holy' producer Herbie Flowers, with another seasoned session-player, Clem Cattini, who has worked with David before, on drums.

This is the first time Noone has met David, though he admitted in 1983: "I was probably his biggest fan then. David had some trouble playing it through completely, so we recorded it in three sections, something Mickie Most helped arrange."

Also recorded is David's song 'Right On Mother'

but a different song is selected for Noone's B-side.

During this period, on a journey into central London from Haddon Hall, David is involved in an accident when his 1932 Riley Gamecock car stalls in Lewisham High Street.

Accidentally he leaves the car in gear while cranking the engine, and it lurches forward, sinking the starting handle into his upper thigh and narrowly missing an artery.[1]

Fortunately he is outside Lewisham hospital, and onlookers help ferry him immediately to the emergency bay. David remains in hospital for a few days, where his presence causes some excitement and he is interviewed by DJ Chris Warbis for Lewisham Hospital Radio.

"[The Riley] stalled outside Lewisham police station one day," said David in 2003. "I had really long hair in those days, so I was standing round the front of the car, trying to pump it back into life again and all the cops were at the windows laughing at me and the bloody thing started up. I'd left it in first gear and it came at me [laughs]. The crankshaft went through my leg and I was pumping blood like a fountain and I cracked both my knees as the bumper had got me pinned to another car just behind it."

On his return home from hospital, David parts with the Riley.

1. David would have another serious car incident the following year. (▸ 17.7.72)

Thursday 1 April

Among a clutch of new songs registered at Chrysalis[1] is 'Ziggy Stardust'.

In the US, *Rolling Stone* headlines a story by John Mendelssohn 'David Bowie? Pantom me Rock'. This portrays a star on the rise ready with an outrageous quote: "Tell your readers that they can make up their minds about me when I begin getting adverse publicity; when I'm found in bed with Raquel Welch's husband."

1. As of 2010, Chrysalis retains an interest in 75 of David's songs, all of which have been released. Any unreleased titles were returned to David's company as part of a later arrangement.

Friday 9 April

Just a few months into their working relationship, publicist Ron Oberman tells David by letter he is leaving the label to manage Wilderness Road (the band he took David to see in Chicago in February): 'I can't tell you how much I enjoyed working with you... I know that you are going to make it very big in the States in just a matter of time, and I am sorry I won't be with the company when it happens.'

Saturday 10 April

Review copies of *The Man Who Sold The World* have finally been sent to the UK press ahead of its British release this month. *Disc & Music Echo* is positive: 'There is a fleeting glimpse of Velvet Underground influence in some of the songs which is all to the good. Quality: good value for money: definitely worth it.'

The Man Who Sold The World press kits have been produced by rock design specialists CCS Advertising. Gem Management orders 500, with each kit containing a folder, photos, biog sheet, lyric sheet and facsimiles of two newspaper cuttings.

Saturday 17 April

Melody Maker's Chris Welch is taken aback at David's style, and asks – in an article headed 'Why does David Bowie like dressing up in ladies' clothes? – Just what happened after Bowie's hit, and why did he sink into renewed obscurity?'

David replies: '"It's very weird. My father died and a week later I had a hit record. The juxtaposition was like a pantomime, a comic tragedy. Since that time I've had a complete change of management and have started writing again."'

Friday 23 April

David is interviewed at Chrysalis's offices by George Tremlett and then heads for Trident Studios to produce a session for his new friend from The Sombrero, male escort Micky King.

King confidently takes the lead vocal on David's new song 'Rupert The Riley', an affectionate tribute to David's old banger written before the painful incident in Lewisham High Street.[1]

David also sings backing vocals and plays sax, with Herbie Flowers on bass, fellow Blue Mink member Barry Morgan on drums and Mark Pritchett on guitar. The session is credited, tongue-in-cheek, to Micky King's All Stars[2] and, now as a producer, David works for the first time with engineer Ken Scott.

As well as 'Rupert The Riley' another track, 'The Man',[3] is recorded with David on lead vocals. Both are mixed to stereo.

Bob Grace is at the studio and listens as David outlines plans for King's first single. "It was a serious attempt to get something going for him," said David of King in 1994. "He had a real attitude and I thought he had what it took to get somewhere."[4]

With the same musicians, King also records David's song 'How Lucky You Are' (initially titled 'Miss Peculiar').[5]

1. David had acquired two classic 1932 Rileys, the first black and the second red, from which he used parts to create a running model with the assistance of neighbour/roadie Roger Fry. On a visit, Mark Pritchett witnessed Fry removing the exhaust pipe from the black car to intensify the sound of the engine. David asked Pritchett to fetch his Revox tape recorder and it was outside Haddon Hall that the start of 'Rupert The Riley' was recorded, as Roger Fry drove off down Southend Road. Widely bootlegged, it has never been released.

2. A tape-box from this session notes the performer as 'Nicky King'. This contains a quarter-inch two-track tape with two versions of 'Rupert The Riley', one rough mix and one final stereo version.

3. 'The Man' (not to be confused with another track of David's from 1971, 'Shadow Man') was later retitled 'Lightning Frightening'. The track was not released at the time, but a mono version was included on the 1990 *The Man Who Sold The World* reissue.

4. In 1983 David gave Bob Grace a horrific account of King's murder at the hands of a client.

5. The end section to 'How Lucky You Are' resembles 'Revolutionary Song', David's contribution to *Just A Gigolo*, the soundtrack to the 1979 movie in which he co-starred with Marlene Dietrich.

MERCURY RECORD PRODUCTIONS, INC.

35 East Wacker Drive, Chicago, Illinois 60601 • DEarborn 2-5788 • Cable Address: "Merrec"

April 9, 1971

Mr. David Bowie
c/o Kenneth Pitt Ltd.
35 Curzon St.
Mayfair
London W.1, England

Dear David:

I am enclosing some more press clippings that have come in since your tour. As you can see, the press has been quite excellent.

Thought you would like to know that this is my last week at Mercury. I have resigned to become manager of WILDERNESS ROAD, the group you saw at the Quiet Night in Chicago. I am really looking forward to working with them as I will be able to devote all my time to one area. The group has the talent and I am quite certain (although nothing is certain in this business) that Wilderness Road will become quite successful.

Mike Gormley, a very fine person from Detroit, is taking over my position. If there is ever anything you need, please let Mike know.

I can't tell you how much I have enjoyed working with you while I have been with the company. I know that you're going to be making it very big in the States in just a matter of time, and I am sorry I won't be with the company when that happens. However, I am sure we will be seeing each other in the coming months.

Paul Nelson is remaining in New York, and I am sure he will be able to help you out with anything you need. David, I will be working out of my apartment at 329 W. Armitage, Chicago 60614; phone 312/929-0828.

Also, the books and records you left with me are on the way to you. I have sent them c/o Nick Massey at Philips in London, with instructions to call you when they arrive.

Sincerely,

Ron Oberman
Publicity Director

A NORTH AMERICAN PHILIPS COMPANY

Mercury RECORDS

ABOVE: The infamous 'dress cover', the first of many Bowie LP sleeves to court controversy. The romantic Rossetti imagery gave little clue to the uncompromising heavy rock and dark, troubled lyrics contained within

THE MAN WHO SOLD THE WORLD Released Saturday 10 April

Side One

1. THE WIDTH OF A CIRCLE (Bowie) (8.05)
David Bowie (vocal, guitar)
Mick Ronson (guitar, vocal)
Woody Woodmansey (drums)
Tony Visconti (electric bass)

2. ALL THE MADMEN (Bowie) (5.38)
David Bowie (vocal, guitar, all extra voices)
Mick Ronson (guitar, Moog synthesiser, recorder, vocal)
Woody Woodmansey (drums)
Tony Visconti (electric bass, recorder)

3. BLACK COUNTRY ROCK (Bowie) (3.32)
David Bowie (vocal, guitar)
Mick Ronson (guitar, vocal)
Woody Woodmansey (drums)
Tony Visconti (electric bass, piano)

4. AFTER ALL (Bowie) (3.51)
David Bowie (vocal, guitar, Stylophone)
Mick Ronson (guitar, vocal)
Woody Woodmansey (drums)
Tony Visconti (electric bass, recorder)
Ralph Mace (Moog synthesiser)

Side Two

1. RUNNING GUN BLUES (Bowie) (3.11)
David Bowie (vocal, guitar, harmonica)
Mick Ronson (guitar, vocal)
Woody Woodmansey (drums)
Tony Visconti (electric bass)
Ralph Mace (Moog synthesiser)
Unknown female vocalist

2. SAVIOUR MACHINE (Bowie) (4.25)
David Bowie (vocal, guitar, harmonica)
Mick Ronson (guitar, vocal)
Woody Woodmansey (drums)
Tony Visconti (electric bass)
Ralph Mace (Moog synthesiser)

3. SHE SHOOK ME COLD (Bowie) (4.13)
David Bowie (vocal, guitar)
Mick Ronson (guitar, vocal)
Woody Woodmansey (drums)
Tony Visconti (electric bass, piano)

4. THE MAN WHO SOLD THE WORLD
(Bowie) (3.55)
David Bowie (vocal, guitar)
Mick Ronson (guitar, vocal)
Woody Woodmansey (drums, percussion)

Tony Visconti (electric bass)
Ralph Mace (Moog synthesiser)

5. THE SUPERMEN (Bowie) (3.38)
David Bowie (vocal, guitar)
Mick Ronson (guitar, vocal)
Woody Woodmansey (drums)
Tony Visconti (electric bass)

Produced by Tony Visconti
Recorded at Trident and Advision Studios
Engineered by Ken Scott and Gerald Chevin
Album photographed and designed by Keef
(Mercury 6338041)

BELOW LEFT TO RIGHT: Ralph Mace, the man who played the Moog on *The Man Who Sold The World*, Robert A. Heinlein's 1953 sci-fi novel *The Man Who Sold the Moon*, which inspired David's title, Greta Garbo, inspiration for cover imagery on this album and David's next, *Hunky Dory*.

BELOW: David photographed shortly after the dress cover photo session, this time in his civilian uniform.

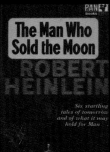

ABOVE: 'Peculiar to Mr Fish' – David in the lounge of Haddon Hall, photographed by Keith MacMillan in summer 1970.

Disliked on release by certain executives at his record label Mercury, *The Man Who Sold The World* *(TMWSTW)* proved important in raising David's profile. Its heavy rock content stirred interest among US radio stations and helped establish an influential underground following for his work, laying solid foundations for the 1972 release of *Ziggy Stardust*. At last David had found a simpatico ally in producer Tony Visconti, who rated his writing skills so highly they had even discussed the idea of making this their *Sergeant Pepper*, meaning "each song would have a completely different theme", as Visconti later explained.

But the making of *TMWSTW* was at times arduous for Visconti, who found himself in charge not only of budget and production, but also in maintaining David's interest. Visconti felt that much of the creative work was made his responsibility while David idled and socialised in Trident Studios' reception space, much preoccupied with his new wife. This view was later disputed by Ronson, whose overwrought guitar-playing and multi-instrumentality are showcased throughout.

However, there is little doubt that David felt overwhelmed by the process. "It was a nightmare, that album," he told BBC Radio One's Stuart Grundy in 1976. "I hated the actual process of making it. I'd never done an album with that kind of professionalism, and that scared me a lot. I felt invalid somehow. I wished I were doing it on four-track at the time. We were on eight tracks and it all seemed too glossy. And also the subject matter was very telling for me. It was all family problems and analogies put into science fiction form."

> 'In Bowie's mood and verse the disjointed images and random allusions reflect an internal torment and confusion that is the microcosm of the world around him.'
> *LA News Advocate*

Along with drummer Mick Woodmansey, the album included another newcomer to the fold – Ralph Mace, A&R man turned synthesiser player who had impressed David and Visconti with his contribution to 1970's two-part single version of 'Memory Of A Free Festival'.

Ronson's employment of volume for his guitar sound took its cue from Eric Clapton's work with Cream and was extended to the other musicians, as Visconti recalled: "He coached Woody to play like Ginger Baker and me to play like Jack Bruce."

This ensemble approach is seen best on the extended showcase 'The Width Of A Circle', part of which was premiered on the February 1970 session for Radio One. The album version is three minutes longer, with the inclusion of fresh lyrics and melody, linked by an acoustic bridge and vocal. This was based on a jam created by the trio.

It is here that *TMWSTW*'s sinister underbelly is revealed: the Aleister Crowley-referencing lyric was also influenced by the regular visits during this period of David's half-brother Terry Burns to Haddon Hall.

Burns' presence was a regular reminder

to David that he could face similar problems.

Whether intentionally or not, *TMWSTW* engaged many of the demons that threatened David's personal well-being. Unlike other family members, however, he was able to exorcise dark thoughts through creativity, and nowhere is this more evident than on this often dark and emotionally charged record.

Take, for example, 'All The Madmen', on which the voice of a little girl whispers: 'He followed me home Mum – can I keep him?' In fact, as Mick Ronson later recalled, it was David who committed this convincing vocal to tape (applying a similar technique on 'Baby Grace Blue' on 1995's *Outside*).

And the song ends with the surreal, quasi-French refrain 'Zane, Zane, Zane, ouvre le chien...' ('Zane, Zane, Zane, open the dog')...

David's on-off relationship with Marc Bolan is to the fore on 'Black Country Rock', for which he had only written a single verse and chorus. The original vocal take was approximately 40 seconds longer, with David's Bolan impersonation continuing to the end. Visconti later said that he and David liked this, but decided that the vocal should be re-recorded with David's voice also thinned out in the mix.

The hand-keyboard Stylophone which appeared on David's biggest hit to date, 'Space Oddity', makes a return on the merry-go-round melody incorporated in the haunting 'After All' (actually inspired by David's memories of popular BBC radio programme *Children's Hour*).

Meanwhile, the origins of 'Saviour Machine' can be traced back to 'Ching-A-Ling', the saccharine folk tune written in 1968 for David's mixed-media/Arts Lab trio Feathers.

At the time of recording, a key literary influence was German philosopher Friedrich Nietzsche, whose *Beyond Good and Evil* is cited in the foreboding closing track 'The Supermen'.

While the album proved problematic in the making, the sleeve design proved an equal frustration for David, who came up with the whole concept. The saga began when he asked Philips to book a photographer to take the cover shots, whilst at the same time commissioning local Arts Lab artist and friend (and fellow Bromley Tech alumnus) Mike Weller to create an illustration for the front cover.[1]

Philips art director Mike Stanford contacted photographer Keith MacMillan (who worked under the moniker 'Keef') and informed him that David wanted to be photographed in a 'domestic environment'. But David was now basing his wardrobe on more outrageous daywear, including two medieval-style velvet gowns recently purchased from boutique Mr Fish. David's school-friend Geoff MacCormack, who worked for designer Michael Fish at his boutique in Clifford Street, Marylebone, had introduced David.

Weller listened to the album tracks and produced rough sketches before proceeding with a finished design: a drawing of a cowboy in front of Cane Hill (the local psychiatric hospital where David's brother Terry had stayed) was chosen by David and Angie.

The illustration of a cowboy with a rifle resting on his shoulder (inspired by the album track 'Running Gun Blues'), was modelled on a publicity photograph of John Wayne from an old film annual. The cowboy's head appeared to be exploding under his hat, a suggestion of David's based on designs Weller had displayed at the Arts Lab. There was also a speech bubble in which Weller wrote 'Roll up your sleeves and show us your arms', and his artwork was completed with David's chosen album title *Metrobolist*.

When Keef arrived at Haddon Hall, he was informed that David would be wearing both of the gowns for the photo shoot, which took place in the lounge and hallway. David adopted louche poses, sometimes holding a pack of playing cards and throwing them at the camera. The chaise longue in the front room was used by David to recreate a setting in the style of pre-Raphaelite Dante Gabriel Rossetti, the room featuring the spoils of antique shop excursions.

On receipt, executives at Philips were not impressed and there was debate about whether the images should be used at all. But David was undeterred and proposed that the entire inner gatefold be dedicated to the Rossetti-style chaise longue shot and that Mike Weller's brightly coloured pop-art cartoon be used on the front cover.

The back was to feature a montage of images including a Byron Newman photo from his most recent Roundhouse appearance, a Keef photo of David in beret and another Weller drawing.

David personally handed over the completed artwork to Philips with clear instructions to be passed to Mercury's art department in Chicago. But when the package arrived in Chicago, the whole cover was immediately amended. Unimpressed with photos of David in a dress and also with his chosen title, they completely ignored David's suggestion and simplified the whole package. Without David's knowledge, they ran with just Mike Weller's drawings (and even edited his work too).

Concerned that the message in the speech bubble was a coded drug-associated slogan, they removed it entirely, leaving the speech bubble blank and meaningless.

The title *Metrobolist*, set out by Weller in black Gothic lettering above the illustration, was also removed and replaced with alternative lettering and new title *The Man Who Sold The World*.

Gone also was the artist's credit 'Mike Weller – Artist Union'. In fact he receives no credit at all.[1]

Angry and frustrated with the truncated US album design, David insisted the UK artwork revert to the photos taken by Keef. Philips relented. At this point the illustrations provided by his Beckenham Arts Lab pals were dropped.

On the front David reclined in his gown in the lounge of Haddon Hall in a photograph printed on textured card to enlarge on the grandiose theme of the central image. The back featured a black and white shot of David in a black beret, wearing a plainer gown (with unseen, a heavily embroidered back), recalling a pose by Greta Garbo in a favourite photo propped up on a mantelpiece at Haddon Hall.[2] David lost the Mr Fish dress used on the front cover during the 70s, but

The adventurous 'round cover'. This German LP is harder to find than the dress cover.

a biography

From the Publicity Department of the Mercury Family of Labels
MERCURY · PHILIPS · SMASH
FONTANA · LIMELICHT

Mercury Record Productions Inc.
35 E. Wacker Dr.
Chicago, Illinois 60601
(312) 332-5788

DAVID BOWIE

David Bowie is one of those Englishmen who has happened upon the pop scene and captured the hearts and minds of nearly all of the audiences that have heard him.

He is also one of the most thoroughly rounded, solid artists to come out of Britain in a long time. His first Mercury LP, "David Bowie" (SR 61246), a record that includes "Space Oddity," Bowie's controversial English hit tune, adequately proved that statment. And now with the release of "The Man Who Sold the World," (SR 61325), Bowie's reputation is certain to soar even more.

TOP LEFT: The first *The Man Who Sold The World* album cover, commonly referred to as the 'cartoon cover'. The original artwork by Mike Weller featured different typography and was titled *Metrobolist*.

TOP RIGHT: John Wayne from a 1950s film annual, the photograph on which Mike Weller based his drawing.

MIDDLE LEFT: Cane Hill Hospital, as featured on the cartoon cover. This is the hospital where David's brother Terry spent much of his adult life.

MIDDLE RIGHT AND BELOW: Biography and David at Haddon Hall.

BOTTOM: 'Oh By Jingo' detail, illustration by Mike Weller.

still owns the blue design.

The 'dress cover' subsequently became the most collectable of David's albums. The German version is also particularly sought-after; the inner has a photo of David wearing a beret at the centre of a fold-out clock-face and the cover is a gaudy painting by Witt Hamburg depicting David as part-eagle/part-human hand nonchalantly flicking the earth away.[3]

In 1972 the album was reissued by RCA and featured a Brian Ward Ziggy-era black and white photograph on the cover.

There was no single release to promote *TMWSTW*; Mercury had received a poor response to circulation of a US promo of 'All The Madmen'. Advertising was scant and the staggered transatlantic release, with the album surfacing in the UK six months after America, put paid to domestic success.

However, the greater US exposure and the work of the label's enthusiastic east coast A&R Robin McBride[4] secured enough interest to merit David's month-long promotional visit there

at the beginning of 1971. It was this trip which dragged David out of the emotional doldrums surrounding the recording of *TMWSTW* and gave birth to the new persona, Ziggy Stardust.

1. Weller's drawing was reproduced on the 1990 reissue, though again he was not credited. This was rectified on the 1999 reissue.

2. When journalist Michael Watts visited Haddon Hall in July 72 he noted: 'On the mantelpiece are framed photographs of Rudolph Valentino, Marilyn Monroe and Greta Garbo, wearing a beret in an almost identical pose as on the back cover of one of his old albums, *The Man Who Sold The World*. On the table are stacks of glossy pictures of Jimmy Dean.'

3. There is a slight edit at the end of side two that doesn't feature on any other version of this album. As 'The Supermen' ends, approximately four seconds of 'Saviour Machine' play out the album.

4. Robin McBride served as A&R Vice President at Mercury Records between 1968 and 1978.

MICK RONSON

MICHAEL Ronson was born on 26 May 1946, the eldest of three children in a practising Mormon family in Beverley Road, Kingston-upon-Hull, Yorkshire.

Never overt about his religious beliefs, Ronson remained true to the faith up to his untimely death from cancer in April 1993.

With a natural gift for music (Ian Hunter said Ronson had 'perfect pitch'), at school he learned to play the recorder and violin, the latter in order to progress to cello. He disliked the sound of the violin so much that he preferred to play the instrument by plucking the strings. Ronson learnt the harmonium in church, and was later to skillfully play keyboards on recordings with David.

Although Ronson became renowned internationally as a guitarist, in fact his first musical love was the drums, which he played privately all his life. "I couldn't afford to buy a set of drums, so I bought a guitar," he said in 1991.

In the early 60s he appeared in a number of local band line-ups, included The Mariners, The Buccaneers and The Crestas. But, in 1966, Ronson moved south and lived first in Harlow, Essex, before taking a bedsit in Gloucester Avenue, Primrose Hill, north London, and joining an outfit called The Voice. This was followed by a stint in Tamla Motown-style band Wanted, but a lack of success forced a dejected return to Hull.

Once home, he joined the city's new and highly-rated band The Rats in line-ups which included drummers Mick 'Woody' Woodmansey and John Cambridge, and also took a day-job working for Hull City Council's parks department as a gardener and groundsman.

In 1969, a break occurred when former bandmate in The Mariners, Rick Kemp, got him session work on singer Michael Chapman's debut album *Fully Qualified Survivor*. While working on this he was introduced to rising young producer Gus Dudgeon. "I was driving down Hull's main thoroughfare when I spotted Mick tending a flower bed on a roundabout," said Kemp in 1991. "I pulled over and said, 'Hey Mick, do you want to make a record?'"

By early 1970, John Cambridge was working with David in Hype and recommended Ronson to both him and Visconti.

"I wasn't so sure because I'd been down to London earlier on and got very sort of heartbroken and disappointed because nothing worked out," said Ronson in 1991.

Cambridge was certain that the match was right, and made the 300-mile round trip to collect Ronson and bring him to London in his car.

"I found Mick marking out the football pitches, painting the lines," said Cambridge. "I said: 'Why not come down for a couple of days? If you don't like it, come back with nothing lost.' So he did."

Two days later Ronson was recording his first national radio show, one of his favourites, John Peel's BBC Radio 1 *Sunday Show*. Soon after, Ronson moved into Haddon Hall and, on the departure of John Cambridge, brought Woodmansey on board.

Their first stint as David's backing musicians was to record *The Man Who Sold The World*, though Ronson also took the opportunity to work with other musicians when he could. In May 1970 he even recorded a demo with Elton John of his track 'Madman Across The Water', (playing both acoustic and electric guitar) at the invitation of John's producer Gus Dudgeon.

But with work thin on the ground, money tight and tension rising, Ronson and Woodmansey abruptly returned to Hull for nine months without any communication with David.

TOP: Mick Ronson in 1972, a Spider From Mars.
ABOVE: Mick Ronson in 1968.

Ronson, Woodmansey and their friend from The Rats Benny Marshall formed side-project Ronno, and signed a deal with Philips which resulted in just one single release on their Vertigo imprint.

When David resumed contact in May 1971, Ronson and Woodmansey were ready to rekindle their musical relationship. Fired by David's renewed confidence and the songs pouring from his pen, *Hunky Dory* and *Ziggy Stardust* were swiftly recorded before the year-end.

During this period, David and Ronson also played occasional gigs as a duo, developing an intuitive bond which would serve them well in the studio. Ronson's unique guitar technique shaped David's early 70s sound.

When David announced his 'retirement' on stage in the summer of 1973, his work with Ronson was just about done.

In the preceding two years, they had recorded five career-defining albums, appeared live together more than 200 times and been the twin-pronged frontline in a series of key TV and radio sessions. They had also fitted in collaborations with Dana Gillespie, Lou Reed, Mott The Hoople and Lulu.

Ronson's 1974 debut album *Slaughter On 10th Avenue* was well received and made the top 10 in the UK album charts. After *Play Don't Worry* in 1975, he embarked on one short-lived musical association after another. That year, Bob Dylan unexpectedly enlisted him in his Rolling Thunder Revue tour band, in which he played alongside such luminaries as Bobby Neuwirth, Roger McGuinn, Joan Baez, Ramblin' Jack Elliott and Ronnie Hawkins.

Subsequently, Ronson produced, amongst many, John Cougar (arranging the US hit 'Jack & Diane'), Roger McGuinn, Ellen Foley, David Johansen, Lisa Dalbello, The Rich Kids and Annette Peacock. He also collaborated with Roger Daltrey, David Cassidy, John Cale, Slaughter & The Dogs and Meat Loaf.

In contrast, Ronson's association with Ian Hunter was long-lived. Having met in 1972, Ronson was fleetingly a member of Mott The Hoople in 1975 before they formed a series of bands together, releasing five albums and ending with a live appearance at Freddie Mercury's Wembley memorial concert in 1992.

From the mid-70s to the mid-80s, Ronson lived with his wife Suzi Fussey – with whom he had a daughter, Lisa – in Woodstock, upstate New York.

Ronson died before his final album could be fully completed, on 29 April 1993 at his London home, 34 Hasker Street. Eerily, Tony Defries' partner Melanie McDonald had died at the same address from cancer seven years earlier.

The album was released, entitled *Heaven And Hull*, in 1994.

A year to the day after Ronson's death, a memorial concert was held at London's Hammersmith Apollo (the former Odeon), where many of his closest friends and colleagues paid tribute.

Saturday 24 April

David's appearance garners national press interest, with a half-page feature in the *Daily Mirror* scored by the publicist he has retained, Bill Harry (ex-editor of *Merseybeat* who cut his teeth with The Beatles).

David employs Harry himself, paying the former art school friend of John Lennon £7 a week. This is symptomatic of Defries' inability to grasp David's potential at this stage in his career.

"I thought David was very interesting, much more thoughtful than your regular artist," said Harry in 1998. "He was really thinking ahead [and] realised that, if he didn't sort things out himself, no one else would. I didn't even think he had a manager – he never mentioned Defries to me."

The piece in the *Daily Mirror* is headlined 'Dressed for the Bowie life', and accompanied by a photograph taken in the back garden of Haddon Hall the previous Tuesday. Don Short's article proclaims: 'When you're a fella, you wear a frock!'

David tells Short that, even though he wears a dress, he isn't "queer and all sorts of things. My sexual life is normal." David's mother says: "As long as he remains a boy, I can't see any harm in it."

Friday 30 April

Mickie Most's label RAK releases Peter Noone's debut single, the double A-side 'Oh You Pretty Thing'[1] and 'Together Forever' written by Vangarde/Fishmann.

From the outset, David's song is chosen as the focus of promotion, and radio stations soon pick up on its unusual melody and catchy chorus.

Meanwhile promo copies are circulated of The Arnold Corns single 'Moonage Daydream'/'Hang Onto Yourself'. Bob Grace has reached an agreement with A&R man Sandy Robertson to release the material on the Charisma label's distribution offshoot B&C Records (which will later license the Mark Pritchett composition 'Man In The Middle'). (▸11.8.72)

Also featured on this recording are session men Herbie Flowers and Clem Cattini. Clem, who had previously worked with David, particularly remembers an evening at London's Wigmore Hall:

"I can't remember who we were backing but I clearly remember David on stage with us just dancing. It was a semi-poetic evening and he was just dancing ballet style, not singing. It's funny because my memory of David is as a piano player and a dancer, not a singer." (▸22.5.69)

1. 'Oh! You Pretty Things' was covered in 1971 by the City Of Westminster Band (released on *4D Quadraphonic Sampler*) and the Alan Caddy Orchestra & Singers. Caddy had been a member of Johnny Kidd & The Pirates and The Tornados.

Saturday 1 May

With The Arnold Corns single being readied for release, David and Burretti – now anointed Rudi Valentino – do the rounds of the music press, turning up for interviews in a Carnaby Street pub in head-

David Bowie wrote "Oh You Pretty Things".

His self-penned album entitled:- **'The Men Who Sold the World'** is available on Mercury Records 633 8041

also his songs **'MOONAGE DAYDREAM'** c/w 'Hang on to Yourself' Recorded by ARNOLD CORNS on B & C Records CB149

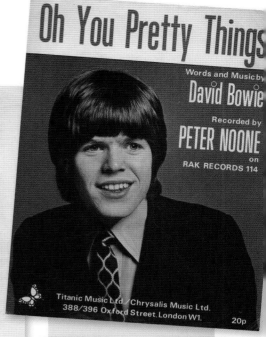

turning 'men's dresses'.

Record Mirror's Lon Goddard reports: "'Rudi will be the new Mick Jagger," said David Bowie. Rudi blushed. "This whole thing has been put together in six days – all on impulse."'

Burretti makes the point that the release targets London's burgeoning but still underground gay scene: "'Really, I'm just a dress designer. Our record will be mainly for discotheques. It will be a hit in the 'specialised clubs'".'

To *Record Mirror*, David announces: "'I believe that Rudi will be the first male to appear on the cover of *Vogue* magazine.[1] I believe that The Rolling Stones are finished and that Arnold Corns will be the next Stones, if we must make a comparison at all."'

1. In fact David nearly became the first man to appear on the cover, in 1973, as the photo used on the cover of *Pin Ups* was originally meant for *Vogue*. (▸19.10.73)

Thursday 6 May

Preparations are made for another BBC radio session, and Bob Grace informs producer Jeff Griffin

TOP RIGHT: 'Oh You Pretty Things' sheet music.

TOP LEFT: Advert featured on the reverse side of 'Oh You Pretty Things' sheet music.

BELOW RIGHT: The original Radio Luxembourg studio 'Lady Stardust' and 'Rupert The Riley' tape box.

BOTTOM LEFT: David in front of 'Oh! You Pretty Things' billboard, 1971.

BOTTOM RIGHT: Noon's version was titled 'Oh You Pretty Thing' and, apart from the billboard display and sheet music, appeared as such in all territories.

by letter that David has chosen drummer Terry Cox, bassist Herbie Flowers and guitarists Tim Renwick of Quiver and High Tide's Tony Hill as his backing musicians. [1]

David invites his former Turquoise bandmate Hill to Haddon Hall to discuss the possibility of working together again. Hill is accompanied by fellow High Tide member, bassist Pete Pauli.

"He played us some ideas he was working on," said Hill in 1992. "Angela was bombing around, full of life, eight months pregnant. She said to me when I arrived, 'Oh, Tony, I've heard so much about you!'"

Hill and Pauli tell David they feel they are 'too experimental', thus incompatible musically with his vision.

"He drove us back to the station in his funny Noddy car [the Riley]; I don't think I saw him after that," said Hill. "My wife Jackie spoke to him a couple of times when he was depressed. He once told her, 'I don't know what to do, I'm never going to make it.' Jackie said to him, 'You're made for the part, you're going to make it,' which bucked up his confidence I think."

Tim Renwick[2] is also unavailable due to commitments to his band Quiver.

1. These same musicians were mentioned in *Disc & Music Echo* as backing David for a gig at the Roundhouse in late April 1971 which didn't transpire.

2. In the US in February 1971, David told *Circus* magazine that he was working with Renwick, who was at that point a member of Quiver, while Hill was still in High Tide: "All the people I want are with other bands at the moment, and I don't want to start breaking them up. I'd like to use Rick Wakeman and the guitarist from High Tide. There are very few good bass players. The only truly fantastic one I have come across is Herbie Flowers."

Friday 7 May

B&C release 'Moonage Daydream'/'Hang Onto Yourself' single.

⊙ **The Arnold Corns**
A **'Moonage Daydream'** (Bowie)[1]
B **'Hang On To Yourself'** (Bowie)
David Bowie (guitar, lead vocal)
Mark Carr-Pritchard (guitar)
Pete De Somogyl (bass)
Tim Broadbent (drums)
Produced by David Bowie for Butterfly Record Productions
(B&C CB.149)

The Arnold Corns do not stir up much commercial or critical interest, yet the project is an important staging post in David's development, providing him with an outlet at a time when he is unwilling to provide Mercury with new material. The name was inspired by David's favourite Pink Floyd song, 'Arnold Layne'.

David uses the Radio Luxembourg studio, where The Arnold Corns single was recorded, to work on demos of new songs[2] with drummer Harry Hughes and bassist Ian Ellis, both members of Clouds.

The other Clouds[3] member, keyboard player Billy Ritchie, declines David's invitation to play on these demo sessions. He is still sore over a fall-out with David backstage at a gig at the Brighton Dome in 1969. (▶19.11.69)

1. Lyrically this version of 'Moonage Daydream' is almost identical to that on *Ziggy Stardust*, while that album's 'Hang On To Yourself' is quite different from this single's B-side. The Arnold Corns song makes no reference to the Spiders From Mars and contains the line 'And me I'm on a radio show'. This is David tipping his hat to the Velvet Underground's 'Sweet Jane' from 1970's *Loaded* (in which Lou Reed sings: 'And me I'm in a rock'n'roll band'.)

2. Including 'Star', which appeared on *Ziggy Stardust*. To date, none of these demos have been made public.

3. Signed to Chrysalis by Terry Ellis, Clouds disbanded in October 1971. Hughes and Ritchie left the music business (the latter to become a property developer) and Ellis is a member of Pink Floyd tribute act Ummagumma.

Saturday 8 May

In the *NME*, David's friend Dave Cousins of The Strawbs selects his three favourite singers: Neil Young, John Lennon and David Bowie.

Wednesday 12 May

David and Angie attend George Underwood's marriage to Danish-born Birgit Graversen at Bromley Register Office.

In this year...

Wednesday 5 May
OPENING of Andy Warhol's controversial play *Pork* for a two-week run at La Mama, New York. The performance is based on many hours of taped telephone conversations between Warhol and Brigid Berlin (aka Brigid Polk).

Friday 7 May
PERFORMANCE by Ronno at the London Temple Club, housed in the basement of the premises of legendary mod hang-out The Flamingo in Soho's Wardour Street.
Support was prog-rock group Beggar's Opera. David attends with publisher Bob Grace.

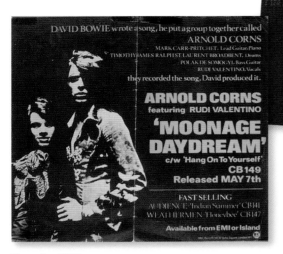

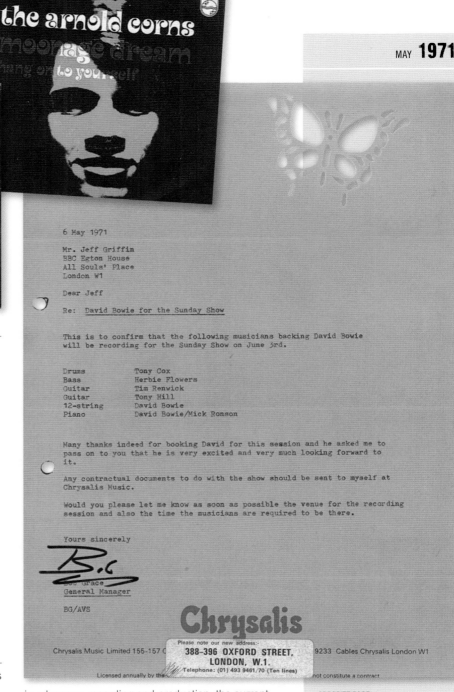

Thursday 13 May

In the US, Stevie Wonder's 21st birthday triggers the expiration of his contract with Tamla Motown, enabling the blind soul singer to gain full financial and creative control over his career.

No longer a minor, he is free to appoint a new manager, a role for which Tony Defries has been pitching.

'Tony's associate, Don Hunter,[1] worked at Motown and knew Wonder,' wrote Defries associate Tony Zanetta in 1986. 'His [Defries'] plan was to take Wonder from Motown and manage him. He was going to make his own record deal for Wonder, a deal of major proportions commensurate with Wonder's stature on the American entertainment scene.'

However, Wonder opts against Defries and stays with Motown on new and enhanced terms.

This is pivotal; with radio play and sales of 'Oh You Pretty Thing' picking up, it is becoming increasingly clear to Defries that he should channel all his energies into David's career.

1. Hunter produced and wrote songs for Wonder in the late 60s.

Friday 14 May

David, Angie and Tony Defries meet Mercury Records executives Irwin Steinberg, Robin McBride and Charlie Fasch at The Londonderry Hotel,[1] near Hyde Park, Mayfair.

Over lunch in the hotel's French restaurant, they listen as Steinberg and McBride outline their intention to improve David's deal and re-sign him for a further three years.

Defries is blunt in his response, telling the Americans that the contract must be terminated without delay.[2] It is due to expire in June but Mercury holds an option to extend it for a third year, and McBride hopes to sign David to a new three-year contract on improved terms, having talked Steinberg into this before leaving Chicago.

McBride is particularly upset when Defries announces that David will not record another note for Mercury, but Steinberg reluctantly agrees at this meeting that, after repayment of all monies spent

in advances, recording and production, the current contract will be terminated.

In the US, *Circus* magazine runs an interview David conducted with journalist Patrick Salvo earlier in the year under the heading 'David Bowie – man for McLuhan', referring to David's interest in the philosopher Marshall McLuhan's ideas about media and society.

David is photographed with his former girlfriend and fellow Gem Management client Dana Gillespie (who is now Defries' partner). Brian Ward takes the photographs.

Around this time, Ward also shoots David in clothing and jewellery styled in the fashion of ancient Egypt.

David considers the look for live work; in his recent *Rolling Stone* article John Mendelsohn had

TOP LEFT: The Egyptian look 1971: "We didn't run with it. Probably a good idea."

TOP RIGHT: David and friend Dana Gillespie in May.

ABOVE: David and Burretti, *Curious* magazine, issued May/June. Photography by Brian Ward.

mentioned his plans 'to appear on stage decked out rather like Cleopatra'.

In 1993, David said: "I did a lot of trying out of images with Brian around that time. This one was actually his idea. He bought a bunch of stuff and I put it on. We didn't run with it, as they say. Probably a good idea."

1. Reopened in the mid-90s as The Metropolitan.

2. In January 1972 David told *Phonograph Record Magazine* that Mercury's interference over the US sleeve design was the main reason for his decision to leave the company.

Monday 17 May

Defries registers a new company, Minnie Bell Music Ltd. In time this will be renamed MainMan.

Fired up with the break from Mercury and with promises from Defries to land a major recording deal, David takes action. After nine months of no contact, he calls Mick Ronson – now living back with his parents in Hull after the failure of the Ronno single – and asks him to return to the fold.

"That was the lowest point, I couldn't have got any lower," Ronson said in 1986. "Then I had a phone call. It was David. He said, 'Aren't you fed up with being back in Hull? Why don't you come back down?' So I said, 'Great, when?' and he said, 'Why don't you just catch the first train?' I did. I met David and he said, 'Let's stop messing about,' and that was it."

With the BBC session looming, the pair agree that Mick Woodmansey should rejoin as drummer, and Ronson returns to Hull to scout for a bass player to take the place of Tony Visconti (since there has been no rapprochement between him and David).

The idea is that Ronson will form a reconstituted Ronno which will simultaneously act as a backing unit for David. It is at these informal auditions that Woodmansey and newcomer Trevor Bolder meet for the first time.

To that end, Ronson puts the word out among local musicians, inviting them to audition for 'David Bowie's new backing band' at the village hall in the appropriately named Woodmansey, just outside Hull.

Ronson's friend Rick Kemp is among those who audition, and journeys south to meet David.

"I'd heard that David was looking to form a new band and decided to travel down to Beckenham with drummer Richie Dharma,"[1] said Kemp in 1991. "We went to Haddon Hall for a not particularly impressive meeting. David sat on the couch and hardly moved; he wasn't much like a pop star. He thought I might be related to Lindsay Kemp."[2]

In the event the bass player's position is taken by an acquaintance of Ronson's, Trevor Bolder, who witnessed David live the previous year in 1970 and even visited Haddon Hall when Ronson was first there.

Bolder – a former hairdresser and piano tuner – is particularly adept, his childhood experience as a trumpeter in Yorkshire brass bands enabling melodic bass lines.

1. Dharma subsequently moved closer to London to Ilford, Essex, and became better acquainted with David, performing on sessions for him and Ronson, including some of those for 1972's Ronson-produced Lou Reed album *Transformer*.

2. Rick Kemp became a founder member of folk/rock group Steeleye Span. David contributed sax to a track on their 1974 album *Now We Are Six*. (▶ 15.3.74)

Saturday 29 May

In an interview with *Record Mirror*, Noone praises David's honesty:

"He talks about his brother who's in a mental institution. He'll say 'He's in an institution because he's a bastard and he can't face up to it'. And I think that's great that he can be that honest."

Sunday 30 May

David is at home listening to a Neil Young album when the call comes through from Bromley Hospital in Blyth Road: Angie has given birth, to their son Duncan Zowie Haywood Jones.[1]

Accompanied by Bob Grace, David heads to the hospital. Much to his amusement, David spends a few minutes admiring the wrong baby before the nurse points Zowie out to him.

To commemorate the birth David completes 'Kooks', a song he has been working on for more than a year. In 1973, David would tell David Wigg (▶ 17.1.73):

"I got the name [Zowie] from a Batman comic. I'm going to tell him later he can call himself anything he wants if he doesn't like the name."

1. Duncan Jones was in advertising directing commercials before he made his big screen directorial film debut, with the acclaimed sci-fi thriller *Moon*, starring Sam Rockwell, in 2009.

Thursday 3 June

At the BBC's Paris Studios in Regent Street for the recording for John Peel's radio show *In Concert*, David is joined by friends Dana Gillespie, Geoff MacCormack, Mark Pritchett and George Underwood as well as the trio who will form his musical backbone for the next three years: Mick Ronson, Mick Woodmansey and Trevor Bolder.

This is Bolder's first appearance with David, and he is startled when David begins the performance in a dress before changing into a pair of voluminous yellow Oxford bags. "I didn't really know David properly; we'd only just met," said Bolder in 1995. "When we rehearsed he was just another guy, dressed in jeans and T-shirt. But when he came out of his dressing room for the Peel show he was wearing a dress and was covered in make-up, the full bit! I couldn't believe my eyes, and didn't know what to say. He had been 'normal' the day before."

In the main, new material which will appear on David's next album are showcased, a particular strain on Bolder who has learnt the basslines to 12 songs in the preceding 48 hours.

"During rehearsals I got 'Song For Bob Dylan' wrong," said Bolder. "David shouted at me, so I went away and practised alone for half an hour. I made sure I could play it. I did the whole set without making a mistake. It was a big thing for me."

Peel points out that Bolder, Ronson and Woodmansey make up Ronno along with an absent Benny Marshall, whom he mistakenly introduces (Marshall rehearsed for the broadcast but has returned home to Hull).

All the songs are David's apart from a cover of Chuck Berry's 'Almost Grown' and Ron Davies' gospel track 'It Ain't Easy'.

The performance starts with 'Queen Bitch' and 'Bombers', both of which Peel says will be on the next album. From *The Man Who Sold The World*, they perform 'Supermen', and also The Arnold Corns numbers 'Moonage Daydream', and 'Looking For A Friend', with David on lead vocals.

Underwood takes the lead on 'Song For Bob Dylan'[1] and Gillespie sings David's pop-artist tribute 'Andy Warhol'. Both are posited as new singles.

'Kooks' is given its first outing as a tribute to his new-born son, but the show's recording is interrupted when David loses his voice attempting 'Oh! You Pretty Things'; a lack of live performance over recent months has affected his vocal stamina.

The session ends with an ensemble rendition of the rousing 'It Ain't Easy' but afterwards David is in tears, as his friends try to console him in The Captain's Cabin bar in nearby Norris Street.

"He was in a real state," said Bob Grace in 1985. "He thought his career was over."[2]

He is soon over the upset caused by his vocal problems, and talks about revisiting the idea of a travelling Bowie Roadshow featuring his friends.

1. In the summer of 1971 David produced Underwood singing 'Song For Bob Dylan' during sessions at Advision, with Rick Wakeman on keyboards. Underwood also took lead vocals on a track with the working title 'We Should Be On By Now'. Modified, this became 'Time' on 1973's *Aladdin Sane*.
2. Five tracks from this session appear on EMI's 2000 compilation *Bowie At The Beeb*.

Friday 4 June

Bolder, Ronson and Woodmansey return to Hull with news of David's plans for a roadshow. "Trevor was quite excited about it, how it would enable Ronno and other special guests to tour with David as a big show," said Benny Marshall in 1990. "They were even planning for me to go and see Lindsay Kemp for lessons in projection."

On Bolder and Woodmansey's return to London, they stay with David; Ronson has already taken up residence in the 'minstrel' gallery above the central hall. For a short time they each create their own living spaces with mattresses on the gallery floor before moving together to a flat in Beckenham.

The cramped basement room at Haddon Hall is used as a useful rehearsal space. The space is so small and badly ventilated that rehearsals are kept to a minimum before the sound equipment is moved to the large ground-floor hallway and set up around the base of the stairs.

Ahead of a new deal and funded by Gem, Defries encourages David to record new material. Within a couple of days Dana Gillespie begins recording a version of David's song 'Andy Warhol' at Trident.[1] Co-produced by David and Ronson, this is for a double-sided promotional album featuring both David and Gillespie.

1. Released as a single by RCA in 1974.

Tuesday 8 June

David, Bolder, Ronson and Woodmansey gather at Trident for their first recording session to work on the tracks which will appear on the next album. Today they start recording 'Song For Bob Dylan'. Ken Scott engineers and co-produces with David and recording is carried out at a swift pace. "Almost everything was done in one take," said Ken Scott in 1999.

In 1983 Ronson described *Hunky Dory* as 'very much a duo record. We just added bass and drums but it was just like the things we did as a duo. It was very spontaneous – we hardly did any retakes'.

During the sessions, demos of other new songs are regularly recorded. These are tracks destined to appear on *Hunky Dory's* successor, *Ziggy Stardust*.

For Bolder, recording with David for the first time was a nerve-wracking experience. "When that red light came on in the studio it was, God, in at the deep end or what!" he said in 1993.

Wednesday 9 June

Peter Noone mimes 'Oh You Pretty Thing' on *Top of the Pops* (broadcast 10 June) with David playing piano and Tony Wilson of Hot Chocolate on bass.

TOP: Ronno, left to right: Trevor Bolder, Benny Marshall, Mick Ronson, Tony Visconti and Woody Woodmansey.
ABOVE: Trevor Bolder from 1972.

In this year...

Wednesday 12 May
MARRIAGE of Mick Jagger and Bianca Macias at the town hall in Saint-Tropez in the south of France. Jagger soon became a close friend of David's. In the late 70s David dated Bianca.

FIRST London fashion show titled *Kansai In London* is staged by 27-year-old designer Kansai Yamamoto at the Great Gear Trading Company, 85 King's Road. Coverage of the kabuki-inspired event attracted David's attention and he purchased a Kansai design in 1972 at the boutique Boston 151, at 151 Fulham Road, London SW3.

ABOVE: David emerges from the Eavises' farmhouse at the Glastonbury Festival wearing Angie's blue 'magician's' cloak. Angie remembers: "I was encouraging him to dress up. I was sick of seeing him in T-shirts." Photographs by Gabi Pape.

BOTTOM LEFT: Detail of the organiser's timetable. David's evening set was eventually moved to the following morning.

BOTTOM RIGHT: David in his 'magic cloak', minutes before taking the stage at Glastonbury for the very first time which is also his first UK appearance of 1971.

For the appearance David again wears one of his man-dresses.

Saturday 12 June

Peter Noone's 'Oh You Pretty Thing' peaks at number 12 in the UK singles chart.

Noone tells the *NME*: "We recorded it in a week. It's not one of those that you sit around and say 'Is it or isn't it good enough to record?' I don't think it's complicated, just a bit different.

"My view is that David Bowie is the best writer in Britain at the moment... certainly the best since Lennon and McCartney, and in fairness you don't hear so much of them nowadays."

Meanwhile, producer Mickie Most tells *Disc* he would like an entire album of David's compositions for the former Herman's Hermits frontman: "I'm hoping to persuade David to write a concept LP, with each song linked to the next."

Income from the sales of the single flow to Chrysalis Music, where David's publisher/confidante Bob Grace would be expected to be congratulated. However, co-owner Terry Ellis harbours hippy ideals which do not accommodate mainstream success and even contemplates changing the company name to dissociate the company from the hit.

```
TUESDAY 22nd
BRONCO              2 00pm -  3 00pm
TERRY REID          3 30   -  4 45
X MOUSEPROOF        5 00   -  6 00
  LEAFY LIMBO, TOAD 6 15   -  7 00
DAVID BOWIE         7 30   -  8 30
DAEVID ALLEN + GONG 9 00   - 10 15
TRAFFIC            10 45   - 12 15am
X PINK FLOYD        1 00am
```

Thursday 17 June

'Man In The Middle' and 'Looking For A Friend'[1] are recorded at Trident.

Mark Pritchett sings 'Man In The Middle' with David and possibly Ronson joining in enthusiastically on the chorus, while Freddie Burretti makes his one and only vocal appearance on 'Looking For A Friend'. For most of the sessions Ken Scott is the engineer; today his duties are taken by Roy Thomas Baker.[2]

1. There were a number of versions of 'Looking For A Friend' recorded during 1971, all with David on lead vocal apart from this.
2. Baker made his name as co-producer of the first three Queen albums in the early- to mid-70s.

Saturday 19 June

David and Angie travel with Defries, Gillespie, Ronson and Bob Grace to Somerset for his first live performance in 10 months at the Glastonbury Fayre, a free festival to be held over the weekend's summer solstice at Michael Eavis' Worthy Farm, six miles to the east of Glastonbury.[1]

Taking the train from Paddington, they arrive at Castle Cary station and decide to walk to the site through apparently endless country lanes.

David wears a loose white shirt and yellow, high-waisted, 20s-style, wide-legged Oxford bags, as does Angie.

"It was a very warm summer's day and David and Angela were [dressed] like strange twins," said Gillespie in 1985.

Since the group are visiting the site of King Arthur's Avalon, Angie has made David a deep blue 'magician's cloak'. He tops off his outfit with a broad, floppy-brimmed hat bought – like his electric blue fur coat – from Paul Reeves' Fulham Road shop The Universal Witness.

David has been invited to appear at Glastonbury by DJ/promoter Jeff Dexter, who recommended him to organiser and *Friends* magazine music editor John Coleman (who is also an acquaintance of Ronson's, having admired his work on Michael Chapman's 1970 album *Fully Qualified Survivor*).

David isn't booked to perform until 7.30pm and the weather takes a turn for the worse. There is much merriment when the urbane Defries trips and falls into the mud.

"I hated Glastonbury," said Ronson in 1983. "It was so cold and I had to try and sleep in a little tent on the grass. It wasn't much fun."

Dexter said in 1995: "David surprised me by keeping himself to himself at the festival. He stayed in the farmhouse and just drank tea continually. He didn't mix with his friends, like [singer] Terry Reid, at all."

Yet in 2000, David said that one of his few memories of the event was meeting Reid in the farmhouse "along with a crew of latter-day hippies, and all kinds of mushrooms".

1. Billed as the Macrobiotic Festival, the line-up included the Pink Fairies, Melanie, Fairport Convention, Gong, Traffic, Brinsley Schwarz,

Hawkwind, Arthur Brown, The Edgar Broughton Band and Skin Alley. The Grateful Dead were scheduled to make an appearance but were forbidden by their record company, Warners.

Sunday 20 June

▶ When performers seriously over-run, David's 7.30pm slot has already been delayed to midnight. But his set is postponed to ensure that the festival abides by a sound curfew imposed by the local authorities.

"There was chaos over who was playing," said Gillespie in 1985. "Everyone was on acid – not David or Angie or Defries I hasten to add, or even me, for once."

Determined to perform, David and Ronson take to the stage at 5am, greeting the dawn with a short set.

David plays organ, guitar and harmonica and Ronson harmonises on vocals and alternates between guitar and bass on a selection of old and new songs – 'Bombers', 'Oh! You Pretty Things', 'Quicksand', 'Kooks', 'Changes', 'Amsterdam' and 'Song For Bob Dylan' – as well as 'The Supermen'[1] from *The Man Who Sold The World* and 'Memory Of A Free Festival' from its predecessor.

As David and Ronson launch into the refrain of the 'Free Festival', 'The sun machine is coming down and we're gonna have a party', the sun breaks over a hilltop, its rays shining off the sides of the silver pyramid constructed in the valley especially for the event.

"People were waking up in their sleeping bags having been frozen all night in the mud," said Gillespie. "It was quite extraordinary. He didn't have a full audience in attendance, but the ones he did have, he completely won over."[2]

In the evening the recent *In Concert* session is broadcast by Radio One and, on the journey back from the festival, Gillespie senses that Glastonbury has been a turning point in David's career: "That trip was really the last time we just messed around. It all got a lot more serious after that weekend."[3]

Defries is certainly more serious about his involvement in David's career. Shortly after their return from Glastonbury, he arranges a meeting with Terry Ellis, Bob Grace's boss at Chrysalis.

"Defries was in a rage," said Grace in 1985. "He said, 'You've been trying to steal my client', which I hadn't. He realised that David was a lot closer to me than him. I apologised and said, 'I'm just trying to do my job as a publisher.'"

1. David contributed a studio recording of 'The Supermen' to the 1972 triple album *The Glastonbury Fayre*, released by festival organisers Revelation Enterprises to recoup losses made the year before as a result of a no-show by The Grateful Dead.
2. Footage shot by a film crew – including Nic Roeg (who later directed David in his film debut *The Man Who Fell To Earth*) as cinematographer – was hastily released as an X-rated film entitled *Glastonbury Fayre* in July 1971. David is not featured, since his performance was too early in the day to be captured. Among those who do appear are Terry Reid, Linda Lewis, Fairport Convention, Family, Melanie, Arthur Brown, Kingdom Come, Daevid Allen and Gong, Quintessence and Traffic.
3. David returned to perform at the Glastonbury Festival in 2000, his hair almost as long as it had been in 1971.

BELOW: David reunited with Jeff Dexter at Glastonbury Festival in 2000. Photo by Mark Adams.

THIS PAGE

TOP: The Glastonbury pyramid stage, 1971.

UPPER MIDDLE: Glastonbury audience and stage.

LOWER MIDDLE: Audience as seen from the Glastonbury stage.

BOTTOM: Excerpt from a letter from David to Benny Marshall, 29 June.

OPPOSITE PAGE

TOP RIGHT: Mick Ronson and friend on the steps of Haddon Hall.

TOP LEFT: At Haddon Hall's old piano in late 1970. This was a gift from a neighbour and the instrument on which David wrote much of *Hunky Dory*.

MIDDLE: Rick Wakeman: "I learned more from David Bowie than anybody else in the studio as regards professionalism and how to work."

BOTTOM: David and Angie with Zowie, in their back garden.

658 -1577.

HADDON HALL, 42, SOUTHEND RD.
BECKENHAM
KENT
BOWIE

Dear Benny,

Just a few ====='s to let you know what's happening down here. Mick is fast becoming a great arranger and I think his mind's opening out to all kinds of influences a change that pleases and excites me as I think he is fated to be a great musician and good person. Benny, I want you to know one thing and its very important that you know it. Both Bob Grace and myself have complete faith in the band and in yourself as lead singer. The last thing either of us want is for you to feel out of things. Ronno as a band, because of its contractual hang-ups, must disapear for a bit, then as soon as my mess is rubbed out, Tony Defries (lawyer) will be work...

Saturday 26 June

Disc & Music Echo publishes an article headed 'Mum taught him all he knows' about The Arnold Corns.

Freddie Burretti is in his guise as Rudi Valentino: '"The rest of the group don't talk much to me," says Rudi, "but I don't get on very well with younger people." He is making a lot of headway in the [clothes] designing business, and all his designs are exclusive and pricey. As a present, Bowie is having some special labels made for him to put on his creations.'

Tuesday 29 June

Benny Marshall receives a letter from David confirming his interest in both Benny and Ronno.

In the letter, David refers to Defries as his lawyer. Defries is actually working on clearing David and Ronno of their separate commitments to Mercury[1] and Philips to make way for a new deal. Among those he is courting is RCA, recommended to David by staff producer Tom Ayres on his US trip at the beginning of the year.

1. Mercury reported that, by the end of June 1971, *The Man Who Sold The World* had sold 1,395 copies in the US since release in November 1970.

Wednesday 30 June

In a letter on Gem Group notepaper, Tony Defries serves notice to Mercury's Irwin Steinberg that David no longer considers himself a Mercury recording artist.

Publicist Bill Harry has engineered more coverage in the *Daily Mirror*, which runs a full-page feature headed 'Right then, which one is Dad?' Ron Burton's photograph shows David and Angie from behind pushing Zowie in his pram outside Haddon Hall in Southend Road.

This is the last publicity Harry realises for David. Shortly after, he receives a call from Defries informing him he is no longer David's PR. "He said he was in charge and would be taking over everything," said Harry in 1998. "I wasn't needed any more. After that call I never heard from, or saw, David again."

In Harry's place, Defries appoints an in-house publicist, trainee journalist Dai Davies, on David's recommendation. They have been introduced by Davies' girlfriend Anya Wilson, who is David's radio plugger.

Davies, who interviewed David for *Music Now* magazine at the beginning of the year, soon scores a front cover feature in tame British sex magazine *Curious*, for which Davies writes the article.

Davies also secures coverage in monthly magazine *Beat Instrumental*. Journalist Steve Turner interviews David and writes: 'Dressed in old jeans and with a day's growth of stubble on his chin, he drove me over to his residence at Haddon Hall. Pages of notepads lay around his home with ideas or rough lyrics jotted down. He played me some demos he had made the same day.'

Another visitor to Haddon Hall (which he dubs 'Beckenham Palace' because of its size) is keyboard player Rick Wakeman, who has agreed to play on the current sessions.

'He then proceeded to play the finest selection of songs I have ever heard in one sitting in my entire life,' wrote Wakeman in 1995. 'I had been given the honour of hearing tracks like 'Life On Mars' and 'Changes' in their raw brilliance. I couldn't wait to get into the studio and record them.'

Friday 9 July

Wakeman joins David and his fellow musicians at Trident, playing harpsichord on 'It Ain't Easy',[1] with Dana Gillespie joining in on backing vocals.[2] Two takes of 'Bombers'[3] are also recorded.[4]

1. This track appeared on *Ziggy Stardust*. David's handwriting credits the recording on the multi-track tape box as 'David Bowie + Ronno' and lists the first track as 'It Ain't Easy (continuation)'.

2. Gillespie received her credit on the 1999 *Ziggy Stardust* reissue.

3. 'Bombers' did not make the final cut of *Hunky Dory* and first received official release as a bonus track on the album's 1990 *Hunky Dory* reissue.

4. Wakeman's recollection in his 1995 autobiography, *Say Yes!*, that David delivered a severe dressing down to the musicians for not being prepared during this session has been disputed by everyone else present, including Trevor Bolder: "That's rubbish. David would never have told the band off in the studio. Especially as Mick and Woody had already left him once and everyone was now getting on. The band would not have survived that – it definitely didn't happen.

"We basically didn't rehearse the material for *Hunky Dory*, apart from a very short run-through in the basement of Haddon Hall, and just the two or three songs we did on the radio show. The rest David had demoed or he showed us what he wanted in the studio. Rick Wakeman was only with us for two days at the most," Bolder concludes. Ken Scott, who naturally attended every session, said in 2002: "I definitely don't remember that and it's not something I would forget. I would definitely dispute that one."

Wednesday 14 July

Tony Defries writes to comedian/pianist Dudley Moore[1] with a request: 'I have approached your office today to try and arrange for you to play piano on a session for David Bowie who is currently making an album of which this session will form a part.

'I appreciate that you will be busy in the next few weeks but the material in question is deserving of the best possible musician and David and I would be extremely grateful if you could do a three-hour session some time during the next few weeks.'[2]

The musicians record four takes of 'Quicksand'[3] at Trident. Among visitors to the sessions is LA DJ Rodney Bingenheimer, on a visit to the UK with his girlfriend Melanie McDonald. Defries has taken a shine to McDonald,[4] so encourages them to hang out.

To clinch a deal for both David and Dana Gillespie with RCA, Defries plans a privately pressed promotional album featuring tracks by each artist.

1. A gifted jazz pianist and composer, Dudley Moore (1935–2002) came to prominence in the early 60s as one of four writer/performers of satirical revue *Beyond The Fringe*, on which he worked with comedy partner Peter Cooke. In the 80s he appeared in such hit films as *10* and *Arthur*.

2. There is no record of a response from Moore. It is likely that David had earmarked him to play the elaborate piano figures on the still-to-be-recorded 'Life On Mars?'.

TOP RIGHT: Rehearsals in Victoria; David, Woody and Mick, July. Photo by Rodney Bingenheimer.

TOP LEFT: Advert for Country Club, 21 July.

MIDDLE: The Gem promo album featuring David and Dana Gillespie, pressed in the summer of 1971.

BOTTOM: Country Club set list for David and *Mark* Ronson.

3. Take four was the version which appeared on *Hunky Dory*.
4. McDonald became Defries' partner for 10 years, giving birth to their daughter Fleur (the name of his music publishing company) in 1975. McDonald died in London in 1989.

Friday 16 July

Tony Defries sends Mickie Most three songs by George Underwood which have been written and produced by David: 'Song For Bob Dylan', 'Hole In The Ground' and 'We Should Be On By Now'.[1]

Defries[2] writes that these tracks 'are available worldwide as is the artiste on which David intends to make further product. The intended A-side was 'Song For Bob Dylan'. I enclose a photograph of George Underwood (Calvin James),[3] who sang on the David Bowie tracks.'

1. Some of this material was recorded for the Bell label in late 1970.
2. It is clear that Defries was unaware that Most produced Underwood's 1965 single 'Some Things You Never Get Used To'.
3. David was keen for Underwood to resume his recording career as Calvin James, though Underwood preferred to work under his own name.

Sunday 18 July

As well as visiting Trident – where there is a six-hour mixing session today – Rodney Bingenheimer witnesses band rehearsals at rooms near Victoria railway station for forthcoming appearances[1] at north London's Country Club and Soho's the Marquee.

At the rehearsals studio David is introduced to young band Chameleon by Bob Grace (who is considering releasing their music via Chrysalis' Butterfly Productions). David gives them a demo of new song 'Star'. The Aylesbury-based group record their own version.[2]

1. Assertions that this period witnessed a heavy bout of gigging by David and his fellow musicians are incorrect. Certainly there were a few low-key appearances, some where David played solo, some as a duo with Ronson. During a solo performance at Walthamstow Assembly Hall, David played keyboards but nervousness or illness led to stage exits between songs.
2. Chameleon's version never received official release. David's demo, which he supplied on reel-to-reel, surfaced in 2000 when it was auctioned for £1,527 at Christie's by Chameleon singer Les Payne.

Wednesday 21 July

▶ David Bowie, The Country Club, Haverstock Hill, London NW3.

During the day there is a three-hour mixing session at Trident, and in the evening David, Ronson (who plays bass on some numbers), Woodmansey and Rick Wakeman are supported by Irish singer/songwriter Jonathan Kelly at the hut-like venue in north London's Belsize Park.

Some songs are performed by David with Ronson as a duo and others with the full band. There are some technical problems – the sound balance is out – but Ronson's growing presence is clearly evident.

Aside from *The Man Who Sold The World*'s 'The Supermen' and 'Memory Of A Free Festival' from 1969's *David Bowie*, the core of the set is a clutch of songs bound for *Hunky Dory*: 'Fill Your Heart', 'Oh! You Pretty Things', 'Eight Line Poem', 'Quicksand', 'Song For Bob Dylan', 'Kooks' and 'Andy Warhol'. There are three covers – Biff Rose's 'Buzz the Fuzz', Ron Davies' 'It Ain't Easy' and Jacques Brel's 'Amsterdam' – as well as new composition 'Gonna Rain Again'.[1]

Wakeman is astonished by David's stagewear: "The most wild outfit I had ever seen, including giant blue feathers protruding from a Tiller-girl style head-dress."[2]

After the show David tells Wakeman he is forming a new band in which he will become a frontman called Ziggy Stardust. Inviting Wakeman to join on keyboards and also to handle all musical arrangements, he confides that the pay will be good since Defries is negotiating a new album deal and world tour.

'David told me to take a couple of days thinking about it and then to call him.' wrote Wakeman in 1995. 'I told him there and then that it sounded great and I really fancied the whole idea, but David insisted I took my time over the decision. The following night, or three o'clock in the morning to be precise, the telephone rang with the other call. This one was from Chris Squire of Yes.'

Wakeman plumps for the progressive rock group, taking him on a path to success as a member of Yes and as a solo star.

1. Also called 'It's Gonna Rain Again', recorded during the *Ziggy Stardust* sessions of November 1971 but not released.
2. David wore this head-dress for Brian Ward's 'Egyptian' photoshoot, though there were no feathers.

Thursday 22 July

Another three-hour mixing session takes place at Trident on tracks for the dual-artist promotional album. This is followed by a seven-hour mixing session on 24 July.

Monday 26 July

Another seven-hour mixing stint at Trident finalises the promotional album, which is privately pressed with a green Gem label[1] and given the matrix numbers BOWPROMO1A1/1B1.

David's side comprises seven songs: 'Oh! You Pretty Things'; 'Eight Line Poem';[2] 'Kooks';[3] 'It Ain't Easy'; 'Queen Bitch'; 'Quicksand'; and 'Bombers'.[4]

As well as David's 'Andy Warhol', Gillespie's side contains four of her own compositions: 'Mother, Don't Be Frightened';[5] 'Never Knew'; 'All Cut Up On You'; and 'Lavender Hill'.

1. White label copies are less collectible than the extremely rare albums bearing the Gem label.

2. This has a different vocal take and minor lyrical changes to the track on *Hunky Dory*.

3. The mix on 'Kooks' is slightly different to that on *Hunky Dory*. The acoustic guitar features throughout the song, whereas the *Hunky Dory* version has the guitar edited out of the choruses.

4. 'Bombers' – here featuring an extended ARP synth outro similar to that which eventually linked into 'Andy Warhol' – was replaced in the final track listing of *Hunky Dory* by 'Fill Your Heart'. The track received its first official release as a bonus track on the 1990 *Hunky Dory* reissue. David said in an early 1972 US radio interview: "'Bombers' is a kind of skit on Neil Young, it's quite funny."

4. This and 'Andy Warhol' were co-produced by David and Ronson. The other three Gillespie tracks were produced by Ronson alone.

Friday 30 July

Two takes of 'The Bewlay Brothers'[1] are recorded at Trident over a tape containing rejected versions of 'Song For Bob Dylan' and 'Fill Your Heart'.

1. Take 2 is the version on *Hunky Dory*.

Sunday 1 August

▶ David Bowie & Mick Ronson, the Marquee, Wardour Street, London W1.

During the day David signs a six-year recording agreement with Gem. This effectively gives his management company the power to license his recordings instead of David signing direct with a record company.

At the Marquee, David and Ronson perform as a duo. The venue is only two-thirds full, though this is an improvement – if only marginal – on attendance a few weeks before at the Country Club.

Monday 2 August

Tony Defries writes to Bob Grace about plans for Peter Noone to release David's song 'Right On Mother': 'David and I have decided that we do not want 'Right On Mother' released by Peter Noone at all unless it is released as a single in Europe or until we have the opportunity to record it as a single here or until we have seen exactly what happens to 'Pretty Things' in the States.'

Andy Warhol's play *Pork* opens for a four-week run at the Roundhouse in Camden, north London.

Edited from 200 hours of Warhol's taped telephone conversations by director Anthony Ingrassia, *Pork*'s erotic and bizarre content – with simulated masturbation, hetero- and homosexual intercourse and defecation – provides the British press with salacious copy.

Invaluable publicity is granted by the *News of the World*: 'A new low in permissiveness... the most amazing scenes, of nudity and immorality ever performed on stage... it made *Oh! Calcutta!* and *The Dirtiest Show in Town* look like a vicarage tea party.'

In the cast are several individuals who will become close to David: Tony Zanetta plays the Warhol character B. Marlow, Cherry Vanilla[1] is the lead as 'Pork', Wayne County is a loud-mouthed transvestite called Vulva and Trash star Geri Miller is a breast-twirling prostitute who cares about the welfare of her clients. Behind the scenes Leee Black Childers is assistant stage director.

During its London run, *Pork* is regularly interrupted by outbursts from angry audience members who presumably have not seen the caution printed on the posters: 'Warning: this play has explicit sexual content and "offensive" language. If you are likely to be disturbed, please do not attend.'

1. Real name Kathy Dorritie.

Friday 6 August

David and his musicians record one of the most important tracks of his career, 'Life On Mars?'[1]

Guiding the session, Ronson sits among the musicians and counts in each take, later adding guitar along with strings, Mellotron and David's vocal.

They also record 'Song For Bob Dylan' one more time, and the album recording is deemed complete. David and Bob Grace then visit Ken Scott at his home in Crofton Park, south-east London, to select tracks for inclusion on the new album.

1. The 'Life On Mars?' master tape contains one vocal master with another complete take and around 10 incomplete instrumental takes.

Saturday 7 August

Today is supposed to be the start of a series of European dates by David and the band, taking in Belgium and France and starting tonight at The Paradiso[1] in Amsterdam.

"David told us to get our passports organised," said Trevor Bolder in 1995. "I was quite excited because it was going to be the whole band." However, the dates are cancelled at the last minute.[2]

1. The Paradiso, at Weteringschans 6-8, is a notable rock venue. Ken Pitt approached the club's promoter about the possibility of David appearing there in 1969.

2. The cancelled appearances included a festival in Belgium on 21 August (possibly the Bilsen Jazz Festival where The Faces performed on that date that year) and appearances in the south of France, between 26-29 August. David was also offered £500 and expenses for three consecutive nights towards the end of October 1971 at the Zoom Club in Frankfurt, Germany. Recording commitments prevented him from accepting the booking.

Wednesday 11 August

▶ David Bowie & Mick Ronson, The Country Club, London NW3.

Rodney Bingenheimer is present but the gig is poorly attended, though the proximity of the venue to the Roundhouse draws a contingent from *Pork*.

They have been persuaded by Leee Black Childers, who notices an advert for the show and recalls David from John Mendelssohn's *Rolling Stone* article (and, in particular, the fact that the unusual Englishman was wearing a dress in the photograph).

Having scored guest passes, Childers is accompanied by Wayne County, Tony Zanetta,

ABOVE: At Gem's central London office.

In this year...

Marie Helvin's big break, modelling Kansai Yamamoto's startling new fashion in London. Helvin reluctantly shaved her eyebrows for the session, a trick David would later use.

Thursday July 8
PUBLICATION of *Harper's & Queen* cover feature on Kansai Yamamoto. The magazine featured outfits from Kansai's first UK show in London. The session was the first modelling work for Marie Helvin. (▶ 13.4.73)

PRESS conference given by the cast of Andy Warhol's *Pork* at London's Mayfair Gallery, promoting a forthcoming run at the Roundhouse.

Saturday 24 July
SINGLE 'Get It On' by Marc Bolan's T Rex reaches the Number 1 spot in the UK chart.

Thursday 29 July
RELEASE of Peter Noone's single 'Oh You Pretty Thing' in the US by Bell Records.

TOP: Tony Defries's rough plans for David's aborted 1971 dates in Europe.

MIDDLE: Andy Warhol's *Pork* makes its mark on Roundhouse history.

BOTTOM: *Pork* programme.

Geri Miller and Cherry Vanilla (who said in 1986 "David had his hair down over his shoulders and Angie was working the lights").

David recognises members of the group when they arrive during the performance and, pausing only to introduce them to the rest of the audience, sings 'Andy Warhol'.

After the show Childers and Vanilla invite David, Angie and Dana Gillespie to *Pork* the following night.

Support at the Country Club is heavy rock band Tucky Buzzard,[1] whose soundman, Robin Mayhew, Angie approaches after David and Ronson once again experience technical difficulties.

1. Tucky Buzzard's line-up included Nicky Graham, who played piano for David in 1972, and guitarist Terry 'Tex' Taylor, who was a member of Bill Wyman's group Willy & The Poor Boys at the memorial concert staged for Mick Ronson at the Hammersmith Apollo in 1994.

Thursday 12 August

Defries officially assumes the role of David's manager as they sign a management contract with Angie as witness. The agreement is backdated to the date when their association began, April 1970, and its duration is without limit.

In the evening David, Angie, Gillespie, Defries and Freddie Burretti see *Pork* at the Roundhouse. The timing is immaculate; here is a milieu which slots neatly into the vision for *Ziggy Stardust* which David is currently developing.

Friday 13 August

Armed with the promotional album featuring David and Gillespie, Defries flies to the US for 10 days of negotiations for new recording deals for both of them.

It is a measure of his confidence that Defries is not now considering a British label for his clients (though David has mentioned that Chrysalis is interested in his new material).

In David's case, Defries has excited interest from five labels: CBS, Columbia, Bell, United Artists and RCA.

The last is the preferred choice since it is not only one of the most important record companies in the world, but has a long-standing relationship with Elvis Presley and his shrewd manager Col Tom Parker, appealing to David and Defries' ambitions for international success.

While Defries has been building a relationship with RCA's recently appointed A&R head Dennis Katz, he has sent acetates to Katz's UA counterpart Martin Cerf.

David's acquaintance and Cerf's friend Screaming Lord Sutch is visiting the West Coast and hears some of the new tracks.

"I said, 'That's David Bowie – he's quite well known in England'," said Sutch in 1992. "I told Martin I thought that David was going to be massive, he was writing such original material. Martin was also keen but was worried that David was completely unknown in America."

Saturday 14 August

In *Sounds*, David's depiction of himself in an interview with Steve Peacock is far removed from the machinations taking place across the Atlantic.

"'I'm not writing very deeply at the moment," he says as he sits in the opulent surroundings of his manager's office in Regent Street. "I'm just picking up on what other people say, writing it down, and making songs out of it. I suppose I'm a disillusioned old rocker. I'm sure that if I'd made it I would have adored it all – all the gold lamé and everything, it would have been fabulous. Then I found myself in a mime company, that made me a clown, and I came out of it a clown/songwriter."'

Simultaneously, *Melody Maker* provides a wealth of coverage, with an interview in a James Johnson feature headed 'The Space Oddity comes down to earth', and several mentions in Michael Watts' profile of Rodney Bingenheimer:

'The day (Bingenheimer) enters the *MM* office carrying a David Bowie album and a briefcase full of sepia-tinted close-ups of the above, he is wearing shiny silver pants and an emerald and silver shirt. David Bowie is English and he likes him a lot. I expect you are wondering by now about David Bowie. Well, the truth is that when Rodney worked for Philips Mercury he held a party for David attended by the underground. "My, were they all surprised when he walked in with these clothes on, they just couldn't believe it! Nobody spoke for several seconds. But that's really him. I don't think it's a gimmick. You know, he really digs Andy Warhol, and the Velvet Underground, Iggy and The Stooges and Kim Fowley. It's really strange; here they hardly look when he walks down the street."

"'David Bowie and Christopher Milk are very close, Christopher Milk, you should understand, are up there with Alice Cooper and Iggy purveying Outre Rock."'

Sunday 15 August

At a meeting with Bell Records executives in Los Angeles, Defries plays the promotional album. Meanwhile, Angie invites Tony Zanetta to Haddon Hall for Sunday lunch. "And there I discovered a different David," said Zanetta in 1986. "In the Sombrero he always seemed a little shy and quiet and Angie was very much more the one who was in the forefront. But in Haddon Hall he took the lead.

"He was very charming, intense and curious. He wanted to know about everything, so our meeting at Haddon Hall was really about me telling him about New York and Andy Warhol and pop culture in New York City."

Thursday 19 August

Defries has another meeting with Bell, this time discussing David's future with the company's Irving Biegel at its New York offices.

Friday 27 August

At United Artists, Martin Cerf persuades the company's president Mike Stewart to make an offer to Defries, and contracts are drawn up.

At the last minute the UA bid is topped by a more sizeable advance from RCA, whose A&R executive, Dennis Katz, has recently been brought in to inject new blood into the company's ageing roster.

Only vaguely aware of David as the person behind 'Space Oddity' (and as a man who wears a dress), Katz is persuaded the company needs this new star by the quality of songs on the Gem private pressing.

"After that David did become massive and Martin Cerf was treated with great respect at United Artists, going on to sign some very important acts," said his friend Screaming Lord Sutch in 1992.

Laurence Myers and Tony Defries receive a telegram from their new US associate Normand Kurtz (the lawyer who negotiated the solid publishing contract for Chrysalis the previous year).

This confirms David's freedom from Mercury and that RCA is his new label: 'Have confirmed with Steinberg release of David Bowie on payment of 17,843.41 Dollars, return of all masters and artwork and am forwarding him cable to that effect. Also confirmed RCA deal.

'Congratulations, you are out of hell reaching for heaven.'

Saturday 28 August

Melody Maker is taking a shine to the camper aspects of David's image. Its Raver column carries an item written by Michael Watts offering readers a photograph: 'Thanks Sandra Wood, of Gem, for sending us three sepia snaps of that famous and much sought after pash...'

In the evening David and Angie are in the audience for the final performance of *Pork* at the Roundhouse and, after the backstage party, join the cast for drinks at the newly opened Hard Rock Cafe in Old Park Lane, Mayfair.

Thursday 2 September

According to a Gem memo generated by Anya Wilson, 'David is to contact John Muir, producer of *Sounds Of The 70s* tomorrow afternoon 3/9/71 re: recording for 3 1/2 hours on 21/9/71.'

Wednesday 8 September

David flies to New York to sign the contract with RCA, accompanied by Angie, Mick Ronson, Tony Defries and his associate Don Hunter, staying at the Warwick Hotel on West 54th Street – in the same suite occupied by The Beatles during their 1965 visit to the east coast for their historic performance at Shea Stadium.

Pork actor Tony Zanetta visits the Warwick, where David reintroduces him to Defries as 'the actor who played Andy Warhol'.

Zanetta – who becomes known as 'Z' – is popular with his new English friends, and is appointed Gem's New York liaison person, taking them around New York and providing entrées into the city's buzzing underground art, music and fashion scenes.

"There was a feeling of real positive energy around David and a belief and faith," said Zanetta in 1986. "I was excited by the intensity that surrounded him. Defries and Angela were very intense and very supportive people. I hadn't experienced a group that worked so closely together as a team before. Everything was certainly focused around David; he could do no wrong.

"They were certainly spinning myths about the future and about destiny, this cosmic destiny. Somehow it didn't seem selfish. It didn't seem like the usual, 'I'm gonna be a star' thing. It felt almost like a spiritual quest. Here was this person who was about to fulfil his destiny on this planet, and it was exciting."

Thursday 9 September

David signs the RCA contract, committing himself to recording three albums over a two-year period with an advance of $37,500 per album. David's royalty is 11 per cent.

The contract is endorsed by label president Rocco Laginestra. At the signing, David is introduced to a number of the label's executives, including in-house RCA producer Richard Robinson, the husband of music journalist Lisa Robinson.

RCA holds a reception for David at The Ginger Man on East 36th Street. Among the invited guests are Lou Reed and his girlfriend Bettye Kronstadt.

Taken with David's new material, particularly 'Queen Bitch',[1] Reed visits David and Ronson at their hotel and plays them songs for his first solo album, which he is planning to record in London, with Richard Robinson producing.

At The Ginger Man, David also meets Lisa Robinson. Instigator of the city's close-knit writing group Collective Conscience, she contributes a column to the UK's *Disc & Music Echo* and is ideally positioned to encourage media interest.

When David mentions he is a fan of The Stooges, Lisa calls her friend, journalist/A&R executive Danny Fields, who signed the band to Elektra and, coincidentally, has frontman Iggy Pop staying with him.

Told by Fields that he should meet this English guy who has been singing his praises – and pausing only to watch the end of a TV screening of Frank Capra's *Mr Smith Goes To Washington* – Pop joins the party at New York's counter-cultural mecca, the back room of Max's Kansas City on Park Avenue South.

With The Stooges dissolved the previous month amid multiple alcohol and drug problems and several line-up changes, Pop's recording contract with Elektra has lapsed and his career, after just two

Bowie at RCA

British composer / performer David Bowie was in New York recently to sign an exclusive recording contract with RCA Records. Bemused by his own joke he is seen here (center) flanked by (from left) Mort Hoffman, Division VP, Commercial Operations; Rocco Laginestra, President; Dennis Katz, Division VP, Contemporary Music; and Tony DeFries, Bowie's manager. His first RCA LP will be out in November, with a tour to coincide.

TOP: David and Mick Ronson at the RCA signing.

MIDDLE: David signs with RCA Records in New York, his most important recording contract, 9 September.

BOTTOM: *Record World* records David's new deal, published 16 October.

In this year...

Tuesday 13 August
MURDER in New York of saxophonist King Curtis, aged 37. Curtis was an early hero of David's.

THIS PAGE

TOP: Gem Management New York point-person and MainMan vice president Tony Zanetta (far right), playing Warhol in *Pork* in 1971. Future MainMan PR Cherry Vanilla kneels behind him.

ABOVE: "It's Andrew Warhola actually." Andy Warhol, in the late 60s.

OPPOSITE PAGE

TOP: Aylesbury Friars, September. Between songs, unsurprisingly, David's main topics were the US and New York: "Anyway, that's where we're going. America – land of the living, land of the dead. They've got lots of murders, killings as you probably read about in the papers."

MIDDLE: David's set list notes, probably drawn up from memory after the gig for Tony Defries to collect his songwriters' performance fee, but it is slightly inaccurate.

BOTTOM: Just before opening his set with 'Fill Your Heart', David comments: "As you all know, it's a long way down. Anyway, I'm back..."

In this year...

Tuesday 14 September
SIGNING of Iggy Pop to Tony Defries' Gem Music Publishing, in his birth-name James Newell Osterberg.

Tuesday 12 October
DEATH of Gene Vincent in Hollywood from heart failure, aged 36. Vincent had considered recording David's 'Hang On To Yourself'.

albums, has come to an apparent dead-end.

1. 'Queen Bitch' was written under the influence of The Velvet Underground's 1970 album *Loaded*.

Friday 10 September

Pop joins David and Defries for a breakfast meeting at the Warwick where they discuss the latter taking over management of his career while options are sought for a new record deal.

Pop is given a room at the hotel next to Ronson's, where he locks himself away and embarks on a strict physical regimen in an attempt to kick his serious heroin addiction.

Tony Zanetta[1] takes David to meet Andy Warhol[2] at his studio, The Factory, in the Decker Building, 33 Union Square West (the meeting is a culmination of Ken Pitt's foresight. Having visited Warhol's studio in 1966 he then introduced David to the artist and The Velvet Underground).

David is accompanied by Angie, Ronson and Defries, the last pitching to arrange UK distribution of Warhol's films with the pop artist's film director and collaborator Paul Morrissey.

For the majority of their time at The Factory, David and Angie sit quietly on a couch while Defries also tells Morrissey about David's wish that Warhol accompany him on a US tour, just as he did for dates by The Velvet Underground in the 60s.

"Tony says (about David), 'We think he's gonna go through the roof. He's big,'" said Morrissey in 1996. "'And RCA has given me a lot of money, so my idea to promote Bowie is that Andy Warhol come with us on the US tour.'

"There's Andy in one corner, and this shy little Bowie thing in another corner – they're sort of eyeing each other across the room, and here's Defries proposing that Andy be paid as a groupie!

"It was all stupid – to take a fee for promoting somebody if you're not part of it, just because Defries wanted David Bowie to be the next Velvet Underground. So I said, 'Gee, I don't think so. We're just a little too busy right now.'"

David gives the artist an acetate of 'Andy Warhol', but Warhol isn't sure how to respond to it and leaves the room for a while without saying a word.

"I wasn't aware that, like most of us, Warhol was very sensitive about what people said about him," said David in 1993. "I'd bought the whole pop-art thing that he wasn't a real person, that he was just this creation."

In fact Warhol will come to intensely dislike the song. "He hated it so much he always made us change stations when it came on the radio," wrote Warhol associate Bob Colacello in 1999. "'Can he use my name without permission?' he would ask. 'Shouldn't he pay us royalties?'"

The encounter is stilted. There is no conversation between David and Warhol for an hour, so the artist's friends start talking among themselves.

A cameraman shoots a black and white video in

which both Warhol and David look noticeably bored. "He had nothing to say at all, absolutely nothing," said David in 1999.[3]

Just as the meeting appears to be at an end, Warhol notices David's Anello & Davide yellow buckled shoes. The former footwear illustrator and shoe collector takes a number of Polaroids of David, focusing on the Anello & Davide creations.

Peeling the negative from each photo, Warhol sets them out carefully on a table. Before leaving, David is coerced into taking one of Warhol's celebrated 'screen tests', in which a camera is directed at an individual and they are left to their own devices. David attempts a few basic mime moves.[4]

Later in the evening, David and Ronson meet Lou Reed at Max's Kansas City.

1. "He [Zanetta] got in real quick with that one," Leee Black Childers said in 1985, referring to the introduction to Warhol.

2. The Andy Warhol Museum notes the meeting taking place on 14 September but it is more likely that it took place on this date.

3. David and Warhol met many more times before the artist's death in February 1987. David played Warhol in fellow New York artist Julian Schnabel's *Basquiat*, his 1996 biopic of their doomed friend and sometime Warhol collaborator, Jean-Michel Basquiat.

4. Far from being a disaster the Factory visit proves to be a turning point in David's career. Within a month of meeting Warhol he begins to radically change his image and by November plans for a new sound, styling and hairstyle are underway. Stage costumes and a slick new show are also planned.

After David had found great success, he gave his friend Mark Pritchett a book about Warhol, telling him "This is what started it all."

Tuesday 21 September

Back in London after their eventful American trip, David and Mick Ronson record an acoustic set for Radio One's *Sounds of the 70s* slot at Kensington House studios in Richmond Way, Hammersmith, west London.

The session is produced by John Muir, who initially asks David to perform a solo set and arranges for him and Ronson to be paid £15 and £10 respectively.

Ken Scott approves an acetate of David's new album, which is still without a title. Although close to the final running order, it doesn't include 'Eight Line Poem' and the length of some tracks has yet to be finalised.[1]

1. Side One: **1** 'Changes' (as LP) **2** 'Oh! You Pretty Things' (longer version) **3** 'Life On Mars?' (as LP) **4** 'Kooks' (as LP) **5** 'Quicksand' (much longer).
Side Two: **1** 'Fill Your Heart' (much longer) **2** 'Andy Warhol' (shorter) **3** 'Song For Bob Dylan' (as LP) **4** 'Queen Bitch' (as LP) **5** 'The Bewlay Brothers' (much longer).

Saturday 25 September

▶ David Bowie, The Friars Club, Borough Assembly Hall, Aylesbury, Bucks.

David and Angie travel with Ronson and Woodmansey to Aylesbury for their first gig with Bolder, who arrives at the venue with former Rats roadie, Pete Hunsley.[1]

"They had all been to Kensington Market and had new jeans, fashionable wooden clogs, the lot," said Bolder in 1995. "I really felt out of it, so I borrowed Pete Hunsley's jeans. He was about 6ft 2in and I was about four sizes smaller, so it looked like I had clown's feet.

"This was one of the first times David put on some make-up – though not as much as he had done on the Peel radio show – and suggested we should think about doing the same."

With Angie working the lights again, the quartet are accompanied by pianist Tom Parker (who has previously played with The Animals).[2] Support acts are saxophonist Lol Coxhill,[3] folk singer Mick Softly and an unbilled Tucky Buzzard.

Billed as the 'Only current British appearance of David Bowie', this was due to have been a co-headliner with America, who are managed by his DJ friend Jeff Dexter and have pulled out.[4]

With the club filled to its capacity of around 250 people (with many sitting cross-legged on the floor in the manner of the day), David performs some songs solo in the style of his appearances in late 1969 and early 1970, as well as others with Ronson on bass and electric guitar and six tracks with the full band.

In the Friars[5] audience are archivist, author and *ZigZag* magazine founder Pete Frame and local lad and Queen drummer Roger Taylor, who recalled in 2002 that David "had long hair and wore a dress" (in fact he is wearing his voluminous Oxford bags).

The set is similar to that played by the group at London's Country Club in the summer, with the addition of 'Space Oddity', and The Arnold Corns number 'Looking For A Friend', as well as new songs 'Changes' and 'Queen Bitch' and covers of Chuck Berry's 'Round And Round' and The Velvet Underground's 'I'm Waiting For The Man'.

"David was very friendly and jokey with the audience," said Frame in 1992. "It was a great performance."

Before the show, club promoter Dave Stopps' wife Budget talks to David about his song 'Star', since a version has now been recorded by local band Chameleon at the suggestion of publisher Bob Grace.

Defries requests that David's £150 performance fee be paid in cash. Stopps acquiesces, and pays the full amount in 50p pieces.

1. Pete Hunsley was David's stage manager until early 1974. Hunsley is photographed backstage with David in the Bowie/Rock book *Moonage Daydream* on page 206.

2. An ex-member of The Mark Leeman 5, in 1972 Parker was a member of Apollo 100, who reached the Top Ten in the UK that year with single 'Joy'.

3. Born Portsmouth 1932, Coxhill was a freeform jazz performer and London street entertainer. "David would occasionally say hello to me when I was busking. He was always very friendly with me," said Coxhill in 1999. "Years later he pulled up in a limo and got out for a chat."

4. The following January, America's 'Horse With No Name' reached number three in the UK singles chart.

5. Friars opened in 1969; promoter Dave Stopps was a local record shop owner and entrepreneur who managed British synth-pop star Howard Jones in the 80s.

Sunday 26 September

▶ David Bowie & Mick Ronson, the Roundhouse, London NW1.

This is another Implosion night promoted by Jeff Dexter with Ian Knight, and also on the bill are Sam Apple Pie, Hackensack,[1] Tír na nÓg and Day.

This is David's last appearance at the Camden venue, though he and Ronson give a couple of other performances as a duo around this time, including a pub gig at which they both wear dresses. In 1986 Ronson said that his only concern was that his gown "was straight at the back".

1. Hackensack's line-up included drummer Simon Fox, a member of British 70s post-glam group Be Bop Deluxe.

Monday 27 September

Mercury Records issues a 'termination' contract, freeing David from the label on the basis that it receives the $17,884.41 calculated to have been its investment in his career.

Significantly, the agreement grants Gem ownership of the masters of both Mercury albums, which Defries licenses to RCA for an advance of $20,000.

In a separate move, Gem pays David's Arts Lab friend, puppeteer Brian Moore, to work on a project called *Curbie & The Princess*. Moore stores his puppets at Haddon Hall for a period.

Monday 4 October

▶ David Bowie & Mick Ronson, Seymour Hall, Seymour Place, London W1.[1]

Tonight is a benefit for homosexual campaign group the Gay Liberation Front. Also on the bill are Third World War, Good Habit and The People Band.

In the evening, Radio One broadcasts the *Sounds Of The 70s* session recorded on 21 September. This is hosted by DJ Bob Harris and produced by John Muir, whom radio plugger Anya Wilson[2] credits with championing David's new direction at an important juncture in his career.

"It had been really hard to get anyone on radio or TV to acknowledge David's new material at the time," said Wilson in 2001. "John Muir kept his door open for me and became a real ally of mine and David's. I credit him with helping to get others interested in David again."

1. This is the last documented live appearance by David and Ronson as a duo.

2. On 5 October John Muir receives flowers from a grateful Wilson, who writes on the card: 'For John, I'll never forget you for being the first.'

Friday 15 October

Mickie Most's label RAK releases Peter Noone's version of David's song 'Right On Mother' with 'Walnut Whirl' as a double A-side single. This will fail to replicate the success of Noone's version of 'Oh! You Pretty Things'.

Tuesday 19 October

Gem presses a preview copy of the new album, now entitled *Hunky Dory,* with a final track listing and mix.

The following day, in a letter to Mickie Most, Tony Defries offers 'Bombers' as a potential single or

TOP: David's new haircut.

MIDDLE: David with Angela.

BOTTOM: Trevor Bolder also cut David's hair in November 71. This new hairstyle was modified in January 72 for the *Ziggy Stardust* album photo session, but already hints at this new style.

album track for Peter Noone, enclosing an acetate of the song.

Tuesday 26 October

Following a meeting with Christopher Lee (who has ambitions to record an album), Gem's Laurence Myers sends a draft contract with a covering letter to the British horror film actor's address in Mayfair's Cadogan Square: 'I would like you to listen to the enclosed records that were written and produced by David Bowie, who is also the artist. I think David has the talent and imagination to come up with something for you. Perhaps you will be kind enough to give me a ring when you have had a chance to hear the records and we could maybe arrange a meeting between David and yourself.'

David and Lee subsequently meet. 'We both got on very well together and after David had played a bit on his guitar and I had sung, he asked me if I would like to make records with him,' wrote Lee in 2003.

'I said that I would be delighted to do so, providing we could find the right material and this is where the whole idea came to a dead stop.'

At this time David and his band are wrapped up in two weeks of rehearsals before commencing recording of *Hunky Dory*'s follow-up, *Ziggy Stardust*.

These are held at Underhill, a two-roomed rehearsal studio literally sited under the hill in Blackheath, south-east London, not far from Beckenham in the basement of a chemist shop at 1-3 Blackheath Road.

The studio proprietor is Will Palin,[1] who has converted the space from a Co-op grocery store, and charges just £1 an hour.

1. Palin became a member of David's road crew in 1972–1973.

Tuesday 2 November

In a letter to Mr J. Morris, manager of north London's newly reopened art deco Rainbow Theatre,[1] Defries proposes the venue book David and his band for an appearance.

Defries says that David is interested in seeing new US shock-rocker Alice Cooper's forthcoming performance at the Rainbow:

'David has expressed considerable interest in seeing Alice Cooper who I understand is appearing on the 7th November and I will arrange for my office to book tickets. I should like you to meet David as he is very interested in this type of project.'

1. Opened as a lavishly appointed Astoria cinema in 1930, this was also an Odeon and in the 60s a music venue. On reopening in 1971, the Rainbow became a London rock landmark as the site of

performances by The Who, Bob Marley & The Wailers, The Clash, and David and the Spiders From Mars before closure in 1982. Since 1995 it has been a religious temple.

Sunday 7 November

David and his bandmates are at the Rainbow for Alice Cooper's theatrical stageshow,[1] which is performed complete with lurid make-up and outrageous set-pieces including one where Cooper wraps his body in his pet boa constrictor.

British shock-rocker Arthur Brown is support for this, the last night of the band's European Love It To Death tour.

"It was very theatrical and we all thought it was great, but David said, 'Wait till you see what we can do,'" recalled Trevor Bolder in 1995.

Cooper's act assists David in persuading his colleagues to adopt more flamboyant appearances on stage.

"They were wearing make-up and were a really heavy band," said Bolder. "The music was great, I thought at the time, and it looked good, so we went along with it too. It was a big jump from being a blues band in T-shirts and jeans, long hair and beards to wearing make-up and flashy clothes."

1. This has been incorrectly listed as taking place the night before, 6 November.

Monday 8 November

With *Hunky Dory* being readied for release in less than two weeks, recording begins at Trident on new tracks, engineered by Mike Stone,[1] 'Rock'n'Roll Star' and 'Hang On To Yourself' for its successor *Ziggy Stardust*.

"You're not going to like it, it's much more like Iggy Pop," David tells co-producer Ken Scott about the rougher, rock sound he is aiming for.

1. Stone was later engineer on recordings by Queen and co-produced Queen's 1977 *News Of The World* album.

Wednesday 10 November

After two days, David is unhappy with the results and the work recorded so far is scrapped.

"At first David brought demos which Mick, Woody and I re-did," said Bolder in 1995. "But David thought that it didn't sound right, so we started again."

Thursday 11 November

A busy day at Trident as the musicians re-record several takes of 'Star'[1] and 'Hang On To Yourself'.[2]

They also record takes of 'Looking For A Friend', 'Velvet Goldmine'[3] and 'Sweet Head'.[4]

"We recorded a lot of material," said Woodmansey in 1994. "A lot of it didn't work and was scrapped, but over the years turned into something else. Like the song he recorded with Queen, 'Under Pressure'. I recognised that melody line from a very early idea we worked on but never used. There must be a lot of material around still."[5]

1. Titled on the tape-box 'Rock 'n' Roll Star'. This tape also contains take 10 of the song 'Ziggy Stardust'.
2. Take 8 is the released version on the album *Ziggy Stardust*.
3. This appeared on an RCA maxi-single released in 1975. The original song was 'He's A Goldmine'.
4. Take 7 of this appeared on the 1990 reissue of *Ziggy Stardust*.
5. A demoed and unreleased track from 1971 is 'Don't Be Afraid'.

Friday 12 November

Two takes of 'Moonage Daydream', one take of 'Soul Love', two takes of 'The Supermen'[1] and two of 'Lady Stardust' are recorded at Trident.

1. One of these appeared on 1972's triple album *The Glastonbury Fayre*.

Monday 15 November

'Five Years', 'It's Gonna Rain Again'[1] and 'Shadow Man'[2] are recorded at Trident, but all but the first will remain unfinished.

The opening line of 'Five Years', 'Pushing thru the market square', is likely to have been inspired by Aylesbury's picturesque Market Square, site of the Friars club.

A running order for *Ziggy Stardust* is drawn up, including songs which won't make the final release: Chuck Berry's 'Round And Round' and Jacques Brel's 'Amsterdam', a new version of 'Holy Holy' and 'Velvet Goldmine'.

Absent from the list is the rousing version of Ron Davies' 'It Ain't Easy' recorded during the *Hunky Dory* sessions. During recording sessions, publicist Dai Davies is invited to Haddon Hall to discuss plans for a forthcoming tour over dinner. David tells Davies that he plans to reveal his bisexuality to the press.

"That night David convinced me he was going to be massive," said Davies in 1998. "I was really flattered to be included in his plans."

Photographs taken at Haddon Hall of David at home with Angie and Zowie reveal that David is preparing for the transformation into his new Ziggy persona, having had his hair cut by the former hairdresser Trevor Bolder. The feather cut retains the length at the back and sides and the crown is cut shorter for maximum effect.

1. The title was inspired by the looped vocal recording 'It's Gonna Rain' from experimental composer Steve Reich's 1965 album *Live/Electric Music* (also an influence on David's 70s collaborator Brian Eno).
2. In 2000 David re-recorded 'Shadow Man' for *Toy*, the unissued album of new versions of his own early compositions. This was released as a bonus track on the 2002 CD single 'Slow Burn'.

Wednesday 17 November

Hunky Dory is released by RCA in the UK and is out this month in the US, where it is greeted with a feature in rock magazine *Creem* headed 'David Bowie – The Rock Oddity'.

Sunday 21 November

Tony Defries forwards a copy of *Hunky Dory* to A&M Records with a suggestion: 'I personally feel that the fourth track on side one entitled 'Kooks' would make a tremendous single for The Carpenters as it has not been released by David in the US.'

Monday 22 November

It seems that producer Mickie Most is considering repromoting Peter Noone's recent single with David's song as the lead track. Bob Grace writes to Defries: 'At long last, Mickie Most has decided to go wholeheartedly on 'Right On Mother' as the A-side of Peter's current single.'

Tuesday 23 November

The plans for David and actor Christopher Lee to collaborate on an album come to nothing. Lee, in Panama City, Mexico, receives an abrupt telegram from Gem: 'Cancel Bowie session.'

On 25 November photographer Brian Ward and his studio team prepare press kits for the promotion of *Hunky Dory*; these are widely distributed in the US.

Monday 4 December

Hunky Dory is released in the US. In an extremely positive review, music business bible *Billboard* hails the album as 'a heavy debut for RCA, loaded with the kind of Top 40 and FM appeal that should break him through big on the charts. Strong material, his own, for programming includes "Changes", "Oh! You Pretty Things", and "Life On Mars?".'

During December 'Changes'/'Andy Warhol' is released in the US.

Monday 17 December

David's contract with RCA is amended to accommodate licensing the two Mercury albums from Gem.

Saturday 25 December

David, Angie and Zowie spend Christmas in Cyprus with her parents. It is David's first visit to the island[1] and the first time he has met his in-laws. During the trip David drives Angela to Lefkara to buy the local speciality, hand-made lace, for covering their dining table and bedroom vanity unit at Haddon Hall.

For the trip, David has his hair cut again so that it is much shorter at the back and sides. Although it is without a particular style and in his natural light brown, the switch from the Greta Garbo look which has dominated this year is but one indicator of the changes to be rung – not only to David's appearance – over the coming months

1. Although a Cypriot driving licence application form was completed in 1970 with David's details, this was filled out by Angie when she travelled to Cyprus without David.

TOP: David and Zowie in Cyprus, Christmas 1971.

MIDDLE: Alice Cooper – David's biggest rival in rock theatre. David would later replace Cooper's boa constrictor with a feather version.

BOTTOM: Puppeteer Brian Moore and Angela Bowie.

ABOVE: *Hunky Dory* UK LP sleeve. Photography by Brian Ward, concept by David, artwork by Terry Pastor – partner of George Underwood at Main Artery.

HUNKY DORY Released Friday 17 December

Side One

1. Changes (Bowie) (3.33)
David Bowie (vocal, alto and tenor sax)
Mick Ronson (guitar, vocal)
Trevor Bolder (bass)
Woody Woodmansey (drums)
Rick Wakeman (piano)
String ensemble
(Arranged by Mick Ronson)

2. Oh! You Pretty Things (Bowie) (3.12)
David Bowie (vocal, piano)
Mick Ronson (guitar, vocal)
Trevor Bolder (bass)
Woody Woodmansey (drums)

3. Eight Line Poem (Bowie) (2.53)
David Bowie (vocal, phased piano)
Mick Ronson (guitar)

4. Life On Mars? (Bowie) (3.48)
David Bowie (vocal)
Mick Ronson (guitar, Mellotron)
Trevor Bolder (bass)
Woody Woodmansey (drums)
Rick Wakeman (piano)
String ensemble
(Arranged by Mick Ronson)

5. Kooks (Bowie) (2.49)
David Bowie (vocal, guitar)
Mick Ronson (guitar, vocal)
Trevor Bolder (bass, trumpet)
Woody Woodmansey (drums)
Rick Wakeman (piano)
String ensemble
(Arranged by Mick Ronson)

6. Quicksand (Bowie) (5.03)
David Bowie (vocal, guitar)
Mick Ronson (guitar)
Trevor Bolder (bass)
Woody Woodmansey (drums)
Rick Wakeman (piano)
String ensemble
(Arranged by Mick Ronson)

Side Two

1. Fill Your Heart (Rose/Williams) (3.07)
David Bowie (vocal, sax)
Trevor Bolder (bass)
Woody Woodmansey (brushes)
Rick Wakeman (piano)
String ensemble
(Arranged by Mick Ronson)

2. Andy Warhol (Bowie) (3.58)
David Bowie (vocal, guitar)
Mick Ronson (guitar, vocal)
Ken Scott (spoken intro, ARP synth)

3. Song For Bob Dylan (Bowie) (4.12)
David Bowie (vocal, guitar)
Mick Ronson (guitar, vocal)
Trevor Bolder (bass)
Woody Woodmansey (drums)
Rick Wakeman (piano)

4. Queen Bitch (Bowie) (3.13)
David Bowie (vocal, guitar)
Mick Ronson (guitar, vocal)
Trevor Bolder (bass)
Woody Woodmansey (drums)

5. The Bewlay Brothers (Bowie) (5.21)
David Bowie (vocal, guitar, treated piano)
Mick Ronson (guitar, vocal)

Produced by Ken Scott (assisted by The Actor)
Recorded at Trident Studios
(RCA SF8244)

LEFT TO RIGHT: *Hunky Dory* producer Ken Scott. *Hunky Dory* advertising (middle), complete with David's hand-written explanation of each track. Far right, David in Oxford Bags "My Evelyn Waugh/Oxbridge' look...".

ABOVE: The original black and white image transferred to a sepia card and hand-coloured by artist Terry Pastor. MIDDLE: *Hunky Dory* session out-take. FAR RIGHT: Greta Garbo inspired David's second album sleeve in a row.

Suffused with David's first-hand experiences of America, *Hunky Dory* consolidated the role of Mick Ronson as his indispensable sideman of the period and provided a brief snapshot of the live set they worked up between them in 1971.

The sessions were completed quickly, particularly since nearly half were recorded in order to secure the RCA deal and most had been sculpted during demo sessions at Radio Luxembourg's central London studios and rehearsals at Haddon Hall.

In August 1971, David discussed how his approach to songwriting had changed: "Two years ago I used to be the most serious of serious people. I used to come out with great drooling epics which were really tedious and boring.

"Since I got back from the States my material has become a lot lighter. Before I went over there I used to think that I had problems! I decided it wasn't worth singing about myself so instead I decided to write songs about anything that came to mind."

And he said of *Hunky Dory*: "It's been the easiest album I've ever done. It's been gloriously easy to record, certainly the best stuff I've been involved with. And there's a vast difference between this and *The Man Who Sold The World*. This one is a totally different concept."

Listening to a playback of one of his new *Hunky Dory* tracks in the control room at Trident Studios. The polaroid was taken by Rodney Bingemheimer during his first trip to London.

A confidence booster had been the spring 1971 success of Peter Noone's single version of 'Oh! You Pretty Things', and its inclusion on *Hunky Dory* displayed David's newly acquired self-assurance as a songwriter.

Meanwhile 'Life On Mars?' (with its title addendum 'inspired by Frankie') referenced a time when his compositional abilities were not so widely recognised – 1968, when his lyric for the Claude François song which became 'My Way' was rejected by the French publisher.

In 1972 David announced that he had written 'Life On Mars?' around the same chord sequence as 'My Way'.

"I couldn't believe those lyrics. You know, I'll get pissed my way, and I'll knock you about the place my way, and you're gonna dig it

my way. Really evil. I love the arrangement on 'Mars'."

David's gift for bringing together influences and references came to the fore with the inclusion of the line 'Look at those cavemen go' from the Hollywood Argyles' 1960 hit 'Alley Oop', produced by Kim Fowley, to whom he had been introduced in California at the start of 1971.

It was during this trip that David wrote the thought-provoking and powerfully delivered side one closer 'Quicksand', and also witnessed a performance by the singer Biff Rose, who co-wrote *Hunky Dory*'s 'Fill Your Heart' with songwriter/actor Paul Williams.

'Fill Your Heart' first appeared on Rose's 1968 album *Biff Rose Is The Thorn In Mrs Rose's Side* on Tetragrammaton Records, and featured as the B-side to that year's hit by Tiny Tim, 'Tiptoe Through The Tulips'.

Rose's album also featured 'Buzz The Fuzz', covered by David in concert and sometimes accidentally accredited to him.

In fact, as David's writing became more piano-oriented in early 1971, his approach and delivery began to reveal a definite Rose influence.

Another powerful musical figure is the subject of 'Song For Bob Dylan', not so much a homage as a lament for his past form, pastiching his 1962 'Song To Woody' and expressing David's frustration with his 70s direction.

When they met in 1973, David spent most of the conversation telling Dylan what he should be doing and where he was going wrong. Just as he had after meeting another hero, Andy Warhol, he came away

frustrated (though his Warhol encounter spurred his creativity).

"The lyrics in that song are not my thoughts," said David in 1971. "It's just that people had told me they felt angry at Dylan for deserting them and I felt it was the moment to write a song about that."

Like *Hunky Dory*'s other 'tribute' track, 'Andy Warhol', 'Song For Bob Dylan' was inspired by blues singer Ron Davies and in particular his compositions 'Lover And The Loved' and 'Silent Song Through The Land' (the guitar riff of which drove 'Andy Warhol' and the end of which was appropriated for the climax of 'Song For Bob Dylan').

Another song title that may have caught David's eye from *Silent Song Through The Land* (also the title of the album) was 'Change'.

These days Davies, from Shreveport, Louisiana, is best remembered for his much covered spiritual 'It Ain't Easy' (which David intended for *Hunky Dory* but included on *Ziggy Stardust*).

During the *Hunky Dory* sessions 'Song For Bob Dylan' was recorded by George Underwood, who performed it on the June 1971 Radio One broadcast. This has never been issued.

David designed the intriguing album closer 'The Bewlay Brothers' mainly to engage and perplex American journalists, whom he found were over-analysing his lyrics.

On this he had a field day painting metaphors and laying false trails. Many concur that its central theme is his relationship with half-brother Terry Burns, and these days David maintains this is true, but this wasn't always so.

This is nevertheless a magnificent work, paying tribute to a brother lost to mental illness many years before his death in 1985.

With a direct link to the back cover of the UK issue of previous album *The Man Who Sold The World*, *Hunky Dory*'s cover image took its cue from photographs of Greta Garbo, finished off with Pre-Raphaelite colouring flourishes.

The image of David was taken by Brian Ward at his Heddon Street photographic studio in central London, where he later captured Ziggy Stardust in all his glory.

George Underwood and his business partner Terry Pastor retouched the image by colour tinting a 12-in square black and white print on a cartridge stock (this technique also being used on *Ziggy Stardust*). Pastor actually airbrushed the cover at his flat in Blackheath, south London, where he worked from a small home studio.

On the rear of the sleeve, in his neatest left-handed script, David wrote out the song titles and acknowledgments. For the arrangement of 'Fill Your Heart', he added: 'Mick and I agree that the 'Fill Your Heart' arrangement owes one hell of a lot to Arthur G. Wright and his proto-type'.

Arthur G. Wright had made the original arrangement for the Biff Rose album which became such a rich source of musical ideas.

The original US *Hunky Dory* front cover[1] featured the framed hand-

tinted photo design without text. The title was printed on a sticker and applied to the cellophane wrapping. Its 1971 UK counterpart, although based on US-supplied film separations, included the album title and artist's name on the cover. Initial UK pressings, now quite sought after, were laminated, which enhanced the front cover's colour to create a superior finish.

Hunky Dory's advertising campaign was hampered when RCA was informed that David would soon be altering his image. "We soon knew we were in a situation where the artist was going to change like a chameleon from time to time," said the label's marketing manager Geoff Hannington in 1986.

With Tony Visconti out of the frame following disagreement over David's appointment of Tony Defries as manager, the recording of *Hunky Dory* saw engineer Ken Scott step up to the plate as a key figure in realising the sound of David's early 70s work.

Trained as one of EMI's engineers, Scott had learnt his trade under the tutelage of George Martin at Abbey Road.

"I started there just as The Beatles started recording side one of *A Hard Day's Night*," Scott said in 1999.

Moving on to work with Jeff Beck, Procol Harum, The Hollies and The Pink Floyd, in the late 60s Scott was invited by Gus Dudgeon to join newly opened Trident, the only facility in London at that time to offer eight-track recording, which had been set up by brothers Barry and Norman Sheffield.

Scott was taken on as a partner in an associated company called Nereus and worked on the 1969 *David Bowie* album and *The Man Who Sold The World*.

"I came into Bowie's life when I did some engineering for him on some of those early sessions," said Scott in 2002. "He could see that I was bored, so he asked me to become his co-producer. I was knocked out."

In turn, David was impressed with Scott's professionalism.

"I'd been used to engineers like Ken Scott," he said in 1993. "You know, who goes home to his wife at night, tie and shirt, a very professional person. Sort of my George Martin in a way."

Scott also co-produced *Ziggy Stardust*, *Aladdin Sane* and *Pin Ups*, and in gratitude David presented him with an inscribed chunky gold bracelet.

Yet it is the sum total of *Hunky Dory*'s Anglo-American pop art mix (with the songs delivered throughout in an unmistakably English accent) which makes this album David's first true masterpiece.

And the title has much more prosaic roots than some of its content. It was suggested by publisher Bob Grace and appealed since this Americanism was a rarely used idiom in Britain at the time. Grace subsequently said he picked up the expression from the landlord of the

TOP: A costume experiment arranged and photographed by Brian Ward. BELOW: (clockwise from top left): Lou Reed, whose Velvet Underground influence was acknowledged on 'Queen Bitch', Bob Dylan, Frank Sinatra, part-inspiration for 'Life On Mars?', Biff Rose, composer of 'Fill Your Heart', Greta Garbo ('I'm the twisted name on Garbo's eyes,' – 'Quicksand'), Andy Warhol 'like hole hole'.

Bear public house in Esher, where he sometimes drank.

1. US copies featured the lyrics printed on the inner sleeve, not a separate sheet. The lyric artwork and setting were also subtly different to its UK counterpart.

Saturday 25 December

Disc and Music Echo review *Hunky Dory*. 'Forget the "Spacey" David and Enjoy This Offering'.

'As one of our more talented eccentrics, it's to be hoped that his songs will have as much success for himself as they have for other people. He has included 'Oh You Pretty Things' with an arrangement not too different from Peter Noone's. However, his voice makes the difference, being sharper and more effective. He has used Rick Wakeman on piano, not being too confident of his own ability in that field, and the musicians from the abortive group he tried to get off the ground a few months ago. They seem to have reached the right understanding of Bowie's songs, but unless they get radio airing and Bowie doesn't take them out in concert, he may well lose out again.'

ABOVE: Aleister Crowley (1875–1947), controversial English occultist and writer. David namechecks Crowley on *Hunky Dory* in 'Quicksand' (I'm closer to the Golden Dawn, immersed in Crowley's uniform of imagery...). In 1976, David also referenced the author on the title track of his album *Station To Station*, namely Crowley's 1895 book of erotic poetry *White Stains*.

CHANGES reviews

50¢

December 15, 1971

HUNKY DORY
DAVID BOWIE
RCA LSP-4623

Mr David Bowie is not just another pretty face. And that's saying something in an age in which beauty is only skin deep, and more than enough to get anybody almost anything. David's flaxen hair, his piercing blue eyes, his blush red lips, have made him the inevitable envy of the world's aspiring starlets. Happily, however, these purely physical traits are attached to a sensibility, and that special Essence of David makes *Hunky Dory* a special record indeed.

I am sure that, one day, the fist of the Almighty invaded the boy's skull, plucked his brain from his cranium, and after gingerly admiring and caressing it, decided it was too precious to share, and smashed it to smithereens. The result is much like the outpouring of a gayly colored kaleidoscope, fragmented but dazzling, jagged bits and pieces of unusually shaped objects, incessantly changing patterns with every gust of wind, each one a very special Bowie song.

These special musical crystals seem to be made of the hallmarks of the age and culture in which Bowie lives and functions. They also possess the timelessness that always marks the work of the true balladeer Bowie is a pop overso.l, introspecting the environment and helping to create 'i through his very special reverberations. It is not surprising that his voice can easily transform itself into Dylan's or even Tiny Tim's while maintaining its own distinctive sense of truth. The fragmented environment is the perfecting hunting ground for the contemporary artist of fragmentation.

David is Greta Garbo, and Bob Dylan, he is Andy Warhol, and Winston Churchill. He creates a self-legend composed of legends; his unique *personnae* is based on the fact that he understands contemporary phenomena. That kind of crinkly intelligence is, in itself, phenomenal. Listen to his Chanson de David, "The Bewlay Brothers." Observe how Bowie leads his listeners through journey which is traditional psychic narrative, and yet is a purely personal and well-observed journey Notice that "Queen Bitch" frankly states that its author-voyeur-progenitor states that he could probably drag it up better than the drag acts on the street.

Drag is important to David Bowie. It is one way of pulling the pieces of a slivered mind into a whole, which is itself another sparkling illustration of fragmentation. Bowie writes: "Time may change me/But I can't trace time." It is a peculiarly sensitive, hard-edged, precise, and truly shimmering perception.

Yes, folks, David Bowie is not just another pretty face.

by Henry Ed wards

'David is Greta Garbo, and Bob Dylan; he is Andy Warhol and Winston Churchill. He creates a self-legend composed of legends, his unique persona is based on the fact that he understands contemporary phenomena.'
Changes magazine

NEW MUSICAL EXPRESS ALBUMS
Bowie at his brilliant best

DAVID BOWIE: " Hunky Dory" (RCA Victor SF 8244; £2.29.)

January 29, 1972

DAVID BOWIE is a million different people and each one is a bit more lovely than the one before. But for Christ's sake don't think he's a gimmick or a hype! Instead, enjoy him as he is; a surreal cartoon character brought to life for us all to enjoy.

Apart from all that, David Bowie has delivered " Hunky Dory," an album which is a breath of fresh air compared to the usual mainstream rock LP of today. It's very possible that this will be the most important album from an emerging artist in 1972, because he's not following trends — he's setting them.

Changes is a fantastic pop song, even if Tony Blackburn does play it. Changes is Bowie's life story. All he ever does is change. That's why there's never an identifiable direction. He's everything, all at once. Every song is a different side of Bowie and the world he sees.

Oh! You Pretty Things is a completely different story from Peter Noone's bopper version, until you hear that catchy chorus which gets an extra push from drummer Woody Woodmansey. Eight Line Poem mellows the mood to prepare the listener for the intense emotionalism of Life On Mars. David's painting the picture as he pleads in top form: Is there life on Mars? The strings help to pull you into his comic strip of life.

Kooks is dedicated to Zowie Bowie, David's seven-month old son. He takes the position of a dad who has good old-fashioned love for his family. As of yet, Quicksand, the final cut on side one, hasn't reached me yet. but I'll give it time.

Fill Your Heart is a pleasant, light little ditty which originated from the pen of Biff Rose (the only song not written by Bow Wow). There's a nice acoustic guitar riff running through Andy Warhol, with a catchy chorus for all you simpletons. (Don't worry, we're all there). David wrote a Song For Bob Dylan, asking him to come out of hiding as well as managing to sound quite a lot like the real

thing.

Queen Bitch is the perverted Velvet Underground-ish shitty city song, complete with Mick Ronson's powerhouse guitar. It's high energy all the way as Bowie camps Lou Reed out of existance. But it's a tribute, not a put-down. The Bewlay Brothers closes the album with turned-on, mind-warping session with Mr Bowie at the helm, directing and misdirecting and telling us where it's at and lying etc. etc. It's all good fun.

Anyone who believes in pop music enough to wish to save it from swallowing it's own excretion should buy this album. " Hunky Dory" is a masterpiece from a mastermind. — D. H.

MIDDLE LEFT: Henry Edwards *Hunky Dory* review, *Changes* magazine, 15 December. RIGHT: Detail from *Hunky Dory* advert featuring David's hand-written comments about each song on *Hunky Dory*. ABOVE: *Hunky Dory* NME review, 29 January 1972.

1972

DAVID sees Kubrick's *A Clockwork Orange* and, ahead of a photoshoot that will give birth to one of the most celebrated album covers of all time, garners valuable style ideas.

The revelation of his bisexuality makes headlines as he and the band, clad in new glam costumes, kick off a tour that will unveil the Ziggy Stardust character and make David a superstar.

An extraordinary *Old Grey Whistle Test* appearance is followed by the release of 'Starman' as a single and the first appearance of *Hunky Dory* in a US chart.

Meanwhile, David and Mick Ronson are working with Mott The Hoople on 'All The Young Dudes', a single that will revivify the flagging rockers.

The word is out, and disappointed fans are being turned away from sell-out shows. David drapes an arm around Ronson as he sings 'Starman' on *Top Of The Pops*.

The album *The Rise and Fall of Ziggy Stardust and The Spiders From Mars* is launched and starts selling immediately.

Lindsay Kemp is working with David once again for three spectacular shows at London's Rainbow Theatre that confirms David's star status.

David sets sail for New York and embarks on a tour that will see him zigzagging across the US by Greyhound bus and train. He is, according to one American critic, a 'certified, genuine, blue-ribbon star'.

Lou Reed's celebrated *Transformer* album, co-produced by David and Ronson, is released and David makes the cover of *Rolling Stone* magazine.

'The Jean Genie' follows 'John, I'm Only Dancing' into the charts as earlier work of David's is rush re-released.

By year-end, *Ziggy Stardust* has sold close to 100,000 UK copies and Bowiemania has gripped the nation.

PREVIOUS SPREAD: "The idea of fame was an obsession - until it happened." Ziggy's first photo call, January 1972. Photo by Brian Ward.

THIS PAGE

TOP: The first and original Ziggy quilted suit. Inspired by Kubrick, designed by David and Burretti and made at Haddon Hall by seamstress Sue Frost.

ABOVE: German issue of 'Changes'/'Andy Warhol' single.

Tuesday 4 January

David and the band are back rehearsing for three days at Will Palin's Underhill Studios in Blackheath, south-east London, in preparation for a final round of recording for *Ziggy Stardust* and a UK tour which will transform his career.

Meanwhile Lou Reed is in town, making his first visit to Britain to record his eponymous debut solo album at Morgan Studios[1] in Willesden, north-west London, with RCA staff producer Richard Robinson.

1. Reed chose Morgan because Rod Stewart's recent transatlantic hit album *Every Picture Tells A Story* was recorded there the previous year.

Friday 7 January

RCA release 'Changes'/'Andy Warhol' single in the UK.

⊙ **David Bowie**[1]
A **'Changes'** (Bowie)
B **'Andy Warhol'** (Bowie)
David Bowie (vocal, guitar, alto and tenor sax, Mellotron)

Mick Ronson (guitar, vocal)
Trevor Bolder (bass on A-side)
Woody Woodmansey (drums on A-side)
Rick Wakeman (piano on A-side)
Session orchestra on A-side
Produced by Ken Scott (assisted by The Actor)
(RCA 2160)

'Changes' is not to be a commercial success but the release stokes interest in David at a crucial time. BBC Radio One's breakfast DJ Tony Blackburn makes it his single of the week, ensuring regular airplay on the national pop station.

1. In France, although the label stated that the B-side was 'Andy Warhol', it was actually 'Song For Bob Dylan'. In the US, 'Changes' was David's chart debut, reaching number 66.

Saturday 8 January

Melody Maker runs a full-page ad for *Hunky Dory*: notes about each album track hand-written by David on Warwick Hotel stationery during his recent trip to New York are included.

A party is held at Haddon Hall for David's 25th birthday (for which he is presented with a battery-powered razor by his band).[1] Lionel Bart and Lou Reed are among the guests who witness David's entrance on the grand staircase.

David is wearing a light green, quilted Ziggy suit he has designed with Freddie Burretti and had made for him from 30s furniture fabric by seamstress friend Sue Frost. David complements this with a short back-combed haircut akin to the one he sported in his days as a mod.

This has been cut by local hairdresser Suzi Fussey in preparation for a photo-session for a forthcoming feature in *Melody Maker* as well as another shoot with Brian Ward for the *Ziggy Stardust* album cover. David has yet to dye his hair; it is still his natural light brown.

Fussey works at Evelyn Paget's Ladies' Hairdressers[2] at 224 Beckenham High Street, opposite The Three Tuns. Angie is a customer and the salon's staff often run to the window to catch the couple's latest 'look' as they shop in the High Street.

After a while the birthday party shifts location from Haddon Hall to the Sombrero, where David's crowd stays until the early hours of the morning.

1. As David's fame rises the band could finally afford their own accommodation and move to a flat nearby at 6 Beckenham Road. David's bodyguard Stuey George also lodges there.
2. Now called Gigante, though still in the same location in Beckenham High Street.

Tuesday 11 January

David and the band record their first BBC radio session for John Peel's *Sounds Of The 70s* Radio One show at Studio T1, BBC Kensington House in west London.

Thursday 13 January

Stanley Kubrick's film version of Anthony Burgess's novel *A Clockwork Orange* opens in London.

David sees *A Clockwork Orange* soon after its release with Ronson, Bolder and Woodmansey at the ABC cinema in Catford, south-east London.

Struck by the attire of the gang of 'droogs' led by the film's anti-hero Alex, David incorporates elements into his and the band's stagewear.

In particular, their brightly coloured patent leather, mid-calf length, (zip-sided) lace-up boots are modelled on those worn by the gang. These are designed and made by local manufacturer/retailer Russell & Bromley.[1]

Ward shoots the band at his Heddon Street studio off Regent Street, and David also poses for the famous shots with an archetypal red London phone box. David becomes confident enough to talk about and appear as his new incarnation during interviews with journalists at Haddon Hall and Gem's offices in London's West End.

This is a risky ploy, and one which frustrates RCA since it renders the recently released *Hunky Dory* of passing interest, in favour of speculation about the *Ziggy Stardust* album (not scheduled for issue until mid-way through the year).

1. Today a High Street chain in the UK. David asked local shoe manufacturer Stan 'Dusty' Miller to design the band's boots. Trevor Bolder recalls that they were made bespoke and fitted by Russell & Bromley in Beckenham High Street.

Tuesday 18 January

David and the band record five tracks at the BBC's Maida Vale Studios in west London for Bob Harris's Radio One show *Sounds Of The 70s*.[1]

1. *Sounds of the 70s* was a series presented by a number of different DJs. The reason David did the same show for different DJs in a short space of time was because producers would pounce when an interesting artist became available for sessions and promotion.

Wednesday 19 January

Ahead of the UK tour, five days of intensive rehearsal take place at Stratford's Theatre Royal in east London.[1]

For the tour, Angie is to continue working the lights using a basic but effective rig, which she is responsible for hiring.

Journalist George Tremlett interviews David during the rehearsals, but is not given a clue about his Ziggy Stardust plans. "He said he didn't know if they were going to wear costumes or just jeans and T-shirts," said Tremlett in 1996.

The band's live sound is now overseen and maintained by Robin Mayhew,[2] who is appointed via his connection to sometime support band Tucky Buzzard. Before the tour, David asks Mayhew to demonstrate it to him and Defries at Beckenham Rugby Club in the suburb's Balmoral Avenue.

Defries promptly buys the stage equipment from Tucky Buzzard and employs Mayhew.

1. Rehearsals were also held at the Royal Ballroom in north London's Tottenham High Road.
2. Mayhew was David's head of sound on the road until 1973, when he moved on to work with a number of other acts, including punk band The Vibrators.

Friday 21 January

Tony Defries buys a duplex apartment at Gunter Hall Studios in Gunter Grove, on the borders of Chelsea and Fulham in west London. He pays £18,000 for the property and £2,000 for the furniture and fittings.

Saturday 22 January

David causes public consternation with his admission in *Melody Maker* to journalist Michael Watts, "I'm gay and always have been."

With the headline 'Oh! You Pretty Thing', the piece reverberates around the music business, and it is clear that David has reserved this attention-grabbing announcement for the country's biggest-selling music paper (today's *Disc & Music Echo* interview with Rosalind Russell carries no such references).

However, Defries is not happy when Watts informs him ahead of publication that it is not the front-page splash.

"Tony only wanted front pages and major coverage or nothing," said Gem promotions person Anya Wilson in 2001. "There was a big row, a monumental

TOP: A complex hybrid; David's most famous character, Ziggy Stardust.

ABOVE: Photographer Brian Ward's business card.

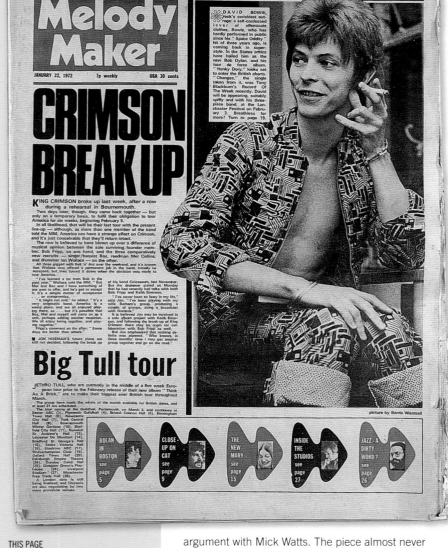

Melody Maker

JANUARY 22, 1972   7p weekly   USA 30 cents

DAVID BOWIE, rock's swishiest outrage: a self-confessed lover of effeminate clothes, Bowie, who has hardly performed in public since his " Space Oddity" hit of three years ago, is coming back in super-style. In the States critics have hailed him as the new Bob Dylan, and his tour de force album, "Hunky Dory," looks set to enter the British charts. "Changes," the single taken from it, was Tony Blackburn's Record Of The Week recently. David will be appearing, suitably spiffy and with his three-piece band, at the Lanchester Festival on February 3. Breathless for more? Turn to page 19.

CRIMSON BREAK UP

KING CRIMSON broke up last week, after a row during a rehearsal in Bournemouth.

Two days later, though, they came back together — but only at a temporary basis, to fulfil their obligation to tour America for six weeks, beginning February 5.

In all likelihood, that will be their last tour with the present line-up — although, as more than one member of the band told the MM, America can have a strange effect on Crimson, and it's just conceivable that they'll return intact.

The row is believed to have blown up over a difference of musical opinion between the sole surviving founder member, Bob Fripp, on one hand, and the three comparatively new recruits — singer/bassist Boz, reedman Mel Collins, and drummer Ian Wallace — on the other.

All three gigged with Bell 'n' Arc over the weekend, and it's known that Wallace was offered a permanent job in the band. Initially he accepted, but then turned it down when the decision was made to tour America.

"I've learned a lot from Bob in the past year," Wallace told the MM. "But Mel and Boz and I have something of our own to offer, and he's got to accept it. It's a simple matter of acceptance — or compromise.

"It might not end," he added. "It's a very enigmatic band. America is a weird place, and we all enjoyed playing there, so ... but it's possible that Boz, Mel and myself will carry on as a unit, perhaps adding another musician. We all enjoy being together, and playing together."

Fripp's comment on the affair: "Some days are better than others."

Jon Hiseman's future plans are still not decided, following the break up of his band Colosseum, last November. But the drummer stated on Monday that he had recently had talks with both Bob Fripp and Keith Emerson.

"I've never been so busy in my life," said Jon. "I've been playing with my wife Barbara's group, producing a couple of groups, doing a broadcast with Nucleus."

It is believed Jon may be involved in a solo album project with Keith Emerson, and following the break-up of King Crimson there may be room for collaboration with Bob Fripp as well.

But Jon emphasised that nothing definite was planned. "Who knows, in three months' time I may get another group together and go on the road."

Big Tull tour

JETHRO TULL, who are currently in the middle of a five week European tour prior to the February release of their new album "Thick As A Brick," are to make their biggest ever British tour throughout March.

The group have made the whole of the month available for British dates, and at least 21 are scheduled.

The tour opens at the Guildhall, Portsmouth, on March 2, and continues at Exeter ABC (3), Plymouth Guildhall (4), Bristol Colston Hall (5), Birmingham Town Hall (6), Newcastle City Hall (7), York Central Hall (8), Bournemouth Winter Gardens (10), Sheffield City Hall (11), Newcastle St Andrew's Hall (13), Leicester De Montfort (14), Bradford St George's Hall (15), Stoke Victoria Hall (16), Stockton ABC (17), Wolverhampton Civic (19), Oxford Town Hall (20), Edinburgh Empire Theatre (24), Dundee Caird Hall (25), Glasgow Green's Playhouse (26), Liverpool Stadium (27), Manchester Free Trade Hall (28).

A London date is still being finalised, and Chrysalis are also negotiating for two more provincial venues.

BOLAN IN BOSTON see page 5

CLOSE-UP ON CAT see page 9

THE NEW MARY see page 15

INSIDE THE STUDIOS see page 27

JAZZ - A DIRTY WORD ? see page 26

picture by Barrie Wentzell

THIS PAGE

TOP: The legendary *Melody Maker* issue, with the interview that nearly didn't appear.

BELOW: Nearly a Spider From Mars, singer/guitarist Laurie Heath. Photo by Marty Kristian.

OPPOSITE PAGE

Photographed by Michael Putland, David first appearance as *Ziggy Stardust*, Aylesbury Friars Club, 29 January.

argument with Mick Watts. The piece almost never happened."

Nevertheless, the timing is crucial; Britain's gay movement initially embraces David as a figurehead, and his revelation of bisexuality will not only draw immediate attention to his tour dates but also trail the summer release of the ambiguous sexuality contained on the *Ziggy Stardust* album and the single 'John, I'm Only Dancing' later in the year.

Some close friends regard it as without substance, a mere publicity stunt.

"I don't know if David was really bisexual," said Mick Ronson in 1991. "He may have been. David likes to shock people. Whether he had genuine feelings about it, I'm not so sure. Perhaps it was just a game?"

"It was probably the best thing I've ever said," David said in 1978, though this was countered in 1983 by his view that it was "the biggest mistake I

ever made". By 1993 his summary was: "It wasn't something I was comfortable with at all, but it had to be done." The following day David receives his first mention in the *Los Angeles Times,* with a review of *Hunky Dory*.

Wednesday 26 January

The band commence three more days of pre-tour rehearsals at Stratford's Theatre Royal.

For a while rhythm guitarist Laurie Heath,[1] an actor in the 60s who was a member of the New Seekers and is in Gem-managed Milkwood,[2] takes part and is considered for David's backing band for the tour, with a stage costume already made and fitted.

But by the end of rehearsals it is decided Heath's services are not required. "He was a good-looking lad and a good singer," said Bolder in 1995. "I think the worry was he may have detracted from David, so he went."

1. David first encountered Heath in 1971 when he was taken to a Milkwood performance at a club in Piccadilly, central London.

2. Released in 1971, Milkwood's first single 'Watching You Go'/'Here I Stand' was produced by Gem's Don Hunter. The musical arrangement of the A-side was handled by Mick Ronson. Heath later wrote 'This Is For You' for Ronson, who recorded it for his 1975 solo album *Play Don't Worry*.

Saturday 29 January

▶ David Bowie, The Friars Club, Borough Assembly Hall, Aylesbury, Bucks.

On the day David and his band return to Friars,[1] the *NME* publishes an interview with Penny Valentine in which David talks about the last appearance there: "We did this gig in Aylesbury before Christmas and got such a great reception, it got us off."[2]

Also in the *NME* David tells Danny Holloway:

"I'm not ashamed of wearing dresses, but unfortunately it's distracted from the fact that I'm a songwriter."

Tonight, with support from Grand Canyon, David and the band make their first public performance in the new glam costumes, for the gig where David is billed as 'The Most Beautiful Person in the World'.

David wears his new patterned, quilted suit, and, in the audience again, Queen drummer Roger Taylor (who has driven in his Mini Cooper to the show with bandmate Freddie Mercury) is struck by the transformation which has taken place; at their previous Friars show, David wore his *Hunky Dory* cover clothes, while the band were in jeans and T-shirts.

The set kicks off with 'The Supermen', and there is an acoustic interlude preceded by the full ensemble performing a version of Cream's 'I Feel Free' during which David changes costume into a cream satin blouse and sequinned trousers.

For the dates in the first half of the year David's fellow musicians are not billed with the name of Ziggy Stardust's band, The Spiders From Mars.

The previous night Radio One had broadcast the recent John Peel *Sounds Of The 70s* session.

THE DARLING OF THE AVANT GARDE

DAVID BOWIE

THIS PAGE

TOP RIGHT: David and the boys photographed for the first time in full stage regalia, January.

ABOVE: *Phonograph Record Magazine*, 'The Darling of the Avant Garde'. Last year's model; the media found it hard to keep up with David's changing image, January 1972 issue.

OPPOSITE PAGE

TOP: Nicky Graham's rough accounting for the first Ziggy tour.

TOP LEFT: The first Ziggy tour begins at the Toby Jug, Tolworth, 10 February.

UPPER MIDDLE RIGHT: Nicky Graham.

LOWER MIDDLE: Ziggy goes Iggy in London West 1. David tries to emulate an Iggy Pop moment.

BOTTOM: Finale; David, Ronson and Woodmansey on stage at Imperial College. Parts of the show were filmed for French TV.

In this year...

February

PERFORMANCES by Syd Barrett with the band Stars at three UK venues. Following these, the former Pink Floyd frontman abandoned his musical career.

Thursday 3 February

RECORDING of two tracks for the album *Slider* by Marc Bolan and his T.Rex bandmates at the Château D'Hérouville in northern France. David recorded *Pin Ups* at the studios on Bolan's recommendation in 1973.

1. The contract with Friars – for a performance fee of £110 – was signed by Gem's Don Hunter.
2. In 1977 David played keyboards in Iggy Pop's band for a performance at the nearby Friars Hall, and was saddened to find Ziggy's birthplace, the Borough Assembly Hall, had become a furniture store.

Wednesday 2 February[1]

'Starman' replaces Chuck Berry's 'Round And Round' in a new running order for *Ziggy Stardust*.

1. The following day, an appearance at the Lanchester Polytechnic Arts Festival in Coventry was cancelled as Defries didn't want David to play festivals.

Friday 4 February

More takes of 'Rock 'n' Roll Suicide', 'Starman' and 'Suffragette City' are recorded at Trident.[1] David sends a copy of the last to Ian Hunter,[2] whose rock group Mott The Hoople[3] he much admires.

'Starman' has been written as a direct response to RCA A&R head Dennis Katz's request for a track suitable for single release.

1. The versions of all three tracks which appear on *Ziggy Stardust* were recorded during this session. David's exclamation "Ah! Droogie don't crash here" (in the teen argot of *A Clockwork Orange*) during 'Suffragette City' was the album's only explicit reference to the film.
2. Born Ian Hunter Patterson, Shrewsbury, Shropshire, 1939.
3. Launched in 1969 under the aegis of producer Guy Stevens, Mott The Hoople had released four well-received but poor-selling albums by the beginning of 1972.

Saturday 5 February

In *Disc & Music Echo*, Martin Marriott's review of the recent Friars show details the band's visual impact. Marriott writes that the audience were 'at first unresponsive and mouths ajar', while David looked 'dazzling' and the band were 'equally stunning in their *Clockwork Orange* bovver spacesuits'.

Monday 7 February

A show at Southampton's Guild Hall is cancelled to make way for recording of an important showcase; on the same day that BBC's Radio One broadcasts the recent Bob Harris-presented *Sounds Of The 70s* session, David and the band tape three songs for BBC TV's late-night rock programme *The Old Grey Whistle Test*.

Gem promotion executive Anya Wilson has been plugging away for an appearance by David on BBC TV for a year, but executives have been put off by his appearance.

"[Series producer] Mike Appleton was really apprehensive," said Wilson in 2001. "When David wore the Mr Fish dress, that threw any TV show out the window. I was told point blank by another producer: 'We don't have perverts on our show.'"

By lobbying Appleton's office every week Wilson has built up a friendship with his assistant Jenny Evans, who alerts her to an opportunity when another act cancels.

"Jenny made sure I had David available and ran into Mike offering Bowie for the show," said Wilson. "With some arm twisting and the fact they were really under the gun, we were on. As soon as the show was in progress and they found out they were dealing with an extremely talented, charismatic professional with showmanship galore, they fell in love with David and we never had a hard time with the show again."

Recorded in the tiny studio on the fourth floor of the BBC's Television Centre in west London, the appearance is ostensibly to promote *Hunky Dory*, though David and his cohorts are dressed in their glamorous new threads and, as well as performing 'Oh! You Pretty Things'[1] and 'Queen Bitch' from the current album, take the opportunity to play 'Five Years' from the next.

With the piano being played by Mick Ronson on 'Five Years' and David on 'Oh! You Pretty Things', the band record backing tapes for two takes of each song, to which David performs the vocals live. This is the first time David and the band appear on TV.[2]

The following evening David and the band excitedly watch their *Old Grey Whistle Test* performance at home in Beckenham. The show is introduced by Richard Williams. The following day another *Ziggy Stardust* master tape is prepared with a revised running order.

1. Not broadcast by the BBC until the 80s.
2. Takes unused at the time have since been broadcast; all three performances are included on EMI's *Best Of Bowie* DVD, along with the alternate take of 'Oh! You Pretty Things'.

Thursday 10 February

▶ David Bowie, Toby Jug, Hook Rise South, Tolworth, Surrey.

During the day David is interviewed by Johnny Moran for Radio One's magazine show *Scene & Heard*, and his new agents at the London branch of the prestigious William Morris Agency seek to capitalise on *The Old Grey Whistle Test* screening by writing to Johnny Stewart, producer of BBC's early evening chart show *Top Of The Pops*, in an attempt to secure a performance of the recently released single 'Changes'.

In the evening[1] the Ziggy Stardust tour, which will take in 45 dates and transform David into a rock'n'roll star, begins in less than glamorous circumstances with a pub[2] gig (David's last) to the south of London.

Augmented on piano by Nicky Graham (who has recently left Tucky Buzzard[3] and works by day at Gem[4] arranging the tour's bookings),[5] David delivers a 'very good, tight show' according to two audience members: his former backing musicians from The Buzz and his 1967 debut album, John Eager and Dek Fearnley.

David notices them in the crowd and introduces Eager and Fearnley from the stage. They meet up for the first time in five years after the performance.

"He introduced us to the band and asked us what we were doing," said Fearnley in 1991. "He was polite but not particularly interested really. He is so creative, always pushing forward and the past doesn't really interest him."

"When we came away from the dressing room we both felt he'd been OK but we knew that basically he hadn't been that interested, which is fair enough," said Eager in 1991. "That's David."

Angie again works the lights but, as the tour progresses, specialist company Heavy Light is engaged, with the rig overseen by Nigel Olaf.

1. A German promoter attempted to book David for a festival in Essen on this date.

2. Briefly turned into a MacDonald's restaurant but demolished in 2008, the Toby Jug had employed John Lennon's errant father Freddie in the mid 60s as a barman, around the time he attended the launch party for David & The Lower Third's 1966 single 'Can't Help Thinking About Me'.

3. A pet project of Bill Wyman's, both Tucky Buzzard's early 70s albums were produced by The Rolling Stones bassist.

4. Graham had been introduced to Laurence Myers and Tony Defries by his girlfriend, their secretary Diana Mackie.

5. Some of the shows on this tour were promoted by Gem.

Friday 11 February

❱ David Bowie, High Wycombe Town Hall, Queen Victoria Road, High Wycombe, Bucks.

Today at Croydon Register Office, David's half-brother Terry marries Olga, a fellow patient at Cane Hill Hospital near Croydon in Surrey.

Saturday 12 February

❱ David Bowie, Imperial College Union, Great Hall, Prince Consort Road, London SW7.

Radio One broadcasts Johnny Moran's interview with David for *Scene & Heard*. He tells Moran: "I don't sing very well. I don't sing like anybody else. It's kind of a bleating goat voice."

During the Imperial College show, which has an entrance fee of 50p, David dedicates 'Queen Bitch' to Lou Reed and attempts to emulate a trick he has seen Iggy Pop performing on film: walking into the audience hoisted upright by crowd members.[1]

Unable to recreate Pop's showmanship, David stumbles and falls into the audience, but not before he is captured in photographs by friend Ray Stevenson.

Part of tonight's show is filmed for French TV show *Pop 2*, which screens the performance of 'Suffragette City'.

Queen drummer Roger Taylor is again in the audience, accompanied by the group's founder and Imperial College student Brian May.[2] After the show May and Taylor hang around the stage, quizzing the roadies about Mick Ronson's equipment and looking for tips on how he creates his guitar sound.

Supporting are folk/rock siblings The Sutherland Brothers,[3] – bassist Gavin and guitarist Iain, who share vocals.

1. During The Stooges' set at the Cincinnati Pop Festival on 13 June 1970, Pop was hoisted in the air by audience members and, flinging peanut butter from a giant pot, gave the impression of walking on the audience's hands. This was televised live by a local TV channel, and subsequently broadcast on national TV, and has become a YouTube favourite.

2. May delivered his completed astronomy PhD thesis to Imperial College in 2007, 36 years after abandoning his studies for music.

3. In 1973 The Sutherland Brothers joined forces with Quiver, whose guitarist Tim Renwick was in David's backing band Junior's Eyes and played on David's 1969 Mercury album.

FOX at the TOBY JUG 1 HOOK RISE SOUTH TOLWORTH
TONIGHT—Thursday. Feb. 10th   D.J. Rick Hawkins
DAVID BOWIE
Feb. 17th., Pink Faries

Bowie's Gigs
Aylesbury (Friars Club) 29. Jan. 150.
Toby Jug. Tolworth. 10 Feb. 100 approx
Brighton Dome. 14 Feb. 125.
Imperial College. 12. Feb. 250
Sheffield Univ. 18 Feb. 175.
Wellington Public. 24 Feb. £76
Cash to Tim

DIRECTORS: VIC LEWIS A. M. HOWARD P. R. SAUL
G. T. WHYTE R. WILLIS B. L. WARMINGTON NEIL WARNOCK

(Licensed annually by Westminster City Council)
MEMBERS OF THE ENTERTAINMENT
AGENTS' ASSOCIATION

NEMS ENTERPRISES LTD.
NEMPEROR HOUSE, HILL STREET, LONDON W.I.
TELEPHONE: 01-629 6341
TELEX No. 21716
204 HN/A 9545/HP

This Agency is not responsible for any non-fulfilment of Contract by Proprietors, Managers or Artistes, but every reasonable safeguard is assured.

An **Agreement** made the _____1st_____ day of _____February_____ 19 72
BETWEEN _____Phillip Haines_____ hereinafter called the
Management of the one part, and _____Gem Management_____
hereinafter called the Artiste of the other part.

Witnesseth that the Management hereby engages the Artiste and the Artiste accepts an engagement to present

DAVID BOWIE

(or in his usual entertainment) at the Dance Hall/Theatre and from the dates for the periods and at the salaries stated in the schedule hereto.

SCHEDULE

The Artiste agrees to appear for _____one_____ evening performance(s) at

£225

a salary of _____ % of the gross Advance and Door takings.
The Management guarantees a minimum of £

VENUE	DATE
Pier Pavilion Southsea Pier SOUTHSEA	4th March 1972

ADDITIONAL CLAUSES

1. The Artistes agree to arrive at the venue by 3.00p.m. and to perform 1 x 60 minute spot. The Management to provide a concert grand piano tuned to concert pitch on the day of the engagement.

2. The Artiste shall not without the written consent of the management appear at any place of public entertainment within a radius of _____ miles of any of the venues mentioned herein for _____ weeks prior to and _____ weeks following this engagement.

3. The management agree to provide suitable and adequate dressing room facilities.

4. Payment is to be made to Nems Enterprises Limited by cheque, within 3 days of the completion of the engagement. The Artiste by cheque on the night.

Wallington Public Hall
STAFFORD ROAD, WALLINGTON

Thursday 24th Feb.

DAVID BOWIE

Bar   7-30 p.m.   D.J. Rick Hawkins

★ ADMISSION ONLY 50p with this Invitation ★

BUSES: 154, 157, 234   WALLINGTON STATION
Thursday 2nd March . . STRAY

THIS PAGE
TOP: All at sea, Ziggy makes his one and only end-of-the-pier appearance in Southsea, 4 March.

ABOVE: Wallington Public Hall promotional ticket.

OPPOSITE PAGE
TOP: Mick Rock's first casual photo session with David. One of the shots later became the *Space Oddity* album cover. © Mick Rock

UPPER MIDDLE: The amazing Daniella Parma. Her changing hair colour convinced David "of the importance of a synthetic hair colour for Ziggy".

LOWER MIDDLE: Suzi Fussey, the local Beckenham hairdresser who, with David's guidance, created the famous Bowie hairstyle. © Mick Rock

BOTTOM: David and Mick at Wallington Public Hall, 24 February.

Monday 14 February

▶ David Bowie, Brighton Dome, Church Street, Brighton, East Sussex.

During the afternoon David makes a personal appearance at Brighton record shop Exspantion Records[1], signing copies of *Hunky Dory*.

Tonight the band are supporting blues act The Groundhogs.

Before the show, in his dressing room, David eagerly opens fan mail, which has been arriving following his *Whistle Test* performance the previous week. "They think I'm from space!" he declares to his bandmates. "Looking at one of the letters David said to me, 'This guy is telling me what my songs mean, it's all news to me'," said Trevor Bolder in 1995.

1. Spelt thus because the owner also managed R&B act Mike Stuart Span.

Friday 18 February

▶ David Bowie, University of Sheffield Rag Ball, University Park, Sheffield, Yorks.

Billed as 'Special Guest Star' David and band support pop-soul singer Labi Siffrie on a diverse bill including poetry/comedy trio The Scaffold, rockabilly act Shakin' Stevens and the Sunsets, roots rockers Brinsley Schwarz,[1] Spencer's Washboard Kings and Bronx Cheer.

Tony Defries writes to Gem's New York publisher representative Normand Kurtz, suggesting 'Life On Mars?' as a cover single for Barbra Streisand.[2]

1. Brinsley Schwarz was fronted by bassist Nick Lowe, later to make a name for himself as producer of Elvis Costello, Graham Parker and The Damned, and a solo singer-songwriter in his own right.
2. Streisand's version appeared on her 1974 album *Butterfly*.

Wednesday 23 February

▶ David Bowie, Chichester College of Further Education, Main Hall, College Lane, Chichester, West Sussex.

Mick Ronson's reputation for his guitar volume drowning out fellow musicians is tackled by the road-crew. Unbeknown to him, they adjust Ronson's Marshall Major amp so that, when he cranks the dial up to 10, it is in fact reaching a maximum of eight.

Thursday 24 February

▶ David Bowie, Wallington Public Hall, Stafford Road, Wallington, Surrey.

The gig features a disco as support, but the venue is only half full, although only a short distance from Beckenham.

An associate of David's, Kenny Bell is now employed by Chrysalis, and helps out booking some of the early dates on this tour, just as he had done for David & The Lower Third in 1966.

Friday 25 February

▶ David Bowie, Avery Hill College, Eltham, Bexley Road, London SE9.

Tony Defries' ambitions are that David and the band would be performing live in the US by now; a date has been pencilled in for New York's Carnegie Hall tonight, with arranger Arthur Greenslade consulted by David over supplying orchestration.[1]

But Carnegie Hall's loss is south London's gain. With an entry fee of 60p, tonight's gig[2] proves a slight financial setback when the promoter's cheque bounces.

1. David had planned to include orchestration through much of the show.
2. Newspaper adverts listed the support act as Armada but the contract named Principal Edwards Magic Theatre and Gordon Giltrap.

Saturday 26 February

▶ David Bowie, Mayfair Suite, Belfry Hotel, Lichfield Road, Wishaw, Sutton Coldfield, Birmingham.

At the venue – situated within the grounds of a the famous golf course – support is provided by 'progressive group' Money Jungle.

A proposed appearance in Newcastle the following day is postponed for a month.

Monday 28 February

▶ David Bowie, Glasgow City Hall, Candleriggs.

This first appearance by the band in Scotland (with support from The Nicholsons) is cancelled just hours before they are due on stage.

Concerned that the band's PA is too large for the stage, the venue attempts to impose restrictions and, as outlined in a letter to Gem from venue manager Thomas MaLarkey, this results in a stand-off:

'The reason that the concert did not take place was that the main attraction – David Bowie and group – refused to go on stage with the permissible amount of equipment and it was on their intimation that they would not go on. I, after consulting you (Gem) and your fellow promoters, advised the queues of perhaps 200/250 persons outside Candleriggs entrance that the concert was cancelled. The queue dispersed in an orderly fashion within a few minutes.'[1]

As he leaves the building, David explains the problem to a group of fans waiting for him.

Gem pulls the following night's gig at The Locarno in the north-eastern coastal city of Sunderland as unsuitable for David.[2] Support was to have been The John Miles Set and Brass Alley.

1. The venue refused to pay Gem's costs, which included return flights for the band, accommodation at Glasgow Central Hotel, wages for roadies and equipment transportation.
2. A letter from Gem to the promoter explained: 'Sunderland Locarno was to have been a civic function of some kind which would have been entirely the wrong type of performance for David. As a result, we did not play the venue.'

Wednesday 1 March

▶ David Bowie, University of Bristol, Queens Road, Clifton, Bristol, Avon.

Early on in the tour many shows are under-subscribed, but low attendances do not affect performances as the band's confidence grows ahead of the release of *Ziggy Stardust* (the completed master tapes and artwork of which Tony Defries takes to New York for RCA's approval).

Saturday 4 March

▶ David Bowie, South Parade Pier, Southsea, Hampshire.

The omens are not positive in the afternoon for this end-of-the-pier show when the Southsea-to-Isle of Wight hovercraft flips over in a storm a mile off the coast, killing five passengers. "We all drove down the coast to have a look," remembered Trevor Bolder in 1995.

The audience is scant for the performance in the Gaiety Lounge Show Bar (Bolder recalled the proverbial 'one man and his dog') and the unloading proves a logistical nightmare since all equipment has to be hauled the length of the pier.[1]

"It was hell!" said roadie Will Palin in 1993. "We couldn't roll it on the pier's open decking, so we carried everything by hand. Absolutely exhausted, we had to do the same again after the gig."

David's friend singer/songwriter Bridget St John is support; she has not seen him live since the Regent Street Polytechnic show in 1970.

"That was such a weird night," she said in 2004. "And there was David in his platform heels. I remember thinking 'Oh, that's not the same guy I remember'."

1. In June 1974, the pier venue was damaged by fire during filming for Ken Russell's cinematic version of The Who's rock opera *Tommy*.

Tuesday 7 March

▶ David Bowie, Yeovil College, Mudford Road, Yeovil, Somerset.

Saturday 11 March

▶ David Bowie, Southampton Guild Hall, West Marlands Road, Southampton, Hants.

David is invited via a letter from film-makers David Tringham and Adrian Hughes to be interviewed for, and supply the soundtrack to, a film about Dutch abstract artist/writer Jan Cremer. He declines the offer.

A performance planned for the previous evening in High Wycombe has been advertised by a local promoter but does not take place since contracts aren't exchanged.

Tuesday 14 March

▶ David Bowie, Chelsea Village, Bournemouth, Dorset.

Friday 17 March

▶ David Bowie, Town Hall, Victoria Street, Birmingham.

Tonight's show – with support from Mr Crisp

– is only half-full. After the performance David is interviewed by photographer Mick Rock, who is engaging in a spot of journalism for adult monthly *Men Only*.

This, their first encounter, continues back at Haddon Hall where they talk until the early morning.

"We hit it off straight away," said Rock in 1992. "I mentioned I liked Lou Reed and Syd Barrett and that cemented it."

Rock will soon become part of David's entourage as his official photographer, documenting his changing appearance over the coming months.

For tonight's show his hair has been dyed a light red and slightly restyled by Suzi Fussey, but David tells Rock he is going to make his hair 'even redder'.

Swayed by his Sombrero friend Daniella Parmar's use of different hair dyes (which, he said in 2002 "convinced me of the importance of a synthetic hair colour for Ziggy"), not long after the Birmingham performance David shows Fussey the exact tone he desires in a photograph of model Marie Helvin in a recent fashion magazine.

Modelling the latest styles by Japanese designer Kansai Yamamoto, Helvin appears to have a mane of bright red hair.

"It was a man's traditional kabuki wig and was very heavy," said Helvin in 2009. "I had to swing it around; it nearly damaged my neck."

Fussey applies a bright red colourfast dye and spikes the crown with Guard, a strong setting lotion and dandruff treatment. The Ziggy hairstyle is born.[1]

When Rock returns to Haddon Hall a few days later for a daytime photo session, David is in his dressing gown and the new style and deeper colouring have been achieved.[2]

1. David chose vivid red stage lighting for the majority of Ziggy performances, which exaggerated his hair colour, even before a stronger red dye was applied.

THIS PAGE

TOP LEFT: UK issue of 'Starman'.

TOP RIGHT: 'Starman' sheet music.

MIDDLE: RCA advert for *Hunky Dory* and 'Starman', 22 April.

BOTTOM: Avery Hill College, 25 February.

OPPOSITE PAGE

TOP: At home lounging in his stage uniform, photographed by Michael Putland.

MIDDLE: Ziggy promotion.

BOTTOM: David and journalist Rosalind Russell at Haddon Hall.

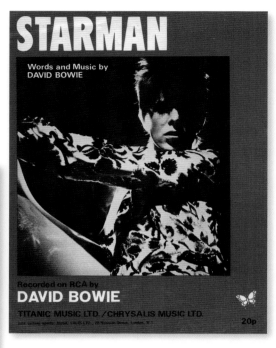

2. A close-up from this session became the cover shot of RCA's 1972 *Space Oddity* reissue of his 1969 Mercury album. Published in the summer of 1972, Rock's *Men Only* feature included his photographs of David taken over a few days from Birmingham and Haddon Hall, effectively tracking the progress of his haircut's style and colour.

Friday 24 March

▶ David Bowie, Mayfair Ball, Newcastle.

David and the band fly to Newcastle to fulfil the engagement postponed the previous month. Support for the show – which unveils the new hairstyle – are Armada and Patch.

Sunday 26 March

After a particularly dispiriting gig while on tour in Switzerland, one of David's favourite bands, Mott The Hoople,[1] decide to call it a day after they have completed live commitments back in the UK.

On his return home and seeking session work, bassist Pete 'Overend' Watts informs David of the decision during an hour-long phone conversation.

Two hours later David returns Watts' call, telling him he has just written a new song for the group. They meet and David plays Watts 'All The Young Dudes' on his acoustic guitar, though the lyrics are not yet complete.

Excited at the quality of the song, Watts arranges for all of the members of Mott to meet David at Gem's Regent Street offices. Sitting cross-legged on his manager's floor, David plays them the song and says he will help out producing the track as a single. Defries says that he will become their manager.

Recognising a hit and stunned that David is prepared to donate it to them, the Mott members resolve to stick together after their forthcoming Rock & Roll Circus tour.

At Trident the following day, David, Mick Ronson

and Ken Scott work together on the remix of 'Starman' for single release.

1. At this point the Mott The Hoople line-up was Ian Hunter (vocal, guitar, keyboard), Mick Ralphs (guitar), Verden 'Phally' Allen (organ), Peter 'Overend' Watts (bass) and Terence Dale 'Buffin' Griffin (drums).

Ian Hunter first saw David perform in 1969, as he recalled in 1993: "It was at some university or other when he was doing mime to a tape machine and a guy playing acoustic guitar [Hutchinson]. We didn't know what to make of him. Totally weird."

Friday 31 March

David renews his contract with Gem for a 10-year term. This is on the basis of providing the company with the exclusive services of 'writing lyrics and/or music, composer, arranger, etc' in return for £300 per week.

Sunday 9 April

David and Tony Defries visit Mott The Hoople for their date at Guildford Civic Centre in Surrey on the Rock & Roll Circus tour (which features jugglers and ill-received support from British music hall veteran Max Wall).

David joins the band on stage for the encore. Defries, meanwhile, is working on snaring Mott a new record deal with CBS (since their contract with Island has expired).

Monday 17 April

▶ David Bowie, Lord's Club, Civic Hall, Windmill Street, Gravesend, Kent.

The Ziggy tour resumes with a date in the coastal town where, on Halloween just over two years ago, the drunken audience had flicked lit cigarettes at David during his solo performance.

Thursday 20 April

▶ David Bowie, The Playhouse, Playhouse Square, Harlow, Essex.

Ticket prices for tonight's show are 75p, 60p and 30p.

Friday 21 April

▶ David Bowie, Free Trade Hall,[1] Peter Street, Manchester.

The Sutherland Brothers are supporting, and the audience includes future Joy Division members Ian Curtis[2] and drummer Stephen Morris.

Curtis manages to meet David after the gig; David asks him if there is a club nearby which plays Northern soul.

1. Now the Radisson Edwardian Manchester Hotel, retaining the original Free Trade Hall façade.

2. Ian Curtis (1956–1980) joined Joy Division in 1976 as vocalist and songwriter. He committed suicide just before the band was due to start a US tour.

Tuesday 25 April

Ken Pitt's management contract with David officially expires today (though Pitt has long since waived the arrangement).

Friday 28 April

RCA release 'Starman'/'Suffragette City' single in the UK.

⊙ **David Bowie**
A **'Starman'** (Bowie)
B **'Suffragette City'** (Bowie)
David Bowie (vocal, guitar)
Mick Ronson (vocal, guitar, piano)
Trevor Bolder (bass)
Woody Woodmansey (drums)
Session orchestra on A-side
Produced by David Bowie and Ken Scott
Arranged by David Bowie and Mick Ronson
(RCA 2199)

'Starman' is David's take on Judy Garland's 'Over The Rainbow' (which David planned for the climax of his cabaret set back in 1968).

In terms of sales the single is a slow-burner, but will benefit from the TV and radio exposure achieved by Gem's Anya Wilson.

Meanwhile Gem's staff is bolstered by the recruitment of Nicky Graham's friend Hugh Attwooll.[1]

Attwooll, who starts off helping Graham with tour bookings, soon gains an insight into Defries' business acumen.

"He was an amazing guy to work for," said Attwooll in 1986. "Coupled with David's talent it was a marriage made in heaven. Defries was a million times more intelligent than most other people he encountered in the music business."

Across the Atlantic, *Hunky Dory* peaks at 176 in the US album charts. This is the first time an album of David's has charted anywhere in the world.

1. The pair were at school together and also in a band, The End.

Saturday 29 April

An appearance by David and The Spiders at the town hall in High Wycombe, Bucks, is cancelled.

'Starman', meanwhile, is garnering David his best critical reception since 'Space Oddity' nearly three years before.

In his *Disc & Music Echo* column, John Peel writes: 'Now this is magnificent – quite superb. David Bowie is, with Kevin Ayers,[1] the most important, under-acknowledged innovator in contemporary popular music in Britain and if this record is overlooked it will be nothing less than stark tragedy.'

Melody Maker's Chris Welch predicts: 'David is taking longer than most to become a superstar, but he should catch up with Rod and Marc soon.'

1. Kevin Ayers, born Kent 1944, founder member of UK psychedelic group Soft Machine. Launched solo career in 1969 with the release of album *Joy Of A Toy*. Ayers met David and Brian Eno in Berlin in 1978 but the three never collaborated.

Sunday 30 April

◗ David Bowie, Guild Hall, Guildhall Square, Plymouth, Devon.

Booked by local promoter Greg Van Dyke, the show is billed as 'David Bowie and Friends' on a poster

featuring a line drawing of David in his *Hunky Dory* look.

Wednesday 3 May

◗ David Bowie, Aberystwyth University, Wales.

David returns to a venue he played with The Buzz in 1966. On this tour David plays sax on one number, soloing on a version of James Brown's 'Gotta Get A Job'[1] (which segues into the melody from Brown's 'Hot Pants').

1. Actual title is 'You've Got To Have A Job', the single released by Brown and Marva Whitney in 1969. David considered performing 'Gotta Get A Job' and 'Hot Pants' on 1974's Diamond Dogs tour.

Saturday 6 May

David Bowie, Kingston Polytechnic Main Hall,[1] Penryhn Road, London.

Disc & Music Echo publishes another feature on David, written by Rosalind Russell after an interview at Haddon Hall.

The *Disc* photographs have been taken by Michael Putland, who said in 2007: "I'd photographed [David]

before, at a small club in Aylesbury, when he was wearing a catsuit in a very tasteful shade of lime-green. When I arrived at his home, there he was: on the top of a ladder, painting his ceiling with a can of Dulux, and wearing the same catsuit with a matching hat."

With the assistance of George Underwood, David decorates his bedroom and living room like a stage set, with silver ceilings and giant blue circles.[1]

The evening's gig at Angie's alma mater marks a turning point in David's popularity.

After the sound-check, pianist Nicky Graham and soundman Robin Mayhew leave the venue to flypost the neighbourhood with posters illustrated with a cartoon rendition of David as Ziggy.

On their return, their access is blocked by the queue which tails around the block. "I had to call friends to act as extra security," said Graham in 1990. "It was about this time we really knew we were on to something."[2]

The set now consists of 'Hang On To Yourself', 'Ziggy Stardust', 'The Supermen', 'Queen Bitch', 'Song For Bob Dylan', 'Changes', 'Starman', 'Five Years', 'Space Oddity', 'Andy Warhol', 'Amsterdam', 'I Feel Free', 'Moonage Daydream', 'White Light/White Heat', 'Gotta Get A Job', 'Suffragette City', 'Rock 'n' Roll Suicide' and 'I'm Waiting For The Man'.

In the audience is David's acquaintance Alan Mair, formerly of The Beatstalkers.

Customers and fellow stall-holders in Kensington Market have been raving about David's latest releases, and Mair is curious to check out the latest from his fellow former client of Ken Pitt's.

"When we got there I was amazed to see the

queue," said Mair in 1992. "We didn't have tickets, so I asked one of the bouncers on the door if he would get a message to David that Alan Mair was outside with friends. He returned and said we could get in through a side entrance.

"We had to pass the dressing rooms on the way to the auditorium. I could hear David singing so I knocked on the door and walked in.

"He immediately said 'Hi Alan!' and threw his arms around me.

"The show itself was absolutely amazing and I could immediately see what all the fuss was about. Afterwards I said to him, 'David, you're fucking brilliant!' That was the last time I saw him; my friends still talk about it to this day."

Also on the bill is Scottish electric folk quintet The JSD Band,[3] who impress David so much they become a regular support act.

1. After David and Angie moved from Haddon Hall in the spring of 1973 the owner, Mr Hoy, pursued them for defacing his property by painting the interior in a 'garish and unsightly fashion'. This, he claimed, made him unable to rent out the ground floor for nine months. In May 1976, on David's return to the UK for his Thin White Duke tour, Hoy took legal action.

2. During this period the first official national David Bowie Fan Club was founded in Aylesbury with the involvement of local journalist Kris Needs (later to edit rock magazine *ZigZag*, which is based in the town). This distributes official photos, newsletters and postcards. Another fan club created fabric Ziggy dolls in 1972, using remnants from material for David's original Ziggy costumes.

3. Des Coffield (guitar, banjo, vocal), Sean O'Rourke (guitar, flute, vocal), Lindsay Scott (violin, vocal) Jim Divers (guitar, bass) and Colin Finn (drums). Formed, Glasgow, in 1969 as a traditional folk group, they released debut album *Country Of The Blind* on Regal Zonophone in 1971 and eponymous follow-up in 1972, when they adopted amplification. The band broke up in 1974.

Sunday 7 May

▶ David Bowie, The Pavilion, Marlowes, Hemel Hempstead, Herts.

With entry at 75p, this is another sell-out show. Support is provided by Lee Riders.

Thursday 11 May

▶ David Bowie, Assembly Hall, Stoke Abbot Road, Worthing, West Sussex.

Tickets are 50p and support is from Steel Mill. Meanwhile, discussions are under way for David to appear in a one-off TV special to be hosted by his friend DJ Bob Harris. In a letter to Chris Pye at Granada Television, Tony Defries writes: 'We shall need £100 for David Bowie to include expenses and £50 for Bob Harris also to include expenses, in order to do the pilot. Please confirm that the pilot will not be used for transmission at any time and that it will be destroyed on the making of the series.'

Friday 12 May

▶ David Bowie, Polytechnic of Central London, 115 Cavendish Street, London W1.

Billed as 'The Only Central London Performance of David Bowie', the gig features support from Good Habit. Members of T.Rex (not including Marc Bolan) are in the audience.

For a while, T.Rex bass player Steve Currie styles his hair like David's, until a furious Bolan asks him to change it.

During this, 'the slickest show in town' according to journalist John Ingham, Mick Rock photographs the performance from stage level.

Rock is also editing 16mm film footage he has shot of David on and off stage to the track 'Moonage Daydream'.

Trainee journalist Steve Harley, who has visited Haddon Hall and been an Arts Lab attendee, sneaks in and watches the sound-check with a few of his friends before seeing the show which will prompt him to form glam-pop act Cockney Rebel. "It was amazing, like David was moving around the stage on ice skates," said Harley in 1994.

Saturday 13 May

▶ David Bowie, Slough Technical College, Willington Street, Slough, Berks.

Carillion and Heavy Eric support at the college's summer ball, where entry is 60p. David and The Spiders have been booked at the suggestion of fan and student Bob Lewis, who designs a poster.

Sunday 14 May

David and Mick Ronson are at Olympic Studios in Barnes, west London, to co-produce Mott The Hoople's recording of 'All The Young Dudes' in the facility's Studio 2.

During the session, engineered by Keith Harwood (who also mixes the track), David records a guide vocal for Mott frontman Ian Hunter,[1] and Nicky Graham and security man Stuey George are seconded to add hand-claps.

Rather than being about his teenage fans, 'All The Young Dudes' sums up the nightclubbing coterie which surrounds David; Sombrero regulars Silly Billy, Wendy Kirby and Freddie Burretti all feature in the lyrics.

1. David's vocal was remixed with Mott's original backing track for 1998's *All The Young Dudes: The Anthology* box-set.

Tuesday 16 May

The band record a session for John Peel's Radio One show *Top Gear* at the BBC studios in Maida Vale, west London.

Friday 19 May

▶ David Bowie, Oxford Polytechnic, Gipsy Lane, Headington, Oxford.

Nicky Graham drives Bob Harris – who is the compère at many gigs on the tour – and CBS A&R head Dan Loggins to the show.

Saturday 20 May

The A-side of this month's US release of 'Starman'/'Suffragette City' is slightly different: David's spoken intro is edited out and, to comply with the preferred

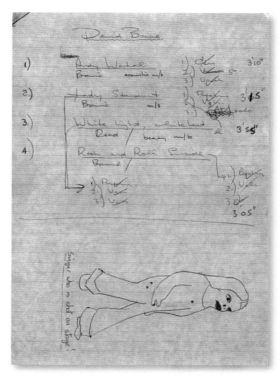

duration among American radio stations, RCA's Dennis Katz ensures the song is cut by 10 seconds.

Monday 22 May

The band are back at the BBC's Maida Vale studios to record four tracks for daytime broadcast on DJ Johnnie Walker's Radio One lunchtime show: 'Starman', 'Space Oddity', 'Changes' and 'Oh! You Pretty Things'.

Tuesday 23 May

First thing in the morning David and The Spiders return once more to the Maida Vale studios to record another *Sounds Of The 70s* for broadcast by Radio One's Bob Harris in June. Their recent John Peel session is broadcast in the evening.

Gem plugger Anya Wilson is there "buzzing around the studio keeping everyone in an up frame of mind", according to producer Jeff Griffin in 2000.

However, the morning call puts off David from recording another session for the BBC. "It's not surprising he didn't come back again," said Griffin. "BBC admin didn't seem to realise that rock'n'roll bands weren't necessarily at their best at 9.30am."

In the evening David and Mott The Hoople hold a party in London to celebrate completing the recording of 'All The Young Dudes'.

Thursday 25 May

▶ David Bowie, Chelsea Village, Bournemouth, Dorset.

The bill includes the Rosko Roadshow, a DJ set by Emperor Rosko,[1] the Radio One DJ whose assistant is David's friend Geoff MacCormack.

1. Born Mike Pasternak, Los Angeles, 1942.

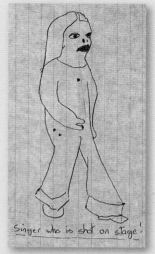

OPPOSITE PAGE

LEFT: Michael Putland contact sheet.

RIGHT: Slough College poster designed by Bob Lewis. It was Lewis who originally suggested to the Student Union that they should book David.

THIS PAGE

TOP LEFT: Jeff Griffin's running order for David and The Spiders Maida Vale BBC radio session on 23 May, with David's drawing titled 'Singer Who Is Shot On Stage!'.

TOP RIGHT: Drawing detail.

MIDDLE RIGHT: Hemel Hempstead, 7 May.

BOTTOM: Ebbisham Hall, 27 May.

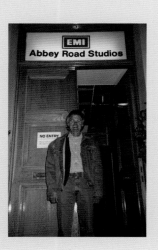

Saturday 27 May

▶ David Bowie, Ebbisham Hall, Epsom, Surrey.

This is one of the gigs promoted by Gem and MC-ed by Bob Harris, who brings along the BBC's Jeff Griffin.

Soundman Robin Mayhew leaves immediately after the show to attend the birth of his son Olly at Epsom district hospital at 11.10pm. Angie and David send flowers.

Monday 29 May

Plans for David's first tour of the US are delayed from late May to September by Defries, who splits with Laurence Myers after his partner expresses concern at the mounting debt accrued from breaking David, compared with the relatively low returns (*Hunky Dory* has sold just 11,000 copies by this point).

After protracted negotiations, Defries pledges to cover the £29,000 invested by Gem in David's career thus far, and to pay a further $500,000 from David's future earnings to Myers for helping relaunch his career.

With Myers concentrating on MoR acts – achieving success with The New Seekers, featuring Ken Pitt's protégé Marty Kristian – Gem is reformulated as the Gem Toby Organisation (GTO).

Friday 2 June

▶ David Bowie, City Hall, Northumberland Road, Newcastle, Tyne and Wear.

David takes a flight to the venue in the north-eastern city where he played on a package tour with The Manish Boys in 1964. The JSD Band are the support act and in the audience is future Pet Shop Boy Neil Tennant,[1] who secures an autograph from David outside the stage door.

1. Tennant and fellow Pet Shop Boy partner Chris Lowe remixed David's 'Hallo Spaceboy' in 1996. The single reached number 12 in the UK.

Saturday 3 June

▶ David Bowie, Liverpool Stadium.

During the Liverpool show, as the band launches into 'Gotta Get A Job', there is a power cut.

"We had so much equipment plugged into the mains, everything blew," said road manager Will Palin in 1993. "We were learning as we went along."

David entertains the crowd on his acoustic guitar for the time it takes to hook up the electricity, and the band surges into a powerful 'Suffragette City' to end the show.

Melody Maker reports: 'David Bowie helping Mott produce LP'.

Sunday 4 June

▶ David Bowie, Preston Public Hall,[1] Lune Street, Preston, Lancashire.

The JSD Band are support; tickets are 60p each.

1. Now known as the Preston Corn Exchange.

Monday 5 June

'Oh! You Pretty Things' is broadcast on Radio One's lunchtime show hosted by Johnnie Walker as a teaser to new single 'Starman' being played every day on the programme for the rest of the week. These are the versions recorded for the show on 22 May.

Tuesday 6 June

▶ David Bowie, St George's Hall, Bridge Street, Bradford, West Yorks.

Today sees the release of *The Rise and Fall of Ziggy Stardust and The Spiders From Mars*, the album which will break David into mainstream success.

In Bradford an increasingly familiar event occurs; following the afternoon sound check, David and the band are at first refused entry to a restaurant because their attire is deemed improper.

Pianist/booker Nicky Graham helps smooth the way and eventually they gain access.

Wednesday 7 June

▶ David Bowie, City Hall, Barkers Pool, Sheffield.

Thursday 8 June

▶ David Bowie, Town Hall, Albert Road, Middlesbrough, North Yorks.

The JSD Band support.

A feature by Mick Rock appears in *Rolling Stone* under the heading 'David is just not Serious' with quotes delivered in Cockney tones: "I'm gettin' all this confidence again. I thought it 'ad gone for good."

Friday 9 June

David, Defries and Ronson fly to New York for a three-day trip for promotion for *Hunky Dory* and *Ziggy Stardust* and negotiations for record company support for David's first US tour in the autumn.

On arrival, the three are driven straight from the airport to Madison Square Garden,[1] where Elvis Presley[2] is performing. They take their seats after the show has started.

"I had the humiliating experience of walking down the centre aisle to my very good RCA-provided seat while Elvis performed 'Proud Mary'," David later said. "As I was in full Ziggy regalia by this time – brilliant red hair and kabuki platform shoes – I'm sure many of the audience presumed Mary had just arrived. He looked at me and, if looks could kill… We nearly stopped the show. He was fantastic."

RCA's attempts to set up a post-concert meet between the label's latest signing and most celebrated artist are unsuccessful but, though disappointed, David is dazzled by the King's 'sexy' performance.[3]

After the concert, David is interviewed by Lillian Roxon in his suite at the Helmsley Park Lane Hotel.

1. David subsequently appeared at Madison Square Garden on a number of occasions, including his 50th birthday concert on 9 January 1997.

2. David and Presley never met, though rumours of a collaboration circulated during David's spell in Los Angeles in the mid-70s. David told Pete Frame in 1993: "Presley's management at one time offered the idea that it might be interesting to update Elvis if I got involved with his production, but nothing ever came of that. But he did send me a telegram when I was on tour once, saying that he would really like to meet me. So I never found out really where that would have

gone, whether he did want somebody to work with him." During an interview in 2002, David said: "I would have loved to have worked with him. God, I would have adored it. He did send me a note once – (imitates Presley's drawl) 'All the best, and have a great tour.' I still have that note."

3. In *Interview* magazine in May 1993, David told writer Hanif Kureishi: "At no point did I ever doubt I would be as near as anybody could be to England's Elvis Presley. Even from eight or nine years old, I thought, well, I'll be the greatest rock star in England. I just made up my mind."

Saturday 10 June

The hastily arranged New York visit – which has necessitated interrupting the UK tour and cancelling a performance at Leicester Polytechnic tonight – enables David to reconnect with Leee Black Childers and Wayne County, who are enlisted to circulate copies of *Ziggy Stardust* to influential and taste-making friends.

During the trip David invites Lou Reed to play his first gig in the UK at a charity concert at the Royal Festival Hall which he and the Spiders are headlining.

In the UK the media is picking up on David's challenge to Marc Bolan's pop supremacy. In her review of the Liverpool Stadium show, Barbara Drillsman writes in *Melody Maker*: 'David has come a long way since 'Space Oddity', far enough to make me think that Marc Bolan won't be clinging on to the top superstar label for very much longer.'

OPPOSITE PAGE

TOP LEFT: Full-page *Melody Maker* tour itinerary with George Underwood drawing.

TOP RIGHT: David preparing for showtime, photographed by Byron Newman.

MIDDLE: Liverpool Stadium leaflet, 3 June.

BOTTOM: Producer of four BBC Bowie sessions in 1971–1972; Jeff Griffin during editing of *Bowie At The Beeb* in 2000.

THIS PAGE

TOP: Recording 'Starman' for ITV's *Lift Off With Ayshea* (in front of a small studio audience), 15 June.

LEFT: Oxford Town Hall, 17 June.
© Mick Rock

In this year...

Saturday 10 June
ENTRY into the UK singles chart of 'Rock And Roll (Parts 1 & 2)' by Gary Glitter, a client of Tony Defries' partner Laurence Myers. David and Glitter occasionally met at the Gem offices in this period and later while on the road in the US in 1974 and Australia in 1978.

RELEASE of album *Vince Is Alive, Well And Rocking In Paris* by Vince Taylor, one of the inspirations for the Ziggy Stardust character.

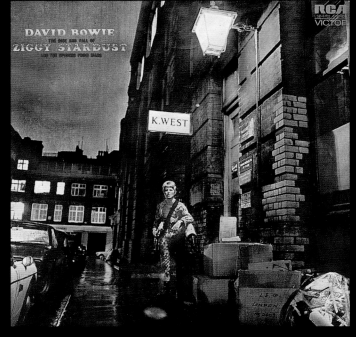

ABOVE: Ziggy Stardust front cover. I could make a transformation as a rock 'n' roll star… RIGHT: The original back cover artwork. Faux diamond beads are sown into the costume's crutch (to mimic a 'Droog' cod-piece). Another subtle *Clockwork Orange* reference, though rarely referred to. BELOW: Live in London, 1972. BOTTOM: The original front cover artwork, which managed to survive and was found with the master tapes.

THE RISE AND FALL OF ZIGGY STARDUST AND THE SPIDERS FROM MARS Released Tuesday 6 June

Side One

1. FIVE YEARS (Bowie) (4.42)
David Bowie (vocal, guitar)
Mick Ronson (guitar, piano, vocal)
Trevor Bolder (bass)
Woody Woodmansey (drums)
Session orchestra

2. SOUL LOVE (Bowie) (3.33)
David Bowie (vocal, guitar, sax)
Mick Ronson (guitar, vocal)
Trevor Bolder (bass)
Woody Woodmansey (drums, percussion)

3. MOONAGE DAYDREAM (Bowie) (4.37)
David Bowie (vocal, guitar)
Mick Ronson (guitar, piano, vocal)
Trevor Bolder (bass)
Woody Woodmansey (drums)
Session orchestra

4. STARMAN (Bowie) (4.16)
David Bowie (vocal, guitar)
Mick Ronson (guitar, vocal, Mellotron)
Trevor Bolder (bass)
Woody Woodmansey (drums)
Session orchestra

5. IT AIN'T EASY (Ron Davies) (2.57)
David Bowie (vocal, guitar)
Mick Ronson (guitar, vocal)
Trevor Bolder (bass)
Woody Woodmansey (drums)
Rick Wakeman (harpsichord)
Dana Gillespie (backing vocal)

Side Two

1. LADY STARDUST (Bowie) (3.21)
David Bowie (vocal, guitar)
Mick Ronson (piano, guitar, vocal)
Trevor Bolder (bass)
Woody Woodmansey (drums)

2. STAR (Bowie) (2.47)
David Bowie (vocal, guitar)
Mick Ronson (guitar, piano, vocal)
Trevor Bolder (bass)
Woody Woodmansey (drums)

3. HANG ON TO YOURSELF (Bowie) (2.38)
David Bowie (vocal, guitar)
Mick Ronson (guitar, piano, vocal)
Trevor Bolder (bass)
Woody Woodmansey (drums)

4. ZIGGY STARDUST (Bowie) (3.13)
David Bowie (vocal, guitar)
Mick Ronson (guitar, vocal)
Trevor Bolder (bass)
Woody Woodmansey (drums)

5. SUFFRAGETTE CITY (Bowie) (3.25)
David Bowie (vocal, guitar, sax)
Mick Ronson (guitar, piano, ARP synth, vocal)
Trevor Bolder (bass)
Woody Woodmansey (drums)

6. ROCK 'N' ROLL SUICIDE (Bowie) (2.57)
David Bowie (vocal, sax)
Mick Ronson (guitar, piano, vocal)
Trevor Bolder (bass)
Woody Woodmansey (drums)
Session orchestra

Produced by David Bowie and Ken Scott
Arrangements by David Bowie and Mick Ronson
Recorded at Trident Stud os
Photographed by Brian Ward
Original Artwork by Terry Pastor (Main Artery)
A GEM Production
(RCA SF8287) – UK   (RCA LSP.4702) – US

LEFT: Ziggy cover experiment shot, Brian Ward, January 1972. David wears the jump suit he co-designed with Freddie Burretti and Kansai Yamamoto's patent leather platform boots (a snip at £28 from Boston-151 in Fulham). RIGHT: *A Clockwork Orange* style inner sleeve images of David, Trevor Bolder, Woody Woodmansey and Mick Ronson. BELOW: Heddon Street signage.

CREATED around a concept seeded during his American visit of February 1971, the *Ziggy Stardust* album had a stratospheric effect on David's life and career.

Replete with sci-fi imagery and religious allegory, the album had as its central character David's metaphor for the ultimate rock star, a role for which he was simultaneously presenting his candidacy.

Interest in David and the album escalated with the release of 'Starman' in April 1972, and went nationwide with his beguiling appearance performing the song on *Top Of The Pops*. One wonders how David and *Ziggy* might have fared had RCA A&R executive Dennis Katz not intervened on hearing the draft track-listing of December 1971 and insisted that it needed to be lifted with a song with more immediacy than those already recorded.

Among tracks worked up in the aftermath of David's return from the US promotional trip were 'Moonage Daydream' and 'Hang On To Yourself', both first recorded at demo level with a cast of trusted musicians and given limited release under the guise of The Arnold Corns.

Although these recordings suffered from the fact that David's fashionista friend Freddie Burretti was a no-goer as a credible frontman, once lyrically revised and given the total Ziggy treatment they became glittering glam gems in the context of this album.

And 'Hang On To Yourself' became a live mainstay, as the opening number of performances by David and The Spiders until their final appearance at Hammersmith Odeon in July 1973.

Trevor Bolder realised they were creating music of a very superior quality during the Trident sessions.

"When I walked into the control room and heard 'Moonage Daydream' played back through the speakers for the first time I knew then we really had something special," said Bolder in 1993. "I'll never forget it."

HEDDON STREET W1
CITY OF WESTMINSTER
HEDDON STREET

'David Bowie has pulled off his complex task with consummate style, with some great rock & roll with all the wit and passion required to give it sufficient dimension.' *Rolling Stone*

The only non-original, US singer-songwriter Ron Davies' 'It Ain't Easy', had been ousted from preceding album *Hunky Dory*, yet sits perfectly at the end of the first side, channelling the gospel flavour of Davies' recording as featured on his 1970 A&M album *Silent Song Through The Land* (with one of David's heroes, Leon Russell, on piano).

While publisher Bob Grace was keen that every track on *Ziggy* should be written by David (thus maximising royalty income), David was adamant about including Davies' song, possibly to signify the debt that *Hunky Dory* owed to *Silent Song Through The Land*.

In recent years two other people have been discovered to have played on this track: Dana Gillespie on backing vocals and Rick Wakeman on harpsichord.

The brief oscillating sound which kicks off the song is a heavily echoed vocal.

While the ARP synthesiser on 'Suffragette City' was programmed by Scott and played by Ronson to replicate the sound of a bank of saxophones, a character mentioned in the title track, 'Ziggy Stardust', can be traced back to David's schooldays. In 1971, David's artist friend from Bromley Tech, George Underwood, mentioned a biker called Gilly (an abbreviation of Gilbert) who attended the rival Bromley Grammar School.

"He became a bit of a local hero when he told the headmaster where to go when he tried to force him to shave his sideburns," said Underwood in 1994.

'...was really impressed with Gilly, thought he was great.' And so this long-lost suburban rebel was incorporated in the line: 'Jamming good with Weird and Gilly...'

As for the dramatic torch song which closes the album, 'Rock 'n' Roll Suicide' included components of soul singer James Brown's overblown performance of 'Lost Someone' and 'Try Me' on one of David's favourite albums, *The Apollo Theatre Presents: In Person! The James Brown Show* from 1963.

But these are elevated by a Parisian influence. "There was a sense of French chanson in there," said David in 2003. "It wasn't an obvious 50s pastiche," revealing that it contained "an Edith Piaf nuance". His delivery of the line 'Oh no love, you're not alone' echoes the passion of Piaf's 'Non, je ne regrette rien'.

The compelling front cover stemmed from a shoot with photographer Brian Ward one afternoon in January 1972 at his studio at 29 Heddon Street, just off central London's busy Regent Street. Ward had spent the afternoon shooting David and The Spiders in various poses, including the monochrome close-ups featured on the original inner sleeve. When he suggested they go outside for more photographs before the natural light was lost, The Spiders opted to stay inside and only David braved the drizzle which had started to fall.

Not willing to venture far, David was photographed just a few doors down outside number 21,[1] the home of furriers K. West.

Over time, K. West (or 'kwest', as David once called it), has become part of the iconography, though little is known about the company itself. The 'K' actually stands for Konn, and the 'West' a reference to the West End. The company was set up in 1903 by a Polish émigré called Henry Konn and the name originated when imported fur bundles were marked 'K West' to indicate that it was Henry Konn's. (Presumably there was a 'K East' too which indicated a different company.)

Konn worked out of various addresses in London's West End, taking the lease of the first floor of Burlington Buildings[2] at number 21. At one time three generations of the family worked there: Henry, his son Ludy and grandson Victor. In the 1980s, when Heddon Street was sold by Sir Richard Sutton's Settled Estates, the property changed hands a number of times until K. West vacated in 1991.

"My grandfather had marvellous taste in everything, women and beautiful objects included," said Victor Konn in 2007. "The business interior was beautifully furnished and fitted, with a show room and workrooms leading off. The walls were oak-panelled and there were very valuable Grecian-styled carved chairs in red leather and a grand inlaid table. Everything had to be sold to get us out of the lease in the end. The chairs sold for more than £30,000 each."

However, back in 1972, the K. West directors were not impressed when their name was emblazoned on the front of a best-selling pop album.

Within a month, solicitors acting for them contacted RCA: 'Our clients are Furriers of high repute who deal with a clientele generally

wish to be associated with Mr. Bowie or this record as it might be assumed that there was some connection between our client's firm and Mr. Bowie, which is certainly not the case.'

Soon, however, the company adjusted to its building being photographed by Bowie fans and tourists.

Now, in 2010, the tenants are proud of the association, displaying a copy of the album cover in a corridor.

The colour retouching and typography on the *Ziggy* sleeve was carried out once again by Terry Pastor, George Underwood's partner in design studio Main Artery.

Pastor airbrushed the colours directly on to Ward's photograph, which had been printed on uncoated sepia card. The lettering was initially applied using Letraset, then traced and airbrushed red and yellow and inset with small white stars.

"David phoned to ask how it was going," said Pastor in 1997. "I told him the front was done and I had started on the photo for the back sleeve and he was really surprised there would also be a retouched photo on the back. He was excited and said 'I can't wait to see it'."

Just as on the *Hunky Dory* sleeve, David's blond hair on the *Ziggy* cover is due to re touching; at this point his hair was still its natural light brown. In Ward's front-cover photograph he is pictured holding Mark Pritchett's Gibson Les Paul guitar, which was also colour tinted from its original red to match David's hair. This was the instrument used by Pritchett on The Arnold Corns recordings, including 'Hang On To Yourself' and 'Moonage Daydream'.

David wore the cover's geometric patterned 'boiler suit' not only throughout the subsequent UK tour but also off stage. Identical sets of trousers and jackets were run up but lost as the tour progressed, while some were even torn from him bodily as his popularity increased.[3]

The back-cover photograph was taken at the north end of Heddon Street, which forms part of an alley leading back on to Regent Street.[4] For a short time the familiar red phone box was replaced with a modern BT telephone booth, but the growing significance of the *Ziggy* cover (which helped gain the street Westminster Conservation Area status) forced the reinstatement of a box in the original style (though not the exact model) in 1997 when the cul-de-sac was renovated.

The K. West sign was later concealed by another company's and acquired by a fan in the late 80s. The lamp above David was a converted gas lamp and is still in situ.

In 1981 David made a return visit to Heddon Street, where he encountered writer/performer Tim Whitnall – who played the role of the young Elvis Presley in late-70s West End musical *Elvis* – taking photographs.

To Whitnall's astonishment, David arrived and then obligingly posed for him under the sign, his hair by that point styled and coloured in a similar fashion to the *Ziggy* cover image. It is understood that David has made occasional visits since then, to show close friends 'David's London'.

Unfinished tracks from the *Ziggy* sessions include: 'It's Gonna Rain Again', 'Shadow Man', 'Only One Paper Left' (originally recorded by Hype), 'Black Hole Kids' and a re-working of The Arnold Corns recording 'Looking Fo

TOP: K. West Furriers founder Henry Konn in the workroom at 21 Heddon Street, circa 1932. MIDDLE: David Hemmings looking towards Brian Ward's studio in Heddon Street in Michelangelo Antonioni's 1966 film *Blow-Up*. ABOVE: David returns to Heddon Street and the scene of his legendary *Ziggy Stardust* cover image. Photo by Tim Whitnall, February 1981.

ZIGGY STARDUST

TOP: Terry Pastor's original lettering. TOP LEFT: *Ziggy Stardust* and *Hunky Dory* cover artist Terry Pastor. "David told me he had started to receive a lot of fan mail and that they believed he was from out of space. That made both of us laugh." ABOVE MIDDLE AND RIGHT: Ziggy cover contact strip images. ABOVE LEFT: Mark Pritchett in 1971 playing the Les Paul he would lend to David for the *Ziggy Stardust* cover photo session. BELOW LEFT: Ziggy cover out-take shot. BELOW RIGHT: Ken Scott in 1972.

The bonus tracks on 1990's Ryko reissue were culled from the November 1971 Trident sessions, supplemented by a couple of earlier demos.

One of those completed at the November sessions, 'Velvet Goldmine', was released by RCA in 1975 as a track on the *Space Oddity* EP, though David had not approved the mix.

Another completed track, 'Sweet Head', was not released because RCA was uncomfortable that the lyric was such a direct paean to oral sex. 'John, I'm Only Dancing' was a variation from the spring 1972 Olympic sessions, from which the initial single came. (▸ 24.6.72)

The Ryko 1990 set includes the previously unreleased original demo of 'Ziggy Stardust', recorded in February 1971 on David's return from America. Like most of his demos of this period, it was taped at Radio Luxembourg's London studio, where the early demo version of 'Lady Stardust' was recorded the following month.

In 2002, to celebrate the 30th anniversary of the album's release, EMI produced a remastered version with a bonus CD including studio banter before the intro to 'Sweet Head' and a version of 'Moonage Daydream' on which Ronson's guitar is to the fore.

This version was used to accompany a series of dramatic TV ads for Dunlop tyres in 2000, remixed by British producers Alan Moulder and Andy Wright.

In 1986, David said of *Ziggy Stardust*, "I acknowledge it was

my moment", yet he often felt that the final mix was not as heavyweight as he would have wished, and certainly not a match for its successor, *Aladdin Sane*.

"I'll never forgive my ex-management company in those days, MainMan, for losing my 24 tracks," he said in 1993. "They don't exist any more. I would give my right arm to remix that album, because I know with today's technology I could bring out a lot of what Mick was playing, and give a lot more resonance to the bass and the bass drum."

In fact, in the interim the majority of the multi-tracks have surfaced. Maybe one day the full majesty of David's vision will be heard.

1. K. West was based at 21 Heddon Street, not at 23.

2. Burlington Buildings backs on to the site of Apple Corps' headquarters in Savile Row, where The Beatles' last live performance was filmed on the roof for documentary *Let It Be* in 1969.

3. David no longer has this or any of the other early 1972 Ziggy outfits.

4. The alleyway from Regent Street into Heddon Street appears in Michelangelo Antonioni's film *Blow-Up*. In one scene, lead actor David Hemmings briefly looks down it, towards the telephone box and Ward's photographic studio.

ABOVE: David performs 'Starman' on *Lift Off With Ayshea*, broadcast 21 June.

In this year...

Monday 26 June
RECRUITMENT of bass player Rik Kenton to Roxy Music. Kenton's first band, Mouseproof, started out at David's Beckenham Arts Lab in 1969.

July
RELEASE of triple album *Revelations – A Musical Anthology For Glastonbury Fayre* by the concert's promoters in an attempt to recoup £5,000 lost at the previous summer's concert. All featured artists contributed their work for free, David's offering being his and The Spiders' update of 'The Supermen' recorded during the *Ziggy Stardust* sessions.

Glastonbury promoter and *Frendz* music editor John Coleman had asked David for permission to include at least one song performed live at the event but, on David's instruction, Tony Defries denied the request and demanded the master tapes were handed over. "Angie was dispatched to pick them up, and then she lost them," recalled Coleman in 2000.

Monday 12 June

On returning from New York, David is greeted with the news that *Ziggy Stardust* has sold 8,000 copies in the week since release – a highly respectable figure.

David has a meeting with Ringo Starr during which the former Beatle asks him to co-star in the comedy/horror film *Son Of Dracula* Starr is producing for Apple Films.[1]

David politely turns down the role as Dracula's son, cornily named Count Down.

1. At the time Starr had already started work on the film *Born To Boogie* with Marc Bolan and was also appearing in the in-production *That'll Be the Day*.

Tuesday 13 June

▶ David Bowie, Colston Hall, Colston Street, Bristol, Avon.
The JSD Band support.

Thursday 15 June

A show in Coventry is cancelled to enable David and the band (without Nicky Graham) to fly to Manchester to record a performance of 'Starman' on Granada TV children's pop show *Lift Off With Ayshea* (presented by Ayshea Brough, whom David met as a performer doing the round of continental TV appearances in 1969).

Friday 16 June

▶ David Bowie, Town Hall, Main Street, Torquay, Devon.
The *NME*'s Gig Guide page describes David as 'a major world talent – and it can't be long now before the world realises it. He's what's happening, baby, and you'd better get into it before he leaves you behind.'

Saturday 17 June

▶ David Bowie, Town Hall, St Aldate's, Oxford.
The JSD Band support.

To a packed venue, during the 'Suffragette City' finale, David gains immediate notoriety by simulating fellatio on Mick Ronson's guitar.

This outrageous act of showmanship is captured by photographer Mick Rock (who has been forewarned by David) and the image will help raise David's public profile immeasurably.

Concert booker Nicky Graham initially found good venues hard to interest as David was still comparatively unknown. When a venue was pleased and eager to re-book (like Oxford), Graham was quick to capitalise.

In *Disc*, Rosalind Russell reviews *Ziggy Stardust*, awarding the album a maximum four stars.

Monday 19 June

▶ David Bowie, Civic Centre, Southampton, Hants.
The JSD Band support.

The musicians return to the city where they played the adjacent, and much smaller, Guild Hall only three months earlier, while the BBC broadcasts the Bob Harris-presented *Sounds Of The 70s* session.

During the tour, on a brief return to Haddon Hall, David and some bandmates discover his prize record collection scattered across the living room floor, with covers and vinyl scrawled on with ballpoint pen. Left unattended for a brief while, Zowie has comprehensively trashed his father's record collection. David is not amused.

Wednesday 21 June

▶ David Bowie & The Spiders From Mars, Civic Hall, Dunstable, Herts.[1]

In the afternoon, thousands of British children witness the recent recording of 'Starman' when *Lift Off With Ayshea* is broadcast in the post-school slot.[2]

The evening gig is the third booking by Aylesbury's Friars promoter Dave Stopps. This is the first show where The Spiders From Mars are officially billed as David's backing band.

The ticket price is 75p. Proclaimed as the 'Flame Of The Home Counties', David's support is provided not by the JSD Band, as on several recent dates, but San Francisco rockers the Flamin' Groovies (whose producer is Lou Reed's ex-manager and producer Richard Robinson).

David climaxes the show by ripping up his white silk shirt and throwing it into the audience.

The encore is 'I'm Waiting For The Man' during which there are more outrageous antics when David chases Ronson around the stage trying to press his naked torso against his guitarist's body.

Mick Rock is on hand to film and photograph the show and the backstage preparations.

1. This concert is almost cancelled when security man Stuey George accidentally sets off the sprinkler system during the set-up, flooding the stage and backstage area. "I can still remember the water dripping on Woody's head during the show," said roadie Will Palin in 1993.
2. Granada TV subsequently erased the broadcast.

Saturday 24 June

In an interview with Roy Hollingworth in *Melody Maker*, Lou Reed sings David's praises: "He's the only person around. Everything has been tedious, rock'n'roll has been tedious, except for what David has been doing. There's a mutual empathy between us. That's hard to find these days."

Today David and The Spiders are at Trident to record new single 'John, I'm Only Dancing', which will further underline his ambivalent sexual predilections.

The two-chord acoustic guitar riff which underpins the song is based on Sonny Boy Williamson's 'Pontiac Blues' as performed backed by The Yardbirds and released on his 1963 album recorded at London blues venue The Crawdaddy.

Two takes are taped with co-producer Ken Scott, along with a version of The Who's 1965 mod anthem 'I Can't Explain',[1] which will become an occasional part of the live set.

1. This version was far rowdier than the one which appeared on

1973's *Pin Ups*. David rejected Rykodisc's request to include this as a bonus track on the 1990 reissue of *Pin Ups*.

Sunday 25 June

▶ David Bowie & The Spiders From Mars, The Greyhound, Park Lane, Croydon, Surrey.

The frenzy around David continues to build. It is later reported that up to 1,000 ticketless fans are turned away from the venue in the south London suburb tonight.

There is also a lot of interest in Roxy Music, who are supporting along with Trapeze, and have recently made their TV debut on *The Old Grey Whistle Test*.[1]

Bryan Ferry's new band have been recommended by David's Beckenham friend Mark Pritchett, a Dulwich College schoolmate of Roxy guitarist Phil Manzanera. Tonight is the occasion of David's first meeting with Brian Eno.

"This was a hell of a gig," said Nicky Graham in 1990. "David was just breaking and so were Roxy. It was a really hot night but a really great atmosphere."

1. Broadcast by BBC2 on 20 June 1972.

Monday 26 June

An appearance at Guildford Civic Hall is cancelled as David and his fellow musicians shift base to Olympic Studios at 117 Church Road in the south-west London suburb of Barnes to record nine takes of 'John, I'm Only Dancing'.

Ken Scott is not involved[1] so David is in sole charge of production, assisted by engineer Keith Harwood. On this session, Lindsay Scott (no relation) of the JSD Band plays violin note-for-note with Ronson's guitar solo.[2]

To achieve sufficient echo on the track's handclaps, these are overdubbed in the studio's entrance hall where David and The Spiders are enthusiastically joined by arriving members of The Faces.

1. Ken Scott was unaware until 1999 that it was re-recorded at Olympic Studios, so similar is it to the Trident version.
2. Lindsay Scott received his credit on the 30th anniversary reissue of *Ziggy Stardust* in 2002. His input can clearly be heard from the middle of the first verse and thereafter in the song. David was friendly with Scott and was keen to involve him in one of his sessions.

Thursday 29 June

Four instrumental takes of 'Starman' are recorded for the forthcoming *Top Of The Pops* performance. Musicians' Union rules dictate that the music must be freshly recorded, while the vocal may be performed live.

Friday 30 June

Today Tony Defries lays the foundations for his growing music business empire by changing the name of the company he acquired in 1971 from Minnie Bell Ltd to MainMan Ltd.[1]

Defries retains 99 of MainMan's 100 shares, with the remaining one held by Gem's former accountant and MainMan employee Peter Gerber. David is not asked to become a partner, though he believes he

holds an equal stake with Defries.

Another live performance is cancelled – at Queen's Hall in High Wycombe, Bucks. Booking agent/pianist Nicky Graham is unhappy with the promoter, who continues to advertise David's appearance even after he is told that this will not happen. Replacement headliner is the support act, folk singer Jonathan Kelly. Alone he faces an unhappy audience of 2,000 who are informed of David's no-show on arrival.

David, Iggy Pop and Mick Rock attend the final date of Alice Cooper's Killer tour at north London venue Wembley Empire Pool.

The support act is Roxy Music. After the show David, Pop and Rock meet Cooper. "David really got the taste to do something more theatrical after this show," said Rock in 1994. "The Rainbow booking happened very quickly after this."[2]

Pop, who has known Cooper since his band was on the same Detroit rock circuit, has become frustrated at the lack of development in his career since signing with Defries the previous autumn.

Having been brought over to England to record a new album, Pop resists David's suggestion that he employ British heavy rockers the Edgar Broughton Band as backing musicians for him and guitarist James Williamson.

Instead he insists that MainMan pay for former Stooges members Ron and Scott Asheton to join them in London.

1. MainMan became the vehicle for at least three different companies: in the UK MainMan Artistes Ltd, in the US MainMan Ltd and in Switzerland MainMan SAAG.
2. In July 1972 at Aylesbury Friars, David utilised a trick from Cooper's 1971 Love It To Death tour by throwing promotional posters into the audience at the end of performances. Cooper's 1975 Welcome To My Nightmare dates also gave David the idea of allowing extended drum and individual musician solos mid-way through the sets on his 1976 Station To Station tour.

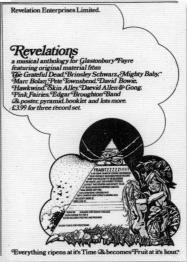

LEFT: Early Ziggy live.

TOP: *Revelations* compilation album advert.

ABOVE: Civic Hall Dunstable, 21 June.

Saturday 1 July

◗ David Bowie & The Spiders From Mars, Winter Gardens Pavilion, Royal Parade, Weston-super-Mare, Somerset.

'Starman' rises to number 41 in the UK singles chart, resulting in a breakthrough: an invitation to appear on BBC's all-important *Top Of The Pops*.

This month US magazine *Words & Music* includes a detailed appraisal of David's albums by Ron Ross under the heading 'David Bowie: Phallus in Pigtails, or the Music of the Spheres Considered as Cosmic Boogie'.

Sunday 2 July

◗ David Bowie & The Spiders From Mars, Rainbow Pavilion, Harbour site, Torbay, Devon.

The JSD Band support.

Up until now David has travelled with the rest of the band in a cramped minibus to most gigs (echoing those days on the road in the 60s in the back of a converted ambulance). From now on David travels separately in a hired Jaguar.

Wednesday 5 July

David and The Spiders are at BBC TV Centre to record their performance of 'Starman' on *Top Of The Pops*. On keyboards is Nicky Graham, while road manager Will Palin dances in the crowd wearing a yellow suit (he can be seen stage right).

David matches a brightly patterned Burretti two-piece with his red vinyl boots, while The Spiders are in pink, blue, scarlet and gold velvet ensembles. Bolder has grown his sideburns and dyed them white, creating an alarming contrast with his thatch of dark hair.

In 2009 Mick Woodmansey recalled waiting to appear on the set with British boogie band Status Quo: "We were dressed in our clothes and they had on their trademark denim. Francis Rossi looked at me and said: 'Shit, you make us feel old'."

Thursday 6 July

A large primetime UK audience watches David on the *Top Of the Pops* broadcast drape his arm around Mick Ronson's shoulder, exposing his white-painted fingernails and driving home the ambiguous glamour of the Ziggy persona.

With Nicky Graham on keyboards and David totally relaxed and confident in his performance, the appearance proves memorable to many viewers, from Boy George, Adam Ant and Spandau Ballet's Gary Kemp to Mick Jones of The Clash and Ian McCulloch of Echo & The Bunnymen, who said in 2007: "As soon as I heard 'Starman' and saw him on *Top Of The*

Pops, I was hooked. I seem to remember me being the first to say it, and then there was a host of other people saying how the *Top Of The Pops* performance changed their lives."

Friday 7 July

Lou Reed joins David and The Spiders for rehearsals at Underhill in Greenwich, south-east London, in preparation for tomorrow's joint performance at the Royal Festival Hall.

Tony Defries confirms MainMan's inception and growing stable of artists in a letter to American music rights body BMI in New York:

'As of 30 June 72 I will be dealing with all the activities of the artists whom I represent, namely: David Bowie, Mott The Hoople, Iggy Pop and the Stooges and Dana Gillespie, which were previously dealt with by the Gem Group.'

Saturday 8 July

◗ David Bowie & The Spiders From Mars, Royal Festival Hall, South Bank, London SE1.

As 'Starman' rises to number 29 in the UK charts, *Melody Maker* reporter Michael Watts visits Haddon Hall where he finds Angela feeding David nutritional supplement Complan "to keep his strength up". David returns to the front page of *Melody Maker*, which announces: 'The man most likely to has gone and done it, just as we predicted when we front-paged him back in January.'

Tonight's concert is in aid of environmental charity Friends of the Earth, with proceeds from the 50p-£2 tickets going to the 'Save the Whale' fund.[1]

Support acts are Marmalade and the JSD Band,[2] with comic DJ Kenny Everett compèring.

The performance is heralded by Walter Carlos' electronic version of Beethoven's 'Song Of Joy' from the *Clockwork Orange* soundtrack.

An intoxicated Lou Reed – who is surreptitiously steered on and off stage by Will Palin – makes his first UK appearance as David's 'very special guest' mid-way through the set, playing rhythm guitar and singing his songs 'White Light/White Heat', 'I'm Waiting For The Man' and 'Sweet Jane'.

Mick Rock is present, as is Japanese photographer Masayoshi Sukita, who does not have his camera with him.

Noting David's impact on the audience, Sukita – who has made his name as a fashion photographer and has arrived in the UK looking for cutting-edge subject matter – subsequently has a meeting with Rock and Tony Defries and outlines his plans for a shoot with David.

Defries, already looking into ways to fulfil David's wish to tour Japan, is intrigued.

"Mick and Tony really liked my photos, for which I am very grateful because that helped introduce my work to David," said Sukita in 2003.

Borrowing the London studio operated by his friend Hiroshi Yoda, Sukita photographs David in the first

DAVID BOWIE: glitter, panache and pace

A star is born

WHEN a shooting star is heading for the peak, there is usually one concert at which it's possible to declare: "That's it — he's made it." For David Bowie, opportunity knocked loud and clear last Saturday at London's Royal Festival Hall — and he left the stage a true 1972-style pop giant, clutching flowers from a girl who ran up and hugged and kissed him while a throng of fans milled around the stage. It was an exhilarating sight.

Bowie is going to be an old-fashioned, charismatic idol, for his show is full of glitter, panache and pace. Dressed outrageously in the tightest multi-coloured gear imaginable, Bowie is a flashback in many ways to pop star theatrics of about 10 years ago, carrying on a detached love affair with his audience, - wooing them, yet never surrendering that vital aloofness that makes him slightly untouchable.

On Saturday, the magic was boosted by an unadvertised appearance by Lou Reed. The American jammed with David and his group, and although mutual admiration societies like this are often disappointing ego

Surprise of the night were compere Kenny Everett's latest raves, the JSD Band. The commercial presented them as the most exciting discovery since early Fairport or Steeleye, and so great was their impact that no one will quarrel. They went down a storm with their unique mixture of Scottish reels and hard rock and Lindsay Scott's violin was absolutely...

of a series of sessions. He then photographs David on and off stage at the Rainbow in August and the following year in New York and Japan. Not long before the shoot with Sukita, David is photographed by David Bailey at his studio in Gloucester Avenue, Primrose Hill. For this rarely seen session, David wears a white ruffled shirt and bespoke matching striped satin trousers and waistcoat.

1. A large double-sided red and white poster promoting the event credited, among others, David's friend Lesley Duncan and her producer Jimmy Horowitz, though the exact nature of their contribution isn't known.

2. Mott The Hoople were originally lined up as support.

Monday 10 July

The Royal Festival Hall gig is covered by the British daily papers. The *Guardian* music critic Robin Denselow predicts: 'For the next few months his picture will be in every magazine. And yet – amazingly enough – he is a remarkable performer.'

ABOVE: Ziggy under the microscope. Close-up images of David were projected onto a screen during parts of the Rainbow shows. © Mick Rock

Friday 14 July

Journalist Michael Watts puts together a press release for MainMan headed 'A Profile of Rock Star David Bowie'. This is culled from interviews at Haddon Hall with David and Angie, as well as Defries, who describes David as 'the-beginning-of-an-empire-syndrome'.

Today David receives a letter from Christina Shand of Friends of the Earth, who sends 'a thousand thanks' for the performance and notifies him that the concert has raised around £1,000.

Late in the evening Lou Reed performs solo for the first time in Britain, at the King's Cross Cinema[1] in Pentonville Road, north London, with the Flamin' Groovies and Brinsley Schwarz supporting.

David, Angie and Ronson are in the audience. Among the photographs taken by Mick Rock is a portrait which will be used as the cover image of Reed's next album, *Transformer*.

1. Renamed The Scala later in the 70s.

Saturday 15 July

▶ David Bowie & The Spiders From Mars, Friars Borough Assembly Hall, Aylesbury, Bucks.

'Starman' continues its rise, to number 20 in the UK charts.

US media are flown to the UK especially for the show as part of an RCA-funded MainMan initiative to prepare the way for David's first US tour.

Dennis Katz, who signed David to RCA, is in town for the show and, with superb timing, the two biggest-circulation UK music weeklies pull out the stops.

A *Melody Maker* headline proclaims 'A Star is Born' while the *NME*'s front page announces a debut at the north London venue The Rainbow and dates for the autumn American tour with the banner: 'Rainbow, US for Britain's high priest of camp-rock'.

To ram the point home to the trans-Atlantic visitors, Tony Defries books a full-page space in *Melody Maker* for Mick Rock's photograph of David 'fellating' Ronson's guitar. This is adorned with a message written by David in Tippex.

Nicky Graham hires a Cadillac to transport David to Aylesbury, but it doesn't show, so a pink Rolls-Royce is booked as a last-minute substitute.

Tonight – the last time the JSD Band supports David – is the finale of the first Ziggy tour of the UK, taking place at the venue where it began six months previously.

David had wanted to relay the concert to a large video screen erected in the Market Square, but the idea is not pursued due to costs.

After the concert, as David exits the venue for the pink Roller, he is mobbed by an excited crowd and, in the scrum, is accidentally hit in the face, resulting in a bloody nose. David remains unfazed on the return journey to the King's Cross Cinema, where Iggy & The Stooges are succeeding Lou Reed in making their UK debut.

In silver leather jeans, his hair also sprayed silver, Pop leads the band into a 2am set during which photographer Mick Rock captures yet another iconic rock photograph – the image of the bare-chested Pop which becomes the cover of new album *Raw Power*.

Sunday 16 July

Before heading off on a two-week holiday, David conducts a busy schedule of press interviews at the Dorchester Hotel, Park Lane, Mayfair.

He also gives a press conference which is attended by Reed, his band and road crew and Iggy Pop.

Throughout the day, David plays tapes from recent Mott The Hoople studio sessions, since their album is now completed.

David shares the news with journalists that he has been asked to produce Lou Reed's next album, telling them that the forthcoming sessions will include contributions from a friend of John Lennon, bassist and record producer Klaus Voorman, and The Who's Keith Moon.[1]

Unhappy at the way he has been portrayed in the 'guitar fellatio' advert, Mick Ronson skips the press conference and flies to Toronto to work with American country rock band Pure Prairie League. The RCA act are recording a new album with producer Bob Ringe.[2]

1. Moon was unable to play on the *Transformer* sessions, which began on 11 August, since The Who started a 16-date European tour the same day.
2. Ronson contributed string arrangements and bass on the Pure Prairie League's *Bustin' Out* LP track 'Amie'. He also later covered two songs from the same album: 'Angel No.9' and 'Leave My Heart Alone'.

Monday 17 July

David and Angie are accompanied by Woodmansey and Bolder on a trip to Cyprus for a two-week summer break at a rented villa in the coastal resort of Kyrenia. Zowie remains in the UK with Haddon Hall neighbours the Frosts.

But any relaxation the holiday offers is interrupted when David, while driving a rented car, is involved in a head-on collision with another vehicle at a level-crossing outside Kyrenia.

Shaken up and with the rental car a write-off, he is charged with dangerous driving and is forced to attend a court hearing. All charges are dropped when he pays for the other car owner's damages, but he is lucky to walk away from such a serious accident without injury or further legal action.

Tuesday 18 July

Tony Defries writes to lawyer Alan Siegel about the deal for David to produce Lou Reed's new album: 'Unfortunately, Bowie has gone to Cyprus for the next two weeks so I will not be able to have the agreement signed until he returns. In addition, there has been a reorganisation between myself and Gem. I would suggest the new contract is made between RCA and MainMan Ltd.'

Thursday 20 July

In *Rolling Stone*, *Ziggy Stardust* receives a favourable review from Richard Cromelin: 'It's all tied up with the one aspect of David Bowie that sets him apart from both the exploiters of transvestism and writers/ performers of comparable talent – his theatricality.'

Saturday 22 July

'Starman' rises to number 18 in the UK charts.

Melody Maker's Michael Watts catches Marc Bolan in a chippy mood about David's new-found success: "Obviously we're very much bigger because we're two years ahead of him, and it's not the same riff either.

"David is into a whole different school to us. I think if Alice Cooper ever happens David Bowie would be much stronger 'cause he's a much better writer. I've always said he should stay there on one line, but he tends to lose interest. If he can hang out long enough he'll be fine. I think 'Prettiest Star' is one of the best things he's ever done. It was daring at the time, because after 'Space Oddity' it would have been easier to put [out] something with a string Mellotron sound. But I'm pleased it's happening for him."

The following day Ken Scott works on a remix of 'Starman' at Trident.

Tuesday 25 July

David's *Sounds Of The 70s: Bob Harris* session recorded in May is broadcast on Radio One.

Friday 28 July

CBS releases Mott The Hoople's new single, 'All The Young Dudes'[1] (Bowie)/'One Of The Boys' (Hunter).

Marc Bolan confides in George Underwood that he isn't happy about the song's lyric 'Oh man I need TV when I got T.Rex'. In 1998 George Underwood said Bolan had believed it was 'David's way of putting him down in public'.

When Mott have to change the reference to 'Marks & Sparks' (Marks & Spencer) to abide by BBC airplay guidelines on advertising, they take David up on his suggestion 'unlocked cars'.

1. In 1992, David and Mick Ronson joined Ian Hunter and members of Queen to perform 'All The Young Dudes' at the Wembley Stadium tribute concert to Freddie Mercury. Two years later, Hunter, Mott's Morgan Fisher and Queen drummer Roger Taylor performed the song at the Hammersmith Apollo during the Mick Ronson tribute concert.

Saturday 29 July

'Starman' peaks at number 10 in the UK charts.

Lou Reed appears at the Friars Club in Aylesbury and *Melody Maker*'s Alan Levin reviews 'All The Young Dudes': 'Long time Hoople supporters may be disappointed to find that the record really tells us more about its producer, arranger and writer, David Bowie, than it does about the band.'

Sunday 30 July

David and his party return to the UK on a storm-tossed flight from Cyprus.

Following on so soon after the car accident, this proves particularly harrowing for David. "The storm picked up the closer we got to England," said Trevor Bolder in 1995. "The plane was being thrown all over the place, with lightning bouncing off the wings. David was terrified by premonitions of his death. Angie freaked out too."

On reaching terra firma, David vows never to fly again.[1] Seriously concerned about his mortality, he will soon introduce Jacques Brel's 'My Death' into his live set.

1. David travelled by plane for the first time since this flight on 10 March 1977 from London to New York, accompanied by Iggy Pop.

Wednesday 2 August

David is at the BBC's Television Centre in west London for Mott The Hoople's recording of 'All The Young Dudes' for *Top Of The Pops*.

Thursday 10 August

David and his retinue set up camp at north London's Rainbow Theatre for intensive rehearsals and preparations for three extravagantly staged shows starting in nine days' time. Tickets for appearances on 19 and 20 August have sold out within hours so an additional date is booked for 30 August.

Today David and The Spiders work on the music.

Promoter Mel Bush has offered a fee of £1,000 for the first night at the venue. "It was an offer we couldn't refuse," said one-time MainMan employee Hugh Attwooll in 1986.

Hastily put together, the Rainbow shows are conceived in part as a response to Alice Cooper's theatricality, which is why Lindsay Kemp is called in to stage direct and visualise the *Ziggy Stardust* concept.

Angie is dispatched to Scotland to accompany Kemp back to London, where he finds David much changed.

"I was overwhelmed with his success. It's just that I was living in Scotland and Bowie had been in London for six months and it was extraordinary," said Kemp in 1991. "In six months he had become acclaimed."

The two theatrical Rainbow shows kick off the second phase of the Ziggy 72 UK tour, with an additional 10 massively over-subscribed performances (including a return to the Rainbow due to popular demand).

Friday 11 August

Woodmansey and Bolder continue rehearsals to backing tapes at the Rainbow. David and Mick Ronson meanwhile move into the Grosvenor House Hotel in Mayfair and head for Trident to co-produce Lou Reed's new album.

Managed by Trident's owners Norman and Barry Sheffield, Queen are recording their first album during downtime at the studio (mainly in the early hours), so David and singer Freddie Mercury have an opportunity to renew their friendship.[1]

ABOVE: David and Lou Reed at the Dorchester, 16 July. "Any society that allows people like Lou Reed and I to become rampant is really pretty well lost." © Mick Rock

Handwritten set list notes:

LADY STARDUST. DAVID. CO in frieze.
HANG ON TO YOURSELF. DAVID.
ZIGGY STARDUST DAVID MICK CO enter.
LIFE ON MARS DAVID CO. (possible change)
SUPER MAN DAVID TRAPEZE
FIVE YEARS. DAVID CO
SPACE ODDITY. DAVID MICK.
Andy WARHOLE. DAVID
MY DEATH. DAVID
WIDTH OF the Circle. DAVID.
WILD EYED BOY. DAVID ? CO?
Queen Bitch. DAVID CO
Suffragette city. DAVID CO
WAITING FOR MY MAN. DAVID CO
WHITE LIGHT. WHITE Heat. DAVID. CO

TOP: Lindsay Kemp's original set list notes, made during rehearsals for the Ziggy Stardust show at the Rainbow.

ABOVE: Rainbow foyer, 19 August.

RIGHT: David's notes for images he wanted projected during his Rainbow shows.

BELOW. *Rolling Stone* Brazil, August issue.

Mick Rock visits Trident to photograph David for a series of close-ups of facial details to be projected during the Rainbow shows.

Keen to cash in on David's new-found popularity, B&C Records release a second Arnold Corns single, 'Hang On To Yourself'/'Man In The Middle'.

The B-side features the song's author and David's friend Mark Carr-Pritchard on lead vocal (not Freddie as it is generally believed), but neither he nor David sanction the release. However, the recording is very important as it bridges between David's developing sound and songwriting style.

⊙ **The Arnold Corns**
A **'Hang On To Yourself'** (Bowie)
B **'Man In The Middle'** (Carr-Pritchard)[2]
(A-side musicians as 7 May 1971)

B-side:
David Bowie (vocal, guitar)
Mark Carr-Pritchard (lead vocal, rhythm guitar)
Mick Ronson (guitar)
Trevor Bolder (bass)
Mick Woodmansey (drums)
A-side Produced by David Bowie for Butterfly Record Productions.
B-side Produced by Roy Thomas Baker.
(B&C CB 189)

Recorded in June 71, 'Man In The Middle' is the final track recorded as The Arnold Corns but the musicians have predominantly changed to the future Spiders From Mars, which can clearly be detected in the rhythm.

'Man In The Middle' is the first hint of the new sound David and Ronson have been searching for (to which Mark Pritchard clearly contributes). In retrospect, the song provides a musical bridge between *Hunky Dory* and *Ziggy Stardust*.

1. In 1981, David's Queen collaboration 'Under Pressure' went to number one in the UK singles chart, making Queen's second and David's third number one UK single.

2. This track has been credited to David but was written by Mark Pritchett (as it was easier for David to collect the royalties for Mark if it was a hit).

Saturday 12 August

Lindsay Kemp and his five-strong troupe arrive at the Rainbow for three days of rehearsals to backing tapes and, occasionally, with accompaniment from Bolder and Woodmansey.

Meanwhile, David and Ronson divide their time between the Rainbow and stints at Trident producing Lou Reed's new album, which is completed in 10 days of six-hour sessions.

"Working with Lou Reed was very different from working with David," said engineer Ken Scott in 2001. "Lou was so out of it the whole time, which David never was. I recently met Lou in New York for a TV documentary, the first time since we made the LP. It was so funny because he hadn't a clue who I was, he just had no memory of me at all."

Ronson drives the production of the album, though there are communication problems between him and Reed, who said in 2000: "He had such a strong Hull accent he had to repeat things about five times, but he was a really sweet guy."

For the baritone sax break which ends the track 'Walk On The Wild Side' David called on Ronnie Ross, the man who gave him lessons in the instrument back in the early 60s.

When he receives the call, Ross[1] has never heard of Lou Reed and fails to recognise David at the studio. "He had make-up on and it didn't register at first," said Ross in 1986. "I think he's incredible. I love people who are that positive about their way of life."

Drummer on 'Walk On The Wild Side' is Richie Dharma, formerly of The Mick Abrahams Band, who was introduced to David by producer Gus Dudgeon in 1969 and also played on Michael Chapman's debut album *Fully Qualified Survivor*, to which Mick Ronson contributed.

When the sessions aren't progressing to his satisfaction, Reed occasionally adopts an abusive attitude to both David and Ronson, though he said in 1984: "The only person in the world with a temper more vile than mine is David Bowie."

There are lighter moments, however, when Reed makes a return visit to the Bowies at Haddon Hall.

As if this welter of activity isn't enough, today Mott The Hoople's 'All The Young Dudes' enters the UK charts for the first time at number 22. "We owe a big debt to David, because without it we'd have been finished," said Ian Hunter in 1973.

In the music press, *Record Mirror* heads an interview with David 'On Death and Drugs', while Rod Stewart tells *NME* journalist Nick Logan that glam rock will quickly fade: "Like Bowie's band, they so obviously don't belong in all that gear. It won't last. It'll get back to denims and jeans.

"I saw Bowie the other day actually. He's a bit snotty now. I saw him down at Olympic and he looked the other way. But he's got talent, when he gets himself in the right direction. Personally I don't care for all that stuff about stars and planets, it just doesn't work with me."

1. Ross also contributed sax to George Harrison's song 'Savoy Truffle' on The Beatles' 1968 *White Album* (also recorded at Trident).

Wednesday 16 August

Three more days of rehearsals commence at the Rainbow now that the theatre has been practically block-booked for the period. "We lived there for ages," said Will Palin in 1993.

Two days later David conducts a breakfast interview with Andrew Tyler from *Disc & Music Echo* in which he says: "I'm rarely David Robert Jones any more. I think I've forgotten who David Jones is."

Saturday 19 August

▶ David Bowie & The Spiders From Mars, the Rainbow Theatre, 232-236 Seven Sisters Road, Finsbury Park, London N4.

Melody Maker enables David to continue in the

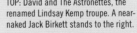

TOP: David and The Astronettes, the renamed Lindsay Kemp troupe. A near-naked Jack Birkett stands to the right.

MIDDLE LEFT: The multi-level structure was based on a Living Theatre production David had seen at the Roundhouse. It was used by Kemp and his troupe to enhance each of David's songs.

MIDDLE RIGHT: Rainbow ticket, 19 August.

BOTTOM RIGHT: David premières his first Kansai Yamamoto costume (a one-off design from Kansai's 1971 collection). The designer was flattered that David wore one of his designs and would prepare a whole range of new stage-wear for his next tour. (▶ 5.2.73/7.4.73)

All three photos listed above © Mick Rock

BOTTOM LEFT: Lou Reed stops backstage after David's first night at the Rainbow, photographed by Masayoshi Sukita.

DAVID BOWIE IS ZIGGY STARDUST AND THE SPIDERS FROM MARS

"The Rise and Fall of Ziggy Stardust and the Spiders From Mars" is already being hailed as a classic on its celestial rise to the top. Included is the hit single "Starman."

Available on
RCA Records and Tapes

TO APPLY:
1. Cut out decal.
2. Remove waxed paper.
3. Submerge in warm water for about 20 seconds.
4. Place decal side to skin.
5. Press with palm.
6. Slide off paper.
7. Let dry.

TO REMOVE: Use cold cream or scrub off with soap & water or use nail-polish remover.

© 1972 RCA RECORDS PRINTED IN U.S.A.

DAVID BOWIE at the RAINBOW

THE SPIDERS
Mick Ronson
Woody Woodmansy
Trevor Bolder

THE ASTRONETTES
Annie Stainer   Ian Oliver
Barbara Ella   Carling Patton

Guest appearance of Lindsay Kemp

Lighting: Heavy Light
Piano: Nicky Graham · Sound: Ground Control
Stage Production: Lindsay Kemp & David Bowie
Stage Management: Robert Anthony

We would like to thank everyone involved in our production and special thanks must go to our guest Lindsay Kemp

ZIGGY CHARACTERS BY GEORGE UNDERWOOD

THIS PAGE

TOP: George Underwood's Ziggy Stardust transfer designs.

ABOVE: The Rainbow concert's programme, the inside designed by George Underwood, the outside a reproduction of the *Ziggy Stardust* cover. George's Ziggy and the Spiders transfers were inside the programme.

OPPOSITE PAGE

TOP: 'John I'm Only Dancing' promo film, shot at the Rainbow Theatre, north London. © Mick Rock

BOTTOM LEFT: 'John I'm Only Dancing' *Disc & Music Echo* review.

BOTTOM MIDDLE. *Cream* (UK) magazine cover with Ian Beck illustration.

BOTTOM RIGHT: David and Mick Ronson with Lindsay Kemp. © Mick Rock

tit-for-tat engagement with Marc Bolan with a feature headed 'Bolan isn't camp says Bowie. He's prissy, and fey, and engrossed in his own image'.

In the evening there is the rather more serious matter of the opening of the second phase of the Ziggy tour with the first of three dates at the north London venue.

For the first two shows at the Rainbow, David and the band are augmented by former Procol Harum keyboard player Matthew Fisher on piano; Nicky Graham, who handled these live duties on the first six months of the Ziggy tour as well as working on bookings for Defries, is out, having been dismissed by Defries a couple of days earlier following a disagreement with Angie.

David's production partner Ken Scott recommends Fisher, whom he worked with as an engineer on Procol Harum's 1969 album *A Salty Dog*. Fisher (who co-wrote and performed the classic organ solo on Harum's 'Whiter Shade Of Pale') said in 1992, "I really enjoyed the Rainbow gig. I can't say I understood what was going on, but I'm very glad I did it."

On arrival the audience is greeted by a giant close-up of David's face taken by Sukita and positioned on the balcony in the foyer.

The show and stage-set betray many of the theatrical influences David has gathered over the years. "The lighting was budget *Cabaret*," said David in 2002. "I had seen that particular production when it was staged in London a number of years before. The sets and lighting were just astounding and, along with other works, including *Oliver!* – which featured lighting by Sean Kenny – revolutionised British stage productions.

"During rehearsals for an early tour with Humble Pie, I had the great good fortune to get to know Sean a little and grilled him mercilessly on his work. I kept every word he uttered filed away for the future so, with the assistance of Lindsay Kemp's sure eye, by the time Ziggy came around I pulled my Kemp/Kenny

one-two punch and put on what I believed to be a pretty spirited and different-looking show to anything I had seen up until that point."

The stage set is scaffolding (painted silver by Palin) which is connected by ladders providing different raised levels for performance.

This snakes and ladders staging was used by US performance art group The Living Theatre for their show *Frankenstein* in the late 60s, when David saw them perform in London.

The stage floor is covered in sawdust, at Kemp's suggestion, to emphasise movement by his company, who are given the name The Astronettes.

Wearing flesh-revealing spider-web costumes designed and made by Natasha Kornilof, The Astronettes include Kemp regular Jack Birkett and Annie Stainer (who appeared with David in the 1970 Scottish TV production of *Pierrot In Turquoise*) as well as Ian Oliver, Barbara Ella and Carling Patton.[1]

Both Rainbow shows open with the Bunuel/Dali 1929 surrealist short *Un Chien Andalou* (as screened at the Arts Lab in 1969).[2]

Opening dramatically with 'Ode To Joy', David enters the stage swathed in dry ice and begins the show by singing 'Lady Stardust' as a photograph of Marc Bolan is projected on to the screen.

David & The Spiders' set includes 'John I'm Only Dancing', 'Life On Mars?' and 'The Supermen', complemented by the choreographed Astronettes interacting with David, who displays his own mime movements.

During 'Starman' David reveals the song's roots by singing "Somewhere over the rainbow…" and there is extensive use of projected images gathered by Mick Rock to David's brief. These include recent and archive shots of David himself, photographs of trees and the sky and art, from Magritte to Warhol.

Having filmed the rehearsals, Rock also shoots parts of both shows and, helped by Dai Davies, interviews fans and guests, including Elton John.[3]

Arriving for the first night, John tells them: "I think I'll see an amazing show. I've followed him since he was doing gigs at the Marquee, years ago. I remember him from The Lower Third and all that rubbish. I just think he's great. I think *Hunky Dory* and *Ziggy Stardust* are masterpieces."

However, Mott's Ian Hunter said in 1992: "I remember Elton John left during the show. I asked him why he was going and he said it wasn't rock. He didn't like it at all."

Also in the audience and at the backstage party are artist Roger Lunn as well as George Underwood and his business partner Terry Pastor.

"Ziggy backstage was like a Fellini movie, normal during the day, strange cosmic people at night," said Pastor in 1997. "David was surrounded by a lot of very weird characters."

But Defries upsets David by telling him after the show that he doesn't think that Kemp's involvement has worked. "David was shattered, really crying," said

Bolder in 1995. "He was very sensitive like that."

1. Stage production by Lindsay Kemp and David Bowie. Stage management by Robert Anthony.

2. This also opened dates on David's Station To Station tour of 1976.

3. Rock assembled from this footage a rough cut of a documentary which he entitled *Ziggy Across The Rainbow*. It has not been shown in public.

Sunday 20 August

◗ David Bowie & The Spiders From Mars, Rainbow Theatre, London.

Support acts on both nights at the Rainbow are blues singer Lloyd Watson and Roxy Music, who are introduced by the exotic fashion model and Roxy singer Bryan Ferry's friend Amanda Lear.[1]

Tonight's show is exactly the same as last night's.

George Underwood has designed the programme for the Rainbow dates, along with a series of posters. Underwood's cartoon figures of David and the band are also made into transfers and are included with the programme.

1. Lear appeared on the cover of Roxy's second album, 1973's *For Your Pleasure*. David missed Roxy's set both nights, and was unaware until 2003 that Amanda Lear had introduced the band: "I never knew she was there. Should have got there earlier I suppose."

Friday 25 August

Since they are already occupying the Rainbow, it makes sense to use the venue for a promo film to accompany the release of new single 'John, I'm Only Dancing'.

With a budget of £100, Rock enlists the help of a cameraman and films David and The Spiders miming to the single, which he plays through the Rainbow's sound-system on the house record player.

In blue vinyl jacket and shot in the half-light, David has a tiny anchor tattoo drawn on his cheek. Rock inter-cuts sequences of The Astronettes dancing during the Rainbow shows.

In the afternoon David meets stage designer Sean Kenny at the Rainbow to discuss lighting ideas for the short tour, since some gigs will be in nightclubs or the popular Top Rank Suites. "David didn't want any coloured lights, just white lights for these gigs," said road manager Will Palin in 1993. "It was decided not to dress up either, but do them casually." David refers to them as 'Top Rank white-light gigs'.

Saturday 26 August

In his review of the two Rainbow shows in *Disc*, Gavin Petrie says that Kemp's company 'detracted from a really great visual and musical band and that their illustrative attempts didn't always come off'.

David and The Spiders are joined in rehearsals at the Rainbow by keyboard player Robin Lumley, a Beckenham resident who has been working with avant-jazz couple and near-neighbours Keith Tippett and Julie Driscoll.

With Matthew Fisher unable to fulfil the tour commitments, David's first choice as a more permanent replacement for the dismissed Nicky Graham has been Bob Sargeant,[1] whose work he knows through the Mick Abrahams Band.

David calls Sargeant's friend, drummer Richie Dharma. "Bob was away so I mentioned I had been working with Rob Lumley on some ideas.[2] I called Rob and said: 'Do you want a gig with David Bowie?' He jumped at it."

1. In 1973, Bob Sargeant co-wrote 'Play Don't Worry' with Mick

SINGLE

David only dancing

DAVID BOWIE—"John I'm Only Dancing" (RCA 2263) on sale from September 1. This single does not have the lush production and strings of "Starman" nor the wealth of lyrics but is a tight little combo (as they are reputed to have said in the days of Rock-n-Roll) and, in fact has a number of Rock-n-Roll echoes.

It starts with the Bowie 12-string and the drumming is the slapping Buddy Holly sound, with David's voice held far back and echoey. The whole thing is basic but bizarre in how it has been recorded.

It's so different from most of Bowie's stuff that I would hazard a guess that David is following through with the concept of adapting the music and presentation to the media (i.e. the theatrical mime show for the Rainbow Theatre but a straight rock concert for the Manchester Hardrock) and that this is a basic, simple and frenzied boogie for discotheques and the BBC.

The other side is another frenzied boogie from the Ziggy album: "Hang On To Yourself" which, nevertheless, could be severe competition to the "A" side, and is my preference.—GAVIN PETRIE

Ronson. This became the title track of Ronson's second album.

2. Dharma and Lumley later formed jazz outfit Brand X with Genesis drummer/vocalist Phil Collins.

Sunday 27 August

▶ David Bowie & The Spiders From Mars, Electric Village, Locarno Bristol Centre, Bristol, Avon.

With support from fellow RCA act Gnidrolog and Thin Lizzy, the band returns to the south-western city for the third time this year, including a cover of The Beatles' 'This Boy' in their performance, while the road crew tests out David's new 'white-light' stage set.

The following day, back at the Rainbow, preparations are made for the forthcoming extra date at the venue.

Wednesday 30 August

▶ David Bowie & The Spiders From Mars, Rainbow Theatre, London.

Tonight's show includes the elaborate stage design and the choreography of Lindsay Kemp and his troupe, though this is the last occasion on which he and David will work together.

Thursday 31 August

▶ David Bowie & The Spiders From Mars, Starkers, Royal Ballrooms, Boscombe, Dorset.

During the day MainMan Ltd is incorporated in New York, with a new office secured by Tony Zanetta at 240 East 58th Street.

Zanetta is made the company's president, and fellow *Pork* cast member Leee Black Childers will soon become vice-president.

Like MainMan's UK base in Gunter Grove, west London, the New York office contains an apartment where Tony Defries and girlfriend Melanie McDonald will generally reside.

In the evening David and the band start the UK mini-tour with a low-level appearance at a nightclub in the coastal town of Boscombe, a couple of miles from Bournemouth.

Like the rest of the dates on this tour, they perform a set of just an hour.

Friday 1 September

▶ David Bowie & The Spiders From Mars, Top Rank Suite, Silver Street, Doncaster, South Yorks.

Today RCA release 'John, I'm Only Dancing'/'Hang On To Yourself' single in the UK and Europe.

⊙ **David Bowie**
A **'John, I'm Only Dancing'** (Bowie)
B **'Hang On To Yourself'** (Bowie)
David Bowie (vocal, guitar, saxophones)
Mick Ronson (guitar)
Trevor Bolder (bass)
Woody Woodmansey (drums)
Lindsay Scott (violin) (A-side)
A-side Produced by David Bowie for MainMan
B-side Produced by David Bowie and Ken Scott
(RCA 2263)

David's first solo production, 'John, I'm Only Dancing', does not receive a US release since its title and subject matter are considered too risqué.[1]

David is quoted in *Beat Instrumental* saying, "I'm a practising bisexual although I've never tried to put it over and make a meal of it."

In 1993 he added: "It was my attempt to do a bisexual anthem, and it was incredibly successful. I was amazed that the Beeb played it."

In the evening David becomes the main feature of the local St Leger Festival when he and The Spiders play the town where his father was born.[2] In the audience is local songwriter/guitarist Bill Nelson.[3]

1. The song's first official US release was on 1976 compilation *ChangesOneBowie*.

2. The venue was just two streets from David's father's birthplace.

3. Two months later Nelson played the same venue with his band, Be Bop Deluxe, performing material from debut album *Axe Victim*.

Saturday 2 September

▶ David Bowie & The Spiders From Mars, Hardrock Concert Theatre,[1] Greatstone Road, Stretford, Manchester.

This is the opening night of this new venue, where support is provided by Iguana, featuring piano player Roy Young.[1] Local DJ Andy Peebles[2] is the compère.

For the performance David is in his Ziggy stagewear and makes regular costume changes.

1. Young played piano on David's 1977 album *Low*.

2. In 1980 Peebles was the last person to interview John Lennon in New York for the BBC. During the same trip he also interviewed David.

Sunday 3 September

▶ David Bowie & The Spiders From Mars, The Hardrock, Manchester.

First thing in the morning, Tony Defries summons band and crew to a meeting at Manchester's Excelsior Hotel and announces: "Everybody in this room will be in America in about two weeks time."

David's first US tour is on.

In the evening, Iguana are supporting again. In contrast to the previous night, David takes to the stage in faded blue jeans, white T-shirt and minimal make-up.

Monday 4 September

▶ David Bowie & The Spiders From Mars, Top Rank Suite, St John's Precinct, Liverpool.

The support act is Geordie folk-rock outfit Lindisfarne.

Tuesday 5 September

▶ David Bowie & The Spiders From Mars, Top Rank Suite, Park Lane, Sunderland.

As the band play the north-eastern city, this month's edition of *Harpers & Queen* features an article on David's rise to fame by author and journalist Nik Cohn,[1] who reports how the interview was delayed when David's appearance resulted in the pair being refused a table at The Ritz: "David turned up in

TOP: Helping the coffers prior to the first US tour and originally referred to by David and road crew as the 'White-Light' tour, the Top Rank late-evening performances and Hardrock Manchester gigs ran for just an hour.

MIDDLE: George Underwood-designed Live Ziggy poster.

BOTTOM: Bristol Electric Village, 27 August.

full slap and tat and we were instantly ejected. A cafe around the corner gave us sanctuary and there we spent an hour in gentle sparring.

"His idols were Edith Piaf and Anthony Newley, and he was fascinated by Elvis Presley, and in their tradition he wanted to turn his stage performances into total theatre. He also wanted to be a star."

1. Born London 1946, Cohn's illustrious career includes coming up with the concept for The Who's rock opera *Tommy* and also writing a piece on the disco scene for *New York* magazine which became the basis for the hit 1977 movie *Saturday Night Fever*.

Wednesday 6 September

▶ David Bowie & The Spiders From Mars, Top Rank Suite, Arundel Gate, Sheffield, Yorks.

The support act is founding father of the British blues scene Alexis Korner.

Thursday 7 September

▶ David Bowie & The Spiders From Mars, Top Rank Suite, Hanley, Stoke-on-Trent, Staffs.

This is the last night of the short UK tour; next stop America.

Since it is also Robin Lumley's last appearance with The Spiders, David holds auditions for a keyboard player for the upcoming US tour at London's Lyceum Theatre, but fails to find a suitable candidate. Among those rejected is Dave Clarke (who goes by the name Dave Carlsen and joins Jimi Hendrix's former bassist in The Noel Redding Band instead).

Friday 8 September

CBS releases Mott The Hoople's new album *All The Young Dudes*, produced by David and Ronson over the course of 20 studio sessions. On David's recommendation, the album includes a cover of The Velvet Underground's 'Sweet Jane' (for which Lou Reed recorded a guide vocal for Ian Hunter).

The following day Mott's 'All The Young Dudes' peaks at number three in the UK charts, making it David's highest charting composition so far.

Sunday 10 September

Iggy & The Stooges begin four weeks of recording for new album *Raw Power* at CBS Studios in Whitfield Street, central London.

During their stay in the UK, Pop and his band lodge in a basement flat in Seymour Walk, off Fulham Road, in west London, a few minutes from MainMan's London HQ.

Tuesday 12 September

Accompanied by George and Birgit Underwood, David and Angie board the *QE2* at Southampton for the voyage to New York.

The Underwoods are last-minute replacements for Lindsay Kemp, whose participation in the US tour has been cancelled in the light of Tony Defries' objections to the choreography at the Rainbow shows.

At dinner on the first night, David appears in the

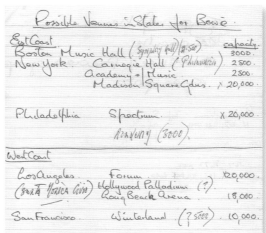

restaurant dressed in his Ziggy costume, attracting uncomfortable stares from fellow passengers (whose number include actor Alan Bates). For the remainder of the voyage, David takes his meals in his cabin.

Underwood has been working on a Ziggy Stardust TV cartoon series with Terry Pastor and Roger Lunn, with whom he has roughed out ideas, and makes presentations to Hanna Barbera and Disney.[1]

1. The cartoon series proposal was later abandoned at the behest of Tony Defries.

Thursday 14 September

The strategy of increasing interest in David by reducing his availability gathers pace. An application for an interview by a journalist, one M. Vaughn of Connaught Square in central London, receives the following reply from MainMan: 'We are in receipt of your letter dated 11 September 72, in which you request an interview with David Bowie. Unfortunately David Bowie does not do interviews.'

Friday 15 September

After much negotiation and correspondence between MainMan and Phonogram (which is part of the Philips Group), the master tapes of David's two Mercury albums, *David Bowie* and *The Man Who Sold The World*, are delivered to MainMan with the original artwork and film separations.

Sunday 17 September

On arrival in New York, David and his party are greeted at the Manhattan dockside by RCA's Gustl Breuer, who is to liaise between RCA and David's tour management.

Breuer is vice president of the record company's classical imprint Red Seal, and has never heard of David before his appointment to the tour.

David, Angie and the

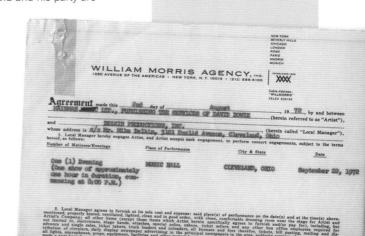

TOP RIGHT: Mott The Hoople in 1972. Left to right: Peter 'Overend' Watts (bass), Verden Allen (keyboards), Mick Ralphs (guitar), Ian Hunter (vocals, guitar), Dale 'Buffin' Griffin (drums).

TOP LEFT: Tony Defries' notes relating to possible US venues for David.

MIDDLE: Mott's *All The Young Dudes*. Sleeve concept and art direction by Mick Rock.

LOWER MIDDLE: The Hardrock Manchester.

BOTTOM: William Morris contract for David's first-ever US live appearance. The Music Hall in Cleveland, 22 September.

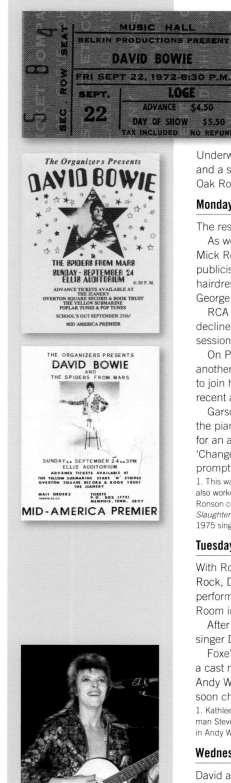

Underwoods check into The Plaza on Central Park and a small welcome party is held in the hotel's Oak Room.

Monday 18 September

The rest of the tour entourage arrive in New York.

As well as The Spiders, their number includes Mick Rock and his photographer wife Sheila, publicist Dai Davies, road manager Will Palin, hairdresser Suzi Fussey and security men Stuey George and Tony Frost.

RCA avant-jazz singer-songwriter Annette Peacock declines David's invitation to play synthesiser on sessions for his next album.

On Peacock's recommendation, David recruits another jazz-trained keyboard player, Mike Garson, to join his live band. (Garson has contributed to her recent album *I'm The One*.)[1]

Garson, who has never heard of David, cancels the piano lesson he is giving and leaves immediately for an audition at RCA. Shown the sheet music for 'Changes', he plays the opening chords and Ronson promptly announces: "You've got the gig."

1. This was co-produced by RCA house producer Bob Ringe, who also worked with Ronson on the Pure Prairie League's *Bustin' Out*. Ronson covered Peacock songs 'I'm The One', on his 1974 album *Slaughter on 10th Avenue*, and 'Seven Days', as the B-side of his 1975 single 'Billy Porter'.

Tuesday 19 September

With Ronson, Woodmansey and Mick and Sheila Rock, David and Angie see The New York Dolls perform at the Mercer Arts Centre's Oscar Wilde Room in the Broadway Central Hotel.

After the show David meets the Dolls and lead singer David Johansen's girlfriend Cyrinda Foxe.[1]

Foxe's beauty and sense of style (first displayed as a cast member of the original New York production of Andy Warhol's *Pork*) impress David and Angie, who soon changes her hairstyle to match Foxe's.

1. Kathleen Hetzekian (1952–2002) later married Aerosmith front-man Steven Tyler, with whom she had a daughter, Mia. She appeared in Andy Warhol's 1977 film *Bad*.

Wednesday 20 September

David and tour personnel board a chartered Greyhound bus to Cleveland, stopping overnight at Erie, Pennsylvania. Traversing the US by bus and train David will notch up 22 shows in 17 cities (nearly all attended by George and Birgit Underwood, who travel with him). On this tour, David will write many of the songs which will appear on his next album.

The following day David and The Spiders take over Cleveland's Music Hall for a seven-hour rehearsal.

Friday 22 September

▶ David Bowie & The Spiders From Mars, Music Hall, 1228 E. 6th Street, Cleveland, Ohio.

For the duration of the tour Cherry Vanilla and Leee Black Childers travel ahead, checking halls for suitability and drumming up pre-publicity from local radio stations and newspapers.

In Cleveland WMMS DJs Denny Saunders and Kid Leo have proved helpful, trailing David's first live performance in the US with extensive airplay of tracks from *Hunky Dory* and, in particular, *Ziggy Stardust*.

And David himself has done his bit to engender interest in the city. Alerted by RCA New York that Cleveland resident Brian Kinchy has set up the International David Bowie Appreciation Society, he called Kinchy before he left England and asked him about the potential local interest in a performance there.

The Music Hall David and The Spiders play tonight is within a complex containing a much larger venue.

All 3,200 seats have sold out for tonight's show, which includes support from British folk-rockers Lindisfarne.

At the end of the gig the excited audience rushes the stage, and a triumphant after-show party is held at the Hollenden Hotel.

After the show David rewards his US fanclub founder Brian Kinchy's support by meeting him.

"The audience was amazing," said Trevor Bolder in 1995. "Afterwards Defries said, 'The next time you come you'll be playing the large one.' We all thought 'Oh yeah?', but he was right, we did."

Saturday 23 September

David, band and crew travel by bus from Cleveland to Memphis.

During these overland journeys, the passengers adopt the chant 'We're going busin', bus, bus, busin'!' to the riff of The Yardbirds' 1965 version of Bo Diddley's 'I'm A Man'.

It is not long before David absorbs this rhythm into new composition 'The Jean Genie'.

Back in the UK, the popular preoccupation with David reaches new highs. In *NME*, Roxy Music guitarist Phil Manzanera tells Ian MacDonald: "David Bowie songs I like a lot too. His management was rather disagreeable at the Rainbow, but Bowie and The Spiders are very nice people and I enjoyed what they were doing."

In the same issue, Elton John discusses a recent meeting with David: "I heard Mott's single on the radio one morning and I thought it was tremendous, so I phoned Bowie up and invited him for a meal."[1]

1. In 1976, John told *Rolling Stone*: "I first met David when I took him out to dinner when he was Ziggy Stardust. We had a nice time. He was with Angie and I was with Tony King, who's now with Rocket

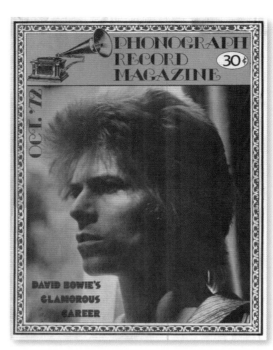

OPPOSITE PAGE
FROM TOP TO BOTTOM:

Cleveland ticket, 22 September.

Ellis Auditorium promotion. Two handbills exist for this appearance, one listing the show time as 3.00pm, the other 6.30pm.

In performance on his first US tour.
© Mick Rock.

THIS PAGE

LEFT: David in rehearsal.
© Mick Rock.

MIDDLE: US *Phonograph Record Magazine*, complete with report by Ron Ross of David's performance at Aylesbury Friars and the Dorchester Hotel press conference.

RIGHT: Prior to his first New York concert, David is photographed at the Plaza Hotel by the late Gloria Stavers, the influential editor of *16 Magazine*. Ken Pitt had made her aware of David as early as 1967.

BOTTOM: *After Dark* magazine also picks up on the growing interest in David in the US, October issue.

Records. And all I remember is his horrible manager walking in with half the cast of *Jesus Christ Superstar* and they all had dinner and left me to pay the bill."

Sunday 24 September

▶ David Bowie & The Spiders From Mars, North Hall, Ellis Auditorium, Poplar Avenue, Memphis, Tennessee.

This is another sell-out gig, with 4,335 tickets bought for a performance which starts at 6.30pm.

A post-concert party is held at the Memphis Downtowner Motor Inn, at which David is snapped flanked by his security guards Stuey George and Tony Frost.[1] Mick Rock also photographs David with the normally camera-shy Tony Defries.

1. Frost became a Scientologist following this tour, as did Mick Woodmansey.

Thursday 28 September

▶ David Bowie & The Spiders From Mars, Carnegie Hall,[1] 57th St, New York.

David, band and crew stay at the classy Plaza Hotel on 5th Avenue and Central Park South.

During the day RCA announces that it has received 400 applications for the 100 available press passes for what is a sell-out appearance. In fact, the show is 'papered' (tickets are given away by the handful by MainMan's promotional team to ensure full attendance by Manhattan's most colourful individuals for this important debut).

ABC Evening News broadcasts a backstage interview with David and films the sound-check. When reporter Scott Osborne asks him to describe himself, David says: "Partly enigmatic, partly fossil."

David dines with influential newspaper columnist Al Aronowitz, who decides not to attend the show and sends junior reporter Bob Weiner (who later

pans the performance).

Supported by Ruth Copeland, David's New York debut is the talk of the town, despite the fact he is suffering from a bout of flu. The contrast with the unveiling of Ziggy Stardust eight months before in a pub in Surrey could not be more pointed.

During the encore, Warhol actress Gerri Miller leaves her seat to present David with a bouquet of flowers.

In the UK, *Top Of The Pops* executives replace Mick Rock's promo for 'John, I'm Only Dancing' with their own cheesy clip of leather-clad bikers chasing a member of regular dance troupe Pan's People, since Defries has demanded they pay £250 for use of the MainMan film.[2]

1. The Beatles were one of the first rock bands to play at the Carnegie Hall, in February 1964, while T.Rex played there in February 1972.
2. In 1979, when David's 'John, I'm Only Dancing (Again)' was released (with the original 1972 track on the B-side), *Top Of The Pops* finally aired the Mick Rock film.

Friday 29 September

With an appearance tonight at the JFK Centre for the Performing Arts in Washington DC cancelled before they even left the UK, David spends the morning in New York working on new song 'Watch That Man', inspired by the previous evening's after-show party, particularly after watching Angela dance with Cyrinda Foxe (who is 'Lorraine' who 'shimmered and strolled like a Chicago moll' in his lyric).

Saturday 30 September

Disc publishes an interview with Marc Bolan by Lisa Robinson which appears to escalate the war of words with David: "I'm far bigger than David Bowie. They're putting us together in a category in England because the press is basically bored with Bolan I think.

TOP LEFT AND RIGHT: Ziggy Stardust descends on the Beverly Hills Hotel – the pre-punk cosmic yob. © Mick Rock

ABOVE: *Let It Rock* magazine, October issue.

"I am what I am. If people don't like what I am, that's OK but I know who I am. David doesn't really know what he is. He steals identities, I create them.

"But he's been slagging me in the press right and left and it's sad. He wasn't even on that session – 'The Prettiest Star' – Tony Visconti did all that.

"Anyway, David sent me a telegram, and it said, 'Darling, they're trying to start a war between us'. I never read telegrams."

While in the US, around this time David signs a new MainMan contract dated 'September 31' (there is no such date). He believes it is a management agreement making him a partner in the company; in fact it is a contract of employment, in effect rendering him a MainMan employee.[1]

1. This agreement became a major sticking point in David's split with MainMan in 1975.

Sunday 1 October

▶ David Bowie & The Spiders From Mars, The Music Hall, 268 Tremont St, Boston, Massachusetts.

Tonight's show is the first of three which are being recorded for a proposed live album.[1]

A positive appraisal of David's New York debut appears in the *New York Times* by Don Heckman, headed 'Rock Music: A Colourful David Bowie'.

The following day David and tour personnel return for four days to New York, where David and Ronson briefly work on mixing Lou Reed's forthcoming album *Transformer*.

1. Shows in New York and Los Angeles were also recorded for this project, which was shelved when the focus moved to releasing *Aladdin Sane* at the beginning of 1973.

Wednesday 4 October

▶ David and The Spiders record an untitled track at RCA Studios New York, with engineer Mike Moran.

The following day recording continues at RCA Studios, with engineer Joe Lopes.

On this day Defries' company Minnie Bell Music Ltd is officially incorporated into MainMan Ltd.

Friday 6 October

'The Jean Genie' (or 'Dream Genie' as it is called on the tape-box) is recorded in RCA's Studio D with David producing.

While the song's main riff emulates The Yardbirds on 'I'm A Man', the track's closing crescendo is taken from a section of another staple of the early 60s British R&B scene: The Yardbirds' version of Howlin' Wolf's 'Smokestack Lightning'.

Trevor Bolder's bass line mimics that of Yardbird Paul Samwell-Smith on their recording of the song.

"We did it as a laugh at the start of the session, but David said 'I like that, let's keep it'," said Bolder in 1995. "We did it in just one take, adding some harp and other things and that was it. It took about one-and-a-half hours from start to finish and the single was being pressed in Eng and within weeks."

The song's lyrical content is preoccupied with Iggy Pop, while its title plays with the name of France's leading outsider dramaturge and novelist, Jean Genet (whose work has often been interpreted by Lindsay Kemp's company).[1]

By this time David has met Genet, approaching him to play the role of Divine in a film version of his book *Our Lady Of The Flowers*. In 1989 one of Genet's closest friends, Paul Thevenin, recalled: "Genet and Bowie agreed to meet at a particular restaurant in London. The others in Genet's group looked around for Bowie in vain, but sharp-eyed Genet spotted an attractive looking woman sitting by herself and went up to her and said, 'Mr Bowie I presume.' His presumption was accurate."

'The Jean Genie' is of such obvious commercial viability that the decision is taken to capitalise on the growing media interest in David and release it as a single as soon as possible.

In the evening the musicians and crew leave New York on the Greyhound bus to resume the tour in Chicago. In the UK David's former record company Pye attempts to exploit his new-found popularity by releasing an EP of 1966 material comprising 'Do Anything You Say'/'I Dig Everything'/'Can't Help Thinking About Me', and 'I'm Not Losing Sleep'.

Saturday 7 October

▶ David Bowie & The Spiders From Mars, Chicago Auditorium Theatre, 50 East Congress Parkway, Chicago, Illinois.

During the day David, The Spiders and Lou Reed install themselves in RCA's Chicago studio, and record yet another version of 'John, I'm Only Dancing', together with Lou Reed's new song 'Vicious'. With David producing, the latter features Reed on lead vocals.

Before the concert starts, Mick Rock photographs

David changing into his costume in his Chicago hotel room.

The venue is practically full (3,982 of the 4,300 seats have been sold) and during the finale ('Rock 'n' Roll Suicide') MainMan staff encourage the audience to approach the stage, provoking a heavy-handed response from security guards. Chaos ensues and an upset David exits the stage, bringing the evening to an abrupt and sour end.

Meanwhile, *Melody Maker* reports on Tony Defries' criticism of the BBC for refusing to show Mick Rock's promo for 'John, I'm Only Dancing'. He says of the film: "It's a bit ethereal, not a straightforward band doing their numbers. It's as if it were a work of art."

A MainMan spokesman points out that the promo has been shown on US national network NBC without any problems.

The British music press's enthusiastic coverage of David's Stateside progress helps fuel interest in him on both sides of the Atlantic. While Lisa Robinson tells *Disc* readers that Andy Warhol was only able to obtain two tickets for the Carnegie show and wasn't allowed backstage, Linda Solomon in *NME* reports: 'In the confrontation between Marc Bolan and David Bowie, Bowie comes away the winner in an undeclared contest.'

Sunday 8 October

❱ David Bowie & The Spiders From Mars, Fisher Theatre, Fisher Building, 3011 West Grand Blvd, Detroit, Michigan.

Music-mad Detroit, home to Motown and the garage rock of the Stooges, MC5 and Alice Cooper, welcomes David with open arms.

Tickets for tonight's show sold out within four days and promoter Nederlander Theatre Promotions is keen to immediately book David again.

Iggy Pop has been flown in by MainMan with the master tapes of *Raw Power*. After the show he talks with David into the small hours, recounting stories about his youth in and around the city. This inspires David to write a new song, 'Panic In Detroit'.

The following day *Newsweek* runs a feature entitled 'Enter David Bowie'.

Wednesday 11 October

❱ David Bowie & The Spiders From Mars, Kiel Auditorium, 1400 Market Street, St Louis, Missouri.

This is one of a handful of late additions to the itinerary which suffers from lack of publicity.

Even hastily booked ads on St Louis' KSHE Radio announcing the gig, and attempts by MainMan staff to paper the show, cannot raise the turnout above 1,000 attendees for this 10,000-seater.

David makes the most of the evening by inviting the audience to cluster around the stage.

Thursday 12 October

The Bowie tour decamps to Kansas for a three-day break ahead of a show there, while David and Ronson head for Nashville to work on mono and stereo mixes of 'The Jean Genie'.

On 13 October work in RCA Studio B, 222 Fifth Avenue South, Nashville (where Elvis recorded many tracks), includes mixing live recordings from the previous week's concert in Boston: 'John, I'm Only Dancing', 'Changes', 'The Supermen' and 'Life On Mars?'.[1]

The following day, 'John, I'm Only Dancing' peaks at number 12 in the UK singles chart.

1. The first three of these were released on Rykodisc's 1989 *Sound + Vision* box set CDV (*Sound + Vision Plus*). All four were bonus tracks on the *Aladdin Sane* 30th anniversary reissue of 2003.

Sunday 15 October

❱ David Bowie & The Spiders From Mars, Memorial Hall, 600 N. 7th Street, Kansas City, Kansas.

This is another late addition to the tour schedule, and again is poorly attended. Disconsolate at the prospect of playing a second near-empty venue, David performs drunk and at one point takes a tumble from the stage.

"The pressure occasionally got to David, as you would expect," said George Underwood in 1995. "He even smashed a hotel room up once, or at least broke quite a few things in one. He had to cope with a lot of stuff, he knew it was all on his shoulders."

Monday 16 October

The majority of the entourage (by now 46 strong) take flights from Kansas and check into the Beverly Hills Hotel on Sunset Boulevard, Los Angeles. David and friends, including George and Birgit Underwood, take the Super Chief luxury sleeper train and are photographed in an observation car by Mick Rock.

Already the tour is making huge losses. Takings are being consumed not only by the high cost of maintaining a crew of this size, but also by the downtime caused by the inept booking policy which has left huge gaps in the schedule (such as the five days between Kansas and the next two dates at the Santa Monica Civic on 20 and 21 October).

With no ready cash and Defries elsewhere, everything is charged to room service at the expensive Beverly Hills Hotel.

David is occupied remixing *Raw Power* at Western Sound Studios in Hollywood. This proves a difficult task since balance has been lost during the recording in London by Iggy Pop's insistence that most of the instruments are mixed on to one channel, with the vocals on the other.

British pop star Lulu is also recording at Western Sound, and bumps into David and Pop. "I ran late into the wrong studio, and he was in there mixing Iggy Pop," said Lulu in 1992. "David was, as he can be, incredibly charming and very British, and Iggy Pop was very forbidding, very dark and sinister-looking. I thought, 'Oh, I'd better get out of here quick!'"

Other guests at the Beverly Hills Hotel include veteran US singer Perry Como and Elton John, who

RIGHT: On stage at Santa Monica: "I asked for lobster tail but they brought me a piece of palm tree."

BELOW: Tony Defries tour personnel conference document, 22 October.

BOTTOM: RCA memo and band itinerary from Roy Bottocchio in Hollywood, 20 October.

PRIVATE AND CONFIDENTIAL INFORMATION

MEMO

TO: David Bowie and The Spiders from Mars, Zee, Robin, and everyone else on USA Tour 1972

FROM: MainMan

RE: Conference of Sunday, October 22, 1972

As you know, I have now given Zee the task of coordinating all your activities and making all necessary decisions and plans concerning the tour. In short, treat Zee as you would me! Zee is in overall charge. Robin will take responsibility as General Manager of all transportation, venue and technical requirements. I would like to establish now clearly that communication within groups of people working together and overall is essential as is planning. All information should be given to Zee and all inquires should be addressed to Zee, who should have your entire cooperation. Everybody should be prepared to extend themselves beyond the areas that they are specifically concerned with and an effort should be made internally to remove any element of competition among groups of people working together. MONEY SHOULD NOT BE SPENT UNNECESSARILY. All money will come from Zee including any necessary transportation or equipment expenses which Robin will determine. Entertainment is an item which should not cost us anything at all if properly planned. Cash will only be available for real needs as opposed to individual wants. Travelling should be done economically and in a planned fashion. We should not use limousines other than to and from gigs or to and from studios or for transportation of Bowie when it is necessary for him to move about. Shopping expeditions or any expeditions of any sort should be done in cabs.

We are attracting too many followers and carrying them with us. Every extra person who stays with us at a hotel is an extra room service charge. In addition, you should be aware that people's motives are very often potentially harmful to us. If we are to be inaccesible then we must maintain a degree of privacy which should extend to groupies. GROUPIES SHOULD BE SENT HOME WITHOUT BREAKFAST!

People should stay in the Hotel provided for them and should be available at all times. Personnel on this tour should not make private arrangements which [...] them unavailable. This extends to all days. Whilst on tour, there [...] nel should eat in Hotel whenever possible unless [...] that I am feeding, clothing [...]

Correspondence

RCA

To: DISTRIBUTION   Location   (Page 2)   Date October 20 1972

From: Roy Battocchio   Location   Telephone

Subject: DAVID BOWIE TOUR (continued)

Transportation

The party is arriving in each city in two groups. David and a group of five which will include either myself or Gustl Breuer will be traveling by a special sleeper-bus and going directly to the hotel. Naturally it is difficult to judge when we will arrive and of course there is no need for us to be met.

The larger group consisting of approximately 12 will arrive by plane. Listed below is the arrival time in each city: (Ask for Stuart George or Tony Frost)

Wed. Oct. 25	LA-SanFrancisco	Lv 11am	Arr 12noon	Western 72
Sun. Oct. 29	SanFrancisco-Seattle	Lv 12noon	Arr 1:42PM	United696
Thur.Nov 2	Seattle-Phoenix	Lv 11am	Arr 3:45PM	Western 629
Sun. Nov. 5	Phoenix-Dallas	Lv 12:50PM	Arr 1:46PM	Delta 526
Sun. Nov. 12	Dallas-Houston	Lv 11am	Arr 11:47AM	Braniff 103
Mon. Nov. 13	Houston-New Orleans	Lv 10am	Arr 10:53AM	Delta 964
Wed. Nov. 15	New Orleans-Miami	Lv 11:15am	Arr 1:45PM	Braniff 259
Sat. Nov. 18	Miami-Nashville	Lv 1:50PM	Arr 3:33PM	Eastern 894

Arrangements should be made for them to be met with some form of ground transportation to handle the group and luggage. In most casesan airport limo or small bus will be adequate.

In addition to transportation for the above mentioned party limos will be needed.
1. At approximately 4pm on the day of the concert 1 limo must be at the hotel to take Bowie and group to the concert hall for a sound check. It should wait and return them to hotel.
2. At approximately 8pm the same evening 2 limos should be at hotel to take entire group and others to the concert, wait and return to hotel. More then likely they will no longer be needed after that.

BILLING INSTRUCTIONS FOR LIMOS, BUS ETC.

Bills to be sent to my attention.

RECEPTIONS

No receptions should be planned. Once we are all in if we feel a gathering might be in order we can discuss it. Controll, security and the right kind of guests are important. No TV or press interviews. We have our own photographer and he is the only one to be cleared for pictures.

---

black trousers and his blue plastic bomber jacket, set off with a shock of red hair.

Rock also takes photographs of David in a similar outfit (with a yellow bomber jacket) with Cyrinda Foxe in an LA bar.

Friday 20 October

▶ David Bowie & The Spiders From Mars, Civic Auditorium, 1855 Main Street, Santa Monica, Los Angeles, California.

Broadcast live – with support from a group called Sailcat[1] – by Santa Monica station KMET-FM,[2] the show is peppered with David's off-the-cuff remarks; referring to "a pair of pliers" as Will Palin effects a running repair on his guitar and impersonating Andy Warhol during the introduction to the song about the pop artist, apparently unaware that the great man is in the audience (though Warhol apparently feels he is being ignored).

After the gig David, band and crew attend a party thrown by veteran DJ Wolfman Jack, where David again meets lanky producer/performer Kim Fowley.

1. Second support Elijah were dropped by Defries due to budget constraints.

2. The show became a popular bootleg and received official release by EMI in 2008 as *Live Santa Monica '72*.

Saturday 21 October

▶ David Bowie & The Spiders From Mars, Santa Monica Civic Auditorium, Los Angeles.

With Rodney Bingenheimer drumming up support and local interest over recent days, another show is booked at the Civic and is again a sell-out.

Behind the scenes, Angie is causing friction. In *Disc*'s Hollywood column, Judy Sims reports: 'That old devile [sic] grapevine told me Angela Bowie and her son Zowie left the Bowie caravan to return to England, possibly because her antics were not universally appreciated (is that vague enough?). "It's a touchy situation," said my Bowie tour spy, but she wouldn't elaborate. The implication was obvious: Angie didn't just leave, she was banished.'

Ahead of his album release, Lou Reed is already chafing at the media casting of him as David's acolyte. "I'm not going in the same direction as David," Reed tells Ray Fox-Cumming in *Disc*. "He's into the mime thing and that's not me at all. I know I have a good hard rock act."

Monday 23 October

In the *Los Angeles Times*, music critic Robert Hilburn raves about David in his review of the Santa Monica shows: "He's a certified, genuine, blue-ribbon star."

In the UK the following day, the clip featuring 'Space Oddity' from 1969 film *Love You Till Tuesday* is given its first public airing on BBC's *The Old Grey Whistle Test*.

In Los Angeles Cherry Vanilla (using her birth name Kathy Dorritie), telegrams RCA's commercial operations VP Mort Hoffman about plans to release 'Space Oddity' as a single with 'The Man Who Sold

---

have each taken exclusive bungalows. David takes afternoon tea with John, who is on his way to a gig at San Francisco's Winterland. Much of the daytime is spent lazing around the hotel pool, while nights are generally reserved for Rodney Bingenheimer's newly opened E Club at 8171 Sunset Blvd.

Bingenheimer's partner in the venture – which quickly becomes known as Rodney's English Disco[1] – is the man who took David to RCA, Tom Ayres. It has been inspired by a conversation Bingenheimer had with David in the summer of 1971 about the new music bursting out of the UK.

"In 1972, David Bowie was Jesus Christ, and Rodney's was the Sistine Chapel," said Bingenheimer's friend Kim Fowley in 1992.

Mick Ronson suffers personally; he is lobster pink from sunburn, while the chlorine in the hotel pool has turned his blonde-dyed hair green.

1. Rodney's English Disco became a haunt of rock luminaries, from Elvis Presley to Led Zeppelin, and was the scene of much debauchery in the early to mid-70s.

Wednesday 18 October

Tony Defries arrives in LA and coolly solves the financial crisis by persuading RCA to settle all bills for the rest of the tour.

During the week-long stay at the hotel, David is photographed in the grounds by Mick Rock in a new look which predates punk by several years: black platform shoes, tight

the World' as its B-side to promote the forthcoming reissue of David's two Mercury albums. 'Do not wish to delay single (Space Oddity) but Bowie and I feel picture sleeve is essential.'

Friday 27 October

▶ David Bowie & The Spiders From Mars, Winterland Auditorium, Post & Steiner, San Francisco, California.

Two shows are booked at the Winterland, and support is provided by future disco star Sylvester and his band, as well as comedy duo Flo & Eddie[1] in their guise of The Phlorescent Leech & Eddie (though the gig poster bills them as 'Phlorescent & Eddie').

Their backing group includes British drummer Aynsley Dunbar,[2] who will soon work with David.

Defries demands that promoter Bill Graham builds a wall inside the auditorium so that David can enter and leave the stage unseen by the audience. A temporary screen is erected.

Mick Rock cuts footage he shoots at the Winterland shows into a new promo for 'The Jean Genie' he oversees in a hired studio in San Francisco. Cameraman is Jerry Slick, ex-husband of SF band Jefferson Airplane's singer Grace Slick.

The clip also features Rock's film of David and Cyrinda Foxe outside the deco Mars Hotel[3] on 4th Street.

1. Mark Volman and Howard Kaylan, who found success as The Turtles in the mid-60s and joined Frank Zappa's Mothers Of Invention before striking out on their own and recording nine albums, also providing backing vocals for recordings by Alice Cooper, John Lennon, T.Rex and others.
2. Born Liverpool, 1946. Unsuccessfully auditioned for The Jimi Hendrix Experience when the US guitarist flipped a coin in Mitch Mitchell's favour. Went on to form Aynsley Dunbar's Retaliation before backing Frank Zappa and playing on sessions for Robert Fripp's King Crimson, Lou Reed, Mick Ronson and on David's *Pin Ups* (1973) and *Diamond Dogs* (1974).
3. A couple of blocks from CBS Studios, this establishment gave its name to the June 1974 album *Grateful Dead From The Mars Hotel* by San Francisco's biggest band. Their film *The Grateful Dead Movie* includes footage of the hotel being demolished in 1974.

Saturday 28 October

▶ David Bowie & The Spiders From Mars, Winterland Auditorium, San Francisco.

The road is taking its toll: a San Francisco seamstress is called on to make replacements for The Spiders' worn-out costumes. This new set of clothes is worn by the band in the studio sequences in Rock's promo for 'The Jean Genie'.

Tom Ayres has been seconded by RCA to accompany David in the city by the bay.

"I was worried no one had heard of David," said Ayres in 1996. "We went for a walk around the streets and people were following us around, but kept in the shadows so we couldn't see them. They kept singing 'Ch…Ch…Ch…Changes…' Then I knew David was making an impact."

However, like last night, the Winterland is only half-full for this evening's show. The decision is taken to cancel bookings in Dallas and Houston on 11 and 12 November as these dates are late additions and

ticket sales in those cities are also poor.

Back in the UK, Mott The Hoople members attempt to pacify their original fan-base following the mainstream success of 'All The Young Dudes'.

Drummer Dale Griffin tells Chris Welch in *Melody Maker*: "We're no different from working with Bowie. We don't wear earrings and have new hairstyles every week. And our stage act is no different from how it has been in the last five years. We do more quality things now. The main effect has been that David gave us our self-respect back."

And British fans are left in no doubt that David is outstripping Marc Bolan in terms of impact across the Atlantic. In her Hollywood column in *Disc*. Judy Sims writes: 'Perhaps Marc isn't quite outrageous enough to stir the American imagination.'

The tour party leaves for Seattle the following day, and 'The Jean Genie' is released as David's new single in the US by RCA, with *Ziggy Stardust* track 'Hang On To Yourself' on the B-side.

For RCA US this is a stop-gap move, since it decided against issuing 'John, I'm Only Dancing' as a single; in the UK, where this has recently charted, 'The Jean Genie' will be released in a month's time.

Wednesday 1 November

▶ David Bowie & The Spiders From Mars, Paramount Theatre, 911 Pine Street, Seattle, Washington.

Yet again there is a low audience turnout, with around a third of the venue full to see David and The Spiders and support Sweet Talkin' Jones, featuring former Paul Revere & The Raiders' guitarist Jim Valley.

During the journey to Phoenix the next day, David is inspired to start on a new song, 'Drive-In Saturday'.

Friday 3 November

Tony Defries raises the prospect of a David Bowie doll in a memo circulated to MainMan staff: 'This is another merchandising idea and I am having sent over one of the dolls which can be used as a manufacturer's prototype. I would like to keep it to a fabric doll with perhaps better features but following this line with identifiable clothing and body contours and jewellery, etc. I should obviously meet with whoever is going to produce the dolls to have detailed discussions on exactly how they will be manufactured, merchandised, etc. Possibly a colour photographic reproduction of Bowie's face on fabric could be used for the face of the doll.'

Saturday 4 November

▶ David Bowie & The Spiders From Mars, Phoenix Celebrity Theatre, 440 N.32nd, Arizona.

David and the band perform in the round, surrounded by a large number of empty seats, though at least support act, Brit soul/R&B outfit The Spencer Davis Group, are more sympathetic than most of those booked for the tour.

"There were hardly any people there," confirmed

TOP: Santa Monica Civic Auditorium, Los Angeles.

UPPER MIDDLE: Santa Monica ticket, 20 October.

LOWER MIDDLE: David checks into Mars, San Francisco. © Mick Rock

ABOVE: Plucked his eyebrows on the way... © Mick Rock

BOTTOM: Winterland poster, 27-28 October.

TOP: *Rolling Stone*, November issue.

RIGHT: A *Record Mirror* special; a 28-page large format publication published in November.

MIDDLE: Lou Reed's *Transformer*, with another timeless Mick Rock photograph.

ABOVE: Phil Spector. David approached the controversial producer to work with him on *Aladdin Sane*.

Trevor Bolder in 1995. "It was desperate. But that was the only show where I can remember the support working with us."

The gaps between bookings are becoming serious; Defries' attempts to attract venues in El Paso and Oklahoma City over the next week prove unsuccessful, so the tour party is forced to stay put in Phoenix for six days before heading east to Dallas.

The heat is intense and the tour principals stay in chalets in the grounds of the hotel.

David blocks out all light from the windows to his chalet to maintain his snow-white tan and stays inside for the most part.

One day he is visited by Underwood and Defries. "He suddenly appeared from the bedroom, waiting for a reaction from us," said Underwood in 2001. "It took me a few seconds to work out his eyebrows had gone. It was very striking."

According to a 1997 account by David, he had become "roaringly drunk" one night and woke up the following morning minus an eyebrow, so finished the job by shaving off the other one.

In 1999 David said that the act had been provoked by Mott The Hoople's rejection of the newly written 'Drive-In Saturday' as a follow-up single to 'All The Young Dudes':[1] "I was so angry, I shaved my eyebrows off. I kid you not."

David may also have been influenced by Japanese designer Kansai Yamamoto's demand to his models at his 1971 debut London show that they shave off their eyebrows. Whatever the reason, David will maintain the look for the next three years.

The following day David tells Robert Hilburn of the *LA Times* the way the media has him aligned with Alice Cooper: "We spearheaded the glamour rock thing in England and, as there was an equivalent

show-time look about the bands in America that Alice had spearheaded, it was obvious we were going to be thrown together even though the American reviewers hadn't seen us and the English reviewers hadn't seen Alice."

1. In 2007 Ian Hunter said: "David Bowie is fond of saying he offered it to us and we turned it down. To my recollection, that wasn't the case at all. We never turned it down. We had this arrangement of that song which was completely different and we wanted to do it. The only thing I can think of is that Tony Defries told David one story and us another."

Monday 6 November

Defries contacts 'wall of sound' producer Phil Spector to gauge his interest in producing David. Since Spector has recently been working with John Lennon and George Harrison, a letter is sent care of their company Apple at 3 Savile Row in London: 'As manager for RCA Recording Artist, David Bowie, I write to inquire if you are interested in working with him on his next album to be recorded at Trident Studios in London January 1973. I have enclosed four of David's albums so that you may become familiar with his work before our next contact.'[1]

1. Spector did not respond to this inquiry.

Wednesday 8 November

RCA releases Lou Reed's album *Transformer* in the UK and US.[1]

As well as co-producing[2] the album with Mick Ronson,[3] David contributed to the writing of 'Wagon Wheel' (though he is not credited) and supplied backing vocals, some with the vocal trio known as Thunderthighs: Karen Friedman, Dari Lallou and Casey Synge (real name Annette Casey).[4]

David had also brought in Klaus Voorman on bass, having been introduced to him by John Lennon's assistant Tony King.[5]

Initially the gender-reversal scene portrayed on the back – Karl Stoecker's stylised photographs of androgynous model Gala Mitchell in a diaphanous black gown and a street hustler in skin-tight jeans, muscle shirt and leather cap – was to be the front cover until Reed[6] replaced it with one of Rock's shots of his performance at the King's Cross Cinema in July.

To promote the album, RCA releases 'Walk On The Wild Side'[7]/'Perfect Day'[8] as a single in the UK.

1. *Transformer* remained in the UK album chart for seven months, peaking at number 13 in September 1973. In the US chart it reached a respectable number 29, even though it was largely panned by the US music press.

2. Since *Transformer*, David has only produced releases for two other artists: Lulu's 1974 single 'The Man Who Sold The World' and Iggy Pop's *The Idiot* (1977), *Lust For Life* (1977) and *TV Eye* (1978).

3. Ronson appeared on Reed's 1974 live set *Rock & Roll Animal*, recorded at New York's Academy Of Music.

4. Thunderthighs appeared on Mick Ronson's 1974 debut album *Slaughter On 10th Avenue*.

5. David was introduced to King (who was a close associate of John Lennon's) by Elton John over lunch in August 1972.

6. Reed and David have remained close; both live in New York, Reed with his wife, multimedia artist Laurie Anderson. In 1997 Reed appeared at David's 50th birthday concert at Madison Square Garden and, in 2002, David was a guest vocalist on Reed's album *The Raven*.

7. 'Walk On The Wild Side' was written by Reed for an unrealised play of the same name. The title was based on Nelson Algren's 1956 novel *A Walk On The Wild Side*.

8. In 1997 'Perfect Day' was used for a promotional film for the BBC. Featuring Reed with David and other performers such as Suede's Brett Anderson and Dr John, it was released as a Christmas single and reached number one.

Thursday 9 November

David makes the all-important front cover of *Rolling Stone*, with a close-up taken by Mick Rock in Chicago announcing 'David Bowie in America'.

The feature by Timothy Ferris is headed 'The Iceman, Having Calculated, Cometh', based on David's description of himself: "I'm a pretty cold person. A very cold person, I find. I have a strong lyrical, emotional drive and I'm not sure where it comes from. I'm not sure if that's really me coming through in my songs. They come out and I hear them afterward and I think, well, whoever wrote that felt really strongly about it. I can't feel strongly. I get so numb. I'm a bit of an iceman.

"I rarely have felt like a rock artist. I don't think that's much of a vocation, being a rock and roller."

Friday 10 November

David's two Mercury albums are reissued by RCA in the UK and the US, both with contemporary covers and poster inserts of David in his Ziggy get-up.

David Bowie (1969) is retitled *Space Oddity* [1] with a new sleeve consisting of two colour photographs taken by Mick Rock at Haddon Hall earlier in the year. The front is a close-up of David's face, while the back shows him sitting on a chair in a silver/grey lurex suit and the red vinyl platform boots.

The track-listing is the same as the 1969 release apart from the exclusion of 20-second filler track 'Don't Sit Down'.[2]

Another Mick Rock photograph of David is on the back of the new sleeve for *The Man Who Sold The World*.[3] The front features a dynamic Brian Ward monochrome shot of David, guitar at his side and throwing a high kick.

David had asked George Underwood to paint a new cover design, based on an idea he came up with during their *QE2* voyage to New York. Underwood was to depict David as a pirate figurehead (with eye-patch and cutlass) on the prow of a square-rigged sailing ship, but RCA was so keen to reissue the albums for the Christmas market that it used the promotional photos already supplied by David and Defries.

1. This peaked at number 17 in the UK album chart and at number 16 in the US.

2. 'Don't Sit Down' was not deliberately dropped from this release, RCA utilised the American masters for the album which didn't feature it.

3. Highest chart positions: UK number 26; US number 105.

Saturday 11 November

The sensitivity Marc Bolan is feeling about the acclaim being heaped on David spills over into print.

In *NME*, James Johnson asks Bolan: "What about the new line in teenage idols? Cassidy,[1] the Osmonds, Bowie, people like that?"

Bolan responds by describing David as "very much a one-hit wonder I'm afraid", adding: "In four or five records' time it may be fair to put him in the same category – statistically speaking that is; it's nothing to do with my own personal taste. I've always thought Mott The Hoople were bigger than David.

"I've never heard a David Bowie album, or at least any of the last four. I'm not saying whether they're good or bad, I just haven't heard them."

And, in *Melody Maker*, Bolan tells Chris Welch: "I haven't seen David for a year. He's a great writer. I think he's being used, but that's only my opinion. He has badmouthed me in the press, but only to make himself a bigger star. I wish him only good."

1. In late 1974, at David's invitation, pop singer David Cassidy flew to New York to discuss David's offer to produce an album by him. This project didn't get off the ground because Cassidy was unwilling to tour again in the wake of the death of a fan at an overcrowded London concert he gave that year.

Tuesday 14 November

▶ David Bowie & The Spiders From Mars, Loyola University, 6363 Saint Charles Avenue, New Orleans.

During his stay in the Crescent City, David sets to reworking 'Time', his song which George Underwood had demoed in 1971.

It is even considered as the title track of David's new album. When he hears of the demise in London of New York Dolls drummer Billy Murcia, resulting from an overdose of sedatives mixed with alcohol, David works a reference into the lyric: 'Time, in Quaaludes and red wine, Demanding Billy Dolls, And other friends of mine...'"

Friday 17 November

▶ David Bowie & The Spiders From Mars, Pirate's World Amusement Park,[1] Sheridan St, Dania, Miami.

Support for tonight's show is billed as local rock band Nitzinger, who are double-booked and replaced with a quartet called Ginger.

During his performance, David accompanies himself on acoustic guitar for the first public rendition of the recently composed 'Drive-In Saturday'.

"I've a new song for you I'd like to do very much," David tells the audience. "I wrote it on the train from LA to Chicago before I came down here, and I tried to write it on the train journey from Chicago to here."

George and Birgit Underwood rejoin the tour from Los Angeles, where George has completed gatefold sleeve artwork[1] for the projected live album, which has the working title *Ziggy Stardust – US Tour Live*.

But the strength of the new songs David is writing persuades him and Defries to abandon the idea and concentrate on progressing with what will become *Aladdin Sane*.

Meanwhile, *Ziggy Stardust* is released in Japan this month, preparing the way for a visit by David and The Spiders in 1973.

1. This artwork was rediscovered in MainMan archives in 2003 and

TOP: RCA's reissue of album *The Man Who Sold The World*, with cover photo by Brian Ward, 10 November.

ABOVE: The RCA reissue of album *Space Oddity* was released at the same time, cover photo by Mick Rock.

In this year...

November
SIGNING of Queen to Trident Management, which was based at David's favourite studio of this period.

Saturday 4 November
ARTICLE published in *Melody Maker*: 'In San Francisco, film maker and artist Andy Warhol revealed that Bowie had contacted him about doing a movie together. Warhol said he was at the concert in LA but felt he was ignored by Bowie.'

Monday 6 November
DEATH by asphyxiation of 21-year-old New York Dolls drummer Billy Murcia in a bath at a west London apartment after a party. David referred to Murcia as 'Billy Dolls' in the song 'Time' from the album *Aladdin Sane* (1973).

TOP: Handbill and free newspaper for *Warehouse* appearance in New Orleans on 22 November.

BELOW: On his first US tour in 1972.

appeared in 2008 with the official release of the Santa Monica Civic Auditorium recordings.

Monday 20 November

▶ David Bowie & The Spiders From Mars, Municipal Auditorium, 417 4th Avenue North, Nashville.

Wednesday 22 November

▶ David Bowie & The Spiders From Mars, The Warehouse, 1820 Tchoupitoulas Street, New Orleans.[1]

Again there is a mix-up over the billing. White Witch, who are billed, pull out and are replaced by folk singer Les Moore.

David is tired and intoxicated, the venue is extremely cold and there are technical problems and the guitars are out of tune for much of the set.

1. Jim Morrison's last concert with The Doors was at the Warehouse on 12 December 1970.

Friday 24 November

RCA release 'The Jean Genie'/'Ziggy Stardust' single in the UK.

⊙ **David Bowie**
A **'The Jean Genie'** (Bowie)*
B **'Ziggy Stardust'** (Bowie)**
David Bowie (vocal, guitar, harmonica)
Mick Ronson (guitar, vocal)
Trevor Bolder (bass)
Woody Woodmansey (drums)
***Produced by David Bowie for MainMan**
****Produced by David Bowie and Ken Scott**
Arranged by David Bowie and Mick Ronson
(RCA 2302) (UK) (RCA 74-0838) (US)

In its advertising, RCA plays up the fact that the new single is the result of David's experiences in the US: 'Written on the road. Recorded in New York. Mixed in Nashville. The first single to come from Bowie's triumphant American tour.'

Saturday 25 November

▶ David Bowie & The Spiders From Mars, Public Auditorium, Cleveland, Ohio.

On this return visit to the city where the US tour

opened, 'special guest' support is provided by fellow Brits, folk-rockers Lindisfarne.

This is the first of two sell-out nights at the 10,000-seater.[1] In the audience is Chrissie Hynde,[2] who wangles a meet with David before the show, and chats with him about her heroes Lou Reed and Iggy Pop.

1. These two Cleveland shows were recorded by local radio station WMMS, but apparently not broadcast.

2. In 1973 Hynde moved to London and worked at the *NME* as a music writer for a spell before appearing on the fringes of the punk scene and forming her own band, the enduring rock act The Pretenders.

Sunday 26 November

▶ David Bowie & The Spiders From Mars, Public Auditorium, Cleveland, Ohio.

With Lindisfarne again supporting, David and The Spiders are treated for the first time to a sea of lit matches and lighters from the audience during their performance.

Meanwhile, Defries writes to David's UK publisher Chrysalis about a New Zealand cover version of 'Life On Mars?' by a singer named Steve Allen. Angie has alerted Defries and David to this in a telex from London. She asks why this release hasn't been stopped, but concedes that it is a 'good recording'.

Tuesday 28 November

▶ David Bowie & The Spiders From Mars, The Stanley Theatre, 719 Liberty Avenue, Pittsburgh.

Support for the show is local act Twheet Twheet. After the gig the entourage visit a local Irish bar, and loyal fan Brian Kinchy is again invited to hang out with David and the band.

Wednesday 29 November

David introduces Mott The Hoople on stage at Philadelphia's Tower Theatre, where he and The Spiders will set up residency tomorrow.

David joins Mott on stage for a rousing version of 'All The Young Dudes' He also contributes sax to their set-closer, a version of The Rolling Stones' 'Honky Tonk Woman'.[1]

1. Released on 1998 Mott compilation *All The Way From Stockholm To Philadelphia*.

Thursday 30 November

▶ David Bowie & The Spiders From Mars, Tower Theatre, 69 & Ludlow Street, Upper Darby, Philadelphia.

The entourage stays at the city's downtown Warwick Hotel and, the evening after Mott's appearance, David is back at the venue[1] which will become a favourite for him over the coming years.

David is introduced to promoter Rick Green's aide Pat Gibbons, who will later become one of his personal assistants.

Meanwhile, an old acquaintance now resident in the city, Calvin Mark Lee, sneaks backstage unannounced. They speak for a few minutes but

David, who has been avoiding Lee's calls, isn't pleased.

1. David's live albums *David Live* (1974) and *Stage* (1978) were both recorded here.

Friday 1 December

▶ David Bowie & The Spiders From Mars, Tower Theatre, Philadelphia.

MainMan's Hugh Attwooll telegrams to book studio time at Trident for David to start work on his new album and for Mott The Hoople to record their next single.

Saturday 2 December

▶ David Bowie & The Spiders From Mars, Tower Theatre, Philadelphia.

During the encore David nearly slips backwards off the stage into the orchestra pit, but manages to deftly save himself by wrapping his legs around the orchestra rail and, while hanging upside down, continues singing as if it was planned all along.

In Britain the *NME* publishes Charles Shaar Murray's article 'Bowie is an Industry'.

Sunday 3 December

▶ David Bowie & The Spiders From Mars, Tower Theatre, Philadelphia.

The band wrap up their stay in Philadelphia and the US tour with a final night at the Tower Theatre, which has been booked at the last minute due to demand for the first two nights there.

David and The Spiders, including Mike Garson, are back at RCA's New York studios the following day, where they are joined by Ken Scott, who has arrived from London to co-produce the new album.

Saturday 9 December

At RCA the band record their version of 'All The Young Dudes' and 'Drive-In Saturday'. David plays sax on both tracks.

On the former David's voice is hoarse from the tour, but all signs of strain are gone from his delivery on what will become his next single.

Sunday 10 December

Taking a break from recording, David spends the evening chatting with Ian Hunter. He plays Mott's singer songs from the new album (at this stage titled *Love Aladdin Vein*), including *Aladdin Sane* (with its dissonant piano solo recorded in a single take by Garson), 'Drive-In Saturday' and his unfinished version of 'All The Young Dudes' (which Hunter thinks is inferior to his band's take on the song).[1]

The two talk all night, dining at 7th Avenue's Stage Deli and parting around 5am.

During this spell in New York, RCA's Gustl Bruer arranges for David to see *The Nutcracker Suite* ballet at Radio City Music Hall.

1. David's version of 'All The Young Dudes' was the preferred version selected by co-director's Ricky Gervais and Stephen Merchant for

their 2010 film *Cemetery Junction*. "His vocal gives the song more of an outsider feel," said Gervais on the film's release.

Monday 11 December

After a final recording session, David holds a late-afternoon press conference at RCA's Studio 3.

Asked about *Transformer*, David says of Lou Reed: "He's very much in charge of what he's doing now. All that I can do is a few definitions on some of the concepts of songs. All Mick can do is arrange them."

One journalist refers to the poor turn-out for the St Louis date on the recent tour. "It made me feel very underground," says David. "I was knocked out we were even considered strong enough to be a headline band on our first tour. I was flabbergasted on the way back with the size of the audiences we drew."

Wednesday 13 December

To promote the reissues of David's earlier albums, RCA releases 'Space Oddity'/'The Man Who Sold The World' single in the US, where it reaches number 15.

During his last day in New York, David is back at RCA's Studio 3 to appear in a Mick Rock promo RCA has requested of 'Space Oddity'.

Tired and wearing minimal make-up, David mimes alone on guitar. A few hours later Rock accompanies David to the docks in Lower Manhattan where he boards the American liner RHMS *Ellinis*, and holds a small 'sailing party' in the Outrigger bar as the ship weighs anchor.

During the week-long passage home, David writes more lyrics and melodies for the song 'Aladdin Sane'. Inspiration is provided by Evelyn Waugh's 1930 satire of London's bright young things, *Vile Bodies*.

"The book dealt with London in the period just before a massive, imaginary war," said David in 1972. "People were frivolous, decadent and silly and were suddenly plunged into this horrendous holocaust. They were totally out of place, still thinking about champagne and parties and dressing up. Somehow it seemed to me that they were like people today."

In the UK, Arcade, a budget label launched by Gem's Laurence Myers, features 'The Jean Genie' and Mott's 'All The Young Dudes' on compilation *20 Fantastic Hits By The Original Artists Volume 3*.

Saturday 16 December

In *Disc*, Ringo Starr enters the Bowie vs Bolan debate: "I think Bowie is a step beyond what Marc is doing and then you've got Alice somewhere in between doing both scenes and trying to make it theatrical in another way."

Thursday 21 December

David arrives back in the UK a superstar. Some venues may not have sold out but, in terms of column inches, the US excursion has elevated David

TOP: Bowie's Back! advert, 16 December.

MIDDLE: 'The Jean Genie' Spanish single release.

BOTTOM: Italian release of 'The Jean Genie'.

In this year...

Monday 11 December
LAST manned moon landing. Two members of Apollo 17 remained on the moon for six days before returning to earth on 17 December, ending America's historic Apollo lunar programme.

Thursday 14 December
PREMIERE in London of Ringo Starr's film *Born To Boogie*, about Marc Bolan and featuring Elton John.

ZIGGY STARDUST

By the end of his first American visit in March 71, David had created his first character, Ziggy Stardust. But it would be a film that would give David the raw material to fully articulate his thoughts.

Stanley Kubrick had already inspired David's first hit record with his *2001: A Space Odyssey*. When his next movie, *A Clockwork Orange*, appeared in preview in 1971, the tabloid press had a field day, highlighting the brutal rape scenes and disturbing casual violence. Mick Ronson (with Bolder and Woodmansey) accompanied David to see the film and 20 years later recalled the event:

"Things came together after we went to see the movie *A Clockwork Orange* – what a great movie. It was basically David and Angela,[1] 'cos Angie was always the real outrageous one. That's how come the Ziggy thing developed.

"It was a timeless movie. I didn't really understand all of it at first."

The most obvious link with *A Clockwork Orange* was the use of the film's music, particularly 'March From A Clockwork Orange' (Ninth Symphony, Fourth Movement – Abridged) by Walter Carlos, later to become Wendy Carlos after sex reassignment surgery. This stirring piece was used as a prelude to David and The Spiders' arrival on stage.

To help complete his new sci-fi creation, David thought back to 1965 and the Giaconda coffee bar in Denmark Street, where he first met Maurice Brian Holden, better known as rocker Vince Taylor. David believed he was American because of his strong accent, picked up from living in California for 13 years. Although Taylor was comparatively unknown in the UK, he became a huge star on the continent (particularly France), stunning the French within weeks of moving there when he began dating Brigitte Bardot, the most famous woman in the country.

In 1975 David released some text for a proposed autobiography, and started with a reference to Taylor:

'Vince was an American and came to England, then went to France and became a star of the dirge. But then he came back to England and we spoke of our findings. He wore a white robe and sandals and we sat in the busy London street with a map of the world and tried to find the people who were passing by and scowling at us. They were nowhere on the map. Vince went back to France, then I heard about the famous show

TOP AND MIDDLE LEFT: The rise and fall of Maurice Holden, aka Vince Taylor (1939–1991). MIDDLE RIGHT: Norman Odam, aka The Legendary Stardust Cowboy – "I have written more space songs than anybody." ABOVE: Iggy's first UK appearance at the King's Cross Cinema, London, July 1972.

where he had told his band to go home and appeared in front of the curtains in that old white robe and sandals telling the French people about the comings and goings due upon us. He was banned from performing.

'I thought of Vince and wrote "Ziggy Stardust". I thought of my brother and wrote "Five Years".'

Towards the end of his life, Taylor's estate was overseen by friend and acquaintance, Roy Williams. Williams recalls once speaking to Taylor about David:

"The only time Vince and I spoke about Bowie was when Vince read an interview where Bowie mentioned him. It read something like, 'Vince Taylor could have been an enormous star, but he became a drug addict and womaniser and was an inveterate name-dropper.' Vince turned to me and said, 'Have you read what this guy has said about me, he's called me a name-dropper!' which I thought was an absolutely hilarious thing to say. He wasn't bothered about being called a womanising drug-taker!"

The Ziggy Stardust name was formed from two American performers, both of whom David discovered on his first US visit.

In California, David was introduced to the music of Iggy Pop and was immediately fascinated. When he returned to the UK, he eagerly spread the word about his latest discovery. ("Apparently I was the first person to mention him over here in England when I got back," David later said.)

Notorious in his hometown for his eccentricities both on and off stage, Iggy was considered one of the main inspirations for the punk movement. He used to cut himself on stage and would often dive into his audience, even walking on their hands and shoulders for a dramatic finale. David was especially fascinated by the aggression and danger of Pop's stage act. Right from his earliest Ziggy appearances, like Iggy, he would often perform bare-chested. In contrast to his theatrical performances, Jimmy Osterberg's early musical activities were fairly run of the mill. Starting out playing the drums in his first band, The Iguanas, in 1964, his later groups included The Prime Movers and The Stooges before becoming solo artist Iggy Pop. It was his fellow Iguana band members that began calling him Iggy.

The most obscure of all the influences on David relating to Ziggy was that of the Legendary Stardust Cowboy. Born Norman Carl Odam in the same year as David, he was also a Mercury recording artist at the time David issued 'Space Oddity'. The Stardust Cowboy, or 'Ledge', recorded two singles for Mercury: his biggest success, 'Paralyzed', and the even stranger 'I Took A Trip (On A Gemini Spaceship)'. This unconventional artist, who worked out of Lubbock, Texas, later described how his stage identity grew:

"I was sitting in my back yard thinking about cowboys and stardust in outer space. I put them together and came up with the Stardust Cowboy. After that I added Legendary, which means I am a legend in my own time."

It was from this performer that David drew part of his own character's name, as he later told Mick Rock: "The name originally came up when I heard a record by someone who called himself the 'Lonesome (sic) Stardust Cowboy'. He was hardly the inspiration for the album, but he was the basis for the title. The Ziggy bit was from Iggy. The Spiders From Mars just came up when I wrote the song. It just all hung together."

1. Although fully supportive of David's Ziggy concept, Angie Bowie was not impressed with *A Clockwork Orange* because of the gratuitous violence.

to the career high he has been seeking since joining The Konrads a decade earlier.

Saturday 23 December

▶ David Bowie & The Spiders From Mars, Rainbow, London.

David and The Spiders – completed by Mike Garson making his UK performance debut – play the first of two triumphant homecoming shows as part of an eight-date mini-tour stretching into the New Year (with support each night from Scottish quintet Stealers Wheel).

Tonight's gig sets a new template; the set is shorter than before, starting with a new version of The Rolling Stones' 1966 hit 'Let's Spend The Night Together', with David playing a Moog VCS3 synthesiser. There are no Velvets songs nor acoustic numbers, and no costume changes.

Four months earlier, Lindsay Kemp had played a major role in David's shows at the same venue; tonight he is turned away at the door.

Sunday 24 December

▶ David Bowie & The Spiders From Mars, Rainbow, London.

The audience for this Christmas Eve show, with support by Stealers Wheel, are asked to bring along a toy for children in care and in hospitals. The following day a large delivery of presents is made to Dr Barnardo's homes in London.

A MainMan Christmas party is held after the gig.

In a heavy snowstorm, Stuey George drives The Spiders home to Hull for Christmas. David returns to Haddon Hall.

Monday 25 December

The band's 'Starman' performance is repeated on a *Top Of The Pops* Christmas broadcast in the afternoon.

With David's fame well and truly established, fans soon begin to invade, camping in his garden or waiting around the driveway. Hoards of fan mail arrive and privacy is sacrificed.

During the day, Ian Hunter and his wife Trudy are summoned to Haddon Hall for an 'urgent' meeting which turns out to be of little importance. Hunter, who has driven, considerably jet-lagged, from Northampton, isn't best pleased.

The February performance of 'Queen Bitch' is repeated the following day on BBC2's Christmas edition of *The Old Grey Whistle Test*.

Thursday 28 December

▶ David Bowie & the Spiders from Mars, Hardrock, Manchester.

Leaving aside their velvet, silk and lurex jumpsuits, David and The Spiders surprise the audience by performing in denim (though in the latter half of the show David removes his jeans to reveal glitter tights).

The set opens with David improvising Beethoven's Ninth Symphony on his Moog synthesiser, a cue for the band to launch into 'Let's Spend The Night Together', with David still at the keyboard (an acknowledgement of Annette Peacock's performance style). As well as Stealers Wheel, retro rock'n'roll band Fumble are support tonight, David having been attracted by their album cover photograph of a Teddy Boy with his hand inside his girlfriend's top.

In the audience is 13-year-old Stephen Morrissey.[1]

The late show at the Hardrock is a set by Edwin Starr. During the soul singer's set, David is interviewed by eight Italian reporters, who have been invited by MainMan to report on the concert. Sixteen journalists had been booked for the press conference, but half haven't shown.

1. In 1992 Mick Ronson produced Morrissey's album *Your Arsenal*. Three years later Morrissey supported David on his UK tour.

Friday 29 December

▶ David Bowie & The Spiders from Mars, Hardrock, Manchester.

Supporting are Stealers Wheel and Fumble. This is David's last live performance of the year. Apart from the unrelaxing Cyprus vacation in July, David has been on the road for 11 months this year, chalking up more than 90 performances, three TV appearances and six radio sessions.

One of the Hardrock concerts is attended by writer Jim White, who will achieve success in 2006 with his TV series *Life On Mars*. In 2007 he recalled: "The sound system was so poor I couldn't make out a word he was singing. Yet, up there on stage, Bowie presented the most visually arresting image I had seen in my adolescent life, a promise of Technicolor in a monochrome world.

"I came out of that concert certain that there must be another universe out there, something beyond the dull, dank, depressing surroundings I was used to."

Saturday 30 December

At year end, *Ziggy Stardust* has sold in excess of 95,000 copies in the UK, and the same amount in the US.

In the *NME*, Charles Shaar Murray notes how David's popularity has grown by leaps and bounds, underlining his position as the most important rock star to emerge in the 70s: 'Just for the record, they've started screaming at David Bowie. It may take some little while to assess the final significance of the event, but at the Rainbow on Christmas Eve young girls were reaching out for our hero's supple limbs and squealing in the customary manner. It is clear that his three-month absence in the States has made the heart grow indubitably fonder.

'So the squealer's seal has been set on the man who is, at least for purposes of reference, Ziggy Stardust. Whether it's Bowiemania or Ziggymania or a combination of the two is not yet apparent, but something is definitely happening, Mr Jones.'

ABOVE: 'Space Oddity' promo film shot on 13 December at RCA's Studio 3, New York. © Mick Rock

In this year...

Tuesday 19 December
APPEARANCE by David's sometime support act Fumble on British rock show *The Old Grey Whistle Test*.

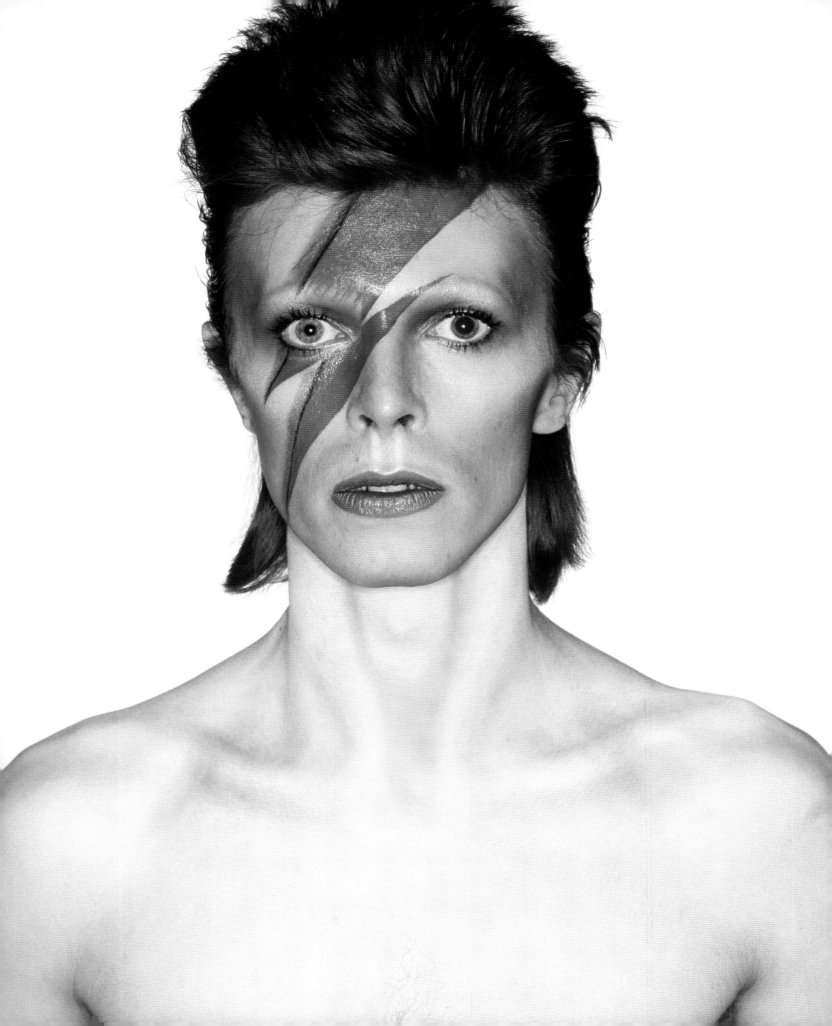

1973

DAVID and The Spiders From Mars are on the road in Britain, as 'The Jean Genie' peaks at number two in the singles chart. Soon, they must depart for a 100-date tour that will see them play to wildly enthusiastic audiences in the US and Japan.

Meanwhile, back in London, work is continuing on tracks for the next album, tentatively titled *Love Aladdin Vein*.

David meets Kansai Yamamoto in New York, and the Japanese designer presents him with garments that will, once again, transform his image.

Amid rumours that the coming UK tour will be his last, and with unease growing among The Spiders, David sets sail for Japan. Here he absorbs further cultural influences, and his Japanese fans go wild. 'Drive-In Saturday' provides more chart success.

Aladdin Sane, largely written in America, showcases a new, raw sound illuminated by Mike Garson's unsettling piano work. It enters the album charts as David returns home from a trans-Russian train adventure.

In his UK gigs, David's new Japanese influence is to the fore. Media frenzy is growing as the tour heads for the final night at the Hammersmith Odeon.

Like Ziggy, David breaks up the band, announcing at the Hammersmith show that 'it's the last show that we'll ever do'. Trevor Bolder and Mick Woodmansey, in the dark about the plan to disband, are stunned.

Recording of an album of cover versions takes place in France, where David also works with singer Lulu and Mick Ronson begins work on a solo venture.

Pin Ups is released, as the last performance by the Ziggy Stardust character in London is filmed, for US television, at London's Marquee.

Melody Maker applauds David's position as 'top singles artist of the year', and he is back in the studio recording 'Rebel Rebel'.

PREVIOUS SPREAD: Rare out-take from *Aladdin Sane* photo shoot by Brian Duffy.

THIS PAGE

TOP RIGHT: Photo by Richard Imrie, January.

TOP LEFT AND MIDDLE: Birthday celebrations at RCA's pressing plant in County Durham and visiting the production line at the pressing plant. Left to right: Bodyguard Stuart George, David, Mick Ronson and Woody Woodmansey.

BOTTOM: Photographed for a London *Evening Standard* interview conducted by *That'll Be The Day* writer Ray Connolly, 3 February.

OPPOSITE PAGE

Rehearsing his performance of 'My Death' on *Russell Harty Plus Pop* (in blue jacket) and (left) taping his performance of 'My Death' and 'Drive-in Saturday'.

Wednesday 3 January

David, The Spiders and Mike Garson run through three takes of 'The Jean Genie' for the *Top Of The Pops* cameras at BBC's Television Centre.

Ronson makes the most of the opportunity to play his guitar at top volume. "He loved it," said road manager Will Palin in 1993. "He cranked it up as far as it would go and blew the television engineers' ears away. Typical Mick."

Dressed in their unusual stage outfits, The Spiders spend time between takes in the BBC bar. "An episode of *Doctor Who* was also being recorded, so there were actors in futuristic costume drinking there," said Trevor Bolder. "People were approaching us asking us what parts we were playing."

In his dressing room, David is interviewed by reporter/DJ Nicky Horne for Radio One's *Scene & Heard* radio show, and RCA presents David with a gold disc for sales of 100,000 copies of *Ziggy Stardust* in the UK.

Thursday 4 January

The *Top Of The Pops* recording is broadcast. The band's third take is chosen, even though it contains a mistake when the musicians fail to start the final section simultaneously.

"Everyone thought it was me," said Bolder in 1995. "The whole band missed the cue, it was a real mess."

Friday 5 January

❯ David Bowie & The Spiders From Mars, Green's Playhouse, Renfield Street, Glasgow. (Two shows)
Support is Fumble and Stealers Wheel.

A pattern is established of maximising ticket sales by playing two shows a night at a single venue: matinee and evening.

The late Sean Mayes,[1] the pianist in Fumble, said about David's appearance in 1991: "No one looked like that then. Not just that there were no Bowie look-a-likes, but no one was looking that kind of way. He

looked extraordinary; he'd plucked his eyebrows right off and he'd got a very pale face, sort of translucent skin, and then this shock of wonderful hair."
1. Mayes died in 1995 aged 49.

Saturday 6 January

❯ David Bowie & The Spiders From Mars, Empire Theatre, Edinburgh.
Support is Fumble and Stealers Wheel.
Radio One broadcasts the *Scene & Heard* interview during which David still refers to the new album as *Love Aladdin Vein*.

Sunday 7 January

❯ David Bowie & The Spiders From Mars, City Hall, Northumberland Road, Newcastle.
Support is Fumble and Stealers Wheel.

Monday 8 January

David celebrates his 26th birthday at RCA's pressing plant in Washington, Co Durham, as a PR stunt initiated by RCA publicist Barry Bethell.

Tuesday 9 January

❯ David Bowie & The Spiders From Mars, Preston Guild Hall, Lancaster Road, Preston, Lancashire.
Support is Fumble and Stealers Wheel.
This is the last date of the mini UK tour. Now the band must focus on completing the tracks for the new album and prepare for a return to the US in just over two weeks. This will be the first leg of a 100-date world tour which will also take in Japan and a return to Britain in little over six months.

Saturday 13 January

'The Jean Genie' peaks at number two in the UK singles chart, ignominiously held off the top spot first by Little Jimmy Osmond's 'Long Haired Lover From Liverpool' and then, ironically, by The Sweet's 'Blockbuster' (a fellow RCA act whose song is inspired by the same Yardbirds riff). In the US, 'The Jean Genie' peaks at number 71.

Wednesday 17 January

David records an appearance as a guest on chat show host Russell Harty's London Weekend Television programme *Russell Harty Plus Pop*, which also features Elton John and Georgie Fame with Alan Price.

David is in yellow platform sandals and a flamboyant brightly-coloured suit designed specifically for the show by Freddie Burretti; in the dressing room he attempts to persuade Mick Woodmansey to wear it but he refuses, so David matches the new clothing with a single chandelier earring (which he gives to Harty at the end of the show).

David and The Spiders perform new single 'Drive-In Saturday', while David performs Brel's 'My Death' solo.

Journalist Charles Shaar Murray is at the TV studio, shadowing David for a piece for the *NME*. Elton John seizes the opportunity to tell Bolder that he noticed the band's miscue on their recent *Top Of The Pops* performance. "Everyone thought it was me. Even Elton John mentioned it to me when we did the Russell Harty show," said Bolder in 1995. The following day the *Daily Express* publishes a feature on David by David Wigg, with the heading 'Zowie! It's the mad, mad world of David Bowie'.

Friday 19 January

Back at Trident, David and The Spiders record new composition '1984', a portent of things to come since it will be central to the theme of the projects he will develop in the latter part of this year.

Meanwhile, his former colleague in The Buzz and Feathers, John Hutchinson, follows up on a report in *Melody Maker* which mentions that David is looking for a rhythm guitarist for the world tour, to give him more freedom on stage.

Still in Scarborough, Hutchinson gets David's Haddon Hall address from John Cambridge and writes to apply for the job.

Shortly afterwards David calls Hutchinson at work. "He said, 'If you can go with us we leave for New York next week'," said Hutchinson in 1983. "The next day I went down to see them. They were just finishing *Aladdin Sane* in the studio. It was strange because that was more or less where I last left him, when we were recording things like 'Ching-A-Ling'."

Saturday 20 January

Russell Harty Plus Pop is broadcast. This includes David's first British TV interview since the 1964 *Tonight* programme about The Prevention of Cruelty to Long-Haired Men.

At Trident, the week-long series of sessions to complete *Aladdin Sane* continues with the taping of the backing tracks for 'Panic In Detroit'; the lyrics have yet to be written.

Pianist Matthew Fisher, visiting the studio, witnesses the taping of another version of 'John, I'm Only Dancing'.[1] "They were recording a piece with some brass players," said Fisher in 1992. "Instead of describing the type of sound he wanted from them in a musical way, David talked about it in terms of colours."

The *NME*'s Charles Shaar Murray is also in attendance, observing that David's notebook betrays the full title to one new song: 'Aladdin Sane: 1913-1948-197? Copyright David Bowie 1972.'

An initial running order is created for the new album, featuring 'John, I'm Only Dancing' as track three and the incomplete 'Zion'[2] as track five on side two.

Queen are also recording at Trident, preparing their second album. They are still recording in downtime (generally the middle of the night). David is again asked to produce them, but his commitments allow

him no time to even consider the offer.

1. This was the third recording of the song by David and The Spiders. He also reworked it into a disco version – retitled 'John, I'm Only Dancing (Again)' – during the *Young Americans* sessions at Philadelphia's Sigma Sound in 1974. Released as a single in 1979.

2. 'Zion' didn't make it on to the release of *Aladdin Sane*. Rykodisc considered it for inclusion on the 1991 *Aladdin Sane* CD reissue, but it was dropped at David's request.

Wednesday 24 January

Final touches are made to 'Panic In Detroit' and, when David adds vocals to the title track, *Aladdin Sane* is completed, now that photographer Brian Duffy has taken the images of David for the cover.

At his studio near Swiss Cottage, north London, Duffy introduces David to former Elizabeth Arden expert Pierre Laroche, who applies the striking make-up, and to Celia Philo, who would oversee the striking sleeve design.

This month Richard Imrie also photographs David, a rare occurrence as MainMan are still maintaining tight restrictions on who can photograph him.

Thursday 25 January

Having invited old friend Geoff MacCormack along as travelling companion and backing vocalist, David boards the SS *Canberra* at Southampton for New York. Mick Rock photographs David in his cabin with MacCormack, who will travel and work with David for the next three years.

Saturday 27 January

The *NME* exclusively reveals David's new persona: 'Goodbye Ziggy and a Big Hello to Aladdin Sane'.

"'Aladdin' is really just a title track," David tells

TOP LEFT: Preparing for US Tour II. Sukita photographs David in rehearsal at RCA. A film crew was also present.

TOP RIGHT: *Hit Parader* magazine, February issue.

ABOVE: Tour itinerary advert from *Rolling Stone*.

In this year...

Friday 9 February

RELEASE of The Edgar Winter Group album *They Only Come Out At Night*, with a sleeve parodying David's *Hunky Dory* and taking a dig at the glam rock scene.

Charles Shaar Murray. "The album was written in America. The numbers were not supposed to form a concept album but, looking back on them, there seems to be a definite linkage from number to number."

David also reaches number three in the newspaper's year-end best male singer category, and *Ziggy Stardust* is listed third album of the year.

Disc quotes soul singer Claudia Lennear, a friend of David's, saying it is "95 per cent settled" that she'll be joining David's US tour in New York.

Tuesday 30 January

David and MacCormack arrive in New York and check into the Gramercy Park Hotel.

With RCA reining in expenditure, the tour entourage has been halved from its Beverley Hills Hotel peak of 46 just three months previously.

Nevertheless, David has brought Pierre Laroche to act as his personal make-up artist for the duration of the tour.[1]

And there is dissent brewing among his most faithful backing musicians, Bolder, Woodmansey and Ronson, following their discovery that relative newcomer Mike Garson is being paid £500 a week, 10 times their salary.

On arrival in New York, The Spiders contact RCA's A&R head, Dennis Katz, who introduces them to friends at rival record label CBS. Ronson has known Katz since 1971, and he and the other Spiders aim to increase their income by signing a record deal as a separate entity.

Katz is enthusiastic, believing that they could command a sizeable advance, but Defries gets wind of it and intervenes, persuading the musicians to hold

out for a better offer.

"Defries said, 'Don't sign with anyone else, RCA will give you more'," recalled Bolder in 1995. "But we didn't want to sign straight away, we weren't ready, and that was our mistake."

Privately, Defries is furious at their actions and has no intention of getting them a deal. Instead, he sets to work on sowing discord among the band by privately offering Ronson a solo deal with RCA.

Publicly, Defries agrees parity with Garson, which Ronson obtains, though Bolder and Woodmansey receive just £200 a week each, with assurances that the difference will be made up on their return to the UK. The following day a master tape of *Aladdin Sane* is completed in London by Ken Scott. This comprises 11 tracks, with side two ending with the new 'sax version' of 'John, I'm Only Dancing'.

1. Laroche went on to work with other rock acts, including Roxy Music and The Rolling Stones. He also created the make-up for Tim Curry in the 1975 film version of *The Rocky Horror Picture Show* and designed album sleeves for Bill Wyman and Hall & Oates. Laroche succumbed to AIDS in the early 90s.

Thursday 1 February

David signs a two-year contract with US booking agent CMA as his American profile goes into overdrive.

This month sees the US release of his mid-60s Decca material by London Records with the double album *Images 1966–1967*, which includes the first release of David's 1967 song 'Did You Ever Have A Dream'. The sleeve notes are supplied by New York journalist Henry Edwards[1] and the cover is drawn by Neon Park XIII.[2]

1. Co-author with former MainMan executive Tony Zanetta of the 1986 Bowie biography *Stardust*.
2. Martin Muller (1940–1993) as Neon Park XIII designed striking covers for Frank Zappa, The Beach Boys, Little Feat and Dr John.

Sunday 4 February

With Sukita taking photographs, rehearsals for the tour commence at RCA Studios in Manhattan.

In 1983, John Hutchinson recalled it as "a huge room that felt like a cinema. It had a full screen, and was used to record soundtracks. Harry Belafonte, who was working upstairs, politely asked us to keep the noise down."

In New York, Hutchinson and David renew their friendship, taking in a gig by jazz giant Charlie Mingus[1] at downtown nightclub The Village Gate.

The previous day, London's *Evening Standard* features an interview with David (headed 'Wowie Bowie') by Ray Connolly, writer of this year's rock'n'roll coming-of-age movie *That'll Be The Day*.

1. In 2005, David named Mingus' 'Hog Callin' Blues' as his all-time favourite jazz track. It featured on the 1962 Mingus LP *Oh Yeah*, which included the song 'Wham Bam Thank You Ma'am', used as a lyric in 'Suffragette City'.

Monday 5 February

David is at the final show of a six-night Max's Kansas City residency by singer-songwriter Biff Rose.[1]

Support is Bruce Springsteen, promoting his debut album. "I hated him as a solo. As soon as the band came on he was like a different person," David said in 1987. "He was marvellous."

1. In 1983, Rose visited London with the intention of meeting David, unaware that he no longer lived in the city.

Monday 12 February

David and Angie are back at Max's Kansas City, where they meet rock star and producer Todd Rungren and his model girlfriend Bebe Buell for the first time.

The following day, David calls Buell and invites her to see Manhattan's premiere dance troupe the Rockettes at Radio City Music Hall, where his tour opens the next day. They go in the evening with Defries and Hutchinson.

During the performance, one of the girls descends to the stage on a silver gyroscope. David announces that he wants to use the same device for his own stage entrance the following evening.

After the show, David joins the other musicians for all-night rehearsals. David is now playing mini-Moog at certain points during the set, with Mike Garson on Mellotron as well as piano. Hutchinson plays rhythm guitar, Geoff MacCormack is on backing vocals and percussion and there is a small brass section: Ken Fordham on tenor, baritone and alto sax and Brian 'Bux' Wilshaw on tenor sax and flute.

While the musicians work, Suzi Fussey, David's personal hairdresser and head of wardrobe, also stays up, restitching The Spiders' costumes which have just arrived from England and don't fit.

The month-long tour takes in 17 shows in six US cities.

Wednesday 14 February

▶ David Bowie & The Spiders From Mars, Radio City Music Hall, Rockefeller Center, Avenue of Americas, New York.

Support group Fumble have encountered visa and work permit problems and do not appear on the first few dates.

The concert is greeted with wild applause as, to the strains of Walter Carlos' Beethoven's Ninth, David is lowered on to the stage via the Rockettes' gyroscope, having been suspended in the flies for over half an hour.[1]

The second half begins in a similarly dramatic fashion as David and group appear on the large stage lift, rising slowly up to performance level.

And drama even consumes the finale, when a fan mounts the stage and runs towards David. Believing he is being attacked, he faints and can't be brought round until he is back in his dressing room.

Tonight's and tomorrow's shows – which are recorded by RCA for potential release – are sell-outs, with attendees including Salvador Dali,[2] actor/singer Rod McKuen and Bette Midler. Kansai Yamamoto is also there and is photographed with Angie in the audience and introduced to David at the small after-show party in the venue.

The prominent Japanese designer has arrived in New York that day, and presents David with a gift of five specially designed garments. He has cancelled all other appointments to be here, after being advised to fly to New York by assistant/stylist Yasuko Takahashi (who attended rehearsals).

Also in New York is photographer Masayoshi Sukita, who is the first to take images of David in his new Kansai wardrobe.

1. A similar entrance was used by David on his 1987 Glass Spider tour.
2. Dali, who saw at least one other show on this US tour, was very impressed with David, though later in the year he told British chat-show host Russell Harty that he "didn't agree" with David's sense of fashion. MainMan even hosted a dinner for Dali in New York, though David did not attend and was never formally introduced to the artist. The closest the two came to meeting was sharing an elevator, though no conversation was exchanged.

Thursday 15 February

▶ David Bowie & The Spiders From Mars, Radio City Music Hall, New York.

In the afternoon a press conference for Japanese media is held at the Gramercy (where *Melody Maker*'s Michael Watts also interviews David). Sukita

TOP LEFT: David performs his feather boa/ boa constrictor Alice Cooper pastiche.

ABOVE: David on the 73 US tour.

TOP: Radio City's stunning architecture (inspired by the Exposition des Arts Décoratifs) was truly home from home for David. He is pictured, resplendent in his latest Burretti creation, in the venue's foyer by Sukita.

TOP RIGHT: Rehearsal at Radio City. David descends to the stage on the Rockettes gyroscope, 13 February.

ABOVE: Tower Theatre press advert, noting David's impressive February sell-out run.

ABOVE RIGHT: David, having just appeared on the *Mike Douglas Show* in Philadelphia.

RIGHT: David and Stevie Wonder in Philadelphia, 16 February.

is in attendance. By now he is building an impressive portfolio which helps boost David's Japanese profile ahead of his visit there in April.

Tonight, rock stars Johnny Winter and Todd Rundgren are in the Radio City audience, as is author Truman Capote.

Friday 16 February

▶ David Bowie & The Spiders From Mars, Tower Theatre, 69th & Ludlow Street, Upper Darby, Philadelphia, Pennsylvania.

Early in the morning, David and the tour entourage leave by Greyhound bus for Philadelphia for seven shows over four nights at the Tower Theatre.

Tonight is the only night they perform once; the rest of the residency includes two nightly shows.

"Bowie stalked his audience like a tiger – by the end he'd be holding them entirely in his sweaty hands," said MacCormack in 2007. "There was the sweet rock'n'roll trick of getting to that moment of thanking the audience and saying good night, pretending not to know there's going to be an encore. Night after night, it would be the best part of the show."

After the show David is at a party for Stevie Wonder

at the city's Genesis nightclub, where he meets cocktail waitress Ava Cherry. They become lovers; she will soon join him as a backing singer.

Saturday 17 February

▶ David Bowie & The Spiders From Mars, Tower Theatre, Philadelphia. (Two shows)

Today the British music press announces that David is to star in a film version of Robert Heinlein's 1961 book *Stranger In A Strange Land*.[1]

1. This did not make it into production. David played a similar role to the book's central character in *The Man Who Fell To Earth*.

Sunday 18 February

▶ David Bowie & The Spiders From Mars, Tower Theatre, Philadelphia. (Two shows)

Support is Fumble. During his stay in Philadelphia, David appears on *The Mike Douglas Show*.

Monday 19 February

▶ David Bowie & The Spiders From Mars, Tower Theatre, Philadelphia. (Two shows)

Support is Fumble. After the second performance a party is held for the band, crew and support act.

Friday 23 February

▶ David Bowie & The Spiders From Mars, War Memorial Auditorium, Capital Boulevard, Nashville, Tennessee.

The show is a sell-out, with 2,000 fans standing on their seats in excitement. Fumble again support.

Saturday 24 February

Melody Maker poses the question 'Bowie's Last Tour?' to flag up Watts' recent interview.

With echoes of Col. Tom Parker, Defries is quoted as saying: "He may not make another British tour after this one for a long, long time, maybe even years, especially if he gets into films."

Sunday 25 February

▶ David Bowie & The Spiders From Mars, Ellis Auditorium North Hall, 74 Poplar Avenue, Memphis, Tennessee. (Two shows)

With Fumble in support, the shows start at 7pm and 10pm.[1] This auditorium was used to stage events by Elvis Presley's high school; he also performed there.

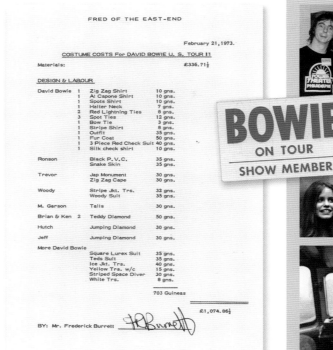

The following evening, artist and teacher Dolph Smith invites David, Ronson and Woodmansey to the Memphis Academy of Art to view work by students.

Meanwhile, plans are firming up for Ronson's solo career, and Defries asks him, Woodmansey and Bolder to sign a letter to RCA's Rocco Laginestra confirming MainMan as their sole representative.

1. A second evening of performances at Ellis Auditorium, although listed in RCA and promoter tour itineraries in early February, did not take place.

Wednesday 28 February

In advance of David's appearance at the Masonic Temple, Detroit newspaper *The South End* reports: 'The bigger timetable for Bowie calls for another US fall tour in 1973, with bigger production than previously, then a solo tour in 1974, featuring Bowie as a solo artist.'

Thursday 1 March

▶ David Bowie & The Spiders From Mars, Masonic Temple, Temple Avenue, Detroit.

During the day, interviews are conducted at the Detroit Hilton, one with *NME*'s Nick Kent.

During the performance, a member of the security staff strikes a girl in the face, Angie intervenes and is throttled by another guard. Leee Black Childers comes to her rescue. Fumble support.

Later David hosts a small party, attended by DJ/publicist BP Fallon and his client Michael Des Barres of glam group Silverhead.

Friday 2 March

▶ Masonic Temple, Temple Avenue, Detroit, Michigan. Fumble are support.

TOP LEFT: The Tower Theatre, listing David's four-night residency, Philadelphia, 18 February.

TOP MIDDLE: Fred Of The East-End; Burretti itemised bill for Bowie tour gear.

TOP RIGHT: Fumble's Des Henley (left) and Sean Mayes with admirer backstage at the War Memorial Auditorium, Nashville. Sean later recalled: "The cops loved Fumble. Loads of them stopped by to see us backstage."

MIDDLE: Bowie meeting fans in LA and a US tour pass.

BOTTOM: Photographed by Sean Mayes heading west in the observation car of an Amtrak Super Chief train.

In this year...

Saturday 24 February

INTERVIEW with Mick Jagger in *Melody Maker*: "All these people have been around for ages. Slade, Rod Stewart, Bolan, Bowie. Rod was overlooked in the old days because he was a solo singer when bands were in. Slade made it when people needed another rocky band."

Would Mick ever consider engaging in erotic tussles with say Bill Wyman or Keith Richard?

"I tried," he said deadpan. "They wouldn't take any notice."

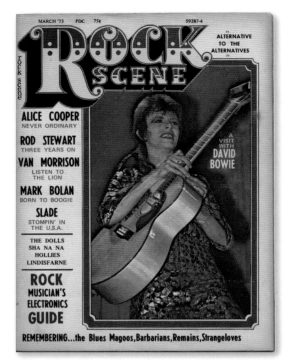

Saturday 10 March

❱ David Bowie & The Spiders From Mars, Long Beach Auditorium, Pacific Terrace Centre, Los Angeles.

Fumble are again supporting and notably Mick Jagger is in attendance. It's the first time David has been formally introduced to Jagger, though they have crossed paths ever since 1963 when The Konrads were initially courted by then-Stones co-manager Eric Easton.

Monday 12 March

❱ David Bowie & The Spiders From Mars, Hollywood Palladium, 6215 Sunset Boulevard, Hollywood.

This final performance of the US leg is added to the itinerary. It is also the last time Fumble support David, though at this stage they are still pencilled in for appearances back in the UK in May. It is also the last time The Spiders will work with David in the US.

David hosts a tour-end dinner party at organic restaurant Lost On Larrabee, with Ringo Starr and Klaus Voorman among the guests.

By this time Claudia Lennear has joined David, and the following evening the pair take in a Bette Midler show at LA's Music Centre, hanging out with the outrageous singer/comedienne afterwards.

While in LA David also catches a performance by singer Sandra Alexandra. A demo of 'Diamond Dogs' is recorded.

Monday 19 March

David and Geoff MacCormack are on board the SS *Oronsay* as it sails from Los Angeles to take them to Japan, where they will meet the rest of the entourage for the next stage of the world tour.

On arrival in San Francisco the following day, unhappy with their berth, David and MacCormack spend the night ashore and meet up again with Bette Midler. Together they visit a small club called The Boarding House.

Wednesday 21 March

Now that improvements have been made to their accommodation, David and MacCormack board the departing *Oronsay*.

Friday 23 March

The ship arrives in Vancouver early in the morning. David is interviewed on the deck by a local TV news team before RCA reps give the pair a guided tour of the city. In the evening the *Oronsay* sets sail again.

Wednesday 28 March

David and MacCormack enjoy a day in Hawaii, arriving first thing in the morning in Honolulu. Greeted in the traditional manner with garlands of flowers, David is given a brief tour of the main island before the ship departs in the early evening.

Thursday 5 April

The SS *Oronsay* docks at Yokohama and David and MacCormack are ferried by limousine from the port to the Imperial Hotel in Chiyoda-ku, Tokyo.

David is greeted at the port by Japanese RCA staff as well as Sukita and Kansai Yamamoto,[1] who, inspired by David's performance in New York has designed a further nine costumes for him.

"The clothes were simply outrageous... nobody

had seen anything like them before," David later said. "[Kansai] contemporised the kabuki look and made it work for rock'n'roll."

These new outfits are also inspired by the Japanese dramatic tradition Noh. David will observe a few Noh performances during his visit: "I found them absolutely fascinating," he said in 1973. "There were an awful lot of very strange ritual dance performances that I hadn't seen before. A lot of them were from Shintoism."

1. Kansai Yamamoto worked uncredited on the production for 1983 movie *Merry Christmas Mr Lawrence*.

Friday 6 April

RCA release 'Drive-In Saturday (Seattle-Phoenix)'/ 'Round And Round' single in the UK, but not the US.

⦿ **David Bowie**
A **'Drive-In Saturday'** (Bowie)
B **'Round And Round'** (Berry)
David Bowie (vocal, guitar, harmonica)
Mick Ronson (guitar, backing vocal)
Trevor Bolder (bass)
Woody Woodmansey (drums)
Mike Garson (keyboards on A-side)
Produced by David Bowie and Ken Scott
Arranged by David Bowie and Mick Ronson
(RCA 2352)

The B-side,[1] the Chuck Berry standard originally titled 'Around And Around', was recorded in late 1971 as a potential track for *Ziggy Stardust*; David and George Underwood performed the song live with The King Bees in the early 60s.[2]

In Japan, Angie and Zowie arrive in the morning, as do the rest of the band and entourage.

David holds a 90-minute press conference in the Fukuno-Ma suite, on the 3rd floor of the recently rebuilt Imperial Hotel.

1. 'Let's Spend The Night Together' was planned for the B-side, before being elevated for inclusion on *Aladdin Sane*.

2. In April 1973 RCA also released a different version of 'John, I'm Only Dancing' in the UK without fanfare; this replaced stocks of the single released the previous year and is the version recorded with a small horn section in January 1973. It was included in error on the 1976 RCA compilation *ChangesOneBowie* and caused a fuss since David wanted the original non-sax version on the album. The record was remastered and created a rush of demand before the new stock arrived.

Saturday 7 April

The musicians prepare for the eight shows they will play in five Japanese cities with an evening rehearsal at RCA Nihon Victor in Tokyo. The record label issues two albums to promote the tour: *David Bowie Rock 'n' Roll Now* features 12 tracks culled from his five RCA albums, and an advance pressing of *Aladdin Sane* has a black and white sleeve featuring a photo from Brian Ward's *Ziggy Stardust* cover session.

Sunday 8 April

▶ David Bowie & The Spiders From Mars, Shinjuku Koseinenkin Kaikan, Tokyo.

OPPOSITE PAGE:

TOP LEFT: Japanese press interview in New York, 15 February.

TOP RIGHT: Continuing to make waves in the US, *Rock Scene* magazine, March issue.

BELOW LEFT AND MIDDLE RIGHT: Arrival at Yokohama on the SS *Oronsay*, 5 April.

LOWER MIDDLE LEFT: Japanese press conference and photo call at the Imperial Hotel, Tokyo, 6 April.

BELOW RIGHT: Yokohama port. RCA and fans wait to greet David's arrival in Japan.

BOTTOM LEFT: Japanese *Music Life* press article, March issue.

THIS PAGE

TOP: In Tokyo, David with legendary designer Kansai Yamamoto, trying on his latest creation. In 1973, Yamamoto said of David: "He has an unusual face, don't you think? He's neither man nor woman, if you see what I mean, which suited me as a designer because most of my clothes are for either sex."

MIDDLE: David in performance.

BOTTOM: David's signature in both English and Japanese.

In this year...

March
SPLIT between Mott The Hoople and manager Tony Defries speculated in a *Melody Maker* report.
THE IMAGE, the 1968 short featuring David, re-run at the Jacey Cinema, Trafalgar Square, sandwiched between two seedy adult films, *I Am Sexy* and *Erotic Blue*.

Saturday 3 March
INTERVIEW with Pete Townshend in *NME*:
"Slade and David Bowie are just so important. If they weren't here now, in England, Christ Almighty, it would just be so sad. I'm so glad that they're there."

Saturday 17 March
INTERVIEW in *NME* with Rick Wakeman, who lists David's 'Wild Eyed Boy From Freecloud' as his favourite recording:
"This is without doubt my favourite song of all time."

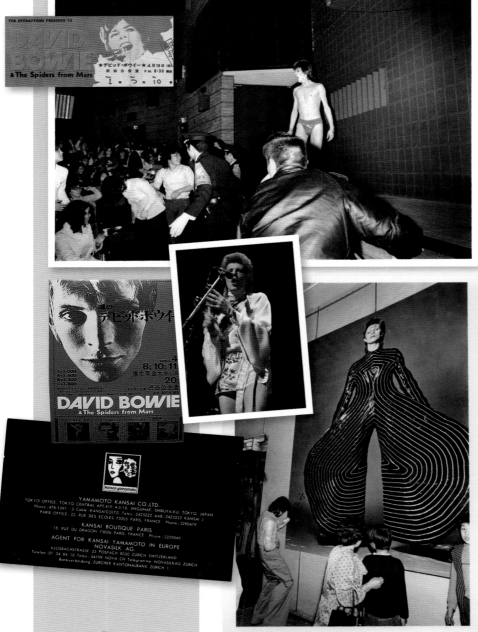

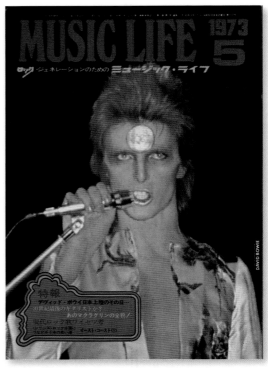

The following evening, David and Angie attend a show by popular kabuki star Tomasa Boru. Afterwards, David is introduced to Boru, who demonstrates how to apply kabuki make-up, a lesson David will apply over the coming months, embracing the theatrical form's richly decorated, heavily powdered cosmetic application. With Ronson, David and Angie also visit a tea ceremony in the Imperial Gardens at the Emperor's Palace.

Tuesday 10 April

▶ David Bowie & The Spiders From Mars, Shinjuku Koseinenkin Kaikan, Tokyo

Mick Ronson picks up a new nickname in Japan – Ricky Monsoon – though the guitarist has more serious matters to consider as Defries continues to press him into pursuing a solo career.

By contrast, the manager steps up his campaign against Woodmansey and Bolder, telling the rhythm section in Japan that the road crew are more important than them. "I was devastated," said Bolder in 2005. "It was also the start of Woody being pushed out of the band."

Wednesday 11 April

▶ David Bowie & The Spiders From Mars, Shinjuku Koseinenkin Kaikan, Tokyo.

The venue is filled to capacity for the three dates, but David is about to find out he is still relatively unknown to the Japanese outside of Tokyo.

Thursday 12 April

▶ David Bowie & The Spiders From Mars, Kokaido, Nagoya.

Final rehearsals are held at 1pm ahead of the 6.30pm show.

Model Marie Helvin – who is a favourite of Kansai Yamamoto – is in the audience. "It was the first time I had seen him in Kansai's clothes," said Helvin in 2009. "I clearly remember Angie walking back and forth in front of the stage. It was almost as if she was stage directing."

The wild reception from the rock-starved audience is matched by the media; *The Japan Times* describes David as 'musically the most exciting thing that has happened since the fragmentation of The Beatles and theatrically he is possibly the most interesting performer ever in the pop music genre'.

TOP LEFT: First night in Japan, 8 April. David is ecstatic. Inset, Tokyo concert ticket.

TOP RIGHT: *Music Life* Japanese magazine.

MIDDLE LEFT AND CENTRE: Nagoya concert promo leaflet and live on stage in Japan.

LOWER RIGHT: David at Seibu Department Store, Ikebukuro, Tokyo, signing a recently taken Sukita giant photograph.

BOTTOM: Kansai Yamamoto promo card.

Leaving Tokyo Yaesu Station, David, band and crew travel on a Tokaido Shinkansen bullet train for the two-hour journey to Nagoya City in central Japan. All stay at the Nagoya Miyako Hotel.

During one bullet-train journey, David leaves his bag containing personal documents and passport in a carriage. It is safely recovered.

Tonight's gig is the first of four consecutive concerts where fewer than 1,000 people turn out at each of the 2,000 seat-capacity venues. Japanese promoter Toa Attractions takes a hit, while MainMan is protected by contractual guarantees.

Friday 13 April

Aladdin Sane is released in the UK to advance orders of 100,000 copies, immediately going gold.

This is the first time pre-order sales of this magnitude have been recorded since The Beatles' albums up until 1969's *Abbey Road*.

Saturday 14 April

◗ David Bowie & The Spiders From Mars, Yuubin Chokin Kaikan, Hiroshima.

In the UK, 'Drive-In Saturday' enters the chart at number 16.

During the Japanese tour, Ronson is summoned to a private meeting with David and Defries in David's hotel room and told that there are plans for an announcement in the summer. "I knew that David was going to retire when we were in Japan," said Ronson in 1984. "I had to swear to keep it to myself."

Monday 16 April

◗ David Bowie & The Spiders From Mars, Kokusai Kaikan, Kobe.

While in Japan, Defries telexes Fumble's manager to inform him that due to additional matinees, there will be no room for the group as a support act on David's forthcoming UK tour, much to their disappointment.

Tuesday 17 April

◗ David Bowie & The Spiders From Mars, Koseinenkin Kaikan, Osaka.

Travels from Kobe to Osaka Grand Hotel by car.

Wednesday 18 April

◗ David Bowie & The Spiders From Mars, Shibuya Kokaido, Tokyo.

In the morning, the party travels from Shin-Osaka station to Tokyo by train, returning to the opulent Imperial Hotel.

Friday 20 April

◗ David Bowie & The Spiders From Mars, Shibuya Kokaido, Tokyo.

The show ends in crowd hysteria, exacerbated after security guards wade in to the audience to break up what they consider to be a riot. The incident is in fact sparked by a ploy of Angie and Tony Zanetta's to create a spectacle during the finale: they swing chairs above their heads.

After two encores the audience demand more, and 15 minutes later the musicians return to the stage and perform 'Round And Round'. Police and venue security struggle to contain enthusiastic fans as they surge dramatically towards the stage.

In the aftermath, it emerges the hall has suffered structural damage. The jumping by exuberant fans has broken the floor joists, and the ceilings of the dressing rooms underneath bow ominously.

The hall's owners are furious and contact the police, who in turn ask RCA Tokyo to pass on the names of the individuals who incited the disturbance. A plan is quickly hatched to enable Angie and Zanetta to disappear, and Tony Defries slips away, for fear of being held personally responsible for the damage.

David is not troubled by the police and spends a quiet evening with MacCormack at a traditional kaiseki-ryori restaurant.

The following day Angie, Zowie and Zanetta discreetly leave Japan on a flight to the US via Honolulu, while police – armed with arrest warrants – mistakenly monitor direct flights to the West.

Accompanied by MacCormack and Childers, David boards liner the *Felix Dzerzhinsky* at Yokohama, where he is seen off by crowds of fans gathered at the dockside.

The ship is heading for Russia's commercial port of Nakhodka to pick up a train to Vladivostok. On the boat David and MacCormack improvise a cabaret act and perform songs, including 'Space Oddity' and 'Amsterdam', for fellow passengers.

Tuesday 24 April

The *Felix Dzerzhinsky* arrives in Khabarovsk, Russia. After a two-hour stopover, the trio join the Trans-Siberian Express,[1] travelling 'soft' (the Russian equivalent of first class).

David shares a compartment with MacCormack for the week-long, 6,000-mile journey to Moscow via Irkutsk, Novosibirsk and Ekaterinburg.

Along for the ride is newsman Bob Musel of the UPI agency. Musel had seen David's performance at Aylesbury in July 1972, and uses this journey as material for his syndicated newspaper series Great Train Journeys. David occasionally films parts of the trip, and considers writing it up as a book.

1. Scott Walker, one of David's heroes and equally wary of flying, took the same Trans-Siberian route after a tour of Japan in 1968, stopping off in Leningrad and Moscow before returning to the UK via Paris.

Monday 30 April

The Trans-Siberian Express arrives in Moscow, where the three are booked in to the Intourist Hotel.

The following day, David, MacCormack, Childers and Musel attend Moscow's May Day Parade, which David films.

TOP: Breakfast on the Trans-Siberian Express. David with journalist Bob Musel. Photo by Leee Black Childers.

ABOVE: Travelling in Siberia. Photo by Leee Black Childers.

In this year...

April
ALBUM *Aladdin Sane* and single 'The Jean Genie' are banned in Rhodesia (now Zimbabwe) before release, since the authorities considered them 'undesirable'.

Monday 9 April
LAUNCH of Queen by EMI Records with a showcase gig at the Marquee Club, London.

ABOVE: The famous *Aladdin Sane* sleeve was a joint concept designed by David, Brian Duffy, Celia Philo, Pierre Laroche and Philip Castle. Photographed in London in January 1973, the graphics were designed by Duffy and Philo for Duffy Design Concepts. The artwork was put together in Switzerland, where the sleeve was printed in seven colours. BELOW: Fan club promotional leaflet included with initial copies of the album.

ALADDIN SANE Released Friday 13 April

Side One
1. WATCH THAT MAN (New York) (Bowie) (4.30)
David Bowie (vocal, guitar, saxophone)
Mick Ronson (guitar, piano, vocal)
Trevor Bolder (bass)
Woody Woodmansey (drums)
Mike Garson (piano)
Ken Fordham (saxophone, flutes)
Brian 'Bux' Wilshaw (tenor sax, flute)
Juanita 'Honey' Franklin/Linda Lewis/
Mac Cormack (vocal backup)

2. ALADDIN SANE (1913-1938-197?)
(RHMS *Ellinis*) (Bowie) (5.15)
David Bowie (vocal, guitar, saxophone)
Mick Ronson (guitar, vocal)
Trevor Bolder (bass)
Woody Woodmansey (drums)
Mike Garson (piano)
Ken Fordham (saxophone, flutes)
Brian 'Bux' Wilshaw (tenor sax, flute)

3. DRIVE-IN-SATURDAY[2] (Seattle–Phoenix) (Bowie)
(4.38)
David Bowie (vocal, guitar, Moog synthesiser,
saxophone)
Mick Ronson (guitar, piano, vocal)
Trevor Bolder (bass)
Woody Woodmansey (drums)
Mike Garson (piano)

4. PANIC IN DETROIT[1] (Bowie) (4.30)
David Bowie (vocal, guitar)
Mick Ronson (guitar, vocal)
Trevor Bolder (bass)
Woody Woodmansey (drums)
Mac Cormack (percussion, vocal backup)
Juanita 'Honey' Franklin/Linda Lewis (vocal backup)

5. CRACKED ACTOR[1] (Los Angeles) (Bowie) (3.01)
David Bowie (vocal, guitar, harmonica)
Mick Ronson (guitar, vocal)

Trevor Bolder (bass)
Woody Woodmansey (drums)

Side Two
1. TIME[1] (New Orleans) (Bowie) (5.10)
David Bowie (vocal, guitar, saxophone)
Mick Ronson (guitar, vocal)
Trevor Bolder (bass)
Woody Woodmansey (drums)
Mike Garson (piano)
Ken Fordham (flutes)

2. THE PRETTIEST STAR[2] (Gloucester Road)
(Bowie) (3.28)
David Bowie (vocal, guitar, saxophone)
Mick Ronson (guitar, piano, vocal)
Trevor Bolder (bass)
Woody Woodmansey (drums)
Mike Garson (piano)
Ken Fordham (saxophone, flutes)
Brian 'Bux' Wilshaw (tenor sax, flute)

3. LET'S SPEND THE NIGHT TOGETHER[1]
(Jagger/Richards) (3.10)
David Bowie (vocal, guitar, Moog synthesiser,
saxophone)
Mick Ronson (guitar, vocal)
Trevor Bolder (bass)
Woody Woodmansey (drums)
Mike Garson (piano)

4. THE JEAN GENIE[3] (Detroit and New York)*
(Bowie) (4.06)
David Bowie (vocal, guitar, harmonica)
Mick Ronson (guitar, vocal)
Trevor Bolder (bass)
Woody Woodmansey (drums)

5. LADY GRINNING SOUL[1] (London) (Bowie) (3.53)
David Bowie (vocal, guitar, saxophone)
Mick Ronson (acoustic guitar)
Trevor Bolder (bass)

Woody Woodmansey (drums)
Mike Garson (piano)
Ken Fordham (saxophone, flutes)
Brian 'Bux' Wilshaw (tenor sax, flute)
Juanita 'Honey' Franklin (vocal backup)

*Produced by David Bowie
Produced by David Bowie and Ken Scott
Arranged by David Bowie and Mick Ronson
Engineered by Ken Scott and Mike Moran
Cover design by Duffy and Celia Philo
Make-up by Pierre Laroche
1 Recorded at Trident Studios
2 Recorded at RCA New York
3 Recorded at RCA Nashville

A MainMan Production
(RCA RS 1001) – UK   (RCA LSP.4852) – US

(Highest position in UK number one) (US number 12)

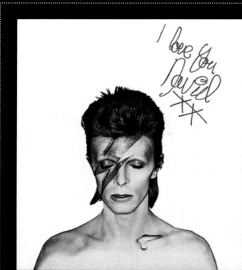

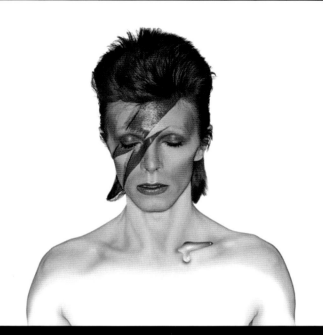

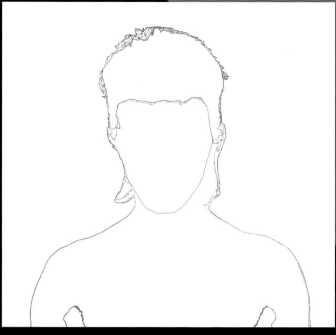

ABOVE: The original *Aladdin Sane* finished artwork. The print is a dye transfer and was developed and printed in Switzerland. The original remains in the Duffy archive. BELOW LEFT: Brian Duffy (1933-2010). BELOW RIGHT: Album sleeve co-designer Celia Philo in 1973.

Crucially, *Aladdin Sane* was the first collection of songs David wrote from the twin vantage points of critical acclaim and commercial success, in the knowledge that the lyrics and music would be evaluated in terms of whether he offered long-term star potential.

And, though Trident was the only studio credited on the original album sleeve, *Aladdin Sane* was also recorded at Olympic in London as well as in the US at RCA's studios in New York.

'The Jean Genie' was mixed in Nashville, Tennessee, underlining the fact that many of the songs were written on the road as David traversed the subcontinent on his first American tour.

"Here was this alternative world that I'd been talking about and it had all the violence and the strangeness and bizarreness and it was really happening," said David in 1993. "Suddenly my songs didn't look out of place. I think any English band that goes to America, or any English artist that goes to America for the first time, probably write some of their best stuff."

Album opener 'Watch That Man' records the raucous after-show party held at New York's Plaza Hotel following his very first performance in the city, an occasion on which he was particularly taken with Cyrinda Foxe's provocative style dance moves.

David's voice was deliberately low in the mix so that the track could be dominated by Mick Ronson's raw, full-volume guitar.

Indeed, at one stage, RCA asked for engineer Ken Scott to remix it and bring David's vocal to the fore. But, on receipt of the new mix they were forced to agree that the original was superior.

The song's lyric conjures up other-worldly revelry: the 'Reverend Alabaster dancing on his knees' line is evocative of scenes in David's favourite surreal movie, Dali/Bunuel's *Un Chien Andalou*, as is the Benny Goodman fan who 'painted holes in his hands'.

The mention of 'Tiger Rag' refers to the 1917 dance tune first recorded by the Original Dixieland Jazz Band.

The title track, with its curiously bracketed dateline, 'Aladdin Sane (1913-1938-197?)', takes its dissolute cue from the book that inspired it, Evelyn Waugh's *Vile Bodies*. David's title alludes to the imminence of

an imaginary war; and Waugh's book examines the 30s milieu in which people socialised madly rather than confront social and economic realities.

The track is dominated by Mike Garson's fractured and unsettling piano break. Garson's avant-garde vamp was recorded in just one take at Trident Studios, and his solo is one of the album's highlights. For David it perfectly captured the unstable make-up of his new character, while at the same time compounding the spirit of Waugh's effete jazz age testimony.

'Drive-In Saturday' had already introduced listeners to David's developing lyrical style, its abstract imagery seamlessly depicting bursting hands and limbs and melting telephones

in a surreal landscape. Jagger and Twiggy are also name-checked and add a touch of glamour, the latter flattered enough to make contact with David shortly after the album's release. (▶ 19.10.73)

'Panic In Detroit' and 'Cracked Actor' referenced David's latest Stateside adventures, the former inspired by a conversation with Iggy Pop which actually took place in Detroit, the latter David's impressions of the seamier side of Hollywood.

Opening side two in dramatic style, 'Time' is based on a tune David had initially given to George Underwood to record. With revised lyrics it recalled the recent sudden death of New York Dolls drummer Billy Murcia, and was laden with preoccupations with mortality. For roadie Will Palin, this particular track reminds him of life on tour with David: "I always thought that 'Time' was Bob See, our lighting man," Palin said in 1994. "He always worked in the wings, not at the back of the hall. He

would shout his lighting directions into a head mic – which only the lighting guys understood – hence, 'He's waiting in the wings – He speaks of senseless things..'."

'The Prettiest Star' was a new take on David's March 1970 single, with Mick Ronson confidently taking Marc Bolan's lead role on guitar. For this album, David reinvented the song as a sentimental hybrid of American 50s doo-wop (in the style of Fumble) and 20s lounge music.

The *Aladdin Sane* promotional material provided extra insights into each track. David added location details revealing where each song was written or inspired. The most curious entry was against 'The Prettiest Star', which David had dedicated to Angela in 1970. Perhaps the Gloucester Road reference hinted that the song was now dedicated to his first love, Hermione Farthingale? Their flat in Clareville Grove was just off Gloucester Road.

Jagger & Richards' 'Let's Spend The Night Together' had been a number three hit for The Rolling Stones in 1967. David pumps a glam urgency into his cover, and The Spiders ably take up the challenge, with both Garson and Woodmansey leading the fray. And, prior to the album's release, 'The Jean Genie' had proved its credentials as a number two UK hit.

The initial Aladdin Sane master closed with the sax-led version of 'John, I'm Only Dancing'. However, it was usurped at the final hour by the melodramatic and moving 'Lady Grinning Soul'. Garson's Chopinesque piano flourishes and Ronson's delicately applied flamenco guitar combined to support David's epic, heartfelt vocal. Lifted by Juanita Franklin's backing vocal as the track tails away, this is a rare song of love and seduction – perhaps the best ballad David has ever written.

As David had clearly been unashamedly influenced by The Stones in creating Aladdin Sane, it comes as no surprise that 'Lady Grinning Soul' was written for Claudia Lennear, the woman who had also famously inspired Jagger and Richards to write 'Brown Sugar' in 1969. David had also fallen under her spell when they met during the tour.

Lennear, having already worked with the likes of Joe Cocker and Ike and Tina Turner, very nearly became a backup singer for David in both 1973 and 1976, but missed out each time. In 1974 she made an appearance in the Clint Eastwood/Jeff Bridges film *Thunderbolt & Lightfoot*, playing a provocative secretary.

Among other backing vocalists is Brit-soul singer Linda Lewis, who, in the summer of 73, had her own UK top 20 hit with 'Rock-A-Doodle-Do'.

She had known David since the late 60s when he had occasionally visited her and friends at the Hampstead commune where she lived. With

Lewis, New Jersey-born Franklin added impressive backing vocals on 'Panic In Detroit', the track in part offering a foretaste of David's mid-70s *Young Americans* material.

Of minor note is the fact that a printing error led to the first few words of 'Cracked Actor' being deleted from the lyric sheet on the inner sleeve. It should have read: 'I've come on a few years from my Hollywood Highs...'

The sleeve of *Aladdin Sane* carried one of the key images of the 70s. This was photographed in his north London studio at 151a King Henry's Road, Swiss Cottage by the late Brian Duffy, with whom Tony Defries had come into contact in the 60s while representing the UK organisation the Association of Fashion & Advertising Photographers. Duffy also photographed David's sleeves for 1979's *Lodger* and 1980's *Scary Monsters*.

Defries asked Duffy to make the sleeve as costly as possible since he wanted to ensure RCA's full commitment to its marketing. To achieve this Duffy set about starting a small design company with Celia Philo – who assisted Duffy as the sleeve's co-designer – and created the cover to be printed in seven-colours.[1]

The *Aladdin Sane* print owes much of its striking tonal quality to the method of production: a dye transfer. This is an expensive and time-consuming process, not much used today – Kodak ceased producing the paper and chemicals for such photographic work in the early 90s.

The 16 x 12 inch print was completed with a 'Duffy 73' signature bottom right, and framed. The original *Aladdin Sane* cover artwork remained on display on the wall of Duffy's London basement workshop, where he worked as a specialist furniture restorer after a career change.

In 2005, he briefly offered it for private sale but quickly changed his mind and retained it.

The *Aladdin Sane* lightning bolt was also applied by Kansai Yamamoto to his 1971 British collection which first brought the Japanese designer to David's attention. Yet Duffy credited the inspiration elsewhere in 2009, "Bowie was interested in the Elvis ring which had the letters TCB (Taking Care of Business) as well as a lightning flash. I drew on his face the design... and used lipstick to fill in the red."

With make-up artist Pierre Laroche, Duffy in fact directly copied the red and blue flash from a National Panasonic rice-cooker in his studio.

Francis Newman, Duffy's assistant and later his studio manager, said in 2009: "I was there that Sunday when the *Aladdin Sane* pic was taken and well remember Duffy drawing the outline of the flash on his face. What to me is more technically interesting is the back cover, with the outline of Bowie's face, which we painstakingly produced photographically. Today it would be so quick and easy to do in Photoshop."

This was the only time that David wore the design on his face, but the logo was retained as part of a hanging backdrop for live performances

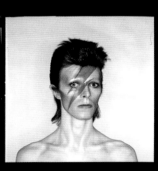

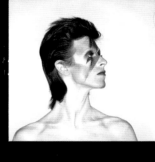

OPPOSITE PAGE: TOP LEFT: Evelyn Waugh's 1930 satire *Vile Bodies* – prime inspiration for the *Aladdin Sane* title track. MIDDLE: Out-takes from Brian Duffy's *Aladdin Sane* session taken at his studio near Swiss Cottage, London, January 1973. BOTTOM: Claudia Lennear, the inspiraton for 'Lady Grinning Soul'. THIS PAGE: ABOVE LEFT: Out-take photo for the *Aladdin Sane* inner gatefold. ABOVE MIDDLE: The final gatefold artwork, airbrushed by Philip Castle. ABOVE RIGHT: A Duffy photograph for Pirelli's 1973 calendar, designed by Allen Jones, airbrushed by Philip Castle. The Duffy/Allen Jones concept inspired David's inner sleeve design. BELOW LEFT: Marie Helvin wearing a Kansai costume, designed for his 1971 London collection. For his show Kansai asked all of his models to shave off their eyebrows. Photo by Clive Arrowsmith. BELOW RIGHT: The *Aladdin Sane* lightning bolt was applied by make-up specialist Pierre Laroche pictured with David below right (© Mick Rock). Duffy himself intensified the red lightning bolt with lipstick.

The cover make-up was completed with a deathly purple wash, which, together with David's closed eyes, evoked a death mask.[2] The collective idea had been to create a statuesque effect, and a droplet of water was airbrushed on to David's collarbone by Philip Castle to complete the illusion. Castle also helped create the silvered effect to David's body on the inner sleeve, similar to designs he had worked on with Duffy and artist Allen Jones for Pirelli's 1973 calendar.[3]

On release, the cover divided opinion. Some reviewers were bewildered and even offended by David's macabre appearance, others applauded his daring, since Duffy had captured David exaggerating the make-up tricks he developed with Lindsay Kemp in the 60s. Today, it can be seen as a risky move for an artist whose success was still relatively recent.

In 2001, Celia's daughter Phoebe Philo took over from Stella McCartney as chief designer for fashion house Chloe.

1. The original gatefold sleeve was printed in seven colours: to the usual four-colour process were added tones of blue, red and silver. In fact, apart from the silver, this could have been achieved out of the usual four-colour process, but added considerably to David and MainMan's costs as such expenses were nearly always deducted from artist royalties. However, it should be noted that the album carried a higher than usual retail price on issue.

2. Having first used masks on stage with Lindsay Kemp in 1967, David has also been the subject of a number of life masks, the first made in Hollywood in 1974 for use as a stage prop and filmed being applied for BBC's *Omnibus* documentary screened the following year.

3. Castle is best known for creating Stanley Kubrick's poster for his film adaptation of *A Clockwork Orange*.

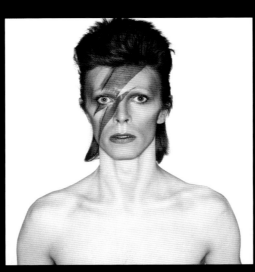

TOP LEFT: *Melody Maker* cover feature, 12 May.

TOP RIGHT: Being mobbed on arrival at Charing Cross station, 4 May.

ABOVE: *Cream* magazine, May issue.

MIDDLE RIGHT: A few days after his world trip, David arrives for the première of the film *Hitler: The Last 10 Days*, in London's West End, 7 May.

BOTTOM RIGHT: David with Peter Cook and Dudley Moore after one of their manic *Behind The Fridge* performances at the Cambridge Theatre. David had invited Moore to play piano on *Hunky Dory*.

Wednesday 2 May

David and MacCormack board the train again for the final leg of the journey to Paris (Childers has opted to take a flight).

While travelling through Poland they are forced to barricade themselves in their compartment as a train guard insists – to the point of violently attempting to break down the door – that they produce documents they haven't got. The situation is resolved when soldiers are summoned and the guard is made to back off.

Thursday 3 May

After the tiring passage across Russia and a short stop in West Berlin (where more fans greet David), they arrive in Paris.

After meeting up with Angie in the luxurious George V Hotel, a reception is held in the hotel's Rouge Room, along with a press conference, at which David is photographed by Claude Gassian.

Friday 4 May

David leaves Paris by train with Angie, MacCormack, Childers, Cherry Vanilla, *NME*'s Charles Shaar Murray, *Melody Maker* journalist Roy Hollingworth and photographer Barry Wentzell (who borrow £30 from David to cover their tickets home after staying at the George V with just three francs between them).

The party takes the hovercraft from Boulogne to Dover and the train to London's Charing Cross station, where fans mob David as he runs from the platform to a waiting car.

By now David and MacCormack have completed a land journey of more than 8,000 miles.

Saturday 5 May

In the UK, 'Drive-In Saturday' reaches its chart peak of number three, while *Aladdin Sane* enters the UK album charts at number one, where it remains for the next month. In the US the album peaks at number 12.

While *Melody Maker* reports David has requested a block of tickets for Liza Minnelli's forthcoming concert at the Rainbow, *Mirabelle* begins publication of a weekly David Bowie diary column titled 'My World' (written by Cherry Vanilla and other MainMan staff).

In the evening, David and Angie hold a homecoming party at Haddon Hall. Guests include Lindsay Kemp, Mick Ronson, George and Birgit Underwood, Freddie Burretti, Daniella Parmar, Suzi Fussey, Ken Scott and Charles Shaar Murray.

Tony Visconti arrives with his wife, the singer Mary Hopkin; this is the first time he and David have met since recording *The Man Who Sold The World* in 1970.

The party marks the final gathering for David at Haddon Hall and the end of his life in this area of England. The ground-floor flat is now besieged by fans on a daily basis, obstructing the driveway and peering through David and Angie's bedroom window.

A move is swiftly effected, supervised by roadie Pete Hunsley. Daniella Parmar has become Zowie's de facto nanny, so she and the boy are moved into the Park Lane Hotel while a new base is sought.

Monday 7 May

David is at the première of the Alec Guinness film *Hitler: The Last 10 Days* at the Empire Cinema in

Leicester Square, where the guest of honour is Princess Margaret.

The following evening, David, Angie, Visconti and Hopkin attend Peter Cooke and Dudley Moore's revue *Behind The Fridge*[1] at the Cambridge Theatre in Covent Garden. The evening seals the renewed friendship with Visconti, and David takes to visiting the producer at his home at Flat 11, 77 Courtfield Gardens in west London's Earls Court.

1. The show's title appeared as part of the opening lyric of David's 1975 hit 'Young Americans'.

Thursday 10 May

David, Angie and bodyguard Stuey George make a surprise visit to Ken Pitt at 39 Manchester Street and invite him to the forthcoming Earls Court show.

Friday 11 May

David is interviewed for Radio One's *Scene & Heard* programme by Stuart Grundy.

Saturday 12 May

▶ David Bowie & The Spiders From Mars, Earls Court, Warwick Road, London SW5.[1]

Melody Maker headlines a report by Roy Hollingworth 'Bowie Mad'. As well as admitting "I just want to bloody well go home to Beckenham and watch the telly," David discusses his wish that the final tour date be at the Friars Club, Aylesbury.

In the evening, the fourth leg of the 1973 world tour – which will include 41 dates promoted by Mel Bush with at least 15 matinee shows – begins at Earls Court. For these dates RCA again maintains strict control over the budget, with artist relations manager Barry Bethell[2] charged with guarding their interests.

Bethell also warms up the audience nightly in the guise of a Teddy Boy quickly nicknamed 'The Ted from Islington', announcing David's arrival on stage at the start of each performance.

Before the show, David greets Mick Jagger and other special guests backstage.

On stage, the Japanese influence is evinced by the new Kansai costumes and David's kabuki-inspired make-up. Mime is reintroduced after David sees it used in a video of one of Kansai's fashion shows.

The minimalist stage set consists of two large white circular discs, each decorated with the *Aladdin Sane* signature red lightning flash and suspended on wires. These have been painted by south-east London musician Chris Difford (later to lead British act Squeeze) at the request of acquaintance and road manager Will Palin. Difford and Squeeze co-founder Glenn Tilbrook attend many of the shows on the tour, the venues of which have been checked out by Palin prior to David's arrival.

Tonight there are crowd problems caused by the low positioning of the stage; David is forced to wait 15 minutes as security tussle with excited fans who have run to the front and refuse to return to their seats. For many in the hall, the stage is obscured for

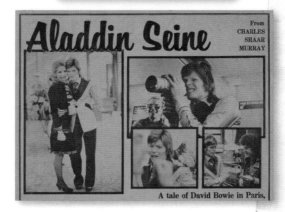

most of the concert.

In addition, the PA is inadequate. "It was a big gig and we simply didn't have enough power," said Trevor Bolder in 1995.

London newspaper the *Evening News* runs a souvenir issue to coincide with the first night, including an interview with David by pop journalist John Blake.

1. David returned to the venue in 1978 for his Isolar II tour, during which he showcased many songs from *Ziggy Stardust*.
2. Bethell became a local radio DJ and was known for advertising diet aid Slim-Fast in the early 90s.

Tuesday 15 May

David is mobbed by teeming fans at Charing Cross station as he leaves for Aberdeen with The Spiders and Mick Rock. In contrast, arriving at Aberdeen Station after the 10-hour journey he is met by less than a dozen fans before being driven just 50 yards to the Imperial Hotel in Stirling Street.

Later in the evening David is interviewed at the Imperial by Ray Fox-Cumming for *Disc*. Journalist Martin Hayman is also there, preparing an article for *Sounds*.

Wednesday 16 May

▶ David Bowie & The Spiders From Mars, Aberdeen Music Hall, Union Street, Aberdeen. (Two shows)

Again there are sound problems for both of tonight's shows, though not on the scale of Earls Court. Tickets have sold out in two hours and the fans are delighted when David mimes squashing an insect underfoot and subsequently aping its flight around the stage.

TOP RIGHT: At the start of his UK 73 tour, photographed in Scotland by Roger Bamber.

TOP LEFT: 'I'm With David Bowie Aren't You?' rare 1973 promo sticker.

ABOVE RIGHT: The 1973 tour programme.

ABOVE LEFT: Charles Shaar Murray *NME* article, 12 May.

In this year...

Tuesday 1 May
APPEARANCE by Lou Reed on BBC TV's *The Old Grey Whistle Test*.

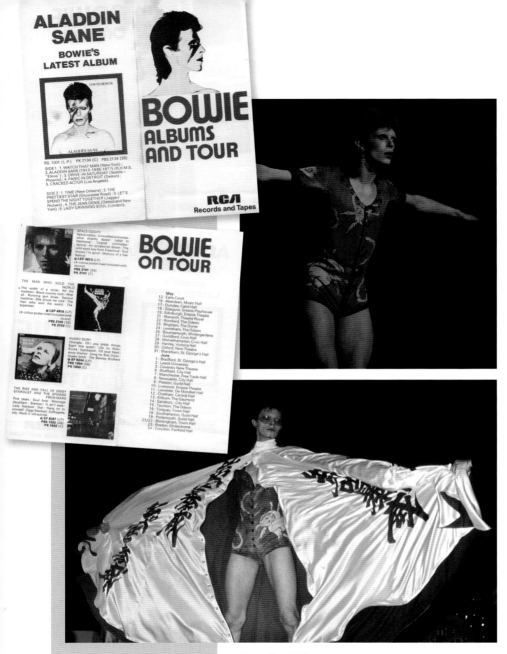

TOP LEFT AND MIDDLE: Promotional tour leaflet.

TOP RIGHT: The Kansai 'woodland creature' outfit. Wear and tear each night began to damage it, as Leee Childers recalls: "Suzi Fussey also had the duty of hand recolouring this little suit with red magic marker after Bowie had performed the ink out of it each night." Natasha Kornilof also created an exact copy so that the original be preserved.

BOTTOM: Another kabuki theatre concept and an idea Kansai had used in his London fashion show. David's cape was two garments connected by studs. Just before 'Ziggy Stardust' Suzi Fussey and Linda Maloney would rip the cape apart and reveal another Kansai costume beneath.

Thursday 17 May

▶ David Bowie & The Spiders From Mars, Caird Hall, City Square, Dundee.

After the show, David is trapped by a mob of admirers outside the stage door until Stuey George pushes him to safety into the waiting limo.

Friday 18 May

▶ David Bowie & The Spiders From Mars, Green's Playhouse,[1] Renfield Street, Glasgow. (Two shows)

Radio One broadcasts the recent interview with David on its *Scene & Heard* slot.

During the second performance, a fan falls from the balcony and injures his ribs and the night ends chaotically with the destruction of chairs, said to be a mark of approval at the venue. In light of the previous evening's post-show incident, David is whisked away under police escort.

"We had, I think, four couples making it in the back row which was fabulous," said David later.

"It's the first time I've heard of that happening. There was also a whole row of seats physically torn out of the floor, which sounds like the 50s to me. Can you imagine how much energy has to be used to tear out a theatre seat?"

1. Green's closed the following month, reopening as the Glasgow Apollo in late 1973. David returned to the venue for four consecutive nights in June 1978. The building was demolished in 1989.

Saturday 19 May

▶ David Bowie & The Spiders From Mars, Empire Theatre, 13-29 Nicholson Street, Edinburgh.

Melody Maker and *NME* focus on the technical problems on the tour's opening night; the former proclaims 'Bowie Blows It' and the latter asks 'Bowie Fiasco, What Went Wrong?' as a trail to a negative review by Nick Kent headed 'Aladdin Distress'.

North of the border, the concert begins at 11.30pm to allow for the venue's regular bingo session.

After the show, David and Angie visit an Edinburgh gay club where their reserved table has been bagged by Monty Python member Graham Chapman, in town for the comedy troupe's First Farewell tour, and his partner David Sherlock.[1]

"Angie said to us, 'Do you know who we are?'" wrote Sherlock in 2005.

David and his entourage are sharing the Post House Hotel with the Python team, whose Michael Palin is kept awake by the late-night partying.

1. In 1983 Sherlock co-wrote the film *Yellowbeard* with Chapman, in which David made a cameo appearance as a character known as 'The Shark'.

Monday 21 May

▶ David Bowie & The Spiders From Mars, Theatre Royal, Theatre Street, Norwich, East Anglia. (Two shows)

Again, tickets for both shows have sold out in record time and the crowd becomes so hyper that four females and one male are treated after fainting.

Tuesday 22 May

▶ David Bowie & The Spiders From Mars, Odeon Theatre, South Street, Romford, Essex.

More scenes of crowd exuberance lead to ambulances ferrying those with minor injuries to the town's Old Church Hospital.

Wednesday 23 May

▶ David Bowie & The Spiders From Mars, Brighton Dome, 29 New Road, East Sussex. (Two shows)

A BBC TV crew with *Nationwide* reporter Bernard Falk film David and the band on and off stage, following David as he arrives at the Bedford Hotel in full stage costume after the show. Fans are also interviewed outside the door to his room.

Following this appearance, David – along with Led Zeppelin and Slade – is banned for life from appearing at the Dome because of damage caused by fan pandemonium.

Thursday 24 May

▶ David Bowie & The Spiders From Mars, Lewisham Odeon, 1 Loampit Vale, London SE13.

During this date – which is a late addition to the tour schedule – David tells the audience, "It's nice to be home," a reference to the venue[1] where he witnessed rock'n'roll gigs in the 50s and the area where he hung out as a teenager.

In the audience is 12-year-old George O'Dowd, the future Boy George, who wrote in 1994: "I'll never ever witness anything like that again."

1. Lewisham Odeon was demolished in 1991.

Friday 25 May

▶ David Bowie & The Spiders From Mars, Winter Gardens, Exeter Road, Bournemouth, Dorset.

Part of the concert is filmed for the BBC's *Nationwide*. Fans and bemused passers-by are also filmed and interviewed outside the venue for their thoughts on David.

The following day Mick Ronson celebrates his 27th birthday and a late-night party ensues.

A *Melody Maker* report infers that there are cracks appearing in the MainMan set-up, reporting the abrupt departure from the tour of Leee Black Childers and publicist Cherry Vanilla to the US. In reality, Childers has been seconded to look after signings Iggy & The Stooges in LA, while Vanilla is to return in a couple of weeks.

Sunday 27 May

▶ David Bowie & The Spiders From Mars, Civic Hall, London Road, Guildford, Surrey. (Two shows)

For much of the tour, Trevor Bolder is accompanied by his wife Anne and their children and, when possible, returns home to Hull between gigs.

Monday 28 May

▶ David Bowie & The Spiders From Mars, Civic Hall, North Street, Wolverhampton, West Midlands.

Zowie Bowie's second birthday is celebrated and David is an hour late on stage at the venue, filled to its capacity of 2,000.

Tuesday 29 May

▶ David Bowie & The Spiders From Mars, Victoria Hall, Albion Street, Hanley, Stoke-on-Trent, Staffs.

Producer Bob Ezrin contacts MainMan to tell them he is producing Lou Reed's next album, and request David be involved in an unspecified capacity.

Wednesday 30 May

▶ David Bowie & The Spiders From Mars, New Theatre, George Street, Oxford.

David makes a return visit to the theatre where he appeared with Lindsay Kemp's company in 1967.

US music trade publication *Billboard* records *Aladdin Sane*'s chart positions in several countries:

number 10 in Belgium and France, nine in Australia and six in Spain.

Thursday 31 May

▶ David Bowie & The Spiders From Mars, King George's Hall, Northgate, Blackburn, Lancs.

With many fans ignoring pleas to sit down, practically everybody in the packed hall views the gig standing on their seats. At one point, two female stage invaders are bodily removed by stewards.

Friday 1 June

▶ David Bowie & The Spiders From Mars, St George's Hall, Bridge Street, Bradford, West Yorkshire.

RCA release 'Time'/'The Prettiest Star' single in the US.

  ⊙ **David Bowie**
A **'Time'** (Bowie)
B **'The Prettiest Star'** (Bowie)

TOP: Glam pantomime in Scotland. David's kabuki space-face, photo by Roger Bamber.

LEFT: Boy George attended the Lewisham show: "I've never seen anything more exciting since."

RIGHT: Even rock'n'roll has to make way for bingo. David's appearance at the Empire, Edinburgh is delayed for the game.

In this year...

Friday 25 May
INTERVIEW with Ian Hunter in *Melody Maker* confirming that Mott The Hoople have split with Tony Defries and that they won't be working with David again: "David helped us, but I think we gave him as much as he gave us, for reasons I won't go into now."

Friday 1 June
RELEASE in the UK of Iggy and the Stooges album *Raw Power*, which David is credited with mixing, along with Iggy Pop.

Saturday 2 June
CHARTING of Lou Reed's single 'Walk On The Wild Side' at number 10 in the UK, produced by David and Mick Ronson.

Saturday 9 June
INTERVIEW with David Essex in *Disc*: 'David used to do dates with Bowie in the pirate radio days. "We're still friendly, except I've probably only seen him a couple of times since."'

Monday 11 June
DEATH of stage designer Sean Kenny at the age of 41. Kenny had advised David on the lighting of his late 72 UK shows less than a year before.

BELOW: *Let It Rock* magazine, June issue.

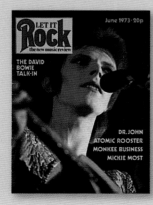

David Bowie (vocal, guitar, saxophone)
Mick Ronson (guitar, piano, vocal)
Trevor Bolder (bass)
Woody Woodmansey (drums)
Mike Garson (piano)
Ken Fordham (saxophones)
Brian 'Bux' Wilshaw (saxophones)
Produced by David Bowie and Ken Scott
Arranged by David Bowie and Mick Ronson
(RCA APBO.0001)

The A-side features a considerably edited version of the album track, and a promo single includes both regular and truncated tracks.

With just over a month to go, there is still some confusion over the venue for the final date of the tour. It is now clear that David's wish for it to be Aylesbury Friars will not be fulfilled. A MainMan telex sent today points out that the Roundhouse is unavailable on 1 July, though promoter Mel Bush says that the Hammersmith Odeon is available on that date and also the previous night.

Saturday 2 June

Melody Maker announces that a return Earls Court concert is cancelled. In *Disc*, Kansai Yamamoto reveals that it was Tony Defries who first saw a video of one of his shows and played it for David: "More than the actual clothes themselves he was apparently very impressed with the staging of the show, the colour, the fantasy and the imagination and the rock'n'roll backdrop supplied by local Japanese session men; but most of all the obvious parallels in the use of mime for dramatic impact."

Tonight's gigs at Leeds University are cancelled just hours before due to poor stage and dressing room facilities. A MainMan spokesperson says: "It would have meant David walking through the audience to get to the stage, which is out of the question."

Sunday 3 June

▶ David Bowie & The Spiders From Mars, New Theatre, Coventry, West Midlands.

Monday 4 June

▶ David Bowie & The Spiders From Mars, Worcester Gaumont, Foregate Street, Worcester, West Midlands.

This is yet another date added after the tour schedule had been drawn up.

Meanwhile, the September 1971 contract for David between RCA and Gem Music is revised, with MainMan Ltd replacing Gem and it being backdated to 1 January 1973.

Tuesday 5 June

BBC early evening magazine programme *Nationwide* includes a 10-minute segment about the tour.

Wednesday 6 June

▶ David Bowie & The Spiders From Mars, City Oval Hall, Barkers Pool, Sheffield. (Two shows)

Between tonight's two shows, which are attended by future members of The Human League and Heaven 17, David encounters singer Lulu by chance in the Hallam Tower Hotel. She is in town for a live show and, accompanied by producer John Ammonds,[1] attends the second performance, later joining David at a small party back at the hotel where they explore ideas for recording together.

"David was serious about me recording one of his songs," said Lulu in 1993. "He chose 'The Man Who Sold The World'. I went along with the choice."

Cherry Vanilla reports to New York: 'Sheffield was fabulous, reminiscent of Glasgow minus the blood.'

1. Ken Pitt had written to Ammonds in December 1969 with a request that he consider including David for a spot on comedy programme *The Morecambe And Wise Show*.

Thursday 7 June

▶ David Bowie & The Spiders From Mars, Free Trade Hall, Peter Street, Manchester. (Two shows)

Another tempestuous gig is interrupted when David and bodyguard Stuey George are forced to stop the house manager from strangling over-excited local celebrity David Eager[1] (who has dyed his hair blue).

1. DJ and a presenter of Tyne Tees Television *The Geordie Scene*.

Friday 8 June

▶ David Bowie & The Spiders From Mars, City Hall, Northumberland Road, Newcastle. (Two shows)

David is an hour late for the first of the two shows tonight and the atmosphere boils over after David hits a security staff member over the head for karate chopping a stage-invading fan.

David stops the performance and announces: "There are two stars in rock'n'roll – me and the audience – and if these stewards don't stop and get out, the stars are going to make this place into a match box."

The gig resumes, though promoter Mel Bush fears a huge damages bill and the venue's house manager is furious at the slight on his staff.

Saturday 9 June

▶ David Bowie & The Spiders From Mars, Guild Hall, Lancaster Road, Preston, Lancashire.

Trevor Bolder celebrates his 23rd birthday with a small party at the hotel.

Sunday 10 June

▶ David Bowie & The Spiders From Mars, Empire Theatre, Lime Street, Liverpool. (Two shows)

More mayhem during both shows, resulting in at least one hospitalisation. David leaves the stage in tears at one point when a bouncer flings a girl from the stage, refusing to return until all security is cleared from the area. This results in the crowd pouring into the orchestra pit. They damage a grand piano, and there are signs that the floor may give way. Vanilla notes the following day, 'It scared David. He'll think twice before asking for no security again.'

Once again the show is halted. To cheers, David tells a heckler: "When you entered the theatre you must have seen the sign 'Artist at Work'. Well, you came to see us. When you go to work we will come to see you. Until then fucking shut up."

In the crowd is 14-year-old Ian McCulloch, later to front post-punk act Echo & The Bunnymen, and 15-year-old Marc Almond, later to form Soft Cell and achieve considerable solo success.

Due to his appearance, Almond has been attacked on the way to the concert. During 'Rock 'n' Roll Suicide' he is one of those who takes hold of David's hand. "It was a moment of epiphany," Almond said in 2007.

Monday 11 June

▶ David Bowie & The Spiders From Mars, De Montfort Hall, Granville Road, Leicester.

At the end of the main section of the show, the PA is hit when a transformer cuts out. The encore is performed on a hastily rigged microphone.

Tuesday 12 June

▶ David Bowie & The Spiders From Mars, Central Hall Theatre, 170 High Street, Chatham, Kent. (Two shows)

David is in a playful mood; not for the first time, he introduces Mick Ronson as 'Suzi Quatro' and also bends over and moons at the audience, lifting his Kansai-designed short tunic from behind.

Wednesday 13 June

▶ David Bowie & The Spiders From Mars, The Gaumont State, Kilburn High Road, London NW6.

David is keen to perform at this classically-designed venue (which is another last-minute addition), where Buddy Holly had appeared in 1958.

During a chaotic exit from the building, David's limousine runs over the foot of a policeman, who has to be taken to a nearby hospital.

Thursday 14 June

▶ David Bowie & The Spiders From Mars, City Hall, Malthouse Lane, Salisbury, Wiltshire.

David dramatically stage-dives into the excited audience, who enthusiastically catch him. He then makes one of his regular climbs atop one of the tall PA stacks, landing awkwardly as he jumps, retiring hurt for a period.

On his return for an encore, he performs 'Round And Round' sitting in a chair and tells the audience: "I think I've broken my ankle. Not really, but it hurts a bit."

Friday 15 June

▶ David Bowie & The Spiders From Mars, Odeon, Corporation Street, Taunton, Somerset. (Two shows)

David is seen by a doctor but ignores advice that he should have an x-ray. He performs much of both shows seated. At one point he falls into the audience

again, and then hops down the aisle, sitting midway and singing, much to the astonishment of the audience. At the end he is carried off stage amid speculation that the following day's gig will have to be cancelled.

Saturday 16 June

▶ David Bowie & The Spiders From Mars, Town Hall, Torquay, Devon. (Two shows)

The shows continue and there are no more reports about his ankle injury.

Monday 18 June

▶ David Bowie & The Spiders From Mars, Colston Hall, Colston Street, Bristol, Avon. (Two shows)

Members of Fumble attend the second show and meet up with David backstage. "He was clearly exhausted and losing his voice," Sean Mayes[1] wrote in his diary that day.

1. Mayes was recruited by David for his 1978 world tour; their next encounter was in March of that year at band rehearsals in Dallas.

Tuesday 19 June

▶ David Bowie & The Spiders From Mars, Guild Hall, West Marlands Road, Southampton, Hants.

A previously scheduled show at Portsmouth Guild Hall has been cancelled in favour of this appearance.

Thursday 21 June

▶ David Bowie & The Spiders From Mars, Town Hall, Victoria Street, Birmingham. (Two shows)

TOP RIGHT: *Record Mirror*, 16 June.

TOP LEFT AND ABOVE: David on tour in the UK (top pic with Mick Ronson).

TOP: David arriving at the stage door of Hammersmith Odeon.

MIDDLE: Hammersmith Odeon exterior. Angie Bowie signs autographs for fans.

BOTTOM: *Beat Instrumental* magazine, July issue.

Friday 22 June

▶ David Bowie & The Spiders From Mars, Town Hall, Birmingham. (Two shows)

RCA release 'Life On Mars?'/'The Man Who Sold The World' single in the UK.

⊙ **David Bowie**
A **'Life On Mars?'** (Bowie)
B **'The Man Who Sold The World'** (Bowie)
David Bowie (vocal)
Mick Ronson (guitar, Mellotron, vocal on B-side)
Trevor Bolder (bass)
Woody Woodmansey (drums)
Rick Wakeman (piano on A-side)
Tony Visconti (bass on B-side)
A-side produced by Ken Scott assisted by the Actor
A-side arranged by Mick Ronson
B-side produced by Tony Visconti
(RCA 2316)

Released due to its strong reception on tour, 'Life On Mars?' is issued, initially, in a picture sleeve. It is supported by another Mick Rock-directed promo film: David in a blue suit and heavy Laroche make-up, shot during a day off from the tour in a warehouse near Westbourne Grove, west London.

Rock adds audience footage to one version and there is another edit without.[1]

1. Excerpts were used in 1990's Sound & Vision stage show. The over-exposed print, most commonly seen, resulted from an inferior, duplicated copy, not from the superior quality 16mm master.

Saturday 23 June

▶ David Bowie & The Spiders From Mars, Gliderdrome, Starlight Rooms, Boston, Lincs.

Sunday 24 June

▶ David Bowie & The Spiders From Mars, Fairfield Halls, Park Lane, Croydon, Surrey. (Two shows)

Monday 25 June

▶ David Bowie & The Spiders From Mars, New Theatre, Oxford. (Two shows)

The tour returns to the New Theatre for two shows tonight and one more tomorrow, with tickets having sold out immediately the previous month.

This month Mick Woodmansey reminisces: "In some ways it was more fun in the early days when we used to sleep on Dave's floor. And no one had any money and no one knew what was going to happen."

Tuesday 26 June

▶ David Bowie & The Spiders From Mars, New Theatre, Oxford.

The band are on the home straight row; it has been decided the tour will end not at Earls Court on 30 June but with dates at London's Hammersmith Odeon on 2 and 3 July.

Wednesday 27 June

▶ David Bowie & The Spiders From Mars, Top Rank Suite, Doncaster, South Yorks.

Blood is shed during the show when the venue's stewards beat up a drunken fan.

Thursday 28 June

▶ David Bowie & The Spiders From Mars, Bridlington Spa Ballroom, South Marine Drive, Bridlington, Yorks.

This is the closest The Spiders will play to their home town, Hull.[1]

In the audience is Gina Riley from Hull, the 100,000th to buy a ticket for the tour. She wins a night in London with two tickets to the final show at Hammersmith Odeon and a late dinner with David.

1. Ronson's band The King Bees supported The Rolling Stones here on 11 July 1964.

Friday 29 June

▶ David Bowie & The Spiders From Mars, Rolarena, Kirkstall Road, Leeds, Yorks. (Two shows)

Replacing the cancelled dates at Leeds University, both shows are poorly attended and the venue is also picketed by disgruntled students.

"We were completely sold out everywhere else but because we had cancelled the original Leeds gig, most people decided to stay away," said Trevor

Bolder in 1995. "It was odd suddenly playing to a small audience again, but it was fair enough. You should never cancel a gig."

Saturday 30 June

▶ David Bowie & The Spiders From Mars, City Hall, Northumberland Road, Newcastle, Tyne & Wear. (Two shows)

David and band return to Newcastle City Hall a few weeks after their previous appearances there.

Monday 2 July

▶ David Bowie & The Spiders From Mars, Hammersmith Odeon, 45 Queen Caroline Street, London W6.

There are no matinees for tonight or tomorrow's shows. (The venue is also reserved for 4 July, but the option is not taken up.) With filming planned and other commitments, David is forced to decline a dinner invitation from Barbra Streisand, who says she will be at tomorrow's show.

The set list includes a medley of 'Wild Eyed Boy From Freecloud', 'All The Young Dudes' and 'Oh! You Pretty Things', and climaxes with 'Let's Spend The Night Together', 'Suffragette City', 'White Light/White Heat' and 'Round And Round' before the finale of 'Rock 'n' Roll Suicide'.

Tuesday 3 July

▶ David Bowie & The Spiders From Mars, Hammersmith Odeon, London.

Tonight is one of the most momentous of David's career, and the tension is heightened by the fact that he and his fellow musicians are nearing exhaustion, this being their 61st performance in just seven weeks.

Adding to the carnival atmosphere are rock aristocracy well-wishers such as Mick and Bianca Jagger and Rod Stewart, and film director D.A. Pennebaker[1] and crew are on hand to record this special occasion. On arrival in the UK, Pennebaker is unaware of David's work, mistakenly thinking he is Marc Bolan. Defries ensures he talks to Mick Rock, who clues Pennebaker in and introduces him to the cameramen he has used in David's promo shoots.

Rock also photographs David backstage with Ringo Starr and Defries, while Pennebaker films David as he prepares to go on stage assisted by Suzi Fussey and Linda Maloney.[2]

David and The Spiders are joined on stage by guitarist and former member of The Yardbirds Jeff Beck, who joins them on 'The Jean Genie' and a verse of 'Love Me Do'. They also perform 'Round And Round' together.

Immediately before 'Rock 'n' Roll Suicide', David steps up to the mic and announces: "Not only is this the last show of the tour, but it's the last show we'll ever do."

While Ronson has known about David's plans to withdraw from live work since the Japanese tour, this stuns Bolder and Woodmansey as much as it does the audience. "We didn't know a thing," said Bolder in 1995. "Woody and I were the only two in the whole party who didn't know."

In 1993 David said: "About 48 hours later, I'm sitting there thinking 'What have I said? I don't think I really meant that at all. I'm feeling better already'. But too late. I know I really pissed off Woody and Trevor. They were so angry, I think, because I hadn't really told them that I was splitting the band up. But that's what Ziggy did, so I had to do it too. And Vince Taylor had done the same thing. He just stopped – and then they carted him away! I'd forgotten that bit!"

Woodmansey[3] is particularly upset. "I think that David forgot that we were so useful to him, with all the previous experiences he had with other musicians that hadn't worked out," said the drummer in 1997. "What he could do with us he couldn't do with other musicians."[4]

Directly after the concert, a retirement party held for David at the Café Royal in Piccadilly becomes one of the social events of the decade. Among those gathered are the cream of the rock elite and include Mick and Bianca Jagger, Ringo Starr, Paul and Linda McCartney, Keith Moon, Cat Stevens, Lou Reed, Jeff Beck, Sonny Bono and Barbra Streisand. Also in attendance are actors Britt Ekland, Tony Curtis, Elliott Gould and Ryan O'Neal, and comedians Spike Milligan, Peter Cook and Dudley Moore.

David and Angie's entrance is announced over the PA to wild applause.

Also present is Lulu, who has maintained contact with David as they cook up plans for a collaboration.

Trevor Bolder is there, though, hurt at the deception over David's retirement, Woodmansey is not.[5] Significantly, drummer Aynsley Dunbar is.

TOP: Make-up specialist Pierre Laroche prepares David for his last performance with The Spiders From Mars, Hammersmith Odeon, 3 July.

MIDDLE: Ringo Starr visits David backstage at Hammersmith Odeon during the intermission.

BOTTOM: Arriving at the Café Royal for Ziggy's wake, 3-4 July.

In this year...

Saturday 23 June
RELEASE by UK Records of Simon Turner's version of 'The Prettiest Star', produced by the label's boss, Jonathan King. Turner became friendly with Angie and, whilst dating Freddie Burretti's muse Daniella Parmar, was a frequent visitor to the Bowies' homes in Chelsea and later in Switzerland in the mid-70s.

TOP LEFT: With Ringo Starr, Lulu and Cat Stevens.

TOP RIGHT: "*Pin Ups* was really to give the Spiders something to do. I didn't quite know how to fit them into the next thing."

MIDDLE LEFT: At the royal première of *Live And Let Die*, with Tony Defries far right.

BOTTOM: How did it go again? David listens to his own version of 'The Man Who Sold The World' while recording Lulu's single.

BOTTOM RIGHT: David and Lulu listen to a playback of 'The Man Who Sold The World'.

John Hutchinson attends, and the brief exchange they have on the dance floor is the last time he will see David.

Among those invited but not in attendance is British pop singer Cliff Richard, a devout Christian who has recently criticised David's lifestyle. David is also reported in the *Evening News* to have personally dispatched a couple of tickets for the Hammersmith Odeon concert to Richard.

Dubbed 'the last supper', the party includes live music supplied by New Orleans pianist Dr John, who plays his biggest hit, 'Right Time Wrong Place'.

The celebration winds down around 5am. In 2002 David said: "I remember nothing of this party, absolutely nothing."

1. Pennebaker later claimed that Marlene Dietrich attended the concert, though this is unsubstantiated. His film, *Ziggy Stardust – The Motion Picture*, was released in 1983 along with a live double album on RCA. It was remixed and reissued by EMI in 2003.

2. A colleague of Fussey's at the Evelyn Pagett salon in Beckenham High Street.

3. In 1976 Woodmansey formed U-Boat with Phil Murray (vocals), Frankie Marshall (keyboards), Phil Plant (bass) and Martin Smith (guitar, vocal). Bronze released U-Boat's eponymous album in 1977. Subsequently, Woodmansey formed the Screen Idols with Keith 'Ched' Cheeseman, former bassist with The Rats.

4. According to Bolder, an approach was made by an unidentified backer for him, Ronson and Woodmansey to reform The Spiders in 1991, though this fell through. Bolder and Woodmansey have occasionally worked together as The Spiders live, twice with Joe Elliott and Phil Collen at the Mick Ronson Memorial concerts in London (1994) and Hull (1997). In 2001, with Elliott, Collen and keyboard player Dick Decent, they toured Japan as The Cybernauts.

5. Woodmansey pressed for the return of his drum kit after the tour but, much to his chagrin, he was informed that MainMan intended to sell it.

Wednesday 4 July

In the evening BBC1's *Nationwide* broadcasts a news item about David's retirement, interviewing Angie, Lulu and Tony Curtis arriving at the venue. This is added to the film shown by the programme in June.

Friday 6 July

David – wearing the flamboyant Freddie Burretti suit from his appearance on the Russell Harty show earlier in the year – Angie and Defries are at the Odeon cinema in Leicester Square for the royal première of Bond movie *Live And Let Die*. Princess Anne is the guest of honour.

David is staying at the Hyde Park Hotel, as is Mick Ronson. David begins to select tracks for a new album project, *Pin Ups*, aided by Scott Richardson, an old friend of Iggy Pop's and someone Angie has recently met and dated in the US.[1]

Pin Ups will be an album consisting entirely of covers from London's 60s mod heyday, to be recorded in France.

Among visitors is Lulu, with whom plans for a single are firming up. "We listened to quite a few tracks," she said in 1993. "David decided that 'The Man Who Sold The World' would be a good one." The following day, an interview with David with *Disc*'s Ray Fox-Cumming is published: "All I can say is that at this time I do not want to do live concerts again for a long, long time – not for two or three years at least."

In *NME*, Charles Shaar Murray's feature on Ronson and Mike Garson is headed 'Say hello to Weird and Gilly'. Garson tells Murray about the piano arrangements of David's songs he played on the final night at Hammersmith Odeon: "We were down in the bar last week, me and Dave, and I'd worked out these jazz arrangements of 'Ziggy Stardust' and 'Life On Mars?' with really plush chords, and I obscured the melody. I said to Dave, 'Tell me what song this is,' and I played Ziggy with all these beautiful jazz chords.

"He said, 'I don't know what the hell you're playing, but it's a good jazz piece. Play it again.' I played it five times. Finally he got it and flipped."

Meanwhile, David visits Morgan Studios in Willesden, where Lou Reed is recording his new album *Berlin* with producer Bob Ezrin.

1. Richardson was vocalist in Michigan band SRC (originally The Scott Richard Case), whose eponymous debut album was released in 1968. Richardson also wrote the lyrics to 'Only After Dark' and 'Pleasureman' for Ronson's debut album.

Monday 9 July

David leaves Victoria Station on a train to Dover before crossing the English Channel and heading for Strawberry Studios[1] at the Château d'Hérouville, Pontoise, to the north east of Paris.

For these sessions, Bolder is on bass but Woodmansey has been replaced by Aynsley Dunbar. In 1976, David said that "*Pin Ups* was really to give The Spiders something to do. I didn't quite know how to fit them into the next thing."

Over a three-week period there are many 12-hour sessions, including the taping of a backing track of The Velvet Underground's 'White Light/White Heat'.[2] David also considers recording a new version of his 1966 song 'The London Boys'.

Any spare time is spent mixing tapes from the final show at Hammersmith Odeon.

1. Commonly known as the Château, the studio had recently hosted Elton John and his producer Gus Dudgeon recording the 1973 album *Honky Chateau*. The Château consisted of two recording facilities, one named after one-time owner Frederic Chopin and the other after fellow resident, the 19th-century novelist George Sand. In late 1973 financial problems forced the Château to close for a year. In 1976 David returned to produce Iggy Pop's album *The Idiot* before working on his own album *Low* with Brian Eno and Tony Visconti. The studios were closed in 1985.

2. This was used by Mick Ronson for his version on the 1975 album *Play Don't Worry*.

Wednesday 11 July

David is interviewed at the Château by Radio Luxembourg's Kid Jensen, who is accompanied by former Velvet Underground member Nico.

NME's Charles Shaar Murray is also among the journalists who interview David at the studios.

Ava Cherry tracks David down and joins him there, having met him in Detroit earlier in the year. David works with her on a demo at the Château, and their meeting marks the beginning of a two-and-a-half-year relationship.

Another guest is guitarist June Millington[1] of Detroit all-female rockers Fanny, whom David praises.

1. Millington's sister and Fanny bandmate Jean contributed backing vocals to 1975's *Young Americans*, and married David's *Station To Station* guitarist Earl Slick.

Saturday 14 July

The music press publishes its obituaries for Ziggy Stardust. In the *NME* David reflects on his past: "I knew that being a mod meant that I had to wear clothes that no one else was wearing. In those days I was in the audience, but I never dressed like anybody else in the rock business."

'Life On Mars?' reaches its highest UK chart position at number three, going silver with sales in excess of 250,000 copies. 'Let's Spend The Night Together'/'Lady Grinning Soul' also enters the US

singles chart this month.

David's interview with Kid Jensen is broadcast by Radio Luxembourg.

Monday 16 July

The *Pin Ups* sessions are put on hold to make way for the recording of two of David's songs with Lulu: 'The Man Who Sold The World' and 'Watch That Man'.

The completed multitrack tape contains one take of 'The Man Who Sold The World' (on which David's guide vocal is overdubbed with backing vocals) and two takes of 'Watch That Man'.

The musicians are Ronson, Bolder, Dunbar, Garson and David on sax and backing vocals, working with house engineer Andy Scott, rather than Trident's Ken Scott (no relation), who said in 2002: "I was only contracted to work with David on the album, nothing more. I just set the levels for the Lulu session and left the room until it was over."

Lulu is accompanied by her manager Marion Massey and is impressed at the work rate, though less so by the studio accommodation, which she described in 1993 as "kind of like dormitories, like a boarding school.

"I smoked at the time and David made me smoke more and more and more. He wanted a certain sound from my voice."

Lulu[1] and backing vocalist Geoff MacCormack's loud vocal warm-ups interrupt the main business of recording *Pin Ups* tracks. "We had to stop because we could hear them, but couldn't find them," said Bolder in 1995. "Eventually they emerged from the reverb room (a confined space used mainly to record vocals), which half-deafened them I think."

Mick Rock also spends a few days at the studios, photographing the *Pin Ups* and Lulu sessions. He is told about new group Queen by Ken Scott and, on his return to London, forms a working relationship which will result in photographing the quartet for the cover of 1974's *Queen II*.

Another photographer visitor to the Château is Terry O'Neill, who captures David and Angie modelling clothes for the *Daily Mirror*.

1. In 1974 Lulu worked with David in New York on two or three more of his songs, including 'Can You Hear Me'.

Wednesday 18 July

David takes a trip into Paris[1] for a British *Vogue* cover shoot with model Twiggy, posing for her partner Justin de Villeneuve.

During the session David and Twiggy[2] discuss collaborating on possible film or TV projects.

1. In 2002 David said: "I can't remember Twiggy coming to Paris at all."

2. The model and Villeneuve's company Twiggy Enterprises was paid £393 for this session.

Monday 23 July

Today all five of David's RCA albums are in the UK top 40, with three in the top 20, an unprecedented

TOP: "We played to 137,000 people, which is more than any act has played to on a single tour of Britain."

ABOVE: At the *Live And Let Die* première.

In this year...

Monday 2 July
INTERVIEW with Van Morrison, who told the *NME*:

"David Bowie's just doing what Phil May of The Pretty Things used to do. He's just wearing different clothes."

Saturday 7 July
CHARTING of Elton John's single 'Saturday Night's Alright For Fighting' at number 36 in the UK. Lyricist Bernie Taupin later stated he wrote the words for the song as a 'sequel' to David's 'Hang On To Yourself'.

Saturday 21 July
DEPARTURE of Brian Eno from Roxy Music announced in the British music press.

TOP: Freddie Burretti and Daniella Parmar waiting to collect David's awards at the *Melody Maker* Awards ceremony, October.

MIDDLE: Dutch release of 'Sorrow' single.

ABOVE: French release of single 'The Laughing Gnome'.

achievement by a solo artist.

A MainMan telex to New York confirms: 'Justin has taken pictures of Twiggy and David in Paris which will be the cover for *Vogue* hopefully sometime in October.'

Starting today, the *Daily Mirror* runs a two-day Terry O'Neill fashion spread from the Château, in which Angie announces that she wishes to pursue a modelling career with a new name. The headline is: 'Have You Met Jipp Jones?'

Tuesday 31 July

Today is the final day at the Château as recording of *Pin Ups* is completed.

Meanwhile, by telex, MainMan's London office informs the New York HQ that *Top Of The Pops* has declined screening Mick Rock's promo for 'Life On Mars?': 'Their words (*Top Of The Pops*) "we decide what goes on our programme and will not use your film".'

Thursday 2 August

Having departed Paris on an overnight sleeper the previous evening, David, Angie, MacCormack, his girlfriend Desna Briggs and bodyguard Stuey George arrive for a holiday in Rome.

The party is installed at the spacious Villa Ofmilla, just outside Rome in Tenuta San Nicola, Via Braccianese La Storta, and are joined from London by Daniella Parmar, Zowie and David's personal assistant Gloria Harris.[1]

Meanwhile, Aynsley Dunbar, Ronson and hairdresser Suzi Fussey (who is by now Ronson's girlfriend) fly in from Paris with tour chef Anton Jones (who was part of David's personal security on the 1972 US tour).

During the break David works on his next project, one he intends to be solo. Initially, his premise is to create an album and stage a musical version of George Orwell's novel *Nineteen Eighty-Four*, partly inspired by his recent train journey through Russia and Eastern Europe.

Meanwhile, Ronson is also preparing a solo project, his first album, for which David suggests that he considers covering Richard Rodgers' show tune 'Slaughter On Tenth Avenue'. Ronson's sister Maggi is also a guest and observes amps and musical equipment in the villa's main room. "David and Michael were still working together," she said in 1993.

1. Harris is seen briefly in Pennebaker's *Ziggy Stardust* film, handing David a telex backstage at the Hammersmith Odeon. She later married chef Anton Jones.

Saturday 4 August

The *NME* publishes a second feature based on Charles Shaar Murray's interview at the Château, with insights into David's workload: 'The session finally breaks up at around three in the morning. Ronson goes to bed, still declaring his intention to write some more string parts. Bowie commandeers the piano in the dining room to work on a new song, and by eight o'clock he's still working.

'He genuinely doesn't know when to stop. After all, there's another album to come after the live tapes (provisionally called 'Bowie-ing Out') are released and already there's a backing track laid down for one of the songs, not to mention the production of Mick Ronson's solo album, and the movie, and God knows what else...'

Tuesday 7 August

After barely a week in Italy, a restless David is keen to get back to work and decides to return to England. He, Angie and Stuey George journey by train and boat back to London. The rest of the party remains at the villa for another two weeks. (Angie returns to Italy for one night on 13 August, while David works at Trident with Ken Scott mixing *Pin Ups*.)

Wednesday 22 August

Dramatist Nicholas Salaman's new play *Mad Dog* opens at London's Hampstead Theatre starring Denholm Elliott and Marianne Faithfull. David has asked Faithfull to appear in the stage show he is developing.

David is in the audience for a performance, sitting next to pop impresario Simon Napier-Bell. Coincidentally, Napier-Bell had watched one of David's shows from the wings in Tokyo earlier in the year and then bumped into him in May when both were checking into the George V in Paris.

Tuesday 4 September

Mick Ronson starts work on recording his album *Slaughter On 10th Avenue* at Château d'Hérouville. The album will be released by RCA with Ronson as a solo artist within the MainMan stable.

Ronson is at the Château for a month, during which time David visits to deliver the song he has written specifically for the project, 'Growing Up And I'm Fine', and lyrics for Ronson's 'Hey Ma Get Papa'.

David also writes an English lyric for 'Music Is Lethal' (based on Italian song 'Io Me Ne Andrei', with Italian lyrics by Giulio Rapetti).

Friday 7 September

Due to demand, Decca repromotes the 1967 Deram single 'The Laughing Gnome'/'The Gospel According To Tony Day', much to David's embarrassment.

The single, which sells more than a quarter of a million copies, is not a reissue but a timely repromotion since it remained undeleted on the catalogue following its initial release.

In the evening, David is at The Rolling Stones concert at the Empire Pool in Wembley, north-west London,[1] and visits the band backstage. The Stones' are riding high in the UK charts with their single 'Angie'[2] (incorrectly rumoured to be about David's wife).

The following day, *Melody Maker's* front cover announces 'Bowie's Back', claiming that he will return to the UK stage for at least one appearance this month, possibly at a Lou Reed gig.

1. In May 1976 David played a triumphant six nights at the venue. These were his first British shows since July 1973.

2. 'Angie' was demoed by Keith Richards in November 1972 before David and Angie Bowie's association with the band. "The basic melody and the title were mine," said Richards in 1993. "I'd recently had my daughter born, whose name was Angela, and the name was starting to ring around the house. Angie just fitted."

Thursday 13 September

At Mick Jagger's invitation, David travels to Newcastle with Scott Richardson, to see The Rolling Stones at the City Hall.

After the gig, David, Richardson and the Jaggers gamble and party the night away at a casino.

Tuesday 18 September

David is at the Royal Albert Hall in Kensington for a Diana Ross concert.

Saturday 29 September

David sweeps up in *Melody Maker's* annual reader's poll, voted number one in the categories for British singer, international singer, best single (top with 'The Jean Genie', and number two for 'Drive-In Saturday'), international producer and international composer.

Aladdin Sane takes second place in both album and international album of the year, as does David for arranger (with Mick Ronson) and live act. Meanwhile, he and The Spiders come sixth in group of the year.

The same issue reports that David is working on a revue to be staged in London's West End the following year.

Now that *Pin Ups* has been finalised, David spends time at Trident working on demos for the show, including new song 'Dodo',[1] complete with a brass section.

MainMan's request to license *Nineteen Eighty-Four* for the musical is refused by Orwell's widow, Sonia Brownell.

David adapts some of the material he has written into a new concept, *The 1980 Floor Show*, and a deal is struck for this to be televised in the US as part of NBC rock series *The Midnight Special*.

1. This was issued as a bonus track for the first time by Rykodisc/EMI on *Diamond Dogs* in 1990.

Thursday 4 October

In France, Mick Ronson completes recording sessions for his first solo album and, as David moves out of Trident, Ronson arrives to begin mixing.

MainMan receives a letter of complaint from Aquis Property, managers of actress Diana Rigg's Vale Court[1] property in Hall Road, Maida Vale: 'We have again received complaints regarding excessive noise. Would you inform your client, Mr Bowie, that if the nuisance continues we will have no alternative but to place the matter in the hands of our solicitors.'

This prompts David and Angie to start searching for new accommodation.

1. Vale Court is the property where Soft Machine drummer and solo artist Robert Wyatt fell from a third-storey window, breaking his back, on 1 June, a few weeks before the Bowies moved in.

Friday 12 October

RCA release 'Sorrow'/'Amsterdam' single in the UK and the US.

⊙ **David Bowie**
A **'Sorrow'** (Feldman/Goldstein/Gottehrer)
B **'Amsterdam'** (Brel/Shuman/Blau)
A-side:
David Bowie (vocal, guitar, saxophone)
Mick Ronson (guitar, piano, vocal)
Trevor Bolder (bass)
Aynsley Dunbar (drums)
Mike Garson (piano, electric piano)
Ken Fordham (baritone sax)
Geoff MacCormack (vocal back-up)
B-side:
David Bowie (vocal)
Mick Ronson (guitar)
Produced by David Bowie and Ken Scott
Arranged by David Bowie and Mick Ronson

Originally scheduled for release on 28 September, this has been delayed by a couple of weeks.

The A-side was first recorded by Liverpool band The Merseys in 1966, while the B-side is the Jacques Brel song David has included in his live set on and off for four years.

On the same day London Records follows Decca's lead in the UK by issuing 'The Laughing Gnome', though it fails to make an impact in the US, much to David's relief. The following day, the single reaches number six in the UK singles chart.

During October, Freddie Burretti accepts a collective *Melody Maker* award on David's behalf. It is presented by jazz singer/art critic George Melly during a ceremony at the Global Village, London, which is filmed by ITV Southern for its news slots.

Wednesday 17 October

David, Angie, Zowie, Burretti, Parmar (by now Angie's assistant) and Zowie's nanny Marion Skene[1] move to 89 Oakley Street[2] in Chelsea, just around the corner from the Jaggers' home in Cheyne Walk and a short distance from Defries' Gunter Grove base.

This also houses residential staff, including David's secretary Ava Clarke,[3] who moves into the basement flat, and personal chef Anton Jones.

The new abode is also handy for rehearsals for *The 1980 Floor Show*, which are conducted in nearby Fulham in a building owned by prog-rockers Emerson, Lake & Palmer.

1. Skene – who was secretary to RCA publicist Barry Bethell – worked for David in Switzerland until the late 90s. As of 2010 she remains a Swiss resident.

2. They rented Oakley Street until 16 December 1974.

3. Clarke later became an actress, notably starring in British drama *Widows*. She died of an overdose in 1988.

THIS PAGE

TOP LEFT: David on stage at the Marquee recording *The 1980 Floor Show*.

MIDDLE: 'Sorrow' sheet music.

ABOVE: The Astronettes at the Marquee for *The Midnight Special*. Left to right: Geoff MacCormack, Jason Guess (aka Jason Carter) and Ava Cherry.

TOP MIDDLE: *Record & Radio Mirror*, 29 December.

TOP RIGHT: *Midnight Special* Marquee club audience ticket.

OPPOSITE PAGE

TOP RIGHT: End of an era, the Marquee club is burnt out and reduced to rubble, 1991. (Below) *Midnight Special* promo ticket.

TOP LEFT: David and William Burroughs, photographed by Terry O'Neill.

BOTTOM: Jacques Brel (1929–1978).

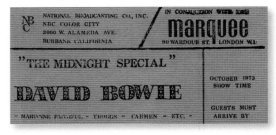

Thursday 18 October

▶ The first of three days of filming of the *Midnight Special* show begins at the Marquee.

"I wanted to go back there because I had so many good memories over the years," said David in 2001.

Produced by Burt Sugarman, this features David backed by Ronson, Bolder, Dunbar and, on rhythm guitar, David's neighbour from Beckenham and one-time member of The Arnold Corns, Mark Pritchett.

Also on the bill are 60s rockers The Troggs, Marianne Faithfull and new Latin American group Carmen,[1] David having been introduced to the last by Tony Visconti, who is handling the sound.

Also taking part are the newly formed The Astronettes (who are not connected to the Lindsay Kemp dancers of the same name who performed at the August 1972 Rainbow shows).

These are led by David's paramour Ava Cherry, with Jason Carter (aka Jason Guess) and Geoff MacCormack (who has adopted the name Warren Peace).

Today the writer Tony Ingrassia arrives from New York to work on stage production ideas with David for the West End show in development, provisionally titled 'Ziggy Stardust'.

1. Visconti was producing Carmen's album *Fandangos In Space* in 1973 and introduced them to David when he visited recording sessions at London's Air Studios.

Friday 19 October

RCA releases *Pin Ups* in the UK and US, with advance sales of 150,000.

▶ Much of the day is taken up filming *The 1980 Floor Show* guest appearances, including Marianne Faithfull's performance of her 1964 Jagger/Richards-penned hit, 'As Tears Go By'.

David's 'Time' sequence, complete with choreographed male dancers, is also filmed. The cast's costumes are designed by David's friend from his Lindsay Kemp days, Natasha Kornilof.

Faithfull's friend Amanda Lear compères the show and appears on stage with David during his performance of 'Sorrow'.

For her duet with David on Sonny & Cher's 60s hit 'I Got You Babe', Faithfull is shaky of voice and wearing a backless nun's habit.

Over the three days the audience is made up of David Bowie fan club members, 200 of whom are randomly selected daily and granted free tickets.[1]

1. At this stage the fan club was run by Sue Townsend.

Saturday 20 October

▶ In many ways today marks the end of an era for David. It is the last time he will appear in the UK with the identifiable Ziggy haircut and garb, and also the final performance with members of The Spiders.

This is also the last time he appears at the Marquee, venue of many a gig in the 60s, so it is fitting that so many of the tracks performed for *The 1980 Floor Show* date from that decade.

Songs also recorded for the NBC broadcast are 'Everything's Alright', 'Space Oddity', 'I Can't Explain' (which David announces as 'The Laughing Gnome'), 'The Jean Genie' and – the only new track – '1984'/'Dodo'.

He tells the audience, which includes Lionel Bart, Dana Gillespie (who first met David at the club eight years earlier), Mary Hopkin, Wayne County and Angie and Zowie: "We've written a musical and this is the title song called '1984'. We'll be doing the show in March next year."

The performance is interrupted by Ronson's guitar going out of tune. Then, when one of the guitarist's strings breaks, David leaves the stage in a huff.

Filming ends at midnight.

Saturday 27 October

Disc reports 'Bowie 1984 A.D.', including a brief interview with Tony Ingrassia.

David begins work on his new album around this time, working at Olympic Studios in Barnes. Keith Harwood engineers the album, having previously worked on Mott The Hoople sessions at the studio and has also recently worked with The Rolling Stones on *It's Only Rock'n'Roll*.

This is the start of five months of sessions, which

will include a rotating cast of contributors, including guitarists Ron Wood, Keith Christmas and Alan Parker, keyboard player Mike Garson, drummers Aynsley Dunbar and Tony Newman and bassist Herbie Flowers.[1]

Also at work at Olympic is Brian Eno, mixing his debut album *Here Come The Warm Jets*.

At least one early *Diamond Dogs* session is conducted at Morgan Studios in north London. In need of a bass player, due to Herbie Flowers' absence, David calls Bolder for their last recording session together. Also present are drummer Tony Newman and keyboard player Mike Garson. However, the session isn't a success, and, in anger, David calls an abrupt halt to the work and leaves without saying farewell to Bolder.[2]

1. Newman and Flowers were Marc Bolan's rhythm section in 1977.
2. In 1976 Bolder teamed up with John Hutchinson and drummer John Cambridge for a trial jam before joining the line-up of heavy rockers Uriah Heep. In 1976 Bolder recorded the album *The Spiders From Mars* with Woodmansey. Bolder's final meeting with David took place after a 1978 show at Newcastle City Hall. "He asked me what I thought of the gig," he said in 1995. "I told him that the sound had been poor, which it had, but before I could say anything else he walked away."

Monday 29 October

MainMan receives a telex request via RCA Paris from songsmith Mort Shuman, who asks whether David would perform Brel's 'Amsterdam' (for which he wrote the English lyrics) for a French TV crew.[1]

The telex reads: 'Mort Shuman doing very important TV show in November. He strongly wishes (exceptionally) David Bowie to perform 'Amsterdam'. TV team could go and film David in London.' But David is unable to fulfil the request.

1. With composer Doc Pomus, Shuman (1936–1991) formed the highly successful team which penned hits such as 'A Teenager In Love', 'Turn Me Loose', 'Save The Last Dance For Me' and 'Viva Las Vegas', as well as the off-Broadway production with Eric Blau, *Jacques Brel Is Alive And Well And Living In Paris*.

Wednesday 31 October

Bowie fans are denied the chance to see David perform 'Sorrow' on *Top Of The Pops* at the eleventh hour when producer Robin Nash pulls his appearance, insisting on a live performance when David has supplied backing tapes to sing over.

'As you probably know, *Top Of The Pops* was cancelled today causing short nerves and large headaches,' reads a telex from MainMan London to New York. 'Barry Bethell had it all in hand (we thought). Robin (Mayhew) informed me this morning when he arrived with the equipment that it was all going to be done live. From what I have been able to understand only Bowie's voice and strings were to be live. Bethell had informed Robin Nash, producer of *Top Of The Pops*, that it was all going to be live. Bowie said this was out of the question.

'MU (Musician Union) rules have it that a backing track must be taped in their studio or with one of their members present.

'Our backing track had been done at Trident with nobody present (well, Bowie was there) and Bowie did not feel that the hour allotted to him at *Top Of The Pops* to remedy the affair was sufficient. So as already said, it was cancelled at the nth hour and everybody was blaming everybody else.'

In Japan, RCA Victor releases David Bowie *Best Deluxe*, a double album compiled from 21 album tracks up to and including 'Aladdin Sane'.

Saturday 3 November

'Sorrow' reaches number three in the UK charts today; it is David's sixth top 10 single in four years.

Saturday 10 November

In the *NME*, some of those who originally recorded songs covered on *Pin Ups* give their verdict: Pink Floyd's Nick Mason says 'See Emily Play' is "rather nice"; Tony Crane of The Merseys opines that 'Sorrow' "could have been more powerful"; and Stu Slater of The Mojos deems 'Everything's Alright' "very good… he has treated it quite respectfully".

Friday 16 November

The 1980 Floor Show is broadcast in the US on NBC's *The Midnight Special*.[1] David is credited with the show's 'concept and design'.

1. To date this hasn't been screened in the UK, though many sequences are available for viewing online.

Saturday 17 November

David is interviewed with writer William Burroughs at Oakley Street by Craig Copetas for *Rolling Stone*. Terry O'Neill photographs the pair together.

Burroughs subsequently visits the sessions at Olympic, as David starts to create lyrics in 'cut-up' form, in line with Burroughs' literary technique (as displayed in the 1965 Burroughs/Anthony Balch film *Cut-Ups* later screened on London's Arts Lab circuit).

In this year...

October
LAUNCH of London commercial station Capital Radio. RCA secured David's place on the playlist of top 10 featured artists, and between 1976 and 1979 David rewarded them with a number of exclusive live interviews with DJ Nicky Horne.

November
RELEASE by label Editions EG of *No Pussyfooting*, a collaboration between Brian Eno and Robert Fripp.
CLOSURE of underground magazine *Oz* after six years.
WITHDRAWAL by director Stanley Kubrick of his film *A Clockwork Orange* from British cinemas after hostile press reports and personal threats.

Saturday 10 November
ENTRY of Kiki Dee's single 'Amoureuse'/'Rest My Head' at number 13 in the UK charts. Impressed with the A-side, David contacted the singer. "He wrote to me saying he liked the single and he sent me a song," said Dee in 2003. "I think at the time I was so thrilled to have a hit record I didn't appreciate how fabulous it was to hear from him."

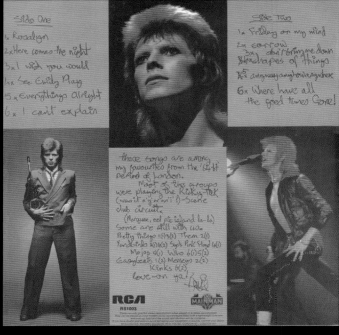

ABOVE: David and Twiggy are photographed by Justin de Villeneuve. The *Pin Ups* cover photo was originally intended as a cover shoot for *Vogue* UK. Taken at *Vogue*'s Paris studio on 18 July 1973, this was de Villeneuve's last session with Twiggy. The back sleeve photography was by Mick Rock. Both the saxophone session and the live photo, bottom right, were contenders for the front design before David asked de Villeneuve if he could instead use a shot from the *Vogue* session.

PIN UPS   Released Friday 19 October

Side One
1. ROSALYN (Duncan/Farley) (2.27)
David Bowie (vocal)
Mick Ronson (guitar)
Trevor Bolder (bass)
Aynsley Dunbar (drums)

2. HERE COMES THE NIGHT (Berns) (3.09)
David Bowie (vocal, guitar, alto and tenor saxes)
Mick Ronson (guitar, backing vocal)
Trevor Bolder (bass)
Aynsley Dunbar (drums)
Mike Garson (electric piano)
Mac Cormack (vocal backup)

3. I WISH YOU WOULD (Arnold) (2.40)
David Bowie (vocal, guitar, alto and tenor saxes, harmonica, Moog synthesiser)
Mick Ronson (guitar, backing vocal)
Trevor Bolder (bass)
Aynsley Dunbar (drums)
Mike Garson (electric piano)
Michel Ripoche (violin)

4. SEE EMILY PLAY (Barrett) (4.03)
David Bowie (vocal, guitar, Moog synthesiser)
Mick Ronson (guitar, piano, backing vocal)
Trevor Bolder (bass)
Aynsley Dunbar (drums)
Mike Garson (piano, electric piano, harpsichord)
Mac Cormack (vocal backup)
Session orchestra

5. EVERYTHING'S ALRIGHT
(Crouch/Konrad/Stavely/James/Karlson) (2.26)
David Bowie (vocal, guitar, alto and tenor saxes)
Mick Ronson (guitar, piano, backing vocal)
Trevor Bolder (bass)
Aynsley Dunbar (drums)
Mike Garson (piano)
Ken Fordham (baritone sax)
Mac Cormack (vocal backup)

6. I CAN'T EXPLAIN (Townshend) (2.07)
David Bowie (vocal, guitar, alto and tenor saxes)
Mick Ronson (guitar, backing vocal)
Trevor Bolder (bass)
Aynsley Dunbar (drums)
Mike Garson (piano)
Ken Fordham (baritone sax)
Mac Cormack (vocal backup)

Side Two
1. FRIDAY ON MY MIND (Young/Vanda) (3.18)
David Bowie (vocal, guitar, alto and tenor saxes)
Mick Ronson (guitar, piano, backing vocal)
Trevor Bolder (bass)
Aynsley Dunbar (drums)
Mike Garson (piano, electric piano)
Ken Fordham (baritone sax)
Mac Cormack (vocal backup)

2. SORROW (Feldman/Goldstein/Gottehrer) (2.48)
David Bowie (vocal, guitar, alto and tenor saxes)
Mick Ronson (guitar, piano, backing vocal)
Trevor Bolder (bass)
Aynsley Dunbar (drums)
Mike Garson (piano, electric piano)
Ken Fordham (baritone sax)
Mac Cormack (vocal backup)
Session orchestra

3. DON'T BRING ME DOWN (Dee) (2.01)
David Bowie (vocal, guitar, alto and tenor saxes, harmonica)
Mick Ronson (guitar, piano, backing vocal)
Trevor Bolder (bass)
Aynsley Dunbar (drums)
Mike Garson (piano, electric piano)
Ken Fordham (baritone sax)

4. SHAPES OF THINGS
(Samwell-Smith/McCarty/Relf) (2.53)
David Bowie (vocal, guitar, alto and tenor saxes)
Mick Ronson (guitar, backing vocal)
Trevor Bolder (bass)
Aynsley Dunbar (drums)
Ken Fordham (baritone sax)
Mac Cormack (vocal backup)
Session orchestra

5. ANYWAY, ANYHOW, ANYWHERE
(Townshend/Daltrey) (3.04)
David Bowie (vocal, guitar, alto and tenor saxes)
Mick Ronson (guitar, backing vocal)
Trevor Bolder (bass)
Aynsley Dunbar (drums)
Mike Garson (piano, electric piano)
Mac Cormack (vocal backup)

6. WHERE HAVE ALL THE GOOD TIMES GONE?
(Davies) (2.35)
David Bowie (vocal, guitar, alto and tenor saxes)
Mick Ronson (guitar, piano, backing vocal)
Trevor Bolder (bass)
Aynsley Dunbar (drums)
Mike Garson (piano)
Ken Fordham (baritone sax)
Mac Cormack (vocal backup)

Produced by Ken Scott and David Bowie
Engineered by Denis Blackeye
Recorded at the Château d'Hérouville, France
Front cover photo by Justin de Villeneuve
Mask make-up by Pierre Laroche
Back cover photos and sleeve design by Mick Rock
Lettering by Ray Campbell
A MainMan Production
(RCA RS 1003) – UK (RCA APL.I.0291) – US

Highest position: UK number one, US number 23.

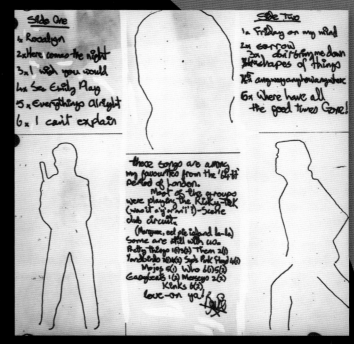

On the back of the *Pin Ups* sleeve, David outlined in longhand his reasons for recording an album of covers: 'These are all songs which really meant a lot to me then, they're all dear to me. These are all bands which I used to go and hear down at the Marquee between 1964 and 1967. Each one meant something to me at the time. It's my London of the time.'[1]

A couple of days after the final concert of his 1973 world tour, with recording in France barely a week away, David and his friend the Detroit singer Scott Richardson worked through a stack of records and selected 12 tracks for *Pin Ups*.

Like David, Richardson was a Pretty Things fan, which explains why two of their tracks are featured. And two more of David's favourite 60s bands were complimented with two covers apiece: The Yardbirds ('Shapes Of Things' and 'I Wish You Would')[2] and The Who ('Anyway, Anyhow, Anywhere' and 'I Can't Explain').

Mick Ronson didn't contribute to the selection, though David and The Spiders had performed 'I Can't Explain' live at least once in 1972 and had also previously recorded the song.

Ronson was the only ex-Spider David had planned to include in the sessions, having invited ex-Cream member Jack Bruce to play bass. When Bruce announced he was not available, Trevor Bolder was once again enlisted.

Although he was thrilled to be working with a musical hero – drummer Aynsley Dunbar – Bolder did not feel comfortable.

"They didn't really want me to hang around for the whole time," he said in 1995. "I did all my work at the earlier sessions and left."

A constant presence, however, was Geoff McCormack, credited as 'Mac Cormack' as he had been on *Aladdin Sane*, and by now David's travelling companion.

One of the LP's highlights was David's rendition of The Pink Floyd's Syd Barrett composition 'See Emily Play'. Although David had often seen the Barrett-era Floyd play, he had only met the band's one-time frontman a couple of times. "We didn't get on all that well. But I'm a great fan of his," he announced during the promotional rounds for *Pin Ups*.

The only lyrics reproduced on the album's illustrated insert were, appropriately, for Ray Davies' relatively unknown composition 'Where Have All The Good Times Gone?'

"I would often try to go for a more obscure song because I felt it would give me more freedom to play around with the arrangement," David later said. "In that particular case, I think I stayed pretty close to the original arrangement. But the idea of doing the more obscure songs was something that really appealed to me."

For years, there were rumours that many more songs were recorded during these sessions for a *Pin Ups II* project, but these proved unfounded when the album was reissued in 1990.

Only one more unreleased song, Bruce Springsteen's 'Growin' Up', was included.[3] This recording, which featured Ronnie Wood,[4] was actually recorded later in the year during the early stages of *Diamond Dogs*.

Springsteen's original appeared on his January 1973 debut *Greetings From Asbury Park NJ*, which David had picked up on his US visit a month after release.

Jacques Brel's 'Amsterdam', also recorded at the château, was used as the B-side of the October 1973 single 'Sorrow' and demonstrated the panache with which David had handled the song many times in concert. It is not confirmed whether he recorded a studio version of another Brel live favourite from this period, 'My Death', but it is highly likely.

During the *Pin Ups* sessions an incomplete backing track was recorded for a

composer Johnnie Dee at the Giaconda in 1965. He later lost his much prized, intricately tooled Tibetan boots when he loaned them to Dee in late 67 and never saw them again.

4. 'Shapes Of Things' – Yardbirds (Paul Samwell-Smith/Jim McCarty/Keith Relf)

'Shapes Of Things' became a number three hit for the band in March 66. The Yardbirds single featured Clapton's replacement and Mick Ronson's hero, Jeff Beck. David was particularly impressed with Keith Relf, whom he had occasionally met on the road and around London in 65/66. It's also possible the song reminded him of an early TV show he appeared on when the Yardbirds were promoting this song. (▸ 4.3.65)

5. 'Anyway, Anyhow, Anywhere' - The Who (Pete Townshend/Roger Daltrey)

Released in June 65. When the group's US label received the master tape they returned it thinking the feedback was a fault on the tape. The single reached number 10 in the UK and was adopted by TV show *Ready, Steady Go!* as its theme tune. Produced by Shel Talmy.

6. 'Where Have All The Good Times Gone?' – The Kinks (Ray Davies) [1]

With obvious significance for David, 'Where Have All The Good Times Gone' was the only track on *Pin Ups* to feature the lyrics on the album's pull-out sheet. Ray Davies was a mid-60s acquaintance of David's, having first met him during his stint with The Manish Boys. In late 65/early 66, this song was the B-side of The Kinks' number 8 Pye hit 'Till The End Of The Day' (and would also make number 50 in the US). Produced by Shel Talmy. (▸ 10.11.73)

1 At a benefit concert in New York in 2003, David performed a duet with Ray Davies of his 1967 classic 'Waterloo Sunset'. Also in 2003 David recorded his own version of the track and included it as a B-side of single 'Never Get Old'.

Tracks featured on *Pin Ups* were originally recorded by:

1. 'Rosalyn' – The Pretty Things (Duncan/Farley)

Co-written by the group's manager, Jimmy Duncan, this song was the first hit for David's friends The Pretty Things when released in June 64 (but only made number 41). The song was evidently based on Benny Spellman's 'Fortune Teller'. The lyrics were supplied by Denmark Street studio owner Bill Farley who made them up on the spot when asked by the band for an idea. Also in 64, Farley, engineered on the Stones' debut LP.

2. 'Here Comes The Night' – Them (Bert Berns)

Irish band Them featured Van Morrison on lead vocals. This song was their biggest hit, making number 2 in April 65. It was written by Bert Berns, who also wrote 'Twist And Shout' and 'Hang On Sloopy'.

3. 'I Wish You Would' – Yardbirds (Billy Arnold)

Another debut single. The Yardbirds' cover of a Billy Boy Arnold song was not a chart success for the group when released in June 64, but was obviously a hit with Davie Jones. Eric Clapton featured on the Yardbirds version.

4. 'See Emily Play' – The Pink Floyd (Syd Barrett)

Originally released in July 67, 'See Emily Play' reached

number six in the charts and was the last chart hit single for Floyd until 'Another Brick In The Wall' in December 79. Syd (real name Roger Barrett) was asked to leave the band in March 1968.

5. 'Everything's Al'right' – The Mojos (Crouch/Konrad/Stavely/James/Karlson)

The first of two Liverpudlian bands to be acknowledged on the album. *Pin Ups* drummer Aynsley Dunbar was an ex-member of the Mojos, but didn't feature on their earlier recording of 'Everything's Al'right' (which was recorded during a residency at the Star Club, Hamburg). Highest position number nine in March 64.

6. 'I Can't Explain' – The Who (Pete Townshend/Roger Daltrey)

Recorded by The Who in January 65 with producer Shel Talmy overseeing (he actually produced four tracks covered on *Pin Ups*), Townshend is augmented on guitar by session-man Jimmy Page. The song was The Who's first single and was also a hit, making number eight.

David and the Manish Boys were also working with Talmy around this time recording 'I Pity The Fool' (also featuring Jimmy Page).

On David's version, Mick Ronson interjects at the end with the instantly

recognisable 'Shakin' All Over' riff created by Johnny Kidd and the Pirates (and session guitarist Joe Moretti), a UK number one single for them in 1960.

Side Two

1. 'Friday On My Mind' – The Easybeats (George Young/Harry Vanda)

The only non-UK band covered on *Pin Ups*, The Easybeats hailed from Sydney, Australia. This song became their second number 1 hit in their home country and made number six in the UK in December 66. (The song also went Top 20 in the US the following year.) Produced by Shel Talmy.

2. 'Sorrow' – The Merseys (Feldman/Goldstein/Gottehrer)

Originally recorded by Rick Derringer's McCoys, 'Sorrow' became a number four hit in June 66 for The Merseys (previously known as The Merseybeats). Songwriters Feldman, Goldstein and Gottehrer were better known as group The Strangeloves. David's version was the only track selected as a single from *Pin Ups*.

3. 'Don't Bring Me Down' – The Pretty Things (Johnnie Dee)

The second of two Pretty Things tracks, this single originally peaked at number 10 in November 64. David met the song's

cover of The Velvet Underground's 'White Light/White Heat'. This was later completed by Mick Ronson and included on his second album, *Play Don't Worry* (released in 1975).

The sleeve for *Pin Ups* was originally destined for the autumn or Christmas cover of *Vogue* UK, and was to be the first time a man had featured on the front of the fashion magazine.

The image was photographed by Twiggy's partner/manager Justin de Villeneuve mid-way through the *Pin Ups* sessions in France.

"Twiggy and I had first heard David mention her on *Aladdin Sane* (the 'Twig The Wonderkid' lyric to 'Drive-In Saturday'), while we were staying at the Bel Air Hotel in Hollywood," said de Villeneuve in 2010. "We loved the album so much I called David and asked him if he would like to do a shoot with Twiggy. He jumped at the idea. *Vogue* flew us to Paris with Pierre Laroche and we stopped by the château first to say hello.

"The photographic studio in Paris, which was owned by *Vogue*, was smaller than I was used to, but the type of shot I had in mind was a closely cropped image, so the ceiling height didn't really matter. My assistant Chris Killip set up the lighting and I posed David and Twigs, and then quickly shot one frame after another. I didn't vary the pose as I knew exactly what I wanted, but used plenty of film to make sure the image was safe."

David and Twiggy's faces were adorned with carefully applied make-up masks by Pierre Laroche. The model and de Villeneuve "had just returned from a tropical island and were as brown as berries," said de Villeneuve, who was shocked at the depth of David's Ziggy pallor.

"I couldn't believe how pale he was when he took off his shirt," he said. "The masks balanced the obvious skin-colour clash between them yet remained enigmatic and strange."

According to Twiggy, the photograph appeared on the album cover because of *Vogue*'s apprehension. "The circulation manager of English *Vogue* started to get nervous about putting a man on the cover," said Twiggy in 1975.

"I said they were crazy because they would sell more issues of that issue – because Bowie was on the cover – than they'll ever sell in their lives. While he was thinking about it, David said, 'Look this is lovely, why don't we use it on the album cover?' I know it doesn't really look like me. In fact there are still a lot of people who don't know it's me. It's still one of my favourite pictures."

In contrast, de Villeneuve says David convinced him the image would have far more exposure as an album cover. "*Vogue* didn't talk to me for years," said de Villeneuve. "They were very angry."

Mick Rock had originally been asked to create the cover and came up with two options for the front which were, in the event, used on the back. The image of David on stage thrusting himself forward with leg trailing was a

conscious tribute to one of his idols, Gene Vincent.

'Back in the 60s, Vincent was to co-star with Little Richard on a whirlwind package tour of the UK,' wrote David in 2002. 'Someone forgot to get his work permit together so he was not allowed to sing from the stage itself. To get over this, he sang his spot from the aisle. Ludicrous but very exciting for us fans. At the time, Vincent had been wearing a leg brace, the result of a car accident. It meant, to crouch at the mike, as was his habit, he had to shove his injured leg out behind him, to what I thought great theatrical effect. This position became position number one for the embryonic Ziggy.'

For the other shot, in which he cradles a saxophone, David wore a box-jacketed brown suit bought at City Lights Studio, the pioneering boutique run by fashion entrepreneur Tommy Roberts in Shorts Gardens, off Drury Lane in London's Covent Garden.

1. David's sleeve notes also mention some of the venues he visited in the formative years of his career. The Eel Pie Island Club was situated on a small island on the Thames near Twickenham, at the Eel Pie Island Hotel, a Victorian building which burnt down in 1971. David performed at the venue with The Manish Boys. The 'Ricky Tik' club (correctly spelt Ricky Tick) operated from several venues in and around London, including one at Hounslow, the Thames Hotel in Windsor, in Newbury, in Aylesbury and also at the Plaza Ballroom, Guildford. A recreation of the Windsor Ricky Tick featured in Antonioni's 1966 film *Blow-Up*, including rare footage of The Yardbirds featuring both Jimmy Page and Jeff Beck on guitar.

2 Michel Ripoche, a violinist and saxophonist from the French band Zoo sessioned on one track, 'I Wish You Would' but was uncredited.

3. David was the first artist to record a cover of a Springsteen song. He would also record a second Springsteen number, 'It's Hard To Be A Saint In The City' in 1974. That year he was introduced to the singer-songwriter for the first time.

4. Ron Wood didn't attend any sessions at the Château d'Hérouville. His contribution was overdubbed later in the year while David was working on *Diamond Dogs*. Wood also contributed to that album, working on early sessions with David and Tony Newman at the Olympic Studios, though didn't feature on final mixes. He also worked on some additional unreleased songs while recording with David in LA during the 1975 *Station to Station* sessions.

TOP: Photographed in Soho, Mick Rock's first studio session with David, Autumn 1973 © Mick Rock. MIDDLE LEFT: American singer and composer Scott Richardson helped David select songs for *Pin Ups*. MIDDLE RIGHT: Live in 72, David emulates Gene Vincent. This photo was also considered for the front cover © Mick Rock. ABOVE: *Pin Ups* promotional leaflet and stickers.

ABOVE: Full page *Melody Maker* advert promoting *Pin Ups*, 24 November.

TOP MIDDLE: Lindsay Kemp and David, photographed together at the Bush Theatre, London, 21 November.

TOP RIGHT: Lindsay, Sheila Rock (Mick's ex-wife) and David at Bush Theatre, London.

BOTTOM: David recording NBC TV's *Midnight Special* show at the Marquee. Behind are Mick Ronson with Mark Pritchett, formerly of The Arnold Corns.

Wednesday 21 November

David videos Lindsay Kemp's *Mermaids* at the Bush Theatre on Shepherds Bush Green, west London.

This is a one-off production brought from Edinburgh and staged for invited guests since Kemp has been unable to obtain a licence (another production is already running in the West End).

Around this time, David introduces the documentary *Lindsay Kemp's Circus,* directed by Celestino Coronado, on stage at London's National Film Theatre.

Monday 3 December

Continuing with his own recordings, David embarks on a side project at Olympic, producing sessions for The Astronettes and working on a Lulu backing track.

Tuesday 4 December

David escorts Amanda Lear to a performance of John Osborne's *A Patriot For Me* at the Palace Theatre, Watford.

They arrive in a white limousine and visit the lead, Marianne Faithfull, backstage after the production. With Angie, David often socialises with Faithfull and her antique dealer partner Oliver Musker.

The following day, David receives a dressing down in the Hertfordshire *Evening Echo* from Watford's Labour MP Raphael Tuck for leaving his car on double-yellow lines throughout the previous night's three-hour play.

Saturday 8 December

Disc reports that David is working on two stage musicals: '*1984* and a Ziggy Stardust show, though which of them will be staged first remains anybody's guess.'

Friday 21 December

In the company of Mick Jagger, David is at the Hammersmith Odeon for a Mott The Hoople gig. After the show a young fan is seriously injured trying to gain access through a dressing-room window.

In *Disc* the following day, David tells Ray Fox-Cumming that he has bought a "fantastic house" in Kensington which he has been keen on since his teenage years.[1]

Meanwhile, singer-turned-actor Adam Faith makes an approach for David to play guitar on his new album. David replies: "I'm not much of a guitarist, are you sure you wouldn't rather I did some sax? I'm much better at that."

David is invited to north London's Morgan Studios by Jethro Tull frontman Ian Anderson, who is producing sessions by folk-rockers Steeleye Span for their new album *Now We Are Six*. Among Steeleye Span's number is bassist Rick Kemp, a Hull acquaintance of the Spiders who met David at Haddon Hall in 1971.

"I ran into Steeleye Span when we were signed to the same label and ended up mixing an album they were a bit stuck on," said Anderson in 1994. "My major contribution was to hire David Bowie to play alto sax on it."

On TV, a celebration of 10 years of *Top Of The Pops* includes David and The Spiders' 1972 performance of 'Starman'.

1. Although *Disc* also reported that 'he and his family will move in on 1 March 1974', the move didn't take place and David didn't buy the house.

Tuesday 25 December

David and Angie host Christmas dinner for Mick and Bianca Jagger at Oakley Street. Daniella Parmar and Freddie Burretti also share in the festivities as Zowie plays with the Jaggers' daughter Jade. At the party, David presents Jagger with a rare and expensive gadget, a video recorder.

Thursday 27 December

Between Christmas and New Year, David is again drawn into the studio and, in his last known visit to Trident, he starts laying down initial ideas for a song which becomes 'Rebel Rebel'.

Saturday 29 December

Melody Maker announces that David is the 'top singles artist of the year'.

In London's Pall Mall, a 10ft-high colour billboard is erected featuring a large drawing of David from *The 1980 Floor Show* by George Underwood. The display wishes Londoners a happy Christmas and New Year.

In Olympic's studio 2, The Astronettes' recording sessions resume with the recording over the next few days of four new David Bowie-penned tracks: 'I Am Divine', 'I Am A Laser',[1] 'People From Bad Homes',[2] and 'Things To Do'.

1. The basis for 'Scream Like A Baby' from 1980's *Scary Monsters* album.

2. This includes lyrics which appear in 'Fashion', also on *Scary Monsters*.

Sunday 30 December

Recording with The Astronettes includes their version

Bowie's quiet night out

David Bowie arrives at the Palace Theatre wearing make-up to match girl friend. *Picture: MARK LEWIS*

SATIN-SUITED SUPERSTAR 'DOESN'T WANT ATTENTION'
by STEPHEN PILE

of The Beach Boys' 'God Only Knows',[1] arranged by Tony Visconti.

David and Visconti also discuss plans for Puerto Rican arranger Luis Ramirez to contribute to the sessions, but these are abandoned before he can become involved.[2]

1. Covered by David on his 1984 album *Tonight*.

2. In 1995, MainMan issued a 12-track CD from these sessions. Credited to Ava Cherry And The Astronettes, it was titled *People From Bad Homes*.

Monday 31 December

RCA throws a press lunch with David as guest of honour at Rules Restaurant in Covent Garden (where David and Angie modelled for *Fabulous 208's* Christmas magazine cover in 1969).

Since signing with RCA in September 1971, David's sales have totalled 1,056,400 albums and 1,024,068 singles.

David is awarded a large commemorative plaque for having six different albums in the charts for 19 weeks during the year.

ABOVE: Receiving a special award from RCA at Rules in Covent Garden, 31 December.

TOP LEFT: 'Bowie's quiet night out', David with Amanda Lear in Watford on 4 December.

BOTTOM: Bowie at Watford's Palace Theatre being interviewed for local radio.

In this year...

Monday 12 November
LAUNCH of UK tour by Mott The Hoople to promote new single 'Roll Away The Stone' at Leeds Town Hall. Support is Queen, who later celebrated the tour in their song 'Now I'm Here' with the line: '... down in the city with Hoople and me'.

December
RELEASE of cult movie *The Wicker Man*, starring Edward Woodward, Britt Ekland, Christopher Lee and Lindsay Kemp.

Saturday 1 December
START of UK tour at Derby College of Art by rock/flamenco band Carmen, who featured in David's TV extravaganza *The 1980 Floor Show*. Carmen were promoting their Tony Visconti-produced album *Fandangos In Space*. Contrary to rumour, David did not record with the band, though he did attend one of their shows and was photographed with the band at a press launch. Carmen bassist John Glascock later joined prog-rockers Jethro Tull.

1974

DAVID maintains a cracking pace in recording new material, both for his next album and for The Astronettes.

Lulu's version of 'The Man Who Sold The World' provides the writer with more chart exposure.

Recording of *Diamond Dogs*, which has been inspired by George Orwell's cautionary novel *1984* and draws on other influences such as Fritz Lang's film *Metropolis*, is close to completion.

So, it seems, is David's time in the UK.

David travels to the Netherlands for TV work and further recording, and RCA releases 'Rebel Rebel', which signals a departure from the glam rock sound that has made him a global superstar.

Working with the Belgian artist Guy Peellaert (creator of the acclaimed book *Rock Dreams*) for the cover of *Diamond Dogs*, David is also in further studio collaboration with Lulu.

But when he leaves Britain's shores again, two months ahead of the release of the new album, it is for the last time as a resident. By the time the SS *France* docks in New York, he has dined with harmonica virtuoso Larry Adler, performed with the ship's crew and left his London roots far behind.

They have nurtured, nourished and inspired much of his artistic growth for 27 years, and they will continue to do so despite his absence.

But the May release of *Diamond Dogs* confirms that the constantly mutating David has launched himself confidently into a new era.

Just as he has distanced himself from the city he grew up in, so he has dispensed with much of what was previously familiar in musical terms: producer, studio and musicians.

The self-produced album proclaims David Bowie, London boy turned global citizen, as the master of his own fate.

PREVIOUS SPREAD: Photographed by Terry O'Neill for the cover design of *Diamond Dogs*.

TOP LEFT: Glasgow's Marie McDonald McLaughlin Lawrie returns to the Top 10 with a Bowie classic.

TOP RIGHT: Performing 'Rebel Rebel' on Dutch TV's *Top Pop*, 13 February. Photo by Roger Bamber.

ABOVE: Spanish single release of 'The Man Who Sold The World' by Lulu.

BOTTOM RIGHT: David conducting a press conference at the Amstel Hotel, Amsterdam, 13 February.

In this year...

Friday 15 March
RELEASE of folk-rock group Steeleye Span's album *Now We Are Six*, featuring David playing sax on their version of Phil Spector's 'To Know Him Is To Love Him'.

Saturday 16 March
RONSON's *Slaughter On 10th Avenue* peaks at number nine in the UK album chart.

Tuesday 1 January

Eager to maintain the pace on *Diamond Dogs*, David is back at Olympic for several days, with Keith Harwood engineering, assisted by the studio's Andy Morris.

New songs 'Take It In Right'[1] and 'Candidate'[2] are recorded, the former a basic acoustic track with lyrics still in progress.

Over the next five days, David also takes time to produce The Astronettes in Olympic's studio 2.

1. 'Take It In Right' evolved into 'Right' on 1975's *Young Americans*.
2. 'Candidate' was first released as a bonus track on the 1990 reissue of *Diamond Dogs*, and included on the 2004 *Diamond Dogs* anniversary edition as 'Alternative Candidate'. Apart from a single line of the lyric – 'I'll make you a deal' – there is nothing linking it to the latter part of the 'Sweet Thing'/'Candidate'/'Sweet Thing' medley which appeared on the 1974 album. An earlier demo version of 'Candidate' was recorded as a guide for David's *1984* musical project in 1973 but remains unreleased.

Monday 7 January

The owners of Olympic are threatening to ban David from recording at the studio if an outstanding bill of £4,935 isn't settled immediately. A MainMan telex from Cherry Vanilla to Tony Defries urges: 'Pay Olympic, harassing David. He is still recording there for several weeks.'

Tuesday 8 January

On his 27th birthday, David visits friend George Underwood's home in Well Walk, Hampstead, accompanied by Amanda Lear.[1] They drop by the local art-house cinema, the Everyman, to catch a screening of Fritz Lang's 1927 bleak expressionist masterpiece *Metropolis*.

The film is by now a major inspiration for *Diamond Dogs* and will influence the staging of David's tour of the US later in the year, as will Robert Wene's 1920 masterpiece *The Cabinet Of Dr Caligari*.

During the day, David mentions an idea he has for creating a film project for Lear based on Petr Sadecky's Russian underground comic book heroine Octobriana.[2]

An unnamed telex to Tony Defries in New York reads: 'Bowie will not be sending you the rough mixes of his new material as he feels this is not yet ready for anyone over there to hear.'

1. David and Lear collaborated on and demoed a song of Lear's entitled 'Star' which remains unreleased. In 2009 she released the *Brief Encounters* album, which included her take on 'Sorrow'.
2. Sadecky published his book *Octobriana And The Russian Underground* in 1971.

Wednesday 9 January

The Astronettes are back at Olympic for three more days of sessions produced by David.

Lulu records her vocal for a performance of her new single 'The Man Who Sold The World' for *Top Of The Pops*. David helps her to record the backing track for the appearance and advises on the sound at the BBC's studios in west London.

Friday 11 January

Polydor releases Lulu's 'The Man Who Sold The World'/'Watch That Man'.

This is one of the last releases to feature a production credit[1] for David; he is becoming concerned that his involvement may have hindered the artists he has produced.

Referring to his work with Lulu, Mott The Hoople and Lou Reed, David said in 1976: "I made them into the picture of what I thought they should be, not what they really were. I was trying to be a Svengali."

1. For Iggy Pop's *The Idiot* (1977) David was credited as having 'recorded' the album, while the same year's *Lust For Life* carries the same credit with the producers as 'The Bewlay Brothers' (generally accepted to be David and Tony Visconti). 1978's live set *TV Eye* carries a co-production credit with Pop.

Saturday 12 January

'Sorrow' re-enters the UK charts at number 30.

Monday 14 January

Photographer Kate Simon, visiting Olympic with a friend, captures David at work recording 'Big Brother' with Mike Garson.

Friday 25 January

Tony Defries' master plan to launch Mick Ronson in the wake of David's 'retirement' gets under way with the RCA release of Ronson's debut solo single, 'Love Me Tender'/'Slaughter On 10th Avenue'.

Saturday 26 January

The *NME* reports that among the songs David has been working on at Olympic are 'Big Brother' and 'Are You Coming? Are You Coming?'

Sunday 27 January

Ronson is interviewed about his new album by Bob Harris on BBC2's *The Old Grey Whistle Test*.

Tuesday 12 February

It is becoming increasingly clear that, with *Diamond Dogs* now complete and new single 'Rebel Rebel' ready to go, David's time in the UK is coming to an end. A MainMan telex states: 'David has to be out of the country for tax reasons and it seems an ideal time for him to go to Holland.'

With writer Tony Ingrassia back in the US, the Ziggy Stardust stage musical idea appears to have withered on the vine. Around this time, Tony Defries telexes MainMan's London office with the following message about David's control of *Diamond Dogs* masters: 'If he doesn't wish me to listen to the material or is reluctant to send me the takes please have him advise me accordingly. All of this applies equally to his notes on the Ziggy Stardust project, if indeed they exist. If they do not exist or he does not wish to part with them, please advise.'

A three-day trip to Holland to promote the new single, pick up a music industry award and check out a studio is organised, with RCA picking up the tab.

David leaves for Amsterdam with a large retinue consisting of Angie and Zowie, Tony and Mary Visconti and their baby Delaney, Freddie Burretti,[1]

Tuesday 15 January

With The Astronettes sessions wrapped inconclusively today, David and his team make headway completing five tracks: 'Rock 'n' Roll With Me', 'Candidate', 'Big Brother', 'Take It In Right' and 'Diamond Dogs' (written as 'Diamond Dawgs' on the tape box).

Wednesday 16 January

Recording 'We Are The Dead' at Olympic. During this period David contacts Tony Visconti for advice on the final mix of *Diamond Dogs*. Visconti is in the process of building a small studio at his home in Hammersmith, so David visits with the master tapes, which they listen to in the half-finished recording room.

During the *Diamond Dogs* sessions, David has covered Bruce Springsteen's 'Growin' Up', with the Faces' Ron Wood contributing guitar.

When Wood starts recording his solo debut, *I've Got My Own Album To Do,* at his home, The Wick in Richmond, with a cast of contributors[1] including Mick Jagger and Keith Richard, David is on hand to sing backing vocals with Wood to a song which will become The Rolling Stones hit 'It's Only Rock'n'Roll'.

1. Bassist Willie Weeks, who played on Wood's sessions, was recruited by David for the recording of *Young Americans* in 1974.

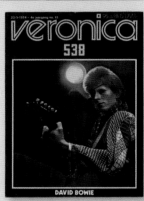

TOP LEFT: David, minus eye patch, relaxing in Amsterdam.

TOP RIGHT: Angie, Zowie and David at the Amstel Hotel in Amsterdam, February.

MIDDLE: *Veronica* magazine, March issue.

BOTTOM: German release of Mick Ronson's single 'Love Me Tender'.

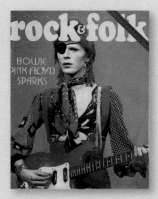

TOP: *Rock & Folk* magazine, May issue.

ABOVE: *Music Scene* magazine, February issue.

In this year...

Wednesday 10 April

LAUNCH of Mick Ronson's first and only solo UK tour in Preston. Free Trade Hall, Manchester (11 April), Odeon, Edinburgh (12), City Hall, Newcastle (13), Caird Hall, Dundee (16), Apollo, Glasgow (17), Hammersmith Odeon, London (19), Colston Hall, Bristol (22), Town Hall, Birmingham (23), Winter Gardens, Bournemouth (24), Pavilion, Hemel Hempstead (27), De Monfort Hall, Leicester (28), City Hall, Sheffield (29).

Tuesday 23 April

ART event by performance artist Chris Burden in Venice, California, centres on Burden being nailed to the top of a Volkswagen car. This contemporary interpretation of the crucifixion was referred to in the lyrics of David's 1977 song 'Joe The Lion', which appeared on "Heroes".

DJ Barry Bethell and chauffeur Jimmy James.[2]

1. By this time Burretti had his own label, Fred Of The East-End, and provided David with on- and off-stage attire for his two 1974 US tours, including the ice-blue suit worn on the cover of *David Live*. After a financial disagreement with MainMan, Burretti cut his association with David and left the US to work for Valentino in Italy. He and David never met again.

In 1978 Burretti was living in Tel-Aviv, Israel, and by 1986 in Rome, where he lost his possessions, including a prized design portfolio, in a fire. Shortly afterwards he moved to Paris to work in fashion. Burretti died of cancer in a Paris hospice on 11 May 2001, a few weeks short of his 50th birthday. He is buried in an unmarked grave.

2. Nicknamed 'Jim the Lim', James appears driving in the BBC's 1975 documentary about David's life in the US, *Cracked Actor*.

Wednesday 13 February

During the day, David is presented with the Netherland's version of the Grammy, the Edison award, for most popular male vocalist by Ad Visser, presenter of music show *Top Pop*.

After the award ceremony at the Amstel Hotel, a tipsy David is interviewed by Lutz Wauligmann for Dutch/German magazine *Muziek Expres*.[1]

Later David appears on *Top Pop* miming to 'Rebel Rebel'. He crowns his Burretti-designed pirate-style outfit with a patch over his right eye, just as rocker and acquaintance Johnny Kidd had done in the 60s.

In the evening, David and Angie attend the televised Edisons award ceremony. When pop act Tony Orlando & Dawn perform their evergreen 'Tie A Yellow Ribbon' the lead singer spots David in the audience. Orlando halts the band mid-song and asks him: "Is that you? Is that really you? The fantastic star David Bowie?"

The following day, David is at Studio L Ludolf in Nederhorst den Berg, close to Hilversum, location of the major Dutch radio station, and then returns to London.

1. Wauligmann's article was published in *Muziek Expres* in May 1974.

Friday 15 February

RCA release 'Rebel Rebel'/'Queen Bitch' single in the UK and US.[1]

⦿ **David Bowie**
David Bowie (vocal, guitar)
Alan Parker (guitar)
Herbie Flowers (bass)
Mike Garson (piano)
Aynsley Dunbar (drums)
Produced and Arranged by David Bowie

'Rebel Rebel' signals David's departure from the glam rock sound with a more ragged rock attitude influenced by The Rolling Stones and paving the way for punk.

Advertising has billed the single as a Valentine's Day release, though this plays with the truth since singles are generally sold from Friday onwards at this time.

1. In May, RCA deleted this in the US and replaced it with a different version of 'Rebel Rebel' featuring a heavily phased remix, with new lead and backing vocals and flamenco/latin-style percussion by Geoff MacCormack. On the B-side, 'Queen Bitch' was substituted by 'Lady Grinning Soul'.

Saturday 16 February

'The Man Who Sold The World' peaks at number three in the UK singles chart, giving Lulu her biggest hit since 1969's Eurovision Song Contest entry 'Boom Bang-A-Bang'.

Friday 22 February

David is at north London's Rainbow Theatre for the first of two nights there by Mick Ronson, who is making his first solo appearance to promote new album *Slaughter On 10th Avenue*. In Ronson's band are Trevor Bolder, Mike Garson,[1] Mark Pritchett on rhythm guitar and Richie Dharma on drums.

1. After touring with Ronson, Garson returned to the US where he worked with David until late 1975, appearing on that year's *Young Americans* and the *David Live* double set. Along with Ronson, he made a guest appearance on David's 1993 album *Black Tie White Noise* and contributed to such studio and live projects as David's 1993 album *The Buddha Of Suburbia*, the *Outside* album and tour (1995) and the *Earthling* album and tour (1997). Garson also appeared on the 1999 *Hours* tour (but was not on the album) and *Reality* album and tour in 2003.

Saturday 23 February

'Rebel Rebel' enters the UK singles chart at number six.

Thursday 28 February

Rolling Stone publishes Craig Copetas' interview with David and William Burroughs, whose literary style David describes as a 'wonderhouse of strange shapes, colours, tastes and feelings'.

Friday 1 March

RCA release Ronson's *Slaughter On 10th Avenue* album in the UK and US.

This features David's track 'Growing Up And I'm Fine', 'Music Is Lethal' (the Italian song to which he contributed the English lyrics) and the album's only Bowie-Ronson co-write, 'Hey Ma Get Papa'.

Having recommended the Richard Rogers title track to Ronson, David has included a hook line from the Rogers and Hart classic 'Bewitched, Bothered and Bewildered' on the *Diamond Dogs* intro 'Future Legend'.

Saturday 2 March

'Rebel Rebel' peaks at number five in the UK charts.

Sunday 3 March

David shares a box with Mick Jagger at the Theatre Royal, Drury Lane, for a Monty Python show.[1]

1. Michael Palin wrote in his diary (published in 2006) that the close presence of David and Jagger was 'rather off-putting'.

Friday 8 March

Belgian artist Guy Peellaert launches his first book, *Rock Dreams* (written by Nik Cohn), with an exhibition at the Rainbow Room[1] on the top of the six-storey glam department store Biba.[2]

Mick Jagger, who has commissioned Peellaert

to create the artwork for the front cover of The Rolling Stones' next album, *It's Only Rock 'n' Roll*, had introduced the artist's work to David, who then immediately made contact with and persuaded Peellaert to supply the sleeve for his next album too.

The night before Peellaert's show opened at Biba's, David met the artist there and collected the artwork.

David laughed as he told journalist Mia Scammell "I've got problems," as he looked at the painting of himself depicted as half-man/half-dog, but added "It's fantastic".

1. In 1984 director Julien Temple used the Rainbow Room as the cabaret venue for David's 'Blue Jean' video. Bryan Ferry's 1976 'Let's Stick Together' video was also shot there.
2. Biba's founder, Barbara Hulanicki, remembers David and Angela taking tea while watching the pink flamingos on the building's fashionable roof gardens.

Thursday 14 March

In a bid to build up the promotion of 'Rebel Rebel', Tony Defries urges the London MainMan office: 'Try and get Bowie on *Russell Harty Show* [1] before he leaves London.'

1. David didn't appear on Harty's programme again until December 1975, when he was interviewed via satellite to publicise single 'Golden Years', imminent album *Station To Station* and the world tour which started in Vancouver in February 1976.

Monday 18 March

MainMan's New York office sends a message to London about the fact that prominent US lighting and set designer Jules Fisher is visiting the UK.

Friday 22 March

RCA releases Dana Gillespie's *Weren't Born A Man*, another album from the MainMan stable.[1] This features two tracks produced by David and Ronson: 'Andy Warhol'[2] and 'Mother, Don't Be Frightened'.[3]

1. Gillespie didn't work with David again, although, during an evening socialising at her Knightsbridge apartment in 1977, she taped a makeshift jam with David and Marc Bolan. On stage she appeared in productions of *Jesus Christ Superstar*, *The Tempest* and *Tommy* and in such films as *The Hound Of The Baskervilles* (1977), *Bad Timing* (1978), *Scrubbers* (1982) and *Strapless* (1988). In recent years, Gillespie has carved out a niche as a jazz and blues singer.
2. 'Andy Warhol' was recorded by Gillespie in the summer of 1971, when Defries instructed David and Gillespie to record a clutch of songs each for a one-off promo album he used in talks with record companies.
3. 'Mother, Don't Be Frightened' was recorded during the 1971 *Hunky Dory* sessions.

Monday 25 March

David is at Olympic working with Lulu on new song 'Can You Hear Me',[1] producing and playing guitar. Tony Newman (whom David has known since he was a session player and member of 60s band Sounds Incorporated) is on drums.

A MainMan telex notes: 'David has met Jules Fisher and they are both excited about the prospect of working together.'

1. Ronson added a string arrangement to the Lulu version, which remains unreleased. David recorded a new version of the track at Sigma Sound in Philadelphia later in 1974 for inclusion on *Young Americans*.

Friday 29 March

David leaves Britain.

First he travels with Geoff MacCormack to Paris, where he is to meet film director and stage producer John Dexter[1] to discuss presentation ideas for touring *Diamond Dogs*.

David and MacCormack are initially booked for a one-night stay at the Hotel Raphael, where they meet up with Ron Wood and decide to stay for a few extra nights.

1. John Dexter (1925–1990), a National Theatre producer in the early 60s, made his directorial debut in 1969 with *The Virgin Soldiers*, in which David appeared as an extra.

Wednesday 3 April

Arriving in Cannes by train, David and MacCormack's two-night stay at the Carlton Hotel on the French Riviera is curtailed to a stopover of a couple of hours before they board the SS *France* for New York.

The liner docks at Madeira, where the pair spend a few hours ashore.

On board they dine with harmonica-playing legend Larry Adler and attend a recital he is giving during the journey.

David also gives an impromptu performance for the ship's crew in the canteen after he hears they are disappointed he isn't going to perform while on board.

"We enjoyed more than 10 songs and especially 'Space Oddity', which was the first one," recalled ship receptionist Bruno Rabreau in 2006. "A few crew members took instruments and played with him."

Thursday 11 April

The SS *France* docks in New York and David checks into the Sherry-Netherland Hotel on 5th Avenue.

Today RCA releases 'Rock 'n' Roll Suicide'/ 'Quicksand' in the UK and US as another stopgap single ahead of the release of the more commercially challenging *Diamond Dogs* on 31 May.

By the time his new album is released, David has left London far behind.

He will return to the city of his birth many times, but never again become anything more than a temporary resident. Yet the 26 years he has spent in and around the metropolis will forever inform his life and artistic world view.

TOP LEFT: Guy Peellaert, Angie and David at Peellaert's one-day exhibition at the Rainbow Room, atop Biba's department store, London.

TOP RIGHT: *Muziek Expres*, Holland.

UPPER MIDDLE: Mick Ronson's first solo album *Slaughter On 10th Avenue*.

LOWER MIDDLE: David's old flame Dana Gillespie. 'Weren't Born A Man' featured the earliest recorded version of 'Andy Warhol'.

ABOVE: Dana Gillespie's 'Andy Warhol' single.

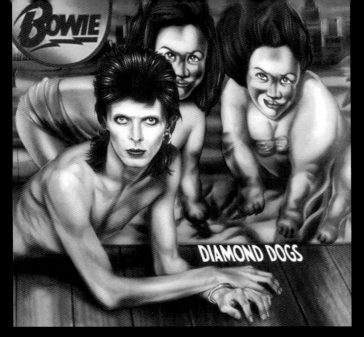

ABOVE: *Diamond Dogs* are real... Guy Peellaert's controversial and censored cover. The artwork was completed by the artist in Paris in February/March 1974.

DIAMOND DOGS   Released Friday 31 May

Side One

1. FUTURE LEGEND (Bowie) (1.07)
David Bowie (vocal, phased guitar)
Mike Garson (Mellotron, Moog)
Aynsley Dunbar (percussion)

2. DIAMOND DOGS (Bowie) (5.56)
David Bowie (vocal, phased guitar, sax)
Herbie Flowers (bass)
Tony Newman (drums)

3. SWEET THING (Bowie) (3.38)
David Bowie (vocal, guitar, sax)
Herbie Flowers (bass)
Mike Garson (piano, mellotron)
Tony Newman (drums)

4. CANDIDATE (Bowie) (2.40)
David Bowie (vocal, phased guitar, sax)
Herbie Flowers (bass)
Mike Garson (piano)
Tony Newman (drums, percussion)

5. SWEET THING (reprise) (Bowie) (2.32)
David Bowie (vocal, phased guitar, sax)
Herbie Flowers (bass)
Mike Garson (piano, Moog)
Tony Newman (drums)
Unknown session player (flute)

6. REBEL REBEL (Bowie) (4.30)
David Bowie (vocal, guitar)
Alan Parker (guitar)
Herbie Flowers (bass)
Mike Garson (piano)
Aynsley Dunbar (drums)

Side Two

1. ROCK 'N' ROLL WITH ME (Bowie/Peace) (4.02)
David Bowie (vocal, guitar, sax)
Alan Parker (guitar)
Herbie Flowers (bass)
Mike Garson (piano)
Aynsley Dunbar (drums)

2. WE ARE THE DEAD (Bowie) (4.54)
David Bowie (vocal, guitar, sax)
Herbie Flowers (bass)
Mike Garson (keyboards)
Aynsley Dunbar (drums)

3. 1984 (Bowie) (3.27)
David Bowie (vocal, guitar, sax)
Alan Parker (guitar)
Herbie Flowers (bass)
Mike Garson (harpsichord, Moog)
Aynsley Dunbar (drums)
Session orchestra

4. BIG BROTHER (Bowie) (3.20)
David Bowie (vocal, guitar, sax, percussion)
Herbie Flowers (bass)
Mike Garson (Mellotron, Moog)
Aynsley Dunbar (drums)

5. CHANT OF THE EVER CIRCLING SKELETAL FAMILY (Bowie) (2.04)
David Bowie (vocal, guitar, sax)
Herbie Flowers (bass)
Aynsley Dunbar (drums/percussion)

Written, arranged and produced by David Bowie
Recorded at Olympic and Island Studios and
Studio L Ludolf, Hilversum, Holland
All tracks mixed by David Bowie and Tony Visconti
except tracks 6 (Side One) and 1 & 2 (Side Two)
mixed by David Bowie and Keith Harwood
'1984' string arrangements by Tony Visconti
Artwork by Guy Peellaert
A MainMan Production
(RCA APLI 0576) – UK   (RCA CPLI 0576) – US

RIGHT: Guy Peellaert hands David the completed cover artwork for *Diamond Dogs*, 7 March.

FAR RIGHT: Terry O'Neill's photoshoot was used by Peellaert as the basis for his cover design.

The album's original April release date was delayed until 31 May.

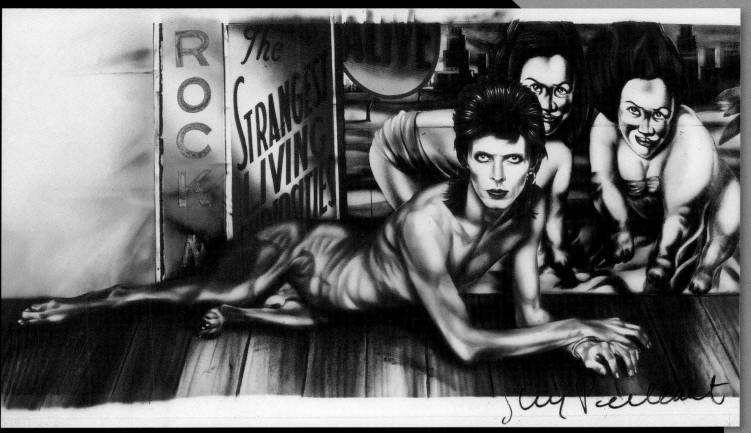

Alzoria and Johanna
WORLD'S STRANGEST FAMILY
Cavalcade Variety Show
1116 SURF AVENUE
CONEY ISLAND, N. Y.

TOP: The cover concept was initially based on a photo of Josephine Baker. Terry O'Neill photographed David in Great Marlborough Street in a similar pose for Guy Peellaert to base his artwork on. ABOVE LEFT: Josephine Baker, photographed by designer Paul Colin in Paris in 1926. ABOVE MIDDLE AND RIGHT: Coney Island Cavalcade Variety artistes Alzoria Lewis (right) and Johanna Dickens. Peellaert would extend their strange headwear and make it bright red hair to match David's, turning them into the Diamond Dog figures on the right of the sleeve.

Diamond Dogs, the title David bestowed upon the album after George Orwell's estate had refused to allow him to call it *1984*, was a brilliant flash of inspiration and has since been appropriated for film and book titles, hard-man movie characters, band names, company identities, and any number of other projects.

Even though the original 1949 source material was duly abridged, songs like '1984', 'Big Brother' and 'We Are The Dead' deftly captured the atmosphere of Orwell's work. From the ruin of an abandoned project David realigned his material into a fresh, complete and consistent composite. The result was more Bowie than Orwell and far more of a concept album than anything else he had created, including *Ziggy Stardust*.

The process was also cathartic, as David stripped away much of what had previously surrounded him, including musicians, studio and producer. He felt confident enough to take the producer's helm alone and also, without Mick Ronson, arranged every song, though with some help on '1984'. Again without Ronson, David played as much lead guitar as he could manage, as well as sax, and took on the majority of vocals. The strong impression given by this sudden shift from the familiar was that he felt there was a lot to prove, that he wasn't reliant on success with, in particular, Ronson and Ken Scott. He wasn't even reliant on a studio,

> 'Maybe it'll turn out to be *The Dark Side Of The Moon* of 1974. Maybe it's actually *The Dark Side Of Aladdin Sane*.'
> Ian MacDonald
> *NME*

even one as successful for him as Trident.

Most of the album was recorded at Olympic, the studio a short distance from David's Oakley Street residence. But this studio was also where engineer Keith Harwood[1] was based. He had recently worked with both Led Zeppelin and The Rolling Stones (he had just engineered on *It's Only Rock 'n' Roll*). He would prove the perfect soundman for David's continued fascination with the Stones, but would also help to fashion a sound that was uniquely David's.

After recording some of David's Tower Theatre Philadelphia performances in July 74, Harwood oversaw the final mixing and additional overdubs of Led Zeppelin's *Physical Graffiti*, rounding off an incredible year of classic recordings. His last work was in New York engineering the Stones' *Love You Live* mixing sessions in early 1977, shortly before his death. That album was dedicated to his memory.

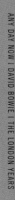

Certain parts of *Diamond Dogs* were recorded at Island Studios in Notting Hill – where David had worked in 1970 – and a small amount for tax reasons in Holland in Studio L Ludolf (which later became Bullet Sound Studios and is in Nederhorst den Berg, close to Hilversum).

David was encouraged to visit the studio because Mick Jagger had worked there, though it was booked for just one day so, any recording was limited. Trident Studios isn't mentioned in the credits, although 'Rebel Rebel' was recorded at his one-time favourite facility over Christmas of 1973.

Alan Parker[2] added guitar to *Diamond Dogs*, in particular on the ambitious 'Big Brother'. David also called in Keith Christmas, who had last sessioned for him on his 1969 *David Bowie* LP. But *Diamond Dogs* would predominantly feature electric guitar, which Christmas wasn't used to playing, but he did supply some guitar parts which David liked and may have absorbed into the album.

Later in the year, David invited Christmas to New York to rehearse for his live band. The two socialised a great deal but Keith couldn't adjust to the band (again because of the need for electric guitar) and returned to the UK.

Aynsley Dunbar was retained after his work on *Pin Ups*. Dunbar, a prolific session man, flew back and forth from LA each week to work with David while continuing his work with Frank Zappa and Flo and Eddie.

Tony Newman (ex Sounds Incorporated) would also session on the album, and with Herbie Flowers would later tour Canada and the US with David.

David's 'Future Legend' opens the record with a howl. Its bleak narrative is mixed with the distorted hook line from 'Bewitched, Bothered and Bewildered' (a popular show tune from the 1940 Rodgers and Hart musical *Pal Joey*). While forgotten, vicious children wail and taunt from the shadows with a premonitory threat, the grim scene is set and the cast introduced.

The live audience at the start of 'Diamond Dogs' was taken from the 1974 Faces live album *Coast To Coast: Overture And Beginners* (the 'Hey' sung over the opening guitar intro is actually Rod Stewart's). This song, together with 'Future Legend', proves to be the album's manifesto. Its scratchy, fractured guitar style is full of portent and invitation and will prove an inspiration for an army of young musicians in waiting.[3]

Having just met William Burroughs, David incorporated his (and Brion Gysin's) famous 'cut-up' technique in his own writing style to brilliant effect. This is particularly evident on 'Sweet Thing/Candidate/Sweet Thing (reprise)'. The song is packed with allegorical images and juxtaposed references, including the French Revolution (les tricoteuses),[4] Perry Como ('On The Street Where You Live'), The Beatles

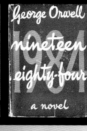

TOP LEFT: David and Great Dane, photographed by Terry O'Neill. TOP RIGHT: Guy Peellaert's original inner gatefold artwork. This was later used as a promotional poster instead. TOP MIDDLE: Tod Browning's 1932 shock film *Freaks* contained all manner of real-life 'strangest living curiosities' and was notably namechecked on the album's title track. TOP MIDDLE RIGHT: Alzora Lewis, depicted as one of the Diamond Dogs on the sleeve. MIDDLE BELOW LEFT: David discreetly included a copy of Walter Ross's 1958 novel, *The Immortal* in some of the photos. Inspired by the life of James Dean, David was already setting his sights towards Hollywood. MIDDLE BELOW AND RIGHT: George Orwell and the novel that provided the early inspiration for *Diamond Dogs*. ABOVE: Leee Black Childers original montage, as featured in the album's inner gatefold.

('Let It Be'), and Rodgers and Hammerstein ('On Broadway'), as well as the more obvious Charlie Manson/Cassius Clay namechecks.

Side One ends with the album's biggest hit, 'Rebel Rebel', its rough garage rock hook line a gift to the composer, his sexually equivocal lyrics maintaining his media infamy. 'You've got your mother in a whirl She's not sure if you're a boy or a girl...'

Opening Side Two, 'Rock 'n' Roll With Me' began life as some basic chords played by Geoff MacCormack on the piano at Oakley Street, which David immediately connected with and expanded. Even though the song's lyrics only partly link it with the overall theme, its pathos and delivery suit the sombre mood perfectly.

The remaining tracks formed the bulk of David's original Orwell concept: 'We Are The Dead', '1984', and 'Big Brother' are all titles directly appropriated from his novel but cleverly woven with David's own inspired wordplay.

Like 'Sweet Thing',[5] 'We Are The Dead' is based on the cut-up technique and is centred on a memorable line by Orwell's protagonist, Winston Smith, in a desperate conversation with secret lover Julia. Realising the end is near, he tells her 'We are the dead...', David eloquently prefacing the legend, 'Because of all we've seen, because of all we've said...'

'Chant Of The Ever Circling Skeletal Family' concludes the album with echoes of William Golding's *Lord Of The Flies*, the primal whoops and mantras of the malnourished Diamond Dogs skilfully realised in full liturgy, with the boys working themselves up into a shamanistic frenzy. Without saying anything of substance, David conjures up fire, ritual and human sacrifice and leaves us with an apocalyptic vision in which mankind has returned to the beginning of time. Its trance-induced climax repeats a double message as one voice shouts 'Riot!', the other 'Bro' (uniquely, listeners either hear one message or the other but rarely both).

If he felt under great pressure to prove himself, it didn't show. *Diamond Dogs* is arguably David's most significant album, a pivotal work and the most 'solo' album he has ever made.

For the cover, he did not use any of the photographers who had provided images for his recent albums but instead plumped for the then cult artist Guy Peellaert, whose collection of airbrushed and manipulated images *Rock Dreams* was making waves as *Diamond Dogs* was completed.

In the spring of 1974, David invited Peellaert to a breakfast meeting at his hotel, then persuaded the Belgian to accompany him to a photo session with Terry O'Neill at a hired photographic studio in Great Marlborough Street, close to Liberty store.

The *Diamond Dogs* sleeve concept was partly based on a photo of the black American singer, dancer and actress Josephine Baker

ABOVE LEFT: Guy Peellaert (1934–2008) in his central Paris studio in 2000. Peellaert said of David in 1974 "I thought he'd be an image, but he's human and very very warm. I was terribly nervous of meeting him but he only looks mysterious." TOP RIGHT: Peellaert's finished design for The Rolling Stones' *It's Only Rock 'n' Roll*. Their artwork was started before David's commission and came out after *Diamond Dogs*. ABOVE RIGHT: Detail from Peellaert's *Rock Dreams* book cover. BELOW: A major hand-painted promotion for *Diamond Dogs* in Los Angeles, made to coincide with David's week-long run at the city's impressive Universal Ampitheater, September 1974.

taken in Paris in 1926. At the studio, David was photographed in the pose adopted by Baker in that shot.

In some shots (intended as the basis for the inner sleeve), there is a book placed by David: *The Immortal* by Walter Ross, a 1958 fiction inspired by the life of James Dean.

A Great Dane was included in the shoot (O'Neill didn't arrange for the dog and thinks that either David or Tony Defries must have). Once the session was over, David made his move and asked if Peellaert could work with the photographs and create for him a unique cover design, just like he was doing for the Stones.

By this time, David had storyboarded his concept for the sleeve: a *Rock Dreams*-style painting combining his head and torso with the dog's hindquarters.

"David tricked me into doing the cover artwork," said Peellaert in 2000. "It was only when we were at the session that he finally asked me if I would do a painting for him. The idea was so interesting I couldn't refuse."

Returning to his studio near the Bastille in Paris, Peellaert used the O'Neill photographs to transform David into a lithe, anthropomorphic *Island Of Dr Moreau*[6] type creature.

Peellaert's studio was crammed with a vast library of periodicals, projectors and enlargers. It also housed large, carefully indexed volumes of visual source material and memorabilia, collected over many years for his stylish and particularly impressive photo-realistic paintings.

Although already quite a size, the dog was still juvenile and was feisty and difficult to control. "He launched himself at me a few times whilst I was shooting," said O'Neill in 2010. "He was being playful but he was a large animal. David calmly reined him in. It was quite eventful."

In these particular photos, David wears the Burretti outfit he had recently worn when accepting his Edison Award in Amsterdam. Burretti's designs were inspired by the costumes worn by the colourful flamenco rock band Carmen, as was David's gaucho hat.

The *Diamond Dogs* backdrop mixed fairground and freak show imagery, based on a book owned by Peelleart about Coney Island Pleasure Park. The grinning flame-haired 'dogs' seated behind David were interpretations of Coney Island freak show performers Alzoria Lewis (the Turtle Girl) and Johanna Dickens (the Bear Girl). Billed as the 'World's Strangest Family', they were a feature of the Island's

Cavalcade Variety Show.

The *Diamond Dogs* cover artwork caused a stir because, of all things, the dog's genitalia. Peellaert's original artwork included the animal's practically unnoticeable penis, and some covers were initially printed uncensored (and now exchange hands for considerable amounts). But RCA ceased production and airbrushed out the offending item, in the process making the most of the ensuing publicity.

Other cover changes included the replacement of the front cover badge legend 'Alive' (the traditional freak-show advertisement for live human acts) with a stylistic and acceptable 'Bowie' design.

There was also discussion – instigated by David – that his figure should have a dog collar. He was keen that the artwork "be altered as little as possible" and preferred "a slap-on dog tag" sticker, but this was deemed too expensive.

One of the shots from the O'Neill session of David with the jumping dog was considered for the inner gatefold. In the event, an apocalyptic photo-montage by David's friend Leee Black Childers occupied this space.

1. Keith Harwood died in a drug-induced car accident in New York in 1977.

2. One of the guitars Alan Parker used on *Diamond Dogs* was Jimi Hendrix's vintage Epiphone FT79 acoustic. Hendrix had given it to Parker as a gift in 1970. In 2001 it was sold at auction for £55,000.

3. *Diamond Dogs* was often cited by punk bands as an important inspiration. Manchester-formed group Slaughter and The Dogs took their name partly from *Diamond Dogs* and partly from Mick Ronson's *Slaughter On 10th Avenue*.

4. Les tricoteuses were the women who sat around the guillotine knitting during the French Reign of Terror in the 18th century. The women were paid to give their casual deliberation on the accused, which usually ended in execution.

5. In 2004, British SAS soldier turned author Andy McNab chose 'Sweet Thing' as his one musical luxury items on BBC Radio's *Desert Island Discs*.

6. 'Not to go on all-fours; that is the Law. Are we not men?' HG Wells. *The Island Of Dr Moreau* (1886).

APPENDIX 1962-73

LIVE PERFORMANCES

THE KONRADS
16.6.62 Bromley Tech School
10/11.62 Croydon, Shirley Parish Hall
17.11.62 Cudham Village Hall
62/63 Chislehurst, Ye Olde Stationmaster
.63 Farningham Country Club
15.6.63 St George's Church Hall
7.63 Biggin Hill, Hillsiders
21.9.63 Orpington Civic Hall
24.10.63 West Wickham, Wickham Hall
2.11.63 Croydon, Shirley Parish Hall
24.11.63 Catford, Lewisham Town Hall
14.12.63 Biggin Hill, Hillsiders
31.12.63 West Wickham, Justin Hall

**DAVE'S REDS AND BLUES/
THE HOOKER BROTHERS**
63/64 Bromley, The Bromel Club

THE KING BEES
4.64 London, Jack Of Clubs, private party
7.6.64 London, The Bedsitter
.64 West Wickham, Justin Hall
.64 London, Bricklayers Arms

DAVIE JONES AND THE MANISH BOYS
25.7.64 USAF Chicksands, Beds
26.7.64 Twickenham, Eel Pie Island
1.8.64 Caterham, Valley Hotel
17.8.64 Deal, Astor Theatre
19.8.64 Twickenham, Eel Pie Island
30.8.64 Ipswich, Savoy Ballroom
2.9.64 Twickenham, Eel Pie Island
9.9.64 Braintree, RAF Wethersfield
19.9.64 London, The Scene
21.9.64 Chatham, Invicta Ballroom
23.9.64 Chatham, Medway County YC
25.9.64 Romford, Willow Rooms
26.9.64 London, Acton Town Hall
28.9.64 London, The Jolly Gardeners
29.9.64 Isleworth, Middlesex
2.10.64 Borehamwood, Herts
7.10.64 Twickenham, Eel Pie Island
9.10.64 London, Finchley
10.10.64 Newmarket, Suffolk
13.10.64 London, Putney
17.10.64 Lee-on-the-Solent, Tower Ballroom
21.10.64 Chatham, Medway County YC
25.10.64 Lee-on-the-Solent, Tower Ballroom
31.10.64 West Wickham, Justin Hall
6.11.64 London, Marquee Club
7.11.64 Conservative Hall, Beds
8.11.64 Twickenham, Eel Pie Island
13.11.64 St Leonards-on-Sea, Witch Doctor
14.11.64 Maidstone, The Royal Star
20.11.64 West Wickham, Justin Hall

DAVIE JONES AND THE MANISH BOYS
On tour with Gene Pitney, The Kinks, etc
1.12.64 Wigan, ABC Cinema (2 shows)
2.12.64 Hull, ABC Cinema (2 shows)
3.12.64 Edinburgh, ABC Cinema (2 shows)
4.12.64 Stockton, ABC Cinema (2 shows)
5.12.64 Newcastle, City Hall (2 shows)
6.12.64 Scarborough, Futurist (2 shows)
(Tour ends)

10.12.64 London, Marquee Club
13.12.64 Conservative Club, Beds
17.12.64 Brighton, Brighton College
18.12.64 Hertford, Corn Exchange
19.12.64 Maidstone, Corn Exchange
31.12.64 London, Finchley
9.1.65 Hitchin, Hermitage Ballroom
18.1.65 Welwyn Garden City, Herts
23.1.65 Maidstone, Star Hotel
30.1.65 St Leonards, The Witch Doctor
6.2.65 Bletchley, Buckinghamshire
8.2.65 London, Marquee Club
13.2.65 Dunstable, California Ballroom
15.2.65 Welwyn Garden City
17.2.65 Chatham, Medway County YC
20.2.65 Boston, Gliderdrome
4.3.65 Cambridgeshire, RAF Wyton
6.3.65 Sevenoaks, Kent
8.3.65 London, Mayfair Hotel, private party
10.3.65 Bromley, The Bromel Club
13.3.65 Coleford, Royal British Legion Hall
14.3.65 Cromer, The Olympia Ballroom
16.3.65 Southsea, Southsea Pier
20.3.65 Newmarket, Suffolk
11.4.65 Trent Bridge, Nottingham
24.4.65 Bletchley, Bucks

DAVIE JONES AND THE LOWER THIRD
1.6.65 Birmingham, The Tower Ballroom
4.6.65 Bournemouth, The Pavilion
11.6.65 Brighton, The Starlight Rooms
10.7.65 Bournemouth, The Pavilion
14.7.65 London, Bata Clan
17.7.65 St Leonards-on-Sea, Witch Doctor
23.7.65 Bournemouth, The Pavilion
24.7.65 Isle of Wight, Ventnor Winter Gdns
25.7.65 Bournemouth, The Pavilion
30.7.65 Bournemouth, The Pavilion
31.7.65 Isle of Wight, Ventnor Winter Gdns
1.8.65 Bournemouth, The Pavilion
6.8.65 Bournemouth, The Pavilion
7.8.65 Isle of Wight, Ventnor Winter Gardens
19.8.65 London, 100 Club
20.8.65 Bournemouth, The Pavilion
26.8.65 London, 100 Club
4.9.65 Cheltenham, Blue Moon
5.9.65 Bournemouth, The Pavilion
7.9.65 London, 100 Club
14.9.65 London, 100 Club
21.9.65 London, 100 Club
8.10.65 London, Marquee Club
31.10.65 Portsmouth, The Birdcage
5.11.65 London, Marquee Club
13.11.65 Brighton, The 'New' Barn
19.11.65 London, Marquee Club
10.12.65 London, Marquee Club
11.12.65 Brighton, Florida Ballroom
31.12.65 Paris, Golf-Drouot
1.1.66 Paris, Golf-Drouot (matinee)
1.1.66 Paris, Bus Palladium (2 shows)
2.1.66 Paris, Golf-Drouot (2 shows)
7.1.66 London, Marquee Club
8.1.66 London, Marquee Club
19.1.66 Birmingham, Cedar Club
28.1.66 Stevenage, Town Hall
29.1.66 London, Marquee Club (afternoon)
Bromley, The Bromel Club
1.66 Harrow, Newmarket and Carlisle

DAVID BOWIE AND THE BUZZ
10.2.66 Leicester, Mecca Ballroom
11.2.66 London, Marquee Club
12.2.66 London, Marquee Club (afternoon)
12.2.66 Stevenage, Bowes Lyon House
15.2.66 Bournemouth, The Pavilion
19.2.66 Crawley, The Boys' Club
25.2.66 Southampton, The Kasbah Club
26.2.66 Chelmsford, The Corn Exchange
28.2.66 Eastbourne, Club Continental
4.3.66 Chislehurst Caves, Kent
5.3.66 Nottingham, Rowing Club
10.3.66 Peterborough, Cambs
12.3.66 Brighton, One-O-One (afternoon)
12.3.66 Newmarket, Suffolk
18.3.66 High Wycombe, Target Club
(afternoon promo)

18.3.66 London, Marquee Club (evening)
21.3.66 Basingstoke, The Galaxy Club
25.3.66 Wealdstone, Railway Hotel
3.4.66 Dundee, Top10 Club
4.4.66 Hawick, Scottish Borders
7.4.66 Venue unknown
8.4.66 Venue unknown
9.4.66 London, Marquee Club (afternoon)
10.4.66 London, Marquee Club
(Showboat) (afternoon)
14.4.66 London, Marquee Club
15.4.66 Greenford, Starlight Ballroom
17.4.66 London, Marquee Club
(Showboat) (afternoon)
23.4.66 Dunstable, California Ballroom
24.4.66 London, Marquee Club
(Showboat) (afternoon)
25.4.66 Chester, Wallaby Club
30.4.66 Newmarket, Drill Hall
1.5.66 London, Marquee Club
(Showboat) (afternoon)
7.5.66 Leeds, University of Leeds
8.5.66 London, Marquee Club
(Showboat) (afternoon)
14.5.66 London, Hampstead, private party
15.5.66 London, Marquee Club
(Showboat) afternoon performance
20.5.66 Birmingham College of Education
22.5.66 London, Marquee Club
(Showboat) (afternoon)
23.5.66 Dunstable, California Ballroom
29.5.66 Blackpool South Pier
3.6.66 Ramsgate, Pleasurama
4.6.66 Cambridge, Dorothy Ballroom
5.6.66 London, Marquee Club
(Showboat) (afternoon)
6.6.66 Dunstable, California Ballroom
10.6.66 Catford, Co-Op Hall
11.6.66 Dunstable, California Ballroom
12.6.66 London, Marquee Club
(last Showboat) (afternoon)
18.6.66 Thetford, Norfolk
19.6.66 Brands Hatch, Big 'L' meeting
20.6.66 Dunstable, California Ballroom
25.6.66 Lowestoft, Suffolk
27.6.66 Dunstable, California Ballroom
2.7.66 Warrington, Lion Hotel
3.7.66 London, Marquee Club (evening)
9.7.66 Cheltenham, Blue Moon
15.7.66 Loughton Youth Centre, Essex
16.7.66 Brighton, Club One-O-One
17.7.66 London, The Playboy Club
23.7.66 Chepstow, Monmouthshire
24.7.66 Hassocks, Downs Hotel
30.7.66 London, Marquee Club (afternoon)
Bishops Stortford, Rhodes Centre (evening)
31.7.66 Nottingham, Rowing Club
4.8.66 Southampton, Adam and Eve
12.8.66 Leicester, Latin Quarter
13.8.66 Coventry Air Display, Baginton
18.8.66 Southampton, Adam and Eve
21.8.66 London, Marquee Club (evening)
26.8.66 Ramsgate, Coronation Ballroom
27.8.66 Wembley, Starlite Ballroom
28.8.66 London, Marquee Club (afternoon)
3.9.66 St Leonards-on-Sea, Witch Doctor
4.9.66 Great Yarmouth, Britannia Pier
6.9.66 Grays, The Civic Hall
10.9.66 Norwich, Orford Arms Jazz Cellar
11.9.66 London, Marquee Club (afternoon)
Gillingham, The Central Hotel (evening)
12.9.66 Welwyn Garden City, Community
Centre
15.9.66 Southampton, Adam and Eve
16.9.66 Hanley, Stoke-on-Trent, The Place
17.9.66 Lyme Regis, The Ballroom
22.9.66 Southampton, Adam and Eve
23.9.66 London, Marquee Club
& Ramsgate, Coronation Ballroom
24.9.66 Ashford, 2B's Club
25.9.66 London, Marquee Club
27.9.66 Southampton, Adam and Eve
30.9.66 Wimbledon, Southlands College
1.10.66 Wembley, Starlite Ballroom
6.10.66 Southampton, Adam and Eve
8.10.66 Catford, Witch Doctor Club

11.10.66 Aberystwyth University, Dyfed
21.10.66 Newmarket, Drill Hall
22.10.66 Brighton, University of Sussex
27.10.66 Southampton, Adam and Eve
28.10.66 Eastbourne, Catacombe
29.10.66 Wembley, Starlite Ballroom
(band only)
& Bognor Regis, Shoreline Club (solo)
12.11.66 Bournemouth, Le Disc A Go Go
13.11.66 London, Marquee Club
19.11.66 Cromer, Royal Links Ballroom
26.11.66 Gosport, The Community Centre
27.11.66 King's Lynn, The Maid's Head
2.12.66 Shrewsbury, The Severn Club
3.12.66 Starlite Ballroom (solo)
10.12.66 Eastbourne, Expresso Club (solo)
17.12.66 Lewes Town Hall (solo)

RIOT SQUAD & SOLO
21.1.67 London, Bricklayers Arms (guest)
28.3.67 Harrow, Kodak Social Club
13.4.67 London, Tiles Club
4.67 Maldon, Swan Hotel, Down Beat Club
18.6.67 Brands Hatch, Big 'L' meeting
(solo guest)
19.11.67 London, Dorchester Hotel (solo)

**Pierrot In Turquoise
with LINDSAY KEMP THEATRE GROUP**
28.12.67 Oxford, New Theatre
3,4,5.1.68 Whitehaven, Rose Hill
5-16.3.68 London, Mercury Theatre
26-30.3.68 London, Palmers Green,
Intimate

DAVID BOWIE
30.4.68 London, Nags Head (mime)
19.5.68 London, Gancalf's Garden Benefit
(mime)
3.6.68 London, Royal Festival Hall (mime)
1.8.68 London, Marquee Club (solo)

**TURQUOISE
with Hermione Farthingale and Tony Hill**
14.9.68 London, Camden, The Roundhouse
16.9.68 London, Wigmore Hall
20.10.68 London, Hampstead, Country Club

**FEATHERS
with Hermione Farthingale and John
Hutchinson**
17.11.68 London, Hampstead, Country Club
6.12.68 London, Covent Garden, Arts Lab
7.12.68 Brighton, University of Sussex
24.12.68 Falmouth, The Magician's
Workshop (solo)
26.12.68 Falmouth, The Magician's
Workshop (solo)
11.2.69 Brighton, University of Sussex
(with Hutch)

DAVID BOWIE – Tyrannosaurus Rex Tour
(15.2.69-8.3.69) (solo support)
15.2.69 Birmingham, Town Hall (mime)
16.2.69 Croydon, Fairfield Halls (mime)
21.2.69 Manchester, Magic Village
(solo acoustic)
22.2.69 Manchester, Free Trade Hall (mime)
23.2.69 Bristol, Colston Hall (did not appear)
1.3.69 Philharmonic Hall, Liverpool (mime)
8.3.69 Brighton, Dome (mime)

DAVID BOWIE and HUTCH
11.3.69 London, University of Surrey
15.3.69 Guildford, Surrey
21.3.69 Lincoln, Bishop Grosseteste College

DAVID BOWIE
(Arts Lab, occasionally with backing
musicians)
29.4.69 London, Ealing College
4.5.69 Beckenham Arts Lab
6.5.69 London, Hampstead, Three
Horseshoes
11.5.69 Beckenham Arts Lab
18.5.69 Beckenham Arts Lab
22.5.69 London, Wigmore Hall
(dance/mime)
25.5.69 Beckenham Arts Lab

1.6.69 Beckenham Arts Lab
8.6.69 Beckenham Arts Lab
11.6.69 Cambridge, Open Air Festival
15.6.69 London, Marquee Club
29.6.69 Beckenham Arts Lab
6.7.69 Beckenham Arts Lab
13.7.69 Beckenham Arts Lab
15.7.69 Hounslow Arts Lab, White Bear pub
(+ mime)
20.7.69 Beckenham Arts Lab
26.7.69 Malta Song Festival, Hilton Hotel
27.7.69 Malta Song Festival, Hilton Hotel
1.8.69 Monsummano Terme, Italian Song
Festival
2.8.69 Monsummano Terme, Italian Song
Festival
3.8.69 Beckenham Arts Lab
10.8.69 Beckenham Arts Lab
16.8.69 Beckenham Free Festival
17.8.69 Beckenham Arts Lab evening
22.8.69 Wolverhampton, Catacombs Club
(mime) (2 performances)
24.8.69 Beckenham Arts Lab
31.8.69 Beckenham Arts Lab evening
9.69 London Whitechapel Hospital Medical
College
7.9.69 Beckenham Arts Lab evening
13.9.69 Bromley open air pop concert,
Library Gardens (compèred and solo)
14.9.69 Beckenham Arts Lab evening
21.9.69 Beckenham Arts Lab evening
23.9.69 London, Hampstead,
Three Horseshoes Folk Club
24.9.69 Beckenham Arts Lab evening
28.9.69 Beckenham Arts Lab evening
1.10.69 Bromley, Bal Tabarin
5.10.69 Beckenham Arts Lab evening

CHANGES '69 TOUR (8.10.69-26.10.69)
8.10.69 Coventry Theatre (Changes '69)
9.10.69 Leeds Town Hall (Changes '69)
10.10.69 Birmingham Town Hall
(Changes '69)
11.10.69 Brighton Dome (Changes '69)
12.10.69 Beckenham Arts Lab evening
13.10.69 Bristol Colston Hall (Changes '69)
17.10.69 Exeter, Tiffany's
19.10.69 Birmingham, Rebecca's Club
21.10.69 London, Queen Elizabeth Hall
(Changes '69)
23.10.69 Edinburgh, Usher Hall
(Changes '69)
25.10.69 Manchester, Odeon (Changes '69)
26.10.69 Liverpool, Empire (Changes '69)
31.10.69 Gravesend, General Gordon
and Gillingham, Aurora Hotel

DAVID BOWIE backed by JUNIOR'S EYES
(& solo appearances)
(mini tour 7.11.69-20.11.69)
7.11.69 Perth, Salutation Hotel, Blue Web
8.11.69 Auchinleck, Community Centre
(afternoon)
Kilmarnock, Grand Hall (evening)
9.11.69 Dunfermline, Kinema Ballroom
14.11.69 Kirkcaldy, Adam Smith Hall
(evening) (solo)
Edinburgh, Frisco's Club (midnight) (solo)
15.11.69 Dundee, Caird Hall (solo)
18.11.69 Croydon, Gun Tavern, Egg Arts Lab
19.11.69 Brighton Dome (solo)
20.11.69 London, South Bank, Purcell Room

DAVID BOWIE solo and Arts Lab appearances
21.11.69 Devizes, Poperama (solo)
23.11.69 Beckenham Arts Lab
26.11.69 Bromley, Ripley Centre
27.11.69 Beckenham Arts Lab
30.11.69 London, Palladium (solo)
14.12.69 Beckenham Arts Lab
21.12.69 Beckenham Arts Lab (Christmas
Party)
28.12.69 Beckenham Arts Lab
4.1.70 Beckenham Arts Lab
8.1.70 London, Speakeasy
11.1.70 Beckenham Arts Lab
15.1.79 Beckenham Arts Lab

18.1.70 Beckenham Arts Lab
22.1.70 Beckenham Arts Lab
25.1.70 Beckenham Arts Lab

DAVID BOWIE
(with Tony Visconti & Tex Johnson*)
30.1.70 Aberdeen University*
3.2.70 London, Marquee Club
8.2.70 Beckenham Arts Lab
12.2.70 Beckenham Arts Lab
15.2.70 Beckenham Arts Lab
19.2.70 Beckenham Arts Lab

DAVID BOWIE and HYPE
22.2.70 London, Camden, Roundhouse
28.2.70 Basildon Arts Lab
1.3.70 Beckenham Arts Lab evening
3.3.70 Houslow Arts Lab, White Bear
5.3.70 Beckenham Arts Lab
6.3.70 Hull University
7.3.70 London, Regent St Polytechnic
11.3.70 London, Camden, Roundhouse
12.3.70 London, Royal Albert Hall (solo)
13.3.70 Sunderland, Locarno Ballroom
14.3.70 University of Surrey, Guildford (solo)
19.3.70 Beckenham Arts Lab
30.3.70 Croydon, Star Hotel
12.4.70 Harrogate Theatre (2 solo sets)
27.4.70 Stockport, Poco a Poco (solo)
10.5.70 London, Talk of the Town (solo)
21.5.70 Scarborough Penthouse
16.6.70 Cambridge University
4.7.70 Bromley, Queen's Mead Rec Ground
5.7.70 London, Camden, Roundhouse
18.7.70 Southend-on-Sea, Fickle Pickle
1.8.70 Southend-on-Sea, Rock With Shelter

DAVID BOWIE – US Promotional Tour
23.1.71 Arrive Dulles Airport, Washington (pm)
24.1.71 Washington/Baltimore
25.1.71 Train from Washington/Baltimore to
Philadelphia (pm)
26.1.71 Philadelphia
27.1.71 Train to New York (am)
28-30.1.71 New York
31.1.71 Fly to Boston (pm)
1.2.71 Fly to Detroit (pm)
3.2.71 Fly to Minneapolis (am)
4.2.71 Fly to Chicago O'Hare (am)
5.2.71 Chicago
6.2.71 Fly back to Detroit (am)
Return to Chicago (pm)
7.2.71 Chicago
8.2.71 Drive to Milwaukee (am)
Fly to Atlanta (pm)
9.2.71 Atlanta
10.2.71 Fly to Houston (am)
Fly to San Francisco (pm)
11-12.2.71 San Francisco
13.2.71 Fly to Los Angeles (pm)
14.2.71 Los Angeles, private party
(solo performance)
15-18.2.71 Los Angeles
18.2.71 Arrive back in UK (am)

DAVID BOWIE with Mick Ronson
20.6.71 Glastonbury Fayre, Somerset
21.7.71 London, Hampstead Country Club
(with additional musicians)
1.8.71 London, Marquee Club
11.8.71 London, Hampstead Country Club
25.9.71 Aylesbury, Borough Assembly Hall
(whole band)
26.9.71 London, Camden, Roundhouse
4.10.71 London, Seymour Hall

DAVID BOWIE and THE SPIDERS FROM MARS
UK Tour I (29.1.72-15.7.72)
29.1.72 Aylesbury, Borough Assembly Hall
10.2.72 London, Tolworth, Toby Jug
11.2.72 High Wycombe, Town Hall
12.2.72 London, Imperial College Union
14.2.72 Brighton Dome, East Sussex
18.2.72 Sheffield University Rag
23.2.72 Chichester College, West Sussex
24.2.72 London, Wallington Public Hall
25.2.72 London, Avery Hill College
26.2.72 Sutton Coldfield, Belfry Hotel

1.3.72 Bristol University
4.3.72 Southsea, South Parade Pier
7.3.72 Yeovil College, Somerset
11.3.72 Southampton, Guild Hall
14.3.72 Bournemouth, Chelsea Village
17.3.72 Birmingham, Town Hall
24.3.72 Newcastle, Mayfair Ballroom
17.4.72 Gravesend, Civic Hall
20.4.72 Harlow, The Playhouse
21.4.72 Manchester, Free Trade Hall
30.4.72 Plymouth, Guild Hall
3.5.72 Aberystwyth University, Wales
6.5.72 London, Kingston Polytechnic
7.5.72 Hemel Hempstead, Pavilion
11.5.72 Worthing, Assembly Hall
12.5.72 Polytechnic of Central London
13.5.72 Slough Technical College
19.5.72 Oxford, Polytechnic
25.5.72 Bournemouth, Chelsea Village
27.5.72 Epsom, Ebbisham Hall
2.6.72 Newcastle, City Hall
3.6.72 Liverpool Stadium
4.6.72 Preston Public Hall
6.6.72 Bradford, St George's Hall
7.6.72 Sheffield, City Hall
8.6.72 Middlesbrough, Town Hall
13.6.72 Bristol, Colston Hall
16.6.72 Torquay, Town Hall
17.6.72 Oxford, Town Hall
19.6.72 Southampton, Civic Centre
21.6.72 Dunstable, Civic Hall
25.6.72 Croydon, Greyhound
1.7.72 Weston-super-Mare, Winter Gardens
2.7.72 Torquay, Rainbow Pavilion
8.7.72 London, Royal Festival Hall
15.7.72 Aylesbury, Friars Hall

UK Tour II (19.8.72-7.9.72)
*with Lindsay Kemp and Company
19.8.72 London, Rainbow Theatre*
20.8.72 London, Rainbow Theatre*
27.8.72 Bristol, Locarno Electric Village
30.8.72 London, Rainbow Theatre*
31.8.72 Boscombe, Royal Ballrooms

Mini Top Rank/Hardrock Tour
(an extension of UK Tour II)
1.9.72 Doncaster, Top Rank
2.9.72 Manchester, Hardrock
3.9.72 Manchester, Hardrock
4.9.72 Liverpool, Top Rank
5.9.72 Sunderland, Top Rank
6.9.72 Sheffield, Top Rank
7.9.72 Hanley, Stoke-On-Trent, Top Rank

USA Tour I (22.9.72-3.12.72)
22.9.72 Cleveland, Music Hall
24.9.72 Memphis, Ellis Auditorium
28.9.72 New York, Carnegie Hall
1.10.72 Boston, Music Hall
7.10.72 Chicago, Auditorium Theatre
8.10.72 Detroit, Fisher Theater
11.10.72 St Louis, Kiel Auditorium
15.10.72 Kansas City, Memorial Hall
20.10.72 Los Angeles, Santa Monica Civic
21.10.72 Los Angeles, Santa Monica Civic
27.10.72 San Francisco, Winterland
28.10.72 San Francisco, Winterland
1.11.72 Seattle, Paramount Theatre
4.11.72 Phoenix, Celebrity Theatre
14.11.72 New Orleans, Loyola University
17.11.72 Miami, Pirate's World
20.11.72 Nashville, The Municipal
Auditorium
22.11.72 New Orleans, The Warehouse
25.11.72 Cleveland, Public Auditorium
26.11.72 Cleveland, Public Auditorium
28.11.72 Pittsburgh, Stanley Theatre
30.11.72 Philadelphia, Tower Theatre
1.12.72 Philadelphia, Tower Theatre
2.12.72 Philadelphia, Tower Theatre
3.12.72 Philadelphia, Tower Theatre

UK Tour (23.12.72-9.1.73)
23.12.72 London, Rainbow Theatre
24.12.72 London, Rainbow Theatre
28.12.72 Manchester, Hardrock

29.12.72 Manchester, Hardrock
5.1.73 Glasgow, Green's Playhouse
(2 shows)
6.1.73 Edinburgh, Empire Theatre
7.1.73 Newcastle, City Hall
9.1.73 Preston Guild Hall

US Tour II (14.2.73-12.3.73)
14.2.73 New York, Radio City Music Hall
15.2.73 New York, Radio City Music Hall
16.2.73 Philadelphia, Tower Theatre
17.2.73 Philadelphia, Tower Theatre
(2 shows)
18.2.73 Philadelphia, Tower Theatre
(2 shows)
19.2.73 Philadelphia, Tower Theatre
(2 shows)
23.2.73 Nashville, Tennessee, War Memorial
Auditorium
25.2.73 Memphis, (Ellis) Auditorium North
Hall (2 shows)
1.3.73 Detroit, Masonic Temple
2.3.73 Detroit, Masonic Temple
10.3.73 Los Angeles, Long Beach Arena
12.3.73 Los Angeles, Hollywood Palladium

JAPAN Tour I (8.4.73-20.4.73)
8.4.73 Tokyo, Shinjuku Koseinenkin Kaikan
10.4.73 Tokyo, Shinjuku Koseinenkin Kaikan
11.4.73 Tokyo, Shinjuku Koseinenkin Kaikan
12.4.73 Nagoya City Kokaido
14.4.73 Hiroshima, Yubin Chokin Kaikan
16.4.73 Kobe, Kobe Kokusai Kaikan
17.4.73 Osaka, Koseinenkin Kaikan
18.4.73 Tokyo, Shibuya Kokaido
20.4.73 Tokyo, Shibuya Kokaido

UK Tour III (12.5.73-3.7.73)
12.5.73 London, Earls Court
16.5.73 Aberdeen, Music Hall (2 shows)
17.5.73 Dundee, Caird Hall
18.5.73 Glasgow, Green's Playhouse,
(2 shows)
19.5.73 Edinburgh, Empire Theatre
21.5.73 Norwich, Theatre Royal (2 shows)
22.5.73 Romford, Odeon Theatre
23.5.73 Brighton, Dome (2 shows)
24.5.73 London, Lewisham, Odeon
25.5.73 Bournemouth, Winter Gardens
27.5.73 Guildford, Civic Hall (2 shows)
28.5.73 Wolverhampton, Civic Hall
29.5.73 Hanley, Victoria Hall
30.5.73 Oxford, New Theatre
31.5.73 Blackburn, King George's Hall
1.6.73 Bradford, St George's Hall
3.6.73 Coventry, New Theatre
4.6.73 Worcester, Gaumont
6.6.73 Sheffield, City (Oval) Hall (2 shows)
7.6.73 Manchester, Free Trade Hall
(2 shows)
8.6.73 Newcastle City Hall (2 shows)
9.6.73 Preston, Guild Hall
10.6.73 Liverpool, Empire Theatre (2 shows)
11.6.73 Leicester, De Montfort Hall
12.6.73 Chatham, Central Hall (2 shows)
13.6.73 Kilburn, Gaumont State
14.6.73 Salisbury, City Hall
15.6.73 Taunton, Odeon (2 shows)
16.6.73 Torquay, Town Hall (2 shows)
18.6.73 Bristol, Colston Hall (2 shows)
19.6.73 Southampton, Guild Hall
21.6.73 Birmingham, Town Hall (2 shows)
22.6.73 Birmingham, Town Hall (2 shows)
23.6.73 Boston Gliderdrome, Lincoln
24.6.73 Croydon, Fairfield Halls (2 shows)
25.6.73 Oxford, New Theatre (2 shows)
26.6.73 Oxford, New Theatre
27.6.73 Doncaster, Top Rank
28.6.73 Bridlington, Spa Ballroom
29.6.73 Leeds, Rolarena
30.6.73 Newcastle City Hall (2 shows)
2.7.73 London, Hammersmith Odeon
3.7.73 London, Hammersmith Odeon

NBC TV Midnight Special Filming
18-20.10.73 London Marquee, *1980 Floor
Show*

APPENDIX 1964-74

BBC TELEVISION APPEARANCES

(Recorded at Television Centre, White City, unless stated otherwise.)

1. (BBC1) *Juke Box Jury*: broadcast: 6.6.64
Produced by Barry Langford.
Hosted by David Jacobs.
David made a brief appearance plugging his first single release, 'Liza Jane'.

2. (BBC2) *The Beat Room*: recorded: 23/24.7.64 (approx), broadcast: 27.7.64
Produced by Barry Langford.
Introduced by Pat Campbell.
David and the King Bees performed 'Liza Jane' live.

3. (BBC2) *Tonight*: recorded: 12.11.64, broadcast: 12.11.64
Associate Producer Kenneth Corden.
Cliff Michelmore interviewed David and friends about the '...Prevention Of Cruelty To Long Haired Men', also featured Manish Boys' Paul Rodriguez and John Watson, King Bee George Underwood and his art school friend Stewart Swaine, neighbour Barrie Jackson, together with Nigel Richmond and David Dickats. David invited the latter (who sat to his left), off the street because he looked the part. Recorded at BBC Lime Grove.

4. (BBC2) *Gadzooks! It's All Happening*: broadcast: 8.3.65
Produced by Barry Langford.
Hosted by Alan David and Christine Holmes.
David and The Manish Boys performed their cover of 'I Pity The Fool'. The show opened and closed with a medley performed by all the artists, including David.

5. (BBC2) *The Pistol Shot*: recorded: 31.1.68, broadcast: 20.5.68
Directed by John Gibson.
Produced by Michael Bakewell.
David and Hermione Farthingale performed a minuet with Lindsay Kemp and others to music scored by Humphrey Searle, dressed in period costume. (Repeated 24.12.68)

6. (BBC2) *Colour Me Pop*: recorded: 10.5.69, broadcast: 14.6.69
Produced by Steve Turner.
David performed a mime alongside The Strawbs during their song 'Poor Jimmy Wilson', also featured Paul Buckmaster (cello), Tony Visconti (recorder), Terry Cox (drums) and Roger Coulam (organ).

7. (BBC1) *Top Of The Pops*: recorded: 2.10.69, broadcast: 9.10.69
Produced by Johnnie Stewart.
Orchestra directed by Johnny Pearson.
Introduced by Pete Murray. David performed 'Space Oddity' using both stylophone and acoustic guitar, backed by the *Top of The Pops* studio orchestra. (Repeated 16.10.69) Recorded at BBC Lime Grove.

8. (BBC1) *Top Of The Pops*: recorded: 9.6.71, broadcast: 10.6.71
Produced by Johnnie Stewart.
Introduced by Tony Blackburn.
Peter Noone performed his hit single 'Oh You Pretty Things', inviting David to play piano.

9. (BBC2) *The Old Grey Whistle Test*: recorded: 7.2.72, broadcast: 8.2.72
Produced by Michael Appleton.
Directed by Colin Strong.
Introduced by Richard Williams.
David and the Spiders made their TV debut performing 'Five Years', 'Queen Bitch' and 'Oh! You Pretty Things'.

10. (BBC1) *Top Of The Pops*: recorded: 5.7.72, broadcast: 6.7.72
Produced by Johnnie Stewart.
Introduced by Tony Blackburn.
David and the Spiders (with Nicky Graham) performed 'Starman'.

11. (BBC1) *Top Of The Pops*: recorded:

3.1.73, broadcast: 4.1.73
Produced by Johnnie Stewart. Introduced by Tony Blackburn or Jimmy Savile. Performed 'The Jean Genie'.

12. (BBC1) *Nationwide*: recorded: 23-25.5.73, broadcast: 5.6.73
Reporter: Bernard Falk.
Presented by Michael Barratt, Frank Bough and Bob Wellings.
David was interviewed and filmed live on his 1973 UK tour, in Bournemouth and in Brighton.

13. (BBC1) *Nationwide*: recorded: 23-25.5.73 & 3.7.73, broadcast: 4.7.73
Reporter Bernard Falk.
A report on David's Hammersmith Odeon retirement concert, edited together with *Nationwide*'s earlier film from June. Included are short interviews with Lulu, Tony Curtis and Angie Bowie outside the venue.

BBC RADIO APPEARANCES

(All broadcast on Radio 1 unless listed otherwise. Songs marked ▲ were included on the EMI 2000 compilation *Bowie At The Beeb*.)

1. BBC Radio Africa (World Service): *Turrie On The Go!*: recorded: 20.5.65, broadcast: Not known.
Producer: Colin Wild.
Still as Davie Jones for this appearance, David featured on this show as 'Teenager of the week' and was interviewed by Turrie. He plugged Manish Boys single 'I Pity The Fool'.

2. Radio One Audition: 2.11.65. Audition Manager: Mary Cotgrove.
Producer: Keith Bateson.
Complete with new surname, David Bowie auditioned with The Lower Third for BBC Radio, performing three songs: 'Out Of Sight', 'Baby That's A Promise' and 'Chim Chim Cher-ee'. David and band did not pass the audition.

3. European English Service. *Let's Go*: recorded: 5.9.67, broadcast: Not known
Producer: Tony De Vletter.
Reporter: David Rider.
A fifteen-minute interview recorded at David Rider's central London flat.

4. John Peel and Tommy Vance introduce *Top Gear*: recorded: 18.12.67, broadcast: 24.12.67.
Producers: Bernie Andrews and Bev Phillips.
Panel Engineer: Dave Tate.
'Love You Till Tuesday', 'Little Bombardier', 'In The Heat Of The Morning', 'Silly Boy Blue' and 'When I Live My Dream'.

5. John Peel in *Top Gear*: recorded: 13.5.68, broadcast: 26.5.68, repeated: 20.6.68
Producer: Bernie Andrews.
Engineers: Pete Ritzema/Alan Harris.
▲'In The Heat Of The Morning', ▲'London Bye Ta-Ta', ▲'Karma Man', ▲'Silly Boy Blue', 'When I'm Five'.

6. Radio 2: *Late Night Extra: Barry Alldis*: recorded: 30.5.68, broadcast: 30.5.68
Producer: Richard Willcox.
David was interviewed by Barry Alldis.

7. Radio One Club: broadcast: 28.8.69 (Live).
Producer: Aiden Day.
Interviewed by Dave Cash at Leas Cliff Hall, Folkestone for this midday broadcast.

8. BBC World Service: Programme not known: recorded: 21.9.69
Interviewed at Bush House by Frances Donnelly.

9. Radio One Club: recorded: 25.9.69
Interviewed in London by ex-Radio London DJ Keith Skues about 'Space Oddity'.

10. D.L.T. (Dave Lee Travis Show): recorded: 20.10.69, broadcast: 26.10.69
Producer: Paul Williams.
Engineer: Pete Ritzema.
Backed by Junior's Eyes, David performed 'Unwashed And Somewhat Slightly Dazed', ▲'Let Me Sleep Beside You' and ▲'Janine'.

11. Top Of The Pops Transcription Disc: recorded 20.10.69
▲ An interview with Brian Matthew, combined with tracks recorded for the *DLT* show and recorded for this BBC Transcription Disc series (used by broadcasters worldwide).

12. Radio One Club: broadcast: 14.11.69 (Live)
Midday broadcast from the Electric Garden, Glasgow. David performed live and is interviewed by Dave Lee Travis.

13. BBC Glasgow: recorded: 14.11.69
Interviewed by Ben Lyon, (live transmission).

14. The Sunday Show introduced by John Peel: recorded: 5.2.70, broadcast: 8.2.70
Producer: Jeff Griffin. Sound balance: Tony Wilson. Assistant: Chris Lycett.
▲'Amsterdam', ▲'God Knows I'm Good', 'Buzz The Fuzz', 'Karma Man', 'London Bye Ta-Ta', 'An Occasional Dream', ▲'The Width Of A Circle', 'Janine', 'Wild Eyed Boy From Freecloud', ▲'Unwashed And Somewhat Slightly Dazed', 'Fill Your Heart', 'The Prettiest Star', ▲'The Cygnet Committee' and ▲'Memory Of A Free Festival'.

15. Sounds of the 70s: Andy Ferris: recorded: 25.3.70, broadcast: 6.4.70
Producer: Bernie Andrews.
Executive Producer: Jimmy Grant.
Engineer: Nick Gomm.
'The Supermen', 'I'm Waiting For The Man', 'The Width Of A Circle', ▲'Wild Eyed Boy From Freecloud'.*

16. Sounds of the 70s: Dave Symonds: recorded: 25.3.70, broadcast: 11.5.70
Producer: Bernie Andrews.
Executive Producer: Jimmy Grant.
Engineer: Nick Gomm.
Culled from the March Andy Ferris session. Only one new track broadcast.*
'The Width Of A Circle', 'Wild Eyed Boy From Freecloud'.*

17. The Ivor Novello Awards For 1969/70: broadcast: 10.5.70 (Live)
Producer: Jack Lynn.
Performed 'Space Oddity' live during the Ivor Novello Awards ceremony at the Talk of the Town, London and collected his award for the most original song. (Radio 1 & 2)

18. Scene And Heard: recorded: 5.71, broadcast: 5.71
Producer: Stuart Grundy.
Engineer: Pete Harwood.
Grundy later recalled that David "came into the BBC in a lovely salmon pink dress".

19. In Concert: John Peel: recorded: 3.6.71, broadcast: 20.6.71
Producer: Jeff Griffin. Sound balance: Chris Lycett. Assistant: John Etchells.
'Queen Bitch', ▲'Bombers', 'The Supermen', ▲'Looking For A Friend', ▲'Almost Grown' (featuring Geoffrey Alexander on backing vocals), ▲'Kooks', 'Song For Bob Dylan' (vocal George Underwood), 'Andy Warhol' (vocal Dana Gillespie), and ▲'It Ain't Easy' (vocals David, Alexander (MacCormack) and Underwood).

20. Sounds of the 70s: Bob Harris: recorded: 21.9.71, broadcast: 4.10.71
Producer: John F. Muir.
Engineers: John White/Bill Aitken.
A duo performance by David and Ronson.
▲'The Supermen', ▲'Oh! You Pretty Things' segued into ▲'Eight Line Poem', 'Kooks'. Other tracks recorded but not broadcast are; 'Fill Your Heart', 'Amsterdam' and 'Andy Warhol'. Repeated: 1.11.71 with the inclusion of 'Fill Your Heart'.

21. Sounds Of The 70s: John Peel: recorded: 11.1.72, broadcast: 28.1.72
Producer: John Muir. Engineer: Nick Gomm.
The first Radio 1 performance by David and the Spiders from Mars.
'Hang On To Yourself', 'Ziggy Stardust', 'Queen Bitch', 'I'm Waiting For The Man' and 'Lady Stardust'.

22. Sounds Of The 70s: Bob Harris: recorded: 18.1.72, broadcast: 7.2.72
Producer: Jeff Griffin. Sound balance: Chris Lycett. Assistant: John Etchells.
▲'Hang On To Yourself', ▲'Ziggy Stardust', ▲'Queen Bitch' and ▲'Five Years', ▲'I'm Waiting For The Man' was also recorded but not broadcast.

23. Scene And Heard: Johnny Moran: recorded: 10.2.72, broadcast: 12.2.72
Producer: John Walters.
David was interviewed for seven minutes by Johnny Moran.

24. Sounds Of The 70s: John Peel: recorded: 16.5.72, broadcast: 23.5.72
Producers: Pete Ritzema.
Engineer: Nick Gomm.
▲'White Light/White Heat', ▲'Moonage Daydream' ▲'Hang On To Yourself', ▲'Suffragette City' and ▲'Ziggy Stardust'. Repeated 25.7.72. with the previously unbroadcast 'Moonage Daydream'.

25. Johnnie Walker Lunchtime Show: recorded: 22.5.72, broadcast: 5.6.72
Producer: Roger Pusey.
▲'Starman', ▲'Space Oddity', ▲'Changes', and ▲'Oh! You Pretty Things' are recorded for lunchtime broadcast. 'Oh! You Pretty Things' was played to remind listeners about David's work, prior to 'Starman' being run on four forthcoming lunchtime spots.

26. Johnnie Walker Lunchtime Show: recorded: 22.5.72, broadcast: 6-9.6.72
Producer: Roger Pusey.
'Starman' recorded for daily broadcast over four days.

27. Sounds Of The 70s: Bob Harris: recorded: 23.5.72, broadcast: 19.6.72
Producer: Jeff Griffin. Sound balance: Chris Lycett. Assistant: John Etchells.
▲'Andy Warhol' (featuring just David and Mick Ronson on acoustic guitars), ▲'Lady Stardust', 'White Light/White Heat', and ▲'Rock 'n' Roll Suicide'. (whole group)

28. The Sounds Of The 70s: Bob Harris: recorded: 16.5.72, broadcast: 25.7.72
Producer: Jeff Griffin.
Made up of tracks recorded for a previous *Sounds Of The 70s: John Peel*, first broadcast in May: 'Moonage Daydream', 'White Light/White Heat' and 'Suffragette City'.

29. Scene And Heard: Johnny Moran: recorded: 3.1.73, broadcast: 6.1.73
Producer: Stuart Grundy.
A four minute interview by Nicky Horne, conducted in David's dressing room at the *Top Of The Pops* studio in Television Centre.

30. Scene And Heard: Johnny Moran: recorded: 11.5.73, broadcast: 18.5.73
Producer: Stuart Grundy.
David provided a ten minute interview the day before his largest ever UK tour. In June he also provided Steve Dickson with a 15 minute interview about the *Aladdin Sane* and UK tour (programme not known).

GENERAL TV APPEARANCES

1. Ready Steady Goes Live!: recorded: 19.6.64, broadcast: 21.6.64 (UK)
Directed by Rollo Gamble.
Programme Assistant Vicki Wickham.
Introduced by Keith Fordyce and Cathy McGowan.
Davie Jones and the King Bees performed 'Liza Jane' for David's TV performance debut. Recorded in central London.
(ITV – Associated-Rediffusion Network)

2. Ready Steady Go!: recorded: 5.3.65, broadcast: 5.3.65 (UK)
Programme Assistant Vicki Wickham.
Introduced by Cathy McGowan.
David was briefly interviewed by Cathy McGowan. Recorded in central London.
(ITV – Associated-Rediffusion Network)

3. Ready Steady Go!: recorded: 4.3.66,

broadcast: 4.3.66 (UK)
Directed by Michael Lindsay-Hogg.
Produced by Francis Hitching.
Edited by Vicki Wickham.
David and The Buzz performed 'Can't Help Thinking About Me'. Recorded in Wembley.
(ITV – Associated-Rediffusion Network)

4. Fan Club: recorded: 8.11.67, broadcast: 10.11.67 (Netherlands)
Directed by Ralph Inbar. Presented by Sonya Barend. Guest Presenter: Rudi Bennet Performs single version of 'Love You Till Tuesday'. Recorded in Hilversum.
(Nederland 1)

5. 4-3-2-1 Musik für Junge Leute (4-3-2-1 Music for Young People): recorded: 27.2.68, broadcast: 16.3.68 (West Germany)
Produced by Gunther Schneider.
Performed 'Love You Till Tuesday', 'Did You Ever Have A Dream' and a mime of 'Please Mr Gravedigger'. Recorded in Hamburg.
(ZDF – Zweites Deutsches Fernsehen)

6. 4-3-2-1 Musik für Junge Leute: recorded: 20.9.68, broadcast: 9.68 (West Germany)
Produced by Gunther Schneider.
Probably performed 'Love You Till Tuesday'. Recorded in Hamburg.
(ZDF – Zweites Deutsches Fernsehen)

7. Für Jeden Etwas Musik (Music for Everyone): recorded: 11.11.68, broadcast: 11.68 (West Germany)
Produced by Gunther Schneider.
David performed one unknown song (possibly 'When I Live My Dream'), and a 'pantomime' piece, possibly to Igor Stravinsky's 'The Circus Polka'. (Repeated 18.1.69)
Recorded in Munich.
(ZDF – Zweites Deutsches Fernsehen)

8. Commercial: LUV: recorded: 22.1.69, broadcast: 6/7.69 (UK)
Lyons Maid ice cream LUV commercial featured David and others acting as pop stars. Filmed on a double-decker bus and on stage in London.
(ITV regions)

9. Doebidoe: recorded: 25.8.69, broadcast: 30.8.69 (Netherlands)
Produced by Ralph Inbar.
David performed 'Space Oddity'. Recorded in Hilversum.
(AVRO – Algemene Vereniging Radio Omroep)

10. Hits A Gogo: broadcast: 3.11.69 (live) (Switzerland)
Directed by Gianni Paggi. Produced by Mani Hildebrand. Presented by Suzanne Doucet. Recorded in Zurich.
Performed 'Space Oddity'.
(STV – Schweizer TV Gesellschaft)

11. 4-3-2-1 Musik für Junge Leute: recorded: 29.10.69, broadcast: 22.11.69 (Germany)
Produced by Gunther Schneider.
Performed 'Space Oddity'. Recorded in West Berlin.
(ZDF – Zweites Deutsches Fernsehen)

12. Like Now: broadcast: 5.12.69 (live) (Ireland)
Produced by Bil Keating.
Performed 'Space Oddity' on his first trip to Ireland. Recorded in Dublin.
(RET – Raidió Èireann Telefís)

13. Cairngorm Ski Night: recorded: 29.1.70, broadcast: 27.2.70 (UK)
Directed by Tony Harrison.
Designed by Eric Mollart.
Introduced by James Spankie.
Performed 'London Bye Ta-Ta' backed by the Alex Sutherland band.
Recorded in Aberdeen.
(Grampian Television)

14. Gateway: Pierrot In Turquoise or The Looking Glass Murders: recorded: 1.2.70, broadcast: 8.7.70 (UK)
Directed by Michael Mahoney.

David and Trevor Bolder performing 'Starman' on Granada TV's Lift Off with Ayshea, broadcast 21 June 1972.

Designed by Ken Wheatley.
David featured as 'Cloud' in this Lindsay Kemp production. Recorded in Edinburgh.
(STV – Scottish Television)

15. Ivor Novello Awards for 1969: recorded: 10.5.70 (live), broadcast to: US, Europe and Australia. Produced by Jack Lynn.
Received award for Most Original Song and, backed by the Les Reed Orchestra, performed his award-winning song 'Space Oddity'. Recorded at the Talk of the Town, London.
(Broadcast: TVR Ltd)

16. Six-O-One: Newsday: broadcast: 6.70 (live) (UK) Presented by Bob Greaves.
Performed 'Memory Of A Free Festival'. Recorded in Manchester.
(ITV – Granada Television)

17. Ready, Eddy, Go!: broadcast: 18.7.70 (Netherlands)
Presented by: Eddy Becker
Performed 'Memory Of A Free Festival'. Recorded in Hilversum.

18. Six-O-One: Newsday: broadcast: 20.1.71 (live) (UK) Presented by Bob Greaves.
Mimes 'Holy Holy'. Recorded in Manchester.
(ITV – Granada Television)

19. Pop 2: recorded: 12.2.72, broadcast: 3.4.72 (France)
Produced by Maurice Dumay & Claude Ventura. Presented by Patrice Blanc Francard.
David and the Spiders were filmed at Imperial College, London performing 'Suffragette City'.
(ORFT Paris)

20. Lift Off With Ayshea: recorded: 15.6.72, broadcast: 21.6.72 (UK)
Introduced by Ayshea Brough. Produced by Muriel Young. Directed by David Warwick.
Performed 'Starman'.
Recorded in Manchester.
(ITV – Granada Television)

21. ABC Evening News: recorded: 28.9.72, broadcast: 29.9.72 (USA)
Reporter: Scott Osborne
David wass interviewed at Carnegie Hall, New York plus rehearsal footage at the venue.
(ABC)

22. Russell Harty Plus Pop: recorded: 17.1.73, broadcast: 20.1.73 (UK)
Produced by Nick Barrett. Directed by Mike Mansfield. Presented by Russell Harty.
David provided a rare UK TV interview and performed 'Drive-In Saturday' and 'My Death'. Recorded in central London.
(ITV – London Weekend Television)

23. The Mike Douglas Show: recorded: Mid-Feb 73, broadcast: Mid-Feb 73 (USA)
Executive Producer Woody Fraser.
David made an appearance on The Mike Douglas Show, a daytime talk show. Recorded in Philadelphia.
(CBS)

24. The Midnight Special: The 1980 Floor Show: recorded: 18-20.10.73, broadcast: 16.11.73 (USA)
Produced and directed by Stan Harris.
Performed '1984 – You Didn't Hear It From Me', 'Sorrow', 'Everything's Alright', 'Space Oddity', 'I Can't Explain', 'Time', 'The Jean Genie', 'I Got You Babe'. Finale – '1984 – You Didn't Hear It From Me'. Recorded over three days and nights at the Marquee club, London.
(NBC)

25. Top Pop: recorded: 13.2.74, broadcast: 2.74 (UK)
Presented by Ad Visser.
Performed 'Rebel Rebel'. David and Angie also attended the AVRO award ceremony Grand Gala du Disque and were briefly seen on screen in the audience during Tony Orlando and Dawn's performance. Recorded in Amsterdam.
(AVRO-televisie)

GENERAL RADIO APPEARANCES

1. Radio Luxembourg – Ready Steady Go Radio!: recorded: 5.3.65, broadcast: 9.3.65 (UK)
Presented by Keith Fordyce and Dee Shenderry.
With his long hair story in the red tops, David was invited to record an interview without The Manish Boys.

2. Radio Luxembourg: Kenny & Cash: broadcast: 1965 (UK)
Quite possibly David's first appearance on pirate radio. Kenny & Cash was one of the ground-breaking, irreverent new pirate shows which helped to attract large young audiences away from old school pre-Radio 1 BBC broadcasting.

3. Radio Luxembourg: The Friday Spectacular: recorded: 8.65, broadcast: 8.65 (UK)
Presented by Shaw Taylor, Muriel Young and Ray Orchard. Produced by Muriel Young.
Interviewed by Shaw Taylor in the ground-floor studio at EMI House, Manchester Square to promote the new single 'You've Got A Habit Of Leaving'. Each member of The Lower Third was also introduced.

4. Radio London: Harry Fenton (sponsored) trial recording: 24.4.66 (UK)
David was interviewed by Earl Richmond at the Marquee club in London. David and The Buzz were also recorded live and Richmond introduced the new single 'I Dig Everything'.

5. Radio Hilversum III: broadcast: 26.8.69 (Netherlands)
Interviewed near Hilversum for this offshore Dutch pirate station re 'Space Oddity'.

6. Radio Veronica: broadcast: 26.8.69 (Netherlands)
Interview re 'Space Oddity'. Recorded at the villa De Lapershoek in Utrechtseweg, Hilversum.

7. 3XY Melbourne: recorded 22.10.69, broadcast: 10/11.69 (Australia)
Interviewed about the success of 'Space Oddity' for Australian radio by reporter Bill Gates. The interview was conducted at

Manchester Street.

8. BRT Radio: recorded: 11/12.10.69, broadcast: 1.1.70 (Belgium)
Interviewed by Ward Bogaert, who also narrates. The five-minute feature mainly focused on David and the Beckenham Arts Lab:
'The boy is called David Bowie. We saw him as the symbol of youth and the England and the world of tomorrow. With his fanatical following, he reminds me of a prophet...'

9. Promotional Tour: broadcast: 1/2.71 (USA)
David was interviewed on various pan-American radio stations during his first promotional trip, including various East Coast radio stations in Washington and also on 94 WYSP in Philadelphia.
In California David appeared on KMAC in Long Beach, CIMS in Santa Anna, KET in Los Angeles, and was also interviewed in San Francisco. In San Jose he acted as guest DJ (when he discovered the music of Iggy Pop and the Stooges for the first time).

10. Hospital Radio – Lewisham: broadcast: 3/4.71 (UK)
Laid up in Lewisham Hospital with injured legs after being struck by his own car, David was interviewed about his career for the in-house hospital radio service by Chris Warbis. During the interview 'Wild Eyed Boy From Freecloud' was played.

11. Radio Luxembourg: The Kid Jensen Show: broadcast: 4/5.71 (Luxembourg)
David was interviewed in London by Bob Grace to promote The Man Who Sold The World for Jensen's show.

12. US Radio: (station not known): broadcast: 1972
David was interviewed about the recording of Hunky Dory and Ziggy Stardust, prior to the release of the latter.

13. KMET-FM Santa Monica: David Bowie Live: broadcast: 20.10.72.
Introduced by B. Mitchel Reed (USA)
David and the Spiders performed live in concert from the Santa Monica Civic Auditorium for this live broadcast (released on CD in 2008).

14. Rockspeak: broadcast: 6.73 (Germany)
Interviewed by journalist and broadcaster Michael Wale during the UK summer tour.

15. Radio Luxembourg: The Kid Jensen Show: recorded: 11.7.73, broadcast: 14.7.73
A '208 Bowie Special'; Kid Jensen interviews David during the Pin Ups recording sessions at the Château d'Hérouville.

David in a US radio studio during his promotional visit, January 1971.

CREDITS/BIBLIOGRAPHY

Pitt, Kenneth ***The Pitt Report*** (Design) 1983
Gillman, Peter & Leni ***Alias David Bowie*** (Hodder & Stoughton) 1986
Carr, Roy/Shaar Murray, Charles ***David Bowie An Illustrated Record*** (Eel Pie Publishing) 1981
Juby, Kerry ***In Other Words David Bowie*** (Omnibus Press) 1986
Tremlett, George ***The David Bowie Story*** (Futura) 1974
Zanetta, Tony & Edwards, Henry Stardust ***The Life and Times of David Bowie*** (Michael Joseph) 1986
Sukita, Masayoshi Ki ***Spiritual Force*** (Tokyo FM) 1992
Kelleher, Ed ***David Bowie A Biography in words and pictures*** (Sire Books) 1977
Buckley, David ***Strange Fascination*** (Virgin) 2004
Pegg, Nicholas ***The Complete David Bowie*** (Reynolds & Hearn) 2000
Kamp, Thomas ***David Bowie The Wild Eyed Boy 1964 - 1984*** (O'Sullivan,Woodside) US 1985
Paytrass, Mark ***Bolan: The Rise And Fall Of A 20th Century Superstar*** (Omnibus Press) 2006
Hunter, Ian, ***Diary Of A Rock 'n' Roll Star***
Logan, Nick/Woofinden, Bob ***The Illustrated New Musical Express Encyclopedia of Rock*** (Hamlyn) 1976
Rees, Dafydd & Crampton, Luke with Lazell, Barry ***Guiness Book Of Rock Stars*** (Guiness Books) 1989
British Hit Singles 14th Edition (Guiness Books) 2001
Rolling Stone Rock Almanac The Chronicles of Rock Music (MacMillan) 1983
Rogan, Johnny ***Starmakers and Svengalis: The History of British Pop Management*** (Queen Ann Press) 1988
Napier-Bell, Simon ***Black Vinyl, White Powder*** (Ebury Press) 2001
White, Edmund ***Genet*** (Knopf Publishing Group) 1993
Wakeman, Rick ***Say Yes!*** (Hodder & Stoughton) 1995
Rock, Mick ***A Photographic Record 1969-1980*** (Century 22) 1995
Bowie, David & Rock, Mick ***Moonage Daydream - The Life And Times Of Ziggy Stardust*** (Genesis) 2002
Elstob, Lynne & Howes, Anne ***The Glastonbury Festivals*** (Gothic Image) 1987
Wyman, Bill ***Rolling With The Stones*** (Dorling Kindersley) 2002
Lewisohn, Mark ***The Complete Beatles Recording Sessions*** (Hamlyn) 1988
King, Vic/ Plumbley, Mike/ and Turner, Pete ***Isle Of Wight Rock: A Music Anthology*** (Rock Archives) 1996
MacCormack, Geoff ***From Station To Station*** (Genesis) 2007
Thorgerson, Storm & Powell, Aubrey ***100 Best Album Covers*** (Dorling Kindersley) 1999
Gorman, Paul ***The Look: Adventures in Rock & Pop Fashion*** (Adelita) 2006
Eickhoff, Randy Lee & Lewis, Leonard C. Bowie - ***A Novel Of The Life Of Jim Bowie*** (Forge) 1998
McNeil, Legs & McCain, Gillian ***Please Kill Me: The Uncensored Oral History Of Punk*** (Little, Brown) 1996
Lulu ***I Don't Want To Fight*** (Time Warner) 2003
Sherrin, Ned ***The Autobiography*** (Little, Brown) 2005
Helvin, Marie ***The Autobiography*** (Wiedenfeld & Nicolson) 2007
Palin, Michael ***Diaries 1969-1979*** (Wiedenfeld & Nicolson) 2006
Sheppard, David ***On Some Faraway Beach - The Life And Times Of Brian Eno*** (Orion) 2008

KEY SOURCES

Kerry Juby: Childhood/Early family history/Arts Lab
Chrissy Iley (*Sunday Times Magazine*): Childhood
Peter & Leni Gillman (*Alias David Bowie*): Childhood – 73
Barrie Jackson: Childhood – 1970
Stuart Grundy/BBC Radio: 1966–73
Pete Frame & Kevin Howlett/BBC Radio: 1961–73
George Underwood: 1961–72
Melody Maker: 1964–73
Record Mirror: 1964–73
Leslie Conn: 1964–65
Bob Solly: 1964–65
Woolf Byrne: 1964–65
Denis Taylor: 1965–66
Phil Lancaster: 1965-66
Disc And Music Echo: 1966–72
John Eager: 1966–67
Derek Fearnley: 1966–67
Gus Dudgeon: 1966–67 & 'Space Oddity'
Natasha Kornilof: 1967–68
Kenneth Pitt Ltd Archives: 1966–70
Mark Pritchett: 1969–73
John Cambridge: 1969–70
MainMan Files: 1970–74
Anya Wilson: 1970–72
Trevor Bolder: 1971–73
Nicky Graham: 1972
Charles Shaar Murray (*NME*): 1972–73
Mick Rock: 1972–73
Cherry Vanilla (Kathy Dorritie): 1973
Phil Lawton: BBC Radio

PICTURE CREDITS

(t=top, b=bottom, m=middle, l=left, r=right)

Fiona Adams/Getty Images: 65(m); Mark Adams: 221; Roy Ainsworth/David Bowie Collection: 6c, 12, 25, 27(t), 29(t/l), 29(t/r), 31(t/l); Rolf Aldercreutz: 5, 191, 192(t/r); Bernie Andrews: 120(l/b); Cyrus Andrews: 77(t); Cyrus Andrews/Getty: 74(b); Cyrus Andrews/Redferns: 83; Clive Arrowsmith/Celebrity Pictures: 295(b/l); Charlie Auringer: 204(t); Tom Ayres Estate: 206(t/l); Author's Collection: 17(b/l), 18(b/l), 23(b/r), 24(t/l&b/r), 27(m), 28, 29(m), 30(b/l), 34(b/l), 38(b/r), 40(t/l), 44(t/l), 50(t), 53(r/m), 58(r), 58(b), 60(m), 61(m), 66(b), 72(l&r&m), 73, 77(b), 78(l), 80(t/r), 85(t/r), 92(b), 94, 98(b), 103(t), 107(t/b), 110(b), 111(t/r), 113(b/l/r/m/r), 114(b) 120(t/l), 127(b), 128(b), 129(m), 135(t), 149(t/r&m&b), 152(b), 154(r), 155(t&b), 158(l/b), 162(t/l&m), 165(b), 166(m), 172(t/l), 173(b/l), 179, 180(b/l), 193(m&b), 197(b), 198, 202(t/l&b/l), 205(b), 207(m/l), 209(m), 213(t/r&upper/m/r), 215(t/r&t/l&b/r), 217(m), 224(m&b), 226(m&b), 227(m&b), 228(t), 229(m), 234(b/l&r), 235(m), 238(b), 242(l), 243(t), 244(t&b), 246(t/l&r), 249(m), 250(m&b), 253(b), 263(m/r), 262(t), 265(b/m), 268(t/l&m), 269(t/m&b), 270(b), 272(m&b), 276(t&upper/m), 277(m&b), 278(t/l&r&b/r), 284(t/r), 286(l/m), 287(m), 288(t), 289(b), 290(t/l&m/l&b/l), 294(t), 296(b/l&r/m), 297(t/l&b/r), 298(t/l), 300(b), 301(m&b), 302(b), 305(b), 306(t&m&b), 308(m&t/m&r), 309(t/r), 311(b/l&r), 312, 313(lower/m&b), 315(t/l&r), 319(m&b), 320, 321, 322(b/l) 323(b/m&r), 324(t/m&lower/m/l), 325(t/l); Author's Collection/Decca: 35, 36(r), 107(t/l), 326, 329(b/r); Author's Collection/Kerry Juby: 15; Author's Collection/Denis Taylor: 55(b); Author's Collection/EMI: 63(t/l), 66(t); Author's Collection/Natasha Kornilof: 128(m); Author's Collection/Pye: 95(b); Author's Collection/Rosehill Theatre: 125; Avon Publishing: 18(t/l); Roger Bamber/Rex Features: 297(t/r), 299(t), 318(t/r); Barnardo's: 21(t)(m); Dick Barnatt/Getty Images: 245(b); Max Batten: 18 (b/r); BBC: 40 (b/r), 51(t/r); Robin Bean/Mark Hayward: 6a, 9, 108(t/b), 109(t), 112(t), 116(t/r&l/b), 117(t/l); *Beat 64* Magazine/Bob Solly Collection: 31(t/r); 43(t/r); David Bebbington/Retna: 158(t/l&r), 161(l&r), 175(t/r); Jacques Bernard/Rex Features: 267(t); Barrie Bethell: 282(t&m); Rodney Bingenheimer: 206(m), 224(t/r), 233(b); Trevor Bolder: 219(b); Terry Bolton: 55(t/l), 63(b); *Bournemouth Evening Echo*: 58(m), 59(m), 60(r); Angela Bowie: 231(t); David Bowie Archive: 6b, 7b, 11, 14 (l), 16(m), 17(t), 17(b/r), 18 (b/l) 23(t), 117(t/r/b), 168(tl&r), 170, 171(b), 195(t&m), 207(m/r), 210(l&r), 215(b/l), 229(b), 252(t/l&r&b), 255(t), 257(l), 275(t&b), 292(t&r&b), 302(m/l&r), 303(r), 322(t/l&r), 323(t), 324(t/r); David Bowie/Lee Black Childers: 324(b); David Bowie/Brian Duffy: 293(t&r); David Bowie/Justin de Villeneuve: 310(t/l&r); *Bromley & Kentish Times*: 20(t/l); *Bromley & Kentish Times*/David Heath-Hadfield Collection: 29(b), 82; Bromley Technical High School/Ravens Wood School: 24(b/r), 26(b); Burnt Ash School: 18(t); Woolf Byrne/Evening News & Star: 51(b); CBS Records: 266(upper/m), 300(t); CSU Archive/Everett/Rex Features: 274(b); Peter Chasseud: 172(b); *Chatham Standard*: 52(m/l); Lee Black Childers: 291(t&b); Paul Colin Archive: 323(b/l); Columbia Pictures: 139(b); Dell Publishing: 16(l); Deram/Universal Music: 104(tl/r); Vernon Dewhurst/David Bowie: 171(t); *Disc & Music Echo*: 164(t), 169(b/l&r), 182(t/l&b), 202(b/r), 204(b), 265(b/l), 266(t&b), 267(b); Brian Duffy © Duffy Archive: Spine, Front Cover, 7f, 280, 293(b/l&r), 294(m), 295(t/l&t/r&b/m); John Eager: 74(t), 75(t), 78(m/r), 80(t/l), 85(m/r), 88, 89(b); EMI: 6e, 23(m); EMI 46, 60(m), 61(t/b); Essex Music: 117(b/l); *Evening Argus*: (78(t); *Evening Standard*/Getty Images: 48(b/r), 51(t/l), 282(b); *Fabulous 208*: 115(m/r), 118(t/l), 173(t) 175(t/l); Gerald Fearnley: 6g, 76(t/l), 96, 105(t); Helen Fearnley: 105(b); James Fortune/Rex Features: 278(b/l); Chris Foster/Rex Features: 303; Fotex/Hudalla: 7h, 200, 225; Pete Frame: 44(m); Clive Frampton: 24(b/l); © Lynn Goldsmith/Corbis: 285(t/l&r); Nicky Graham: 243(upper/m/r); Dave Graves/Rex Features: 223(r/m); Billy Gray: 86; Dick Greener: 158(m/r); Jeff Griffin: 217(r), 249(t); Grove Press: 18(t/l), 206(b); Gijsbert Hanekroot: 318(b/r), 319(t/l); Tony Hatch: 71(r); David Heath-Hadfield Collection: 30 (t/l) 30 (l/m/t) 30 (l/m/b); *Harpers Bazaar*: 225(b); Dezo Hoffmann/Rex Features: 6d, 32, 34(t/l), 38(t), 78(b), 108(t/r), 113(t/r), 234(upper/m/r), 234(lower/m/r); Hulton-Deutsch Collection/Corbis: 182(t/m); John Hutchinson: 149(l); Richard Imrie/Camera Press: 282(t/r); Interfoto MTI/Hulton Archive/Getty: 168(b/2); ITV/Rex Features: Inside Front Cover Spread, 251(t), 256, 283, 329; Dick James Music Ltd: 38(b/l); Michael John/Martin Argent Collection: 54 (t/r); *Kentish Times*: 160(t), 187(t&b); Lindsay Kemp/Scottish TV: 180(t/l&r); Keystone/Getty Images: 296(b/r); Jak Kilby: 112(m), 121(t), 128(t/l&r); John Lynn Kirk/Getty Images: 276(lower/l&b/r); Victor Konn: 254(t); Marty Kristian: 121(m), 240(b); *LA Modern Architecture*: 273(t); Helene Lancaster: 59(b&m); Robert Landau/Corbis: 325(b); Brian Lane/ Bromley Tech/Ravens Wood School: 19; Barry Langford: 50(l), 53(t/m); Calvin Mark Lee: 168(b/3); Bob Lewis: 24(r); Ralph Mace: 210(b/1); Keith MacMillan/David Bowie Archive: 7i, 176, 197(t/r), 211, 213(lower/m); Benny Marshall: 222(b); Howard Marshall/MainMan: 199, 226(t), 266(t/l&b); Sean Mayes/Author's Collection: 287(t/l&t/r&b); Robin McBride: 178(b); *Melody Maker*: 53(b/r), 56(m), 72(l), 78(m), 87(m/b), 133(t/l), 162(b), 181(t), 183(t/r), 184(t/l&b), 186(t/l&m), 188(t/r), 193(t/r), 224(t), 222(b/m), 240(t), 243(t/l), 246(m/l&b), 250(t), 257(t/r&b), 258(t/r), 259, 314(t/l); John Mendelssohn: 205(tl&r), 216(b); MGM/Premier: 254(m); Mirrorpix: 223(b), 296(t/r), 302(t), 318(t/l); Brian Moody/Rex Features: 234(lower/m/l); Mark Moxon: 14(t/r); *Music Life*: 288(l&m), 290(t/r&upper/m); *Music Now*: 174; Harry Myers/Rex Features: 304(m/l); Byron Newman: 251(t), Inside Back Cover Spread; *New Musical Express*: 71(l), 91(t), 101, 163(t/l&r), 185(b), 235(b), 297(b/l); News Ltd/Newspix/Rex Features: 92; Ron Oberman: 203(tr&mr); Michael Ochs Archives/Getty Images: 207(t), 231(m), 234(upper/m/l), 272(t), 269(t/r), 314(b); Terry O'Neill/Getty Images: 7e, 309(t/l), 316, 322(b/r), 324(t/l; Pan: 22(r), 325(t/r); Gabi Pape: 220, 222(lower/m); Parlophone Records: 52(b); Chas Pearson: 52(t); Tristram Penna: 24(m), 100, 116(t/m), 118(b/l), 128(b/r), 181(b), 189, 202(t/r), 210(b/2), 215(m/r), 218(b/l); Linda Phillips: 53(t/l); © Pictorial Press Ltd/Alamy: 6f, 68, 70(l), 76(r), 91(t), 203(t/l), 210(b/r), 223(t/l); Kenneth Pitt: 6h, 6i, 27(m)(b), 37, 52(m/r), 58(l), 64(t/b), 65(b), 80(m/b), 81, 84, 85(b), 87(t), 89(t), 90, 95(t), 98(t), 110(t), 111(t/l/b), 114(t/l&r), 115(l), 116(t/l), 118(b/m&r/m), 119(t/r&b), 120(b), 121(b), 122, 126, 127(t), 129(b), 130(t/m&b), 131(t&b), 133(t/r), 134(t/l&b), 135(b), 137(b), 138(l&r), 139(t), 142, 144(r), 145(b), 146(b/l), 147(t/r &l/m&b/l), 148(b), 150(t/r), 151, 153, 156(m&b), 157(m&b), 162(r), 163(b&m), 164(m&b), 166(t&b), 167, 168(b/5), 173(b/r), 175(b), 184(b), 186(b), 192(t/l), 209(b); Jon Lyons/Rex Features: 129(t); Daniella Parmar: 207(b), 245(upper/m); Terry Pastor: 255(upper/m/l); Philips Group/David Bowie Archive: 159, 212, 213(t/l); Barry Plummer: 182(t/r); © Neal Preston/Corbis: 285(t), 289; Mark Pritchett: 157(t), 188(t/l), 196(t/l), 209(t), 217(t/l), 255(lower/m/l), 311(upper/m/l); Michael; Putland/Retna: 241, 247(t&b), 248(l); NBC: 308(t/l); RCA Records: 274(m); Radio London: 75; *Rave*: 178(t); *Record Mirror*: 39(t/r), 63(t/r) 103(b), 105(t/r), 249(b), 274(t/r), 277(t), 301(t/r); Redferns/Getty: 286(b); Rex Features: 40(b/l); M. Richardson: 16(b); Stuart Richman/London Features International: 148(t), 165(t); Billy Ritchie: 101(t), 109(b); © Mick Rock: 7d, 194, 245(t&lower/m), 251(b), 260, 261, 262(m/r), 263(t&m&b/r), 265(t&b/r), 268(b), 269(t/l), 270(t/l&r), 273(m), 279, 299(b/r), 301(t/l), 304(t/r&b/l&r), 311(t/r), 313(t&upper/m/r), 314(t/m&r); Mick Rock Collection: 230; Sheila Rock/Rex Features: 132(b); John Rogers/Getty; Images: 303(b), 304(t/l); Rolling Stone: 274(t/l), 284(b); Rolling Stones/Atlantic Records: 325(t/m); Minnie Ronson: 214(b), 227(t); Nicholas Ronson: 184(t/r), 186(t/r); Samye Ling: 112; Carlton Sandercock: 102(t/r); Pete Sanders: 190; Sarah Sapherson-Hine: 223(t/r); Ken Scott: 222(b/l), 255(b/r); © Christian Simonpietri/sigma/corbis: 168(b/1); Bob Solly Collection: 41, 42, 45, 48(t), 49(t)(b), 52(m/t), 53(t/r); Nico Van Der Stam/Maria Austria Institute: 118(t/r), 119(t/l), 195(b); Gloria Stavers: 269(t/r); John Steven: 65(t); Ray Stevenson/Rex Features: 55(m), 115(b), 124, 130(r), 132(t), 136(l&r), 137(t), 140(t/b) 141, 152(t), 156(t), 160(b), 169(b/r), 173(b/r), 183(t/l&b), 243(b&lower/m); Ray Stevenson: 130; Michael Stroud/Getty Images: 218(t/r); Lyle Stuart: 21(t/r); Masayoshi Sukita: 258(t/l&b), 262(l/m) 263(b/l), 284(t/l), 286(t/l&t/r), 288(b), 289(t), 290(t/m&b/m); Sunshine/Retna UK 319(t/r); Shel Talmy Archive: 48(b/l); Denis Taylor: 55 (t/r), 56(t)(b), 57, 59(t), 60(t)(b), 61, 67, 70(r); *TV Times*: 184(m); TVR Ltd: 192(m/b); George Underwood: 20(t), 26(t), 36(l) 39(m/r), 54(t/l), 168(b/4&6), 169(t/l&m&r), 216(m), 262(t&b), 266(m); Universal Music/Decca: 93, 102(b); Universal Music/Kenneth Pitt: 144(l), 145(t), 146(t&b/r), 147(t&b); Mike Vernon: 100(b), 104(b); Justin de Villeneuve/Getty Images: 311(t/l); Santi Visalli Inc/Getty Images: 228(b); Tony Visconti: 150(b); Richard Ward: 29(b); Brian Ward: 231(b), 239(b); Brian Ward/David Bowie Archive/Terry Pastor: 1; Brian Ward/David Bowie Archive: 7g, 208, 216(t/l), 281(t/l), 222(b/r), 233(t/l&m), 234(t), 235(t/l), 236, 238(t), 239(t), 242(r), 247(m), 253(l&r), 255(m&r&b/l); Warner Bros Records: 294(b); *Watford Observer*: 315(b); Mike Weller/David Bowie Archive: 213(t/l&b); Tim Whitnall: 254(b); Anya Wilson: 195(t/r); Shirley Wilson: 85(t/l)

INDEX